Data Matters

Conceptual Statistics for a Random World

Nicholas Maxwell

Key College Publishing
Innovators in Higher Education

www.keycollege.com

Nicholas Maxwell
Maxwell Statistics
Everett, Washington

Key College Publishing was founded in 1999 as a division of Key Curriculum Press® in cooperation with Springer-Verlag New York, Inc. We publish innovative texts and courseware for the undergraduate curriculum in mathematics and statistics as well as mathematics and statistics education. For more information, visit us at *www.keycollege.com*.

Key College Publishing
1150 65th Street
Emeryville, CA 94608
(510) 595-7000
info@keycollege.com
www.keycollege.com

Development Editor: Susan Minarcin
Technical Review: Larry Copes
Production Project Manager: Michele Julien
Copyeditor: Erin Milnes
Production Director: Diana Jean Parks
Text Designer: Kurt Krames
Compositor/Technical Art: ICC
Illustrator: Beatrice Benjamin
Photo Researcher: Margee Robinson
Art and Design Coordinator: Kavitha Becker
Cover Designer: John Nedwidek
Cover Illustrator: Andy Levine
Prepress and Printer: Versa Press

Executive Editor: Richard Bonacci
General Manager: Mike Simpson
Publisher: Steven Rasmussen

Library of Congress Cataloging-in-Publication Data
Maxwell, Nicholas
    Data matters: conceptual statistics for a random world / Nicholas Maxwell.
        p. cm.
    Includes bibliographical references and index.
    ISBN 1-930190-89-1
    1. Statistics. I. Title.

QA276.12 .M295 2002
001.4—dc21

2002034101

Printed in the United States of America
10 9 8 7 6 5 4 3 2 1   07 06 05 04 03

Contents

Foreword

Yet another book for the first course in statistics? Is it possible that a new book could cover the standard topics, be effective for a broad readership, and at the same time do things that are truly distinctive? If I didn't think so, I wouldn't have written this foreword.

The last quarter century has been an exciting time for the introductory statistics course. We have seen the arrival of a half dozen books that deserve to be called groundbreaking. To that select company, I would add *Data Matters* by Nicholas Maxwell. Here are four distinctive strengths that I would urge instructors to consider in deciding whether this book is a good choice for their introductory course.

1. *The prose style is highly readable and engaging*. Maxwell consistently uses short words and simple sentence constructions. I would expect a readability index to show that it is the easiest to read of all books that cover the same content. Yet, remarkably, there is a distinct author's voice. The book is written with grace and wit. More than any other statistics textbook I know, it reads like a trade paperback. Students will find it enjoyable to read.

2. *The technical demands on the reader are modest*. As Maxwell points out, the book is written to be accessible even to students who have trouble with proportions. Nevertheless, his book manages to take readers as far as analysis of variance, which many first courses never get to. This is possible because the use of mathematics is carefully planned and skillfully presented to make minimal demands initially, to escalate only gradually, and to use mathematics only where necessary. Maxwell's step-by-step "quasi-narrative" presentation of longer calculations is without rival among introductory books.

3. *The exposition tells stories based either on "statistics in the news" (Part I) or, later, "statistics in research articles" (Part II)*. Nowadays almost all authors use the media and research articles as sources of examples. What makes

Maxwell's book different is the way he uses the examples. Most books use them as adjuncts, to illustrate the "main" exposition, which is concerned with the abstract concepts, principles, and methods of statistics. Maxwell has a dramatist's ear; he is able to present the abstract ideas as part of the "plot" that unfolds as you follow the story of the examples. He leads with the stories and lets the technical exposition serve as explanation for what students have just read in excerpts from the news. This presentation gives his exposition a much stronger narrative flavor.

4. *The presentation of sampling distributions is the best I have seen at this level.* Experienced teachers generally agree that the hardest concept for students in an introductory course is the sampling distribution. Difficulty with this fundamental concept keeps many beginning students from understanding the logic of statistical inference. Maxwell's treatment of these topics is truly original. For one thing, he spends a lot of time on using the population to predict how the sample will behave. Reasoning from population to sample is easier to understand than the "backward" logic of inference, which goes from sample to population. *Data Matters* spends far more time than other books preparing students for the logic of inference by reasoning from population to sample. With the chapters spent on predicting sample behavior as background, Maxwell's readers are much better prepared to reverse perspective when it comes time for inference. Moreover, Maxwell's inspired use of the language makes it easier for students to focus on the key ideas. For example, most books that treat p-values for significance testing talk about "outcomes at least as extreme as the one we observed." This articulation is correct, direct, and less convoluted than many other possible wordings, but it is still hard for students. Nicholas uses this phrase a couple of times, but talks mostly about "outcomes at least as embarrassing to the null hypothesis." This personification is not only amusing and therefore memorable, but the word "embarrassing" contains within it an effective reminder to students of how the logic of testing works. This kind of effective use of unusual language as well as thoughtfulness about the sequence in which he presents key concepts are typical of Maxwell's approach.

Maxwell's book is not for every introductory course. His approach is, by choice, a strategy of "concrete first, abstract after." Some people come to prefer the opposite order. Nevertheless, I think *all* teachers who read this book will learn new ways to present the ideas of statistics to their students, and many will conclude that their students will enjoy the course more, and learn more, with *Data Matters* as the textbook.

—George Cobb
Mount Holyoke College

Preface

To the Instructor

The first time I taught introductory statistics, the initial chapter of the text I had chosen included this equation:

$$\bar{x} = \frac{\sum x}{n}$$

There was no explanation of the summation symbol. Many of my students could find no clue what it meant. The class went downhill from there.

The text I tried next included almost no equations, but it didn't cover much material either. At the end of the course, a student said, "I'm a little disappointed. I now know something about statistics, but I don't feel like I've taken a whole course in statistics." I agreed.

I searched widely for a text that would support my students' need for a presentation they could understand within the context of a comprehensive course in statistics. I was frustrated by finding that texts either assumed a strong background in mathematics, or almost completely avoided mathematics, as though statistics had little to do with quantity. I decided the book I needed wasn't out there, so I decided to write *Data Matters*.

I developed the plan for *Data Matters* around what students most need from introductory statistics. Every student needs to know enough about statistics to think sensibly about news reports. Some students need to learn enough to read reports in the sciences, and a few need a foundation for further study in statistics. *Data Matters* serves all three types of students. Part I prepares students to read the news. Part II prepares students to learn from reports in the sciences. Each section of each chapter includes a subsection specifically for students who will proceed to further classes in statistics.

Data Matters explains the full logic of statistical sampling and inference in the context of one type of statistic: proportions. Proportions are the most common statistic in the news. Having solidified the students' conceptions of the quirks that arise from how the proportion is calculated, *Data Matters* uses proportions to present sampling distributions, confidence intervals, and statistical inference. After the logic of statistics has been fully revealed for proportions, *Data Matters* proceeds to show how that logic applies to other types of statistics.

In addition to statistics literacy, *Data Matters* encourages critical thinking. Concepts and procedures are almost always presented with some sort of supporting evidence. Much of that evidence is simulations and empirical tests. It is worthwhile to repeat those experiments in class to enable students to see the concepts in action with their own eyes. The goal is to encourage a healthy skepticism. For example, I strongly recommend that at some point you have every student flip a coin 10 times and report the number of heads. The textbook reports on my doing this, but reading about trials in a textbook is not as compelling as seeing them for yourself.

Data Matters is unique in seriously reviewing the foundational mathematics that students must understand before they can learn statistics. This exploration has been carefully tested and adjusted until all of the foundational mathematics in the text is essential. If you skip over chapter sections that look like review to you, I bet you will lose some students who otherwise would have succeeded in your course.

Innovative Pedagogy

Data Matters is divided into two parts, each consisting of five chapters. Each chapter is further broken down into easy-to-digest sections, and each section of the book has a variety of elements to support student learning:

- Textboxes highlight key concepts throughout the text.
- Section summaries review materials and help reinforce key concepts.
- The Algebra and Greek Symbols feature restates each section's material in traditional mathematical and statistical equations to prepare students for further courses in statistics.
- Exercises provide practice on key concepts and work to ensure students' mastery.
- Answers to odd-numbered exercises appear immediately after each section's exercises so that students can learn from their mistakes.
- Each section features a computer project to illustrate the text's key claims and give students a hands-on opportunity to see just how data matters.

Part I focuses on statistics in the news, particularly proportions and statistical analysis of categorical data. The first four chapters follow a very carefully crafted line of argument in order to build a step-by-step knowledge base that will not only help students understand real statistical issues but will also provide a solid foundation for more complex studies. Each concept follows from and builds on the previous concept:

- Calculating a proportion
- Sample statistics versus population parameters
- Random sampling
- Sampling distributions
- Prediction intervals
- Confidence intervals
- Statistical inference
- Test of location
- Test of correlation

Chapter 5 provides a quick introduction to a variety of other statistics concepts that are needed for reading the news. If students were to stop only after Chapter 5, they would be well prepared for statistics in the popular press.

Part II focuses almost exclusively on continuous data in the sciences. Chapter 6 presents exploratory methods, summary statistics, and prediction and confidence intervals. Chapters 7 and 8 present the *t*-test and ANOVA. Chapters 8, 9, and 10 present regression, building up from graphs, and equations of lines.

Sections 8.2 and 10.2 present nonparametric tests. These sections' primary objectives are to emphasize the assumptions of the parametric tests and to highlight how violations of those assumptions affect the parametric tests.

In my classes, I gave a closed-book comprehensive final exam, in which students were provided a tiny (four-observation) data set. In the exam, students calculated summary statistics and performed an ANOVA, chi-square test, and regression test. My students could memorize the equations to do this because *Data Matters* takes the time to explain why the equations are sensible and memorable.

I recommend you give a similar closed-book exam. Students should understand how the statistics are calculated. It is worthwhile pointing out that tiny data sets often violate the assumptions of tests, which assume larger samples, so have your students calculate the statistics on tiny samples and report why the samples are too tiny.

Instructor Resources and Other Ancillary Materials

A complete line of instructor resource material is available.

- *Instructor Resources.* These resources, available in print and Web-based formats, provide section-by-section support for *Data Matters.* This manual also provides a sample syllabus and schedules, answers to homework problems, overall strategies for teaching a conceptual statistics course, and tips on everything from how to foster learning communities to suggestions on handling class demonstrations.

- *Data Matters Resource Center at www.keycollege.com/dm.* Data sets and software-specific instructions for the computer projects that appear in the *Data Matters* text are available to students and educators alike via the *Data Matters* Resource Center. This website features alternative instructions for the text-based **Computer Projects,** allowing students to use a variety of software packages including **Fathom Dynamic Statistics™ software, Microsoft® Excel,** and **SPSS®.** Fathom is a data exploration and analysis software package that facilitates simulation experiments and allows an intimate feel for sampling and sampling distributions. The Web site also includes instructions for SPSS and Excel. SPSS is the statistical analysis software most widely required for employment. To get a feel for the commercial need for SPSS compared to other software packages, visit a job-listing Web site, such as *www.monster.com,* and search for "SPSS" and the other packages. You'll see that the number of jobs that require SPSS is far greater than that of jobs requiring any of the other packages. Despite SPSS's advantages, you'll want to try the projects with Excel also. Although Excel is not well set up for data analysis, and the instructions for the projects in Excel are necessarily longer, most of your students will already have Excel installed on their PCs, and will likely be expected to be familiar with Excel at their workplace.

- *Data Matters with Fathom Dynamic Statistics™ Student Lab Manual.* This hands-on, activity-based manual is an extension of the online computer experiments and is designed to help students deepen their understanding of statistics though challenging, Fathom-based exercises. The lab manual makes running a lab section easier, as students do not have to search through the online instructions.

- *Data Matters Instructor Demonstrations CD.* This exciting new package combines chapter objectives with preset demonstrations in Fathom. Designed for use either with the *Student Lab Manual* or simply for demonstrating concepts in the classroom, this powerful tool provides instructors with a limited use version of the software for those who do not have the full version.

- *Data Matters Test Generator.* Created in conjunction with Renaissance Learning, Inc., the most recognized name in ancillary testing services, this CD-ROM test generator adheres to the unique style and tone of *Data Matters.*

To the Student

Data Matters is organized into fairly bite-sized sections. Don't let the tone of the text fool you—this is important information, but I hope you will find it fun and interesting to read, too. Each chapter is broken into three sections. Each section can be studied on its own and finishes with exercises that enable you to check your understanding of the section before proceeding onward.

I suggest a simple strategy when you work through the exercises. I used to read one-minute mysteries. These are mysteries that are described in a page or two. After reading the mystery, you give yourself a minute to figure out the solution to the mystery, and, when you think you have it, you turn to the next page to see what the right answer is. Throughout this book, at the end of each chapter section, there are exercises that are like 15-minute mysteries. The answers to the odd-numbered exercises appear after the exercises. To check whether you understood the section, try these exercises and check your answers against the provided answers. If you don't see how to answer an exercise within 15 minutes, you might look at the answer to see how it's done. Always be sure to check your answers against those provided; if your answer is wrong you should go back and try to understand why. Ask for help when you need it. These ideas build on each other; make sure you understand the section before reading on.

New material is presented within the text and then summarized at the end of the section to reinforce key ideas. The material is further restated in the Algebra and Greek Symbols subsection. The Algebra and Greek Symbols subsections are designed to prepare you to proceed in other classes in statistics. You could skip them altogether, or use them as a review for each section, or finish the text and then go back and read all of the Algebra and Greek Symbols subsections on their own.

Part I of *Data Matters* presents the statistical concepts you need to be a critical reader of statistics in the news. If your goal is to just be an informed consumer of statistics in the popular press, you needn't read further. If you aim to be a liberally educated person, you will need to be able to read statistics in the sciences. A liberal education examines the natural and social sciences as well as the humanities. Part II will give you enough of a foundation to get you started reading statistics in scientific reports. There is a lot more to statistics than is covered in this book, but, having mastered what is covered here, you will be ready to learn from reports that use other statistical concepts.

Lastly, don't skip the Introduction. It explains why you want to learn statistics in the first place.

—Nicholas Maxwell

Acknowledgments

Many thanks go to the hundreds of students who worked through earlier drafts of this text at the University of Washington, Bothell. Most of these students at Bothell were returning to school in their 30's and 40's. Some had not dealt with mathematics for decades. Most were assertive enough to tell me when I wasn't making sense to them. What clarity this book has is a testament to their feedback. I am very grateful to have had the opportunity to work with them as they learned statistics.

Several people at Key College Publishing and Springer-Verlag deserve thanks for supporting this project as it went from manuscript to published work. Many thanks to Jerry Lyons and Richard Bonacci for launching the publishing project and continuing to support it. Susan Minarcin deserves the credit for overseeing the final revisions and edits. Susan's cheerful and firm insistence kept things moving.

A number of people have commented on or edited drafts of the partial manuscript or the complete manuscript. George Cobb did a wonderful job reviewing the overall concept and providing conceptual advice at various stages of development. My wife, Rachel Maxwell; my in-laws, historian Jim Robertson and novelist Janet Robertson; and my mother, professor Sarah Maxwell, all edited parts of the manuscript at various times. Michael Goldberg read and commented on the first chapters, and Pete Nye reviewed the Algebra and Greek Symbols subsections.

The reviewers of the core text and the ancillaries provided invaluable feedback:

William Duckworth II, Iowa State University
Chris Franklin, University of Georgia, Athens
Daniel A. Griffith, Syracuse University
Susan Herring, Sonoma State University
Larry J. Ringer, Texas A & M University
Nancy Schoeps, University of North Carolina, Charlotte
Lewis Shoemaker, Millersville University
John Stroyls, Georgia Southwestern State University
Engin A. Sungur, University of Minnesota, Morris

INTRODUCTION — *Why Data Matters*

House Hunting

Statistics can change your life.

When my wife and I were looking to buy our first home, we had two kids and one income. This meant we could afford to spend little. What could we buy? The first house our realtor showed us had two bedrooms and high-tension power lines directly over the roof. The next five houses seemed to be made entirely of asbestos: asbestos ceilings, asbestos insulation, asbestos wallboard, and what looked to me like asbestos carpeting.

The realtor explained that, at my salary, we were not supposed to buy a nice house. We were supposed to buy what is called a "starter home," because you start with that, and then later, when you have more money, you commit to a larger mortgage and move out.

My wife was discouraged. Having seen six houses, she wanted to buy one of the asbestos wonders under the power lines. The realtor was not surprised. He let us know that he had shown us all the houses we should consider.

Because I am a statistician, I was not convinced we had seen all there was to see. I had seen only a few houses. I know from statistics that a small number of examples do not give you an accurate idea of what is available. My realtor had picked the examples I had seen. He seemed like a nice guy, but from statistics I know that if you want to get an idea of what is available, you do not want a selected sample—you want a random sample. Even if most of the houses in my price range were like the ones I had seen, I know from statistics that things vary: In general, most items in a group are a lot like one another, but a few are very different from the usual. I knew that most houses in our price range would be like the ones I had seen, but a few would be a lot worse, and a few would be a lot better. It takes some time to find unusual examples, but I know from statistics that all you need to do to find unusual cases is to look long enough.

I found a realtor who gave me access to his realty database to get my random sample. From that sample, I figured out what an unusually good house would be like. I needed to know what it would be like, so that when I found the exceptionally good house, I wouldn't pass it over and keep looking for something better. Finally, I searched.

Two months later, having considered descriptions of more than 2,000 houses and having driven past more than 100 of them, I found our current home: no power lines, no asbestos, four bedrooms, and six years old, with a 160-degree view of the Cascade Mountains. It is a dream.

That story is an example of what this book will teach you: how to find your own best house, or best job, or best investment. Things will be better for you if you understand statistics.

Natural Childbirth

A friend of mine followed a natural-childbirth method during her first pregnancy. The book she was reading said that if you followed the program, you would have a pain-free delivery. The book described many women who had not followed the plan and frightening things that happened to them: days of labor, excruciating pain, cesarean sections, and high-forceps deliveries. "But not to worry," the book explained. "If you follow the program, you will sail through delivery painlessly. You will have trouble only if you cheat on the program."

Apparently, if something went wrong, you could tell whose fault it was. The fault was yours, because you didn't follow the program.

As it happened, my friend had a long and painful labor. Then she had a cesarean section. The baby was not positioned properly in the womb. Nevertheless, the delivery was a great success. The baby was healthy. The mother was never in any danger. They are both now doing magnificently, except that my friend felt guilty after her delivery. The book had said that if you followed the program, you would have a painless delivery. My friend felt that she must have failed, and the delivery trouble was her fault.

Well, the world is not like that. Statistics show us that there are few sure things. Even if Dr. Spock, Marie Curie, Dr. Lamaze, and Jonas Salk all got together to devise a childbirth program, they still could not guarantee that every delivery would happen a particular way. Things vary. Things happen by chance. If the delivery goes badly, you don't know for sure why it went badly, and unless you have some other evidence, it's probably not a good idea to beat yourself up about it.

That's how it is. The world you live in is somewhat random. You don't get credit for everything, but you don't deserve blame for everything either. That is the most important thing you can learn from this book: Many things happen by chance.

Reading the News

You may have heard of the DARE (Drug Abuse Resistance Education) program. The DARE program arranges for police officers to teach students to avoid using illegal drugs. One newspaper article about DARE says the following:

> *About 27,000 Houston fifth-graders and 24,000 seventh-graders participate in DARE programs. . . . "There is very little compelling evidence to suggest that the primary goal of the DARE program is being reached at a statistically significant level."*
> —BARDWELL, *HOUSTON CHRONICLE*, SEPTEMBER 3, 1998

The DARE program is expensive. DARE America, the organization that sells curricular materials to the officers teaching the DARE program, has a multimillion-dollar annual budget, and thousands of American police officers are paid full-time salaries to work in DARE. It's a serious problem if DARE is not effective, which might be what that quote from the *Houston Chronicle* is saying. But is that what the quote is saying? The quote says that there is little evidence that the goals are being reached "at a statistically significant level." What does "a statistically significant level" mean? Does this mean that the DARE program is no good? Or does it mean something else? These are questions you will be able to answer when you have finished this book.

The news is packed with statistics and statistical ideas. Statistical significance is one of the more advanced ideas used in the news, but without understanding statistical significance, you cannot understand important information reported in any typical newspaper. A major goal of this book is to improve your ability to understand the news and other sources that include statistics.

Every chapter section of Part I of this book begins with one or more quotes from a newspaper or other popular press source. The quotes are selected to reveal some aspect of statistics. You might not be able to understand a section's quote when you begin the section, but you will be able to understand it by the section's end. By the time you finish Part I, you will have learned what you need to know to be able to understand the statistics and statistical ideas that appear in the news.

About DARE: We won't cover the concept of statistical significance until a later chapter. However, the gist of the quote about DARE is that, although it's possible that DARE helps some children avoid drugs, studies comparing children who receive DARE training with children who do not reveal no convincing evidence that the program makes a difference.

Quantity

Sometimes people are unable to perceive whole classes of the world's features. A friend of mine lost her ability to smell as a result of a car accident. She cannot smell any foods. She can tell that something is burning only by seeing the smoke or hearing the smoke alarm go off. Her life has its difficulties.

My older brothers are both color blind between red and green (and all shades in between). The only way they can tell a red light from a green light is by looking at the position of the lit bulb on the stoplight. For them, the light on the bottom means "go"; the light on the top means "stop."

Now and then, I meet someone who cannot perceive or work with quantities. Several people who have studied statistics with me have somehow avoided doing calculations their whole life. I asked one of them how she balanced her checkbook. She didn't know what I was talking about. She hadn't heard of "balancing" a checkbook, so I asked her how she avoided bouncing checks. "That's easy," she said. "Every month, the bank sends me a statement. At the bottom is something called the 'balance.' If the balance is under $200, I have to slow down in my shopping. If the balance is over $200, I can have some fun." That works, sort of. But it does rule out making a budget, and you would not be surprised to learn that she had never saved up money for a big vacation or to buy a home. Like my friend who can't smell and like my brothers who are color blind, there is an aspect of the world that this woman cannot perceive or work with. The aspect that she is blind to is quantity.

Many people who pay no attention to quantities avoid math in college. This is not impossible. Some even become professors. I once attended a lecture on Napoleon's ill-fated march into Russia. The professor had previously announced that he could not figure out percentage. It was distressing to hear him talking about the losses to Napoleon's army. "Many, even most, died. I don't mean all of them. Some came back. But lots didn't. Thousands died, and there were thousands in the army. I mean, what with the winter, so many died that Napoleon's army was nowhere near as big as it had been. It was much smaller. It was like a . . . small army." What happened was that Napoleon began with about 453,000 soldiers. During the campaign, he lost about 443,000 men. Napoleon lost 98% of his army. That 98% is an inextricable feature of French history, but as a history student, you might never learn that, depending on your professor.

I have taught statistics to many students who could not balance a checkbook (as well as many students who could), and they have learned a lot. If you usually skip over numbers and avoid calculations, there is a purpose in this book just for you: to bring you gently to quantity. My friend will never smell. My brothers will never see red or green. But you will see quantity. When you are done with this book, the newspaper will look different—it will have quantities in it, and they will make sense. When you are done with this book, you will feel more comfortable with numbers. Maybe you will create a budget. Maybe you will put aside some money and someday take a big vacation. I hope so.

Statistics in the News

Basic Concepts of Statistical Thinking Presented in the Context of Categorical Data

Almost all of the statistics in the popular press are proportions. "64 percent think the Vatican meetings will result in meaningful improvements." "Arenas sold 95.5 percent of tickets." "The wireless equipment maker unexpectedly announced it was shedding up to 17,000 more jobs, about 20 percent of its work force."

Percentages report on the categories into which things fall. If you read that 64% of survey respondents think meetings will help, that tells you the proportion who fall in the *meetings–will–help* category. If you read that 95.5% of tickets were sold, that tells you the proportion of tickets that were in the *sold* category.

Part I of this book is all about statistics in the news. Because most of the statistics in the news are proportions reporting on categories, Part I will focus exclusively on statistical analysis of categorical data. Part II will prepare you to read statistics in the sciences and focuses on statistical analysis of numeric measurements, such as incomes, weights, and ages.

The most important idea in Part I is that some of what you see in reports of proportions is coincidence—nothing more than chance. For example, I just flipped a coin 10 times while singing and 10 times in silence. While singing, I got 50% heads. In silence, I got 80% heads. Can I get more heads by being silent? No. It's a coincidence. By the end of Part I, you will see how to test whether patterns in proportions can be reasonably chalked up to chance variation or whether the patterns are telling you something important.

CHAPTER 1 *Proportions in Samples, Proportions in Populations*

As you read about percentage and numbers in the news, be aware that news writers can spin a story by choosing whether to report the percentage or the raw numbers. Big issues can be made to look small, and small issues can be made to look big. As long as you understand what you're up against, you can protect yourself from being misled. That protection is the topic of Sections 1.1 and 1.2.

The introduction said that things vary. But they do not vary completely chaotically. There are patterns in randomness. As you think about what you can learn from percentage, you need to know something about the pattern that chance puts into percentage. Section 1.3 begins to show you that pattern.

1.1 The Most Popular News Statistics

- Percentage
- Proportions
- Raw Counts
- Pie Charts
- Bar Charts

In 1991, the last year for which statistics are available, 38,317 people in the United States died by gunfire.
—BUTTERFIELD, *NEW YORK TIMES*, SEPTEMBER 21, 1994

[Here are] the leading U.S. causes of death and their 1992 mortality rates per 100,000 people: heart disease, 144.3; cancer, 133.1 . . .
—*ROCKY MOUNTAIN NEWS*, DECEMBER 16, 1994

MORE THAN 38,000 AMERICANS died of gunshots in 1991. Put all those 38,000 together, and you have a town the size of Salem, Massachusetts, or Salina, Kansas. By comparison, about 58,000 Americans died during 12 years of fighting in Vietnam: 38,317 is a lot of shootings, but how does it compare to heart disease?

In 1992, the death rate for heart disease was 144.3 per 100,000 people. You can't immediately compare the 38,317 to the 144.3. They are not the same kind of thing. The 38,317 is a raw count. The "144.3 per 100,000" is a proportion. You can compare a proportion to a proportion, or a raw count to a raw count, but not one to the other.

There are many ways of writing proportions. For example, "50,000 per 100,000" is a proportion—it is one-half. One-half could also be written as "0.5" or "50%" or "one-half." Similarly, "144.3 per 100,000" could be written as "0.001443"or "0.1443%." However you write a proportion, you can't compare it to a raw count.

To compare the two mortality statistics, you could calculate how many people died of heart disease. Then you would have a raw count of heart disease deaths to compare to the raw count of gunfire deaths. Let's do it.

How to Write a Proportion as a Decimal

To write a proportion as a decimal, divide by whatever the proportion is per.

For example, percent means "per 100." To write a percentage as a decimal, you divide by 100. That means that 35% is 0.35. To translate from "per 100,000," divide by 100,000. The proportion "144.3 per 100,000" is 0.001443.

When you start with a proportion and want to find a raw count, you multiply the proportion by the number in the total population. Before you can do that, you need to translate the heart disease proportion into a decimal. To translate a proportion into a decimal, you divide by whatever it is per. The heart disease proportion "114.3 per 100,000" is per 100,000, so you divide by 100,000. You then divide 114.3 by 100,000, and the result is 0.001443. To find how many people died of heart disease in 1992, you multiply 0.001443 by the number of people in the United States in 1992. In the early 1990s, there were about 260 million Americans, so you multiply 0.001443 by 260 million. That's 0.001443 times 260,000,000, which is 375,180.

How to Translate from a Proportion to a Raw Count

To find the raw count of a group that is a part of a larger set, multiply the number in the larger set by the proportion.

For example, in 2001, there were about 281 million Americans. About 51% were female. To find the number of American women, you multiply 281,000,000 by 0.51, getting 143,310,000. In 2001, there were about 143 million American women.

About 375,000 Americans died of heart disease in 1992. (One moral of this story is that you might want to have a calculator handy when you read the newspaper.)

During the early 1990s, there were about 375,000 heart disease deaths and about 38,000 gunshot deaths each year. Now you can compare them: There were about 10 times as many deaths from heart disease as from gunshots.

Expressing the heart disease deaths as a proportion didn't show that many more people died from heart disease than from gunshots. You might wonder why people ever report the death rate rather than the total number of deaths.

There are good reasons to report rates, or proportions, rather than raw numbers. Proportions allow you to compare across different-sized groups. Proportions reveal the nature of groups, independent of the groups' sizes. If one group has five women and five men, and a second group has 1,000 women and 1,000 men, the two groups have similar mixtures of men and women. It is their proportions that reveal that similarity. Both groups are 50% female. Their raw counts look very different (5 versus 1,000), but the proportions reveal the similarity in their natures.

Transformations

To find the proportion of a group that falls in a subgroup, you divide the raw count in the subgroup by the total number in the larger group. It may help you to see that in an equation:

$$\text{Proportion in Subgroup} = \frac{\text{Raw Count in Subgroup}}{\text{Number in Full Group}}$$

To find the raw count in a subgroup, you can multiply the proportion in that subgroup by the number in the full group:

$$\text{Raw Count in Subgroup} = \text{Proportion in Subgroup} \times \text{Number in Full Group}$$

If you know the raw count and proportion in a subgroup, you can find the number in the full group by dividing the subgroup's proportion into the raw count in the subgroup:

$$\text{Number in Full Group} = \frac{\text{Raw Count in Subgroup}}{\text{Proportion in Subgroup}}$$

How to Calculate a Proportion from a Raw Count

To find the proportion that fall in a subgroup, divide the number in the subgroup by the number in the full group.

For example, 14,081 American women were diagnosed with AIDS in 1994. There were then about 132.6 million women in the United States. To find the proportion who were diagnosed with AIDS, you divide 14,081 by 132,600,000. The proportion of American women diagnosed with AIDS in 1994 was 0.0001061, which is about 0.01%, or about 11 per 100,000.

Practice Transforming

Try transforming to make sure you're comfortable with raw counts and proportions. Here is a situation in which you must calculate the proportions and raw counts if you want to understand what's going on:

> *The [Centers for Disease Control and Prevention] said AIDS was diagnosed in 14,081 adult women in the United States last year. . . . More than three-fourths of the women who contracted AIDS last year were black or Hispanic.*
>
> —Reuters, *Rocky Mountain News*, February 10, 1995

How does the spread of AIDS among African American and Hispanic women compare to the spread among other women? To compare the nature of the two groups, you need to find what proportion of each group was diagnosed with AIDS. Here's the equation for finding the proportion:

$$\text{Proportion in Subgroup} = \frac{\text{Raw Count in Subgroup}}{\text{Number in Full Group}}$$

One group is the African American and Hispanic women. The other group is the rest of the American women. To find the proportion in each group, you need to find the raw count of AIDS diagnoses in each group and the total number in each full group.

Finding How Many African American and Hispanic Women Had Been Diagnosed with AIDS

The article says that more than three-fourths of the diagnoses were for African American and Hispanic women. The authors probably wrote "more than three-fourths" because the actual proportion was a little bit higher than three-fourths. We will guess that the actual proportion was about three-fourths. To translate that into a decimal, you divide 4 into 3, and get 0.75. That means that 0.75 of the 14,081 infected women were African American or Hispanic.

To find the raw count of how many of the infected women were African American or Hispanic, start with the equation for finding a raw count:

$$\text{Raw Count in Subgroup} = \text{Proportion in Subgroup} \times \text{Number in Full Group}$$

Then plug in the proportion who were African American or Hispanic (0.75) and the number in the full group of diagnoses (14,081):

$$\text{Raw Count in Subgroup} = 0.75 \times 14,081$$

$$\text{Raw Count in Subgroup} = 10,560.75$$

After rounding, you can say that there were about 10,561 AIDS diagnoses for African American and Hispanic women in 1994. (You could round to 10,600 or 11,000. Rounding numbers is discussed later in this section.)

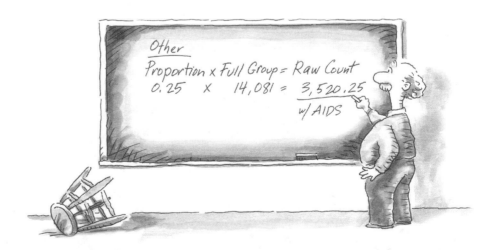

Finding How Many Diagnoses Were for Other Women

If three-fourths of the diagnoses were African American and Hispanic women, the other one-fourth must have been the other women. One-fourth is 0.25. How many diagnoses is that among the other women? To find out, start with this equation:

$$\text{Raw Count in Subgroup} = \text{Proportion in Subgroup} \times \text{Number in Full Group}$$

Plug in the proportion who were other women (0.25) and the number in the full group of diagnoses (14,081):

$$\text{Raw Count in Subgroup} = 0.25 \times 14,081$$

$$\text{Raw Count in Subgroup} = 3,520.25$$

In 1994, there were about 3,520 AIDS diagnoses among the other women.

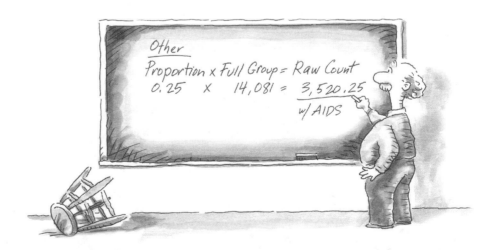

Looking at those raw counts, 3,520 and 10,561, you would say that AIDS is a bigger problem for African American and Hispanic women than it is for others. It looks as though the risk of infection is three times greater for the African American and Hispanic group, but that's wrong. It's a mistake to compare groups using their raw counts. To compare groups, you need to compare their proportions, because it is the proportions that reveal the groups' natures. Before you can compare proportions, you need to know how many women are in each of the two groups.

Women make up slightly over half of the U.S. population, 51%. In the early 1990s, there were about 260 million Americans. How many were women? Here's how to find a raw count:

$$\text{Raw Count in Subgroup} = \text{Proportion in Subgroup} \times \text{Number in Full Group}$$

Plug in the proportion who were female (0.51) and the number in the full group of Americans (260 million):

$$\text{Raw Count in Subgroup} = 0.51 \times 260,000,000$$

$$\text{Raw Count in Subgroup} = 132,600,000$$

There were about 132.6 million American women. Here is some information about the proportion who were African American and Hispanic:

> *African-Americans make up 13 percent of the United States population.*
>
> —STOLBERG, *NEW YORK TIMES*, JUNE 29, 1998

> *Nationwide [Hispanic] numbers total 28.6 million, or 10.7 percent of the U.S. population.*
>
> —MASON-DRAFFEN, *NEWSDAY*, MARCH 23, 1998

We can add those proportions to find the proportion who were African American or Hispanic: 13% plus 10.7% is 23.7%, or about 24%. About 24% of American women were Hispanic or African American in the early 1990s.

Finding the Raw Count of African American and Hispanic Women

Here's the equation again:

$$\text{Raw Count in Subgroup} = \text{Proportion in Subgroup} \times \text{Number in Full Group}$$

Plug in the proportion who were African American or Hispanic (0.24) and the number in the full group of American women (132.6 million):

$$\text{Raw Count in Subgroup} = 0.24 \times 132,600,000$$

$$\text{Raw Count in Subgroup} = 31,824,000$$

This number rounds to 32 million, so according to this calculation, the total number of African American and Hispanic women is about 32 million.

Finding the Proportion of African American and Hispanic Women Diagnosed with AIDS

There were 10,561 AIDS diagnoses among the 32 million African American and Hispanic women. To find a proportion, divide the number in the subgroup by the number in the full group:

$$\text{Proportion in Subgroup} = \frac{\text{Raw Count in Subgroup}}{\text{Number in Full Group}}$$

Plug in the raw count of AIDS diagnoses (10,561) and the number of African American and Hispanic women (32,000,000):

$$\text{Proportion in Subgroup} = \frac{10,561}{32,000,000}$$

$$\text{Proportion in Subgroup} = 0.00033$$

To translate 0.00033 into a percentage, you multiply by 100 and find that 0.03% were diagnosed with AIDS. To express 0.00033 as a proportion per 100,000, you multiply by 100,000. For every 100,000 African American or Hispanic women, 33 were first diagnosed with AIDS in 1994. Note that 0.03% is a very small proportion. Although AIDS may be a bigger problem in the African American and Hispanic communities than in the population as a whole, AIDS cannot be described as "common" in the African American and Hispanic communities.

How does this compare to the frequency of AIDS among other women? To find out, you need the raw count of other women.

Finding the Raw Count of Other Women

Of the total population of women in the United States, 24% were African American or Hispanic. The remaining 76% were the other women. Again, we can use this equation:

$$\text{Raw Count in Subgroup} = \text{Proportion in Subgroup} \times \text{Number in Full Group}$$

Plug in the proportion who were other women (0.76) and the number in the full group of American women (132.6 million):

$$\text{Raw Count in Subgroup} = 0.76 \times 132,600,000$$

$$\text{Raw Count in Subgroup} = 100,776,000$$

After rounding off, this tells you that 76% of 132.6 million women is 101 million other women. There were about 101 million American women who were not African American or Hispanic in 1994.

Finding the Proportion of Other Women Diagnosed with AIDS in 1994

It is out of this group of 101 million that the other 3,520 AIDS diagnoses came. What proportion is that?

$$\text{Proportion in Subgroup} = \frac{\text{Raw Count in Subgroup}}{\text{Number in Full Group}}$$

Plug in the raw count of AIDS diagnoses (3,520) and the number of other women (101 million):

$$\text{Proportion in Subgroup} = \frac{3,520}{101,000,000}$$

$$\text{Proportion in Subgroup} = 0.000035$$

A proportion of 0.000035 of the other women were diagnosed with AIDS in 1994. To translate that to percentage, you multiply by 100, finding that 0.0035% of the other women were diagnosed with AIDS. To translate that figure to a number per 100,000, you multiply 0.000035 by 100,000 and find that 3.5 other women per 100,000 were diagnosed with AIDS in 1994.

Proportion × Population = Raw Count
0.76 × 138.6 million = 101 million

Raw Count ÷ Population = Proportion
3,520 ÷ 101,000,000 = 0.000035
= 35 per 100,000

A proportion of 3.5 per 100,000 is a lot lower than 33 per 100,000. In 1994, AIDS infections were almost 10 times more common among African American and Hispanic women than among other women.

When you read statistics in the newspaper, you often need to transform between raw counts and proportions in order to understand what you read.

Proportions and Raw Counts Change How Things Appear

Proportions look very different from raw numbers, because a proportion is the number in a small group divided by the total number in the big group. In the case of women with AIDS, African American and Hispanic women are a smaller group. When you divide by a smaller number, you get a larger result. (For example, one-half is bigger than one-third.) When you calculated the proportion with AIDS by dividing by the 32 million African American and Hispanic women, you got a much larger number than when you divided by the 101 million other women.

As you calculated proportions and raw counts, did you notice that proportions make things look smaller, and raw counts make them look larger? There were 3,520 AIDS diagnoses among the other women. A number like "3,520 people diagnosed with AIDS" clearly means there are a lot of infected people. When you turned that into a proportion, it became "0.0035%," less than 1/100 of a percent. A proportion like 0.0035% doesn't seem like such a big thing.

This kind of change of appearances is used all the time. With a big group, like 101 million women, raw counts make the numbers look big and important, and percentages make them look small and trivial. You can see this in the heart disease and gunshot statistics too. "There were 144.3 heart disease deaths per 100,000" doesn't seem as frightening as "375,000 people died of heart disease," even though they mean the same thing. And "38,317 gunshot deaths" sounds a lot worse than "0.01% died of gunshots."

The effect of switching between raw counts and proportions is reversed for small groups. Proportions make whatever is happening in small groups look big. Imagine a group of five doctors. That's a small group. Saying "80% of doctors surveyed recommend Zipporac" sounds a lot more impressive than "We surveyed five doctors, and four recommended Zipporac."

What makes a group small or large? It depends on how the proportion is represented. For percentage, 100 is probably the cutoff. The proportion "25%" seems bigger than "20 out of 80 people," but "30 out of 120 people" seems bigger than "25%." For "per 100,000," 100,000 is the cutoff. If a group has fewer than 100,000, then proportions per 100,000 seem larger than raw counts. If a group has more than 100,000, then raw counts seem larger. For example, "50 per 100,000" seems bigger than "40 out of 80,000 people." But "50 per 100,000" seems less than "60 out of 120,000 people," even though these are all the same proportion.

> ### Switching Between Proportions and Raw Counts Can Make Numbers Look Bigger or Smaller
>
> For large groups, proportions make numbers look smaller, and raw counts make them look larger. For example, saying "there are 38 million African Americans" makes the number seem larger than "13% of the population are African Americans." For small groups, the effect is reversed. For example, "75% of the surveyed students liked the cafeteria food" sounds like a bigger number than "three of the four students we surveyed."

When you see that a journalist has chosen to report a proportion or a raw count, think about how the journalist's choice is designed to affect readers' perceptions. For example, in the quote about AIDS diagnoses earlier, the writer chose to write, "AIDS was diagnosed in 14,081 adult women." The writer could have written, "AIDS was diagnosed in 0.01% (1/100 of a percent) of adult women." Reporting the percentage makes the AIDS diagnoses look less important. That author was probably aiming to startle the reader with the number of AIDS diagnoses.

Relative Merits of Proportions and Raw Counts

Which are better, raw counts or proportions? If you are responsible for providing hospital beds for African American and Hispanic women with AIDS, you need to know how many there actually are—you need the raw count. If you are studying how AIDS is moving through our society, you want the proportions. Proportions tell you the nature of things. Raw counts give you the size. Both proportions and raw counts are valuable. Ideally, a report would provide both, as in this example:

> *Approximately 50 million Americans—19 percent of the population— live below the national poverty line.*
>
> —*The Nation, 1997*

In this case, the writer put the proportion between dashes. Sometimes the second form appears in parentheses, as in this rewording: "Approximately 50 million Americans (19%) live below the national poverty line." That quote could also be reworded like this: "Among Americans, approximately 19% (50 million) live below the national poverty line."

All three of these wordings provide the raw count and the proportion clearly. That's good. Providing both the raw count and the proportion lets the reader know what is going on without having to pull out a calculator.

Pie Charts, Bar Charts, and Pictorial Bar Charts

Reporters can do even more when reporting proportions and raw counts. They can also draw pictures. For proportions and raw counts, there are two kinds of pictures, or graphs—pie charts and bar charts.

You have probably seen pie charts. They show circles cut into wedges shaped like pie slices. The size of each slice shows the proportion of the big group that falls into that slice's subgroup. Figure 1.1.1 is a pie chart illustrating a report from the *St. Louis Dispatch* that 19% of Americans live in poverty (June 15, 1997).

Figure 1.1.1* **Pie Chart of American Household Incomes**

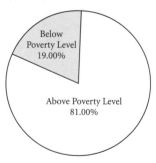

---

*Each graphic in this text that is part of the explanation is called a figure. To make it easier to distinguish between them, the figures have this complicated numbering system. This is the first figure in Section 1.1 and is called Figure 1.1.1. The second figure in Section 1.1 is Figure 1.1.2. The second section of Chapter 7 is Section 7.2, and the fourth figure in Section 7.2 is Figure 7.2.4. It may seem a little goofy, but if you are shouting a question to a professor from the back of a 200-seat auditorium, you'll appreciate being able to explain that you're asking about Figure 4.3.8 and having the professor know what you're talking about.

"Poverty" usually applies to those earning below the federal government's poverty line, which in 1994 was $15,141 for a family of four. To show the proportion living in and out of poverty in a pie chart, you draw a circle for the pie and draw lines to show two slices. For a pie chart of the proportion in poverty, one slice is 19% of the pie. The other slice is the rest: 81% of the pie. For the pie chart to mean anything, you have to indicate what each slice stands for.

A pie chart can show more than two proportions. You can divide the chart into more income groups.

> *The [U.S. Census Bureau] says only one-fifth of all American households [20 million households] earn more than $62,841 a year, and only 5 percent earn more than $109,821. The median household income, meanwhile, remains around $32,000.*
>
> —AUSTIN, *CHATTANOOGA TIMES*, NOVEMBER 7, 1995

The median is what 50% of American households earn less than, so, in 1995, 50% of American households earned less than $32,000, and 50% earned more.

In the above quote, Austin rounds numbers inconsistently. That quote reports that the median is "around $32,000," which is rounding to the nearest thousand, but the other numbers are rounded to the nearest dollar ($62,841 and $109,821). The Census Bureau doesn't know to the dollar what the real amounts are. It is better to say that one-fifth of households earn more than $63,000 and that 5% earn more than $110,000.

To make a pie chart for this report, as shown in Figure 1.1.2, you would need to draw a slice for households that earn less than $32,000, a slice for households earning from $32,000 to $63,000, a slice for households earning from $63,000 to $110,000, and a slice for those earning $110,000 or more.

Figure 1.1.2   **Pie Chart of American Household Incomes**

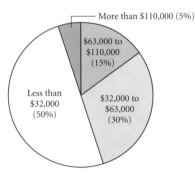

What proportion earned from $32,000 to $63,000? The answer is that 20% earned more than $63,000, and 80% earned less. Since 50% earned less than $32,000, the other 30% earned from $32,000 to $63,000. The same kind of thinking will show you that 15% earned from $63,000 to $110,000.

For the last 20 years, there have been about 100 million households in the United States. That makes it easy to figure out the raw counts for these proportions: 5% of the households is 5 million households. That means 5 million households earned more than $110,000 and 50 million households earned less than $32,000.

Pie Chart

A pie chart uses a diagram of a pie to show proportions. Each slice's area is the proportion of the pie that matches the proportion that slice represents. For example, the pie chart below represents the 13% of Americans who are African Americans. (The Census Bureau's Web site reports that 13% of Americans are African Americans.) The area of the slice is 13% of the area of the pie.

Bar Charts

There is another way to draw a picture of proportions. If you read *USA Today*, you have probably noticed that it puts a graph about the United States on the lower-left corner of every front page. Most of the time, that graph is what is called a "pictorial bar chart." A bar chart uses bars to indicate how many people or things fall in each group. For example, Figure 1.1.3 is a bar chart for the household income report.

To find out how many people fall in each bar, you look at how tall the bar is and compare it to the scale on the side. For example, the top of the tallest bar is

Figure 1.1.3 **Bar Chart of American Household Incomes**

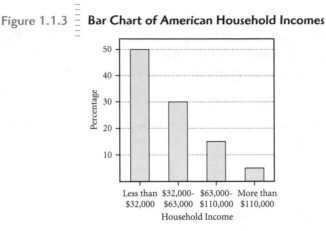

level with 50%. That means 50% of the households fall in that bar. To find out the bar's income, you look at the scale on the bottom. In 1995, 50% of the households earned less than $32,000.

Charts Need All Their Labels

Usually, when a chart maker leaves off labels, you should just ignore the chart altogether, because either the chart is incomprehensible or there is too much risk that the chart maker is misleading you. Consider Figure 1.1.4, a chart of the 80% of American households that earned less than $63,000.

Figure 1.1.4 **Bar Chart of American Household Incomes Less Than $63,000**

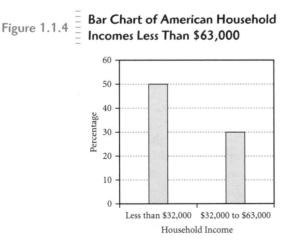

Figure 1.1.5

Bar Chart of American Household Incomes Less Than $63,000

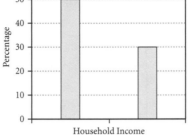

Now consider what happens if you leave off the labels on the *x*-axis (the horizontal bottom of the chart), as shown in Figure 1.1.5. This chart means nothing. Now look at Figure 1.1.6 to see what you can do by leaving off the labels on the *y*-axis (the vertical side of the chart). Suddenly the less-than-$32,000 bar seems so much taller than the other bar. What's the trick? To see, consider Figure 1.1.7, which has the *y*-axis labeled.

Now you can see how the trick is done. I changed the scale of the *y*-axis to start at 25%. The earlier charts started at 0%. Look back at Figure 1.1.6. When I don't label the *y*-axis, there's no way to know that I've made the switch. Beware charts that have unlabeled *y*-axes. When you make charts, be sure to label both axes. If someone shows you a chart with an unlabeled axis, you may need to ignore it.

Figure 1.1.6

Sneaky Bar Chart of American Household Incomes Less Than $63,000

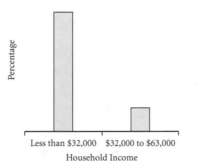

Figure 1.1.7 **Bar Chart of American Household Incomes Less Than $63,000**

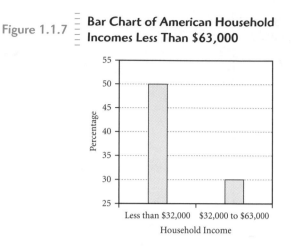

Bar Charts

A bar chart shows proportions or counts by the height of bars. For example, the following bar chart shows that, in 2000, 74% of Americans were 18 years old or older and 26% were 17 years old or younger.

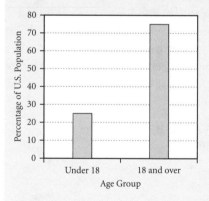

Both the *x*-axis and *y*-axis of a bar chart must be labeled.

Pictorial Bar Charts

USA Today replaces these boring-looking bars with pictures. That's why the graphs it shows are called "pictorial" bar charts. Figure 1.1.8 shows our bar chart with pictures.

Figure 1.1.8   **Pictorial Bar Chart of American Household Incomes**

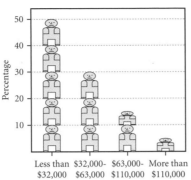

Pictorial Bar Charts

Pictorial bar charts replace the bars with graphics. Every graphic bar should be the same width.

Pictorial bar charts are usually pretty honest, as long as the pictures are all the same width. But pictorial bar charts provide an enormous opportunity to misrepresent what's going on. The trick is, rather than just stretching or shrinking the picture up and down, the graphic artist can magnify it up and down and also expand it side to side. A picture that is twice as tall becomes twice as wide, but when it's stretched in both directions, it has a total area that is four times larger.

Let's say you wanted to redo that last graph for the *Voice of Communist Propaganda*. For that paper, you'd want to make the poorer people really stand out as the great mass of exploited Americans. Figure 1.1.9 shows how it would look.

This figure gives a very different impression. It makes it look like almost nobody earns more than $110,000, and even people earning more than $63,000 don't seem

Figure 1.1.9   **Misleading Pictorial Bar Chart of American Household Incomes with Mixed Picture Widths**

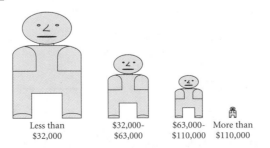

very impressive. The capitalist pigs are keeping all the wealth to themselves. The trick is that the bar for the 50% is almost twice as wide as the other bars and almost twice as tall. Altogether, the 50% looks almost four times larger than the 30%.

Of course, you would never do that yourself. You would always make sure your pictures were equally wide. But if you're looking at someone else's graph, you'll want to take a moment to check whether or not that person is trying to fool you with the widths.

Rounding

At the beginning of this section, you figured out that there were 375,180 American heart disease deaths in 1992. Later in the section, I referred to that as "375,000" deaths. I referred to it as "375,000" because 375,180 can be rounded to 375,000. Throughout this book, you will be rounding numbers.

In rounding, you simplify a number you are working with by substituting a number that has fewer non-zero decimal places that is close to the number you started with (given how many non-zero decimal places you are using). The number 18.4 can be rounded to 18, as can 18.499999. The number 18.6 rounds to 19, as does 18.500001. To give you the idea, Table 1.1.1 shows several numbers and what they could be rounded to.

Table 1.1.1*   Numbers and Rounded Replacements

ORIGINAL NUMBER	POSSIBLE ROUNDED REPLACEMENT
12	10 (rounded to 10's)
14.6	10
15.26	20
1.48	1 (rounded to 1's)
1.56	2
1.5000001	2
1.4999999	1
0.03500001	0.04 (rounded to two decimal places)
0.0349999	0.03
−0.0350001	−0.04
−0.03499999	−0.03

---

*In this text, the tables are numbered the same way the figures are. Table 1.1.1 is the first table in the first section of Chapter 1. Table 8.2.4 is the fourth table in Section 2 of Chapter 8, and so on.

Every once in a while, when rounding, you are faced with a number that is equally far from two possible alternatives. For example, 18.5 is as close to 18 as it is to 19. There are different ways of handling such numbers. Some people suggest keeping a sheet of paper in your pocket and alternating rounding up and down throughout your life. Others suggest flipping a coin. I usually round against the point I'm trying to make. That way, if I succeed in making the point, I know I made it despite my rounding.

Rounding

Replace the number with the closest value on the number line that has the desired number of decimal places. For example, 3.2451 could round to 3.245; 14.4999 could round to 14; and 115.000001 could round to 120.

Ideally, you do not round numbers while you are calculating and round only the final result of your calculations.

I have been often asked how many digits is the right number to which to round. For example, should one say that 64.47 is 64, or 64.5, or 60, or 100? The answer is that you should not report more digits than you know. For example, if all I know is that the population of the United States is somewhere between 283 million and 280 million, I would be making up a figure if I reported that there are 281,434,132 Americans.

Scientific Notation

What proportion of the U.S. population are you by yourself? In 2001, there were about 285 million Americans. As you read this, there are probably about 290 million. To find your personal proportion, you would divide 1 by 290 million. If you type in "290000000" for "290 million," your calculator may say that your proportion is "3.4483e–9" or "3.4483E–9" or even "3.4483–09." That does not mean that you are 3.4% of the U.S. population. On the far right of those readouts, it says "E–9" or "–09." That means that those readouts are in scientific notation. The negative 9 means that, to translate to regular decimal, you would need to move the decimal place to the left nine places. You are 0.0000000034 of the U.S. population. That is 0.000003% of the population, or 0.003 per 100,000 Americans. Table 1.1.2 shows a few more proportions so you can see how scientific notation works in these cases.

Table 1.1.2   Some Proportions of the U.S. Population in Scientific Notation and Percentage

GROUP AND RAW COUNT	CALCULATOR READOUT	PROPORTION AND PERCENTAGE
There are 148 million females in the United States.	5.103E–1	0.51 = 51% of the population
17 million Americans are employed by the government.	5.862E–2	0.06 = 6% of the population
One million Americans have Japanese ancestry.	3.448E–3	0.0034 = 0.34% of the population
175,000 Americans serve in the Marine Corps.	6.034E–4	0.0006 = 0.06% of the population
10,000 Americans are male and more than 100 years old.	3.488E–5	0.000034 = 0.0034% of the population (3.4 per 100,000)

Algebra and Greek Symbols

A trick of mathematics is to use abbreviations (symbols) for concepts. This allows the mathematician to write math in a shorthand that takes less space and is quicker to write. If you proceed to study more statistics after you finish with this book, you will find that other texts use the shorthand symbols of mathematics. To prepare you for these other texts, each section of this book includes an "Algebra and Greek Symbols" subsection to show you the shorthand.

In this section, the mathematical content involved the number of people in a full set (such as Americans), the raw count of people in a subgroup, and the proportion in the subgroup. There is a little flexibility, but the most established symbols for these ideas are as follows:

CONCEPT	SYMBOL
The number in the full group	n
The raw count in the subgroup	c
The proportion in the subgroup	p (e.g., p could be 0.3 or 52%)

Here are the relationships we used and how they would be expressed in the shorthand of math:

$$\text{Proportion of Full Group in Subgroup} = \frac{\text{Raw Count in Subgroup}}{\text{Raw Count in Full Group}}$$

In the shorthand of symbols, that is this:

$$p = \frac{c}{n}$$

Here's another:

Raw Count in Subgroup = Proportion in Subgroup $\times$ Raw Count in Full Group

In the shorthand of symbols, that is this:

$$c = pn$$

In the equation $c = pn$, there is no times symbol between the p and the n. That is because, in algebra, when two things are written immediately next to each other, that means they are multiplied by one another. For example, "$2a$" means "2 times a," and "pn" means "p times n."

Here's another:

$$\text{Raw Count in Full Group} = \frac{\text{Raw Count in Subgroup}}{\text{Proportion of Full Group in Subgroup}}$$

which is the same as this:

$$n = \frac{c}{p}$$

Summary

To calculate what proportion of a large group falls in a subgroup, divide the number in the subgroup by the number in the large group:

$$\text{Proportion of Full Group in Subgroup} = \frac{\text{Raw Count in Subgroup}}{\text{Raw Count in Full Group}}$$

To find the raw count in a subgroup, multiply the proportion in the subgroup by the number in the full group:

Raw Count in Subgroup = Proportion in Subgroup $\times$ Raw Count in Full Group

To find the number in the full group, you can divide the number in the subgroup by the proportion of the full group in the subgroup:

$$\text{Raw Count in Full Group} = \frac{\text{Raw Count in Subgroup}}{\text{Proportion of Full Group in Subgroup}}$$

Before you can multiply by a proportion, you need to transform the proportion into a decimal form. To translate a proportion into decimal form, you divide by whatever the proportion is per. "Percent" is Latin for "per 100," so you transform percentage to decimals by dividing by 100. Proportions per 100,000 are transformed by dividing by 100,000.

Raw counts make subgroups of large populations look larger. Proportions make them look smaller. For subgroups of small groups, proportions can make the subgroup look larger. Ideally, a report would include both the raw count and the proportion.

Pie charts represent proportions by drawings of circles with wedges shaped like pie slices. Each slice's proportion of the full pie represents the proportion that the slice stands for.

Bar charts represent proportions or counts by the height of their bars. Charts must have both axes labeled. Pictorial bar charts are bar charts in which the bars have been replaced with drawings. Ideally, a pictorial bar chart will change only the height of the bars, not the widths, because increasing the widths along with the heights produces misleading increases in area.

Avoiding Common Misunderstandings

The proportion 17% is 0.17; 83.96% is 0.8396; 10% is 0.1. Before you can use a percentage on your calculator, you need to translate it to a decimal. To translate to a decimal, move the decimal point two spaces to the left: 34% becomes 0.34; 93.654% becomes 0.93654.

Try it out. On a calculator, find 24% of 324. If you got 77.76, you've got it. If your calculator tells you 24% of 324 is 7,776, then you're not translating to decimal.

Computer Project

The computer provides some excellent opportunities for learning about statistics. Throughout this text, I will provide you with computer projects that will deepen your understanding. The *Data Matters* Resource Center at *www.keycollege.com/dm* provides specific details for doing the computer projects in several computer packages. You may be able to do these projects without instructions for your specific software.

As you enter data into a computer program, there are some rules you need to follow. Before you can understand the rules, there is some language you must know. Each person who is studied is called a "case," an "observation," or a "subject." If a study looks at sprockets, then each sprocket would be called a "case" or an "observation." A case is a single studied person or object.

Each aspect of the cases that is measured is called a "measure," an "attribute," a "characteristic," or a "variable." "Variable" is actually the most commonly used term. A measurement is called a "variable" because it varies from one case to another.

These are the rules for data entry:

- Each case gets its own row.
- Each variable gets its own column.

For example, this project requires entering data on the last three U.S. presidents. The variables are the presidents' names, political parties, and genders. As I write this, the cases are George Bush, Bill Clinton, and George W. Bush. If I entered these into a computer program, my entered data would look something like this:

NAME	POLITICAL PARTY	GENDER
George Bush	Republican	Male
Bill Clinton	Democrat	Male
George W. Bush	Republican	Male

Each column's variable is identified at the top. The first column is for the name variable. The second column's variable is political party. The first data row's case is George Bush. The second data row's case is Bill Clinton.

For this project, follow these four steps:

1. Open the program you are using.

2. Enter data for the last three U.S. presidents: their names, political parties, and genders.

3. Get your software to calculate the proportions of those three presidents who had each name, the proportions who were in each political party, and the proportion of each gender. Check that the steps you used produced valid answers.

4. Get your software to create a bar chart showing the proportions found in the last step. Check that the steps you used produced valid bar charts.

Exercises

Try rewriting the reports in Exercises 1 through 4 so that they report both raw counts and proportions. This will require translating between raw counts and proportions. In the 1990s, there were about 268 million Americans. It will work fine to use that figure for the total population for these quotes.

1. Rewrite this quote to include the proportion and the raw count.

   41 million Americans have no health insurance.

   —*USA Today*, May 1, 1997

2. Rewrite this quote.

   A Clinton administration task force estimated that 7 million Americans were homeless at some time during the second half of the 1980s.

   —Associated Press, *Los Angeles Times*, November 11, 1996

3. Rewrite this quote.

   Anywhere from 700,000 to 3 million Americans are homeless, according to National Interfaith Hospitality Networks.

   —Cashnelli, *Cincinnati Enquirer*, November 6, 1995

4. Rewrite the following quote. Note that the "mortality rate" in this quote is per living people. For example, the statistic for heart disease, "144.3 per 100,000," is 144.3 per 100,000 Americans. In 1992, there were about 268 million Americans.

   The 10 leading U.S. causes of death and their 1992 mortality rate per 100,000 people: heart disease, 144.3; cancer, 133.1; accidents, 29.4; strokes, 26.2; lung disease, 19.9; pneumonia and influenza; 12.7; diabetes, 11.9; AIDS, 12.6; suicide, 11.1; homicide, 10.5.

   —*Rocky Mountain News*, December 16, 1994

5. Sketch a pie chart to show what proportion of 1992 American deaths were caused by AIDS, suicide, and homicide. (Have a slice for the AIDS deaths, a slice for suicide, a slice for homicide, and one slice for the rest of the deaths.) Because the pie chart shows proportions of deaths, you will need to know that there were about 2,230,000 deaths in the United States in 1992.

6. Sketch a pie chart to show what proportion of 1992 American deaths were caused by heart disease and cancer. (Have a slice for the heart disease deaths, a slice for cancer, and one slice for the rest of the deaths.)

7. Sketch an honest pictorial bar chart showing the proportion of deaths caused by each of the top five causes of death.

8. Resketch that last bar chart to make one that could persuade Congress to appropriate more money to research heart disease and cancer.

9. Here is a report of what the U.S. Census Bureau has found about home ownership in the general and African American populations.

   The U.S. Census Bureau tells us that the rate of homeownership for all Americans is 67 percent. But among African Americans it is only 47 percent.
   —SINGLETARY, *WASHINGTON POST*, OCTOBER 14, 2001

   a. Why would you guess Singletary reports proportions rather than raw counts in this quote?

   b. There are about 100 million households in the United States. About 13% are African Americans. What are the raw counts for home ownership among all Americans and among African Americans?

10. Here is a report on the number of Americans and the number of female Americans.

    There were 138.1 million men in 2000 . . . according to the Census Bureau. . . . Women numbered 143.7 million.
    —ASSOCIATED PRESS, *LOS ANGELES TIMES*, SEPTEMBER 10, 2001

    a. Why do you think the Associated Press writer chose to report raw counts?

    b. What proportion of Americans were women in 2000?

11. Here is a report on the number of Americans who are 100 years old or older.

    [Mrs.] Chorover is one of 50,454 Americans age 100 or older . . . according to a 2000 Census report released last week.
    —TASKER, *MIAMI HERALD*, OCTOBER 7, 2001

    a. Why do you think Tasker chose to report the raw count of Americans over 100 in the above quote?

    b. What proportion of Americans were over 100 in 2000? (You might need to refer back to the numbers in Exercise 10 to do this exercise.)

12. Here is a report of the number of unemployed people collecting benefits.

    The total number of unemployed collecting benefits rose to an 18-year-high of 3.65 million people.
    —CRUTSINGER, ASSOCIATED PRESS, OCTOBER 25, 2001

    a. Why do you think Crutsinger chose to report a raw count in the above quote?

    b. In 2001, there were about 285 million Americans. What proportion were collecting unemployment? (Note that this is not the unemployment rate. We will get to that later.)

13. Here is a chart that appeared on the side of a box of tea I bought recently:

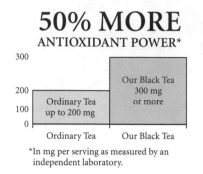

50% MORE
ANTIOXIDANT POWER*

*In mg per serving as measured by an
independent laboratory.

The *y*-axis isn't labeled, but the meaning of the bar heights is indicated by text inside the bars. The bar on the left means "200 milligrams." The bar on the right means "300 milligrams." The chart is extraordinarily misleading. What is very wrong with this chart?

Answers to Odd-Numbered Exercises

1. 41 million Americans, 15% of the population, have no health insurance.

3. Anywhere from 700,000 to 3 million Americans are homeless, according to National Interfaith Hospitality Networks. That is somewhere between 3/10 of a percent and 1% of the population.

5.

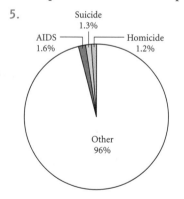

7.

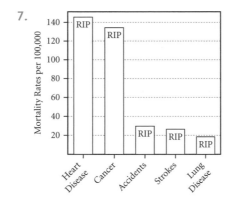

9. a. Singletary wants to compare the nature of home ownership in the two groups. Because the two groups are differently sized, comparing the raw counts would not reveal the nature of the groups. (Singletary might be avoiding the raw counts, because they would make African American home ownership look huge.)

b. 67% of 100 million is 67 million American households that own their own homes. First calculate the total number of African American households and then the number of these that represent homeowners.

Raw Count in Subgroup = Proportion in Subgroup × Number in Full Group

Raw Count in Subgroup = 0.13 × 100,000,000 = 13,000,000

There are 13 million African American households.

Raw Count in Subgroup = 0.47 × 13,000,000 = 6,100,000

In 2000, there were about 6 million African American households that owned their own home.

11. a. It looks as though Tasker wanted to make the number of Americans over 100 years old look big.

b. About 2/100 of a percent were over 100.

$$\text{Proportion in Subgroup} = \frac{\text{Number in Subgroup}}{\text{Number in Population}}$$

$$\text{Proportion in Subgroup} = \frac{50,454}{281,800,000} = 0.000179 \text{, which rounds to } 0.02\%$$

13. The chart maker did not use a number line for the y-axis. The distance from 300 to 200 is twice the distance from 200 to 100. The result is that the bar on the right is twice the size of the bar on the left, greatly exaggerating the difference between the bars.

1.2 How Many People Are There?

- U.S. and World Populations
- Population Growth
- Proportional Changes
- The Unemployment Rate
- X-Y Plots

> *As long as there's access to a television set—as there will be for 800 million people worldwide—all will have a common bond for three hours Sunday when Super Bowl XXXI kicks off.*
> —MARTIN, *CHATTANOOGA FREE PRESS*, JANUARY 26, 1997

> *The Super Bowl is the most watched one-off sports event in the world. Over 750 million people watched it globally.*
> —[LONDON] *DAILY TELEGRAPH*, FEBRUARY 3, 1997

SEVEN HUNDRED FIFTY MILLION. That's a lot. Does everyone in the entire world watch the Super Bowl? Can you tell? Not unless you know how many people there are in the world. There are currently about six billion people. About 12% watch the Super Bowl.

How about access to television? Television is very big in the United States, and I'm sure whoever came up with that "800 million" felt that every American had "access to a television set." But how big is television worldwide? 800 million divided by 6 billion is about 13%. Most people, 87%, do not watch television. In terms of people worldwide, television is not a big phenomenon. It doesn't hold a candle to amusements like drinking and telling jokes.

In Section 1.1, you saw that it helps to know how many Americans there are. A lot of reports do not give proportions as well as raw counts. It's up to you to be able to translate back and forth between raw counts and proportions.

You need to know some of the other populations that appear in the news a lot. The Census Bureau estimates that there were about 285 million Americans in 2001. The U.S. population has been rising by about 3 million people a year, so 285 million will be close to accurate for a few years. If you remember that, and you read that 12% of Americans are African Americans, you can multiply the 12% by 285 million to figure out that there are about 34 million African Americans. (That is about the number of people who live in California.)

Table 1.2.1   Some Populations

PLACE	YEAR	POPULATION
World	2001	6.1 billion
China	2001	1.3 billion
India	2001	1 billion
United States	2001	285 million
California	2000	34 million
New York City metropolitan area	1999	20 million

Note: World and country populations are from the CIA online World Factbook 2001; state and metropolitan populations are from the Census Bureau's Web site, *www.census.gov.*

Table 1.2.1 lists a variety of populations that are worth learning. It shows the populations of the two largest countries in the world, China and India, which each have about one billion people. There are about six billion people in the world. More than a third of the people in the world now live in either China or India. Contrast that with the United States, which has about 4% of the world's population.

Populations change. The United States was estimated to have 258 million people in 1993. By 2001, it was estimated to include more than 285 million. Because populations change, Table 1.2.1 lists the year of each population.

It is worthwhile to memorize a few populations. That way, when you read that 10% of Californians are of Asian descent, you can recognize that that is more than three million people. Compare that to the half million people who live in Wyoming. There are six times as many Asian American Californians as there are Wyomingites of any ethnicity, even though Asian Americans are considered a minority. Three million is a lot of people. If you want to talk about minorities, maybe we should discuss those Wyomingites.

Population estimates are imprecise. They do not have 100% accuracy. Not only does the population change all the time (with births, deaths, and migrations), but also errors creep into any effort to find out the population. There are measurement errors: mistakes in counting people and recording the counts. There are errors in calculation. There are specification errors: mistakes in specifying who should be counted. (For example, do you count people who have homes in the United States but spend most of each week in Canada?)

Because population estimates are estimates, what is really important about populations is the general nature of the numbers. You will do fine to learn the population numbers after rounding them, to think of China and India as each having about one billion people, and the world as having six billion. This is not only simpler but also more honest. You do not know the exact current populations of these places. No one does.

Cities have two kinds of populations. One population is the people who live in the urban area of the city. To find where this population lives, you drive around the city until you bump into farms or wilderness. That is a city. Such a population is the population of the metropolitan area.

Because metropolitan areas grow far beyond the bounds of the original city limits, populations of metropolitan areas are much greater than populations within city limits. For example, 20 million people live in the grid of streets that spreads over Manhattan and around the mouth of the Hudson, but only half of those people actually live in the five boroughs of New York City and pay New York City taxes. Many don't even live in New York State: They live in New Jersey and Connecticut. That's why the New York metropolitan area includes 20 million people, whereas New York State includes only 19 million. On the other side of the country, 16 million people live in the urban sprawl called "L.A.," but only 3.5 million live in a city called "Los Angeles." The rest live in cities like Santa Monica, Culver City, and Beverly Hills.

Unless you know the populations, people can mislead you by using raw counts when comparing one country to another. For example, there are about 300 million Chinese and about 270 million Indians who live in cities and towns, but only about 210 million Americans who live in urban centers. Are China and India more urban than America? Only if you think that having 30% of your population in urban centers (as do China and India) is more urban than having 75% living in cities and towns (as is the case in the United States). Remember that both China and India have about 1 billion people, whereas tiny America has only 285 million. Raw counts in China and India are usually going to swamp raw counts in the United States.

Proportions can also be misleading, if you don't know the population sizes. 2.3% of the folks who live in Wyoming are Native Americans. In contrast, 1% of Californians are Native Americans. Wyoming seems to be a greater center of Native American culture than California. But are there more Native Americans in Wyoming than in California? No. There are 340,000 Native Americans in California and about 11,000 in Wyoming. There are about 30 times as many Native Americans in California as there are in Wyoming.

Whenever people talk about huge places like New York, California, or China, you have to remember that those places have huge populations. In 1996, about 0.5% of New Yorkers were homeless (*Newsday*, March 28, 1996). Does that mean that homelessness was not a big problem in New York? Well, remember that we are talking about 20 million New Yorkers—one half a percent of 20 million is 100,000 people. That's a lot.

Population Growth and the Unemployment Rate

In some ways, the American economy boomed in the late 1990s. Here's one way:

A burst of hiring . . . helped drive down the unemployment rate to 4.8%, the lowest level in more than 23 years. . . . There were 129.6 million Americans working last month and 6.5 million unemployed.

—ROSENBLATT, *LOS ANGELES TIMES*, JUNE 7, 1997

In 1973, the unemployment rate was 4.9%. By 1974, the unemployment rate had risen to 5.6%, and it stayed above 4.9% until 1997. In 1997, the unemployment rate was down again to 4.8%.

Does that mean that there were fewer unemployed people in 1997 than in 1974? No. There were more unemployed in 1997—more unemployed Americans than there had ever been before. There were more unemployed people in 1997 than in 1974, even though the unemployment rate was lower in 1997. To see why, you need to understand what the unemployment rate is and to see how it depends on the shifting size of the population.

The unemployment rate gives some idea about how hard it is to find a job and how easy it is to find someone to fill a job. As the unemployment rate goes up, on the average, Americans have a harder time finding work, because there are more people competing for jobs. High unemployment can make life easier for employers: When they advertise a job, more people answer their ads.

The unemployment rate is a proportion. To calculate the unemployment rate, a federal agency, the Bureau of Labor Statistics, estimates the size of the labor force. The labor force is made up of the people who work at paying jobs and the people who are looking for paying jobs. The labor force does not include people working without pay, such as full-time parents or students, no matter how hard they labor. The unemployment rate is the number of people looking for jobs divided by the number in the total labor force.

The Unemployment Rate

The unemployment rate is the number of people without paying jobs who are looking for paying jobs divided by the number in the labor force. The labor force is the number of people working at, or looking for, paying jobs.

In 1997, 129.6 million Americans had jobs, and 6.5 million were looking for jobs. Add the two groups together, and you get the 1997 labor force: 136.1 million people. Of those 136.1 million, 6.5 million were looking for work, which is about 4.8% of 136.1 million. That's what the Bureau of Labor Statistics meant by an unemployment rate of 4.8%.

In contrast, in 1974, the labor force was about 92 million people. The 1974 unemployment rate of 5.6% meant that 5.6% of the 92 million were looking for work. That's about 5 million job seekers, 1.5 million fewer people looking for work than in 1997.

What's going on here? A big part of what is happening is that the United States grows, and the labor force grows along with it. In 1974, there were 214 million Americans. By 1997, there were 268 million. As the total population grew, the number of people in the labor force grew. This is why, even though the unemployment rate dropped, the total number of unemployed people rose between 1974 and 1997.

Table 1.2.2   U.S. Population

YEAR	POPULATION (MILLIONS)	YEAR	POPULATION (MILLIONS)
1790	4	1920	106
1800	5	1930	123
1810	7	1940	132
1820	10	1950	151
1830	13	1960	179
1840	17	1970	203
1850	23	1975	216
1860	31	1980	227
1870	40	1985	238
1880	50	1990	249
1890	63	1995	263
1900	76	2000	281
1910	92	2001	285

Source: U.S. Census Bureau.

Populations usually grow. The U.S. Census Bureau counts the population every 10 years, and has done so since 1790. Table 1.2.2 shows what the Census Bureau has found about U.S. population growth.

Table 1.2.2 shows a lot of numbers. A picture of those numbers would make it easier to see how the U.S. population has changed. When you want to show how two sets of numbers are related, you can graph them. To do this, you draw two number lines—a horizontal x-axis and a vertical y-axis. Each pair of numbers is represented as a dot on the graph. In this case, there is one dot for each year and its population. The dot's location indicates its two values: Its height represents the dot's value on the y-axis, and the dot's position from side to side represents the dot's value on the x-axis. Figure 1.2.1 shows an X-Y plot of the U.S. population.

The leftmost dot in Figure 1.2.1 is the population for 1790. We can tell it's 1790, because it is above 1790 on the x-axis. There were four million Americans in 1790, so that dot is horizontally aligned with 4 on the y-axis.

The dots get closer together at the upper right. That's because Table 1.2.1 gives populations every five years after 1970. The x-axis is a number line, and numbers that are closer together fall closer together on number lines. When you draw or sketch an X-Y plot, make sure you use number lines and remember that number lines represent differences between numbers by distance, so "10" has to be 10 times as far from 0 as "1" is.

Figure 1.2.1 **U.S. Population Growth (1790–1997)**

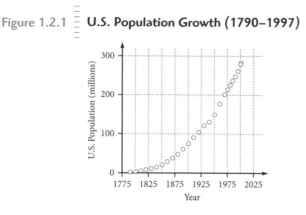

X-Y Plots

An X-Y plot has two number lines: the *x*-axis and the *y*-axis. The value on the *y*-axis that an observation's dot aligns with horizontally is the observation's Y value. The value on the *x*-axis that the dot aligns with vertically is the observation's X value.

For example, the following X-Y plot shows the world population in 1650 (one-half billion), 1800 (one billion), and 1997 (six billion).

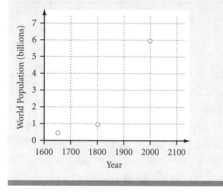

This kind of an X-Y plot is called a "time-series plot," because it represents time on its *x*-axis. In a time-series plot, the dots are usually connected with a line. The line highlights the shape of the changes over time, as you can see in Figure 1.2.2.

Other than the line connecting the dots, a time-series plot is no different from a regular X-Y plot. Each dot still represents one pair of numbers by the dot's location relative to the *x*-axis and the dot's location relative to the *y*-axis.

Time-Series Plot

A time-series plot is an X-Y plot in which the *x*-axis represents time.

Figure 1.2.2  **A Time-Series Plot of U.S. Population Growth**

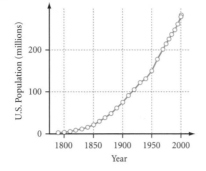

Proportional Change

When thinking about population changes, it's helpful to see how much they change. You might look at the raw counts of the changes, but that can be a little misleading. If you are with a friend, and a third person joins you, it's a big change in the group. By comparison, if one more person joins the 285 million Americans, that's not as noticeable. In both cases, in terms of raw counts, it's an addition of one more person, but the raw counts do not reflect the nature of the change.

To see the nature of the change, you can look at how many people were added as a proportion of the size of the group before the addition. If you divided the number of new people by the original number in the group, you would be calculating what is called the "proportional change." Here is the equation for a proportional change:

$$\text{Proportional Change} = \frac{\text{Raw Change}}{\text{Initial Number}}$$

In terms of proportional changes, the increase from 2 people to 3 people is much larger than the increase from 285 million to 285 million and one. Here are the calculations to find those two proportional changes:

$$\text{Proportional Change} = \frac{\text{Raw Change}}{\text{Initial Number}}$$

Let's look at the jump from 2 to 3 first. That's a raw change of 1, and an initial number of 2.

$$\text{Proportional Change} = \frac{1}{2}$$

One-half is 50%, so the addition of one person to a couple is a 50% increase:

$$\text{Proportional Change} = 50\%$$

How about the addition of one person to 285 million?

$$\text{Proportional Change} = \frac{\text{Raw Change}}{\text{Initial Number}}$$

The raw change is 1; the initial number is 285 million:

$$\text{Proportional Change} = \frac{1}{285{,}000{,}000}$$

The number 1 divided by 285 million is 0.0000004%:

$$\text{Proportional Change} = 0.0000004\%$$

That seems right. The nature of the increase of one person is much smaller when it is to the whole country than when it is to two people. And that fits our impression of the consequences that a single birth has on the country compared to the consequences the birth has on the child's parents. The proportional change reveals the nature of the change.

Proportional changes help reveal how the United States has grown. Between 1790 and 1840, we added 13 million people. Between 1840 and 1890, we added 46 million. Between 1940 and 1990, we added 117 million. It looks as though we are getting larger faster and faster. In a way we are—117 million is more than 46 million, which is more than 13 million. But those are raw changes. The proportional changes show a different picture of what's going on.

To find the proportional change from 1790 to 1840, you divide the additional 13 million by the 1790 population of 4 million. It's a 325% increase.

To find the percentage change from 1840 to 1890, you divide the increase of 46 million by the 1840 population, 17 million. That's a 271% increase.

Table 1.2.3 U.S. Population Growth

YEAR	POPULATION (MILLIONS)	RAW CHANGE (MILLIONS)	PREVIOUS NUMBER (MILLIONS)	PROPORTIONAL CHANGE
1790	4			
1840	17	+ 13	4	3.25%
1890	63	+ 46	17	2.71%
1940	132	+ 69	63	1.1%
1990	249	+ 117	132	0.89%

From 1940 to 1990, there was an 89% increase (a 117-million increase divided by the 132 million people in 1940). In terms of proportional change, U.S. population growth has been slowing down, as shown by Table 1.2.3.

The changes in population pose questions about how we think about ourselves. To paraphrase singer/songwriter David Roth, if you are one in a million, there are 284 more like you in the United States. If you are one in a million, there are 6,100 like you worldwide. In 1776, if you were one in a million, there were two others like you in the United States.

"More . . . Than Ever Before"

You have to be wary of population growth. Whenever someone reports, "There are more than there have ever been before," look out. It may just be that there are more people. For example, there are more car accidents than there have ever been before. There are more people winning lotteries than ever before. And there are more belly buttons too.

Whenever you hear that raw counts have changed over the years, you need to keep in mind that the number of people is changing, and the reported change might not be interesting. It might even reflect that something is becoming less common: For example, as we saw, the number of unemployed was higher in 1997 than in 1974, even though the chances that a worker was unemployed had fallen.

"More . . . Than Ever Before"

If someone tells you that something occurs more than it has ever occurred before, it may be only because there are more people than ever before.

Raw Counts Exaggerate Changes

Sometimes, the image you get from the raw numbers is somewhat honest, in that something is actually increasing, but the raw numbers exaggerate the increase. You can see this in incarceration rates. In 1930, there were 127,000 inmates in U.S. state and federal prisons. By 1960, that number had nearly doubled to 213,000. By 1990, there were 740,000. Table 1.2.4 shows those raw incarceration counts.

In terms of raw counts, the inmate population nearly doubled between 1930 and 1960 and then increased three and a half times by 1990. The raw counts have certainly gone up, but what happened to the nature of America? Were a larger proportion in prison? To find out, we could divide the number in prison by the total population in each year. In 1930, 0.10% were in federal or state prisons. By 1960, that proportion had risen to 0.11%. There had been a 10% increase in the proportion. A 10% increase looks much smaller than the doubling we saw in the raw counts from 1930 to 1960. By 1990, the proportion in state and federal prisons had risen to 0.3%: The proportion in prison had nearly tripled.

Table 1.2.4 — Raw Incarceration Counts

YEAR	NUMBER IN PRISON
1930	127,000
1960	213,000
1990	740,000

Since 1960, it has become more and more likely that an American will be in prison. For the change from 1930 to 1960, raw counts did not entirely mislead, but they greatly overstated the increase. What looked like a near doubling was only a 10% rise. From 1960 to 1990, the raw count understated the increase. Between 1960 and 1990, the raw count did not even double, though the proportion of the population in prison tripled.

There are a variety of ways to report changes in the population honestly. One is to report the change in proportions as well as changes in raw counts. Another way, which is not quite as wordy, is to mention how the population has changed, as in the following quote.

> It [the U.S. military] is far larger—some six times the size of the 244,000-man active-duty military of 1933. (Over the same period the U.S. population has merely doubled in size.)
>
> —ATLANTIC MONTHLY, JULY 1997

The quote lets you see that the proportion of the population in the military is now about three times what it was in 1933.

Algebra and Greek Symbols

Here is the idea of proportional change represented in algebraic symbols: Let us call a first measurement x_1 and a second measurement x_2. The variable x could be a proportion or a raw count. Let's call the proportional change d:

$$d = \frac{x_2 - x_1}{x_1}$$

Summary

When reports fail to provide both proportions and raw counts, you can figure out what was left out if you know the size of the population. Table 1.2.1 provides several important populations that are worth remembering. When people compare proportions or raw counts between places, they may mislead you if you do not recognize how the populations differ.

The unemployment rate is the proportion of the labor force that is looking for a job. The labor force includes the people working in paying jobs and the people looking for paying jobs.

Since 1790, the U.S. population has grown from 4 million to more than 285 million. It has doubled in the last 60 years.

An X-Y plot represents pairs of observations by dots on a graph. A time-series plot is an X-Y plot that represents time with its x-axis.

A proportional change in raw counts or proportions is calculated by subtracting the earlier value from the later value and then dividing that difference by the earlier value.

If someone tells you that there are "more [fill-in-the-blank] than ever before," that is at least partly because there are more people than ever before.

Avoiding Common Misunderstandings

Two hundred eighty-five million is 285,000,000. Six billion is 6,000,000,000. Five hundred thousand is 500,000. A thousand is written with three zeros. A million is written with six zeros. A billion is written with nine zeros.

A bar chart has a number line up the side. An X-Y plot has two number lines, one up the side (the y-axis), and another across the bottom (the x-axis). Number lines represent differences between numbers with distance. For example, on a number line, the distance from 13 to 15 is the same as the distance from 26 to 28.

Computer Project

A very powerful tool built into almost all statistical analysis packages is the random number generator. The purpose of this project is to allow you to learn what the random number generator is and what it produces. For this project, follow these steps:

1. In your software, use the random number generator to create random observations. When you are done, each cell will have a single number produced by the random number generator.

2. Look at the first 20 random numbers. You should not be able to recognize any sequences in them. There are features to how those random numbers were created. Most random number generators have some way to produce random decimals between 0 and 1, for which every decimal is equally likely and shows up an equal amount. Figure out how to get this kind of random number in your software.

3. Repeat these steps to see how the random number generator produces new random numbers.

4. Figure out what the chances are that the random number generator produces a number less than 0.5. (This may be tough, and I strongly recommend you ask friends for help thinking this through.) Write down your answer and how you figured it out.

Exercises

1. Rewrite the following report to reflect the proportion as well as the raw count of people:

   The government [of India] can't afford to buy [AIDS treatments] for the nearly four million Indians infected with HIV.
   —BRENDA WILSON, *MORNING EDITION*, NATIONAL PUBLIC RADIO,
   MARCH 29, 2001

2. Rewrite the following report to reflect the proportion as well as the raw count of people:

   A recent United Nations report estimated that already more than one million Chinese had HIV in January 2001.
   —*MONTREAL GAZETTE*, AUGUST 27, 2001

   Here are two quotes about voting in the United States and in India:

   This week, about 400 million Indians are voting. . . . India's elections are by far the most expansive exercise of democracy in the world . . . the glory of India is that democracy is so routine.
   —SIMON, *ALL THINGS CONSIDERED*, NATIONAL PUBLIC RADIO, MAY 4, 1996

   Curtis Gans, who heads the Committee for Study of the American Electorate, said 19 percent (18 million) of those who voted in the 1992 election were over 65.
   —SHANAHAN AND BENSON, *NEW ORLEANS TIMES-PICAYUNE*, APRIL 28, 1996

3. From the Shanahan and Benson quote, you can figure out what proportion of Americans voted in 1992.

   a. How many people voted in the 1992 election in the United States? (To find out, consider that 19% of the raw count of voters was 18 million people. So, 18 million divided by the number of voters equals 0.19.)

   b. What proportion of the U.S. population voted in the 1992 election?

4. From your last answer and the Simon quote above, you can figure out how American voting compares to Indian voting.

   a. What proportion of the Indian population voted in the 1996 elections?

   b. Do Americans participate in democracy more or less than Indians do?

5. From the following table, draw a time-series plot showing the change in world population between 1650 and 2000.

YEAR	POPULATION (BILLIONS)
1650	0.5
1700	0.6
1750	0.7
1800	1
1850	1.2
1900	1.6
1950	2.6
2000	6

Source: World Almanac Books

The following table shows proportions of American men and women who are in the labor force. These are proportions only of men and women who were neither hospitalized nor in prison.

YEAR	PROPORTION OF WOMEN IN LABOR FORCE	PROPORTION OF MEN IN LABOR FORCE
1960	38%	83%
1970	43%	80%
1980	52%	77%
1990	58%	76%
1995	59%	75%

6. Sketch a time-series plot showing American women's labor force participation from 1960 to 1995.

7. Sketch a time-series plot for American men's labor force participation from 1960 to 1995.

8. How would these changes affect the size of the labor force? And how would the unemployment rate have been affected if the number of jobs held steady?

9. What are the proportional changes in world populations shown in the table in Exercise 5? Make a table showing how the rate of world population growth has changed over the last 300 years.

10. The following table is an abridged version of a table from the *Statistical Abstract of the United States, 1995*. What are the proportional changes in the African American population?

YEAR	NUMBER OF AFRICAN AMERICANS
1790	757,000
1900	8,834,000
1995	33,141,000

11. If Americans were more inspired to vote in 1992, then a larger proportion of the voting age population would have voted. In the following quote, Eagan points out that the raw count of voters was higher in 1992 "than ever before":

> *Of all the fictions . . . one about the 1992 presidential election is the most damaging. It's the one that says Rock the Vote and Motor Voter inspired us to make a difference in our government. . . . This much is true: More of us voted than ever before.*
>
> —EAGAN, *HARTFORD COURANT*, MARCH 9, 1998

Does this mean that Americans were more inspired to vote in 1992 than they had been in the past? Why or why not?

12. What does the following quote tell you about the change in the proportion of Americans who live in apartments?

> *While renting is not necessarily the best housing choice for everyone, the number of apartment residents has doubled in the United States over the last 25 years.*
>
> —O'BERRY, *CHICAGO SUN-TIMES*, MARCH 7, 1999

13. In 1980, there were about 316,000 people incarcerated in the United States. In 1990, there were 740,000. Here is a report on 2000:

> *U.S. prisons and jails now hold a record 1.8 million Americans and may hold 2 million by the end of 2001, according to new Justice Department statistics.*
>
> —CBS NEWS, APRIL 20, 2000

What proportion of the U.S. population was incarcerated in 1980, 1990, and 2000? Draw a time-series plot showing the proportion of Americans who were imprisoned in 1980, 1990, and 2000.

14. What was the proportional change in the proportion of Americans incarcerated from 1980 to 1990 and from 1990 to 2000?

Answers to Odd-Numbered Exercises

1. The government [of India] can't afford to buy [AIDS treatments] for the nearly four million Indians (400 per 100,000) infected with HIV.

3. a. 95 million (18 million divided by 0.19).

   b. About 38% (if you use 250 million for the 1992 population—the 1990 population was 249 million).

5.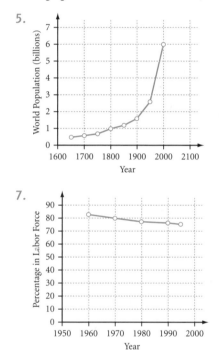

7.

9.

YEAR	POPULATION (BILLIONS)	CHANGE (BILLIONS)	DIVIDED BY (BILLIONS)	PROPORTIONAL CHANGE
1650	0.5			
1700	0.6	0.1	0.5	20%
1750	0.7	0.1	0.6	17%
1800	1	0.3	0.7	43%
1850	1.2	0.2	1	20%
1900	1.6	0.4	1.2	33%
1950	2.6	1	1.6	62%
2000	6	3.4	2.6	137%

11. Not necessarily. Even if the same proportion voted in every election, a greater number would have voted in 1992 than ever before, because the population was greater than it had been ever before.

13.

YEAR	NUMBER OF PRISONERS	U.S. POPULATION	PROPORTION INCARCERATED
1980	316,000	227,000,000	0.14%
1990	740,000	249,000,000	0.30%
2000	1,800,000	281,000,000	0.64%

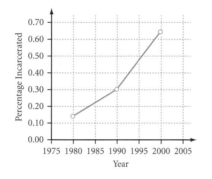

1.3   Things Vary, and Small Samples Vary the Most

- The Law of Large Numbers

> *This year's top [mutual] funds will likely slide in rank next year.*
> —QUINN, *WASHINGTON POST*, OCTOBER 2, 1994

> *Half the time, the [mutual] funds with the worst track records did better [than those with the best track records].*
> —*CHICAGO TRIBUNE*, OCTOBER 2, 1994

> *In 11 of the last 12 years, the fund [Giftrust] has ranked in either the highest or the lowest quartile of mutual funds.*
> —WYATT, *NEW YORK TIMES*, MAY 14, 1995

MORE AND MORE AMERICANS have retirement plans that let them invest their retirement savings—plans like IRAs and 401(k)s. There is talk in Washington, D.C., of having social security participants invest their own social security savings. Investing your retirement savings may be a big part of your life.

A popular approach is to invest in mutual funds. When you buy into a mutual fund, your money is pooled with other investors' money and spread across a variety of investments, like stocks. How do you pick a good mutual fund? You might think that your best bet is to invest in the mutual fund that did best last year. This section begins with what some newspapers have said about such a strategy.

Apparently, last year's best performer cannot be relied on to be this year's best. The top performer could even be like Giftrust, rocketing up and down in performance—some years in the top 25%, other years in the bottom.

Why would the best performer one year perform so badly the following year? To see what is happening, you can make your own test-case mutual funds from the stock exchange reports in your local newspaper. What you do is create an imaginary mutual fund that invests in many stocks and several mutual funds that each invest in just a few stocks. Then watch the funds over the following days. You will see that the many-stock fund varies only a little in its performance. It is never the best, but it's never the worst either. The few-stock funds jump around a lot. From day to day, if a fund goes from best to worst, it's probably a few-stock fund.

To show you this, I looked at the New York Stock Exchange reports for July 9, 10, and 11, 1997. On all three days, of the stocks whose prices changed, about 60% rose in price. In stock lingo, 60% rising and 40% falling would be reported "advancing stocks led decliners 6 to 4." I'm going to simplify the story of mutual fund performance by looking only at what proportion of a fund's stocks rise in value.

I made up three mutual funds: the ABC Fund, the DEF Fund, and the Fuddy Fund. ABC and DEF are few-stock funds. The ABC mutual fund invests in three stocks, the first stock whose abbreviation in the stock listings begins with "A," the first that begins with "B," and the first that begins with "C." The DEF Mutual fund invests in the first stocks listed under "D," "E," and "F." The Fuddy Mutual Fund is a many-stock fund. It invests in the first two stocks listed under every letter of the alphabet, a total of 52 stocks.

I expected the Fuddy Fund to be the most stable, because it is a sample of many stocks. I expected the ABC and DEF funds to vary widely in their performances, because they were samples of few stocks. On July 9, the Fuddy Fund had 41% gainers and 59% losers. That day, the ABC and the DEF Funds were both top performers. For both, 100% of their stocks rose in value. Both funds outperformed the market. On July 10, the Fuddy Fund did better: 82% of its stocks rose in value. Of the ABC Fund's stocks, 100% rose in value. That day, the DEF Fund was the worst performer: 100% of its stocks lost value. On July 11, 52% of the Fuddy Fund's stocks rose. The ABC Fund had a 67% rise, and the DEF Fund continued with 100% losing value. Table 1.3.1 shows how the three mutual funds did during those three days in July.

What you see in these three imaginary funds is what regularly happens. The best and the worst performers are always few-stock mutual funds. Funds that invest in many stocks tend to be more stable.

What is happening here is called "the law of large numbers." The law of large numbers is that, as a sample of events gets larger, the proportion of each type of event will tend to approach the probability that that event would occur on each trial. For example, let's say that I am going to collect a sample of coin flips. In this sample, each trial is a coin flip. In each trial, there are two possible events. One event is a head. The other event is a tail. In each trial, the probability of a head is 50%, and the probability of a tail is 50%. In this situation, the law of large numbers says that, as the sample gets larger, the proportion of trials (flips) that comes up heads will tend to approach the probability of heads (50%), and the proportion of trials that have the other event (tails) will tend to approach the probability of tails (50%).

Table 1.3.1 Hypothetical Mutual Fund Performances: Percentage of Gainer Stocks

HYPOTHETICAL MUTUAL FUND	JULY 9	JULY 10	JULY 11
The Fuddy Fund	41%	82%	52%
The ABC Fund	100%	100%	67%
The DEF Fund	100%	0%	0%
Total Market	60%	60%	60%

The Law of Large Numbers

As a sample of events gets larger, the proportion of each type of event tends to move toward the probability of that type of event occurring on each trial.

For example, the probability of a baby being a girl is about 50%. If you look at a small sample of births, the proportion that is female may be far from 50%, but if you increase the size of that sample, the proportion who are female will tend to get closer and closer to 50%.

In the case of the ABC, DEF, and Fuddy Funds, the chance that a stock would rise in value was slightly higher than 50%, because this data came from a day when 60% of stocks rose in value. Each fund was a sample of stocks. The law of large numbers says that, as each sample got larger, the proportion that rose in value would tend to get closer to the probability that a stock would rise in value. The ABC and DEF Funds did not get large, so the tendency toward the probability was not strong. They were not much constrained to the probability. The result was that their proportions whipped around from 0% to 100%. The Fuddy Fund got larger and larger until it included 102 stocks, and, as it got larger, the tendency to have a gainer proportion close to the probability that a stock would be a gainer got stronger and stronger. The result is that the Fuddy Fund's gainer proportion was more tightly constrained—more tightly hemmed in. That's why a mutual fund like the Fuddy Fund is never the best and never the worst.

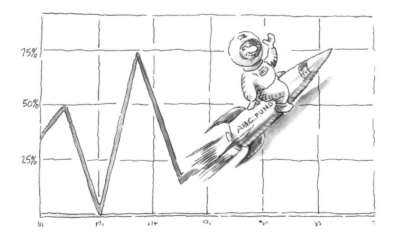

You can test the law of large numbers whenever you are stuck waiting somewhere. All you need is a coin. Flip the coin and keep track of the proportion of heads that appear. Early on, that proportion may be far from 50%, but as you add more and more flips, the proportion will tend to get closer and closer to 50%.

To show you, I will flip a nickel 200 times and record for you how it comes out. The first flip is a head. After that first flip, I have 100% heads, which is far from 50%. On my second flip, I get a second head. On my third flip, I get a tail. I am at 66% heads, closer to 50%. Here's how it goes from there:

After 5 flips: 40% heads

After 10 flips: 60% heads

After 20 flips: 65% heads

After 50 flips: 60% heads

After 100 flips: 47% heads

After 200 flips: 49% heads

Figure 1.3.1 shows how the heads percentage changed over those 200 flips. Figure 1.3.1 has a line at 50%. That reference line lets you see how close to 50% the proportions fell.

Figure 1.3.1 **Proportions of Coin Flips That Came Up Heads (First Series)**

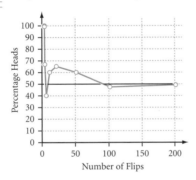

You can see in Figure 1.3.1 that the percentage began far from 50% and initially moved around a lot. As the sample got larger and larger, the sample's proportion tended to vary more and more closely to 50%.

Here's what I found on another 200 flips:

After 1 flip: 0% heads

After 2 flips: 50% heads

After 3 flips: 67% heads

After 5 flips: 40% heads

After 10 flips: 60% heads

After 20 flips: 55% heads

After 50 flips: 54% heads

After 100 flips: 50% heads

After 200 flips: 51% heads

Figure 1.3.2 shows how this series of flips went.

Figure 1.3.2  **Proportions of Coin Flips That Came Up Heads (Second Series)**

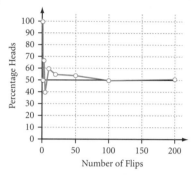

As happened before, the percentage initially varied widely, but then, as the sample size increased, the percentage varied more and more tightly around 50%. That is what the law of large numbers says would happen.

I can test the law of large numbers with dice too. If you roll a die (one dice), there is one chance in six that you will get a "one." That is a 17% chance of rolling a one. Here's what I got:

After 1 roll: 100% ones

After 4 rolls: 25% ones

After 5 rolls: 40% ones

After 10 rolls: 30% ones

After 15 rolls: 27% ones

After 20 rolls: 35% ones

After 50 rolls: 20% ones

After 100 rolls: 22% ones

After 200 rolls: 18% ones

Figure 1.3.3 shows the progression of percentages. Figure 1.3.3 includes a reference line at 17% (the probability of rolling a one).

The pattern shown in all these examples is that, initially, the proportion of an event can be far from the probability of that event, but, as the sample gets larger and larger, the proportion tends to move more and more toward the probability.

Figures 1.3.1 through 1.3.3 show only some of the percentages. Those figures do not give you as complete an image as you might like. Figures 1.3.4 through 1.3.6 show the percentage after each flip in three new samples.

Figures 1.3.7 through 1.3.9 show how the percentage of die rolls that come up as one changes over 100 rolls.

Figure 1.3.3

Changes in Proportions of Die Rolls Coming Up One as Sample Increases

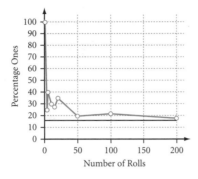

Figure 1.3.6

Heads Percentage After Each of Yet Another 100 Coin Flips

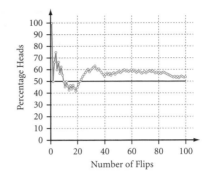

Figure 1.3.4

Heads Percentage After Each of 100 Coin Flips

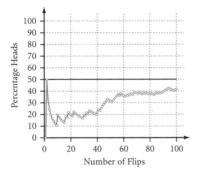

Figure 1.3.7

Ones Percentage After Each of 100 Die Rolls

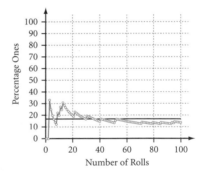

Figure 1.3.5

Heads Percentage After Each of Another 100 Coin Flips

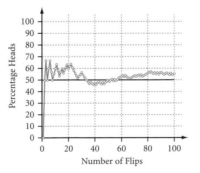

Figure 1.3.8

Ones Percentage After Each of Another 100 Die Rolls

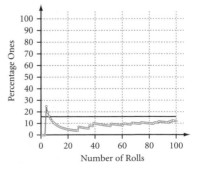

Figure 1.3.9 **Ones Percentage After Each of Yet Another 100 Die Rolls**

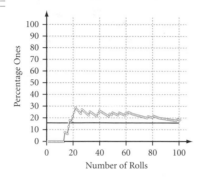

In all of these figures, you can see the law of large numbers in action. Small samples vary widely. As the samples get larger, the proportions continue to vary, but they vary within a range that is closer and closer to the probabilities that are producing them.

The law of large numbers does not appear only in coins and dice. You can see events in everyday life behave like coin flips. One example is births. On Sundays, my newspaper reports local births. Some hospitals are busier delivering babies than others. Table 1.3.2 shows the percentage of babies who were female at each hospital. These numbers are all from the July 13, 1997, issue of the *Everett Herald* (in Washington State).

Table 1.3.2 **Number of Births and Gender Proportions Among Babies Born at Seven Hospitals in Washington State**

HOSPITAL	BIRTHS (NUMBER)	FEMALE BABIES (PERCENTAGE)
Whidbey General	2	100%
Group Health Eastside	3	67%
Arlington Birth Center	3	67%
Valley General	8	50%
Cascade Valley	13	46%
Stevens Hospital	43	65%
Providence General	73	52%

In Table 1.3.2, the number of births at each hospital goes from 2 up to 73. You can see another pattern also. It is inconsistent, but it is there. As you scan from the top to the bottom, the proportion of births that were girls tends to get closer to 50%. Figure 1.3.10 shows how the percentage varies with the number of births.

Figure 1.3.10   **Female Percentage Among Deliveries in Seven Hospitals**

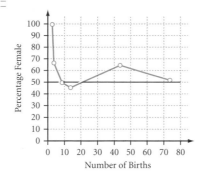

The approach to 50% reflects the law of large numbers. As the sample gets larger, the proportions in the sample tend to get closer to the probability of a baby being female.

Note that the law of large numbers says that the proportions only tend to get more like the probabilities. A larger sample can have proportions that are less like the probabilities than a smaller sample. Look again at Table 1.3.2. Valley General had 8 births with exactly 50% female. Stevens Hospital had 43 births with 65% female. The larger hospital (Stevens) had the more extreme proportion. Proportions can get less like their probabilities, but the general tendency is for proportions to get more like the probabilities, and that tendency gets stronger and stronger as the sample gets larger and larger.

Conversely, the push toward the probabilities is weaker for smaller samples. You can see this in those same births by turning the table upside down. Table 1.3.3

Table 1.3.3   Number of Births and Gender Proportions Among Babies Born at Seven Hospitals in Washington State

HOSPITAL	BIRTHS (NUMBER)	FEMALE BABIES (PERCENTAGE)
Providence General	73	52%
Stevens Hospital	43	65%
Cascade Valley	13	46%
Valley General	8	50%
Arlington Birth Center	3	67%
Group Health Eastside	3	67%
Whidbey General	2	100%

shows the same births, except now the hospitals are sorted from most births to fewest.

In Table 1.3.3, as the number of births goes down, the percentage are freed to vary more and more widely. This is another aspect of the law of large numbers: Smaller samples have proportions that are free to vary more widely away from the probabilities that created them.

You can see that small samples vary more widely in births, and you can see it in baseball statistics. The 1996 baseball season was Alex Rodriguez's first full season in the major leagues, and he came in with a bang, batting better than anyone else that year. His 1996 batting average was .358. Batting averages are proportions—the proportion of times at bat that a batter gets a hit. "Batting .358" means that Alex Rodriguez got a hit 35.8% of the 600 times he came to bat. That is about one-third of the times he got to bat. Did he get a hit every third time he faced a pitcher? No. If you looked at small samples, you find he often hit well above .358 and often hit well below. Small samples are free to vary widely.

> *Alex Rodriguez . . . singled twice and homered in four at-bats [batting .750] against Cleveland.*
>
> —NEWNHAM, *SEATTLE TIMES*, AUGUST 8, 1996

> *Rodriguez was 3 for 5 [batting .600] yesterday against Milwaukee.*
>
> —SHERWIN, *SEATTLE TIMES*, AUGUST 2, 1996

> *Rodriguez, hitless [batting .000] in his 10 previous at-bats.*
>
> —ROCKNE, *SEATTLE TIMES*, JUNE 1, 1996

> *Rodriguez got only his second hit in 12 at-bats [batting .167] during the series.*
>
> —FINNIGAN AND SHERWIN, *SEATTLE TIMES*, SEPTEMBER 16, 1996

> *Alex Rodriguez is batting .407 (22 for 54).*
>
> —FORT-LAUDERDALE SUN-SENTINEL, MAY 26, 1996

On May 22, it was reported that out of his last 22 times at bat, Rodriguez had 11 hits, batting .500. It was reported on August 10 that, out of the last 37 times that he got to bat, he got 15 hits. 15 out of 37 is 40.5%, which is even closer to his average of .358. Table 1.3.4 summarizes these reports. Figure 1.3.11 shows how those batting averages vary relative to the size of the sample.

In these batting averages, you see the same wide variation in small samples and tighter variation in larger samples that we saw in birth patterns, coin flips, and die rolls. All of these examples demonstrate the law of large numbers. As sample sizes increase, proportions in samples tend to become more like the probabilities involved in producing the samples.

Table 1.3.4   Reports of Alex Rodriguez's Batting Sorted by Sample Size

REPORT DATE	AT-BATS	BATTING AVERAGE
August 8	4	.750
August 2	5	.600
June 1	10	.000
September 16	12	.167
May 22	22	.500
August 10	37	.405
May 26	54	.407
Postseason (Entire Season)	600	.358

Figure 1.3.11   **Alex Rodriguez's Batting Averages at Various Sample Sizes**

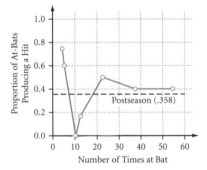

Note: "Batting average" means proportion of at-bats producing a hit.

The Gambler's Fallacy

There is a common misconception about the law of large numbers. The misconception arises from a puzzle. Let us say that you have just flipped five heads in a row—five out of five flips coming up heads. The law of large numbers says that, as you flip the coin more and more, the proportion that comes up heads tends toward 50%. What makes your sample tend toward 50%, after this initial string of five heads? The mistaken conception, called the "gambler's fallacy," is that because the overall proportion tends toward 50%, the chances of flipping a tail are higher when you haven't flipped one in a while. This mistake might seem plausible to you, so let's take a moment to see what is going on.

Gambler's Fallacy

The gambler's fallacy is that, after several appearances of a chance outcome, that outcome is less likely. For example, after two coin flips come up heads, someone persuaded by the gambler's fallacy believes that the chances of a head on the next flip is less than 50%.

The gambler's fallacy would not be a fallacy if the coin said to itself, "Five heads in a row! I'd better try to come up tails now." But the coin does not do that. Coins do not talk to themselves. Coins do not remember how they came up before. The chances do not change. With each coin flip, the chances remain 50/50.

The proportions tend toward the probabilities without any adjustments for previous flips. This happens partly because of how proportions are calculated. To calculate the proportion that came up heads, you divide the number of heads by the number of flips. Let us say you start off with 5 heads in a row. Now imagine you flip 10 more times, and the coin does nothing to adjust for those first 5 heads. It ignores the first 5 flips and gives 50% heads and 50% tails. That would be 5 more heads and 5 tails. After 15 flips, you would have 10 heads and 5 tails. The amount 10 out of 15 is 67% heads, down quite a bit from the 100% heads that showed up in the first 5 flips, even though nothing was done to compensate for

Table 1.3.5   How Proportions Move After a String of Heads Without Adjusting for the Initial String

NUMBER OF FLIPS	WHAT HAPPENED	SUMMARY	HEADS (PERCENTAGE)
After 5 flips	first 5 heads	5 heads	100% heads
After 15 flips	5 heads + 5 heads and 5 tails	10 heads and 5 tails	67% heads
After 25 flips	5 heads + 10 heads and 10 tails	15 heads and 10 tails	60% heads
After 205 flips	5 heads + 100 heads and 100 tails	105 heads and 100 tails	51% heads

the initial string of 5 heads. Table 1.3.5 shows how this would continue if the coin did nothing to adjust for the initial 5 heads.

Although the number of heads stays 5 higher than the number of tails, that difference matters less and less as you divide by a larger and larger number of flips. The proportions tend to go where they are supposed to go, without any adjusting for the initial 5 heads in a row.

The Law of Large Numbers Works Without Any Adjusting for Strings of Outcomes

If I flip a coin 10 times and get 10 tails, the law of large numbers will show up, even if the coin does nothing to adjust for those first 10 flips. If I then flip 20 heads and 20 tails, I will be at 60% tails. After another 20 of each, I'm at 56% tails, and so on toward 50%.

The gambler's fallacy is a fallacy. Proportions tend toward probabilities without chances changing for any given outcome.

Small Samples Vary More Widely

You can also see how proportions in small samples have more freedom to vary with a simple card game. The way you play is, after shuffling, you deal one person 4 cards, and another person 16 cards. Players figure out what percentage of their hands are hearts. Whoever gets closest to 25% wins. Reshuffle the deck before dealing the next hand. Calculating a percentage of 16 cards is a hassle, but there is a compensation for the 16-card player. The 16-card hand will win most of the time. The hearts percentage in the 4-card hand will vary more.

I have played this game with my eldest son. Although he is six, he is tolerant and put up with his dad for 10 hands. Dealing myself the 16-card hand, I won five times. He won three, and we tied twice. Most of the time, he was off by 25%. I was that far off only once.

I recommend that you take a moment with a deck of cards and try it out. Here's why it is worth your time: When we are faced with things like a top-performing mutual fund, a string of six strikeouts in baseball, or seven failed sales calls, we tend to think that these small samples reflect the nature of what's going on. We might think that someone who has won six times in a row at roulette is "lucky" and has a better chance of winning than other people. Playing with cards is one way to get a stronger feeling of how proportions in small samples are often quite different from the probabilities involved in their production. It can be simply chance variation that makes them different. Often there is no more explanation for what happened than that you were looking at a small sample from a chance process—a few sales calls, a few stocks, or a few times at bat.

You can see the extremity of small samples in medical statistics as well. States publish reports on the births and deaths in their counties. These reports are called "vital statistics." Table 1.3.6 shows some statistics from a Washington State report.

What do you see in Table 1.3.6? Garfield County and Wahkiakum County seem to have been the safest places some years and the most deadly in other years. Look at Garfield's row. In 1992 and 1993, Garfield had the lowest rates of death from liver ailments of any county in Washington State. In 1992, it had the lowest death rate from arteriosclerosis, but in 1993, it had the very highest rate. In 1995, its death rate from arteriosclerosis dropped to the lowest again.

Wahkiakum's row in Table 1.3.6 shows similar leaps to the highest rate and drops to the lowest. In 1992, Wahkiakum had the highest rate of death from liver ailments, but its rate then dropped to the lowest in the state in 1993. In deaths from arteriosclerosis, Wahkiakum had the lowest rate in 1992 and 1993, but Wahkiakum's rate leaped to the highest in 1995.

Table 1.3.6 Deaths per 100,000 in Washington State Counties

| | LIVER AILMENTS | | ARTERIOSCLEROSIS | | |
	1992	1993	1992	1993	1995
Garfield County	0*	0*	0*	43.5[†]	0*
Wahkiakum County	29.4[†]	0*	0*	0*	54.0[†]
King County	8.1	8.7	5.9	4.9	4.1
Statewide	9.4	8.7	8	7.4	7

Note: Data from Washington State Vital Statistics, 1996.
*Lowest rate in the state.
[†]Highest rate in the state.

In contrast, King County's vital statistics vary little. King County's rates stay closer to the statewide rates shown on the bottom row of Table 1.3.6.

What is going on here? From Table 1.3.6, you get the impression that Wahkiakum County and Garfield County are unstable places. Their vital statistics zoom about, shooting from the lowest rate in the state to the highest the next year. Meanwhile, King County seems to putter along with proportions that are kind of close to the statewide rates. What gives?

The answer is mostly that King County has about 1.6 million people. Wahkiakum has about 3,700, and Garfield has about 2,400. Garfield and Wahkiakum are the two least populous counties in Washington State. Their statistics zoom around for the same reason you get heads sometimes and tails others. They are like the four-card hand in the card game. Because they are smaller samples, their proportions vary more widely simply by chance.

Uncontrolled Proportions Vary Randomly

If a process produces an outcome only a proportion of the time, and if nothing is fixing the proportion to a particular quota, the proportion will vary from time to time, and that variation will be, at least in part, due to random variation.

For example, basketball players try to have all shots go in, but do not have complete control over whether a shot goes in. For that reason, only a proportion of the shots go in. That proportion varies from one set of shots to another, partly for the same reason one set of coin flips varies from another.

Small samples tend to vary more widely. Try tossing 10 coins at a time. Chances are that you will never see 100% heads or 100% tails. But try tossing two coins at a time. You will get 100% heads or 100% tails pretty often. Similarly, in Wahkiakum, Garfield, and King Counties, chance affects people's health. It is as though each county were flipping coins, but each coin had about an 8 per 100,000 chance of coming up heads and having someone die of arteriosclerosis. It is as if King County is flipping coins for more than 400 times as many people as Garfield and Wahkiakum. Because of their small size, it will be Wahkiakum or Garfield that get the most extreme proportions each year.

Things Vary

There is an obvious point here and a subtle point. The obvious point is that extreme samples tend to be small samples. That is part of the law of large numbers. The subtle point is that things vary. And they do not necessarily vary for any reason that you would be interested in or want to pay attention to. They vary for the same reason flipped coins come up sometimes heads and sometimes tails. It is chance.

"Chance" is a way of saying "factors about which we do not know and about which it may be impossible to know." For example, when you flip a coin, how the coin comes up is completely determined by a large set of factors, including which side it started on, the force of your thumb hitting the coin, where your thumb hit, how low your catching hand was when it caught the coin, the density of the air, and any wind that affects the coin's spin in the air. Then there are the factors behind those factors. For example, the factors that determined the force of your thumb include your previous practice at coin flipping, whether you play the piano, your recent diet, how rested you are, whether you are paying much attention, whether you are trying to produce a lot of force or not, and so on. At our current stage of technological development, these factors are beyond our ability to measure. There is no way we could reveal the influences that determined the coin coming up heads rather than tails. We describe that situation as one of "chance."

Algebra and Greek Symbols

This section talks about proportions and probabilities. In mathematical representations of statistical ideas, it is common to abbreviate values that can be seen with Latin letters (a, b, c, etc.), and values we know or infer, but don't actually ever see, with Greek letters. A proportion is something that appears in a sample, so we abbreviate the proportion with a "p."

A probability is something that we know or infer. We never actually see the probability, so we would indicate the probability with a Greek letter. It makes a lot of sense to call the probability Π, the Greek letter for "P," and we could do that, but I will save Π for something else. We will be talking about population proportions a great deal. Like probabilities, we rarely get to see the actual proportions in a population. The population is usually too big for us to measure it in its entirety. I will use Π to refer to a population proportion.

We need a Greek letter to refer to the probability. Faced with the same issues we face, some statisticians refer to the probability with "θ," the Greek letter theta. That's what we will do here.

Therefore, we can represent the gist of this section with the following symbols:

$$\text{With independence, } p \to \theta \text{ as } n \to \infty$$

"With independence" means that none of the outcomes affect any other outcomes so that the probability remains constant. The arrow means "approaches"; p is the proportion of an outcome in the sample; θ is the probability of the outcome; n is the number of observations in the sample; ∞ is infinity. Saying "as n approaches infinity" is a way of saying "as n gets larger." So "$p \to \theta$ as $n \to \infty$" means "the proportion of an outcome in a sample approaches the probability of that outcome as the number of observations in the sample approaches infinity."

Summary

Unless someone or something holds them steady, proportions vary from sample to sample, and this variation can be partly or entirely random. In small samples, the proportions tend to vary more widely than they do in large samples. The law of large numbers is that, as a sample of events gets larger, the proportions of each type of event tend to approach the probabilities of each event occurring.

Avoiding Common Misunderstandings

The most common misunderstanding is the gambler's fallacy. Just keep in mind that the law of large numbers works, even though the probabilities do not change. In fact, the law of large numbers is based on the concept that the probabilities stay the same.

Computer Project

Use your computer software to simulate flipping a coin. Check whether the law of large numbers describes what happens. For each flip, have your software record in a column what proportion of the flips have been heads. Probably the easiest way to do this is to have your software pick 1's and 0's randomly, and call the 1's "heads" and the 0's "tails."

1. Chart these proportions to produce the sort of charts you saw in this section, with the number of simulated flips along the *x*-axis and the heads proportions indicated on the *y*-axis.

2. Look at the chart. It shows you the law of large numbers. The percentages range widely on the left, when the sample is still small. As the sample gets larger, the proportions tend to get closer and closer to 50%.

3. Have your software rerun these steps, creating and charting new samples of simulated coin flips. Watch how the charts change.

4. Print out some of the charts and write a few sentences explaining what this simulation shows you about where you expect proportions to fall when you flip coins.

Exercises

1. A friend of mine is a doctor in an emergency room. His hospital set up a new evaluation system. The administration decided that each year they would randomly pick a sample of 20 emergency room patients and mail them customer satisfaction surveys. In the past, when they were handing out surveys to every patient, about 10% of the patients had indicated dissatisfaction with their doctors. The hospital proposed a deal with the doctors in which, if the dissatisfied-patient proportion went over 20%, my friend and other ER doctors would be penalized with a pay cut. Why would a statistician say that this was a bad deal for my friend?

2. Let's say you are trying to sell life insurance. You call five people, and they all turn you down—100% rejection. Is that 100% good evidence that you will never sell a policy? Why or why not?

3. Here is a quote showing how one sports writer thinks about chance:

   > *Jason Isringhausen was due for all of the good fortune he received Wednesday in pitching the New York Mets past the San Francisco Giants 15-6. . . . "Through all of the bad luck I've had this year, it's nice to have a little good luck," he said.*
   >
   > —Pedulla, *USA Today,* August 28, 1997

   What do you think of the idea that, after a lot of bad luck, someone is due for some good fortune?

4. Imagine that you are playing Monopoly, and you roll two doubles in a row.

   a. Are the chances of a double different for your third roll of the dice?

   b. What is it called when someone thinks the chances go down?

5. Imagine you hear that a basketball player sank 100% of his shots in one game and none of his shots in the next game. What would you guess about how many shots he attempted in each game?

6. Imagine that at a small hospital, there are about three births each day. On three consecutive days, the babies are 100%, 0%, and then 100% girls. How would you explain this wild variation in percentage?

7. Imagine that, during one week, mothers at a large hospital deliver 100 female babies, and no male babies. Why might you be uncomfortable saying that that pattern was the result of chance variation alone?

8. Cafeterias at two educational institutions keep track of how many people pick the beef course at dinner. Both have a policy to stock enough of each main course so that no dish runs out before 9:30, even though this policy requires cooking more food than will be eaten. One of the institutions is a

college with 100 students. The other is a university with 8,000 students.[1] Which institution's wastes are a larger proportion of the food they cook? And how can you tell?

9. Here is a quote of people trying to talk about the law of large numbers:

   First Baptist Church . . . leaders and members say their hefty representation in politics is natural, the Law of Large Numbers at work. They suggest the church is courted by politicians because it has such massive membership [more than 25,000].

   —Pinzur, *Florida Times Union*, August 26, 2001

   Write a short note to Mr. Pinzur explaining what the law of large numbers is.

10. Here's someone else talking about the law of large numbers:

    In 2000, Waste Connections was the top-performing stock in the "environmental" sector with appreciation of 129 percent. . . . "The law of large numbers eventually does catch up, but we think [Waste Connections] can continue to grow above industry average rates," said Salomon's Young.

    —Walter, *Sacramento Bee*, August 17, 2001

    Waste Connection has been buying other companies and rapidly growing. What does Salomon's Young mean by "the law of large numbers eventually does catch up"? Why might you think that the law of large numbers is about to catch up for Waste Connections?

11. Insurance companies themselves know fairly accurately how much they will have to pay each year. How can this happen, given that each customer cannot know how much misfortune he or she will have each year?

12. The following quote shows some disagreement between the U.S. Census Bureau and Washington State researchers. What would you guess led to the differing numbers?

    According to a U.S. Census Bureau survey [of 623 households]. . . . The percentage of Washington [State] people without health insurance grew 1.4 percent between 1998 and 2000. . . . Aaron Katz . . . said the state's own population surveys [of more than 6,000 households] show rates of uninsured actually dropped steadily from 1998 to 2000.

    —Ostrom, *Seattle Times*, September 28, 2001

---

[1]This exercise is based on a comparison of Haverford College in Pennsylvania and Louisiana State University done by a leading food service company.

Answers to Odd-Numbered Exercises

1. The problem is that a 20-person sample is free to vary widely and will drift over 20%, even if the population's proportion holds steady at 10%.

3. Believing that a string of bad outcomes improves your chances of getting good outcomes is the gambler's fallacy. A given outcome doesn't remember the previous results; there is no overall "balance of luck."

5. In both games, the basketball player took only a few shots. (Small samples are free to vary widely.)

7. I wouldn't explain it as small samples varying widely. It is too extreme for a large sample. That's not what my coin flips looked like. Perhaps this hospital is doing research on the births of female babies and has recruited parents expecting girls. If it were only chance variation, 100% girls in 100 births would be like 100% heads in 100 coin flips. It could happen, but it is mind-blowingly unlikely.

9. What the church leaders are talking about (politicians courting the church because it is large) relates to the large size of the church, but is not an aspect of the law of large numbers. The law of large numbers says that, as a sample of events gets larger, the proportions of the events that are each type of event tend to approach the probabilities of each type of event. The law of large numbers would only suggest that the church's per-member political influence and activity should tend to approach the influence and activity of the general population.

11. Here is an answer from John Gin of the *New Orleans Times-Picayune:*

> *If a company insures a large number of policy holders, it can predict with a high degree of accuracy how many will die in a given year by using "the law of large numbers," a fundamental principle of life insurance.*
>
> —GIN, *NEW ORLEANS TIMES-PICAYUNE*, SEPTEMBER 16, 1997

CHAPTER 2

The Pattern in Random Sample Proportions

Imagine that you need to find a sample of people who are so similar to an entire population that you could study the sample to learn about the population. Your best bet would be random sampling. The superiority of random sampling is something that George Gallup discovered and built a successful polling business on. But Gallup was a fickle devotee, and in 1948 he tried a new approach, to his great embarrassment. The result was President-Elect Harry Truman holding up a newspaper announcing that his opponent, Thomas Dewey, had won the election.

What you get when you do polls without random sampling are inaccuracies. Random sampling is not sloppy sampling, and random sampling is not easy, but it works, as you will see in Section 2.1.

Random sampling does not produce samples with precisely the same proportions that you would find in the total population. There is some variation in random samples. If you create a special kind of bar chart, a histogram, of the proportions that appear in samples, you will see something that so struck Florence Nightingale that she felt it showed the hand of God: a bell shape. This bell shape is approximately what is called a "normal distribution," described in more detail in Sections 2.2 and 2.3.

(2.1) Taking a Good Sample of a Population

- Representative and Biased Samples
- Random Sampling
- Self-Selected Samples

40 percent of American adults engaged in some type of educational activity in 1995, according to . . . the National Center for Education Statistics.

—STEWART, *CHICAGO TRIBUNE*, MARCH 1, 1998

IMAGINE THAT YOU HAVE BEEN ASKED to vote on whether a new community college should be started in your town. How much demand would there be for a community college? What does the preceding quote tell you about your town?

Let's guess that the National Center for Education statistics is right that 40% of American adults received some sort of education in 1995. But what if you want to know what is going on in a smaller sample? For example, what about adults in your town? How many of them engage in educational activities? There is a way to get some sense of the local proportion. If you know that the adults in your town are similar, as a group, to American adults in general, then there is about the same proportion in your town as in the rest of the United States, about 40%. If your town has 10,000 adults, then you would expect about 4,000 to get some sort of education. That number of students might justify a new community college, depending on what else is currently available.

Your town is a portion of the larger population of Americans. A population is a group from which a sample is taken. Our task in this section is to think about how we can infer the nature of a sample from what we know about a population.

Populations and Samples

A sample is a portion of a larger group. In statistics, the larger group is referred to as the "population." This is the case even if the larger group is not made up of people.

For example, if I study 100 cars to learn about cars in the United States, then the 100 cars are a sample, and the total set of all cars in the U.S. is the population.

Here is another task calling for making an inference from the population to a sample: Let's say that your company has declared its building to be smoke-free.

Smokers tend to huddle outside the entrances of smoke-free buildings. Your company has decided to provide a covering so that the smokers stay dry when it rains. How big a shelter will your company need to build? How many smokers are in your company? Let's say that 1,000 people work in your building. How many would you guess are going to be smokers? You might be able to figure that out from the following news item:

> *Americans' adult smoking rate peaked at 42.6 percent in 1966, two years after a landmark Surgeon General's report linked tobacco use to lung cancer. The country's per capita cigarette consumption has declined each year since 1973, and one of four adults now smokes.*
>
> —Rosen, *Sacramento Bee*, May 17, 1998

Let's trust that about 25% of adult Americans smoke. Knowing that does not necessarily tell you that 25% of your coworkers smoke. After all, you might work at an emphysema treatment clinic where hardly anyone smokes. But your company might consist of people who are representative of American adults. If so, then they are like Americans in general.

The similarity between your coworkers and American adults in general tells you something about what proportion of your company's employees smoke. If your coworkers are roughly representative of American adults in general, then they have roughly the same proportions as the general population. That is what "representative" means.

For example, 12% of Americans are African American. But consider Wyoming, where less than 1% of the population are African American. Wyoming is "not representative" of the United States in regard to the proportion of its inhabitants who are African American. In contrast, in Missouri, 11% of the population belong to this group. Missouri, then, is fairly representative of the total U.S. population in this regard. One of the definitions of "representative" is that, if a sample is representative of a population, then the sample has the same proportions as the population. So if you know that you have a representative sample of a population, you can make inferences from the population to your sample. The sample will have roughly the same proportions as the population.

Let's get back to figuring out how many smokers work at your company. Let's say that you cannot think of a more representative sample of Americans than your company. If that is so, then you can use the 25% as an estimate of the proportion of people in your company who smoke. Remember that 1,000 people work at your company. If 25% smoke, there will be 250 smokers. You're going to need a big awning to cover them all.

Here is the rule: If your sample is roughly representative of the population, then your sample will have roughly the same proportions as the population.

Making Inferences About a Representative Sample from Population Statistics

If a sample is roughly representative of a population, you can estimate that the sample has roughly the same proportions as the population.

For example, if you knew that a sample was roughly representative of Americans in general, you could estimate that the sample would be about 51% female, because that is the proportion of Americans who are female.

Let's look at another use of that idea. Imagine that you are considering starting a magazine specifically for Maryland families who do not watch television. How big is your market? According to the Census Bureau, there are about two million households in Maryland, but how many have no television?

> *Some people—about 1.4 percent of American households—live without TV.*
>
> —IMHOFF, *BALTIMORE SUN*, MARCH 1, 1998

If you guess that Maryland households are roughly representative of American households in general, how many would you guess have no television? If Marylanders are representative, then 1.4% of Maryland households have no television. That is 0.014 times 2 million, which is 28,000 households. It is up to you to decide whether 28,000 is a big enough market to support a magazine.

Biased Samples

Doesn't that sound easy? You learn the statistics of the country, and away you go: You know what the people are like before you even talk to them. Yes? Well, maybe, and maybe not. The problem is that not every group is representative of the larger population. For example, with regard to television, the U.S. population is not representative of the world population. In the United States, 98.5% of households watch television, whereas only 13% of people worldwide even have access to television.

The difficulty with using populations to guess what a sample is like is that the sample may not be representative. If your sample were created in a way that would tend to make it unrepresentative, statisticians would say that the sample was created with a "biased" sampling method.

Bias

A method for collecting a sample is considered "biased" if it will usually produce an unrepresentative sample.

For example, if I survey shoppers at a store, asking them whether they like shopping there, I am using a biased method of collecting samples because the fact that they are shopping there suggests that they like shopping there. The sample will tend to be unrepresentative because it does not represent all the people in the community.

The problem of biased sampling methods came up at a school where I used to teach. The school catered to an unusual student population. Most of our students were between 40 and 55 years old. The state of Washington had started the school to serve the adults in the area who had not yet earned their bachelor's degree.

The school did not provide on-campus daycare. The idea that the school should provide daycare so that parents could drop off their children while they attended classes came up every other year. Whenever this idea came up, the school surveyed its current students, asking them whether they needed on-campus daycare to be able to attend classes. Think about it. How do you think this survey came out?

Every time, the students reported that they did not need on-campus daycare in order to attend classes. The school could have figured that out without the survey. Potential students who did need on-campus daycare were not students and could not fill out the survey.

What did that tell us about the adults in our region? Was this sample representative of the people in our region who had not yet earned their B.A. degrees? No. The school's sampling method was biased. Potential students who needed daycare did not appear at all in the sample, because the school didn't provide daycare.

A few years ago, a pregnant student of mine was perturbed by an unrepresentative sample. She had gone to court to fight a traffic ticket for traveling in a carpool lane with only herself and her third-trimester fetus in the car. Washington State law says that a third-trimester fetus is a person, so that there were two people in the car. She concluded and she was then justified in using the carpool lane. The traffic officer didn't see it that way, though, and he gave her a ticket. She took it to court, the news got out, and she was interviewed on national television.

After appearing on the television show, my student received dozens of letters a day from people with very strong views on the issue. She did not know how they had found her address, but they were writing to her at home. The writers all seemed to be extremely excitable. None of them demonstrated any calm consideration of the issue. If the sample of people who wrote to her were representative of the general population, then Americans were a pretty intense bunch.

My student was concerned about this, wondering, "Is this what Americans are like?" I was able to reassure her. These letters were not cause for much worry about the general population because the letter writers were a biased sample. Think about the sample of people who write letters to people who appear on the news. Such writers have extreme views. That is why they are willing to go to the extreme bother of finding a person's mailing address. In this case they were not a representative sample. The sampling method was biased toward people with extreme motivations.

Self-Selected Samples

The letter writers and my university's sample of students have something in common: Both samples were created by the people in the sample themselves. No researcher found them. Instead, the people in the sample included themselves in the sample. The college students chose the college they attended. The letter writers went to the trouble of finding the mailing address.

In the social sciences, such groups are called "self-selected" samples. Self-selection is a biased sampling method. If self-selected samples are not biased in any other way, they are at least biased in that they underrepresent the portion of the population that would not choose to include itself in the sample. My student's letters underrepresented the portion of the population who would not bother to write her a letter. The students at my college underrepresented the portion of the local population who would need on-campus daycare to attend classes.

If you have a self-selected sample, it is always the result of a biased sampling method: It does not have enough of the people who would not select themselves to be in it.

You might think that self-selection wouldn't be a problem for some research questions. For example, think about a study of kidney functioning. You might think that people who volunteer for research are unlikely to have kidneys that function any differently from anybody else's. But consider who would be most interested in volunteering for this type of study. In such a study, doctors would examine how well your kidneys work and pay you for the examination. Who is going to be particularly interested in participating? People in ill health whose doctors have told them they may have kidney trouble. Such a study would lead to the conclusion that people's kidneys do not work as well as we might think.

Self-selected samples cause this kind of trouble for almost any kind of research—the people who volunteer are unlike the general population in that they tend to be more enthusiastic about volunteering for those studies. If you read much in the social and medical sciences, you will notice that many researchers work with self-selected samples. You yourself may have seen advertisements asking for volunteers for such studies on a college campus. Unfortunately, using self-selected samples is very common.

Estimating the Nature of Biased Samples

Even if there is bias in how a sample was created, you can often still use population information to guess something about what samples would be like. If you know that your sample is more extreme than the general population, then you know that the general population is less extreme than your sample. That can tell you something. For example, what proportion of workers at the American Cancer Society smoke cigarettes? If we knew nothing, we would have to say that the smoking proportion at the society is somewhere between 0% and 100%. We can narrow that down a lot. About 25% of U.S. adults smoke. We can be pretty sure that the smoking rate is lower at the American Cancer Society. That tells me that the proportion at the society is somewhere between 0% and 25%. The population proportion, 25%, is an upper limit on the possible proportion in the American Cancer Society, quite an improvement over saying that the proportion falls somewhere between 0% and 100%.

Estimating Proportions in Biased Samples

If you know that a sample is biased in that it underrepresents a particular group, then the proportion of the sample that is part of that group is less than the proportion of the population that is part of that group in the general population. Conversely, if a sample overrepresents the group, then the group's sample proportion is greater than the group's proportion in the general population.

Random Samples

So how do you get a representative sample? The researchers who did the study mentioned in the following quote report that they interviewed a representative sample. How did they get a representative sample?

> *[Previous] studies relied not on random samples but on volunteers who may have been drawn to participate because of a heightened interest in sex.... Using ... interviews and ... questionnaires to survey a random, nationally representative sample ... [researchers] found: 85 percent of married women and 75 percent of married men said they are faithful.*
>
> —SACRAMENTO BEE, OCTOBER 11, 1994

The quote says that the sample was "random" and "representative." That is true, but it is surprising. If you are careless and take whatever sample is convenient, you will get a biased sample. The sample that is convenient is the unusual sample that happens to be nearby and available to you. For example, if you were a psychologist working at a university, your convenient sample would be college students. If you accepted that sample as a sample of people in the United States, you would be startled to discover that everyone in the United States is currently enrolled in classes. And you would be wrong, because a sample of college students is not representative of Americans in general.

The answer to our puzzle is that a "random sample" is not a careless sample. It is not produced by random behavior on the part of the person collecting the sample. A random sample is created by some method that gives every person in the population an equal chance of being selected for the sample. If you are studying sprockets at a bicycle factory, then a random sample is a sample created in such a way that every sprocket has an equal chance of being selected for the sample.

How to Collect a Random Sample

A random sample is any sample created using a method that gives every person or item in the population an equal chance of being included in the sample.

For example, to collect a random sample of people at a party, you could have each person flip a coin and include in your sample everyone who flipped a head.

Let us say that you wanted to get a random sample of Americans. You might write everyone's name on a piece of paper, put the names in a hat, stir them up, and pick slips with your eyes closed. But how are you going to get everyone's names? And where will you find a hat big enough? I can fit about 285 small slips of paper in my hat. To get every American's name in a hat, you would have to have a hat one million times larger than mine. The hat would have to be at least five stories tall and 20 yards across. Creating a random sample is hard work.

Random samples are easier to collect from populations that are smaller than that of the total United States. For example, imagine that you want to know what proportion of your company's employees are planning to resign next year. You could ask everyone in the company, but asking about quitting might be a bad idea. You might put ideas in people's heads. Instead, you could ask just a sample. If there are 1,000 people at your company, it is possible to write every name on a slip of paper, stir them up, and pick out 100 with your eyes closed. If you stir well, the names you pick will be a random sample.

Another approach is to have a computer program pick employees from a database. To do this properly, the computer would have to be programmed to give everyone in the company an equal chance of being selected for the sample.

Here is what is amazing about random samples: If you collected a large random sample, your random sample would most likely be roughly representative of the full population at your company. If 28% of your coworkers are Catholic, then about 28% of your sample will be Catholic. If 57% of your coworkers are Democrats, then roughly 57% of your sample will be Democrats. If 5% of your coworkers read *Cosmopolitan,* then about 5% of your sample will be *Cosmopolitan* readers. Your random sample will become roughly representative without your worrying about it.

Why Random Sampling Works

To see why random sampling works, think about fairground raffles. When you buy a ticket in these lotteries, a stub with your ticket's number is put in a big pot. At the end of the day, the pot is well stirred, and one ticket is picked out. Because every ticket has an equal chance of being pulled, fairground lotteries are random sampling systems.

Let us say that the lottery sells 100 tickets, and you buy one ticket. What is your chance that you hold the winning ticket? The chance is one out of 100, or 1%. What if you buy five of the 100 tickets? Then you have five chances. Your chances of winning are 5%, because you hold 5% of the tickets.

Let us go back and imagine that you buy only one ticket. In fact, imagine that in this lottery each person is allowed only one ticket. Let us say that five (5%) of the people holding tickets are redheads. There are 100 tickets sold. What are the chances that a redhead wins? The chances are 5%, because redheads hold five tickets. The chances that a redhead is selected match the proportion of the population that is redheaded.

Imagine that 35 of the 100 ticket holders are teenagers. Therefore, 35% of the ticket holders are teenagers, and the likelihood that a teenager will win is 35%.

In a fairground lottery, for any characteristic, the proportion of the ticket holders who have that characteristic determine the chances that someone with that characteristic will win the lottery. If 60% of the ticket holders are women, then the likelihood that a woman will win is 60%. If 17% of the ticket holders are left handed, the likelihood that a left-hander will win is 17%.

Each selection for a random sample is like a fairground lottery: Everyone in the population is equally likely to be selected. So, if 50% of the population is female, then there is a 50% chance that a random sample draw will yield a female. If 20% of the population is over 65, then the chances are 20% that a random-sample draw will yield someone over 65. As with the lottery, in any random sampling system, the proportion of the population that has a particular characteristic is the same as the chance that someone with that characteristic will be chosen.

Why does it matter what the chances of getting each type of person are? Because of the law of large numbers. The law of large numbers says that, as the sample gets larger, the proportions of each type will tend to approach the probabilities of each type. For random samples, the probabilities are determined by the population proportions. So, as random samples get larger, the proportions of each type tend to approach the proportions of each type in the population.

That is why a random sampling procedure produces a sample that is roughly representative. The population proportions set the chances, and the chances roughly set the sample proportions.

The Proportions in a Random Sample

The proportions that appear in a large random sample roughly reflect the probabilities of getting each kind of person each time someone is selected for the sample.

For example, if the chances of picking a Californian are 2.8%, then probably about 2.8% of a large random sample will be Californians.

Random sampling requires careful attention to make sure that everyone in the population has an equal chance of being included in the sample. That's it. To create a random sample, you do not need to know what proportion of the population is left handed, female, or redheaded. The left-handers, females, and redheads are likely to appear in about the right proportions. When you create a random sample, you do not pay attention to any of the characteristics of the population or of the people put into the sample. This power of a random sample is not intuitive. It is so nonintuitive that pollsters have had trouble keeping it in mind.

Why Random Samples Become Roughly Representative

Because everyone has an equal chance of being selected, the probability of getting someone from a particular group equals the proportion of the population that is in that group. Because the proportions in a large random sample are roughly determined by the probabilities, the proportion that falls in a subgroup of a large random sample is likely to be roughly the same as the proportion of the total population that falls in that group.

When Pollsters Disregard Random Sampling

At the beginning of the 20th century, a magazine called the *Literary Digest,* conducted massive polls to predict election outcomes. In a typical poll, it would mail millions of postcards, asking Americans how they were going to vote. The *Literary Digest* had a sense that larger samples were better, but it had no understanding of random samples. The *Literary Digest's* calculations were based on the sample of postcards that were mailed back, but that was a mistake. The returned postcards were a self-selected sample. In addition, the *Literary Digest* did not mail the cards to a random sample to begin with. Instead, it collected addresses from telephone listings, automobile registration lists, and club membership rolls, without worrying about whether everyone in the general population had an equal chance of appearing in the sample.

In 1936, George Gallup (of Gallup Poll fame) recognized the mistakes that the *Literary Digest* was making in not using random samples. Before the presidential election of 1936, Gallup wrote to the *New York Times* predicting that Roosevelt would win the election. He also predicted that the *Literary Digest* would predict that Alf Landon would win and by how much the *Literary Digest* would be off.

Gallup made his predictions by gathering a random sample of Americans and asking them who they would vote for and whether they had participated in the *Literary Digest* poll. From this random sample, he was able to estimate the nature of the voting population. He was also able to estimate the nature of the population of *Literary Digest* respondents.

The *Literary Digest* finished its poll and made the predictions that Gallup had said that it would make. The country then went to the polls and reelected Roosevelt, as Gallup had predicted. The *Literary Digest* lost all credibility and went bankrupt soon after.

Unfortunately, Gallup's success in 1936 did not solidify Gallup's commitment to random sampling. Twelve years later, Gallup tried to predict the results of the 1948 presidential race between Harry Truman and Thomas Dewey. In the intervening years, Gallup had lost faith in random sampling and was replacing it with a scheme that looked more sensible to him at the time, quota sampling.

In quota sampling, rather than leaving the sample proportions to chance, you set the proportions to fit what you know about the population. For example, let's say that you were collecting a quota sample with 100 people. If 51% of your population were female, you would interview 51 females. If 2% of your population were Jewish, you would interview two Jews. And so on for everything you know about your population.

You may see why Gallup went for quota sampling over random sampling. Intuitively, it seems wrong to leave the sample proportions to chance. It is hard to imagine that chance might be more accurate than setting the quotas to be precisely right.

But Gallup was mistaken. Random sampling is a better idea. Gallup predicted that Thomas Dewey would win the 1948 election. On election day, Gallup's prediction was printed on the front page of *The Chicago Daily Tribune*: "DEWEY DEFEATS TRUMAN." And then Truman was elected. The following day, Truman

posed for photographs holding a copy of the paper with the headline proclaiming Dewey the winner.

The fault was not really with quota sampling. Using quotas can be harmless, as long as you use random sampling within each quota. For example, 12% of Americans live in California. You could set a quota for your sample of 1,000 that 120 will be from California. If you then took a truly random sample of Californians for that 120, you would have used random sampling within that quota. If you used random sampling within each quota, you would end up no worse off than if you collected a completely random sample.

The problem was that Gallup did not use random sampling. He left the interviewers free to pick people for each quota. The result was a group of interviewer-selected samples, which are just as biased as self-selected samples. Interviewer-selected samples tend to overrepresent people who are pleasant to interview and underrepresent grumpy people.

Gallup never made that mistake again, but many researchers have not learned from Gallup's experience. Gallup and other pollsters are in the business of predicting elections. This gives them lots of clear feedback: If they botch their samples, they discover their mistakes on election day. This feedback has allowed Gallup and Roper and other pollsters to hone their methods.

Some other researchers do not get such clear feedback. Think of researchers studying private activities, like the researchers studying sexual behavior. If these researchers botch their samples, who can tell? No one, not even the researchers.

Algebra and Greek Symbols

To distinguish between population statistics and statistics that appear in samples, it is common to use Greek letters for population statistics and letters of the English alphabet for sample statistics. To indicate the population proportion, you use the capital Greek letter *pi*, Π. To indicate the proportion in the sample, you use *p*. The big point of this section is that with random sampling the sample proportion will be roughly the same as the population proportion. As you will see, this is more and more the case as the random sample gets larger. The mathematical symbol "$\approx$" means "approximately equal to." Right now we can say this: For a large random sample,

$$p \approx \Pi$$

Summary

A sample is a portion of a larger group. A population is any group that a sample has been, or can be, taken from. A sample is representative of its population if the proportion of members in a certain category is the same as the proportion of the larger group that falls in that category.

If you need to guess a proportion in a sample, and if the sample is representative of some population, then you can use the proportion in the population to estimate what is happening in the sample.

A biased sampling method is a method of creating samples that will usually produce an unrepresentative sample. Self-selected samples come from a biased sampling method. Bias does not entirely prevent you from using population statistics to guess the nature of samples, because the population proportion may set an upper or lower limit on possible proportions within the sample.

Random sampling is the best way to get a representative sample. To get a random sample, use a method that gives each member of the population an equal chance of being selected. In random sampling, the proportions in the population determine the probabilities of selecting members from the population's subgroups, and these probabilities then cause the proportions in a random sample to tend to match the probabilities in the population.

Avoiding Common Misunderstandings

Proportions exist in samples and in populations. If the sample is representative of the population, the sample proportion equals the population proportion. In a nonrepresentative sample, the sample proportion does not equal the population proportion. In a biased sample, the sample proportion usually does not equal the population proportion. In a random sample, the sample proportion tends to be close to the population proportion, but does not have to precisely equal the population proportion.

The bottom line is this: The sample proportion may equal or be close to the population proportion, but the sample proportion is not the same thing as the population proportion.

Computer Project

Go to the *Data Matters* Resource Center at *www.keycollege.com/dm*, and download "Representative U.S. Sample of March 2001." Open the data file in your software. The data in that file are from 50,000 Americans surveyed in March 2001. They are a roughly representative sample of Americans who you can think of as a population.

The first column in the data is "ID_Number" and contains an identification number for each person. We are going to take random samples of the population, and we can tell who was selected by looking at the ID numbers. The second column is "Ages." The third column is "Education." This column shows the highest level of education each person has obtained. For example, the first person (ID number 1) is a high school graduate who did not go to college at all. Education was recorded only for people who were over 15 years old.

We want to know about the population. Record several proportions from the population. Include the proportion who have high school diplomas, the proportion who are under 16, and the proportion with bachelor's degrees.

Use your software to take a small random sample of the population. Look at the ID numbers and have your software take new samples several times. Can you see any pattern in which people are chosen? You shouldn't be able to see any pattern. Every person in the population collection is equally likely to be selected for the sample each time.

Take a random sample with 400 people in it.

Before you took a random sample, you recorded some of the proportions in the population in the file. Have your software calculate those same proportions for the 400-person random sample. Because the sample is a random sample, its proportions should be roughly the same. By roughly, in this case, I mean within 5%. For example, the proportion of people in the sample with a bachelor's degree is unlikely to be more than 5% away from the population proportion.

Record the proportions in the sample. Note whether the random samples are actually roughly representative of the population from which they were drawn.

Experiment with this. Try a few more samples. You can leave the proportion screens showing and watch them change. Note that they always stay near the population proportions.

The most important thing to note is that this population contains many proportions, and the random sampling creates a sample that roughly matches all of the proportions simultaneously, without looking at those attributes. All the random sampling does is select people by a system that gives every person an equal chance of being selected for the sample.

Exercises

1. Imagine that you are responsible for organizing services for welfare recipients in California. You need to know how many recipients exist. Here is a report about the United States in general:

   With 12.8 million [welfare] recipients in 1995, the numbers are down compared with 1992.
   —HAVEMANN AND VOBEJDA, *WASHINGTON POST*, MAY 13, 1996

   For this exercise, use the population sizes you learned in Chapter 1. Those figures will produce numbers that are close enough for these exercises. (I hope you remember the size of the American population. You can find the United States population in Section 1.2.)

   a. What proportion of the U.S. population received welfare in 1995?

   b. If California were representative of the country as a whole, about how many welfare recipients would you expect in California?

   c. How does your estimate compare with the number reported in the following quote?

   [California Governor] Wilson wants to drop support checks for California's 2.7 million welfare recipients—most of them children— from $607 to $565 a month in urban areas and from $607 to $538 in rural areas.
   —GUNNISON, *SAN FRANCISCO CHRONICLE*, MARCH 29, 1996

   d. Regarding the proportion on welfare, is California representative of the United States in general?

2. Here is a report on how widespread Alzheimer's disease is:

   About four million Americans suffer from Alzheimer's disease, which results in progressive memory loss and ultimate death from related complications.
   —*NEW YORK TIMES*, MAY 10, 1996

    a. What proportion of the U.S. population has Alzheimer's disease?

    b. Imagine that you are planning to provide a new center to care for Alzheimer's patients in your town (population: 100,000). How many Alzheimer's patients would you expect in your town, assuming that your town is roughly representative of the United States in general?

3. Here is a quote from a letter sent to Ann Landers:

> *Dear Ann: You seem to get a lot of letters from married women who consider sex a bore, a nuisance or a duty.*
>
> —Landers, *Seattle Post-Intelligencer*, October 17, 1996

Here is another report on how American women feel about their sex lives:

> *A standardized sexual function questionnaire was administered to 329 healthy women, aged 18–73 years, all of whom were enrolled in a Women's Wellness Center [in Piscataway, New Jersey]. . . . 68.6% of the sample rated their overall sexual relationship as satisfactory.*
>
> —Rosen, Taylor, Leiblum, and Bachmann, *Journal of Sex and Marital Therapy*, 1993

Which sample would you expect to be more representative of the general female population: the people who write to Ann Landers or 329 women at an HMO in Piscataway, New Jersey, and why?

4. Consider the information you get from news media and gossip about lottery tickets.

    a. Do these sources provide a representative sample of what happens when people buy lottery tickets?

    b. What bias influences the sample of lottery tickets that you hear about?

5. According to the following quote, researchers somehow managed to collect a random sample of public school parents.

> *[Researchers surveyed] over 600 parents in and around six Massachusetts cities. . . . According to the survey, the first of its kind to compare random samples of charter school and district school parents . . . 25 percent of charter school parents hold college or graduate school degrees, compared to 31 percent of district school parents.*
>
> —Peyser, *Boston Herald*, July 10, 1998

Describe a system that might do a good job of producing a random sample of public school parents from the Massachusetts metropolitan areas. (Assume that you have all the assistance from government agencies that you could use.)

6. According to the following quote, surveyors managed to collect a random sample of American adults.

> *A random sample of 1,514 adults was asked 11 general knowledge questions about politics and government. . . . The survey revealed [that] . . . the more you know about government and politics, the more mistrustful you are of government. But . . . more knowledgeable Americans expressed more faith in the American political system.*
>
> —MORIN, *WASHINGTON POST,* JANUARY 29, 1996

   a. If you had the full cooperation of the U.S. Internal Revenue Service, how would you try to create a random sample of adult Americans?

   b. If the researchers mentioned in the preceding quote really did collect a random sample of Americans, each time they picked someone, what were the chances that they would pick someone from the New York metropolitan area? (You can find the New York metropolitan area population in Section 1.2.)

   c. About what proportion of a random sample of Americans would you guess lived in New York State?

   d. Explain your answer to Exercise 6c.

7. The following quote describes how a sample was collected for one study.

> *Charles County elementary school students face some of Maryland's most crowded classrooms while those in neighboring St. Mary's County enjoy some of the state's least crowded, according to a survey of teachers. . . . [The] State Teachers Association . . . distributed 60,000 questionnaires to teachers across the state and got back about 30,000 replies.*
>
> —SHIELDS, *WASHINGTON POST,* JUNE 14, 1998

   Why would this method not produce a random sample?

8. As the following quote reports, pollsters were embarrassed in the 1996 United States elections.

> *In Arizona, exit poll results reaching political campaigns and newsrooms in the late afternoon indicated, erroneously as it turned out, that Mr. Buchanan was winning, and winning big.*
>
> —LINDBERG, *WASHINGTON TIMES,* MARCH 20, 1996

In the 1996 presidential primary in Arizona, Patrick Buchanan came in third, after Steve Forbes and Bob Dole. Election night estimates are based on exit polls. Exit polls are surveys of voters as they are coming out of the polling locations where they voted. To do these surveys, pollsters ask exiting voters to fill out questionnaires about how they voted. Write a short note explaining your guess as to why the 1996 Arizona polls were inaccurate.

9. In preparation for the 2002 Winter Olympics in northern Utah, meteorologists at the University of Utah tried to help the Olympic organizers anticipate the weather during the 2002 games.

   The University of Utah meteorology department has taken a detailed look at northern Utah's weather records during a slightly extended Olympic period (Feb. 5–25). . . . The U. figures put the chance of fog during a four-hour [Olympic opening] ceremony at 10 percent.

   —GORRELL, SALT LAKE TRIBUNE, SEPTEMBER 24, 2001

   What kind of research could researchers do to find the probability of fog? That is, what might they have done as they were trying to discover the probability of fog, and why would that research reveal the probability?

10. The following quote makes a claim about a probability.

    University of Arizona President Peter Likins lifted a ban Thursday on the hiring of adjunct professors for next semester. . . . In the media arts department, students have a 70 percent chance of enrolling in classes taught by nontenure-track faculty members.

    —SKLAR, ARIZONA DAILY WILDCAT, NOVEMBER 16, 2001

    Actually, 70% of Arizona media arts students were enrolled in classes taught by nontenure-track faculty members. What method of class selection would Arizona media arts students have to be using for it to be true that every student had a 70% chance of being taught by a nontenure-track faculty member?

11. Here's another report on the 1996 polling inaccuracies:

    [The networks] all made the same Election Night blooper in 1996— the call that Senator Robert Smith, R-NH, had lost his reelection bid. In fact, he defeated his Democratic opponent. . . . [Political pollster] Edelman speculated that Republicans in New Hampshire . . . were less inclined to fill out exit poll questionnaires.

    —BARNES, PUBLIC PERSPECTIVE, JANUARY 1997

    a. Why does it matter if Republicans are less inclined to fill out exit polls than Democrats?
    b. What kind of sample is used in exit polling?
    c. In a random sample, the proportions in the population determine the probabilities of being selected for the sample, and the probabilities drive the proportions in the sample. In exit polls, which part of that scheme doesn't work: the population proportions determining the probabilities, or the probabilities driving the sample proportions?

12. In your own words, explain why random sampling tends to produce a representative sample in the long run.

13. The following quote reports on the total population.

    In 1992, 38 percent of Americans considered homosexuality "an acceptable alternative lifestyle," according to Gallup polls. By 2001, the proportion had jumped to 52 percent.
    —PADAWER, [BERGEN COUNTY, NEW JERSEY] RECORD, AUGUST 15, 2001

    In previous studies, Republicans have expressed less tolerance of homosexuality than Democrats.

    a. What does this quote tell you about the proportion of Republicans who consider homosexuality "an acceptable alternative lifestyle"?

    b. What does this quote tell you about the proportion of Democrats who consider homosexuality "an acceptable alternative lifestyle"?

14. The following quote indicates that workers who live in remote suburbs (farther-out suburbs) are more likely to drive to work alone than the general population.

    [According to the Census Bureau] nationally, 76 percent of workers 16 and older drove alone to work, up from the 1990 census figure of 73 percent. . . . Farther-out suburbs . . . contributed to the trend despite continued efforts to push public transportation and carpooling, analysts said.
    —ARMAS, *BATON ROUGE ADVOCATE*, AUGUST 7, 2001

    What does this quote tell you about the proportion of workers (16 and older) who live in the farther-out suburbs who drive alone to work?

Answers to Odd-Numbered Exercises

1. a. As you may have read from Table 1.2.2, in 1995, there were 263 million Americans. Of these, 5% received welfare, because 12.8 million is 5% of 263 million. If you used 285 million, you got 4.49%, which rounds to 4%. Either way, you get the idea.

   b. 1.7 million. If California were representative of the country as a whole, the proportion on welfare would be the same in California, 5%. There are 34 million people in California, and 5% of 34 million is 1.6 million. (It would have been impressive if you estimated how many Californians there were in 1995 and used that figure. In 1995, there were 32 million, and we would estimate that 1.6 million were on welfare.)

    c. My estimate, 1.7 million, was much lower than the actual number, 2.7 million.

    d. California is not representative of the general population in terms of welfare. Californians are more likely to receive welfare than the general population.

3. Ann Landers answered this one:

> *Dear T.W.R.: The reason I print so many letters from women who don't get enough or get too much is because the ones who are content don't write me.*
>
> —LANDERS, *SEATTLE POST-INTELLIGENCER,* OCTOBER 17, 1996

The Women's Wellness Center is more likely to be a representative sample. The letter writers who write about their love lives are a self-selected sample of people who are especially concerned about difficulties in their love lives.

5. With help from the Census Bureau and the local vital statistics office, I would create a computerized database listing everyone in the Massachusetts metropolitan areas. Once I had this list, I could use the random number–generating function of a computer program to randomly select my sample.

7. It's a self-selected sample, as was noted by school officials:

> *Charles school officials cast doubt on the results of the survey by the state teachers association. They said bias may have crept in because the study did not use random samples but depended on answers from teachers who chose to reply to a questionnaire.*
>
> —SHIELDS, *WASHINGTON POST,* JUNE 14, 1998

9. The researchers could have checked records of a large random sample of previous four-hour blocks of time in that date range (February 5 to 25). If they found that 10% of the four-hour blocks were foggy, the researchers could infer that the probability of fog was 10%, because the proportion of an event in a large random sample tends to be near the probability of that event.

11. a. If Republicans are less likely to fill out exit polls, then exit polls are biased toward overrepresenting Democrats.

    b. A self-selected sample.

    c. It is the probabilities of getting Democrats and getting Republicans that are not right: They do not match the proportions of Democrats and Republicans in the population.

13. a. Somewhere between 0% and 51% of Republicans consider homosexuality "an acceptable alternative lifestyle."

    b. Somewhere between 53% and 100% of Democrats consider homosexuality "an acceptable alternative lifestyle."

2.2 How Samples Vary

- Histograms
- Bell Curves

Three teams . . . have winning percentages over .550, and only three . . . have winning percentages under .450. . . . Baseball's bell curve always bulges at the middle.

—GEE, *BOSTON HERALD*, MAY 2, 1997

WHAT MICHAEL GEE MEANS by "winning percentage" is the proportion of the games that a team has played that the team won. For example, if the Seattle Mariners play four games and win three, their winning percentage is 75%. Gee would call it ".750." According to Gee, at the end of April 1997, three teams had winning percentages above 55%, three had winning percentages below 45%, and the rest were bunched up between 45% and 55%, a bulge at the middle. Gee seems to be saying that some bulge always happens, but what does he mean by baseball's *"bell curve"*?

The bell curve is a regular pattern that appears in proportions. As you saw in the last section, proportions in samples vary. They vary, but they do not vary completely chaotically.

Proportions tend to hang together. For example, if you had 10 pennies, and you shook them up and tossed them on a table, you could calculate the proportion of heads. You could write down that proportion of heads, pick up your 10 pennies, and toss them again. If you did this several times, you would get a variety of proportions, one from each sample. Sometimes there would be five heads—50% heads. Sometimes there would be 40% heads. Sometimes there would be 60% heads. What you would find is that most of the proportions would be near 50%.

To let you see what this is like, I flipped a set of 10 coins 100 times. I got 10% heads 2 times; 20% heads 3 times, 30% heads 14 times, 40% heads 17 times, 50% heads 25 times, 60% heads 20 times, 70% heads 9 times, 80% heads 8 times, and 90% heads 2 times. Table 2.2.1 shows how many of each percentage appeared.

Histograms

As you scan Table 2.2.1, you can see the number of appearances rises to the 25 appearances of 50% heads and then drops again. Figure 2.2.1 shows a picture of the numbers in Table 2.2.1.

Figure 2.2.1 has a bar for each percentage of heads. A short bar on the far left shows the two times I got only 10% heads. The bar to its right is slightly higher, because it shows the three times I got 20% heads. The tallest bar, over 50%, shows the 25 times I got five heads.

The height of each bar shows how many times each percentage appeared. For example, if I look at the bar for 40% heads, I see that that bar's height matches

Table 2.2.1 Number of Times Each Heads Percentage Appeared in 100 Flips of a Set of 10 Coins

HEADS PERCENTAGE	NUMBER OF APPEARANCES
0%	0
10%	2
20%	3
30%	14
40%	17
50%	25
60%	20
70%	9
80%	8
90%	2
100%	0

Figure 2.2.1 **How Often Each Heads Percentage Appeared**

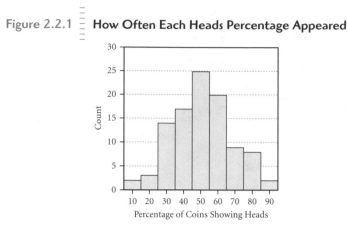

about 17 or 18 on the scale on the left axis, so there must have been about 17 or 18 throws with 40% heads. Looking back at Table 2.2.1, I see that there were 17.

The sort of graph in Figure 2.2.1 is called a "histogram." "Histo" comes from the Greek word *histos,* which means the mast of a sailing ship. In a histogram, the bars that stick up look like ship masts. The second part, "gram," is like the "gram" in "telegram." A telegram is a message sent over a telegraph wire. A histogram is a message written in masts.

Histograms

Histograms are bar graphs that show how often various numbers appeared. A histogram has a number line across the bottom and bars that stick up above the number line. Each bar covers a segment of the number line. As long as every bar is equally wide, the height of each bar indicates how often numbers in that bar's segment appeared.

For example, imagine that four people purchase groceries, spending $1, $2, $11, and $36. The 1, 2, 11, and 36 could be depicted in a histogram like this:

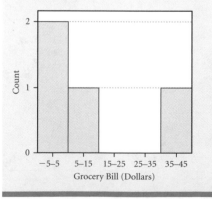

Looking at the histogram in Figure 2.2.1, you can see that there is a tall bar over 50%, which was a very popular percentage. The percentages 30%, 40%, and 60% were all fairly common. It was rare to get 10% or 90%, and there were no tosses with no heads or 100% heads. If you sketched a curve over the outline of the histogram in Figure 2.2.1, you might end up with a drawing like that in Figure 2.2.2.

Figure 2.2.2   **Histogram with Sketched Outline Curve**

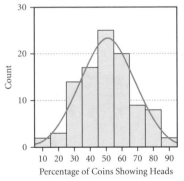

How would you describe the shape in the histogram? It is a little like a bell. It has a mass in the middle and then splays out on either side. The bell shape of such distributions is quite common.

Bell Shape

Histograms of proportions from samples tend to be roughly bell shaped—mounded in the middle and splayed out on either side.

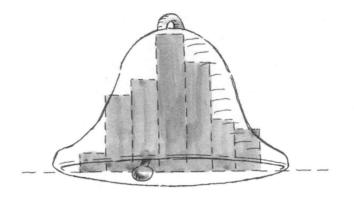

What if I tried the tossing exercise with 20 coins instead of 10? Would a different number of coins produce a very different picture? To show you, I flipped a set of 20 coins 100 times. Table 2.2.2 shows how often each heads percentage appeared.

Figure 2.2.3 shows those percentages in a histogram. This histogram is similar to the histogram in Figure 2.2.2. There is a mound in the center that splays out on either side.

In both histograms, the bells are roughly centered over 50%. That is what will typically happen for proportions. For any set of proportions, the bell has its center at roughly the probability of the outcome. If you were randomly selecting Americans, and you looked at the proportion who lived in California, you'd find that the center of the bell shape was at about 11%, the proportion of Americans who live in California.

Table 2.2.2   Number of Times Each Heads Percentage Appeared in 100 Flips of a Set of 20 Coins

HEADS PERCENTAGE	NUMBER OF APPEARANCES	HEADS PERCENTAGE	NUMBER OF APPEARANCES
20%	1	50%	15
25%	2	55%	16
30%	3	60%	9
35%	7	65%	12
40%	12	70%	4
45%	17	75%	2

Figure 2.2.3

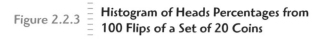
Histogram of Heads Percentages from 100 Flips of a Set of 20 Coins

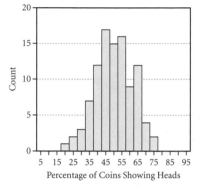

Where the Bell Shape Is Centered

The bell shape in histograms of sample proportions tends to be centered at the proportion of the population from which the sample was drawn.

For example, the chances of rolling a die and getting either a five or a six are 33%. If you roll handfuls of dice, the histogram of the proportions of each handful that came up with fives or sixes would be roughly centered around 33%, as you can see in this histogram of proportions from rolling handfuls of 20 dice 50 times.

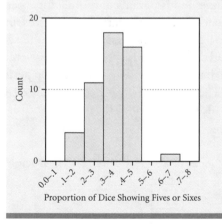

What does this have to do with Michael Gee's comment about "baseball's bell curve"? What Gee is implying is that most teams have something like a 50/50 chance of winning each game. Let's say they have played 30 games, for example. You can think of it as though each team has flipped 30 coins. Some teams end up with only 43% heads. Others end up with 57% heads. Altogether, if you draw a histogram of the winning percentages, you'll see something like a bell curve.

Figure 2.2.4 **Baseball Winning Percentages on July 17, 1997**

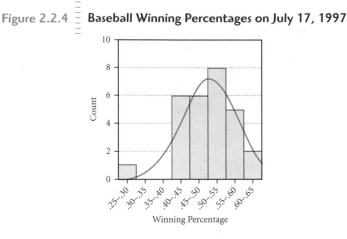

Winning Percentage

Figure 2.2.4 shows a histogram of the National and American League winning percentages on July 17, 1997. In Figure 2.2.4, I have drawn in the bell shape that I can kind of see in the histogram. The histogram itself is the bars. The curve is my effort to show you a bell-like shape in that histogram.

The bell shape that shows up in proportions does not always look particularly well made. The bell shape in Figure 2.2.4's histogram looks a little lopsided. In fact, it has a gap from .30 to .40. That happens. As you add more and more proportions, the bell shape tends to be better and better drawn.

You can see bell curves in histograms of mutual fund performances as well. To show you this, I went back to the stock market report. This time I made up 200 simple mutual funds. The first had the first 10 stocks, the second had the second 10 stocks, the third had the third 10 stocks, and so on. Overall, that day, 70% of the stocks rose in value. In my mutual funds that day, the top performer had 100% of its stocks go up in value. The five worst performers had only 30% of their stocks rise in value. Figure 2.2.5 is a histogram showing the performance of my 200 mutual funds.

Figure 2.2.5 **Histogram of Performances of 200 Hypothetical 10-Stock Mutual Funds**

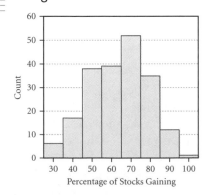

Percentage of Stocks Gaining

Table 2.2.3 Number of Hypothetical 10-Stock Mutual Funds with Each Gainer Percentage

GAINER PERCENTAGE	NUMBER OF FUNDS
30%	6
40%	17
50%	38
60%	39
70%	52
80%	35
90%	12
100%	1

You can check that you understand what a histogram is by looking at Figure 2.2.5 and guessing how many 30% gains there were, how many 40% gains, and so on, and then checking your guesses against the data in Table 2.2.3.

The bell shape that appears in histograms of proportions is a fairly reliable feature of samples that come from systems that involve chance. It doesn't matter whether you're looking at stock prices, mortality rates, birth rates, crop yields, or how many people come into a restaurant. As long as the population being sampled stays roughly the same and the sample size stays roughly the same, as the number of samples gets larger, the bell shape tends to emerge.

Histogram Bar Widths

Histogram bar widths can vary from each other, although they usually do not. For example, one bar could cover from 1 to just under 45, and the next bar could cover from 45 to 50. When bars have different widths, the count of the numbers represented by each bar is indicated by the area of the bar.

Using bars of different widths is unusual, and I won't do it in this book. A histogram with every bar the same width is a type of bar chart, where the count is indicated by the height of the bar.

When you are creating histograms, you will need to choose widths to work with. Histograms with bars of equal widths are usually easier to understand because of their similarity to bar charts. The question of what width to use is up to your judgment. The width you choose will affect how many bars there are. A histogram with wide bars has fewer bars. A histogram with narrow bars has more. A histogram with just one bar doesn't convey any information, and a histogram with 100 bars conveys more information than is useful. Use a bar width that gives you somewhere from 2 to 99 bars. Usually 5 to 20 bars tell a lot.

Assigning Numbers to Bars

Each bar in a histogram represents all of the numbers on the part of the number line that the bar covers. For example, a bar that sits over 0, 1, and 2 also represents 1.3, 1.7, and 0.5.

When you create your own histograms, you will have to assign each number in the data to a bar. For example, if your first bar is from 0 to 10, and your second bar is from 10 to 20, where do you put 10? Does it go in the first bar or the second bar? The answer depends on your judgment. If you decide that your bars are from 0 to *just under* 10 and from 10 to *just under* 20, 10 goes in the second bar. If your bars are from *just over* 0 to 10 and from *just over* 10 to 20, 10 goes in the first bar. It is most common to assign numbers the first way, from 0 to *just under* 10.

Labeling the Bottom of the Histogram

There are several approaches to labeling the bottom of a histogram. You can label each bar by the value in the center of that bar, as in Figure 2.2.6. This is the most common approach. You can label each bar by the range it covers, as in Figure 2.2.7. In Figure 2.2.7, the "25–35" means "from 25 to *just under* 35," and so on for each bar's labels. A less common approach is to label the edges of each bar.

 Figure 2.2.6 **Histogram with Bars Labeled by the Value at the Midpoint of Each Bar**

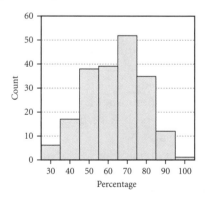

Figure 2.2.7

**Histogram with Bars Labeled by the
Range of Values of Each Bar**

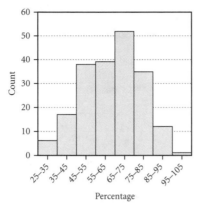

Algebra and Greek Symbols

The statistical jargon for what this section talks about is called a "sampling distribution." A sampling distribution is the way a statistic is distributed (spread out in a histogram) when you calculate that statistic from each of many samples.

In this section, the statistic we looked at is the proportion. This section says that when you calculate proportions from many samples, you will find that the proportions you calculated are distributed in roughly a bell shape, with the center of the bell at roughly the probability that is leading to the proportion. We expect proportions to fall in a particular range. We estimate probabilities, but our estimated probabilities do not determine proportions; actual probabilities do.

Another way to say that is this: If the probability of event X is θ, and p is the proportion of events that are event X, then the sampling distribution of p is roughly bell shaped with a center at θ.

Summary

Histograms are like bar graphs—they show bars over number lines. When every bar is the same width, histograms show how many observations fall in each segment by the height of the bar over that segment.

Histograms of sample proportions will usually be roughly bell shaped, mounding in the center and splaying out on either edge. The center of the bell shape will be at roughly the probability that is expected for that proportion.

Avoiding Common Misunderstandings

When every bar in a histogram is equally wide, the height of each bar indicates how many numbers are on the portion of the number line on which that bar stands. For example, if there are twice as many 2's as 3's, and each has its own bar, then the bar for 2's will be twice as tall as the bar for 3's.

Computer Project

Don't take my word for it. Run some simulations yourself. Using your software, set the probability where you would like it, set the sample size where you would like it, and use the random number generator to simulate taking samples. Record the proportions that appear in the samples and make a histogram of those proportions. You will find that the histograms are roughly bell shaped, with centers at the probability that you chose.

Repeat the process with larger samples. You'll notice that your histograms are narrower with larger samples. That's the law of large numbers.

Exercises

I have a game at home, Yahtzee™, in which you roll five dice at a time. I rolled those five dice 200 times, keeping track of the percentages that came up 1's, and keeping track of the percentages that came up greater than 4. The following table shows how things turned out.

PERCENTAGE OF DICE SHOWING 1'S	NUMBER OF APPEARANCES	PERCENTAGE OF DICE SHOWING NUMBERS GREATER THAN 4	NUMBER OF APPEARANCES
0%	76	0%	26
20%	89	20%	65
40%	31	40%	74
60%	4	60%	26
80%	0	80%	8
100%	0	100%	1

1. Sketch a histogram of the percentages of the dice showing numbers greater than 4. Do not forget to label your axes.

2. Sketch a histogram of the percentages of the dice that came up 1's.

3. Using the histogram you sketched for Exercise 1, you can test the claim about the location of the histogram's center.

   a. When you consider dice rolls, what is the probability of rolling a number greater than 4?

   b. Look at the histogram you sketched for Exercise 1. In that histogram, did the center of the bell shape fall where you expected it?

   c. Write down why you answered Exercise 3b as you did.

4. You can check the center's location by looking at your histogram from Exercise 2.

   a. What is the probability that a rolled die will come up a 1?

   b. Look at the histogram you sketched for Exercise 2. In that histogram, did the center of the bell shape fall where you expected it?

   c. Write down why you answered Exercise 4b as you did.

5. The *Statistical Abstract of the United States, 1995* reports the percentage of total horsepower that was used in propelling automobiles rather than other machines in the United States, as shown in the following table.

   a. Try drawing a histogram of the percentages from the table.

   b. In what ways does that histogram look like a bell?

   c. How does it look unlike a bell?

YEAR	PERCENTAGE OF HORSEPOWER USED BY AUTOMOBILES	YEAR	PERCENTAGE OF HORSEPOWER USED BY AUTOMOBILES
1960	94.2%	1985	94.7%
1965	94.8%	1986	94.6%
1970	94.7%	1987	94.7%
1975	94.6%	1988	94.8%
1980	94.6%	1989	94.8%
1981	94.6%	1990	94.7%
1982	94.6%	1991	94.8%
1983	94.7%	1992	94.7%
1984	94.7%		

6. You can estimate the population proportion from a histogram.

   a. Assume for the moment that there is a constant tendency to have a particular proportion of U.S. horsepower put into cars. If you had to guess one proportion that describes the total population, what proportion would you guess?

   b. Write down why you answered Exercise 6a the way you did.

I shuffle a deck and deal hands of cards. Ten hands have one card each. Ten hands have two cards each. Ten hands have five cards each. The following table shows the percentages of each hand that were red.

DEAL	PERCENTAGE RED IN HANDS WITH ONE CARD	PERCENTAGE RED IN HANDS WITH TWO CARDS	PERCENTAGE RED IN HANDS WITH FIVE CARDS
1	100%	50%	40%
2	0%	0%	80%
3	0%	50%	60%
4	0%	50%	60%
5	0%	50%	20%
6	100%	100%	80%
7	100%	50%	40%
8	100%	50%	60%
9	0%	0%	60%
10	0%	0%	20%

7. Sketch a histogram for the percentages from the one-card hands.

8. Sketch a histogram for the percentages from the two-card hands.

9. Check whether a bell shape appears in the percentages from one-card hands.

   a. Sketch a histogram for the percentages from the five-card hands.

   b. Do you think that the idea that percentages fall into a bell shape depends on the number of observations that went into each proportion?

   c. Write down why you answered Exercise 9b the way you did.

10. On January 21, 1999, the *Hartford Courant* published the Hartford office vacancy rate for 1988 through 1998. The office vacancy rate is the proportion of office space that is available to be rented in a city that has no tenant renting it. In economic downturns, as businesses go under, the office

vacancy rate goes up. A healthy rental market has a low office vacancy rate. The following table shows the office vacancy rates for those years.

a. Sketch a histogram of those rates.

b. Is the histogram somewhat bell shaped?

YEAR	OFFICE VACANCY RATE PERCENTAGE	YEAR	OFFICE VACANCY RATE PERCENTAGE
1988	8.0%	1994	20.8%
1989	14.3%	1995	18.3%
1990	14.7%	1996	16.4%
1991	16.8%	1997	14.7%
1992	19.9%	1998	9.6%
1993	18.2%		

11. I deal 10 hands of cards, shuffling the deck between each deal. Each hand has five cards. The following table shows the percentages of the cards that were aces in each deal.

a. Sketch a histogram of the 10 percentages.

b. There are four aces in a deck of 52 cards, so about 8% of the cards are aces. If a bell shape appeared over a proportion of 8%, why wouldn't it get much splay to the left?

HAND NUMBER	PERCENTAGE OF ACES
1	0%
2	0%
3	0%
4	20%
5	0%
6	20%
7	0%
8	20%
9	0%
10	0%

12. At the end of the 1998–99 season, the *Kansas City Star* published the win-loss record for the Kansas University basketball team for each year from 1988 to 1999. The following table shows the win-loss records along with the percentages of games that Kansas University won each year.

a. Try sketching a histogram of Kansas's winning percentages.

b. In what way is the histogram not bell shaped?

SCHOOL YEAR	WINS	LOSSES	WINNING PERCENTAGES
1988–89	10	4	71%
1989–90	15	1	94%
1990–91	15	0	100%
1991–92	13	1	93%
1992–93	13	2	87%
1993–94	13	3	81%
1994–95	14	0	100%
1995–96	13	0	100%
1996–97	15	0	100%
1997–98	16	0	100%
1998–99	10	3	77%

Answers to Odd-Numbered Exercises

1. **Histogram of Percentages of Five Dice That Showed Numbers Greater Than 4**

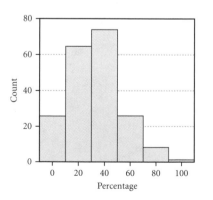

3. a. The chance of rolling a number greater than 4 is the chance of getting a 5 or a 6, which is two-sixths, or one-third, which is 33%.

b. Yes.

c. I was expecting a center of the bell near 33%, and the top of the center lump is somewhere between 20% and 40%, a little closer to 40% than 20%. It looks about right.

5. a. **Histogram of Percentages of Horsepower Used by Automobiles**

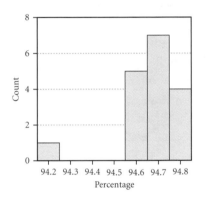

b. It has a mound over 94.6 to 94.8, and you might call the single 94.2 a splay to the left.

c. There is no splay to the right, and 94.2 looks somewhat far away to be called a splay to the left. This looks a lot like a mound without much splay and with a number that lies outside the typical range.

7.

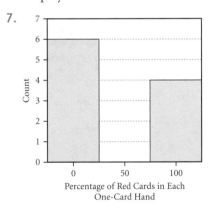

9. a.

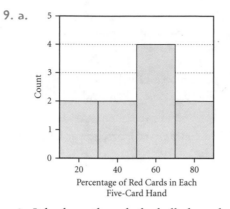

Percentage of Red Cards in Each
Five-Card Hand

b. It looks as though the bell-shaped nature depends at least a little on the number of observations.

c. When there is only one observation in each sample, you can only get a two-pronged histogram with bars over 0% and 100%.

11. a.

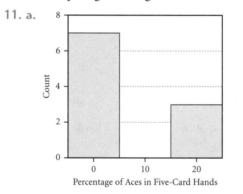

Percentage of Aces in Five-Card Hands

b. If a bell appeared that was centered at 8%, it wouldn't be able to spread much to the left, because percentages cannot go below 0.

2.3 How Widely Samples Vary

- The Standard Error of a Proportion
- The Normal Distribution

The percentage of minority students in the five entering Columbia [Law School] classes between 1991 and 1995 ranged from a low of 28 percent to 39 percent. During the same period, the percentage of minorities in NYU's entering [law school] classes ranged from 22 percent to 27 percent.

—WISE, *NEW YORK LAW JOURNAL*, AUGUST 15, 1996

OVER THE LAST DECADE, some universities have stopped setting quotas for minority student admissions. A quota is a proportion of the class that is set to be drawn from a particular ethnic group. When these quotas are dropped, the press reports that fact, partially because the proportion of students in each class who are minorities change from year to year, as described in the preceding quote.

Why do the percentages of minority students change? One possibility is that the schools change something from year to year so that the chances that an admitted student is part of a minority group rise and fall. But there is another possibility. The shifting around might be due to chance variation (variation due to who happens to appear in each year's sample—each year's class). If there is a constant chance that any given student will be part of a minority group, it is like the constant 50% chance of getting heads when a coin is flipped. Although the chance, or probability, is constant, the sample proportions will not all be the same.

But could chance variation make the proportions jump from 28% to 39%? Each year, Columbia admits 330 students. Surely the law of large numbers would keep the proportions steadier—or would it?

Let's see whether chance would give us this result. Let's guess that Columbia has a steady 33.5% chance of admitting a minority student. I picked 33.5% because it is halfway between Columbia's two extremes, 28% and 39%. Now let's see how chance would affect the variation of the sample proportions when the probability is 33.5% and there are 330 students in each sample.

To find out how chance, or random variation, affects the proportions, we can use a computer to simulate admissions. Most computer programming languages come with a random number generator. For example, the BASIC programming language comes with a function called "RND." RND produces decimals from 0 to just under 1 in a way so that every decimal is equally likely on each draw. RND produces a random sample of the decimals from 0 to 1.

I asked BASIC to print out six numbers from RND, and it gave me these:

0.9723017   0.3894116   0.0428060   0.5109064   0.8048474   0.7027486

Because every decimal from 0 to 1 is equally likely, the probability of getting a number below a particular proportion from RND is the same as that proportion. For example, in the long run, half of the decimals will be below .5, 10% will be below 0.1, 33.5% will be below 0.335 and so on.

Columbia admits 330 students each year. To simulate Columbia's admissions, a computer would pick 330 numbers using RND and check what proportion was below 33.5% (below .335).

The simulation is not a very hard program to write, so I did it for you, and here is how it turned out. The first time I simulated picking 330 students, I got 102 minority students (31%). The next time, I got 110 (33%). The next four times, I got 35%, 35%, 31%, and 34%. Sorted from smallest to largest, the six percentages were 31%, 31%, 33%, 34%, 35%, and 35%. Figure 2.3.1 shows a histogram of those percentages.

Figure 2.3.1 shows a range of only 4% from the smallest to the largest. Columbia had a range of 11%. But there is something unusual about Figure 2.3.1. The histogram is not bell shaped. That is because there are so few samples. To find out if more samples would make the histogram bell shaped and to get a better image of how such percentages would be spread out, or distributed, I repeated the simulation 10,000 times. Figure 2.3.2 shows the distribution of 10,000 simulated minority percentages for a class size of 330 students.

Figure 2.3.1

Six Simulated Minority Student Percentages (Probability = 33.5%; Sample Size = 330)

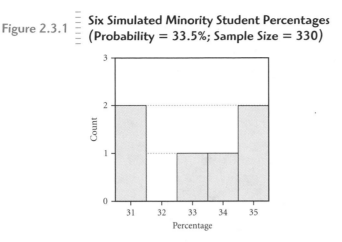

Figure 2.3.2

10,000 Simulated Minority Student Percentages (Probability = 33.5%; Sample Size = 330)

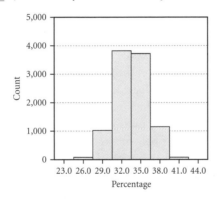

There's the bell curve. Figure 2.3.2 shows how random variation distributes the sample proportions when you have a 33.5% chance of getting a minority student, and you collect classes of 330 students each. In light of Figure 2.3.2, a range from 28% to 39% seems like a possible result of random variation. It is reasonable to guess that the variation in proportions at Columbia is just random variation—like the variations in the proportions of heads that you might see in sets of coin flips.

How about New York University (NYU)? From 1991 to 1995, NYU's minority student proportions ranged from 22% to 27%. For NYU, I ran the simulation again, but this time, I guessed that the probability of getting a minority student was 24.5%. NYU admits about 400 students each year, so I simulated classes with 400 students each. As before, I created 10,000 simulated classes. Figure 2.3.3 shows how the simulated proportions were spread out.

NYU's variation from 22% to 27% seems like something that could result from the distribution shown in Figure 2.3.3. In the case of both schools, the variation in their minority student proportions could reasonably be due to random variation.

It's awkward running a simulation program every time you want to know how proportions in samples would be distributed. Luckily, we don't need to do that, because a lot is known about how chance distributes random sample proportions.

We know that a histogram of random sample proportions displays a bell shape, but there are a variety of bell shapes. Sample proportions tend toward a specific bell shape that is called the *normal distribution*. Figure 2.3.4 shows the outline of a histogram of a normal distribution.

Figure 2.3.3

10,000 Simulated Minority Student Percentages (Probability = 24.5%; Sample Size = 400)

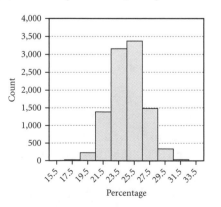

Figure 2.3.4 **The Shape of a Normal Distribution**

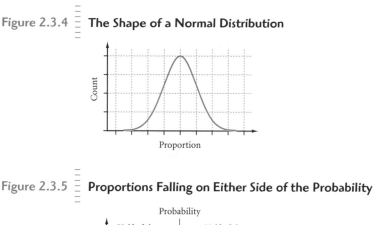

Figure 2.3.5 **Proportions Falling on Either Side of the Probability**

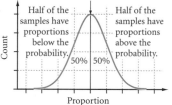

When you gather random samples, their proportions become roughly normally distributed, with the center of their distribution falling at the probability of the proportion's outcome. That means that half of the sample proportions fall at or above the probability, and half fall below, as in Figure 2.3.5.

Proportions Are Approximately Normally Distributed

If groups of samples each have the same number of observations and are all drawn from a system with a steady chance of some outcome, then the proportions in each sample that are that outcome will be distributed in a specific bell shape: the normal distribution.

For example, if the chances of a child having attention deficit disorder (ADD) are 10%, and each of many elementary schools has 300 students, a histogram of the proportions of students at the schools who have ADD would be roughly distributed in a normal distribution.

On either side of the normal distribution, fairly straight diagonal sides spread down before curving outward. The distance along the x-axis from the middle of the bell to about midway along the straight sides is called 1 "standard error," meaning that it is a standard distance off the mark. (We'll talk about how to calculate the standard error a little later.) Figure 2.3.6 shows the normal distribution with lines drawn in marking where the standard errors fall.

Figure 2.3.6 **Normal Distribution Divided into Sections That Are Each 1 Standard Error Wide**

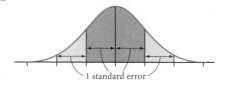

1 standard error

Figure 2.3.7 **Normal Distribution Showing That 95% of Sample Proportions Fall Between 2 Standard Errors Below the Probability and 2 Standard Errors Above the Probability**

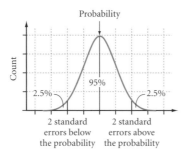

The center lump contains most of the proportions—95% of samples will have proportions that are within the center 4 standard errors. That is, the middle 95% of the sample proportions will fall not more than 2 standard errors away from the probability, as shown in Figure 2.3.7. (Later in this chapter, I will show you how to check these claims for yourself.)

Once you know the standard error, you can figure out where 95% (almost all) of the sample proportions will be. Because the normal distribution is symmetrical, the other 5% of the sample proportions appear evenly on both sides: 2.5% of the sample proportions fall below the middle 95% (more than 2 standard errors below the probability), and 2.5% fall above the middle 95% (more than 2 standard errors above the probability).

Of the samples, 68% will have proportions that fall in the middle 2 standard errors of the normal distribution. So, the middle 68% of the sample proportions will be not more than 1 standard error away from the probability. The amount 68% is just a little more than 1% more than two-thirds, so it's reasonable to think of it as two-thirds falling within 1 standard error of the probability, as shown in Figure 2.3.8.

The normal distribution is symmetrical. If about two-thirds of the proportions fall in the middle, the other third falls on the outside. One-sixth of the sample proportions fall below 1 standard error *below* the probability, and one-sixth fall above 1 standard error *above* the probability. Figure 2.3.9 shows a summary of how many proportions fall in each part of the normal distribution.

Figure 2.3.8

Normal Distribution Showing That the Middle 68% of Sample Proportions Fall Within 1 Standard Error of the Probability

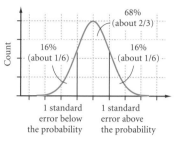

Figure 2.3.9

Where Sample Proportions Fall in a Normal Distribution

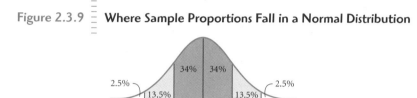

Figure 2.3.9 shows that 2.5% of samples have proportions that fall below 2 standard errors below the probability, 13.5% of samples have proportions that fall between 1 and 2 standard errors below the probability, 34% have proportions that fall between 1 standard error below the probability and the probability, and so on.

The Standard Error of the Normal Distribution

The distance on the number line from the center of a normal distribution to where the diagonal sides of the normal distribution look the straightest is 1 standard error. For proportions,

$$\text{Standard Error} = \sqrt{\frac{\text{Probability} \times (1 - \text{Probability})}{\text{Sample Size}}}$$

In a normal distribution, 68% of the proportions fall within 1 standard error of the center, and 95% of the proportions fall within 2 standard errors of the center.

For example, imagine a football league with many teams. Each team has 25 players. Each player has a 20% chance of having a cold on Thanksgiving Day. On Thanksgiving Day, each team will have some proportion of players who are sick with colds. Those proportions will be normally distributed with a standard error of 8%: 95% of the proportions will be between 4% and 36% (between 20% minus 16% and 20% plus 16%). Two-thirds of the proportions will be between 12% and 28%.

Calculating the Standard Error

All this information about the normal distribution isn't terribly useful if you don't know what the standard error is. Fortunately, you do not need to run a simulation or collect many proportions to find the standard error. Before collecting any samples, if you know the probability and the number of observations in each sample, you can calculate the standard error. Here is how:

$$\text{Standard Error of Sample Proportions} = \sqrt{\frac{\text{Probability} \times (1 - \text{Probability})}{\text{Sample Size}}}$$

The "sample size" is the number of observations in each sample. For this equation to work, you need to have the same number of observations in each sample.

To see what I mean by that equation, let's try it out on the example of Columbia admissions. Our estimate for Columbia was that the probability is 33.5% (.335), and the sample size is 330. To find the standard error, I start with that equation, plug in Columbia's figures, and then do the calculations:

$$\text{Standard Error} = \sqrt{\frac{\text{Probability} \times (1 - \text{Probability})}{\text{Sample Size}}}$$

I plug in .335 for the probability, and 330 for the sample size:

$$\text{Standard Error} = \sqrt{\frac{.335 \times (1 - .335)}{330}}$$

When we calculate, we do what is inside the parentheses first. The value 1 minus .335 is .665:

$$\text{Standard Error} = \sqrt{\frac{.335 \times .665}{330}}$$

The value .335 times .665 is .222775:

$$\text{Standard Error} = \sqrt{\frac{.222775}{330}}$$

The value .222775 divided by 330 is .000675:

$$\text{Standard Error} = \sqrt{.000675}$$

The square root of .000675 is .02598:

$$\text{Standard Error} = .02598$$

We round .02598 to .026, which is 2.6%:

$$\text{Standard Error} = 2.6\%$$

Once we know the standard error, we can predict where the sample proportions will fall. Figure 2.3.10 shows the predictions we would make. The figure

Figure 2.3.10

Predicted Distribution of Sample Proportions (Estimated Probability = 33.5%; Sample Size = 330; Standard Error = 2.6%)

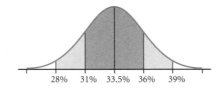

shows half of the sample proportions falling at about 33.5% or lower, and the other half falling at about 33.5% or higher. The middle 95% of the sample proportions range from about 28% to about 39%. The middle two-thirds range from about 31% to about 36%.

Testing the Standard Error and Normal Distribution

You don't need to accept on faith what I have been saying about how proportions in samples vary. You can test whether the equation works. It's a good idea to take the time to do so to make sure that you really understand the ideas. If you can understand them well enough to figure out how to test the predictions they make, you have mastered them.

To test the equation for the standard error, we can compare the predictions to what happened in the simulation of 10,000 Columbia classes. Before we do that, let's make sure we understand what the predictions are. According to the normal

Figure 2.3.11 **Where Sample Proportions Fall in a Normal Distribution by Percentage**

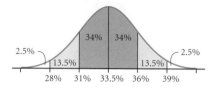

distribution, 2.5% of the proportions will fall at about 28% or below. That is below 2 standard errors below the probability. About 13.5% will fall between 28% and 31%. About 34% will fall between about 31% and 33.5%. About 34% will fall between about 33.5% and 36%. About 13.5% will fall between 36% and 39%, and about 2.5% will fall above 39%. Figure 2.3.11 summarizes the predictions.

To check the predictions, I sort the sample proportions from the smallest proportion to the largest. Once the proportions are sorted, 2.5% from the bottom of the list should be the bottom of the middle 95%. The calculations predicted that the bottom of the middle 95% would be 28%, so the prediction is that the sample proportion that is 250th from the bottom will be about 28%.

When I count one-sixth of 10,000 up from the bottom (1,667 samples from the lowest), I should be at the bottom of the middle two-thirds. The 1,667th sample proportion from the bottom should be about 31%.

The 5,000th sample proportion from the bottom is at the center, and it should be at about 33.5%, the probability in that simulation.

The 8,333rd sample proportion from the bottom should be the top of the middle two-thirds, and I am predicting that it will be 36%.

Finally, the 9,750th from the bottom is the top of the middle 95%, and I am predicting that it will be 39%.

Table 2.3.1 shows the sample percentages from the Columbia simulation. From the table we see that the lowest and second lowest proportions were both 23%. The third lowest was 24%. We predicted that the 250th would be 28%, and it was. We predicted that the 1,667th would be 31%, and it was. We predicted that the 5,000th would be at about 33.5%; it was 33%. We predicted that the 8,333rd would be 36%, and it was. We predicted that the 9,750th would be 39%; it was 38%.

On the last one, we were off by 1%. All estimates from the normal distribution will only be approximately accurate. As the number of observations in the samples gets larger and the number of samples gets larger, the normal distribution gets more and more accurate. In this case, we were looking at 10,000 sample proportions. If we had been looking at 100, or 10, we would have been even further off, but the estimates would have been *roughly* correct. It is partially because these predictions are only approximately correct that it is sensible to think of the middle 2 standard errors as including two-thirds of the sample proportions, rather than 68%.

Table 2.3.1   Simulated Sample Percentages According to Position in Sorted List

LIST POSITION	SAMPLE PERCENTAGE	PREDICTED PERCENTAGE
1st	23%	(not predicted)
2nd	23%	(not predicted)
3rd	24%	(not predicted)
250th	28%	28%
1,667th	31%	31%
5,000th	33%	33.5%
8,333rd	36%	36%
9,750th	38%	39%
10,000th	44%	(not predicted)

Test This on Your Own

All you need to test the claims about the standard error equation and the normal distribution in this section is an easy way to take random samples from a system for which you know the probability. The first prediction is that about half of the sample proportions will fall at or above the probability, and about half will fall below. You can test that without calculating the standard error.

The middle 95% are predicted to fall within about 2 standard errors of the probability. Once you have calculated the standard error, you can add and subtract 2 standard errors to find where the edges of that middle 95% are predicted to be. About two-thirds of the sample proportions are predicted to fall within 1 standard error of the probability.

Once you have the predictions, you can collect your samples and check whether the predictions work. If they do, then you know that you have a powerful way to foresee a lot about how chance events will turn out before they have occurred.

An easy test would be to use 10 coins to collect samples. You could calculate the proportion in each sample that will come up heads when flipped. To collect each sample, you shake the coins up in your hands and then toss them onto a table. Each time you toss them, record the proportion that come up heads.

What are the predictions? The first is that we are predicting that half of the sample proportions will be at 50% or above, and half will be at 50% or below.

What's the standard error? In this case, the probability is 50%, and the sample size is 10. We plug those numbers into the equation, and it will tell us what the standard error is:

$$\text{Standard Error} = \sqrt{\frac{\text{Probability}\,(1 - \text{Probability})}{\text{Sample Size}}}$$

I plug in .5 for the probability, and 10 for the sample size:

$$\text{Standard Error} = \sqrt{\frac{.5 \times (1 - .5)}{10}}$$

The value 1 minus .5 is .5:

$$\text{Standard Error} = \sqrt{\frac{.5 \times .5}{10}}$$

Then .5 times .5 is .25:

$$\text{Standard Error} = \sqrt{\frac{.25}{10}}$$

Then .25 divided by 10 is .025:

$$\text{Standard Error} = \sqrt{.025}$$

The square root of .025 is .15811:

$$\text{Standard Error} = .15811$$

The value .15811 rounds to .16, which is 16%:

$$\text{Standard Error} = 16\%$$

Once we know that the standard error for such samples is 16%, we can predict what will appear in the sample proportions. To predict the middle two-thirds, we add and subtract 16% to and from the probability, 50%:

$$50\% + 16\% = 66\%$$

$$50\% - 16\% = 34\%$$

The middle two-thirds are predicted to fall between 34% and 66%.
To predict the middle 95%, we add and subtract 2 standard errors:

$$2 \text{ Standard Errors} = 2 \times 16\% = 32\%$$

$$50\% + 32\% = 82\%$$

$$50\% - 32\% = 18\%$$

The middle 95% are predicted to fall between 18% and 82%. Figure 2.3.12 shows what we are predicting. Now that you have the predictions, you can go ahead and check how well this works.

Figure 2.3.12

Predicted Distribution of Sample Proportions (Probability = 50%; Sample Size = 10; Standard Error = 16%)

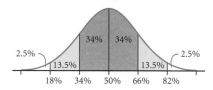

Figure 2.3.13

Proportions of 42 Samples (Probability = 50%; Sample Size = 10; Standard Error = 16%)

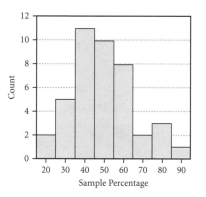

I couldn't bear not trying this myself, so I got 10 coins and shook and tossed them 42 times. Figure 2.3.13 shows how my 42 sample proportions were distributed.

In Figure 2.3.13, there are three taller bars in the center. They are the sample proportions that fell in the ranges 35–45%, 45–55%, and 55–65%. Because there were 42 samples, the bottom half were the bottom 21 sample. After sorting my sample proportions from the smallest proportion to the largest (Table 2.3.2 shows my sorted list), the 21st smallest was 50%, as was the 22nd. The center of my sample proportions *was* 50%. So far so good.

What about the middle 95% of the proportions? How many is 95% of the proportions? There were 42 proportions, and 95% of 42 is 39.9. When we say "the middle 95% of the 42 proportions," we mean "the 40 proportions in the middle." We predicted that those middle 95% would fall between about 18% and about 82%. My middle 40 ranged from 20% to 80%. Not bad.

How about the middle two-thirds that should have fallen within 1 standard error of the probability? How many is that? Two-thirds of 42 is 28, so we are talking about the middle 28. How many does that leave on each side? The value 42 minus 28 is 14, so 7 proportions fall above the middle two-thirds, and 7 fall below the middle two-thirds. If I counted in from the ends to the 8th smallest and the 8th

Table 2.3.2 Percentages of 42 Sorted Samples According to Position in Sorted List (Probability = 50%; Sample Size = 10; Standard Error = 16%)

LIST POSITION	PERCENTAGE	LIST POSITION	PERCENTAGE	LIST POSITION	PERCENTAGE	LIST POSITION	PERCENTAGE
Lowest	20%	12th	40%	23rd	50%	34th	60%
2nd lowest	20%	13th	40%	24th	50%	35th	60%
3rd	30%	14th	40%	25th	50%	36th	60%
4th	30%	15th	40%	26th	50%	37th	70%
5th	30%	16th	40%	27th	50%	38th	70%
6th	30%	17th	40%	28th	50%	39th	80%
7th	30%	18th	40%	29th	60%	40th	80%
8th	40%	19th	50%	30th	60%	2nd highest	80%
9th	40%	20th	50%	31st	60%	Highest	90%
10th	40%	21st	50%	32nd	60%		
11th	40%	22nd	50%	33rd	60%		

largest, I would have the edges of the middle two-thirds, which we predicted would be at about 34% and about 66%. The 8th from the bottom of the list was 40%, and the 8th from the top (the 35th from the bottom) was 60%. We had predicted about 34% and about 66%. In both cases, we were off by 6%. Not bad.

You could also test these predictions by rolling dice. I have a game at home that uses five dice. You could use five dice also, or you could roll one die five times for each sample. How about looking at the proportion of 1's that come up? The probability for a 1 coming from a rolled die is one-sixth, about 16.7%. Here are the calculations to find the standard error, when the sample size is 5:

$$\text{Standard Error} = \sqrt{\frac{\text{Probability} \times (1 - \text{Probability})}{\text{Sample Size}}}$$

I plug in .167 for the probability and 5 for the sample size:

$$\text{Standard Error} = \sqrt{\frac{.167 \times (1 - .167)}{5}}$$

The value 1 minus .167 is .833:

$$\text{Standard Error} = \sqrt{\frac{.167 \times .833}{5}}$$

The value .167 times .833 is .139111:

$$\text{Standard Error} = \sqrt{\frac{.139111}{5}}$$

Figure 2.3.14 **Predicted Distribution of Sample Proportions (Probability = 17%; Sample Size = 5; Standard Error = 17%)**

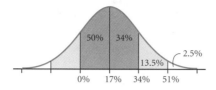

The value .139111 divided by 5 is .0278222:

$$\text{Standard Error} = \sqrt{.0278222}$$

The square root of .0278222 is .1668:

$$\text{Standard Error} = .1668$$

The value .1668 rounds to .17, which is 17%:

$$\text{Standard Error} = 17\%$$

Figure 2.3.14 lets us see what we would predict for the sample proportions. In this case, because the predicted distribution overlaps 0, and proportions cannot go below 0, we expect that the proportions will not go below 0. We still predict that half of the sample proportions will fall at or below about 17%. We predict that 95% of the sample proportions will fall between about 0% and 51%. Finally, we predict that two-thirds of the sample proportions will fall between about 0% and about 34%.

You can do this for yourself if you have some dice handy. Or you can work with something else, figure out the standard error, and see if you can predict how the sample proportions will be distributed.

To compare what you find to the predictions, you have to sort the sample proportions from the smallest to the largest. The middle 95% are all but the bottom 2.5% and the top 2.5% of the sample proportions. The middle two-thirds are all but the bottom one-sixth and the top one-sixth of the sample proportions.

Using the Standard Error to Predict Sales

Once you know the equation for the standard error, you can make sensible predictions about the future. I have heard that life insurance salespeople have about a one-third chance of making a sale each time they are invited to someone's home to pitch their insurance policies. Let's say an agent visits three homes in one day. If her chances hold steady at 33.3% per house call, where do we expect her sales rate to fall? To find out, we substitute .333 for the probability and 3 for the number in the sample. Here are the calculations:

$$\text{Standard Error} = \sqrt{\frac{\text{Probability} \times (1 - \text{Probability})}{\text{Size Sample}}}$$

$$\text{Standard Error} = \sqrt{\frac{.333 \times (1 - .333)}{3}}$$

$$\text{Standard Error} = \sqrt{\frac{.333 \times .667}{3}}$$

$$\text{Standard Error} = \sqrt{\frac{.222111}{3}}$$

$$\text{Standard Error} = \sqrt{.074037}$$

$$\text{Standard Error} = .27$$

About 95% of the time, she'll make somewhere between 0% and 87% sales. If she is about to visit three homes, can she be very sure that she will make at least one sale? No. Zero percent sales is a reasonable outcome to expect.

Algebra and Greek Symbols

When mathematicians write about standard errors, they indicate standard error with a Greek letter, a lowercase sigma (σ). There are standard errors of proportions and standard errors of averages, and many other standard errors. So far, you have seen the standard error of a proportion, or percentage. There are different standard errors for other statistics. To indicate what a standard error is of, mathematicians write a small subscript on the sigma. We indicate a proportion with a p, so the standard error of a proportion is σ_p.

The symbol θ indicates the probability of a particular event, p is the proportion of a sample that is that particular event, and n is the number of observations or trials in the sample. For example, let's say I flip 10 coins and get six heads. In that case, $p = 60\%$, $\theta = 50\%$, and $n = 10$. Here is the formula for the standard error of proportions:

$$\sigma_p = \sqrt{\frac{\theta(1 - \theta)}{n}}$$

Normal Distribution

There is specialized language for normal distributions. The center and width of a normal distribution are all that you need to completely specify what that normal distribution is like, because normal distributions differ from one another only in their centers and in their widths. As the standard error gets larger, the normal distribution becomes wider. There is shorthand for referring to normal distributions. A normal distribution is indicated with a stylized $\mathcal{N}$ along with the distribution's center and standard error. For example, a normal distribution with a center at 0 and a standard error of 1 would be indicated by $\mathcal{N}(0,1)$. To say that proportions are approximately normally distributed with a center at θ and a standard error of σ_p, I could write

$$p \sim \mathcal{N}(\theta, \sigma_p), \text{ approximately}$$

The "~" means "is distributed in a . . ."

To capture the idea that 95% of the sample proportions will be within 2 standard errors of the probability, a mathematician might write this:

$$P(|p - \theta| < 2\sigma_p) = .95$$

$P(. . .)$ is the probability of whatever is in the parentheses. For example, for a coin flip, $P(\text{heads}) = .5$. The expression $|p - \theta|$ refers to the absolute value of a sample proportion minus the probability. The absolute value of something is the positive version of that something. For example, $|5|$ is 5, and $|-5|$ is also 5. The absolute value of a difference between two numbers is how far apart the two numbers are on the number line. The equation preceding this paragraph is saying that the probability that the absolute value of the difference between a sample proportion and the probability is less than 2 standard errors is 95%. (Sometimes these things are a lot easier to say in equations, which is why we have equations.)

Here's the last idea of this section:

$$P(|p - \theta| < \sigma_p) = .68$$

In this equation, the standard error of the proportion (σ_p) does not appear to be multiplied by anything. That is because this equation is about adding and subtracting 1 standard error, and $\sigma_p = 1\sigma_p$.

Summary

When many samples that all have the same number of observations are taken, the proportions in the samples of a particular outcome are roughly normally distributed, with a center at the probability of that outcome. A normal distribution is a symmetrical bell shape. About half of the samples will have proportions at or below the probability, and about half will have proportions at or above the probability. The standard error of sample proportions can be estimated with the following equation:

$$\text{Standard Error} = \sqrt{\frac{\text{Probability} \times (1 - \text{Probability})}{\text{Sample Size}}}$$

The sample size is the number of observation in each sample. If you know the probability and the sample size, you can predict a lot about where sample proportions will fall. You can predict that 95% will fall within 2 standard errors of the probability, and about two-thirds will fall within 1 standard error of the probability.

Avoiding Common Misunderstandings

Proportions of Proportions

What is most difficult in this section is that here we start talking about "proportions of proportions": for example, "95% of the percentages will fall within 2 standard errors of the probability." Let's say we write the proportion of each sample on a slip of paper. We do this for each sample, so we have one slip of paper for each sample. Then imagine that the slips of paper are pasted on a number line over their values: a slip with "30%" over the 30%, a slip with "65%" over the 65%, and so on. Then think about proportions of the slips of paper. Half of the slips of paper are 50% of the slips of paper. If you take away 95% of the slips of paper, you leave 5% of the slips of paper. Now you can think about what this section is saying: When we place the slips of paper on the number line, 95% of the slips of paper will be pasted not more than 2 standard errors away from the probability.

Decimals for Probabilities

A common difficulty in working with the equation of the standard error is remembering to use decimals for the probability. Remember that 50% is .5, 15% is .15, and so on.

Computer Project

In this section, I have made a very strong claim and backed it up with examples of simulations I have run. Don't take my word for it. Test it yourself. Have your computer pick samples in some way so that you can determine the chances of an event. Let's call the event "X." Have the computer pick a lot of samples. Have every sample be the same size and have the computer save the proportion in each sample that is X. Make a histogram of the proportions and a sorted and numbered list of the proportions. Calculate the standard error and compare the predictions of the normal distribution to what you found in your simulation. Make a prediction for the proportion that is 2.5% up the sorted list of proportions from the bottom. Make a prediction for the proportion that is 16% up, 50%, 84%, and 97.5%. At first, this will be easiest when there are 1,000 samples. Then the predictions are for the 25th, 160th, 500th, 840th, and 975th proportions in the sorted list of proportions.

Try changing the probability, the sample size, and the number of samples. How do changing these things affect how accurate the normal distribution's predictions are?

Exercises

Federal statistics released this summer show that women now comprise 57 percent of all college students nationwide.
— KIRK, *PROVIDENCE [R.I.] JOURNAL*, JANUARY 13, 2002

Let's consider the freshman classes at 200 colleges. Each of these colleges admits 150 freshmen a year. And let's consider the freshman classes at 100 universities. Each university admits 2,000 freshmen each year. For the moment, let's guess that the chances that a freshman is female are the same everywhere: 57%.

1. About how many of the 200 colleges have freshman classes that are more than 57% female? Write why you answer as you do.

2. About how many of the 100 universities have freshman classes that are more than 57% female? Write why you answer as you do.

3. For the colleges, what is the standard error of the proportion of freshmen who are female?

4. For the universities, what is the standard error of the proportion of freshmen who are female?

5. Consider the female proportions at the colleges. If I sorted the 200 female proportions from smallest to largest and just looked at the middle two-thirds of the proportions, what would be roughly the lowest of those middle two-thirds of the proportions, and what would be the highest?

6. Consider the female proportions at the universities. If I sorted the 100 female proportions from smallest to largest and just looked at the middle two-thirds of the proportions, what would be roughly the lowest of those middle two-thirds of the proportions, and what would be the highest?

7. For 200 colleges, 95% is 190. For the colleges, where would you expect the middle 190 female proportions to fall?

8. For the universities, where would you expect the middle 95% of the percentages?

9. Try sketching a normal distribution that shows roughly where the female proportions of the colleges' freshman classes would probably fall.

10. Try sketching a normal distribution that shows roughly where the female proportions of the universities' freshman classes would probably fall.

11. In 1999, 55% of the 30,500 students at the University of Georgia were female (according to Mark Clayton, *Christian Science Monitor,* November 13, 2001). Consider the proportions of students who are female at schools with 30,500 students. What is the standard error of such proportions if the probability of a student being female is 57%?

12. Sketch a normal distribution to show where you would expect female proportions to fall for schools with 30,500 students.

13. Compare the University of Georgia's 1999 figure (55%) to your sketch for Exercise 12. Is 55% the sort of proportion you would expect to see if the probability that a student is female were 57%? Explain how you reached your conclusion.

Answers to Odd-Numbered Exercises

1. About half: 100. For these exercises, we are guessing that the chances that a freshman is female are 57%. The female proportions will be normally distributed with a center at 57%, so half will be above 57%.

3. $\text{Standard Error} = \sqrt{\dfrac{\text{Probability} \times (1 - \text{Probability})}{\text{Sample Size}}}$

   $\text{Standard Error} = \sqrt{\dfrac{.57 \times (1 - .57)}{150}}$

   $\text{Standard Error} = \sqrt{\dfrac{.57 \times .43}{150}}$

   $\text{Standard Error} = \sqrt{\dfrac{.2451}{150}}$

   $\text{Standard Error} = \sqrt{.001634}$

   $\text{Standard Error} = .0404$

   The standard error is about 4%.

5. Lowest: 53%. Highest: 61%.

7. From 49% to 65%.

9.
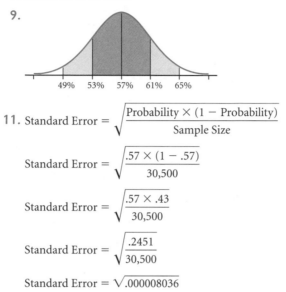

11. Standard Error $= \sqrt{\dfrac{\text{Probability} \times (1 - \text{Probability})}{\text{Sample Size}}}$

Standard Error $= \sqrt{\dfrac{.57 \times (1 - .57)}{30,500}}$

Standard Error $= \sqrt{\dfrac{.57 \times .43}{30,500}}$

Standard Error $= \sqrt{\dfrac{.2451}{30,500}}$

Standard Error $= \sqrt{.000008036}$

Standard Error $= .0028$

The standard error is about 0.3%.

13. No. I would expect to see proportions that range almost all the time between about 56.4% and 57.6%.

By the way, here's some explanation of that 55%: For several years before 2000, the University of Georgia awarded males extra points in the admissions process in order to give them a better chance of being admitted.

> *The [University of Georgia] campus was 45 percent male, and just 42 percent of first-time freshman applicants had been men in recent years. "We just wanted to stop the trend before it became something bad," a high-ranking [University of Georgia] administrator said.*
> —Clayton, *Christian Science Monitor*, November 13, 2001

CHAPTER 3 *Making Inferences*

Statistics have a kind of magic. Statisticians use data to see what cannot be otherwise seen. They forecast the future, as you will see in Section 3.1. Statisticians can also learn about populations that are so large that no one could ever study every person in those populations. Sometimes statisticians even make inferences (deductions) about infinite populations, such as all the people who will ever exist. Sections 3.2 and 3.3 discuss how you can learn about populations that are too large to study directly.

3.1 Forecasting the Future

- Prediction Intervals for Sample Proportions

Strikes threatened significant service cuts. . . . "We expect to provide between 50 percent and 70 percent of service . . . but there may be far fewer trains on some lines," the spokesman said.

—REUTERS FINANCIAL SERVICE, MAY 15, 1996

The convention center's marketing director, Tony Delgado [said], "Next year, we expect to be booked between 55 percent and 60 percent."

—CLANCY, TAMPA BAY BUSINESS JOURNAL, JUNE 7, 1996

GPT Communications Systems . . . expects between five percent and 20 percent of its customers to drop formal maintenance arrangements [during the following year].

—TELECOM MARKETS, SEPTEMBER 12, 1996

THE PRECEDING QUOTES ARE ALL from the business pages of periodicals. They show something about how businesspeople talk. These quotes all contain predictions involving proportions. They mention ranges, for example, "between 50 percent and 70 percent" or "between five percent and 20 percent." Why aren't these predictions more precise?

The predictions are reported with all of the precision that is possible. The planners may have very good ideas about the chances of any particular train line being staffed or the chances of a convention center being filled on any particular day, but those ideas don't tell the planners precisely what will happen in the future. The future contains only a sample of the possibilities. Until you see the future, all you know is that the proportion that interests you will fall somewhere in the normal distribution that describes where sample proportions will fall.

Predicting precise proportions is a common mistake. For example, psychiatrists estimate that about 7% of school age children have attention deficit disorder (ADD). If someone asked how many children with ADD are enrolled in a local elementary school that had 300 students, the usual answer would be something like this: "About 7% of the kids have attention deficit disorder; I would say 21 kids." But what if you had to plan the staffing for that school? Let's say the state tells you that you need to have one learning disabilities specialist for every 15 children with ADD. How many will you have? Do you want to count on having 21 children with ADD? How confident are you that you'll have exactly 21?

You shouldn't be too confident about that prediction. Proportions vary. What's the standard error here, anyway? The proportion in the population is about 7%. If you believe that the school is representative of the general population as far as ADD is concerned, then, for each child in the school, the probability of having ADD is 7%. The sample size is 300. You calculate the standard error like this:

$$\text{Standard Error} = \sqrt{\frac{\text{Probability} \times (1 - \text{Probability})}{\text{Sample Size}}}$$

$$\text{Standard Error} = \sqrt{\frac{.07 \times .93}{300}}$$

$$\text{Standard Error} = \sqrt{\frac{.0651}{300}}$$

$$\text{Standard Error} = \sqrt{.000217}$$

$$\text{Standard Error} = .0147$$

You can be 95% confident that the proportion in the sample will fall within 2 standard errors of the population proportion, 7%. You can be 95% confident that the children with ADD will be somewhere between 4% and 10% of the students. That's between 12 and 30 children. You need one learning disabilities teacher for each 15 students with ADD. To be 95% confident that you will have enough learning disabilities specialists, you should hire two.

That interval, from 4% to 10%, is called a "95% prediction interval," because you can be 95% confident in a prediction that the actual proportion will fall somewhere in that interval. You're 95% confident because 95% of the time the proportion will be inside that interval. Prediction intervals are ranges that you believe (with a certain amount of confidence) contain whatever you are predicting. For proportions, the 95% prediction interval is a range that goes from 2 standard errors below the population proportion to 2 standard errors above the population proportion.

You might be comfortable with a two-thirds prediction interval. A two-thirds prediction interval ranges from 1 standard error below the probability to 1 standard error above the probability. It's a "two-thirds" prediction interval because it will include the predicted sample proportions about two-thirds of the time. In the case of kids with ADD at a 300-student school, the two-thirds interval would be 7% plus and minus 1.5%, or from 5.5% to 8.5%, which is between 16 and 26 kids. One-sixth of the proportions fall below the middle two-thirds. Altogether, you can be 84% confident that no more than 26 kids will have ADD. That might justify having only one learning disabilities teacher.

95% Prediction Intervals

A prediction interval is a section of the number line that has a specified probability of including an observation or a statistic.

For example, the interval that falls between 2 standard errors below the population proportion and 2 standard errors above is a 95% prediction interval for a random sample proportion.

When you need to guess a proportion, prediction intervals can save you a lot of trouble. For example, let's say that you want to get together a team to play basketball in a local league. You know that people twist their ankles, go on business trips, and get sick now and then. The league organizers tell you that on any given game day about 16% of their league members are unable to play. You find six people to be on the team. Do you have enough people? Will you be able to get a whole team of five players on the court at every game?

To determine whether you have enough players, you need to think about how the proportion of the players who will be absent will vary. The normal distribution those proportions fall into will have its center at 16%. The sample size is 6 players. To know how much the absent proportion will vary, we need to calculate the standard error:

$$\text{Standard Error} = \sqrt{\frac{\text{Probability} \times (1 - \text{Probability})}{\text{Sample Size}}}$$

$$\text{Standard Error} = \sqrt{\frac{.16 \times .84}{6}}$$

$$\text{Standard Error} = \sqrt{.0224}$$

$$\text{Standard Error} = .1496$$

The result, .1496, is approximately 15%. You can be two-thirds confident that the proportion will be within 1 standard error of the population proportion, 16%. Your two-thirds prediction interval is that 1% to 31% will be unable to play. If 31% of your six players are unable to play, you have only four people to put on the court. And that's just the two-thirds prediction interval. About one-third of the time, you will have proportions outside the two-thirds interval. About half will be above and half below. About one-sixth of the time, you'll have a proportion above your two-thirds prediction interval, and even fewer than four people will be able to play. A 95% prediction interval would range from 0 to 2 standard errors above 16%. The standard error is 15%, so 2 standard errors is 30%. The 95% prediction interval would be from 0% to 46%. Therefore, it's not unreasonable to think that sometimes you would have only three players.

Would nine players be enough? To find out, we need to recalculate the prediction interval using a sample size of 9. The center of the distribution remains the same, but the standard error changes. Now the standard error is the square root of .16 times .84 divided by 9:

$$\text{Standard Error} = \sqrt{\frac{\text{Probability} \times (1 - \text{Probability})}{\text{Sample Size}}}$$

$$\text{Standard Error} = \sqrt{\frac{.16 \times .84}{9}}$$

$$\text{Standard Error} = \sqrt{.014933}$$

$$\text{Standard Error} = .122$$

The result, .122, is approximately 12%. You can be 95% confident that the proportion will be somewhere within 2 standard errors of the population proportion, 16%. The 95% prediction interval is from 0% to 16% plus 2 times

12%—from 0% to 40%. If you multiply 40% times 9, the result is 3.6, which is about 4. If 40% of your nine players can't play on a given day, you still have five players to take the court. With nine players, you can be 95% confident that you'll have five players who are able to play. Over the course of 100 games, you'll only have to forfeit about two or three because of an insufficient number of players.

Two-Thirds Prediction Intervals

A two-thirds prediction interval for a sample proportion is from 1 standard error below the population proportion to 1 standard error above.

For example, if the population proportion is 20% and the standard error is 12%, you can be two-thirds confident that a random sample will have a proportion between 8% and 32%.

Using prediction intervals highlights something important about human knowledge: We are not certain about most things. We don't know what will happen in the future. For example, when GPT Communications Systems says that it expects 5% to 20% of its customers to drop their maintenance agreements, that statement highlights the company's uncertainty. It also highlights what the company does know: that it is fairly sure that the proportion will be below 21%.

Prediction intervals can be particularly helpful when estimating worst-case scenarios. For example, several years ago, my son's preschool was going to raffle a beautiful quilt. The school had a list of about 500 families to which to try to sell $5 raffle tickets. Over the years, the school has found that about 70% of the calls produce ticket sales, and almost all of the successful calls sell only one ticket each. The school could estimate that it would probably make about 70% of 500 sales, or 350 sales. At $5 per ticket, that's about $1,750. But the school also knew from experience that it often overestimated how much the raffle would raise. The school asked me whether I could provide a reliable minimum estimate.

How would you have answered the school? I used the 95% prediction interval for the proportion of calls that will produce sales and gave the bottom of the interval as a reasonable minimum estimate. To do that, I needed to find the standard error. In this case, it was the square root of .7 times .3 divided by 500:

$$\text{Standard Error} = \sqrt{\frac{\text{Probability} \times (1 - \text{Probability})}{\text{Sample Size}}}$$

$$\text{Standard Error} = \sqrt{\frac{.7 \times .3}{500}}$$

$$\text{Standard Error} = \sqrt{.00042}$$

$$\text{Standard Error} = .02049$$

The result is .02049, or approximately 2%. Now 95% of the time, the proportion would fall no more than 2 standard errors away from the population proportion, 70%. The 95% prediction interval is between 66% and 74%. I said something like this: "You can be 95% confident that about 66% to 74% of your calls will produce sales. You will probably raise roughly somewhere between $1,650 and $1,850. You can be very confident of raising at least $1,650."

I emphasized the bottom of the 95% prediction interval. It's a judgment call how one ought to communicate about 95% prediction intervals to people who don't already understand them. Some people would highlight the top of the interval, saying, "You shouldn't count on more than $1,850." A concern with this approach is that people will count on that $1,850, and you can be almost certain (97.5% certain—remember 2.5% falls below the middle 95%) that the fundraiser will raise less money than the figure you mentioned. Many people would highlight the center of the interval, saying, "You can expect about $1,750, plus or minus a hundred dollars." Again, there is the same problem. The chances are 50% that they will collect less than that center figure and feel that the fundraiser didn't live up to expectations. And what if, in the meantime, they spend the predicted $1,750? That too produces disappointment. In this sort of case, even if I had not been asked for a minimum, I would still have emphasized the bottom of the interval. It is not unreasonable to expect any amount between $1,650 and $1,850. If the school expected only $1,650, I was very confident (97.5% confident) that it wouldn't be disappointed. In fact, it would not be unwise for the school to go ahead and spend the $1,650, but I wouldn't recommend spending more than that for fear of future financial troubles. The way I put it was, "I am sure you will raise *at least* $1,650." The school did raise well over the minimum I calculated, and everyone was pleased.

I have used prediction intervals in dealing with testing situations as well. Many years ago, I moved to Colorado and had to take a written test to switch my driver's license from Pennsylvania to Colorado. My driving education was poor. I'm a cautious but ignorant driver, and I failed the test the first time I took it. The state police gave me a booklet full of facts about good driving and told me to come back no sooner than one hour later, but that if I failed the test a second time, I would have to wait a week before taking it again.

The test had 25 questions, and I needed to answer at least 80% correctly to pass. After an hour of study, I had read 7 of the booklet's 10 chapters and felt that I knew about 70% of the material. Could I pass the test? That would depend on what proportion of the test questions came from the chapters I had worked on memorizing. What would that proportion be? To find out, I calculated the standard error. The probability that a randomly chosen bit of information was one that I knew was 70%. My sample size was 25. The standard error was the square root of .7 times .3 divided by 25:

$$\text{Standard Error} = \sqrt{\frac{\text{Probability} \times (1 - \text{Probability})}{\text{Sample Size}}}$$

$$\text{Standard Error} = \sqrt{\frac{.7 \times .3}{25}}$$

$$\text{Standard Error} = .0916$$

The result was .0916, or approximately 9%. I could be two-thirds confident that the proportion of the questions that I could answer would be within 1 standard error of the proportion for all the material, 70%. I was about two-thirds confident that somewhere between 61% and 79% of the questions would be on material I knew. Remember that these prediction intervals describe the middle of the normal distribution. I was about one-third confident that the portion of questions that I could answer would be outside the two-thirds prediction interval. About one-sixth of such proportions would be below 61% (how embarrassing), and about one-sixth above 79%. So I had about a one-in-six chance of passing the test. That seemed like a good enough chance for me. I gave it a go, got 80%, and got my Colorado license.

Understanding 95% prediction intervals enables you to understand the law of large numbers in more depth. The law of large numbers says that as the number in the sample increases, the proportions in the sample fall closer and closer to the population proportion. Consider the situation in which you're taking a random sample of the U.S. population. According to the Census Bureau, about 20% of the U.S. population is under 15 years of age. When you are taking a random sample, the probability of each type of person is the same as the population proportion of that kind of person, so the probability of someone under 15 is 20%. Say you're taking random samples from the U.S. population. What if you sample 10 people?

$$\text{Standard Error} = \sqrt{\frac{\text{Probability} \times (1 - \text{Probability})}{\text{Sample Size}}}$$

$$\text{Standard Error} = \sqrt{\frac{.2 \times .8}{10}}$$

$$\text{Standard Error} = \frac{\sqrt{.2 \times .8}}{\sqrt{10}}$$

$$\text{Standard Error} = \frac{.4}{\sqrt{10}}$$

$$\text{Standard Error} = .126$$

If your random sample has 10 people, then the standard error will be about 13%, and your 95% prediction interval for the proportion of that sample who are under 15 will be from 0% to 36%.

What if you increase your sample size to 50?

$$\text{Standard Error} = \sqrt{\frac{\text{Probability} \times (1 - \text{Probability})}{\text{Sample Size}}}$$

$$\text{Standard Error} = \frac{\sqrt{.2 \times .8}}{\sqrt{50}}$$

$$\text{Standard Error} = \frac{.4}{\sqrt{50}}$$

$$\text{Standard Error} = .057$$

With 50 people in each sample, your standard error shrinks down to about 6%. About 95% of the time, the proportions in the samples will range between 8% and 32%.

Try increasing your sample to 400 people:

$$\text{Standard Error} = \sqrt{\frac{\text{Probability} \times (1 - \text{Probability})}{\text{Sample Size}}}$$

$$\text{Standard Error} = \frac{.4}{\sqrt{400}}$$

$$\text{Standard Error} = .02$$

Your standard error drops to 2%. About 95% of the time the sample proportions will be between 16% and 24%.

Figure 3.1.1 shows the limits of the 95% prediction intervals for this example for sample sizes up to 500. In the figure, the two curves show the edges of the 95% prediction intervals. The y-axis shows proportions from 0 on the bottom to 1 at the top. With only one person in each sample, the proportions will vary from 0% to 100%. The x-axis shows the sizes of samples. For each sample size, there is a line you could draw parallel to the y-axis showing where the proportions would be 95% of the time. You can see that with samples of 100, 95% of the time the proportions will range between about 11% and 29%. Figure 3.1.2 shows the same graph with a vertical line showing the 95% prediction interval for samples that have 100 observations.

Figure 3.1.3 shows the same graph with a vertical line showing the 95% prediction interval for samples that have 200 observations. By the time you get to sample sizes of 500, the proportions are held pretty much within about 4% of the population proportion.

In Figures 3.1.1, 3.1.2, and 3.1.3, the curves reflect the law of large numbers. They show constraints that tend to hold the sample proportions ever closer to the population proportion as the sample sizes get larger.

Figure 3.1.1 **Edges of the 95% Prediction Interval When the Population Proportion Is .20**

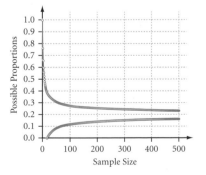

Figure 3.1.2 **95% Prediction Intervals with Interval for 100-Observation Samples Indicated (For a Population Proportion of .20)**

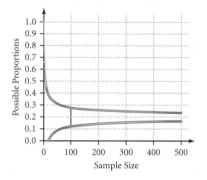

Figure 3.1.3 **95% Prediction Intervals with Interval for 200-Observation Samples Indicated (For a Population Proportion of .20)**

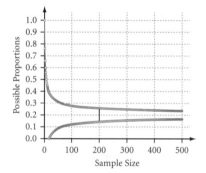

Algebra and Greek Symbols

This section is a restatement of ideas in previous sections. One idea is that, because sample proportions are approximately normally distributed, about 95% of the time, the sample proportion will be within 2 standard errors of the probability, and about two-thirds of the time, the sample proportion will be within 1 standard error of the probability. Here are the equations that make those statements:

$$P(|p - \theta| < 2\sigma_p) \approx 95\%$$
$$P(|p - \theta| < \sigma_p) \approx 68\%$$

We've used a wavy equal sign ($\approx$) before. They mean "is approximately equal to." Here, we use them rather than regular equal signs to signify that the proportions are not perfectly normally distributed. They are only approximately normally distributed (although their distribution does become more and more normal as the sample size increases).

But we can state the section's main idea more generally: With a certain probability, a future sample proportion will fall within a particular range. The way to say that symbolically for the two-thirds prediction interval (68%) is

$$P[p \in (\theta - \sigma_p, \theta + \sigma_p)] = .68$$

"$P[\ldots]$" means "the probability of what is in the brackets." The lowercase p is the sample proportion. $\in$ means "is an element of." The material in parentheses is a range on the number line. For example, "$(1, 3)$" would be the range from 1 to 3. θ is the probability, and σ_p is the standard error of the proportion. So the range in this equation is from the probability minus a standard error to the probability plus a standard error. Here is a translation of that equation: "The probability that the sample proportion is an element of the range from the probability minus a standard error to the probability plus a standard error is 68%." Once again, it may be easier to read the equation than the English translation.

Here's a statement of the idea of the 95% confidence interval:

$$P[p \in (\theta - 2\sigma_p, \theta + 2\sigma_p)] = .95$$

Prediction Intervals for Random Samples

For random samples of a population, the probability that we are referring to as θ is the same as the population proportion, as described earlier. We refer to the population proportion with Π (pi), the Greek letter for "p." This means that for random samples,

$$P[p \in (\Pi - \sigma_p, \Pi + \sigma_p)] = .68$$

and

$$P[p \in (\Pi - 2\sigma_p, \Pi + 2\sigma_p)] = .95$$

Remember that Π in this case is the population proportion, not the value 3.14 that is so important in working with circles.

Law of Large Numbers

Since we have returned to the law of large numbers in this section, it might be nice to restate that law more carefully. Here it is:

$$P(|p - \theta| > \varepsilon) \to 0, \text{ as } n \to \infty, \text{ for any } \varepsilon$$

The variable ε is "some small value." As before, p is the proportion of a sample of events that is a particular event. Let's call it "event X." θ is the probability of event X appearing each time an event is included in the sample. What that equation is saying is that the probability that the distance between the sample proportion and the probability of event X is *larger* than some small value goes toward 0 as the sample size goes toward infinity. That is a hard sentence to read in English. Once again, we see that some ideas are easier to state in mathematical equations.

Summary

When describing where a random sample proportion will be, it is best to give a prediction interval. The prediction interval is an interval within which you have a specified confidence that the sample proportion will fall. The interval from 2 standard errors below the population proportion to 2 standard errors above the population proportion is a 95% prediction interval. You can be 95% confident that that range will include the sample proportion. In the long run, 95% prediction intervals will include their sample proportions 95% of the time and miss the sample proportions 5% of the time. The interval from 1 standard error below the population proportion to 1 standard error above the population proportion is a two-thirds prediction interval.

Avoiding Common Misunderstandings

The most common mistake related to this section is to give a single number when estimating what proportion will appear in a sample. When asked any question about what proportion or percentage will appear, always give some sort of interval. If you don't want to take the time to calculate the standard error, estimate the standard error and use your estimate. An important reason for doing this is to become accustomed to recognizing what you do and do not know. You do not know precisely what the proportion will be, but you do know more than nothing. If we're talking about 50 coin flips, you know the chances are that the heads proportion won't be 2% or 96%. This "knowing" is knowledge of probabilities. It is not knowing with 100% certainty that there won't be 48 heads in 50 flips. There could be 48 heads. What is important is knowing that 48 heads in 50 flips is very unlikely.

Computer Project

For this project, you will need something like a population. The Representative Sample included in the *Data Matters* Resource Center at *www.keycollege.com/dm* includes data on more than 50,000 Americans collected by the U.S. Census Bureau in 2001. You could use that data or get your own. Find out some of the population proportions. Pick a sample size and create prediction intervals for random sample proportions. Have your software take random samples and check what proportion fell within your prediction interval and what proportion fell outside.

Does your prediction interval work correctly? That is, for the 95% prediction interval, do 95% of the sample proportions fall inside the interval and 5% fall outside? Do the sample proportions that fall outside fall evenly, with 2.5% on each side? For the two-thirds prediction interval, do two-thirds fall inside? Do one-sixth fall below and one-sixth above the interval?

Exercises

1. For many years, I taught classes that filled up early in the sign-up period before each quarter. The result was that students asked whether they could get into my classes after the classes were full. My experience of many years was that 10% of any class drop the class when they see the syllabus. Each of my classes had 45 students in it. I told the students who wanted to get into my classes something like this: "I expect that somewhere between 1% and 19% will drop the class. That's my 95% prediction interval. So I expect somewhere between zero and nine spaces to open up in the class during the first week. Because of the possibility that no spaces will open up, if I were you, I would sign up for another class, in case you can't get into this one. If you do get in, you can drop the other class."

   Imagine that a friend of yours has heard this statement and asks you, "What does he mean when he says his '95% prediction interval' is from 1% to 19%?" Write a brief note answering that question.

2. Years ago, I heard a presentation on stocking a cafeteria for dinner. The cafeteria's policy was that most diners should have a choice between the beef and chicken dishes that were offered, even though that meant that the cafeteria had to stock more meals than would be eaten. Previous experience had shown that about 40% of students preferred the chicken dish. Each night, 400 meals were served. The speaker said, "We expect 35% to 45% of the students will choose the chicken dish, and 55% to 65% will choose the beef dish on any given night. Those are our 95% prediction intervals. We stock 180 chicken dinners and 260 beef dinners. That wastes 40 dinners a night, but it's rare that we run out of an option."

   Imagine a friend has heard of this policy and asks you, "What does she mean by '95% prediction intervals'?" Write a brief note answering that question.

3. A friend of mine is an emergency room doctor. The hospital where he works administered questionnaires to emergency room patients about their satisfaction with the doctors. For many years, about 10% of the patients expressed dissatisfaction with these doctors. The hospital decided to randomly survey 20 patients for each emergency room doctor to see what they thought of that doctor's performance. If a doctor's dissatisfaction ratings were more than 20%, that doctor's pay would be docked. Assume that, in fact, year in and year out, 10% of my friend's patients do get annoyed enough to complain on a survey about his work. With the hospital randomly surveying 20 patients each year, about how often will he end up losing pay?

4. Consider this quote:

> *Thirty-four percent of the nation's 46 million smokers try to quit each year, the CDC said. Of those, about 1 million succeed.*
>
> —ASSOCIATED PRESS, DECEMBER 22, 1994

Imagine that I start a smoking-cessation clinic. I will charge a patient only if that patient succeeds in stopping. Assume that my smoking treatment program is about as good as any other quitting strategy, and assume that my patients are a random sample of smokers trying to quit. About how many of the first 100 will stop?

Consider an excellent professional baseball player, such as Roberto Alomar in his prime. Your baseball player is batting .360. That is, out of 100 times at bat, he gets 36 hits.

5. What is a 95% prediction interval for the number of hits your excellent baseball player will get in the next 9 times at bat?

6. What will your excellent baseball player's batting average be over his next 49 times at bat?

7. If you look at the prediction intervals for larger samples, you can see how sample sizes affect prediction intervals.

   a. What is a 95% prediction interval for your excellent baseball player's next 256 times at bat?

   b. As the size of the sample gets larger, what happens to the prediction interval?

8. In the business I currently run, I make sales calls. These are what are called "cold calls" in that the people I'm calling don't know me or anyone I know and are not expecting me to call. After a year of this, I can tell you that 2% of my cold calls lead to new clients. I make about 400 cold calls a month. Let's say I make exactly 400 cold calls next month. How many new clients will I find with those 400 calls?

9. Imagine that I am looking at the last four babies born at a particular hospital.

   a. What is a 95% prediction interval for the proportion who are boys?

   b. If there were 100% boys (four out of four), why wouldn't you be surprised? That is, why would you *not* wonder what that hospital was doing to deliver so many boy babies?

10. Imagine that I am considering the last 100 babies born at a particular hospital.

    a. What is a 95% prediction interval for the proportion who are boys?

    b. If there were 100% boys (100 out of 100), why *would* you be surprised and start to wonder what that hospital was doing to deliver so many boy babies?

11. In Section 1.3, I reported some vital statistics for Washington State. For deaths from liver disease and arteriosclerosis, the proportion dying of each disease were about 10 out of 100,000. King County's proportions each year varied by about 3 per 100,000 from year to year. King County has 1.6 million people. Does that variation look like what you would expect from a constant chance of dying from each disease and random variation?

12. Wahkiakum County and Garfield County each have about 3,000 people. Their proportions varied by about 44 per 100,000.

    a. Does that variation look like what you would expect from random variation and constant chances?

    b. Is it reasonable to think that these wider variations of the smaller counties are due simply to their being smaller?

    c. Jot down how you reached your answer to b.

Answers to Odd-Numbered Exercises

1. "Each time he teaches a class, some proportion of the students drop the class during the first week. He means that 95% of the time he teaches classes of that size, the proportion of students who drop will range between 1% and 19%. For any given class, there is a 95% chance that the proportion who drop will be between 1% and 19%. It's like when a weather forecaster says that there is a 95% chance of rain. In this case, he is saying that there is a 95% chance that the proportion who drop the course will be between 1% and 19%."

Here are some answers you might be tempted to give and why they would be mistaken:

MISTAKEN ANSWER	WHY IT'S A MISTAKE
"He means that the proportion will be between 1% and 19%."	5% of sample proportions will fall outside the 95% prediction interval.
"Either 1% will drop or 19% will drop."	1% to 19% is the *interval* that we are 95% confident will include the sample proportions. The proportions that appear could be 2%, 4%, 7%, and so on to 18%.
"95% will drop."	The "95%" refers to the proportion of *sample proportions* that will appear between 1% and 19%. Given that, in the past, 10% had dropped, it is extremely unlikely that 95% will drop.

3. For that sample size, the standard error would be the square root of .1 times .9 divided by 20:

$$\sigma_p = \sqrt{\frac{.1 \times .9}{20}}$$

$$\sigma_p = \sqrt{.0045}$$

$$\sigma_p = .07$$

That's 7%. The two-thirds prediction interval would be from 3% to 17%. The 95% prediction interval would be from 0% to 24%. So 18% of the proportions would fall above the middle two-thirds; that's above 17%. And 2.5% would fall above the middle 95%, above 24%. Somewhere between about 3% and 18% of the time, my friend would lose pay, simply because of random variation.

5. For 9 times at bat:

$$\text{Standard Error} = \sqrt{\frac{\text{Probability} \times (1 - \text{Probability})}{\text{Sample Size}}}$$

$$\text{Standard Error} = \sqrt{\frac{.36 \times (1 - .36)}{9}}$$

$$\text{Standard Error} = \sqrt{\frac{.36 \times .64}{9}}$$

$$\text{Standard Error} = \sqrt{.0256}$$

$$\text{Standard Error} = .16$$

The 95% prediction interval would be .360 plus and minus .320, from .040 to .680.

7. a. For 256 times at bat:

$$\text{Standard Error} = \sqrt{\frac{\text{Probability} \times (1 - \text{Probability})}{\text{Sample Size}}}$$

$$\text{Standard Error} = \sqrt{\frac{.36 \times (1 - .36)}{256}}$$

Standard Error = .03

The 95% prediction interval would be .360 plus and minus .060, from .300 to .420.

b. As the sample size increases, the prediction interval shrinks.

9. a. $\text{Standard Error} = \sqrt{\dfrac{\text{Probability} \times (1 - \text{Probability})}{\text{Sample Size}}}$

$$\text{Standard Error} = \sqrt{\frac{.5 \times (1 - .5)}{4}}$$

Standard Error = .25

The 95% prediction interval would be 50% plus and minus 50%, from 0% to 100%.

b. With four kids, 100% is inside the 95% prediction interval, given that the probability of getting a boy is 50%. It is a reasonably likely thing to happen.

11. If there is a single constant chance, the chance is about 10 out of 100,000, which is .0001. The sample size is 1,600,000.

$$\text{Standard Error} = \sqrt{\frac{\text{Probability} \times (1 - \text{Probability})}{\text{Sample Size}}}$$

$$\text{Standard Error} = \sqrt{\frac{.0001 \times (1 - .0001)}{1,600,000}}$$

$$\text{Standard Error} = \sqrt{\frac{.0001 \times (.9999)}{1,600,000}}$$

Standard Error = .79 per 100,000

A 95% prediction interval would be from 10 minus 1.6 to 10 plus 1.6 per 100,000. That's from 8.4 to 11.6 per 100,000, or a range of 3.2 per 100,000. Yes. A variation that covers 3 per 100,000 is roughly what I would expect if there were a constant chance.

3.2 What a Sample Reveals About a Population

- Confidence Intervals for Proportions in Populations

Women . . . were more likely than men to support affirmative action for blacks, 61 percent to 47. . . . [The] margin of error [3.5%] means that . . . in 19 of 20 cases the poll results would differ by no more than 3.5 percentage points from [what] would have been obtained by questioning all Kentucky adults.

—EAGLES, *LOUISVILLE COURIER-JOURNAL*, OCTOBER 15, 1995

IN 1995, EAGLES REPORTED THAT 61% of Kentucky women support affirmative action. Eagles also reported that 19 out of 20 times (95% of the time) a survey like the one on which she reported would provide a proportion that was no more than 3.5% away from what you would find if you surveyed all of the women in Kentucky. We call the 61% the sample proportion. The proportion you would find if you surveyed everyone is the population proportion. Eagles said that there is a 95% chance that the sample proportion, 61%, is not more than 3.5% away from the population proportion. That is, we can be 95% confident that the population proportion is somewhere between 57.5% and 64.5%.

In the last section, we saw how you could start with a population proportion and develop a prediction interval for a proportion of a random sample. Eagles reported an interval, but her logic differed from that of a prediction interval. Eagles estimated the population proportion from a sample proportion and provided what is called a confidence interval.

A confidence interval is very like a prediction interval in that you have a particular confidence that your interval includes whatever you are estimating. The difference is the direction of the estimation. When you make inferences from probabilities or population proportions to samples, you are using a prediction interval. When you make inferences from samples to population proportions, you are using a confidence interval. The reason for the switch in language from "prediction" to "confidence" is to help us keep straight the direction of the inference. You use confidence intervals to estimate population proportions; prediction intervals are used to estimate sample proportions.

Confidence Intervals

A confidence interval is an interval on a number line that has a specified probability of including a statistic of a population. In the long run, 95% confidence intervals for population proportions will include the actual population proportions 95% of the time.

For example, one study explored what proportion of college students in New York had downloaded music from the Internet by surveying a random sample of 100 students. The study reports that the 95% confidence interval for the proportion of students who download music is from 40% to 60%. This means there is a 95% chance that, if all of the students had been surveyed, the proportion would fall between 40% and 60%.

Confidence intervals for population proportions can save you a lot of work. If you can use confidence intervals to estimate population proportions, you have a way of studying large populations, like that of the United States, without having to interview every single person in the population.

By estimating the population proportion from a sample proportion, you can also do research that would otherwise be too harmful. For example, imagine that you work at a plate factory. Your boss asks what proportion of plates will break when dropped on concrete. You want to determine that figure for all the plates the factory makes. You could test every plate, dropping them all on a concrete floor. That would give you a result in which you could be very confident, but the factory might go out of business. Instead, you test a random sample of plates and use the results to estimate the nature of the total population of plates.

Let's see how that plate testing would work. Let's say that you test 100 plates and find that 60 of the plates break when they hit the floor. What we've seen so far is that whatever the proportion in the population, we are 95% confident that the sample proportion falls less than 2 standard errors away from the population proportion. Does that tell us what the population proportion is when the sample proportion is 60%? It does: A number line is like a ruler. Distances work both ways. If the sample proportion isn't more than 2 standard errors from the population proportion, then the population proportion isn't more than 2 standard errors away from the sample proportion. Now all we need to know to come up with the confidence interval for the population proportion is the standard error.

Recall the basic equation for the standard error:

$$\text{Standard Error} = \sqrt{\frac{\text{Probability} \times (1 - \text{Probability})}{\text{Sample Size}}}$$

We are talking about random sampling, and with random sampling the probability is the same as the population proportion. So the equation is:

$$\text{Standard Error} = \sqrt{\frac{\text{Population Proportion} \times (1 - \text{Population Proportion})}{\text{Sample Size}}}$$

Here is a problem. We don't know the population proportion. If we knew the population proportion, we wouldn't have to create a confidence interval. The solution is to guess the population proportion while we're estimating the standard error. When guessing the population proportion for estimating the standard error, statisticians have found that it usually works well to use the sample proportion as an estimate of the population proportion. At the end of this section, you will see how you can test this trick. Right now, we will use the sample proportion in the equation.

Here's the equation for the *estimated* standard error. We have replaced the population proportion with our guess, the sample proportion.

$$\text{Estimated Standard Error} = \sqrt{\frac{\text{Sample Proportion} \times (1 - \text{Sample Proportion})}{\text{Sample Size}}}$$

Estimating the Standard Error

To estimate the standard error, temporarily estimate that the population proportion is the same as the sample proportion:

$$\text{Estimated Standard Error} = \sqrt{\frac{\text{Sample Proportion} \times (1 - \text{Sample Proportion})}{\text{Sample Size}}}$$

For example, if a random sample of 100 teens includes 80% who are continuing to college, the estimated standard error would be the square root of .8 times 1 minus .8 divided by 100, which is 4%.

Let's get back to our plate factory. We tested 100 plates, and 60% broke. How many would have broken if we tested all the plates? To find out, we first estimate the standard error by plugging the sample proportion and sample size into the equation for the estimated standard error. The sample proportion is .6.

$$\text{Estimated Standard Error} = \sqrt{\frac{\text{Sample Proportion} \times (1 - \text{Sample Proportion})}{\text{Sample Size}}}$$

$$\text{Estimated Standard Error} = \sqrt{\frac{.6 \times (1 - .6)}{100}}$$

$$\text{Estimated Standard Error} = .05$$

That's 5%. We're 95% confident that the 60% didn't fall more than 10% (2 standard errors) away from the population proportion. We are 95% confident that the population proportion isn't below 50% or above 70%.

95% Confidence Interval for a Population Proportion

To calculate a 95% confidence interval for a population proportion from a random sample, add 2 estimated standard errors to and subtract them from the sample proportion.

For example, if 80% of a random sample of 100 teens are going to college, the estimated standard error would be 4%, and a 95% confidence interval for the population proportion would be from 72% to 88% going to college.

That is how we calculate a confidence interval for a population proportion. The 95% confidence interval is the sample proportion plus and minus 2 estimated standard errors.

Margin of Error

Because 95% confidence intervals are very widely used, there is a special term for 2 estimated standard errors: "margin of error." In our plate-smashing example, the margin of error is 10%. We are 95% confident that the population proportion is less than a margin of error away from 60%.

Margin of Error

The margin of error is 2 estimated standard errors, unless the sample proportion is 0% or 100%.

For example, a survey of teens finds that 80% will go to college. The estimated standard error is 4%. The margin of error is 8%.

In her report on a survey of Kentuckians, Cynthia Eagles reported a margin of error of 3.5%. In that survey, 61% of women reported they were in favor of affirmative action for blacks. If the margin of error was 3.5%, then we can be 95% confident that the proportion in the total population of Kentucky women was somewhere between 57.5% and 64.5%. Now you can see why Eagles wrote that the "margin of error means that . . . in 19 of 20 cases the poll results would differ by no more than 3.5 percentage points from [what] would have been obtained by questioning all Kentucky adults" (19 is 95% of 20). Eagles is saying that she is 95% confident in the confidence interval.

Here is another quote referring to the margin of error:

> [Researchers] asked 1,009 people about this statement: "The U.S. Air Force is withholding proof of the existence of intelligent life from other planets." . . . 24 percent replied "somewhat likely." Saying "very likely" were another 24 percent, give or take the margin of error demonically dictated by lime-green intruders.
>
> —NOLAN, TAMPA TRIBUNE, JULY 15, 1997

Nolan writes that 24% of those interviewed thought it "very likely" that the U.S. Air Force hides the fact that there is intelligent life on other planets. Does that 24% apply to the entire population? No. As Nolan writes, that is 24%, "give or take the margin of error demonically dictated by lime-green intruders."

What is the margin of error for Nolan's report? Nolan reports that the survey involved 1,009 people. To find the 95% confidence interval for all Americans, we first estimate the standard error:

$$\text{Estimated Standard Error} = \sqrt{\frac{\text{Sample Proportion} \times (1 - \text{Sample Proportion})}{\text{Sample Size}}}$$

$$\text{Estimated Standard Error} = \sqrt{\frac{.24 \times .76}{1,009}}$$

$$\text{Estimated Standard Error} = \sqrt{.0001807}$$

$$\text{Estimated Standard Error} = .013$$

Then we calculate the margin of error:

$$\text{Margin of Error} = 2 \times \text{Estimated Standard Error}$$

$$\text{Margin of Error} = 2 \times .013$$

$$\text{Margin of Error} = .026$$

That's 2.6%. If this were a random sample we could be 95% confident that if every American were asked, somewhere between 21.4% and 26.6% would say that it was "very likely" that the Air Force is hiding evidence of alien intelligence.

One-Person Samples

Part of our inheritance from the 1980s is a colossal national debt. Much of this debt was incurred during the presidency of Ronald Reagan, who promised to balance the budget.

> *When Ronald Reagan ascended to the White House . . . [we were told,] just eliminate the "waste, fraud, and abuse" in our welfare system—all those mink-wearing welfare queens driving Cadillacs and buying vodka at taxpayers' expense—and a balanced budget would be in reach.*
>
> —PETERSON, *ATLANTIC MONTHLY,* OCTOBER 1993

> *When Reagan was asked, for example, about areas where he hoped to achieve large-scale savings, he told the congressional leaders his well-worn campaign anecdotes about the "welfare queen" of Chicago who was on the rolls with 100 different names.*
>
> —BRODER, *WASHINGTON POST,* FEBRUARY 15, 1981

The welfare queen who attracted so much of Ronald Reagan's attention was a Chicago woman who used false identification to apply for welfare benefits under many names. Eventually, she was charged with defrauding the state of a total of $8,000 (*New York Times,* January 9, 1977). The administration's claim was that if we tightened up welfare so that people like this woman couldn't bilk the system, we would save lots of money and balance the budget. The federal budget deficit was then $80 billion: That is, the federal government spent $80 billion more than its income in 1980.

Stopping welfare abuse would balance the budget only if a large proportion of welfare recipients were abusing the system. But what proportion of welfare recipients were doing so? Let's try to find out from what we know, and, along the way, you will see how you can be badly misled.

The Chicago welfare queen is our sample of welfare recipients. Is this a random sample? No. The press thought that this woman was an amazing woman and so remarkably unusual that they had to print her story. That's how the news works. The press does not run a story about someone who works hard to find a new job. The Chicago welfare queen was certainly not a random sample.

But let's pretend for a moment that we don't notice that she's not a random sample. For the moment, let's assume she is a random sample of welfare recipients. What's the margin of error?

The proportion in our sample is 100% welfare swindler. The margin of error is 2 times the square root of 100% times 0 divided by the sample size 1.

$$\text{Margin of Error} = 2 \times \sqrt{\frac{\text{Sample Proportion} \times (1 - \text{Sample Proportion})}{\text{Sample Size}}}$$

$$\text{Margin of Error} = 2 \times \sqrt{\frac{100\% \times (1 - 100\%)}{1}}$$

$$\text{Margin of Error} = 2 \times \sqrt{\frac{1 \times 0}{1}}$$

$$\text{Margin of Error} = 2 \times \sqrt{0}$$

$$\text{Margin of Error} = 2 \times 0 = 0$$

Zero times 100% is 0, even after you divide by 1. The square root of 0 is 0, so the estimated standard error is 0, and the margin of error is twice that, still 0. Our 95% confidence interval for the proportion of the general population is from 100% to 100%. This seems great. You can see why Reagan was so excited. Apparently welfare recipients are all cheats. If we get every welfare recipient to chip in $8,000, we will make some progress on the deficit.

But wait. Should you really be 95% confident in a confidence interval that goes from 100% to 100%? It's not even an interval. It's a point. Let's try that another way, this time with coins. I flip a coin once. It comes up 100% heads. Now I do my figuring. The estimated standard error is 0. The margin of error is 0, and I conclude that I ought to be 95% confident that that coin will give me 100% heads forever. There are two-headed coins, but when I look at this one, I can see that it has a tail on the other side. In fact, when I flip it a second time, I get a tail. There's something wrong with the thinking that led to my 95% confidence interval in this example, and there's something very wrong with the margin of error we figured for the welfare recipients based on the experiences of one woman.

The problem is that sample proportions at 100% or 0% cause trouble for us when we use the sample proportion to estimate the population proportion. There is another way to estimate the margin of error that can cope better with very small samples. The other way just considers how the sample size sets the maximum possible margin of error. Here's the equation we can use when the sample proportion is 100% or 0%, or if we just want to be extra careful:

$$\text{Maximum Possible Margin of Error} = \frac{1}{\sqrt{\text{Sample Size}}}$$

Let's see what that tells us about a sample with one person:

$$\text{Maximum Possible Margin of Error} = \frac{1}{\sqrt{\text{Sample Size}}} = \frac{1}{\sqrt{1}} = \frac{1}{1} = 1 = 100\%$$

With only one observation in a sample, the maximum possible margin of error is 100%.

The Maximum Possible Margin of Error

The maximum possible margin of error is the largest margin of error possible for a given sample size and is particularly helpful when working with small samples. At a given sample size, the maximum possible margin of error occurs when the population proportion is 50%. To calculate the maximum possible margin of error, divide 1 by the square root of the sample size:

$$\text{Maximum Possible Margin of Error} = \frac{1}{\sqrt{\text{Sample Size}}}$$

For example, if 400 people are surveyed, the maximum possible margin of error is 5%.

When the sample proportion is 0% or 100%, we use the maximum possible margin of error for our margin of error. So, for our sample of 1, the margin of error is 100%.

A margin of error of 100% is something in which I can have confidence. If I have studied one person, and that person is 100% welfare swindler, I can be 100% confident that the proportion of all welfare recipients who are swindlers is somewhere between 0% and 100%. I'm very sure of that confidence interval, because all proportions fall somewhere from 0% to 100%.

Margin of Error for Sample Proportions at 0% or 100%

If the sample proportion is 0% or 100%, you use the maximum possible margin of error: 1 divided by the square root of the sample size.

For example, if 100% of the first nine people who come into a bookstore buy a book, the margin of error for the population proportion would be 1 divided by the square root of 9, which is 33%.

To see how well this confidence interval does compared to what we know about the population proportion of fraud at the time, consider how much welfare fraud existed. To get an idea, you might consider the sales pitch of a company that sold the state of Connecticut an "anti-welfare queen" system. This system requires every welfare applicant to be fingerprinted. The system then checks records to see whether a new applicant already receives welfare benefits under another name.

> *The State of Connecticut took bold steps . . . in combating fraud by implementing a statewide welfare recipient verification program. . . . Connecticut estimates savings of $7.5 million in the first year of the program.*
>
> —BUSINESS WIRE, FEBRUARY 6, 1996

In 1993, Connecticut spent $2.8 billion on public welfare (Bureau of the Census, *Statistical Abstract of the United States, 1995*). This was one of the first systems to prevent welfare-queen-style cheating, and our first evidence of how many people cheated. The amount of $7.5 million is about 0.3% of the state's public welfare budget. If every welfare recipient collected the same amount, then about 0.3% of welfare recipients were welfare cheats. If welfare swindlers collected more than other recipients, then the $7.5 million savings would come from less than 0.3% of the recipients. We don't know the precise number, but it appears that welfare swindlers are somewhere at or below 0.3% of the total number of welfare recipients.

Even though our sample proportion (100%) was very far from 0.3%, our 95% confidence interval did include the actual proportion. Our 95% confidence interval was from 0% to 100%, and the actual proportion is about 0.3%.

Where the Maximum Possible Margin of Error Comes From

The maximum possible margin of error is the largest margin of error that is possible with a given sample size. To see why, think about the equation for the standard error. Here it is again:

$$\text{Standard Error} = \sqrt{\frac{\text{Population Proportion} \times (1 - \text{Population Proportion})}{\text{Sample Size}}}$$

Let's consider one sample size: 49 welfare recipients. Let's say 2% are swindlers. Then

$$\text{Standard Error} = \sqrt{\frac{.02 \times (1 - .02)}{49}} = \sqrt{\frac{.02 \times .98}{49}} = \sqrt{.0004} = .02$$

That's 2%. When the population proportion is 2%, the standard error is 2%.

What if 20% are swindlers? Then

$$\text{Standard Error} = \sqrt{\frac{.2 \times (1 - .2)}{49}} = \sqrt{\frac{.2 \times .8}{49}} = \sqrt{.00327} = .057$$

That's about 6%. The standard error has gone up.

How about 40% swindlers? Then

$$\text{Standard Error} = \sqrt{\frac{.4 \times .6}{49}} = \sqrt{.004898} = .06999$$

That's 7%.

If the population proportion is 50%, then the standard error is 7.1%:

$$\text{Standard Error} = \sqrt{\frac{.5 \times .5}{49}} = \sqrt{.005102} = .0714$$

If the population proportion is 60%, then the standard error is the same as when the population proportion is 40% (because .6 times .4 is the same as .4 times .6):

$$\text{Standard Error} = \sqrt{\frac{.6 \times .4}{49}} = \sqrt{.004898} = .06999$$

The standard error will continue to fall as the population proportion gets larger, all the way to 100%. Table 3.2.1 shows those proportions and the resulting standard errors.

The graph in Figure 3.2.1 shows the standard errors for all population proportions. In the figure, to find the standard error for any population proportion, you trace up from that proportion to the curve, and then horizontally to the left. For very low population proportions and very high population proportions, the standard error is smaller. The standard error gets larger and larger as you

Table 3.2.1   Standard Errors Resulting from Given Population Proportions (Sample Size = 49)

PROPORTION	STANDARD ERROR
2%	2%
20%	6%
40%	7%
50%	7.1%
60%	7%
80%	6%
98%	2%

Figure 3.2.1   **Standard Errors for Samples with 49 Observations**

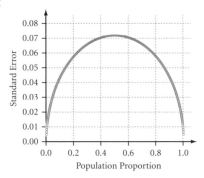

approach 50%, and it is as big as it can get when the population proportion reaches 50%. That is always true. Even if you don't know anything about the population proportion, remember that its standard error cannot be any larger than the standard error for 50%.

One way to make sure you have a large enough standard error is to use 50% to estimate the population proportion. When you calculate the standard error using 50%, your estimated standard error can't be too small, because the standard error associated with 50% is as large a standard error as is possible for a particular sample size.

There is an extra benefit in using 50% to estimate the maximum standard error. It leads to a simple equation for the maximum possible margin of error. To see why, consider the equation for the margin of error:

$$\text{Margin of Error} = 2 \times \sqrt{\frac{\text{Estimated Population Proportion} \times (1 - \text{Estimated Population Proportion})}{\text{Sample Size}}}$$

The maximum possible margin of error would occur when the estimated population proportion is .5. Watch what happens when we plug in .5:

$$\text{Maximum Possible Margin of Error} = 2 \times \sqrt{\frac{.5 \times (1 - .5)}{\text{Sample Size}}}$$

$$\text{Maximum Possible Margin of Error} = 2 \times \sqrt{\frac{.5 \times .5}{\text{Sample Size}}}$$

The square root of a ratio is the same as the ratio of the square roots:

$$\text{Maximum Possible Margin of Error} = 2 \times \frac{\sqrt{.5 \times .5}}{\sqrt{\text{Sample Size}}}$$

$$\text{Maximum Possible Margin of Error} = 2 \times \frac{.5}{\sqrt{\text{Sample Size}}}$$

The 2 can then be multiplied by the .5, which gives us the simple equation introduced earlier:

$$\text{Maximum Possible Margin of Error} = \frac{1}{\sqrt{\text{Sample Size}}}$$

The equation for the maximum possible margin of error makes it easier to see how the sample size is related to the maximum possible margin of error. If you had 49 welfare recipients in your sample, the maximum possible margin of error would be about 14%. If you had a sample of 100 welfare recipients, your maximum possible margin of error would drop to 10%. With 400 welfare recipients, your maximum possible margin of error would be 5%.

Figure 3.2.2 shows a graph of sample sizes from 50 to 1,000 and the relates maximum possible margins of error. To find the maximum possible margin of error for a particular sample size, you trace up from that sample size to the curve and then trace to the left. You can see that with 430 in the sample, the maximum possible margin of error is about 5%. With 1,000, it is about 3%.

Figure 3.2.2 **The Relationship Between Sample Size and the Maximum Possible Margin of Error for Sample Sizes from 50 to 1,000**

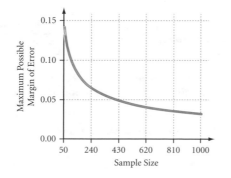

Figure 3.2.3 **The Relationship Between Sample Size and the Maximum Possible Margin of Error for Sample Sizes from 1 to 50**

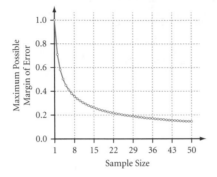

How about if we go the other way? The graph in Figure 3.2.3 shows how the maximum possible margin of error changes as sample sizes go down from 50 to 1. With a sample size of 8, for example, the maximum possible margin of error is about 35%. With a sample size of 43, the maximum possible margin of error is about 15%.

The Information Value of a Sample Size of 1

The equation for the maximum possible margin of error reveals something about how to do research with people. Before studying anyone, you can be certain that the proportions in the population fall between 0% and 100%. After you study only one person, the margin of error is 100%, so the 95% confidence interval is from 0% to 100%. Your confidence interval is unchanged. With a sample of one, you cannot tell whether that person is typical of the general population or unusual.

The fact that samples of one tell you almost nothing doesn't mean that people don't use them. Think of the before-and-after shots in dieting advertisements. They are samples of one. Samples like this are so common that Richard Nisbett and Lee Ross coined a name for them: "man-who statistics" (Nisbett and Ross, 1980), because people often start such stories with "I know a man who . . ."

When the Sample Size Equals One

If a sample contains only one person, for any feature of the sample, 100% of the sample includes that feature, and the margin of error is 100%. Having studied one person, you have learned nothing about how the population varies.

Statistics describing a sample of one are called "man-who statistics."

The conceptions that come from man-who statistics are not reliable. In the case of welfare fraud, man-who statistics implied a much too-high rate of fraud. Welfare reform did not pose a great opportunity to balance the budget.

Algebra and Greek Symbols

This section explains how to estimate the standard error of a proportion, σ_p, when the population proportion, Π, is unknown. In statistics, we indicate an estimated value by placing a circumflex accent ($\wedge$) over the value, so the estimated standard error of a proportion is indicated by $\hat{\sigma}_p$. To calculate $\hat{\sigma}_p$, we substitute the sample proportion, p, into the equation for the standard error:

$$\hat{\sigma}_p = \sqrt{\frac{p(1-p)}{n}}$$

In this equation, n is the sample size.

Now that we have a way to say "estimated standard error of the proportion," we can write out our 95% confidence interval—the idea that 95% of the time the population proportion, Π, will not be more than 2 estimated standard errors from the sample proportion:

$$P(|\Pi - p| < 2\hat{\sigma}_p) \approx 95\%$$

We use an approximately equal sign, because sample proportions are approximately normally distributed.

Summary

When estimating a population proportion from a sample proportion, you calculate a confidence interval, which is a range that you have a specified confidence includes the population proportion.

To calculate the confidence interval, you must estimate the standard error. If the sample proportion is not 0% or 100%, you can use the following equation to estimate the standard error:

$$\text{Estimated Standard Error} = \sqrt{\frac{\text{Sample Proportion} \times (1 - \text{Sample Proportion})}{\text{Sample Size}}}$$

The 95% confidence interval for a population proportion is the sample proportion plus and minus 2 estimated standard errors. The sum of 2 standard errors is called the "margin of error."

For a particular sample size, the maximum possible margin of error is the margin of error associated with a sample proportion of 50% and is equal to 1 over the square root of the sample size:

$$\text{Maximum Possible Margin of Error} = \frac{1}{\sqrt{\text{Sample Size}}}$$

When the sample proportion is 0% or 100%, you must use the maximum possible margin of error, rather than the margin of error you calculate with the equation based on estimating that the population proportion is the same as the sample proportion.

A man-who statistic is a statistic derived from a sample that includes only one observation. For a man-who proportion, the margin of error is 100%, and the 95% confidence interval is from 0% to 100%. A man-who statistic tells you nothing about population proportions. Each additional observation in a sample does less than the previous to diminish the margin of error less and less.

Avoiding Common Misunderstandings

At this point, it is very important to keep several distinctions clear: the distinction between a sample proportion and a population proportion, between a prediction interval and a confidence interval, and between a standard error and an estimated standard error.

This concrete example may make the distinctions clearer. Sue knows that if you looked at all babies, you would find that about 50% are female. Sue works in a hospital, and 75% of the last four babies born there were female. In this story, the population proportion is 50%, and the sample proportion is 75%.

Sue was curious to see whether a prediction interval would have included the sample proportion that she saw, 75%. To determine this, Sue calculated the standard error:

$$\text{Standard Error} = \sqrt{\frac{\text{Population Proportion} \times (1 - \text{Population Proportion})}{\text{Sample Size}}}$$

$$\text{Standard Error} = \sqrt{\frac{.5 \times (1 - .5)}{4}} = .25$$

Sue's 95% prediction interval is 50% plus and minus 50%: It is from 0% to 100%. Sue's prediction interval started with information about the population and predicted what would happen in samples.

Sue wondered whether the sample proportion, 75%, would make a sensible confidence interval. To find the confidence interval, Sue calculated the estimated standard error:

$$\text{Estimated Standard Error} = \sqrt{\frac{\text{Sample Proportion} \times (1 - \text{Sample Proportion})}{\text{Sample Size}}}$$

$$\text{Estimated Standard Error} = \sqrt{\frac{.75 \times (1 - .75)}{4}} = .217$$

Sue's 95% confidence interval is 75% plus and minus 44%: from 31% to 100%. Sue's confidence interval started only with information about the sample and estimated the nature of the population. In this case, Sue's confidence interval was successful: It included the actual population proportion, 50%.

Computer Project

There are two major claims to test in this section. The first is that the estimated standard error is a pretty good estimate. The second is that the margin of error will create a confidence interval that will include the population proportion 95% of the time.

Testing the Estimated Standard Error

To test the estimated standard error, consider a population like the 50,000 people in the Representative Sample included in the *Data Matters* Resource Center at *www.keycollege.com/dm*. Find a proportion in the population and pick a sample size. Calculate the standard error for random samples taken from this population. Then have your software take random samples and calculate the estimated standard error. Make a histogram of the estimated standard errors. How do they compare to the actual standard error?

Testing the 95% Confidence Interval

To test the 95% confidence interval, modify your instructions to your software so that it calculates the 95% confidence interval and records whether or not the interval includes the population proportion. How did the confidence interval do? Did it capture the population proportion 95% of the time, and did it miss the population proportion 5% of the time?

Exercises

1. Here is a report of a large survey on gun ownership:

   A survey of 8,000 randomly selected American households found that 50% of the households had guns, and 21% of those households stored guns loaded and unlocked.

   —ASSOCIATED PRESS, JANUARY 1995

   a. In the preceding Associated Press quote, what is the margin of error for the proportion of American households that have guns?

   b. What is a 95% confidence interval for the proportion of the population that have guns?

   c. There are about 100 million American households. About how many American households have guns?

2. There is a margin of error and confidence interval for the 21% in the preceding Associated Press quote as well.

   a. In the quote, what is the margin of error for the proportion who store guns loaded and unlocked?

   b. What is a 95% confidence interval for the proportion of the population who store guns loaded and unlocked?

3. Here is a report on American sociability:

   Nearly half (47%) chat with neighbors five times or more per month. . . . The poll [surveyed] 1,002 [American] adults.

   —PETERSON, *USA TODAY*, JULY 14, 1997

   a. What is the margin of error for Peterson's quote?

   b. What is a 95% confidence interval for the population proportion?

4. Here's a survey about UFOs:

   One in 10 Arizonans has seen objects in the sky they believe are alien craft. . . . [This] Behavior Research Center poll [surveyed] 709 people.

   —RUELAS, *ARIZONA REPUBLIC*, JULY 26, 1997

   a. What was the margin of error for Ruelas's report?

   b. What is the 95% confidence interval for the proportion that would have been found had the survey included every Arizonan?

5. You're considering buying a car. A *Consumer Reports* survey of car owners indicates that the Zimmer is very reliable, but a friend tells you, "I know a woman who owned a Zimmer. It was a complete lemon." What are you going to guess about the reliability of the Zimmer, and why would you make that guess?

6. You have probably seen advertisements in which the announcer interviews a customer who reports how wonderful some product is.

   a. What is wrong with the advertisements that show someone in a supermarket giving a testimony about how wonderful a product is?

   b. How would you change those testimony advertisements to make them more convincing to someone who has read this book?

7. An aspiring writer submits 4 manuscripts, which are all turned down. Assuming the writer never gets any better or worse, what is your estimate of the proportion of the writer's total production that will be published?

8. The aspiring writer perseveres and submits 12 more manuscripts, all of which are rejected. Now that 16 manuscripts have been rejected, what is your estimate of the proportion of the total production of this writer that will be published?

9. I am going to do a survey for a client, who will be presenting the results to his boss. He tells me, "Nicholas, if the margin of error is larger than 5%, I'm going to look bad." What is the smallest sample size I can use for this survey? How can you tell?

10. The client from the preceding exercise comes back to me the following year. We're redoing the survey. He tells me, "Nicholas, everyone else always reports a margin of error of 2%. Last year, my boss was a little concerned that our survey had a margin of error of 5%. This time I want 2% at most." What is the smallest sample size I can use for this survey? How can you tell?

11. Here is a report on a survey asking Colorado citizens their opinions on a matter of public policy:

    > *Customers of the Arkansas River Power Authority overwhelmingly support the construction of a new, coal-burning energy plant south of Las Animas. Eighty-two percent of the people responding to an authority survey said they favored such a project. The authority queried 500 of its customers and 41 percent responded.*
    >
    > —NESLAND, *PUEBLO [COLORADO] CHIEFTAIN*, NOVEMBER 27, 2001

    a. Assume for a moment that the people who responded to this survey were a random sample of Colorado citizens. What proportion of Colorado citizens favor a coal-burning energy plant south of Las Animas?

    b. Why is this not a random sample?

    c. In what way would you expect this sample to be biased?

12. Here's a report on a union surveying its membership:

> *70 percent of [Texas] educators . . . expressed satisfaction with their jobs. . . . The Association of Texas Professional Educators . . . questioned 1,200 educators by mail, with a 51 percent response rate.*
>
> —*Dallas Morning News*, July 25, 1997

a. A "51 percent response rate" means that 51% responded. How many people answered questions for this survey?

b. What is the margin of error associated with the 70%?

c. In what way would you expect this survey to be a biased sample of Texas educators?

d. How might this bias be related to the answers the surveyors received?

Answers to Odd-Numbered Exercises

1. a. $\text{Margin of Error} = 2 \times \sqrt{\dfrac{\text{Sample Proportion} \times (1 - \text{Sample Proportion})}{\text{Sample Size}}}$

$= 2 \times \sqrt{\dfrac{.5 \times (1 - .5)}{8,000}} = 2 \times \sqrt{.00003125}$

$= 2 \times .006 = .012$

The margin of error is about 1%.

b. The 95% confidence interval is from 49% to 51%.

c. There are about 100 million households, so 49 to 51 million households have guns.

3. a. $\text{Margin of Error} = 2 \times \sqrt{\dfrac{.47 \times (1 - .47)}{1,002}} = 2 \times \sqrt{.0002486} = 2 \times .016$

$= .032$

b. The 95% confidence interval is from 44% to 50%.

5. I would suspect that Zimmers are pretty reliable. *Consumer Reports* bases its reports on large samples. The woman whom my friend knows provides only a man-who statistic.

7. The sample proportion here is 0%, so we need to use the maximum possible margin of error, which is 1 divided by the square root of the sample size. The sample size is 4. The square root of 4 is 2, so the maximum possible margin of error is one-half, or 50%. A 95% confidence interval would be from 0% to 50%.

9. I need to find the sample size so that the maximum possible margin of error will be 5%.

$$\text{Maximum Possible Margin of Error} = \frac{1}{\sqrt{\text{Sample Size}}}$$

So I'm looking for a sample size so that

$$\text{Maximum Possible Margin of Error} = \frac{1}{\sqrt{\text{Sample Size}}} = 5\%$$

The proportion 5% is the same as 1/20, so I am looking for the sample size that will work in this equation:

$$\frac{1}{\sqrt{\text{Sample Size}}} = \frac{1}{20}$$

That's only going to work if the square root of the sample size is 20.

$$\sqrt{\text{Sample Size}} = 20$$

The value 20 squared is 400, so 20 is the square root of 400. I bet 400 will do the trick. Let's check:

$$\text{Maximum Possible Margin of Error} = \frac{1}{\sqrt{\text{Sample Size}}} = \frac{1}{\sqrt{400}} = \frac{1}{20} = .05 = 5\%$$

Yes, I need a sample size of 400. Another way to do this is to algebraically solve for the sample size and then plug in 5% for the maximum possible margin of error.

11. a. The sample size is 41% of 500, which is 205.

$$\text{Margin of Error} = 2 \times \sqrt{\frac{.82 \times .18}{205}} = 2 \times \sqrt{.00072} = .054$$

   If this had been a random sample of 205 Colorado citizens, I would expect that between 77% and 87% of Colorado citizens favor such a plant.

   b. This is a self-selected sample. The majority of the people who were sent the survey did not participate and send answers.

   c. This sample would be biased to people who open junk mail from their energy company. Of those, it would be biased to people who feel strongly about the issue and people who are compliant (who tend to obey when asked to do things like fill out a survey).

(3.3) The Story of Statistical Inference

- Null Hypothesis
- *P*-Value
- Alpha
- Significance

Land O' Lakes High saw about a 5 percent increase in the number of students on the honor roll. . . . "It could be multiple factors," [Principal] Ramos said. "There's always a variance among classes from one year to the next. I don't think that 5 percent would be statistically significant."

—BLAIR, *TAMPA TRIBUNE*, NOVEMBER 25, 2001

IN 2001, THE FLORIDA STATE LEGISLATURE changed the rules for high school grades. Before 2001, test scores from 94 to 100 were A's. After 2001, the A range was from 90 to 100. Principals said that they were unsure whether this change would affect how many students got A's.

Blair's article also reports that, in 2000, 379 of the 1,000 students at Florida's Gulf Middle School were on the honor roll. In 2001, there were 426. That's an increase of 4.7%—roughly the same jump that Ramos reported about Land O' Lakes High. Gulf Middle School's principal reported, "We're excited. That's the most students we've had make the honor roll in the 3 1/2 years I've been here." Blair reports, "Like Ramos, though, Bonti said he can't pinpoint the reason."

What do you think? Can *you* pinpoint the reason for more students on the honor roll? Does this jump from 37.9% to 42.6% show us that the new rules changed a student's chances of getting A's? It's a change, but not every change in proportions indicates that the underlying probabilities have changed. Could this be just random variation, what Ramos calls the "variance among classes"?

This section presents the logic of statistical inference. Statistical inference is how statisticians make inferences. By the end of this section, you will know how to determine the answers to these questions. You will also see what Ramos meant when he said, "I don't think that 5 percent would be statistically significant."

Before we deal with Florida students' grades, let's think about a similar but simpler situation: coin flips. Once we understand how to make a judgment about coin flips, we will come back to the Florida students.

Testing for a Fair Coin

My dad was an amateur magician. He learned how to glance at a flipped coin as he brought his hand over to slap the coin on the back of his other hand. If the coin wasn't going to come out the right way, during the rest of the swing, he could turn the coin over in his palm. After much practice, he could call every flip correctly. Every flip would come up the way he called it, and you couldn't tell how he did it. Imagine that you were watching him. You could tell something funny was going on, but *how* could you tell that something funny was going on?

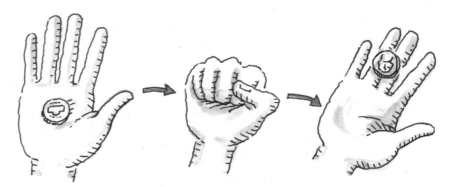

Let's state that question more clearly. Let's say that I am flipping a coin and saying, while the coin is still in the air, which side will land face up. You don't know whether I can do my dad's trick. I flip the coin 10 times and call 9 outcomes correctly. You would probably conclude that I was cheating somehow, but what would your evidence be?

You might say, "Nine out of 10. That can't happen. He must be cheating." That sounds sensible at first, but what do you mean by "that can't happen"? Why would you say, "That can't happen," when you have just seen me call 9 out of 10 correctly? Obviously it *can* happen. It just did. What you mean is "that can't happen *if he's not cheating*."

Your thinking is like this:

If he is not cheating, **then** he can't call 9 out of 10 correctly.

He called 9 out of 10 correctly.

Therefore, he is cheating.

Is that sound reasoning? To see, we can look at the logic of that reasoning in the abstract and see whether it holds up. Here is the logic you would be following:

If A is true, **then** B can't happen.

B happened.

Therefore, A is not true.

We can test that logic by substituting various ideas and events for A and B. If the logic consistently makes sense, then it deserves our respect. Here's an example. For A I could use "it rains," and for B I could have "the ground stays dry." Then our logic would be this:

If it rains, **then** the ground can't stay dry.

The ground stayed dry.

Therefore, it did not rain.

You might quibble with the initial claim about the ground having to get wet if it rains, but the logic is sound. This is a structure of thinking that we all use all the time. Imagine that someone says to you, "It just stopped raining." You look outside, and the ground is completely dry. What would you conclude? You would conclude that the person was mistaken and say, "But the ground is completely dry." To which the person might reply, "Oh, I meant that it just stopped raining in London, not here." That's all sensible, because the logic is respectable.

In the case of the coin flips, your thinking is this:

If he is not cheating, **then** he can't call 9 out of 10 correctly.

He called 9 out of 10 correctly.

Therefore, he is cheating.

But just a moment. I *could* get 9 out of 10 correctly without cheating. It is unlikely, but it can happen. Remember that the coin does not keep track of how it came out on the first 8 flips, and it *can* give me 9 out of 10.

What are the chances of getting 9 out of 10 correct? We can estimate it with the normal approximation. The sample proportion is 90%. The sample size is 10, and the probability is 50%.

$$\text{Standard Error} = \sqrt{\frac{.5 \times (1 - .5)}{10}} = 16\%$$

Figure 3.3.1 shows roughly how the sample proportions would be distributed if there were no cheating. The value of 90% is a little more than 2 standard errors from the population proportion. In fact, it is 2.5 standard errors from the population proportion, out in the tiny triangle on the right. The chances of getting a proportion that is more than 2 standard errors away from the population proportion is 5%. Remember proportions are only *approximately* normally distributed. In fact, with 10 flips, there is a 1% chance of getting 90% correct, which means it happens about once every 100 times someone tries it. There is a 2% chance of getting a proportion at least as far from 50% as 90%—a 1% chance of 90% or higher plus a 1% chance of 10% or lower.

Even though 9 out of 10 correct could happen, it still seems as if something odd was going on when I did it. How can we justify our conclusion that something odd is going on? We can no longer say, "If he's not cheating, then he couldn't call 9 coin flips in a row correctly." We don't have that kind of certainty. How can we adjust our thinking if we don't have certainties? Here is a possible adjustment:

If A is true, **then** B is very unlikely to happen.

B happened.

Therefore, we reject A (respecting that there is a chance that A is true).

Let's try that logic with some idea and event and see whether it seems reasonable:

If Joe is innocent of denting Tom's blue car in the parking lot, **then** it is very unlikely that Joe's car would have chips of blue paint on its bumper.

Joe's car *does* have chips of blue paint on its bumper.

Therefore, the idea of Joe's innocence is rejected (in a way that respects that there is a chance that Joe *might* be innocent).

Figure 3.3.1

Normal Approximation of the Distribution of Percentage of Coin Flips Called Correctly (Sample Size = 10; Standard Error = 16%)

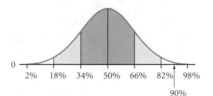

At first, you might think, "Joe *has* to be the one who dented Tom's car. Why do we have to respect some chance that Joe is innocent?" But you would be mistaken. Joe might be innocent. He may have gotten those chips some other way. He may have dented someone else's blue car, someone may have framed him, or something else may have produced the blue paint chips. We don't know for certain that Joe did it, but it is reasonable to reject Joe's innocence, as long as we keep in mind that we are not 100% certain of his guilt. That kind of thinking will rarely get us into trouble. If we have to form some sort of conclusion, we can go ahead and conclude that it's Joe's fault.

Actually, our thinking about the rain was not certain either. We don't know for certain that "If it rains, then the ground will get wet." Someone could have put up a circus tent or awning to keep the ground dry. We might even live where it is very dry. When I lived in Denver, it twice happened that the rain was so light and the air was so dry that the rain evaporated just before hitting the ground. As I walked around in that rain, my hair and shoulders got wet, but my shoes didn't. If you have ever lived at a high altitude, you might have seen what I'm talking about. You can probably think of some other reasons why the ground might stay dry as well.

So, really our thinking about the rain was like this:

If it rains, **then** it's very unlikely that the ground will stay dry.

The ground is dry.

Therefore, we reject the idea that it rained (respecting that there is a chance that it might have rained).

That is not bad thinking, but imagine that I told you this:

If you are not cheating, **then** it's very unlikely that you can call correctly one coin flip in a row.

You called one coin flip in a row correctly.

Therefore, you are cheating.

"Hold on a second," you would say. "It's not very unlikely to call *one* coin flip in a row correctly." We could then argue about that (and you would win the argument). It would be worth arguing, because it's very important what the chances are in the first statement, the one that says, "If A is true, then B is very unlikely to happen." If B isn't very unlikely, the thinking is no good.

How unlikely does B have to be to justify rejecting A? Let's consider a few possibilities. Let's say that B happens. I suppose that it would be wrong to reject A when A gives B a 50% chance of happening. If A gives B only a 1 out of 10,000 chance of happening and B happens, I think A looks bad, and we can reject A. If A gives B a 30% chance of happening, I don't feel comfortable rejecting A when B happens. If A gives B a 1 out of 1,000 chance, I reject A when B happens.

Somewhere between 30% and 1 out of 1,000 (.1%), we have
pens, and the probability of B happening when A is true is bel
reject A. Let's see how that looks in the story in which I have c
10 correctly and use a cutoff at 5%:

> If I am not cheating, **then** there is only a 2% probability of my getting a
> sample proportion at least as far from 50% as 90%.
>
> I call 90% correctly; that is, my sample proportion *is* 90%.
>
> Let's say your cutoff is 5%. Then the value of 2% is below your cutoff for
> likelihood; **therefore,** you reject the idea that I am not cheating.

That seems reasonable. In fact, it is the thinking of statistical inference. If a statistician were faced with my calling 9 out of 10 flips correctly, that is exactly the
line of thinking the statistician would follow.

Here is the thinking in the abstract:

> If A is true, **then** the probability of a result at least as unexpected as B is less
> than my cutoff.
>
> B happened.
>
> **Therefore,** I reject that A is true.

Null Hypothesis

Because statisticians use this kind of thinking all the time, there is associated terminology. The initial claim about what is happening is called the "null hypothesis." That's the "A is true" part of the logic. In the coin-flipping case, the null
hypothesis is that I am not cheating. In the rain case, the null hypothesis is that
it's raining. The null hypothesis is whatever story we start with.

P-Value

The probability of getting a result at least as unlikely as the result that happened,
if the null hypothesis is true, is called the "*p*-value." In our thinking, the *p*-value
was the probability of B happening, if A were true. In the coin-flipping case, the
p-value is the probability of getting a sample proportion at least as far from 50%
as 90%, if the null hypothesis is true. (Remember, the null hypothesis is that I am
not cheating.) In the rain case, the *p*-value is the probability of the ground being
dry, if the null hypothesis that it's raining is true.

Alpha

Our cutoff is called "alpha." The most commonly used alpha is 5%. If the *p*-value is less than the cutoff, alpha, then we reject the null hypothesis. If the *p*-value is greater than alpha, we do not reject the null hypothesis. We will use an alpha of 5%, as is common. In both cases, the *p*-value was smaller than alpha, so we rejected the null hypothesis.

Significant

When we use this kind of thinking and reject a null hypothesis, we say that the data was "significant." In the popular press, this is referred to as "statistical significance." "Significant" is terminology that means "a null hypothesis was rejected." It doesn't matter how silly the null hypothesis is. If a null hypothesis is rejected, statistics says that the results are *significant*. If the *p*-value is less than alpha, we reject the null hypothesis, so, if the *p*-value is less than alpha, the results are significant.

Here is our thinking about the coin-flipping case restated with all this jargon:

If the null hypothesis is true, **then** the *p*-value is 2% for a sample proportion at 90%.

The sample proportion *is* 90%.

The value 2% is below our alpha. **Therefore,** we reject the null hypothesis: We say that the sample proportion is significantly far from 50%.

Summary of Statistical Inference Terms and Their Meanings

TERM	MEANING
Null hypothesis	The initial story that is being tested.
P-value	The probability of the sort of result that happened, *if the null hypothesis is true.*
Alpha	A cutoff for p-values. If the p-value is less than alpha, we reject the null hypothesis. Otherwise, we do not reject the null hypothesis.
Significance	If a null hypothesis is rejected, the data that led to the rejection is "significant." "Significant" means that some null hypothesis was rejected, no matter how silly the null hypothesis was.

Retaining the Null Hypothesis and Not Affirming the Consequent

There is a famous logical fallacy called "affirming the consequent." The fallacious logic of affirming the consequent is this:

If A is true, **then** B happens.

B happens.

Therefore (and this is a fallacious "therefore"), A is true.

To see the foolishness of this kind of thinking, let's try it out:

If it rains, **then** the ground gets wet.

The ground is getting wet.

Therefore, it must be raining.

Can you imagine having a neighbor who believed this? Every time you would water your lawn, the neighbor would think it was raining and go walking with an umbrella.

Such behavior would be foolish. Although it may be generally true that if it rains, the ground gets wet, there are many other reasons why the ground could get wet, so we would need more evidence before we can conclude that it was raining.

Affirming the Consequent

Affirming the consequent is a logical fallacy that has this form:

> If A is true, **then** B will happen.
>
> B happens.
>
> Invalid conclusion: **Therefore,** A is true.

Here is an example of affirming the consequent:

> If I get my MBA, **then** I will get a good job.
>
> I got I good job.
>
> Invalid conclusion: **Therefore,** I must have gotten my MBA.

The two lines of logic can look very similar even though one is valid and the other is not. Here they are again.

VALID

If A is true, **then** B is unlikely to happen.

B happens.

Therefore, we reject A.

INVALID (affirming the consequent)

If A is true, **then** B is unlikely to happen.

B does not happen.

Invalid conclusion: **Therefore,** we conclude that A is true.

Let's try these logic patterns again. For A, we will use "you are shopping in a supermarket." For B, we will use "you are getting a haircut." Here they are:

VALID

If "you are shopping in a supermarket" is true, **then** "you are getting a haircut" is unlikely.

You are getting a haircut.

Therefore, we reject the idea "you are shopping in a supermarket."

Seems reasonable. If your friend calls you from a cell phone and says, "I'm getting a haircut," you would assume that your friend was not shopping in a supermarket. How about the other line of thinking?

INVALID (affirming the consequent)

If "you are shopping in a supermarket" is true, **then** "you are getting a haircut" is unlikely.

You are not getting a haircut.

Invalid conclusion: **Therefore,** we conclude that "you are shopping in a supermarket" is true.

That sounds wrong. For example, right now you are reading this book and presumably *not* getting a haircut. And are you shopping in a supermarket? No. That invalid logic is definitely invalid.

Now look at the invalid logic using the terminology of statistical inference. A is the null hypothesis. B is a particular result, such as a particular proportion in the sample.

INVALID (affirming the consequent)

If the null hypothesis is true, **then** B is unlikely to happen.

B does not happen.

Invalid conclusion: **Therefore,** we conclude that the null hypothesis is true.

That might not sound too bad to you, so let's make it even clearer. Our null hypothesis is that Kenneth is completely honest. Kenneth will flip a coin for us 10 times.

If Kenneth is completely honest, **then** it is unlikely that he will call the flips correctly 9 times.

Kenneth does not call the flips correctly 9 times.

Invalid conclusion: **Therefore,** we conclude that Kenneth is completely honest.

What would things be like if that were valid logic? Instead of lie detectors, we could just have accused criminals flip coins. Every accused criminal who called fewer than 9 heads would get to go home free. No, that's a bad idea, and it's bad thinking.

The Logic of Statistical Inference

Statistical inference uses a very specific logic:

> If A is true, **then** B is unlikely.
>
> B occurred.
>
> Therefore, we reject A, while respecting that there is a chance that A is true.

Or

> If A is true, **then** B is unlikely.
>
> B did not occur.
>
> Therefore, we do not reject A, nor do we take this as evidence that A is true.

Here are examples of the logic of statistical inference:

> If Leslie goes to law school, **then** it is unlikely that she will finish her education before she is 24.
>
> Leslie stopped going to school at 21.
>
> Therefore, Leslie did not go to law school (respecting the possibility that Leslie *might* have skipped a lot of grades).

Or

> If Leslie goes to law school, **then** it is unlikely that she will finish her education before she is 24.
>
> Leslie stopped going to school at 27.
>
> Therefore, we don't make a conclusion about whether Leslie went to law school.

Let's see how this thinking would look in statistical inference. Our null hypothesis is that Kenneth is honest. Kenneth calls 7 out of 10 flips correctly. Our *p*-value is greater than 5%. It would be invalid to conclude that Kenneth is honest; he could be trying to cheat, but simply not be good at the magic trick. Instead, we only decide to *not* reject the null hypothesis. We conclude that the 70% does not justify rejecting the idea that Kenneth is honest.

The bottom line is that when the *p*-value is greater than alpha, if you conclude that that fact is evidence that the null hypothesis is true, you are affirming the consequent. When the *p*-value is greater than alpha, you conclude only that the evidence does not justify rejecting the null hypothesis.

Occam's Razor and Retaining the Null Hypothesis

A general principle of science called "Occam's razor" says that, if there is no other reason to choose one theory over another, it's best to use the simpler theory. William of Occam (pronounced "AH-kum"), a philosopher, suggested that it is a way to cut less helpful theories away from more helpful ones, hence the name "Occam's razor."

Occam's razor makes students' lives easier. If a teacher has no reason to endorse one theory over another, Occam's razor says to go with the simpler theory, and that's the theory that is easier to learn.

Occam's Razor

Occam's razor is a principle that says if multiple theories all have equal evidence to support them, you should use the simplest theory.

For example, if your friend parks your car in a two-hour parking zone and you get a ticket before you get to your car, there are two possibilities.

Possibility 1: Your friend parked the car and left it more than two hours before you got to it.

Possibility 2: Your friend parked the car. The parking official noted the car's presence in the parking spot. Your friend then drove the car away, did some errands, and then brought it back, parking in the same spot. When the parking official returned, the parking official (using Occam's razor, no doubt) assumed that your car had been there all along and gave you a ticket.

If you have no other evidence to decide between these two ideas, Occam's razor would recommend that you go with possibility 1, because it is simpler.

In statistical inference, the null hypothesis is usually the simpler theory. When a sample proportion is not significant, and there is no reason to reject the null hypothesis, Occam's razor recommends that we retain the null hypothesis. So, the tradition is to retain the null hypothesis because it is simpler, but this retention is done with a very strong respect for the possibility that the retention might be a mistake.

Here's how our logic in the coin-flipping case looks with the addition of Occam's razor:

If the null hypothesis that I'm not cheating is true, **then** the *p*-value is 33% for a sample proportion at 70%.

The sample proportion is 70%.

The value 33% is *above* our alpha (which we have set at 5%). **Therefore,** we do *not* reject the null hypothesis: The sample proportion is *not* significant.

We retain the null hypothesis (that I am not cheating), because it is a simpler theory than alternative theories.

Throughout the rest of this book, we will consider tests that find *p*-values for results and decide whether to retain or reject null hypotheses. In all of the tests, the logic is similar to what you have seen in this section.

Retaining the Null Hypothesis

Because the null hypothesis is usually simpler, Occam's razor leads us to retain the null hypothesis when the *p*-value is greater than alpha.

For example, if someone flips a coin and calls 7 out of 10 flips correctly, the null hypothesis is that the person had a 50% chance of calling the flips correctly. The *p*-value is larger than a sensible alpha, so we do not reject the null hypothesis. The idea that there is a 50% chance that the person will call a flip correctly is simpler than alternatives, so we retain the null hypothesis.

The Florida Grade Change

Now we can think sensibly about the proportion of students on the honor rolls in Florida. At a 1,000-student middle school, the proportion of students on the honor roll rose from 37.9% to 42.6%. A principal at another high school remarked that a 5% jump like this might not be statistically significant. Maybe, maybe not. Let's see.

Figure 3.3.2 **The Sampling Distribution of Percentages from Random Samples (Sample Size = 1,000; Probability = 37.9%)**

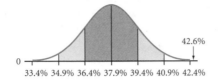

42.6%

0

33.4% 34.9% 36.4% 37.9% 39.4% 40.9% 42.4%

Before I can begin significance testing, I need a null hypothesis. I will start with a null hypothesis that, in 2001, the chance of a student being on the honor roll was 37.9%. Then the question is whether the 42.6% is significantly far from 37.9%. To find out, I need to determine the probability of getting a percentage as far from 37.9% as 42.6% if my null hypothesis is true.

I will need the standard error. The sample size is 1,000.

$$\text{Standard Error} = \sqrt{\frac{.379 \times (1 - .379)}{1,000}} = 1.5\%$$

Figure 3.3.2 shows how sample proportions would be spread out if the null hypothesis were true.

As you can see in Figure 3.3.2, proportions as far away from 37.9% as 42.6% are not likely, if the null hypothesis is true. Our *p*-value is below our alpha of 5%. We reject the null hypothesis that 37.9% is the probability of a student getting onto the honor roll in 2001 at Florida's Gulf Middle School. The 42.6% is statistically significantly greater than 37.9%.

Keep in mind, though, that we didn't know for certain that the probability was 37.9% in 2000. The 95% confidence interval for the probability was from 34.9% to 40.9%, and 42.6% is *not* significantly higher than 40.9%. Whether the 42.6% is statistically significant depends on the figure we use in our null hypothesis.

Algebra and Greek Symbols

Logic

Logic has its own set of symbols. For example, in this section I have been writing, "If A is true, then B will not happen." Using logic symbols "A is true" and "A will happen" would be indicated just by "A." The if-then is noted with a left facing "U" (⊃). So "If A, then B" would be indicated by "A ⊃ B." In logic, "not" is indicated by a tilde (~). So "If A, then not B" would be "A ⊃ ~B."

The following table shows the fallacious thinking of affirming the consequent expressed in logic symbols, with translations on the right.

Logic Symbols	Meaning
A ⊃ B	**If** A, **then** B.
B	B happened.
———	**Therefore**
A	A is true.

Note that the horizontal line means "therefore." In this case, it is a fallacious therefore.

Affirming the consequent is invalid. The valid thinking that we started with was of this form:

A ⊃ B

~ B

———

~ A

In our thinking about coins, A was "he is not cheating." B was "he will *not* call 9 out of 10 coins correctly." It's a little odd that our statements for A and B had a "not" in them (because the resulting double negative makes a sort of positive: "it is not true that he is not cheating"), but the thinking was still of this form. This perticular form of logical conclusion is called "modus tollens."

The *P*-Value

The *p*-value is a conditional probability: the probability of something happening *if the null hypothesis is true*. The null hypothesis being true is the condition of the *p*-value. Conditional probabilities are written with a vertical line (|), which means "given that" or just "if." For example, here's the *p*-value:

$$p\text{-value} = P(\text{something happening} \mid \text{the null hypothesis is true})$$

The "something happening" in the *p*-value is the sort of statistic that actually happened, so

$$p\text{-value} = P(\text{the sort of statistic that happened} \mid \text{the null hypothesis is true})$$

Let's say that the probability of calling a coin flip correctly is θ. In the case of my calling 9 out of 10 flips correctly,

$$p\text{-value} = P(\text{something like 90\% happening} \mid \theta = 50\%)$$

That is, the *p*-value is the probability of a proportion like 90% happening if the probability of the outcome is 50%. In the next chapter, we will get more specific about what we mean by "something like 90% happening."

Summary

Statistical inference starts with an initial idea called the "null hypothesis." Statistical testing then finds the *p*-value, which, for sample proportions, is the probability of getting a sample proportion at least as far from the null hypothesis's population proportion as the sample proportion that was found. If the *p*-value is at or less than a cutoff (called "alpha"), the null hypothesis is rejected, and the data are called "significant" or "statistically significant." If the *p*-value is greater than alpha, the null hypothesis is retained.

When the *p*-value is less than alpha, the null hypothesis is rejected because of a particular logic:

If the null hypothesis is true, **then** it is unlikely that the kind of data that appeared would appear.

The kind of data that appeared did appear.

Therefore, we reject the null hypothesis (while respecting that it may be true).

A *p*-value greater than alpha is not evidence that the null hypothesis is true. To think it is evidence supporting the null hypothesis is a logical fallacy, affirming the consequent.

When there are multiple equally well-supported theories, Occam's razor recommends using the theory that is simplest. In statistical inference, the null hypothesis is usually the simplest. Because of Occam's razor, if the *p*-value is greater than alpha, we retain the null hypothesis.

Avoiding Common Misunderstandings

The *P*-Value Is a Conditional Probability

English makes it hard to understand the *p*-value or any other conditional probability. In English, we don't say the conditions. For example, if someone asks you the chances of winning a lottery, you say something like "about one out of a million." You do not say, "About one out of a million, if you buy a ticket or someone gives one to you," even though you know full well that if you don't get a lottery ticket, your chances of winning are zero. We tend to leave the conditions unspoken, which often leads us to ignore them. But you cannot understand the *p*-value if you ignore its conditions.

The *p*-value is the chance of the sort of thing that happened *if the null hypothesis is true*. In fact, given that what happened happened, I would say that its overall chances are 100%. It happened. Its chances *if the null hypothesis is true* are what may be quite small.

The *P*-Value Is Not What You Most Want

It would be nice if, after we did some research, we knew the probability that the null hypothesis was true. I would be happy with the probability that the null hypothesis was false or the probability that some alternative was true. These are all sensible probabilities that you might want research and statistics to give you.

Statistics does not give you these values. Instead, it gives you the probability of the sort of thing that happened if the null hypothesis is true. Turning that into the probability that the null hypothesis is true requires some assumptions with which statisticians do not feel comfortable. If you would like to learn about how that's done, look up Bayesian inference. This text will not be teaching you Bayesian inference. It is not the dominant thinking in statistics, and William of Occam would not approve of it; it requires complex assumptions and algebra that we won't be using.

As you figure out what the *p*-value is, it may help to understand that it's not the probability you might want most. It is the probability of a kind of outcome if the null hypothesis is true.

Computer Project

The test of the effect of the change in the Florida grading law was not completely satisfactory. We most wanted to know about the change. Was it statistically significant? To find out, in this computer project you are going to do what is called a "Monte Carlo" simulation. In a Monte Carlo simulation, you set your computer to simulate data according to your null hypothesis. Then you consider the distribution of whatever statistic you are interested in. The *p*-value is the portion of simulated samples that have your statistic at the same distance from the center or further from the center than the statistic in your real sample.

In this situation, we have a difference between proportions from two 1,000-student samples. The difference is 4.7%. In this project, you will have the computer simulate collecting pairs of 1,000-observation samples. The computer will record the differences. The *p*-value is the probability of getting a difference at least as large as 4.7%. In your simulation, as long as you take enough pairs of samples, your proportion will fall close to the probability.

What will you use for your null hypothesis? In 2000, 37.9% of the students made the honor roll. In 2001, 42.6% made the honor roll. Your null hypothesis is that the underlying probability has not changed—that both proportions came from a single probability. Let's use the probability that is halfway between the two proportions. It is the overall proportion from the two years: 379 plus 426 divided by 2,000. It is 40.25%, or .4025.

Your task is to set your software to collect pairs of 1,000-observation samples from a system with a 40.25% probability. Have the software find the difference between the proportions in each sample and record those proportions. Your *p*-value is the proportion of differences that are at 4.7% or greater. Report your significance test.

Exercises

1. Consider this story:

   My dad flips a coin 25 times. He calls the coin in the air, and calls it correctly 19 out of 25 times (76% of the time). For a sample of 25 coin flips, if the chance that he can call a coin flip correctly is 50%, the standard error is 10%. The 95% prediction interval for sample proportions would be from 30% to 70%. The value 76% correct is outside of the 95% prediction interval for sample proportions, so the chances are less than 5% of getting a proportion as far from 50% as 76%, if the underlying proportion is 50%. Because the chance is less than 5%, it seems too unlikely an event to happen. I conclude that my dad is using his coin-flipping trick at least some of the time.

   a. In this story, what is the null hypothesis?
   b. What is the *p*-value (in words)?
   c. Is the numerical value of the *p*-value greater than 5%, less than 5%, or exactly 5%?
   d. What is alpha?
   e. How can you tell that I rejected my null hypothesis?
   f. *Why* did I reject my null hypothesis?

2. Here's a variation on that story:

   I flip a coin 25 times. I call the coin in the air, and call it correctly 15 out of 25 times (60% of the time). For a sample of 25 coin flips, if the chance that I can call a coin flip correctly is 50%, the standard error is 10%. The 95% prediction interval for sample proportions would be from 30% to 70%. The value 60% correct is inside the 95% prediction interval for sample proportions, so the chances are more than 5% of getting a proportion at least as far from 50% as 60%. Because the chance is more than 5%, it doesn't seem too unlikely an event to happen. We conclude that I am not using some sort of trick.

   a. In this story, what is the null hypothesis?
   b. What is the *p*-value (in words)?

   c. What can you say about the numerical value of the *p*-value?

   d. What is alpha?

   e. How can you tell that we retained our null hypothesis?

   f. *Why* did we retain our null hypothesis?

> *In Houston between 1995 and 1997, nearly half of all African Americans who applied for a home loan were rejected and more than a third of Hispanic applicants were rejected. . . . Those figures are significantly higher than the 30 percent rejection rate for whites.*
>
> —Yip, *Houston Chronicle*, November 11, 1998

This article by Pamela Yip also reports that, of 2,647 mortgage applications by African Americans in the Houston area, 47.4% were turned down. Of 11,886 mortgage applications by Hispanics, 36.4% were turned down. Let's say that the 30% rejection rate for whites is based on such a massive survey that we know that the population proportion for whites is 30%.

3. Imagine that you are discussing the article with a friend over e-mail.

   a. Your friend asks, "What do they mean that the figures are *significantly* higher?" Write a quick note explaining what "significantly" means.

   b. In your answer to your friend, you may have mentioned a "null hypothesis." Imagine that the term did come up. Your friend asks, "As far as the applications from African Americans go, what is the null hypothesis?" Write a brief note answering your friend.

   c. Your friend asks, "Why do we conclude that the chances of having your application turned down are higher for African Americans than whites?" Write another brief note explaining the logic of the inference.

4. Your friend is still full of questions.

   a. "Regarding the applications from Hispanics, what is the null hypothesis?" Write a brief note answering your friend's question about the null hypothesis.

   b. Your friend asks, "Why do we conclude that the chances of having your application turned down are higher for Hispanics than for whites? After all, the Hispanic proportion is 36.4%, close to that of whites." Write another brief note answering this question.

5. You can see whether African Americans had the same chance as whites (30%) of being rejected.

   a. These statistics are proportions from samples. If the population proportion were 30% for all of these groups, how many standard errors from the population proportion would the African American proportion (47.4%) be?

b. Think about a normal approximation of the distribution of sample proportions. Is a sample with a proportion as far as 47.4% is from 30% likely or unlikely, if the population proportion is 30%?

6. You can also get an idea of whether it is sensible to say that Hispanics had a 30% chance of being rejected.

   a. If the population proportion were 30% for all of these groups, how many standard errors from the population proportion would the Hispanic proportion (36.4%) be?

   b. Is a sample with a proportion as far as 36.4% is from 30% likely or unlikely, if the population proportion is 30%?

7. In 1998, the *Sacramento Bee* reported that a study had examined about 1,500 women admitted to California emergency rooms. The researchers kept track of the proportion of women who "said they had experienced emotional or physical abuse in their lifetimes by a partner."

   About 44 percent of California women reported being victims of such abuse in their lifetimes. . . . The fund's [previous] study, in 1996, showed 24 percent of all [American] women had been abused at some time.

   —STANTON, SACRAMENTO BEE, AUGUST 5, 1998

   a. If you take the 24% as a null hypothesis for the proportion of California women who would report such abuse, how many standard errors away from the null hypothesis's population proportion would the proportion in California (44%) be?

   b. What can you say about the numerical value of the *p*-value?

   c. Would the *p*-value be less than the commonly used alpha (5%)?

   d. If your alpha were 5%, what would you conclude about the null hypothesis in this case?

   e. If you assume that 24% was the rate in the population of women admitted to American emergency rooms in the 1990s, what would you conclude about the California rate in 1998?

8. Let's look more carefully at the study of Californian women admitted to emergency rooms. It's a good guess that the fund's 1996 study included at least 1,500 women. Let's assume that it was a random sample of exactly 1,500 women admitted to American emergency rooms.

   a. What is the 95% confidence interval for the population proportion?

   b. Use the top of the 95% confidence interval as your null hypothesis for a new statistical test of the 44% found in 1998. Write down your null hypothesis.

   c. What can you say about the *p*-value?

d. Use an alpha of 5%. Is the *p*-value less than alpha?

e. What do you conclude about your null hypothesis, and why do you make that conclusion?

9. Imagine I use my computer to take 100-observation samples from a system in which I set the probability to be 70%. For each sample, I am going to test the null hypothesis that that sample came from a system with a probability at 70%. I will use an alpha of 5%. Before I start, I calculate that my 95% prediction interval is 70% plus and minus 9%. That means that the probability of getting a 79% or a greater percentage is 5% (as is the probability of getting a 61% or a lesser percentage). So for all sample proportions at 79% and above and for all sample proportions at 61% and below, I will reject my null hypothesis.

a. In these tests, what is the null hypothesis, and is it true or false?

b. How often will I reject the null hypothesis?

c. When I reject the null hypothesis, is that a success or a mistake?

d. How often will I make mistakes in this situation?

10. Imagine that I do exactly the same thing as described in Exercise 9, but I use 33% as my alpha.

a. How often would I make mistakes when I'm testing the null hypothesis that the probability is 70%?

b. What is the relationship between alpha and the chances of mistakenly rejecting the null hypothesis, when the null hypothesis is true?

11. Imagine that you and your friends are trying to use year psychic power to affect coin flips. You try to psychically cause heads, and you flip a coin 16 times. You get 11 heads (69%). Now you want to use statistical inference to see whether you have psychic abilities.

a. What is your null hypothesis?

b. How many standard errors from 50% is your 69%?

c. What can you tell me about the *p*-value's numerical value?

d. What would you conclude about your null hypothesis?

e. Why did you make that conclusion?

12. Here's another report on Florida's change in grading policy:

> *There were somewhat bigger jumps for students making straight A's, though. At Land O' Lakes, 33 seniors had all A's, compared to 21 for the same grading period a year ago.*
>
> —Blair, *Tampa Tribune*, November 25, 2001

Guess that there are 250 seniors each year.

a. What proportion of seniors had straight A's in 2000?

b. What proportion had straight A's in 2001?

c. When you put the two years together, what proportion had straight A's?

d. Use the proportion you found in Exercise 12c as a null hypothesis for the probability of getting straight A's at Land O' Lakes. If that null hypothesis were true, what would be the standard error for 250-observation samples?

e. In terms of standard errors, how far from the null hypothesis's probability was the 2001 proportion? And how far was the 2000 proportion?

f. What can you conclude about the null hypothesis? And why do you make that conclusion?

Answers to Odd-Numbered Exercises

1. a. The null hypothesis is that my father is not using his magic trick, and the chances of calling a flip correctly are 50%.

b. The *p*-value is the probability of getting a sample proportion at least as far from 50% as 76%.

c. In this story, the *p*-value is less than 5%.

d. In this story, alpha is 5%.

e. The null hypothesis was that he was not using the magic trick, and I concluded that he was using the magic trick.

f. I rejected my null hypothesis, because the *p*-value was less than my cutoff (alpha).

3. a. "Significantly higher" means that the researchers had an initial hypothesis, called a "null hypothesis." In this case their initial hypothesis was that rejection rates were the same for everyone. Their initial ("null") hypothesis suggests that rejection rates at least as high as 47.4% for the African Americans in that sample would be very unlikely, but 47.4% was the rejection rate, so the researchers rejected their null hypothesis. When a statistician uses this kind of thinking and rejects a null hypothesis, the evidence is said to be "significant." That's why they say that the 47.4% was *significantly* higher.

b. For the African American applications, the null hypothesis was that their chances of having their applications turned down were the same as the white applicants' chances (30%).

    c. We conclude that African Americans were more likely to have their applications turned down because of this line of thinking:

> **If** African Americans have the same chance of being turned down, **then** it is extremely unlikely that they would have a proportion at least as far from 30% as 47.4%.
>
> The African American rejection rate *was* 47.4%.
>
> **Therefore,** we reject the idea that African Americans have the same chance of being turned down (respecting that there is a tiny possibility that they do have the same chance).

5. a. There are 2,647 applications from African Americans.

$$\text{Standard Error} = \sqrt{\frac{\text{Population Proportion} \times (1 - \text{Population Proportion})}{\text{Sample Size}}}$$

$$= \sqrt{\frac{.30 \times (1 - .30)}{2{,}647}} = .009 = .9\%$$

The African American rejection rate was 47.4%, 17.4% away from 30%.

$$\frac{17.4\%}{0.9\%} = 19.333$$

The amount 17.4% is 19.333 standard errors. So the African American rejection rate is 19.333 standard errors away from a population proportion of 30%.

    b. It is extremely unlikely to get a proportion as far as 47.4% is from 30% if the population proportion is 30%.

7. a. $\text{Standard Error} = \sqrt{\dfrac{\text{Population Proportion} \times (1 - \text{Population Proportion})}{\text{Sample Size}}}$

$$= \sqrt{\frac{.24 \times (1 - .24)}{1{,}500}} = .01 = 1\%$$

The California rate, 44%, is 20% away from 24%. That's 20 standard errors.

    b. The *p*-value must be a lot less than 5%, because 44% is 20 standard errors from 24%.

    c. Yes, the *p*-value would be less than the commonly used alpha, 5%.

    d. In this case, I can reject the null hypothesis.

    e. The California rate is significantly higher than the national rate.

9. a. The null hypothesis is that the probability is 70%, and it is true.

   b. Proportions will fall outside of the 95% prediction interval 5% of the time. So I will reject the null hypothesis 5% of the time.

   c. It's a mistake.

   d. I will make mistakes about 5% of the time.

11. a. My null hypothesis is that the chances of calling the flip correctly are 50%.

   b. Standard Error $= \sqrt{\dfrac{.5 \times (1 - .5)}{16}} = .125 = 12.5\%$

   $\dfrac{19\%}{12.5\%} = 1.52$

   My 69% is 1.5 standard errors from 50%.

   c. My *p*-value will be greater than 5%, because there is a 5% chance that a sample proportion will be at least 2 standard errors away from the null hypothesis's probability, and 69% is closer.

   d. I would retain the null hypothesis.

   e. There isn't evidence to reject it, and it is simpler than the theory that I do have psychic powers, but they were on the blink today, or being blocked by nefarious unseen forces.

CHAPTER 4 *Testing Locations and Differences of Proportions*

Once statisticians had created the logic of significance testing, all they needed to test a null hypothesis was to find a statistic that reflected how embarrassing the data were for the null hypothesis and determine how that statistic would be distributed if the null hypothesis were true.

One of the first tasks for statistics was to test claims (null hypotheses) about probabilities or about the proportions in populations. For example, a salesperson might say that a fishing lure would attract a fish 80% of the time, or a politician may claim that 90% of the public backs her program. Section 4.1 shows how to test such claims with a z-test. This z-test is called a test of location, because it tests whether the probability or population proportion falls at a particular location on the number line.

Another task for statistics is to test for correlations and the effectiveness of treatments. For example, doctors may claim that a cancer screening will lower your chances of dying of cancer. What that claim is really saying is that a proportion (the proportion dying) in one group (those screened) is different from the proportion in another group (those not screened). Sections 4.2 and 4.3 show how to test such a claim with a chi-square test.

4.1 Testing Where a Proportion Is

- The Z–Test

"A significantly higher percentage of music videos aired on MTV contained one or more episodes of violence or weapon carrying than the videos aired on other networks". . . . In total . . . violence occurs in nearly a quarter—22.4 percent—of the videos on MTV, more than double the violence in videos on three other cable channels.

—CARMAN, *SAN FRANCISCO CHRONICLE*, MAY 15, 1997

PEOPLE LEARN ABOUT HOW TO BEHAVE by watching what other people do. This can make you nervous when you consider how much violence is on TV. As parents and activists try to cope with TV violence, they need to know which networks air the most violent shows. In 1997, the *San Francisco Chronicle* reported that researchers had looked at 130 music videos on MTV and found that 22.4% of MTV's videos contained violence, compared to less than 11.2% on other cable channels.

If the researchers picked another sample of 130 videos, they would probably find a different proportion. If they repeated this process, they would get a variety

of proportions. The proportions would be roughly normally distributed with a center at the population proportion. (In this case, the population is all MTV videos, and the population proportion is the proportion of all MTV videos that include violence.)

What does this study tell us about the population proportion? Is violence any more common in MTV videos than elsewhere? To find out, we are going to test a null hypothesis that the population proportion is 11% (roughly the proportion of videos containing violence on other networks).

To find out whether the sample proportion, 22.4%, would lead us to reject the null hypothesis, we need to know the standard error, which will let us find out the distance, counted in standard errors, 22.4% is from the null hypothesis's population proportion, 11%. This distance is called a "z-value." In our effort to check on MTV, we are testing the null hypothesis's claim that the population proportion is 11%, so we're interested in the distance from 11%.

Here's how we calculate the z-value:

$$z\text{-value} = \frac{\text{Sample Proportion} - \text{Null Hypothesis's Claimed Population Proportion}}{\text{Standard Error}}$$

We subtract the null hypothesis's claimed population proportion from the sample proportion and then divide by the standard error.

We don't know the standard error, but we are testing the null hypothesis, so we will use the null hypothesis to find the standard error. The null hypothesis says that the population proportion is 11%. The sample size is 130. That means that the standard error is the square root of .11 times 1 minus .11 divided by 130, or .027.

Now we can calculate the z-value by plugging in the numbers:

$$z\text{-value} = \frac{\text{Sample Proportion} - \text{Null Hypothesis's Claimed Population Proportion}}{\text{Standard Error}}$$

$$= \frac{.224 - .11}{.027} = 4.2$$

A z-value of 4.2 means that MTV's 22.4% is 4.2 standard errors away from the null hypothesis's claim for the population proportion. What does 4.2 tell us?

Z-Values

A proportion's z-value is the proportion's distance from a hypothesized chance or population proportion in terms of standard errors.

For example, imagine I flip a coin 100 times and hypothesize that the chance of a head is 50%. The standard error is 5%. If I get 55% heads, that 55% has a z-value of 1, because it is 1 standard error above 50%. A 40% would have a z-value of −2, because it is 2 standard errors below 50%.

A sample proportion's z-value indicates where, in the distribution of sample proportions, that proportion falls. MTV's z-value of 4.2 indicates that its proportion would fall to the right of the center of the distribution of sample proportions. Figure 4.1.1 shows how such proportions would be distributed and where a z-value of 4.2 would be. If we relabel the x-axis of Figure 4.1.1, we can show the distribution in terms of z-values, as shown in Figure 4.1.2.

Figure 4.1.1

Normal Approximation of the Distribution of Sample Proportions (Sample Size = 130; Population Proportion = 11%; Standard Error = 2.7%)

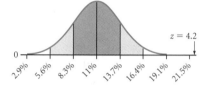

Figure 4.1.2

Normal Approximation of the Distribution of the Z-Values of Sample Proportions

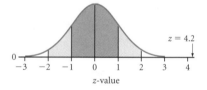

If you fully understand how Figure 4.1.2 was created from Figure 4.1.1, you understand z-values. The z-value of 11% is 0, because we are looking at distances from 11%. The value 13.7% is 1 standard error above 11%, so it has a z-value of 1; 16.4% is 2 standard errors above 11%, so it has a z-value of 2. This is all because the z-value is the distance from the designated proportion, in terms of standard errors.

The Normal Distribution in Terms of Z-Values

All z-values have the same normal distribution, with a center at 0 and a standard error of 1:

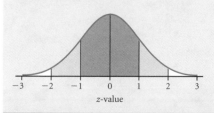

Now we need to figure out the *p*-value for MTV's 4.2 *z*-value. Figure 4.1.2 shows us that everything we know about the normal distribution can be expressed in terms of *z*-values, and that will tell us the *p*-value for any *z*-value. Table 4.1.1 lists prediction intervals in terms of *z*-values. The table includes what we already know about normal distributions. It says that about two-thirds of the proportions fall within 1 standard error of the center (from a *z*-value of −1 to a *z*-value of 1). Table 4.1.1 includes some new details about normal distributions and will lead us to the *p*-value.

The table tells us that 68% of samples will have proportions with *z*-values between −1 and +1. That leaves 32% to fall outside −1 and +1. The proportions of 95% of samples will have *z*-values between −1.96 and +1.96. You already have encountered the normal approximation of the distribution of proportions (in Chapter 3), except that earlier I rounded 1.96 to 2.

What does Table 4.1.1 tell us about the *z*-value of 4.2 for MTV? From the table you can see that only 0.01% of sample proportions fall more than 4 standard errors from the population proportion. That means that the chance of getting a *z*-value at least as far from 0 as 4 is 1 out of 10,000. We got a 4.2, which is slightly further away than 4. It would be slightly less likely to find a *z*-value at least as far from 0 as 4.2, because the values further from 0 are less likely. Remember that the *p*-value is the chance, if you assume that the null hypothesis is true, of having a proportion that is at least as far from the population proportion as the proportion that happened. The *p*-value for 4.2 is less than .01%. We will use an alpha of

Table 4.1.1 Prediction Intervals for Observations from Any Normal Distribution

PREDICTION INTERVAL IN TERMS OF Z-VALUES	PROBABILITY THAT INTERVAL INCLUDES SAMPLE PROPORTION	PROPORTION OF Z-VALUES EXPECTED TO FALL OUTSIDE INTERVAL
0 to 0	0%	100%
−0.5 to 0.5	38%	62%
−1 to 1	68%	32%
−1.5 to 1.5	87%	13%
−1.96 to 1.96	95%	5%
−2 to 2	95.45%	4.55%
−2.5 to 2.5	99%	1%
−3 to 3	99.70%	.30%
−3.5 to 3.5	99.90%	.10%
−4 to 4	99.99%	.01%
−4.5 to 4.5	99.999%	.001%

5%. Our *p*-value (.01%) is less than our alpha (5%), so we reject the null hypothesis that violent videos are 11% of what MTV shows.

Because we rejected a null hypothesis, we can say that MTV's 22.4% is *significantly* (or "statistically significantly") higher than 11%. It seems that MTV is a pocket of high television violence.

Z-Values and P-Values

Every *z*-value has a *p*-value. In Table 4.1.1 the *p*-value for each *z*-value appears in the rightmost column. Table 4.1.2 shows just the *z*-values and *p*-values from Table 4.1.1.

To see how the *p*-values in Table 4.1.2 work, consider this report of a study of the dangers of talking on the telephone while driving a car:

> *[Researchers] randomly selected 100 New York motorists who had been in an accident and 100 who had not. Of those in accidents, 13.7 percent owned a cellular phone, [compared to] 10.6 percent of the accident-free drivers.*
>
> —*GREENSBORO NEWS & RECORD*, MARCH 19, 1996

The quote says that of 100 New York motorists who were in car accidents, 13.7% owned cellular phones. However, there's something unusual about this report. Somehow, these researchers calculated a proportion of 100 people and got 13.7%. What's the .7? If they had 13 people, that would be 13%. If they had 14 people, that would be 14%. Probably what was happening here was that they selected *about* 100 people. Nonetheless, let us take the report at face value and go with the idea that *about* 13.7% owned cellular phones.

Z-Values and P-Values

Z-values can be used to test whether a proportion came from a hypothesized chance or probability. *Z*-values for proportions are approximately normally distributed with a center at 0 and a standard error of 1. For each *z*-value there is a specific proportion of the distribution that falls further from 0 than that value. That proportion is the *p*-value for that *z*-value when you test a hypothesized chance or probability.

For example, if a hypothesized population proportion is true, 5% of the *z*-values will fall at 2 or further from 0, so the *p*-value for 2 is 5%.

Table 4.1.2 *P-Values for Some Specific Z-Values*

Z-VALUES	P-VALUE	Z-VALUES	P-VALUE
0	100%	−2.5 or 2.5	1%
−0.5 or 0.5	62%	−3 or 3	.30%
−1 or 1	32%	−3.5 or 3.5	.10%
−1.5 or 1.5	13%	−4 or 4	.01%
−1.96 or 1.96	5%	−4.5 or 4.5	.001%
−2 or 2	4.55%		

13.7% of 100 Drivers

Does that mean that accident-prone drivers are more likely to own cellular phones? Maybe. Overall, the researchers found that 12% of the people they surveyed owned cellular phones. How does the accident-prone drivers' proportion, 13.7%, compare to that 12%? To find out, let's see what the *z*-value would be if we guess that the population proportion is 12%.

First, we find the standard error. The sample size is 100, and the null hypothesis's guess is that the population proportion is 12%.

$$\text{Standard Error} = \sqrt{\frac{.12 \times (1 - .12)}{100}} = 3\%$$

Now we can figure out the *z*-value.

$$z = \frac{\text{Sample Proportion} - \text{Population Proportion}}{\text{Standard Error}}$$

$$z = \frac{.137 - .12}{.03} = 0.57$$

Figure 4.1.3

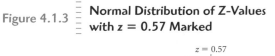

Normal Distribution of Z-Values with $z = 0.57$ Marked

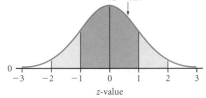

Figure 4.1.3 shows the location of a z-value of 0.57.

A sample proportion at 13.7% is not terribly surprising if the population proportion is 12%. To find the p-value of a z-value at 0.57, we can look at the p-values in Table 4.1.2. The p-value of a z-value at 0.5 is 62%. The p-value for a z-value of 1 is 32%. The p-value for 0.57 would be somewhere between 32% and 62%. It would certainly be greater than 5%. We retain our null hypothesis, which was that the population proportion for the accident-prone drivers was 12%. This means that we do not have evidence against the hypothesis that the population proportion is 12%. We are not affirming that null hypothesis. We are just *not rejecting* it.

What about the no-accident drivers? There were 100 of them. How does their proportion, 10.6%, compare to the possibility of 12%? Their sample size was also 100. If the population proportion were 12%, then their standard error would still be what we just calculated: 3%. What would the z-value for 10.6% be? Here are the calculations:

$$z = \frac{\text{Sample Proportion} - \text{Population Proportion}}{\text{Standard Error}}$$

$$z = \frac{.106 - .12}{.03} = -0.46$$

This z-value is less than 0, because the proportion is less than 12%, even closer to 0 than the last proportion. Its p-value is a little over 62%, much greater than a sensible alpha of 5%. We have no evidence to support rejecting the idea that the population proportion of no-accident drivers who owned cellular phones was 12%. It looks as though the *Greensboro News & Record* jumped the gun. Later

Z-Tests

When z-values are used to test a null hypothesis, the test is called a "z-test."

The z-test begins with a null hypothesis that a chance or population proportion is a specific value. From that hypothesis, the z-value of the observed proportion is calculated. If alpha is 5%, and the z-value is less than -2 or greater than 2, the null hypothesis is rejected.

research might have provided evidence of the dangers of driving while phoning, but this study did not.

Z-Test Summary

Z-Test Use

The z-test is used to test a claim that a probability or a population proportion is a particular value.

Z-Test Requirements

The z-test assumes that the sample being tested is a random sample and that each observation in the sample is independent of the rest. That is, each observation is a random selection from the total population, and making each observation does not change the others.

Z-Test Null Hypothesis

The null hypothesis of the z-test is that the population proportion is a particular value. For example, in this section, the null hypothesis of our first z-test was that the violent proportion of the population of MTV videos was 11%.

The Z-Test Statistic

The statistic used in the z-test is the z-value.

$$z\text{-value} = \frac{\text{Sample Proportion} - \text{Null Hypothesis's Claimed Population Proportion}}{\text{Standard Error}}$$

The P-Value

If the null hypothesis is true, z-values calculated from proportions are roughly normally distributed with a center at 0 and a standard error of 1. The p-value is the probability of a z-value at least as far from 0 as the z-value seen in the sample if the null hypothesis is true. For example, for a z-value of 1, the p-value is 32%. For a z-value of 2, the p-value is 5%.

The Inference

If the p-value is less than alpha, the null hypothesis is rejected. If the p-value is greater than alpha, the null hypothesis is not rejected.

Reporting the Results

When a null hypothesis is rejected, the results are described as "significant." In the popular press, a significant z-test might be reported in this manner.

"MTV's 22.4% is statistically significantly higher than 11%."

Algebra and Greek Symbols

Here is a restatement of the concepts of the z-test. Π is our symbol for the population proportion. We will denote the null hypothesis with H_0, and the null hypothesis's claimed population proportion with Π_0. The null hypothesis can then be stated as H_0: $\Pi = \Pi_0$. The alternative is denoted as H_1 and can be stated as H_1: $\Pi \neq \Pi_0$.

The test statistic for the z-test is z, the z-value:

$$z = \frac{p - \Pi_0}{\sigma_p}$$

Remember that σ_p is the standard error of the sample proportion, if the null hypothesis is true; that is, if H_0 ($\Pi = \Pi_0$) is true,

$$z \sim \mathcal{N}(0, 1), \text{approximately}$$

which is to say that z is approximately normally distributed with a center at 0 and a standard error of 1. A normal distribution with a center at 0 and a standard error of 1 is called a "standard normal distribution." Z-values are distributed in an approximately standard normal distribution.

Alpha (α) is the cutoff for statistical significance. If the p-value is less than alpha, the null hypothesis is rejected, and the results are considered statistically significant.

It is also helpful to determine the z-value that a percentage of proportions equal to *half* of alpha ($\alpha/2$) fall above. We use $z_{\alpha/2}$ to represent that z-value. For example, if α is 5%, then $z_{\alpha/2}$ is $z_{.025}$, which is the z-value that 2.5% of proportions fall above (or you could say it is the z-value that is below 2.5% of proportions). We know that 2.5% of proportions and therefore 2.5% of z-values fall above a z-value of 1.96 in a standard normal distribution, so if $\alpha = 0.05$, then $z_{\alpha/2} = 1.96$. You might also round that figure and say that for $\alpha = 0.05$, $z_{\alpha/2} = 2$.

If $|z| > z_{\alpha/2}$ then we reject H_0. ($|z|$ is the absolute value of z.) Otherwise, we retain H_0. That is, if the absolute value of z is greater than the z-value that is below only 2.5% of z-values, we reject the null hypothesis and conclude that the population proportion (or the probability) is not where the null hypothesis said it was.

Describing the Spread of Z-Values

There is a special term for the standard error of a statistic calculated from samples that have only one observation, the "standard deviation." This text will get to standard deviations when it turns to research on number-line observations, such as prices, ages, and heights. In those contexts, you can describe how widely spread amounts are by describing the standard error of samples where each sample has a single observation. In that case, you would be reporting a "standard deviation." A standard deviation is a standard error calculated when the sample size is 1.

Z-values can be calculated from single observations. For example, a former pro basketball player, Manute Bol, is 7 feet 7 inches tall. Compared to American males in general, his height has a *z*-value of 7.7. That is, if you created a histogram of American male heights, Manute Bol's height would be very far to the right of the central lump. Because *z*-values can be calculated from single observations, statisticians usually report that z-values have a *standard deviation* of 1, rather than saying that they have a *standard error* of one. Because a standard deviation is a kind of standard error, it is not incorrect to say that *z*-values have a standard error of 1, but it is unusual.

One-Sided Significance Tests

This text will only tell you about two-sided significance tests. The *z*-test described in this section is a two-sided *z*-test, because it would reject the null hypothesis no matter which side of the null hypothesis's population proportion (or probability) the data's proportion was on. For example, with 500 observations and a null hypothesis that the probability is 50%, this *z*-test would reject the null hypothesis if the sample proportion were significantly higher than 50%, at 90%, for example, or lower, at 10%.

Some researchers use what is called a one-sided test. For a one-sided test they must commit to retaining the null hypothesis no matter where the proportion is as long as the proportion is on a specified side. For example, they may say, "I don't care about proportions that are low. I believe that the null hypothesis is wrong, and the sample proportion will be higher than 50%." Having said that, they have to retain the null hypothesis even if the sample proportion is 0 and they have 1,000 observations.

You might wonder why anyone would use a one-sided hypothesis. The value to some people is that they get to use a different *z*-value as their cutoff. Rather than using $z_{\alpha/2}$, they can use z_α. The reason is that if the null hypothesis is true, the chances of getting a value higher than z_α is alpha. We don't have to worry about extremely low sample proportions, because we're not going to pay attention to them.

This text does not teach any more about one-sided tests, because using them is almost never justified. For example, I have seen one-sided tests used for reports on global warming, but I suspect that the researchers would have been interested and reported the results if it turned out that the earth was cooling. I can't see them standing in the snow in southern California: saying, "It's not statistically significant, because we used a one-sided test." No, they would say, "We have learned that there is global cooling." And I've seen one-sided tests of whitening agents for toothpaste, but would the researchers really ignore the results if the chemical darkened teeth? I don't think so.

Summary

Each sample proportion has a z-value. The z-value is how many standard errors the sample proportion is from the population proportion:

$$z = \frac{\text{Sample Proportion } - \text{ Population Proportion}}{\text{Standard Error}}$$

Z-values reveal where on the normal distribution a sample proportion falls. P-values are the portions of the normal distribution that are further from the population proportion than the sample proportion. A z-value's p-value is the portion of the normal distribution that falls outside a prediction interval from negative z to positive z.

The z-test can be used to test whether a population proportion falls at the null hypothesis's claimed population proportion. The z-test calculates a sample proportion's z-value based on the null hypothesis's population proportion. If alpha is 5%, and the z-value is more than 2 away from 0, the results are statistically significant. (Notice that when the z-value is more than 2 away from zero, that means that the sample proportion is more than 2 standard errors away from zero.)

Avoiding Common Misunderstandings

The z-value is a measurement in terms of standard errors that indicates how many standard errors from a claimed population proportion a sample proportion is. A z-value of 2.3 means that the sample proportion is 2.3 standard errors above the claimed population proportion. A z-value of -1.4 means that the sample proportion is 1.4 standard errors below the claimed population proportion. Looking back and forth between Figure 4.1.1 and Figure 4.1.2 in this section helps clarify the relationship between the z-value and the standard error.

Computer Project

For the computer project, confirm the values in Table 4.1.2 for yourself. Pick a population proportion (I suggest 50%). Pick a sample size (I suggest 2,500). The normal approximation works better for larger sample sizes. If you would like to see that for yourself, try sample sizes of 2,500 and 4. Have your software create 100 samples and calculate the proportions.

Transform the proportions into z-values. That is, calculate the standard error of the proportions, subtract each sample proportion from your population proportion, and divide by the standard error. You can get your software to subtract and divide each one for you.

Have your software sort your z-values from lowest to highest. Check the entries in Table 4.1.2 against what happened in your simulation. For example, the table shows that for a z-value of 1, the p-value is 32%. Were 32% of your z-values at 1 or further from 0? For more precision, work with a greater number of z-values. A larger number of z-values will give you a better image of how z-values are distributed in this situation.

Exercises

Here is a report on the graduation rates at 10 western universities.

SCHOOL	GRADUATION RATE
Oregon State	58%
Stanford	93%
Oregon	58%
Southern California	66%
UCLA	76%
California	78%
Washington	66%
Arizona	50%
Washington State	59%
Arizona State	45%

—BORST, *NEWS TRIBUNE*, JUNE 28, 1996

Each school admits about 3,000 new freshmen each year. The proportions in the preceding table are calculated from four years of freshman, 12,000 at each school.

1. Sketch a histogram of those proportions. The center of the distribution is near 64%. The question we might consider is whether the variation from school to school is just random or shows that some schools do a better job graduating students than others.

2. Add to your sketch an outline of the approximate normal distribution for proportions from samples that have 12,000 observations and come from a population with a proportion at 64%. Does it look as though we are seeing anything more than just random variation?

3. For Oregon State, do and report a z-test to check whether its graduation rate is statistically significantly lower than the overall rate, 64%. In your answer, state the null hypothesis and show the standard error, z-value, and what that tells you about the p-value.

4. For Arizona State, do a z-test to check whether its graduation rate is statistically significantly lower than 64%. Write down the null hypothesis and show the z-value and what it tells you about the p-value.

5. Make a table of the first five schools' z-values and p-values. For which of those schools can you reject the possibility that the population proportion is 64%?

6. Now consider the last five schools.

   a. Use a null hypothesis that the population proportion is 64% and make a table of the last five schools' z-values and p-values.

   b. For which of those schools can you reject the hypothesis that the population proportion is 64%?

7. Here is a report on African American graduation rates in Arizona public universities.

   $\frac{66}{240} = 27.5\%$

   Just 66 of the 240 African-American freshmen at the [Arizona public] universities in 1989 graduated within six years. That 27.5 percent rate contrasts with a 47.6 percent graduation rate among the 8,956 Anglo students in 1989's freshman class.

   —WEBSTER, ARIZONA REPUBLIC, FEBRUARY 22, 1996

   Imagine that the NAACP wants to know whether the different graduation rates are evidence that African Americans have a chance of graduating that is less than 47%.

   a. If your population proportion were 47.6%, what would be the z-value for the "66 of the 240 African-American freshmen" who graduated in six years?

   b. What does that tell you about the p-value?

   c. What would you conclude for the NAACP?

8. The same article included information on Native American graduation rates:

   Only 38 of the 287 Native Americans who began as full-time freshmen [at Arizona public universities] in 1989 graduated within six years, a drop to 13.2 percent from a 19.5 percent average for the three preceding freshman classes.

   —WEBSTER, ARIZONA REPUBLIC, FEBRUARY 22, 1996

a. What does the "38 of the 287 Native Americans" graduating indicate about the possibility that Native Americans have a 47.6% chance of graduating in six years?

b. What is the z-value of that "38 of the 287 Native Americans"?

c. What can you say about the p-value?

d. What would you conclude about the possibility that Native Americans have a 47.6% chance of graduating in six years from Arizona public universities?

9. Here is a report on graduation rates for football players.

Here's a [ranking] based on the 1997 NCAA graduation-rate report of the percentage of freshmen entering in 1990–91 [with football scholarships] who received degrees: 1–Penn State and Florida State: 71 percent; 3–Nebraska: 63 percent . . . 9–Tennessee: 25 percent; 10–LSU: 20 percent.

—BAGNATO, *CHICAGO TRIBUNE*, SEPTEMBER 3, 1997

The NCAA limits each school to a maximum of 25 football scholarships for freshmen. NCAA graduation rates are the proportion of the scholarship freshmen who graduate within six years. The 1997 graduation rate was based on 25 athletes at each school.

a. Let's assume that the 64% graduation rate we found in Exercise 1 applies. When you consider the possibility that Penn State, Florida State, and LSU each had a 64% chance of having a football player graduate in six years, what are the schools' z-scores?

b. What are their p-values?

c. What would you conclude about the possibility that the population proportion for those schools was 64%?

10. What can we conclude about how well Tennessee and LSU are graduating football players?

a. When you consider the possibility that Tennessee and LSU each has a 64% chance of having a football player graduate in six years, what are the school's z-scores?

b. What are their p-values?

c. What would you conclude about the possibility that the population proportion for those schools was 64%?

11. Here is a report on the graduation rates of basketball players at the University of Maryland.

Maryland's four-year graduation rate for freshmen entering from 1986 through '89 was 15 percent (2 of 13), down from 38 percent in last year's report.

—NAKAMURA AND ASHER, *WASHINGTON POST*, JUNE 28, 1996

Imagine that a University of Maryland administrator has written to you because she is concerned that only 2 out of the 13 basketball players graduated within six years.

a. If we stick with the guess of 64% as a graduation rate, what is the *z*-value in this case?

b. What is the *p*-value?

c. What would you conclude about the claim that these basketball players are running a 64% chance of graduating in six years?

d. Think about your answers for this question and for the previous questions. How does the sample size affect the *z*-value?

e. How does the sample size affect the *p*-value if the proportion doesn't change?

12. Here is a report comparing Wisconsin's universities to the rest of the universities in the United States.

Of the nearly 20,000 freshmen who entered [University of Wisconsin] System schools in 1991, 51.8% graduated from the same school they started at. . . . [Nationally,] 47.6% of students graduated from the school at which they started.

—DURHAMS, *MILWAUKEE JOURNAL SENTINEL*, JUNE 2, 2000

a. Does Wisconsin's 51.8% reflect just random variation, or does it show that Wisconsin is doing a better job graduating students than other university systems?

b. With a sample size of 20,000 and a population proportion of 47.6%, what's the standard error?

c. What's the *z*-value of a test checking whether Wisconsin's 51.8% is significantly higher than 47.6%?

d. Is the *p*-value above or below 5%?

e. Can you reject the null hypothesis that Wisconsin's population proportion is 47.6%?

Answers to Odd-Numbered Exercises

1.

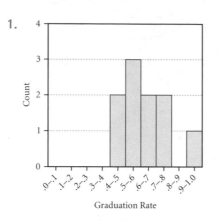

Graduation Rate

3. My null hypothesis is that the chance that an Oregon State student will graduate is 64%.

$$\text{Standard Error} = \sqrt{\frac{.64 \times (1 - .64)}{12,000}} = .0044 = .44\%$$

Oregon State's graduation rate is 58%.

$$z = \frac{.58 - .64}{.0044} = -13.6$$

If we check Table 4.1.2, we see that the p-value is less than the p-value for a z-value of -4.5 is .001% (.00001). The p-value for a z-value of -13.6 must then be much less than .00001. Oregon State is significantly less likely to graduate a student than a school that graduates 64%.

5.

SCHOOL	GRADUATION RATE	Z-VALUE	P-VALUE
Oregon State	.58	−13.6	Less than .00001
Stanford	.93	65.9	Less than .00001
Oregon	.58	−13.6	Less than .00001
Southern California	.66	4.5	.00001
UCLA	.76	27.3	Less than .00001

We can reject the null hypothesis for all of the schools, because their p-values are less than the common alpha, 5%.

7. a. Standard Error $= \sqrt{\dfrac{.476 \times (1 - .476)}{240}} = 3\%$

The graduating proportion equals 66 divided by 240, which equals 0.275, or 27.5%.

$$z = \frac{\text{Sample Proportion} - \text{Population Proportion}}{\text{Standard Error}}$$

$$z = \frac{.275 - .47}{.03} = -6.5$$

b. According to Table 4.1.2, the p-value would be less than .001%.

c. We could reject the idea that there is a 47.6% chance that an African American will graduate in six years. The graduation rate for African American students is statistically significantly lower than the overall rate.

9. a. Standard Error $= \sqrt{\dfrac{.64 \times (1 - .64)}{25}} = \sqrt{.009216} = .096$

$$z = \frac{\text{Sample Proportion} - \text{Population Proportion}}{\text{Standard Error}}$$

For Penn State and Florida State,

$$z = \frac{.71 - .64}{.096} = .73$$

For LSU,

$$z = \frac{.20 - .64}{.096} = -4.58$$

b. According to Table 4.1.2, for Penn State and Florida State, the p-value is greater than 32%. For LSU, the p-value is less than 1%.

c. The information about 25 football players at Penn State and Florida State does not justify rejecting the hypothesis that football players at those schools have a 64% chance of graduating within six years. Football players at LSU are significantly less likely to graduate than the 64%.

11. a. Standard Error $= \sqrt{\dfrac{.64 \times (1 - .64)}{13}} = \sqrt{.0177} = .133$

$$z = \frac{\text{Sample Proportion} - \text{Population Proportion}}{\text{Standard Error}}$$

Of the 13 University of Maryland basketball players, two (15%) graduated.

$$z = \frac{.15 - .64}{.133} = -3.7$$

b. According to Table 4.1.2, the p-value is between .1% and .01%.

c. We can reject the idea that the basketball players had a 64% chance of graduating.

d. As the sample size gets larger, the standard error gets smaller. As the standard error gets smaller, if the difference doesn't change, z gets farther from 0.

e. As z gets farther from 0, the p-value gets smaller. Values of z that are farther from 0 are less likely to appear. That means that as the sample size increases, the p-value gets smaller.

4.2 How to Look for Differences in Chances

- Cross-Tabulations
- Correlation
- The Null Hypothesis of the Chi-Square Test

[College student] binge drinkers experienced many personal and social problems, the researchers said. For instance, 90 percent of those who binged more than once a week said they experienced a hangover and 63 percent said they did something they regretted.

—Talan and Brown, *Newsday*, December 7, 1994

O F THE BINGE-DRINKING COLLEGE STUDENTS mentioned in the preceding quote, 63% said that they did something they regretted. Were they more likely to do things they regretted than students who did not binge drink? Maybe. Table 4.2.1 shows some of the research findings that Talan and Brown were reporting on. It tells us something about whether binge drinkers have more regrets than other college students.

The data in the table are from a survey of American college students done by a team led by Dr. Henry Wechsler. The Wechsler team defined binge drinking as consuming five or more alcoholic drinks in a row for men or four or more in a row for women (Wechsler et al., 1994). Frequent binge drinkers had been binge

Table 4.2.1   Alcohol-Related Problems Among College Students Who Consumed Alcohol in the Past Year

	NONBINGE DRINKERS (n = 6,894)	INFREQUENT BINGE DRINKERS (n = 4,090)	FREQUENT BINGE DRINKERS (n = 3,291)
DID SOMETHING YOU REGRET	14%	37%	63%
MISSED A CLASS	8%	30%	61%
GOT BEHIND IN SCHOOLWORK	6%	21%	46%

Source: Wechsler et al., 1994, p. 1672.

drinking more than twice in the two weeks before they were interviewed. Infrequent binge drinkers reported binge drinking once or twice in the two weeks before the interview, and nonbinge drinkers were those who reported not having been binge drinking at all during the previous two weeks.

Cross-Tabs

Table 4.2.1 is set up like a table in the Wechsler team's report. That table makes it somewhat difficult to see at a glance the overall chances of binge drinking and the overall chances of falling behind in your schoolwork.

Another approach to presenting this information is to make a table with the categories of one measurement listed on the side and the categories of another measurement listed across the top, and then to list how many people appear in each cell of the table. Table 4.2.2 shows an example.

Such a table is called a "cross-tab" or "cross-tabulation." Table 4.2.2 is a cross-tab comparing frequent and infrequent binge drinkers and nonbingers, and whether they reported getting behind in their schoolwork. Wechsler's table indicated that there were 6,894 nonbingers and that 6% fell behind in their schoolwork; 6% of 6,894 is 414. Those 414 appear in the left column (Nonbingers) and in the bottom row (Got Behind in Schoolwork).

The numbers in a cross-tab are counts of how many people are in each combination of categories. For example, the count for frequent bingers who kept up with their schoolwork was 1,777, and that is what appears in the upper-right cell.

Table 4.2.2   Cross-Tab of Drinking and Falling Behind in Schoolwork

	NONBINGERS	INFREQUENT BINGERS	FREQUENT BINGERS
KEPT UP WITH SCHOOLWORK	6,480	3,231	1,777
GOT BEHIND IN SCHOOLWORK	414	859	1,514

Cross-Tabs

A cross-tab is a table that shows the counts for each combination of categories for two sets of measurements.

For example, in Section 4.1, a study was discussed in which 14 out of 100 drivers who had been in accidents owned cell phones, and 11 out of 100 drivers who had not been in accidents owned cell phones. This table is a cross-tab of that data:

	OWNS CELL PHONE	DOESN'T OWN CELL PHONE
HAS BEEN IN ACCIDENT	14	86
HAS NOT BEEN IN ACCIDENT	11	89

Marginal Proportions

Table 4.2.2 still doesn't show the overall chances of falling behind in schoolwork. What we need are the proportions in each row. The proportion in each column would tell us about the chances that a student binge drinks, which would be useful information. To find the proportions in each row, we need to total up each row and then divide by the number in the entire table. Table 4.2.3 shows what we find.

To find the proportion who kept up with their schoolwork, we totaled the counts in the top row (6,480, 3,231, and 1,777). That gave us a total of 11,488, which appears in the margin to the right of the top row. Totaling the counts in the bottom row (414, 859, and 1,514) gave us the total who fell behind in their schoolwork, 2,787, which appears in the right margin of the bottom row. We add those together to get the total for the entire table. In cross-tabs, you put the total of all the cells (called the "grand total") in the lower-right corner to show that it is the total of the row totals and that it is also the total of the column totals. (You

Table 4.2.3 — Cross-Tab of Drinking and Falling Behind in Schoolwork with Marginal Totals and Percentages

	NONBINGERS	INFREQUENT BINGERS	FREQUENT BINGERS	
KEPT UP WITH SCHOOLWORK	6,480	3,231	1,777	11,488 80%
FELL BEHIND IN SCHOOLWORK	414	859	1,514	2,787 20%
	6,894 48%	4,090 29%	3,291 23%	14,275 100%

could check that: Add up the column totals that appear in the margin on the bottom as well as the row totals that appear in the right margin. Both groups of figures add up to 14,275.)

To find the proportion who kept up with their schoolwork (the top row), we divide the row total (11,488) by the grand total (14,275). We get 80%, as is shown in the table. We can do the same to find the proportion who fell behind in their schoolwork (20%).

The same steps can be followed to find the column proportions. The column total for nonbingers is 6,894, which when divided by 14,275 yields 48%. These column proportions appear in the bottom margin of Table 4.2.3.

Now we can see the overall chances. Table 4.2.3 shows that 80% of students reported keeping up with their studies, 48% reported never binge drinking, and 23% reported binge drinking frequently.

Marginal Totals and Proportions

Cross-tabs often provide the totals of each column in the bottom margin under the column, and the total of each row in the margin to the right of the row. These are the marginal totals. Cross-tabs also often include the proportion of the observations in the table that appear in each row and column.

For example, this table includes the marginal totals and proportions:

	OWNS CELL PHONE	DOESN'T OWN CELL PHONE	
HAS BEEN IN ACCIDENT	14	86	100 50%
HAS NOT BEEN IN ACCIDENT	11	89	100 50%
	25 12.5%	175 87.5%	200

Correlation

A cross-tab is a way of checking for a correlation. Two measurements are correlated if knowing one measurement improves your ability to guess the likelihood of the other. For example, many parents follow a tradition of dressing each baby in colors to indicate whether the baby is a boy or girl. Generally, boy babies are dressed in blue and girl babies are dressed in pink. So, for babies, there is a correlation between clothing color and gender.

Table 4.2.4 is a cross-tab from a day at a park. I've included only the babies dressed in pink or blue. There were five girls in pink, three boys in blue, and one boy in pink.

Table 4.2.4 shows a correlation between clothing color and gender, because knowing the clothing color improves the chance of guessing the gender correctly. If you didn't know the color of the clothes, and I told you I held a baby that day at the park, you would guess that there was about a 56% chance that the baby was a girl, because the row proportion for girls is 56%. If I told you the baby I held was wearing pink, you would guess that it was probably a girl. If I told you the baby's clothes were blue, you would guess "boy," and you would be more sure of your guess (because 100% of the babies in blue were boys). That is what is meant by a correlation: some relationship so that knowing one aspect improves your ability to guess the probability of another aspect.

Sometimes things are uncorrelated, or independent. For example, imagine that I roll a die 6 times with my left hand and 12 times with my right, and the results are as shown in Table 4.2.5.

Table 4.2.4 ⋮ Cross-Tab of Baby Gender and Baby Clothing Color

	BLUE	PINK	
BOY	3 (100% of Blues)	1 (17% of Pinks)	4 44%
GIRL	0	5 (83% of Pinks)	5 56%
	3 33%	6 67%	9 100%

Knowing which hand I was using doesn't change your guess about whether I rolled a 1. Similarly, knowing whether I rolled a 1 doesn't change your guess about which hand I was using. For example, let's say I tell you that on one of the rolls the die went off the table, and I ask you to guess which hand I was using. You would say there is a 67% chance that it was my right hand. Then I tell you, "Ah, but this was one of the times when I rolled a *1*." You would still say there is a 67% chance that I rolled with my right hand. That is what is meant by "uncorrelated." These measurements (hand and whether the roll was a 1) are completely uncorrelated. Knowing one measurement doesn't change our guess of the other.

Before we check for a correlation between binge drinking and falling behind in your schoolwork, note that when there is no correlation in a cross-tab, the proportion in a row is the same for every column. In Table 4.2.5, the top row proportion is 67%, and 67% fall in the top row in every column. The bottom row proportion is 33%, and 33% fall in the bottom row of every column.

There is another way to think about that. When there is no correlation, you can figure out how many observations to expect in each cell by multiplying the row proportion by the column total. For example, Table 4.2.6 shows the same

Table 4.2.5 Cross-Tab of Hand and Die-Rolling Outcome

	ROLLED A 1	ROLLED GREATER THAN 1	
RIGHT HAND	2 67% of 1's	10 67% of 1's	12 67%
LEFT HAND	1 33% of 1's	5 33% of 1's	6 33%
	3 17%	15 83%	18

Table 4.2.6 · Cross-Tab of Hand and Die-Rolling Outcome with Counts Expected If No Correlation

	ROLLED A 1	ROLLED GREATER THAN 1	
RIGHT HAND	Observed: 2 Expected: $2/3 \times 3 = 2$	Observed: 10 Expected: 2/3 of $15 = 10$	12 2/3
LEFT HAND	Observed: 1 Expected: $1/3 \times 3 = 1$	Observed: 5 Expected: 1/3 of $15 = 5$	6 1/3
	3 1/6	15 5/6	18

data as Table 4.2.5 and includes the counts you would expect if there were no correlation.

In the upper-left cell, the expected count was 2, because that is 2/3 of the 3 rolls in the left column. In the bottom-right cell, the expected count was 5, because that is 1/3 of the 15 rolls in the right column. I multiplied by 2/3 and 1/3, because those are the row proportions. (To avoid rounding errors, I used fractions.) The expected counts we ended up with precisely matched the counts we actually observed. That makes sense, seeing that our assumption of no correlation was true.

Correlation

Two sets of measurements are correlated if knowing an observation's value for one of the measurements allows you to better estimate the probabilities of that observation's value on the other measurement.

For example, infancy and driver's licenses are correlated. Knowing whether a person is an infant changes your guess about the chances that he or she has a driver's license.

This is another way to look for correlations. If the counts you would expect if there were no correlation are the counts you actually observed, then there is no correlation. If the expected counts are different from the actual counts, then there is a correlation. You can see this in Table 4.2.7, which is the baby data with the counts we would expect if there were no correlation.

When there is a correlation, the expected counts do not match the observed counts. For example, if there were no correlation, we would expect about 1.32 boys in blue, but we observed 3. And we would expect about 1.68 girls in blue, but we observed 0.

Table 4.2.7 Cross-Tab of Baby Gender and Baby Clothing Color with Expected Counts

	BLUE	PINK	
BOY	Observed: 3 Expected: 44% of 3 = 1.32	Observed: 1 Expected: 44% of 6 = 2.64	4 44%
GIRL	Observed: 0 56% of 3 = 1.68	Observed: 5 56% of 6 = 3.36	5 56%
	3 33%	6 67%	9

Why look at it this way? Why not say only that we expected 44% of the babies in blue to be boys, and 100% were? The reason is that it helps to see proportions *and* raw counts. In this case, looking at the raw counts shows us that although the proportions are far apart, the counts are not. Compare the table of colors and baby genders to the same sort of cross-tab for binge drinking and falling behind in schoolwork, shown in Table 4.2.8.

As before, each of the expected counts in Table 4.2.8 was calculated by multiplying the row proportion by the column total. For example, the proportion for the top row was 80% and the total for the center column was 4,090. Therefore the expected count for the top center cell was .8 times 4,090, or 3,272.

Table 4.2.8 Cross-Tab of Drinking and Falling Behind in Schoolwork with Marginal Totals, Percentages and Expected Counts

	NONBINGERS	INFREQUENT BINGERS	FREQUENT BINGERS	
KEPT UP WITH SCHOOLWORK	Observed: 6,480 Expected: 80% of 6,894 = 5,515.2	Observed: 3,231 Expected: 80% of 4,090 = 3,272	Observed: 1,777 Expected: 80% of 3,291 = 2,632.8	11,488 80%
FELL BEHIND IN SCHOOLWORK	Observed: 414 Expected: 20% of 6,894 = 1,378.8	Observed: 859 Expected: 20% of 4,090 = 818	Observed: 1,514 Expected: 20% of 3,291 = 658.2	2,787 20%
	6,894 48%	4,090 29%	3,291 23%	14,275

Expected Counts

Expected counts are helpful indicators of what the count would be if the row proportion applied equally to all the data in it; that is, if there were no correlation between the observations in a cross-tab. The expected counts in each cell are found by multiplying the row proportion by the column total.

For example, this table includes its expected counts:

	OWNS CELL PHONE	DOESN'T OWN CELL PHONE	
HAS BEEN IN ACCIDENT	Observed: 14 Expected: 50% of 25 = 12.5	Observed: 86 Expected: 50% of 175 = 87.5	100 50%
HAS NOT BEEN IN ACCIDENT	Observed: 11 Expected: 50% of 25 = 12.5	Observed: 89 Expected: 50% of 175 = 87.5	100 50%
	25 12.5%	175 87.5%	200

Table 4.2.8 shows huge differences between the expected counts and the observed counts. In the Nonbinger and Frequent Binger columns, the differences between the observed and the expected counts are almost 1,000.

The differences are greater in Table 4.2.8 than in Table 4.2.7, and they deserve more attention. The data in Table 4.2.7 are based on 9 observations. That's not a large enough sample to deserve much attention. The observations in Table 4.2.8 are based on 14,275 observations. That table shows bigger differences, which deserve more attention.

Simply looking at the percentages in each cell of the cross-tab can be misleading, because they hide the sample size. The observed counts and the expected counts help show whether there is a correlation and give some indication of the sample size.

Testing a Null Hypothesis of No Correlation

Table 4.2.8 shows a correlation, but its data is only a sample—a very large sample, but a sample nonetheless. The Wechsler team did not survey the entire population of college students. If they did, would they have found a correlation in the population? To find the answer, we will test a null hypothesis that there is no correlation in the population. If we reject that hypothesis, we have to accept the alternative hypothesis that there is a correlation in the population.

To do our test, we will use the same strategy that we used for the z-test. Our null hypothesis is that there is no relationship.[1] We need to find a special statistic that reveals how embarrassing (unexpected) the current table is for the null hypothesis. That will give us a statistic that indicates how much the null hypothesis did or did not predict this kind of a result.

To translate from a z-value to a p-value, we had to look at how the z-value would be distributed if the null hypothesis were true. We will do the same thing here. We will see how the statistic we come up with is distributed when the null hypothesis is true. Once we know that distribution, we can use it to find p-values. The p-value is the probability, *if the null hypothesis is true,* of getting a statistic at least as embarrassing for the null hypothesis as what was found.

Calculating a Chi-Square Statistic

Around 1900, one of the founders of modern statistics, Karl Pearson, developed the Pearson chi-square test, which is commonly used to test correlations in cross-tabs. This test uses the Pearson chi-square statistic to summarize how much the expected counts differ from the observed counts. This statistic is just what we were looking for.

To get a Pearson chi-square statistic, we find the difference in each cell between the expected counts and the observed counts. Table 4.2.9 shows the same numbers as Table 4.2.8 and includes the differences between the expected and observed counts.

You might think that the thing to do with the differences is just add them up, but notice what would happen if you did:

$$964.8 + (-964.8) + (-41) + 41 + (-855.8) + 855.8 = 0$$

In fact, no matter what is going on in the table, the sum of the differences will always add up to 0. This isn't going to work. Any statistic that is 0 for every table isn't going to tell us much about those tables.

You might say, "The differences only add up to 0 because you left the minus signs on." And that would be true. There's something wrong with just adding up all the errors. For example, if an archer shot one foot to the left of the bull's eye and one foot to the right, altogether, we would say that the archer was two feet off, not zero feet off.

So all differences should be positive before we add them up. Because it works better mathematically, Pearson decided to capitalize on the fact that squares are

---

[1]The "null" in "null hypothesis" is from the Latin word "nullus," which means "nothing." Most null hypotheses are that there is no relationship—that the relationship is null.

Table 4.2.9 Cross-Tab of Drinking and Falling Behind in Schoolwork with Differences Between Expected and Observed Counts

	NONBINGERS	INFREQUENT BINGERS	FREQUENT BINGERS	
KEPT UP WITH SCHOOLWORK	Observed: 6,480 Expected: 5,515.2 Difference: 964.8	Observed: 3,231 Expected: 3,272 Difference: −41	Observed: 1,777 Expected: 2,632.8 Difference: −855.8	11,488 80%
FELL BEHIND IN SCHOOLWORK	Observed: 414 Expected: 1,378.8 Difference: −964.8	Observed: 859 Expected: 818 Difference: 41	Observed: 1,514 Expected: 658.2 Difference: 855.8	2,787 20%
	6,894 48%	4,090 29%	3,291 23%	14,275

always positive. For example, 2 squared is 4, and so is −2 squared. Table 4.2.10 shows the same information as Table 4.2.9 and includes the squares of the differences.

You might think that Pearson would just add up all the squared differences, but he decided also to adjust for the fact that some cells were expected to have many observations and others were not. To do this, he divided each squared difference by the expected count in the cell.

This is a somewhat intuitive thing to do. If the expected count is 4,000, and you get 4,010, that does not seem too far off. If the expected count is 5, and you get 15,

Table 4.2.10 Cross-Tab of Drinking and Falling Behind in Schoolwork with Squared Differences Between Observed and Expected Counts

	NONBINGERS	INFREQUENT BINGERS	FREQUENT BINGERS	
KEPT UP WITH SCHOOLWORK	Observed: 6,480 Expected: 5,515.2 Difference: 964.8 Squared Difference: 930,839.04	Observed: 3,231 Expected: 3,272 Difference: −41 Squared Difference: 1,681	Observed: 1,777 Expected: 2,632.8 Difference: −855.8 Squared Difference: 732,393.64	11,488 80%
FELL BEHIND IN SCHOOLWORK	Observed: 414 Expected: 1,378.8 Difference: −964.8 Squared Difference: 930,839.04	Observed: 859 Expected: 818 Difference: 41 Squared Difference: 1,681	Observed: 1,514 Expected: 658.2 Difference: 855.8 Squared Difference: 732,393.64	2,787 20%
	6,894 48%	4,090 29%	3,291 23%	14,275

that seems like the null hypothesis was pretty far off. In both cases, the difference is 10. However, if you square it and divide by the expected count, the first case is 100 divided by 4,000, which is 0.025. The second case is 100 divided by 5, which is 20.

So, the quantity that Pearson calculated for each cell is how large the squared difference is relative to the expected count.

The final step to find Pearson's chi-square statistic is to add up all the relative squared errors. Their sum is called a "chi-square statistic." "Chi-square" can be written out ("chi-square") or written with the Greek letter chi, which looks like a large capital X, but is more wiggly (χ). Chi-square looks like this: χ^2. Table 4.2.11 illustrates the process of finding the relative squared errors for the data in Table 4.2.2.

$$\chi^2 = \text{Sum of Relative Squared Differences}$$

$$\chi^2 = 168.8 + 0.5 + 278.2 + 675.1 + 2.1 + 1{,}112.7 = 2{,}237.4$$

The chi-square value for Table 4.2.11 is 2,237.4. That is a large chi-square statistic. If the table contained no correlation, the expected counts would be the same as the observed counts, and the differences, and the chi-square would be 0. As the correlation gets stronger, the differences get larger and therefore the chi-square statistic gets larger. A chi-square of 2,237.4 indicates that there is a strong correlation between drinking habits and falling behind in schoolwork.

Table 4.2.11 Cross-Tab of Drinking and Falling Behind in Schoolwork with Relative Squared Differences Between Observed and Expected Counts

	NONBINGERS	INFREQUENT BINGERS	FREQUENT BINGERS	
KEPT UP WITH SCHOOLWORK	Observed: 6,480 Expected: 5,515.2 Difference: 964.8 Squared Difference: 930,839.04 Relative Squared Difference: 168.8	Observed: 3,231 Expected: 3,272 Difference: −41 Squared Difference: 1,681 Relative Squared Difference: 0.5	Observed: 1,777 Expected: 2,632.8 Difference: −855.8 Squared Difference: 732,393.64 Relative Squared Difference: 278.2	11,488 80%
FELL BEHIND IN SCHOOLWORK	Observed: 414 Expected: 1,378.8 Difference: −964.8 Squared Difference: 930,839.04 Relative Squared Difference: 675.1	Observed: 859 Expected: 818 Difference: 41 Squared Difference: 1,681 Relative Squared Difference: 2.1	Observed: 1,514 Expected: 658.2 Difference: 855.8 Squared Difference: 732,393.64 Relative Squared Difference: 1,112.7	2,787 20%
	6,894 48%	4,090 29%	3,291 23%	14,275

Chi-Square Statistic

The chi-square statistic is the sum of the relative squared differences between the expected counts and the observed counts. To find the relative squared differences, the difference in each cell is squared and then divided by the expected count of that cell.

For example, this table shows all the values needed to calculate the chi-square statistic:

	OWNS CELL PHONE	DOESN'T OWN CELL PHONE	
HAS BEEN IN ACCIDENT	Observed: 14 Expected: 12.5 Difference: 1.5 Squared Difference: 2.25 Relative Squared Difference: 2.25/12.5 = 0.18	Observed: 86 Expected: 87.5 Difference: −1.5 Squared Difference: 2.25 Relative Squared Difference: 2.25/87.5 = 0.026	100 50%
HAS NOT BEEN IN ACCIDENT	Observed: 11 Expected: 12.5 Difference: −1.5 Squared Difference: 2.25 Relative Squared Difference: 2.25/12.5 = 0.18	Observed: 89 Expected: 87.5 Difference: 1.5 Squared Difference: 2.25 Relative Squared Difference: 2.25/87.5 = 0.026	100 50%
	25 12.5%	175 87.5%	200

$$\chi^2 = \text{Sum of Relative Squared Differences}$$

$$\chi^2 = 0.18 + 0.026 + 0.18 + 0.026 = 0.412$$

Algebra and Greek Symbols

Cross-tabs are sometimes called "contingency tables," because they can be used to test whether one set of measurements is contingent on another.

To indicate which cell they're talking about, mathematicians use subscripts. C indicates a count. C_{ij} is the count in the cell at the intersection of row i and column j. For example, C_{11} is the count in the cell at the intersection of row 1 and column 1. Table 4.2.12 shows a sample table with each count identified.

Table 4.2.12   Labels for Elements of a Cross-Tab (Contingency Table)

	COLUMN 1	COLUMN 2	
ROW 1	C_{11}	C_{12}	$\sum_j C_{1j}$ = Row Total
ROW 2	C_{21}	C_{22}	$\sum_j C_{2j}$ = Row Total
	Total = $\sum_i C_{i1}$	Total = $\sum_i C_{i2}$	$\sum_i \sum_j C_{ij}$ = Grand Total = n

The totals are indicated with the summation symbol, the capital Greek letter sigma ($\sum$). The row totals are summed over the columns. In this presentation, we are indicating columns with "j," so the summation symbol shows that it is a summation over j by having a j below it. $\sum_j C_{1j}$ means "the sum of all the counts in the first row, for all values of j"; that is, for all columns. For example, if the counts in the first row were 6 and 8, $\sum_j C_{1j}$ would equal 6 plus 8, which is 14.

The calculations for the grand total are indicated by two summation symbols, one for the rows and one for the columns. The grand total is the number of observations, so we could also say that the grand total equals n.

We need to indicate the proportion in the top row. It would be sensible to call it p. The proportion for the top row would be p_1, and the proportion for the bottom row would be p_2. If we also called the column proportions p, that would be confusing. A common solution is to call the column proportions q. So q_1 is the column proportion for the left column, and q_2 is the column proportion for the right column.

E indicates the counts that are expected if the row measurement and the column measurement are not correlated. The E's are called the "expected counts." The expected counts can be calculated by multiplying the column total by the row proportion.

Each column total is that column's proportion times the grand total, so we could also calculate the expected count by multiplying the row proportion by the column proportion by the grand total. That would be written like this:

$$E_{ij} = n p_i q_j$$

The chi-square statistic is the sum of the squares of the differences between expected and observed counts divided by the expected counts. So we can write the equation for the chi-square statistic in this way:

$$\chi^2 = \sum_i \sum_j \frac{(C_{ij} - E_{ij})^2}{E_{ij}}$$

A more precise definition of the null hypothesis that there is no correlation between measurements can be indicated in two ways. In the first way, let I represent row and J represent column. Remember that the null hypothesis is indicated by H_0:

$$H_0: P(I|J) = P(I), \quad \text{for all } I \text{ and all } J$$

That means "the probability of an observation being in a row, given that the observation falls in a particular column, is the same as the overall probability that an observation falls in that row, and this works for any row and any column." This is the definition of statistical independence, the opposite of correlation.

Here is the other way to indicate the null hypothesis that there is no correlation. Π_i is the proportion of the population that belongs in the ith row of the table. Π_j is the proportion of the population that belongs in the jth column of the table. Π_{ij} is the proportion of the population that belongs in the cell that is in the ith row and the jth column. Here is the null hypothesis:

$$H_0: \Pi_{ij} = \Pi_i \Pi_j$$

That says that in the population, the proportion in a cell equals the product of the proportion in that cell's row and the proportion in that cell's column. Earlier we saw that you could find the expected *count* by multiplying the proportion in a cell's column by the proportion in the cell's row and then multiplying the product by the number in the table. The second way we showed to indicate our null hypothesis says that the expected *proportion* of the table's observations in the table that falls in a cell is equal to the product of the row proportion and the column proportion. The expected proportion is what happens when there is no correlation, so this statement of the null hypothesis is just restating, at the level of the population, what we saw about the table.

Summary

A cross-tabulation shows the relationship between two sets of measurements. It lists the possible values for one set of measurements along the top of the table, and the possible values for the other set on the left side. Lines are drawn to create cells. Each cell gets a count to show the number of observations that had that column's value and that row's value.

To say that there is a correlation between the two sets of measurements is to say that knowing an observation's value in one set of measurements improves one's ability to predict the probability of that observation's values in the other set of measurements.

The chi-square statistic summarizes how bad the cross-tab makes the null hypothesis look. The chi-square statistic is the sum of the relative squared differences between the null hypothesis's most expected cell counts and the cell counts actually observed. They are "relative" squared differences, because after squaring, the squared differences are divided by the null hypothesis's expected counts.

Avoiding Common Misunderstandings

The chi-square statistic is the sum of the relative squared differences between the expected counts and the observed counts. "Relative" means that the squared difference from each cell was divided by the expected count of that cell before the summing. The expected counts are the counts that would be expected if the null hypothesis of no correlation were true.

Computer Project

In your software, access the Representative Sample of the United States from March 2001 (from the *Data Matters* Resource Center at *www.keycollege.com/dm*). Several variables have categorical answers, such as marital status and gender. Pick two and use your software to create a cross-tab of them. Make sure you get the marginal totals and proportions. Run a chi-square test to get a chi-square value.

Have your software find the expected counts for you. Where are the big differences between expected and observed? Can you guess why those differences appear in the data?

Exercises

Here is some of the data from Wechsler's study:

	NONBINGE DRINKERS ($n = 6{,}894$)	INFREQUENT BINGE DRINKERS ($n = 4{,}090$)	FREQUENT BINGE DRINKERS ($n = 3{,}291$)
DID SOMETHING YOU REGRET	14%	37%	63%
MISSED A CLASS	8%	30%	61%

1. a. Create a cross-tabulation of binge drinking and doing something you regret. Leave plenty of room in each cell.

    b. Put in the marginal totals.

    c. Put in the marginal proportions.

    d. Put in the expected counts.

2. Repeat the steps of Exercise 1 with a cross-tab of binge drinking and missing a class.

3. In what way does your cross-tab show evidence of a correlation between binge drinking and doing something you regret?

4. In what way does your cross-tab show evidence of a correlation between binge drinking and missing a class?

5. Two researchers wanted to test whether alcohol consumption would be affected by telling undergraduates that the work they needed to do during an experiment would be worsened if they drank alcohol. The participants in one group were told that they should expect that drinking alcohol would impair their performance. The two other groups were told "that alcohol had no effect on performance and . . . that the effects of alcohol were unknown. . . . Subjects who drank no alcohol whatsoever [during the study] were more common in the 'expect impairment' group (chi-square = 7.32, 2 df, $p < .05$)" (Sharkansky and Finn, 1998).

    A friend writes to you about this report, asking, "What is that 'chi-square' that was 7.32?" Write your friend a brief note explaining what the chi-square is.

6. In 1998 and 1999, UCLA was concerned about a basketball referee, Christman. That season, in the games when Christman was referee, UCLA shot 82 free throws, and the school's opponents shot 177. When Christman was *not* refereeing, UCLA shot 126 free throws, and the school's opponents shot 128. Here is a quote from an article about this issue published in UCLA's *Daily Bruin:*

    > *Taking these numbers and using a standard statistical technique, a chi-square analysis, the "p" value is less than .0001. This means that the likelihood of this being due to chance is less than one in 10,000. In medicine, if these were treatment results, they would be considered conclusive.*

    > —LEWIS, *DAILY BRUIN*, FEBRUARY 3, 1999

    Imagine that a friend writes to you about this article, asking, "What is a chi-square analysis? And what's a 'p-value'?" Write your friend a reply. While you are at it, look carefully at Lewis's explanation of what a *p*-value is. It's wrong. This *p*-value is *not* "the likelihood of this being due to chance." As an extra kindness to your friend, explain what the *p*-value of .0001 is and what Lewis's mistake was.

7. Here is a report on a study of gender and salt use.

   In response to the question on use of table salt more men than women replied "always" (39% vs. 24%) and fewer replied "never" (38% vs. 53%).

   —ALDERMAN, COHEN, AND MADHAVAN, *LANCET*, 1998

   In this study, there were 4,478 men, and 6,868 women. Create a cross-tab including the marginal counts and proportions. Each person gave one of three answers: "Never," "Sometimes," and "Always."

   What is the chi-square value for this comparison of men and women on the table salt issue?

8. Consider the data in Lewis's article in Exercise 6. What is the chi-square value for that data? (Each observation is a free throw. The two categorical measurements are whether Christman was refereeing and whether UCLA was shooting the free throw.)

9. This empty cross-tab includes its marginal proportions and grand total:

	LEARNS ALL OF THE MATERIAL	DOES NOT LEARN ALL OF THE MATERIAL	
SETS GOALS FOR HOURS OF STUDYING			50%
DOES NOT SET GOALS FOR HOURS OF STUDYING			50%
	50%	50%	20

   Make a copy of this table and fill in counts that would make a null hypothesis of no correlation look very bad.

10. Here is another cross-tab with its marginal proportions and grand total:

	GETS A HEAD	GETS A TAIL	
WISHES FOR HEADS WHILE FLIPPING			50%
WISHES FOR TAILS WHILE FLIPPING			50%
	50%	50%	20

Make a copy of the table and fill in counts that would make a null hypothesis of no correlation look good.

11. Imagine that a school board allocates funds for a counseling company to bring a drug and alcohol treatment program to a school district that has two high schools. There is not enough money for both high schools, so students at only one of them receive the training. At the end of the school year, seniors at the two high schools are asked whether they drank five or more alcoholic beverages on any night during the previous month. On both campuses, exactly 20% report "yes."

   a. If you created a cross-tab of whether or not students attended the school with the training and whether or not they reported having had five or more alcoholic beverages in one evening in the previous month, what would the chi-square statistic be?

   b. Does this result embarrass a null hypothesis of no correlation?

   c. How low can a chi-square statistic get?

12. As a null hypothesis of no correlation looks worse and worse, how does the chi-square change? Give an example.

Answers to Odd-Numbered Exercises

1.

	NONBINGE DRINKERS	INFREQUENT BINGE DRINKERS	FREQUENT BINGE DRINKERS	
DID SOMETHING YOU REGRET	Observed: 965 Expected: 2,206.08	Observed: 1,513 Expected: 1,308.8	Observed: 2,073 Expected: 1,053.12	4,551 32%
DID NOT DO SOMETHING YOU REGRET	Observed: 5,929 Expected: 4,687.92	Observed: 2,577 Expected: 2,781.2	Observed: 1,218 Expected: 2,237.88	9,724 68%
	6,894 48%	4,090 29%	3,291 23%	14,275

3. Among the nonbinge drinkers, if there were no correlation, we would expect about 2,206 to report doing something they regretted, but only 965 did. Among the frequent binge drinkers, if there were no correlation, we would expect about 1,053 to report doing something they regretted, but 2,073 did. If I knew whether someone was a frequent binge drinker, it would affect my guess about whether that person had done something regrettable. I would guess that the chances of reporting that they had done something they regretted were higher for people who reported being binge drinkers.

5. That 7.32 reflects how much what happened makes a particular idea look bad. The idea is that there is no correlation between instructions and refraining from drinking altogether. As the chi-square statistic gets larger, the "no correlation" idea looks worse and worse. Chi-square is calculated by making a table of how many people fall in each combination of the categories (drink versus no drink, and instructions). The "no correlation" idea makes predictions for how many people will fall in each cell of that table. The chi-square is the sum of the differences between the "no correlation" expected numbers and the numbers of people in each cell who were actually observed after squaring the differences and dividing the squares by the "no correlation" expected numbers. So chi-square gets bigger as the idea of "no correlation" makes bigger mistakes setting expectations for the numbers in the table.

7.

	NEVER	SOMETIMES	ALWAYS	
MEN	Observed: 1,701 Expected: 2,107.97 Difference: −406.97 Squared Difference: 165,622.4 Relative Squared Difference: 78.6	Observed: 1,030 Expected: 1,030.1 Difference: −.106 Squared Difference: .01 Relative Squared Difference: .00001	Observed: 1,746 Expected: 339.5 Difference: 406.5 Squared Difference: 165,216 Relative Squared Difference: 123.3	4,478 39%
WOMEN	Observed: 3,640 Expected: 3,233 Difference: 407 Squared Difference: 165,649 Relative Squared Difference: 51.2	Observed: 1,580 Expected: 1,579.9 Difference: .1 Squared Difference: .01 Relative Squared Difference: .000007	Observed: 1,648 Expected: 2,054.5 Difference: −406.5 Squared Difference: 165,216 Relative Squared Difference: 80.4	6,868 61%
	5,341 47%	2,610 23%	3,394 30%	11,346

$$\chi^2 = 78.6 + 0.00001 + 123.3 + 51.2 + 0.000007 + 80.4 = 333.5$$

9.

	LEARNS ALL OF THE MATERIAL	DOES NOT LEARN ALL OF THE MATERIAL	
SETS GOALS FOR HOURS OF STUDYING	10	0	50%
DOES NOT SET GOALS FOR HOURS OF STUDYING	0	10	50%
	50%	50%	20

11. a. Chi-square would be 0. In case you have doubts about this, here's an example:

	FIVE OR MORE DRINKS	NOT FIVE OR MORE DRINKS	
TRAINING	Observed: 20 Expected: 20 Difference: 0 Squared Difference: 0 Relative Squared Difference: 0	Observed: 80 Expected: 80 Difference: 0 Squared Difference: 0 Relative Squared Difference: 0	100 50%
NO TRAINING	Observed: 20 Expected: 20 Difference: 0 Squared Difference: 0 Relative Squared Difference: 0	Observed: 80 Expected: 80 Difference: 0 Squared Difference: 0 Relative Squared Difference: 0	100 50%
	40 20%	160 80%	200

If you change the number of students in each class, you will find that if the proportions are the same in both schools, the expected counts will equal the observed counts. This is because having the same proportion in both schools is having no correlation.

b. This is as unembarrassing as a result can get for the null hypothesis of no correlation.

c. Chi-square can get as low as 0, but no lower.

4.3 Checking for No Correlation with the Chi-Square Test

- Chi-Square Distribution
- Degrees of Freedom
- Correlation Is Not Causation

Frequent binge drinkers at college also reported vastly more problems ranging from arguments with peers to missed classes to unplanned sexual activity . . . study director Dr. Henry Wechsler said, ". . . there has been an intensification of severe drinking behavior among drinkers."

—MEHREN, *LOS ANGELES TIMES*, SEPTEMBER 28, 1998

IN THE LAST SECTION, we looked at a study that asked college students about their drinking and various aspects of their lives and schoolwork. The preceding quote is from another report on that study. We haven't finished checking whether the relationship between binge drinking and trouble is statistically significant, but it looks as though there is a real correlation in the population.

Table 4.3.1 Results of a Study of Telekinesis

SONG SUNG DURING COIN FLIP	PERCENTAGE OF COIN FLIPS COMING UP HEADS
"Auld Lang Syne"	100%
"O, Danny Boy"	33%

In Section 4.2, we created a cross-tab to check for a correlation between falling behind in schoolwork and binge drinking. It looked as though students who binge drank more were more likely to fall behind in their schoolwork.

At least that's what we saw in the data, but the patterns that appear in data are not always what you would see if you looked at the entire population. For example, Table 4.3.1 shows some data from an experiment I conducted on telekinesis. In this experiment I tried to see whether the outcome of coin flipping was affected by which of two songs I sang.

Whoa! Table 4.3.1 seems to show pretty impressive data. Or does it? Table 4.3.2 shows a cross-tab of the results shown in Table 4.3.1.

Table 4.3.2 Cross-Tab of Telekinesis Study Results

SONG SUNG DURING COIN FLIP	FLIP OUTCOME	
	HEAD	TAIL
"AULD LANG SYNE"	1	0
"O, DANNY BOY"	1	2

Ah. Well, maybe that's *not* so impressive. Do you think that this relationship would hold up if we took a thousand samples? Probably not. There is a correlation in the table, but it is not a significant correlation. That is, the data in Table 4.3.2 do not justify rejecting a null hypothesis that there is no correlation in the population (or probabilities) from which the data were drawn.

Statistically Significant Correlation

A correlation is statistically significant if it justifies rejecting a null hypothesis that there is no correlation in the population.

For example, imagine that a survey of 1,000 randomly chosen Americans finds that 95% of the women own dresses and only 5% of the men do. These data show a statistically significant correlation, because there is adequate evidence to reject a null hypothesis of no correlation in the American population.

What about the Wechsler team's data that we examined in Section 4.2? Did the patterns in their data appear because the population has a correlation between binge drinking and falling behind in schoolwork, or was this pattern simply a coincidence that appeared in a sample drawn from a population without a correlation? That is, was the correlation statistically significant?

To find out whether a correlation is significant, we need the *p*-value. If the *p*-value is less than our alpha, we will reject the null hypothesis, and the correlation will be significant.

To find the *p*-value, we can use a strategy we have used before. We can have a computer create data, using a system in which the null hypothesis is true. We will use each row's proportion to determine the probability of falling in that row, and we will use each column's proportion to determine the probability of falling in that column without any correlation between the rows and columns. We will have the computer do this to fill a cross-tab and calculate the chi-square statistic. Then we will have the computer repeat these steps 10,000 times and save the chi-square values. Finally, we can check how those chi-square statistics (created when the null hypothesis is true) are distributed. The *p*-value for any data's chi-square statistic is the probability of a chi-square value at least as embarrassing for the null hypothesis as that data's chi-square value, if the null hypothesis is true.

In chi-square statistics, 0 is the value that is least embarrassing for the null hypothesis. A chi-square of 0 appears when there is no correlation in the table. The null hypothesis of no correlation in the population cannot look better than if there is no correlation in the table. As the correlation in the table increases, chi-square gets larger, and the results look more embarrassing for the null hypothesis. So the *p*-value of a study's chi-square is the probability of getting that chi-square value or higher (if the null hypothesis is true).

For example, 100% of the chi-square values will be at 0 or higher. If a study had a chi-square value of 0, the p-value would be 100%. If half of our simulated chi-square values are at 1.4 and higher, then, when the chi-square value is 1.4, the p-value is 50%.

Using simulations to figure out the distribution of a test statistic and then to figure out the p-value is called a "Monte Carlo" approach. When Pearson developed the chi-square statistic, he figured out how it would be distributed through mathematical derivation. This text only presents these Monte Carlo derivations.

Monte Carlo Strategy for Finding a *P*-Value

The Monte Carlo strategy simulates trials with a system for which the null hypothesis is true. The p-value is the proportion of simulated test statistics that are at least as embarrassing for the null hypothesis as the data's test statistic.

For example, imagine that a company hires 100 people a year. In 2001, the company hired 51 women. In 2002, the company hired 49 women. A researcher suspects that the company has a quota that is constraining the proportion of women hired to be near 50%. To test this idea, the researcher sets a null hypothesis that there is a single, unchanging probability that women would be hired, 50%, and no artificial constraint to hold the proportion near 50%. The researcher's test statistic is the difference between the two years' proportions: 2%.

The researcher then has a computer create 10,000 pairs of samples. Each sample has 100 simulated hires, and, for every simulated hire, the chance that the hire is a woman is 50%. The computer records the differences between the samples. The p-value would be the proportion of simulated differences that were 2% or smaller.

The researcher found that 28% of her pairs of samples had differences that were 2% or smaller. Her p-value was .28, which is greater than her alpha of .05, and she retained her null hypothesis that the female proportion was not being artificially constrained near 50%.

The Chi-Square Distribution

To find out how the chi-square statistic is distributed for the drinking and schoolwork data when the null hypothesis is true, I had the computer simulate 14,275 students. I used the marginal proportions from the Wechsler study, so for each student, the probability of falling behind in schoolwork was 20%, the probability of not binge drinking was 48%, of binge drinking infrequently was 29%, and of binge drinking frequently was 23%. The null hypothesis was true: Whether or not a student binge drank was not tied in any way to whether or not that student fell behind in schoolwork. Once the 14,275 simulated students were created, the chi-square statistic was calculated and saved. This process was repeated 10,000 times. Figure 4.3.1 shows how 10,000 chi-square statistics are distributed when the null hypothesis is true.

Now let's do those calculations again, using 50% for the probability of falling behind, and 30%, 30%, and 40% for the probabilities of the various binging states. And let's use only 60 people in each table. Figure 4.3.2 shows how the simulation turned out.

The distribution of chi-square statistics (when the null hypothesis is true) is about the same in both simulations. Figure 4.3.1 and Figure 4.3.2 show that Pearson's chi-square statistic is not normally distributed. It has a lump on the left and then a small spread to the right. The two figures do not show all of the chi-square values. Among the 10,000 chi-square values, the maximum was 15, even though most were below 1.5.

Figure 4.3.1

Distribution of 10,000 Chi-Square Statistics When the Null Hypothesis Is True (Using *n* and Marginal Probabilities from Wechsler Data)

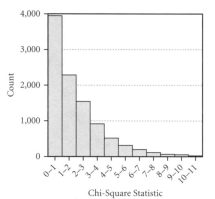

Figure 4.3.2

Distribution of 10,000 Chi-Square Statistics When the Null Hypothesis Is True (*N* = 60; New Marginal Probabilities)

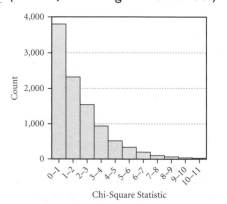

After the 10,000 chi-square statistics in the first simulation were sorted, the 9,500th from the bottom was 5.89. So 95% of the chi-square statistics fell at 5.89 or lower. In the second simulation, it was 5.94. That is a lot of variability, so I reran the simulation. This time, I used 240 simulated people in each table and created 1 million tables. I was thinking about the law of large numbers: As the number of chi-square statistics I collected increased, the proportion at each value would get closer and closer to the probability that that value would show up in a chi-square statistic drawn from a true null hypothesis. After sorting these 1 million chi-square values from smallest to largest, I found that the 950,000th chi-square from the bottom was 5.9928. I ran the simulation again and got 5.99211, which I'll round to 5.99. For this situation, when the null hypothesis is true, and with two rows and three columns (I'll explain why that matters later), about 5% of chi-square statistics fall at 5.99 or higher. That means that for this situation, the *p*-value of 5.99 is 5%. A higher chi-square value would have a lower *p*-value. A lower chi-square value would have a higher *p*-value (and not be significant for alpha equal to 5%).

So far, this sounds easy. If the chi-square value is 5.99 or more, the results are significant. However, when the null hypothesis is true, the distribution of Pearson's chi-square test comes out differently depending on the design of the study, because it matters how many rows and columns the table contains. For example, if you studied the relationship between religion (recorded as "Christian," "Jewish," "Muslim," and "Other") and region (recorded as "Urban," "Suburban," and "Rural"), you would need a four-by-three table to show your data. To show you what the null hypothesis claims for a table such as that, I reran the simulation from Figure 4.3.1, using four rows and three columns, and increasing the number of chi-square statistics simulated.

Figure 4.3.3 shows this second simulation's chi-squares, which ranged from 0.1 to 34. Half of the chi-square statistics fall at 5.4 and lower, and 5% of the

Figure 4.3.3 **Histogram of 30,000 Simulated Chi-Square Statistics When the Null Hypothesis Is True (Cross-Tabs with Four Columns and Three Rows)**

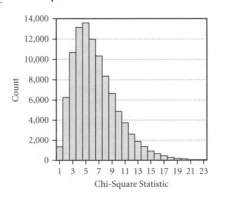

chi-squares fall at 12.583 or higher. The histogram in Figure 4.3.3 is not like the histograms in Figures 4.3.1 and 4.3.2. Pearson's chi-squares are different when they come from cross-tabs with more cells (12 cells as opposed to 6).

What changes the distribution of the chi-square value is something called the "degrees of freedom," or "*df*" for short. The *df* are the product of 1 less than the number of rows and 1 less than the number of columns. For example, if a cross-tab had three columns and two rows, we could find the *df* as follows:

$$df = (\text{Rows} - 1) \times (\text{Columns} - 1)$$

$$df = (2 - 1) \times (3 - 1)$$

$$df = 1 \times 2 = 2$$

There would be 2 *df*. That was the situation when we were considering a possible relationship between binge drinking and falling behind in one's schoolwork. So when there are 2 *df*, if the null hypothesis of no correlation is true, 95% of Pearson's chi-square statistics will fall at 5.99 or lower, and 5% will fall at 5.99 or higher.

The second simulation had four rows and three columns. Here are the calculations to find the *df*:

$$df = (\text{Rows} - 1) \times (\text{Columns} - 1)$$

$$df = (4 - 1) \times (3 - 1)$$

$$df = 3 \times 2 = 6$$

According to Figure 4.3.3, then, when there are 6 *df*, *if the null hypothesis of no correlation is true,* 95% of Pearson's chi-square statistics will fall at or below 12.59, and 5% will fall at or above 12.59. That means that if a cross-tab has four rows and three columns, a chi-square statistic of 12.59 has a *p*-value of 5%. A higher chi-square statistic would have a lower *p*-value. A lower chi-square statistic would have a higher *p*-value.

---

df and Chi-Square Distribution

When the null hypothesis of no correlation is true, the distribution of Pearson's chi-square statistic depends on the degrees of freedom (*df*) of the cross-tab. The *df* are 1 less than the number of rows times 1 less than the number of columns.

For example, with three rows and five columns, *df* equals 2 times 4, which equals 8. With two rows and nine columns, *df* equals 1 times 8, which equals 8. For both cross-tabs, if the null hypothesis is true, 95% of the chi-square statistics will fall between 0 and 15.5. For a table with two rows and two columns, *df* equals 1, and 95% of the chi-square values will fall between 0 and 3.84 (if the null hypothesis is true).

Table 4.3.3 A Few Critical Values for Pearson's Chi-Square Statistic

df = (ROWS − 1) × (COLUMNS − 1)	CRITICAL CHI-SQUARE (FOR ALPHA = 5%)
1	3.84
2	5.99
3	7.81
4	9.49
5	11.07

Table 4.3.3 shows some critical values: the values for which 5% of chi-square statistics fall at that value or above, *if the null hypothesis is true.* Table 4.3.3 shows whether a *p*-value is less than 5%. For precise *p*-values, a statistician would refer to a table showing more details. What does Table 4.3.3 tell us about the chi-square value we found for the relationship between binge drinking and falling behind in one's schoolwork? The cross-tabulation had 2 *df*, and the chi-square value we found was more than 2,000. The *p*-value was much less than 5%. There was a significant correlation between binge drinking and falling behind in one's schoolwork. Students who binge drink are significantly more likely to report falling behind in their schoolwork than students who do not binge drink.

Correlation Is Not Causation

When people see evidence of a correlation, they tend to assume that the correlation tells what is causing what. For example, if there is a correlation between binge drinking and falling behind in classes, some people will jump to the conclusion that binge drinking causes students to fall behind in their classes. They might say, "Let's ban drinking, and the students will do better in classes." Other people, with just as much confidence, will jump to the conclusion that falling behind in their studies causes students to binge drink. They might say, "Let's have the professors assign less schoolwork, and we can deal with the campus's drinking problem." When I look at that correlation, several other things jump to my mind. I wonder whether students who won't admit to overdrinking also won't admit to falling behind in their classes. I also wonder if older students are more likely to binge drink, simply because it's legal, and are more likely to have jobs that prevent them from keeping up with their schoolwork. And I wonder lots of other things about this result.

When there is a correlation between measurements, there are always at least three explanations worth considering. Let's call our measurements "A" and "B." They could be "binge drinking" and "falling behind in schoolwork." They could be "being an infant" and "having a driver's license." They could be "owning a cell phone" and "having an accident." Whatever the measurements are, let's say that we have found evidence of a significant correlation, so we conclude that there is a correlation between A and B in the population.

There are many possible reasons why A and B are correlated. It could be that the correlation is caused by A affecting B, either directly or indirectly, as illustrated by Figure 4.3.4. A affecting B might be binge drinking causing students to fall behind in classes.

Or the correlation could be that B affects A, either directly or indirectly, as illustrated by Figure 4.3.5. B affecting A might be falling behind in classes causing students to binge drink.

Or the correlation could be that A doesn't affect B, B doesn't affect A, but some third factor affects them both, as illustrated by Figure 4.3.6. C affecting both might be students' ages causing more binge drinking and causing them to fall behind in classes.

It wouldn't hurt to keep in mind that there are other possibilities. For example, A, B, and C might all affect one another, as illustrated by Figure 4.3.7. In the case

Figure 4.3.4 **A Affects B**

Figure 4.3.5 **B Affects A**

Figure 4.3.6 **A Does Not Affect B, B Does Not Affect A, and a Third Factor Affects Both**

Figure 4.3.7 **A, B, and C All Affect One Another**

of binge drinking, falling behind in classes, and age, all affecting one another is unlikely, but possible. Here's what it would look like: Binge drinking causes students to fall behind in classes, because they don't pay enough attention to studying. Falling behind in classes makes students drink more, because they regret their poor performance. This happens more for older students, because they can drink legally, which increases their chances of binge drinking, and they are more likely to have more demanding jobs that get in the way, which increases their chances of falling behind. Also, it may be that binge drinkers, attending college mostly to get drunk, are more likely to stick with college for multiple years, while students who are not binge drinkers are more likely to quit college, because they are tired of hanging out with the drunken binge drinkers. This would mean that binge drinking or the lack of it keeps students who are not binge drinkers younger. And it could be that students in their sixth and seventh years of college are students who fall behind in their classes. Perhaps if they hadn't fallen behind, they would have finished earlier. That would be the causation flowing from falling behind in classes to being older.

These causal relationships are not necessarily true; they are only theories. The point is that a significant correlation means only that knowing whether a student is falling behind in classes ought to change your estimate of the chances that a student is a binge drinker, and knowing whether a student is a binge drinker ought to change your estimate of the chances that the student falls behind in classes.

We can't tell which of these ideas is right from the data we have so far. A correlation provides no evidence about what causes what or *why* the features are correlated. All it tells us is that we can improve our predictions of one feature by knowing another feature. Correlation is not causation.

Correlation Is Not Causation

When a correlation appears between two features, there are at least three possible reasons. The first feature might in some way affect the second, the second might in some way affect the first, and they may not affect one another at all, but both be affected by some third factor.

For example, if there is a correlation between owning a cell phone and being in car accidents, it may be because talking on the phone distracts people from driving and raises the chance that they will be in accidents. Or people who have been in a car accident may be more likely to get cell phones, because they see the value in owning a cell phone to call for help. Or it may be that some people drive more than other people, and because they drive more, they are more likely to be in car accidents, and are also more likely to get a cell phone so they can call people while driving.

Experiments

Sometimes we can rule out some possible conceptions of what causes what. For example, a college administrator could flip a coin to assign students to dorms. Students who get heads would be assigned to a no-drinking dorm, which uses a breathalyzer and punishes any student caught drinking. The other dorm has no such system. If students in the strict-alcohol-policy dorm are significantly less likely to have fallen behind in their studies, we have learned that assigning students to such dorms diminishes falling behind. In that situation, we could make a conclusion about the direction of causation.

We know the direction of causation because other possibilities could not have happened (without divine intervention). A student's future school performance

could not affect the coin flip. Coin flips don't work like that. A third factor, such as age or obedience, could not have affected the coin flip. That rules out all causation except causation from the coin flip to the schoolwork achievement.

When people are randomly assigned to experiences in this way, it is called an "experiment." Experiments reveal causation. If you have seen a correlation and need to find out what causation is underlying the correlation, you can use experiments to test the various possibilities.

Experiments Reveal Causation

An experiment involves having the things being studied randomly assigned to be treated differently. If the things being studied end up significantly different, the cause can be attributed to the treatment, because the causation could not be flowing back to the random assignment.

For example, in an experiment we might flip a coin to determine whether retired people are sent a pamphlet outlining the benefits of taking half an aspirin every day. After two years, a significantly higher proportion in the no-pamphlet group has had heart attacks. Because we can rule out the possibility that some aspect of the retired people affected the coin flip, we can conclude that the correlation is due to causation flowing from the coin flip, through the mailed pamphlet, to the lower heart-attack rate.

Chi-Square Test Summary

The chi-square test is the second significance test presented in this book. The first significance test was the z-test, which tested where a probability was on the number line.

Purpose of the Chi-Square Test

The chi-square test checks for a significant correlation between two sets of categorical measurements that appear in a sample. A categorical measurement involves categories that cannot be represented on some continuum—for example, whether you are dead or alive. You are either one or the other. Whether your cells include Y chromosomes is another categorical measurement, and so is whether you have been in a car accident.

The number of car accidents you have had is *not* a categorical measurement. It is a number that falls on a number line; that is, a quantitative measurement. Categorical measurements are measurements that cannot sensibly be placed on a continuum.

Categorical Measurements

Categorical measurements are recorded data reflecting aspects of the studied people (or objects) that cannot be represented as being on a continuum.

For example, citizenship (Canadian, Mexican, German, and so on) is a categorical measurement.

If a group of people were asked about their religions and their genders, a chi-square test could be used to check for a significant correlation between gender and religion. If one or both of the measurements were a number-line measurement (a measurement that can be shown on a number line), such as weight, height, income, or age, other tests would be more appropriate.

The chi-square test looks at the correlation that appeared in the sample and leads to a judgment of whether there is sufficient evidence to conclude that a correlation exists in the population from which the sample was drawn.

Requirements of the Chi-Square Test

The chi-square test works for random samples taken from a population. Sometimes, because of poor sampling, a researcher may not understand which population the sample is a random sample of. For example, psychologists who take a random sample of local college students may mistakenly believe that the sample is a random sample of the human population. The chi-square test will tell the psychologists about the population from which the sample was actually drawn—local college students.

Pearson's chi-square statistic is based on one more assumption: that no expected count is less than 5. If an expected count is less than 5, it is possible to calculate a chi-square statistic, but the mathematical work that led to the derivations in the critical-value table (Table 4.3.3) were based on the assumption that each expected count would be at least 5.

Before any data is collected, you can be sure that at least one expected count will be less than 5 if the number of observations is less than 5 times the number of cells. For example, if there are 4 cells and 19 observations, you should not use the chi-square test.

Chi-Square Test Null Hypothesis

The null hypothesis of the chi-square test is that there is no correlation in the population.

The Chi-Square Statistic

To calculate Pearson's chi-square statistic, we create a cross-tabulation. The cross-tabulation is a table with a row for each value of one of the categorical measurements and a column for each value of the other categorical measurement. For example, a cross-tabulation of gender versus religion could use the following table:

	ROMAN CATHOLIC	PROTESTANT	JEWISH	MUSLIM	BUDDHIST	OTHER
FEMALE						
MALE						

In a cross-tabulation, the value in each cell is the observed count of the number of observations that fell in that cell. For example, if a study found 1,000 female Roman Catholics, then the upper-left cell of the preceding table would contain 1,000. One can sum each column to find the number of observations in that column and calculate the proportions that fall in each row.

If the null hypothesis is true we most expect that the counts in each cell will be equal to the product of the row proportions and the column totals.

Pearson's chi-square statistic is calculated from the squares of the differences between the observed counts and the expected counts in each cell. These squares are each divided by the expected counts, and the resulting proportional squares (the relative squared differences) are summed to create Pearson's chi-square statistic.

The *P*-Value

The *p*-value is the proportion of chi-square statistics that would fall at the sample's chi-square statistic or higher, *if the null hypothesis of no correlation were true.*

When the null hypothesis is true, the distribution of Pearson's chi-square statistic depends on the size of the cross-tabulation table. A value, *df*, is calculated by multiplying 1 less than the number of rows by 1 less than the number of columns. If *df* is 1, 5% of Pearson's chi-square statistics will fall at or above 3.84; the *p*-value of 3.84 will be 5%, and higher chi-square statistics will have lower *p*-values. If *df* is 2, 5.99 will have a *p*-value of 5%, higher chi-square values will have lower *p*-values, and lower chi-square statistics will have higher *p*-values. If *df* is 3, 7.81 will have a *p*-value of 5%, and if *df* is 4, 9.49 will have a *p*-value of 5%.

The Logic of the Inference

There are two possible inferences for the chi-square test. If the p-value is below one's cutoff for significance, alpha, then the null hypothesis is rejected. Here is the logic of that inference:

> **If** the null hypothesis of no correlation is true, **then** a chi-square value at least as embarrassing for the null hypothesis as the sample's chi-square value will be very unlikely to appear in a random sample.
>
> The sample's chi-square value appeared in a random sample.
>
> **Therefore,** we reject the null hypothesis (respecting that there is a chance that the null hypothesis is true).

In this case, we would say that there is a significant correlation (meaning that a significance test was done and a null hypothesis of no correlation was rejected).

If the p-value is greater than alpha, then the null hypothesis is retained. Here is the logic for that situation:

> **If** the null hypothesis of no correlation is true, **then** a chi-square value at least as embarrassing for the null hypothesis as the sample's chi-square value will be *reasonably likely* to appear in a random sample.
>
> The sample's chi-square value appeared in a random sample.
>
> **Therefore,** the data provide no evidence one way or another about the null hypothesis.

In this case, there is not a statistically significant correlation, and the chi-square test does not reject the null hypothesis. If there is no evidence to distinguish between two theories, Occam's razor directs us to proceed with the simpler theory. The null hypothesis of no correlation is usually the simpler theory. Therefore, we *retain* the null hypothesis. *Retaining* the null hypothesis is not the same as saying that the null hypothesis was supported by the data.

Correlation Is Not Causation

In a correlational study, in which the researchers only collect data, a correlation does not reveal causation. A correlation reveals how knowing one of an observation's measurements can help you guess the probabilities of the categories for the observation's other measurement. For example, if significant correlation between gender and religion exists, it could be because having society's conceptions of the genders leads men and women into sympathies with different religions. That would be causation flowing generally from gender toward religion. Or it could be that religions differ in their enthusiasm for and kindness to different genders, driving certain genders away. That would be causation flowing from religion to gender. Or it could be that a third factor is tied to both features. For example, it could be that certain careers attract particular genders and that religions spread through professional contacts.

If an experimenter has determined one of the measurements by randomly assigning groups to various conditions in an experiment, then a correlation would reveal causation. For example, imagine that a researcher randomly assigned students to two groups by flipping a coin. The researchers arrange for one group to have 10 hours per week of supervised study and for the other group to be left alone. If a correlation exists between how the coin flips came out and whether students fall behind in their schoolwork, we can deduce that the line of causation flows somehow from the coin flips to the students' performances. It is not reasonable to think that the factors that determine the coin flips could be determined by students' later performance or anything related to that performance.

Reporting the Results

There are two dramatically different styles of reporting chi-square statistics. One style is that of the popular press, in which a report would only remark that a proportion in one group was "statistically significantly" higher than that proportion in another group. The press would not mention that a chi-square test was done, and would not mention the chi-square value or *p*-value. For example, here is a report of a study that appeared in the *Sacramento Bee*:

> *Of the 3,455 women . . . 36.9 percent . . . said they had experienced emotional or physical abuse . . . by a partner . . . the rate of abuse among California women was significantly higher. About 44 percent of California women reported being victims of such abuse . . . compared to 31 percent in Pennsylvania.*
>
> —STANTON, *SACRAMENTO BEE*, AUGUST 5, 1998

If there is a significant correlation, it makes sense to report proportions in each group, as in this quote. If there were no significant correlation, then we would retain the null hypothesis that the patterns in the sample are only random variation. We would report the proportion of women from each state and the proportion reporting abuse, but not provide the abuse-report rate for each state, because we would have no evidence that the state-to-state differences in abuse-reporting rates were anything more than random variation.

In the sciences, a chi-square test will sometimes be as casually reported as in the popular press, although a science writer typically reports something about the *p*-value, as in the following hypothetical example: "The rate of reporting abuse was significantly higher among California women ($p < .0005$). In California, 44% of women reported being victims of such abuse. In Pennsylvania, 31% of women did so."

The fullest report of a chi-square test reports the chi-square value, the *df*, and the *p*-value. In the test comparing California and Pennsylvania women, the cross-tabulation has two rows (reporting abuse and not reporting abuse) and two columns (the two states), so *df* equals 1. The chi-square value is about 60. A science-style report of that study might look like the following: "The proportion reporting abuse was significantly higher among California women (chi-square(1) = 62.34, $p < .0005$). In California, 44% of women reported being victims of such abuse. In Pennsylvania, 31% of women did so."

In this version, the *df* appears in the parentheses immediately after "chi-square." This version states that the chi-square value was 62.34.

Sometimes "chi-square" is replaced with the Greek letter chi (χ) and a "squared" symbol, as in the following version: "The proportion reporting abuse was significantly higher among California women ($\chi^2(1) = 62.34$, $p < .0005$). In California, 44% of women reported being victims of such abuse. In Pennsylvania, 31% of women did so."

Algebra and Greek Symbols

The chi-square test in this section is a chi-square test of independence between two measurements. There are other chi-square tests, but this text does not discuss them.

The null hypothesis of the chi-square test of independence is that there is no correlation. Another word for correlation is "association." Some researchers prefer to call the correlation found in a chi-square test an "association" and to reserve "correlation" for correlations between two sets of measurements that both fall on number lines.

Pearson's chi-square statistic does not have exactly what statisticians call a chi-square distribution (a χ^2 distribution). Pearson's chi-square statistic is only approximately chi-square distributed. As the number of observations in each contingency table (cross-tab) increases, the distribution of Pearson's chi-square values gets closer and closer to a χ^2 distribution. When the number of observations gets so low that an expected count is less than 5, the distribution of chi-square statistics is enough unlike a χ^2 distribution that the chi-square test gives misleading p-values.

As noted in Section 4.2, expected counts are $p_i q_j n$ (the row proportion times the column proportion times the number of observations). The requirement that all expected counts be at least 5 would be written like this:

$$p_i q_j n \geq 5 \text{ for all } i, j$$

The degrees of freedom are the number of cell counts that are free to vary, once we have determined the marginal counts. If there are x columns in a table, and the row total for row i is y, and the sum of the first x minus 1 cells in row i is z, then the xth cell count is not free to vary: It is determined to be y minus z. Similarly, once we know all but the bottom-most count in a column, the bottom-most count must be the column total minus the sum of the other columns. This tells us that one row and one column are not free to vary, whereas the rest of the cells have counts that are free to vary. We call the number of the free-to-vary cells the "degrees of freedom."

Degrees of freedom are represented by df. To distinguish between χ^2 distributions with varying df values, the df are written in parentheses after the χ^2. For example, $\chi^2(1)$ is the χ^2 distribution for df equal to 1, and $\chi^2(3)$ is the χ^2 distribution for df equal to 3.

Sometimes it helps to have a shorthand for referring to the chi-square value below which a particular proportion of the chi-square statistics fall. For example, 95% of the chi-square statistics fall below the chi-square value for which the p-value is 5%. That value may be referred to as $\chi^2_{.95,\,df}$. For example, $\chi^2_{.95,2}$ equals 5.99 (that is, 95% of chi-square values fall at 5.99 or lower, if df equals 2), and $\chi^2_{.95,3}$ equals 7.8.

Summary

The chi-square test has a null hypothesis of no correlation. A statistically significant chi-square value justifies the conclusion that a correlation exists in the population from which the data were drawn.

A Monte Carlo simulation creates data for which the null hypothesis is true and records statistics that indicate how bad the null hypothesis looks. The *p*-value is the proportion of simulated statistics that are at least as embarrassing for the null hypothesis as the statistic calculated from the data.

When the null hypothesis is true, the distribution of chi-square statistics depends on the *df* (the degrees of freedom). The *df* are the product of 1 less than the number of rows and 1 less than the number of columns. To find the *p*-value for a chi-square statistic, we look in a table showing *df* and the chi-square values that only 5% fall at or above (if the null hypothesis is true).

Correlation is not causation. Every correlation could be the result of at least three lines of causation: A causing B, B causing A, or A and B not affecting one another while a third variable affects both. Experiments involve random assignment to certain experiences. Because experiments preclude concluding that assignment was determined by other factors, experiments allow for conclusions that the random assignment to that experience caused any later significant differences between assigned groups.

Avoiding Common Misunderstandings

In a chi-square test, the *p*-value is the probability if the null hypothesis is true, of getting a chi-square value at least as large as the one seen in the data.

The data in a sample and the statistics that describe it are not the same as those statistics in the population. For example, although 20% of the students in a *sample* are binge drinkers, there may be 25% in the *population* who are binge drinkers. Similarly, if there is a correlation in the sample, there might not be a correlation in the population. That's why we need to perform a chi-square test.

Correlation is not causation. Experiments reveal causation.

Computer Project

Run Monte Carlo simulations to check the distribution of chi-square statistics when the null hypothesis is true. Try different cross-tab designs that have the same *df*, for example, a design with three columns and three rows, and another one with two rows and five columns. Do they have the same distribution when the null hypothesis is true? And are the *p*-values in Table 4.3.3 in this section correct?

Check whether it is true that the expected counts must be at least 5. You can do this by using a design with two columns and two rows with 19 observations in each sample.

In the Computer Project in the last section, you found the chi-square values for tests of correlations in the U.S. population. You were working with the U.S. data from the *Data Matters* Resource Center at *www.keycollege.com/dm*. Determine the *p*-values and report those tests once in the style of the popular press and once in a complete style of the sciences.

Exercises

Here is some more data from the Wechsler team's research:

	NONBINGE DRINKERS (*n* = 6,894)	INFREQUENT BINGE DRINKERS (*n* = 4,090)	FREQUENT BINGE DRINKERS (*n* = 3,291)
DID SOMETHING YOU REGRET	14%	37%	63%
MISSED A CLASS	8%	30%	61%

For a cross-tabulation of binge drinking and doing something you regret, the chi-square statistic is 2,532. For a cross-tabulation of binge drinking and missing a class, the chi-square statistic is 2,000.

1. In the style of the popular press, report the results of a chi-square test of a relationship between doing something you regret and binge drinking.

2. In the style of the popular press, report the results of a chi-square test of a relationship between missing a class and binge drinking.

3. In the style of the sciences, with a full report of the chi-square test, report the results of a chi-square test of a relationship between doing something you regret and binge drinking.

4. In the style of the sciences, with a full report of the chi-square test, report the results of a chi-square test of a relationship between missing a class and binge drinking.

In 1999, the *Irish Times* reported on a study that stopped drivers and asked them how much they had been drinking. The report did not say how many people were stopped. For the following exercises, assume that the researchers stopped 100 drivers: 50 men and 50 women. The report said that 31% of the men reported having been drinking, and 13% of the women reported having been drinking (Humphreys, 1999). If you calculated the chi-square statistic in this case, you would find that the chi-square value was 9.4.

5. Write a report of this study in the style of the popular press.

6. Write a report of this study in the style of the sciences, providing a full presentation of the chi-square test.

7. In a previous section's exercises, we considered the possibility that a campus might ban drinking. College campuses have carried out many such actions, banning drinking, fraternities, or even football. Rarely are such actions based on experimental research. How could administrators go about instituting such bans in a way that would make the banning process itself an experiment that would enable them to make judgments about the value of the ban?

8. One of the explicit claims of this book is that reading it and learning about statistics will improve your life. The claim is that you will be able to make better judgments about what you read and make better decisions in your life. However, I haven't yet tested that claim. Write me a note explaining how I might go about testing whether this book improves people's lives.

9. Here is a report on a 17-year study that asked kids about their television viewing and then watched their lives as young adults:

> *Adolescents who watch more than one hour of television a day are more likely to commit aggressive and violent acts as adults. . . . "It's a very important study . . . it very niftily isolates television as a causal factor," said George Comstock.*
>
> —Mestel, Los Angeles Times, March 29, 2002

A friend writes you, "Hey! You've taken stats. Does this really mean that they showed that TV watching causes violence?" Write your friend a reply. If you think that this study did not show whether TV watching causes violence, describe a study that would be able to show whether TV watching causes violence.

10. Here is a report of a 16-year study from the *Washington Post:*

> *Women . . . were randomly assigned either to receive regular mammograms . . . or not. . . . A statistically significant reduction in breast cancer deaths was seen among women between the ages of 53 and 73 who received mammograms.*
>
> —Washington Post, March 16, 2002

A friend writes to you, "Does this mean that getting mammograms *causes* a reduction in the risk of dying of breast cancer for women who are 53 to 73? I thought correlation wasn't causation?" Write a reply. If you think that this study did not show whether mammograms cause a reduction in breast cancer deaths, describe a study that would be able to show whether mammograms did reduce these risks.

11. The chi-square tests done on the large study of student drinking apply to some population. Think about receiving a survey such as the survey in that study. Think about what would make you willing to return it and what would lead you to ignore it. What does this tell you about the population of which the sample was a random sample?

12. The study of binge drinking was based on students' reports. What reasons might have led students to be less than completely honest, and how might that affect the conclusions you would draw from this study?

Answers to Odd-Numbered Exercises

1. "Researchers found that frequent binge drinkers were statistically significantly more likely to have done something they regretted than students who do not binge drink. Among light drinkers, 14% reported having done something they regretted, compared to 63% of frequent binge drinkers."

3. "As drinking increased, the chances of reporting having done something regrettable increased significantly (chi-square(3) = 2,532, $p < 5\%$). Among nonbinge drinkers, 14% reported doing something regrettable; among infrequent binge drinkers, 37% did so; and among frequent binge drinkers, 63% did so."

5. Here is how the journalist at the *Irish Times* reported the study:

   "Some 22 per cent of car-owners said they had driven soon after consuming two or more alcoholic drinks. A significantly higher proportion of men reported doing this than women, 31 per cent to 13 per cent respectively."

   —HUMPHREYS, *IRISH TIMES,* MARCH 12, 1999

   If I were writing for an American newspaper, I would have called it a "*statistically* significant" result, but perhaps Humphreys can have more confidence that his audience will understand what he means by "significant" than I would.

   Note that Humphreys reported the proportions for each gender. That was a sensible thing to do, because there was a significant correlation between gender and drinking. It would not have been sensible if there were no significant relationship between gender and having been drinking.

7. If the university administrators phased in the ban by randomly selecting half of the college students to experience the ban for four years before making the ban a university-wide requirement, there would be something of an

approximation of an experiment that would enable them to form some conclusions about the value of the ban at the end of the four years.

9. "Not really. The researchers may have done a lot to try to rule out other lines of causation, but a correlational study, as this is, does not provide evidence for causation. In this case, the researchers are probably fairly sure that the violence does not cause the television viewing, since the violence happens when the people are adults, and the television viewing happened when they were adolescents. It's a general rule that causation moves forward in time, not backward. Nonetheless, there are always other factors that might be causing both. For example, TV watching and violence might both be related to children's enthusiasm for violence, families' approval of violence, children's capacity for violence, IQ, attention span, number of friends, how hot their city is, how busy their parents are, how self-absorbed their parents are, how they get along with their siblings, or many other factors. No matter how much they try to track these extra factors down, until they have done an experiment, the researchers do not have compelling evidence about causation. Ideally, they would randomly assign kids to either TV or no TV. That's probably not going to go over well with parents, so the researchers could randomly assign families to no-TV interventions or being left alone. For the no-TV intervention, counselors would visit with the parents and give them all the arguments the researchers are aware of for why children should not watch lots of TV. If kids in the no-TV-intervention group end up less violent, that would be evidence that the no-TV intervention diminishes violence."

11. I wouldn't have bothered with the survey if I were very busy, whether studying or partying. I wouldn't fill out the survey if I thought the researchers had some bone to pick and would be using my answers to foist an objectionable policy on people. It would be pretty clear to anyone taking such a survey that these are not researchers who are going to be advocating increased drinking on college campuses, so I wouldn't be enthusiastic about returning the survey if I felt that drinking was fine. In reality, I think that drinking doesn't work well with college. I tried it in my freshman year, and it seemed a great way to waste tuition. Someone like me would be enthusiastic about returning the survey. This survey was sent to tens of thousands of students, of which about half ended up being analyzed. We can only hope that in the future, researchers will focus on gathering a random sample of perhaps 500 students and making sure to hear from the full sample, rather than working with a self-selected sample.

CHAPTER 5

Averages and Other Number Line Statistics in the News

The average American household earns about 70% of the average income of American households. Sounds nutty, but it's true. The reason is that there are several different meanings of "average." Section 5.1 explains that one average is the arithmetic average, called the "mean," found by adding up all the numbers in a group and dividing by how many there are. Another average is the median, the number that has as many other numbers above it as below it. In 1995, the median American household earned $30,700, and the mean household earned $44,100.

So which is it, $30,700 or $44,100? Which is the best summary of American households? Section 5.2 will tell you the answer.

An average of $30,700 doesn't seem like much. How much money is that now? There has been inflation. The amount $30,700 in 1995 was like $35,676 in 2001. For the last decade, annual inflation has stayed close to 3%, so $30,700 in 1995 is like $37,848 in 2003. That makes more sense. All dollar amounts from the past require adjustments. You also need to consider inflation when you think about dollar amounts in the future, such as what your retirement fund will pay you. Section 5.3 will tell you all about how to adjust for inflation.

5.1 Incomes and Other Quantities

* Medians
* Number Line Observations
* Means

> *Nationally, the 1996 median income [was] $35,492. . . . The median income is the amount earned by the typical family at the center of the income scale: Half the families earn more and half earn less.*
> —FIORE AND BROWNSTEIN, *LOS ANGELES TIMES*, SEPTEMBER 30, 1997

D IFFERENT KINDS OF FAMILIES earn different amounts.

> *Median earnings for [full-time working] women [were] $23,710, while the figure for men [was] $32,144. . . . Median income for Hispanics climbed to $24,906. . . . For blacks the increase was to $23,482. . . . Income for whites climbed to $37,171 . . . and for Asians it rose to $43,276. . . . In the South . . . median household incomes climbed to $32,422 in 1996.*
> —VOBEJDA AND CHANDLER, *WASHINGTON POST*, SEPTEMBER 30, 1997

The preceding quotes talk about "medians." On their Web site, *www.census.gov,* the U.S. Census Bureau reports that the median U.S. household income had risen to $42,148 by 1999 and remained at $42,148 in 2000. Before we can figure out what this tells us, we need to know what a median is.

Medians

The median is the middle number. To find the middle height in a group of five children, you would have them stand in order by height. The median height would be the height of the child in the middle (the height of the child who is third from shortest and third from tallest).

The median is a summary that serves as a model of a group of numbers. Imagine that five families' annual incomes are $5,000, $17,000, $31,000, $50,000, and $120,000. The median is $31,000. As a model of the incomes, it is too high for the two poorest families. The mistakes (or errors) it makes modeling the poorest families are somewhat compensated by the errors it makes modeling the two richest families, for which it is too low.

You may have to sort the numbers before you can find the median. For example, you might be told that three of your friends earned $1,000, $100, and $110 in sales commissions last week. To find the median, you would first sort the numbers from lowest to highest. (The list would become $100, $110, and $1,000.) You would then count halfway up to find the median of $110.

Sometimes there is no middle number, for example, when there are an even number of observations. Let's say that on four different days it takes you 10 minutes, 15 minutes, 20 minutes, and 25 minutes to drive to work. When there are an even number of observations, the median is halfway between the two middle numbers, in this case between 15 and 20 minutes. To find the median, you can add the two numbers together and divide by 2. In this case, 15 plus 20 is 35, which when divided by 2 gives 17.5. Your median commute time would be 17.5 minutes.

How to Find the Median

To find the median, sort your numbers from lowest to highest. If there are an odd number of observations, the median is the middle one, halfway up the list. If there are an even number of observations, the median is halfway between the two middle numbers.

For example, a waiter considers three tips: $4, $5, and $7. The median is $5. If the tips were $4, $5, $6, and $7, then the median would be $5.50. If the tips were $6, $6, $6, $9, and $9, then the median would be $6.

The quote at the beginning of this section reported that the median household income was $35,492 in 1996. That means that if you sorted the incomes from every American family in 1996 and counted halfway up, the middle family earned $35,492. Half of the families earned more than $35,492, and half earned less.

Figure 5.1.1 **Histograms of Salaries for American Men and Women**

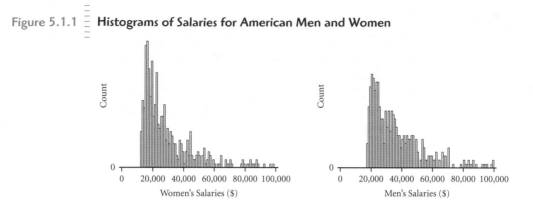

According to the second quote at the beginning of this section, the median income for men was $32,144, and the median for women was $23,710. Figure 5.1.1 shows histograms of women's and men's salaries based on these medians and the distribution of salaries that you can see in the Representative Sample data at the *Data Matters* Resource Center at *www.keycollege.com/dm.*

Each histogram by itself is very interesting. In both, the bulge is around $20,000 and then spreads far to the right. They give you some idea of what is happening in America.

How well do the histograms work for comparing men's and women's salaries? When I calculated the medians, I found that the median of the women's histogram is at about $24,000, of the men's at about $32,000. Is the gap between the men's salaries and the women's visually obvious? Not really.

Histograms do not make it easy to make comparisons like this. Looking at the histograms, it is hard to compare men's and women's salaries. Using the medians of salaries of men and women reveals what you might miss in a histogram: the fact that the typical woman is earning about 74% as much as the typical man.

Number Line Observations

The median is a useful model, but it works only for certain kinds of measurements: numbers from a number line. For example, say you are a doctor, and you have been keeping track of whether your patients are pregnant and how much they weigh. You can report the median weight, but there is no median pregnancy state. Medians apply only to observations that fall on a number line. Weights, heights, distances, loudnesses, and amounts of money are all observations that fall on a number line. With pregnancy, either you are or you are not, so pregnancy does not belong on a number line, and is not modeled with a median.

When you have observations, for example, pregnancy, in which people fall into one category among several, your observations are called "categorical." Categorical observations are summarized with proportions and percentages. Number line observations can be summarized and modeled with medians.

All around you, aspects of your life can be summarized and modeled with medians or proportions. For example, my son got a fish tank. So far we have bought seven fish. One of the things we need to monitor is the water temperature. If it gets too cold, the fish will die. So far, three have died. In talking about the temperature in the tank, I could summarize the temperatures with a median and use that as my model, because temperatures are number line variables. In talking about the health of the fish, medians make no sense. Death is categorical: You are either dead or alive. You can summarize deaths with percentages, not medians. For example, 43% of our fish have died. Medians work for number line observations. Categorical observations require proportions.

Means

The most commonly known average is the mean, which is sometimes called the "arithmetic average" or "arithmetic mean." The median is also an average, but outside of statistics, the word "average" is usually reserved for the mean. If a journalist reports an "average," your best bet is that it's a mean. Journalists usually refer to medians as "medians," but not consistently.

Like the median, the mean is a model and summary of where observations fall on a number line. The mean is also a value at the center of the observations in a set. To find the mean, you add up all the observations and divide by the number of observations.

Finding the Mean

To find the mean of a set of measurements, add up all the observations and divide by the number of measurements in the set.

For example, I keep track of my car's gas mileage. On four fillings, my car got 20, 19, 16, and 21 miles per gallon. The mean mileage is 19 miles per gallon, because 20 plus 19 plus 16 plus 21 is 76, and 76 divided by 4 equals 19.

An example of a mean that many people deal with is grade point averages (GPAs). To see how GPAs are calculated, let us say that you are a college student and have earned three A's and a C, and each course is worth five credits. Before colleges calculate GPAs, a numerical equivalent is assigned to each grade. An A is considered a 4, a B a 3, a C a 2, and so on. With three A's and a C, your grade equivalents would be 4, 4, 4, and 2. Here are the calculations that would find your mean grade:

$$\text{Mean} = \frac{\text{Sum of Observations}}{\text{Number of Observations}}$$

In this case, there are four observations: 4, 4, 4, and 2. We can plug them into that equation:

$$\text{Mean} = \frac{4 + 4 + 4 + 2}{4} = \frac{14}{4} = 3.5$$

The mean and median are usually different, and this provides journalists with an opportunity to mislead you by which average they report. For example, in 1995, the median U.S. household income was $30,700. The mean U.S. household income was $44,100. Imagine a town that was completely representative of the U.S. population in regard to income: Its median income was $30,700 and its mean income was $44,100. To make the town look poor, a journalist could honestly write that in that town the median income ($30,700) was two-thirds the national average ($44,100). Or, to make the town look rich, a journalist could write that in that town the average income ($44,100) was half again higher than the national median ($30,700). A journalist could even call the median an average. The median is a kind of average. So, it would not be a lie to say that the average income in that town ($44,100) is half again higher than the national average ($30,700).

How the Mean Balances Errors

Because of differences in how the mean and the median trade off their too-high and too-low errors, the mean and median can be very different. Because it is the middle number, the median is below about half of the observations in its sample.

Figure 5.1.2 **4, 4, 4, and 2, and Their Mean on the Number Line**

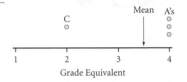

Figure 5.1.3 **The Mean of 4, 4, 4, and 2, and Its Errors**

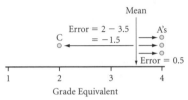

In contrast, the mean can be below most of the observations from which it was calculated. For example, consider again a student with three A's and a C. The student's GPA would then be the mean of 4, 4, 4, and 2, which is 3.5; 3.5 is lower than all three 4s, as you can see in Figure 5.1.2.

Figure 5.1.3 shows the mean's errors. The way that the mean balances its errors is that, if you add up how far off it is when it is too high, the sum equals what you get when you add up how far off it is when it is too low. If you think of the mean's errors as being negative when the mean is too high and positive when the mean is too low, then the mean's errors add up to 0. Table 5.1.1 shows this for our grade example.

The mean's errors add up to 0. For any set of numbers, the mean's errors always add up to 0. That is how the mean balances the errors that it makes in modeling the observations. Because the sum of the mean's errors is 0, the mean of the mean's errors is also 0. The mean is the value that has a mean error of 0.

Table 5.1.1 Three Grades, Their Mean, and the Mean's Errors

GRADE	MEAN	MEAN'S ERRORS (GRADE MINUS MEAN)
4	3.5	0.5
4	3.5	0.5
4	3.5	0.5
2	3.5	−1.5
	TOTAL	0

The Mean's Errors

As a model of the measurements in a set, a mean makes errors. The errors are the differences between the mean and the measurements themselves. The mean's errors always add up to 0.

For example, if two grades have numerical equivalents of 3 and 4, the mean is 3.5. This mean is 0.5 too high ($+0.5$) for the 3 and 0.5 too low (-0.5) for the 4. The mean's errors are $+0.5$ plus -0.5, which equals 0.

Because of how the mean balances its errors, it is the balance point of a histogram. To see what I mean, look at Figure 5.1.4, which shows the histogram of the four grade equivalents we are considering: 4, 4, 4, and 2. If you think of Figure 5.1.4's x-axis as a seesaw and the histogram's bars as blocks on the seesaw, the mean, 3.5, is the point at which the seesaw would balance.

How the Mean Balances Errors

When the mean is used as a model of a set of numbers, the errors it makes when it is too high add up to the sum of the errors it makes when it is too low.

For example, 19 is the mean of my mileages (20, 19, 16, and 21). As a model of each mileage, 19 is too low for the 20 and the 21. For those, 19's errors are 1 and 2, which sum to 3. The mileage 19 is right on for the 19 and is 3 too high for the 16. Its error when it is too high is 3, and its errors when it is too low sum to 3.

Figure 5.1.4 **Histogram of Four Grade Equivalents with Their Balance Point (Their Mean, 3.5)**

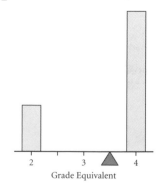

Grade Equivalent

Figure 5.1.5

Used Computer Prices

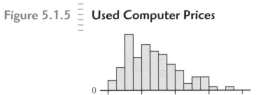

Price ($)

Because the mean is the balance point of a histogram, you can estimate a histogram's mean by guessing where the histogram would balance if it were made of blocks on a seesaw. For example, try estimating the mean for the histogram in Figure 5.1.5., which shows computer prices collected from an online newsgroup.

It might not be immediately obvious that you can find the balance point. Start by considering $1,800. I think you will agree that $1,800 is too high. If a fulcrum were under $1,800, the seesaw would tip to the left. How about $1,000? I think you can see that $1,000 is too low. The seesaw would tip to the right. How about $1,200? That amount looks pretty good to me. In fact, the mean of those prices is $1,268. Figure 5.1.6 shows a fulcrum under the mean, so you can see that the histogram balances at that point.

Figure 5.1.7 shows yearly in-state tuitions from 17 colleges and universities that I found on their Web sites in the late 1990s. For practice, can you estimate the mean?

Each bar represents $2,000. Some of the bars have no height at all and look like gaps. How about $14,000 for the balance point? Too high. $2,000? Too low. $8,000 looks like the seesaw would tip to the right, so $8,000 is still too low. That puts the mean somewhere between $8,000 and $14,000. What's your estimate?

Figure 5.1.6

Used Computer Prices with Fulcrum at Mean

Price ($)

Figure 5.1.7

In-State Yearly Tuition at Colleges and Universities

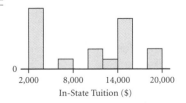

In-State Tuition ($)

Figure 5.1.8

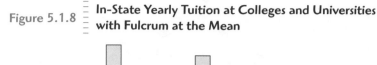

In-State Yearly Tuition at Colleges and Universities
with Fulcrum at the Mean

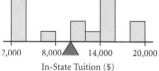

In-State Tuition ($)

The mean of those tuitions is $10,000. Figure 5.1.8 shows the histogram with a fulcrum at the mean. The point to remember here is that the mean is the balance point of the histogram.

Balancing Histograms

If a histogram were a seesaw with blocks on it, the mean would be the balance point.

For example, imagine a histogram of 1, 2, and 6. The mean is 3. The histogram would balance on a fulcrum at 3, as is shown in this figure:

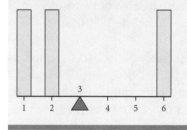

Because the mean is the balance point of the histogram, when the histogram is symmetrical, the mean and the median are the same. A symmetrical stack of blocks balances at its middle, with half of the blocks below and half above. To see this more clearly, consider the symmetrical distributions shown in the histograms in Figure 5.1.9.

The first histogram in Figure 5.1.9 has observations that range from −20 to 80. All of the numbers between −20 and 80 appear equally often. Their probabilities of appearing are all the same. That kind of distribution is called a uniform distribution, because the probabilities of each number appearing are uniform (from −20 to 80). That histogram balances at its middle, 30, which is its median and mean.

The middle histogram in Figure 5.1.9 is a sample from a normal distribution, which is symmetrical. The balance point of this histogram is its center, 40. Half of

Figure 5.1.9   **Histograms of Samples from Three Symmetrical Distributions**

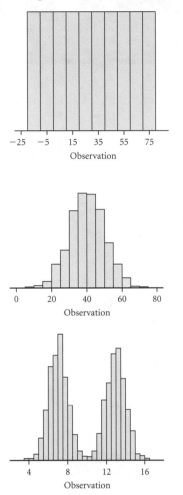

its observations fall below 40, and half fall above. The number 40 is both mean and median for this histogram.

The last histogram in Figure 5.1.9 is less symmetrical than the other two, but it is close to symmetrical. You might see that its balance point, the mean, is 10. Each lump has almost the same number of observations, so the median is somewhere between them, very near the mean. In fact, for this histogram, the median is 9. For roughly symmetrical histograms, the balance point is roughly the observation in the middle. That is, the mean is roughly the same as the median.

Symmetrical Distributions

When a histogram is symmetrical, its balance point is the middle observation. So the mean is the same as the median.

Tails in Distributions

Look again at the normal distribution in the second histogram in Figure 5.1.9. On either side, the histogram gets thinner and thinner. Those thin areas at the edges of a histogram are called the "tails" of the distribution. It is as though the normal distribution were two cats facing each other with their tails spread out on either side.

Tails in Distributions

The part of a distribution that spreads out at the edges of a histogram is called a "tail."

For example, a normal distribution has two tails, as shown here:

A normal distribution is symmetrical, so its two tails are the same size and thickness. When a distribution is not symmetrical, it is said to be "skewed." If a distribution has a long, thick tail on the right but no matching tail on the left, the distribution is said to be right skewed. If there is a long tail on the left but no tail on the right, the distribution is left skewed. Skewed distributions are skewed toward the observations in the longer or thicker tail.

Skewness

Distributions that are not symmetrical are skewed. If a distribution has a larger right tail, it is said to be right skewed.

For example, prices are usually right skewed like this:

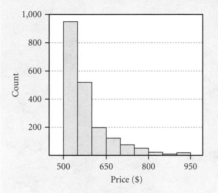

If a distribution has a larger tail on the left, it is left skewed. For example, grades are often left skewed like this:

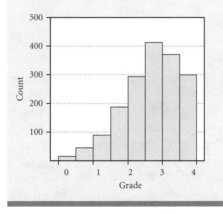

The Mean Follows Skewness

Knowing that the mean is the balance point of a histogram lets us see some important features of the mean. Imagine that you have a seesaw, and you balance some blocks on it. Now take a block on the far right and slide it further to the right. What happens? The seesaw tilts down on the right. How do you adjust for that? You move the balance point to the right also. That is what happens to means as well. When you replace one of the higher measurements with something much higher, the distribution becomes more right skewed, and the mean also moves up (to the right on the number line) a little.

Consider the GPA example from earlier in this section. You can see how the mean would become higher if a high grade were replaced with something higher still. Imagine that you had earned four grades that translated to 1, 3, 3, and 4. Their mean is 2.75. Now imagine that the grade fairy turns that 4 into a 9. The sum becomes 16, and the mean is 16 divided by 4, or 4.0. Congratulations: Your GPA is now 4.0!

Notice how this change in the mean differs from what would happen to the median. Numbers out in the tails of the distribution do not affect the median. Before the grade fairy's magic, the median is 3, and after the magic, the median is 3. The grade fairy could pull your top grade to 1,000, and the median would still be 3. Statisticians say that the median is "robust," because it isn't much influenced by extremely high or low measurements.

You can see the difference between means and medians in statistics about U.S. incomes. In 1995, the median income was $30,700, and the mean income was $44,100 (*Federal Reserve Bulletin,* January 1997). The mean income was about one and a half times the size of the median. It is typical for the mean U.S. income to be higher than the median. Figure 5.1.10 shows a histogram of U.S. incomes up to $400,000. The incomes shown in the figure are from a survey of 57,000 American families reported by the U.S. Census Bureau in March 1997.

Figure 5.1.10 shows that U.S. incomes are far from symmetrical. There is a long tail to the right. In reality, that tail is even longer than it appears in this histogram, which omits some of the highest incomes, because it goes up to only $400,000. Very few families earn more than $400,000 a year, but superstar athletes sometimes earn $10 million. The histogram in Figure 5.1.10 would have had to

Figure 5.1.10

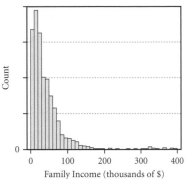

have been 20 times wider to include $10 million. As another example, in 1997 Bill Gates's wealth increased by about $25 billion. To fit Bill Gates's 1997 income on this histogram, you would need to make it 50,000 times wider than it is now: more than a mile wide! The full histogram of everyone's income would have an extremely long tail to the right.

As the extreme cases get more and more extreme, the skewness increases, and the mean moves farther and farther from the median. You can get some idea of how much the distribution is skewed by seeing how far the mean is from the median. American incomes are very skewed.

Estimating the Median from a Histogram

The median is the number above which about half of the observations fall. In a histogram, that means that half of the area of the histogram appears above the median, and half appears below. When estimating the mean and median, take into account the skewness of the histogram. If the histogram is symmetrical, then they should be about the same. If the histogram is right skewed, the mean should be higher than the median. If the histogram is left skewed, the mean should be lower than the median. Figure 5.1.11 shows the computer prices from Figure 5.1.5 again. Try estimating the median price.

Figure 5.1.11   **Used Computer Prices**

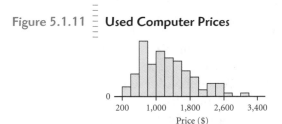

Figure 5.1.12   **In-State Yearly Tuition at Colleges and Universities**

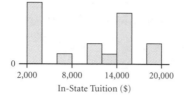

In-State Tuition ($)

As was noted previously, the mean price is $1,268. The prices are right skewed, so the mean price is higher than the median. How much higher? Each bar in Figure 5.1.11 represents $200. $800 looks too low—less than half of the area falls to the left of $800. So the median is somewhere between $800 and $1,268. That's probably as good as you can do without taking out a ruler and calculating the space in each bar. In fact, the median price is $1,100.

How about the in-state tuitions? The mean was $10,000. Figure 5.1.12 shows the tuitions from Figure 5.1.7 again. The tuitions look fairly symmetrically spread out. By looking at the histogram, I would guess the median is probably close to the mean. In fact, the median is $11,500.

The important points here are that the median is that point at which half of the observations fall below it and half fall above it; the mean is the point that balances its errors, so it is the balance point of a histogram; and the mean follows the skewness, whereas the median does not.

Algebra and Greek Symbols

In statistics, the mean of something is indicated with a bar over the value, so the mean x value is $\bar{x}$. The mean of a sample is usually represented by $\bar{x}$, because we think of the observations in the sample as x:

$$\bar{x} = \frac{\sum x}{n}$$

That is, the mean is the sum of all the values divided by the number of observations. The mean of the population is noted with the Greek letter μ, pronounced "mu."

The median must be defined in terms of steps of work. To find the median, first sort the observations by size. Call the lowest observation x_1, the second lowest x_2, and so on up to x_n. If n is odd, the median equals $x_{(n+1)/2}$. For example, if n is 5, the median equals $x_{(n+1)/2}$, which is $x_{6/2}$, or x_3. If n is even, the median equals $x_{n/2}$ plus $x_{(n/2)+1}$ divided by 2. For example, if n is 6, the median equals $x_{n/2}$ plus $x_{(n/2)+1}$ divided by 2, or x_3 plus x_4 divided by 2.

In this book, numbers are called "number line" measurements. It is more common to refer to such values as "continuous," "scale," or "numeric" measurements.

"Continuous" emphasizes that the number line is continuous—for any two numbers, there is a number between them. For example, between 4 and 5, there is 4.5. Between 4 and 4.1, there is 4.05. Between 4 and 4.001, there is 4.0005, and so on. No matter how close two numbers are, there are other numbers between them. They spread continuously from negative infinity to positive infinity. "Scale" emphasizes that what we're looking at is something that was measured by some standard numerical system, such as weight measured on a scale. "Numeric" emphasizes that these are numbers, but that could be misleading. For example, social security and telephone numbers are numeric, and you can't summarize them with averages. "Number line" emphasizes that these are things that exist on a number line. That's why they are referred to as "number line" observations in this text.

If an observation is far out on a tail of a distribution, it is sometimes called an "outlier." Right skewed is sometimes called "positively skewed," and left skewed is sometimes called "negatively skewed." A normal distribution is symmetrical. A chi-square distribution is positively skewed.

Summary

When a researcher collects data, some of the observations are numbers reflecting where things fall on a number line. Other observations reflect categorical features. Categorical features are features that cannot be described on a number line. Categorical observations can be summarized and modeled with proportions. Number line observations are better modeled with medians or means.

Medians are the middle observations in a sorted list of numbers. To find the median of an odd number of observations, you sort the list from lowest to highest and count halfway through the list; the middlemost observation is the median. If there are an even number of observations, the median is halfway between the middlemost two observations.

The mean is found by summing the observations and dividing by the number of observations.

If a histogram were a seesaw with blocks on it, the mean would be the balance point, because the sum of the mean's errors when it is too low equals the sum of the mean's errors when it is too high. In symmetrical distributions, the mean equals the median.

The edges of a distribution are called its "tails." If a distribution has a long, heavy tail on the right, it is right skewed. If the dominant tail is on the left, the distribution is left skewed. The mean is pulled by the tails, and the median is not. In left-skewed distributions, the mean is lower than the median. In right-skewed distributions, the mean is higher than the median. The mean can be used to estimate total outcomes, because it is calculated from a total.

The skewness is determined by the tail. A long tail toward the right indicates right skewness and a mean above the median. A long tail to the left indicates left skewness and a mean below the median.

Avoiding Common Misunderstandings

Both the mean and the median are types of averages.

Numbers exist on an imaginary number line. If you aren't comfortable with the idea of the mean balancing the observations on either side of it, play around with data on a number line. Draw a number line and pick three points. Find their mean and draw in the errors that the mean makes as it models the three numbers. See how some of its errors are positive (it's too low) and some are negative (it's too high).

The median is the middle number in your set of observations; that is, after you sort the numbers from smallest to largest, the median is the middle number in the list. The median is *not* halfway between the largest and the smallest. Halfway between the largest and the smallest is called the "midrange" and is *not* the median. Remember that the median is only the middle number *after* you sort all the numbers from lowest to highest.

Half of the observations fall at or below the median. Half fall at or above the median. If I am looking at how much people earn, and I read that 40% earn below $40,000 and another 20% earn between $40,000 and $51,000, I know that, as I count to the salary that is halfway up a list of salaries, I will pass $40,000 (because that's only 40% up the list), and I will stop before $51,000 (because that's 60% up the list). The median will be somewhere between $40,000 and $51,000.

Computer Project

Use your software to find the mean and median of at least two of the number line observations in the data in the U.S. Representative Sample used in previous computer projects. Note whether they are skewed and which way they are skewed.

Exercises

1. The quotes at the beginning of this section say that, for Hispanic families, the median income was $24,906 in 1996. According to the *Statistical Abstract of the United States, 1996,* about 11% of Americans are Hispanic. There are about 100 million American families. What is the approximate raw count of the number of Hispanic families who earned more than $25,000 in 1996?

2. The quotes at the beginning of this section report that the median African American family income was $23,482 in 1996. About 16% of Americans are African American. How many African American families earned more than $23,500 in 1996?

3. The Census Bureau's *Statistical Abstract of the United States, 1996* reports that 22% of European Americans are under 14 years of age, 46% are between 15 and 44, 20% are between 45 and 64, and 11% are over 65. What does this tell you about the median age of European Americans?

4. The following table is adapted from the *Statistical Abstract of the United States, 1996*.

EDUCATION (YEARS)	EUROPEAN AMERICANS MORE THAN 24 YEARS OLD (PERCENTAGE)	AFRICAN AMERICANS MORE THAN 24 YEARS OLD (PERCENTAGE)
0–8	8.4	10.3
9–11	9.5	16.8
12	34.5	36.2
13–15	24.6	23.8
16 or more	22.9	12.9

The table says that, of European Americans more than 24 years old, 8.4% have less than a 9th-grade education, 9.5% have between a 9th-grade and an 11th-grade education, and so on.

Write a short news paragraph reporting what the table tells you about the median years of education of European Americans and African Americans.

5. Think about the characteristics of U.S. states. They differ in the following ways:

- Size (in terms of square miles)
- Population size
- Region of the country
- Whether you can drink alcohol when you are 19
- The age of consent
- The year in which they were brought into the union
- The party affiliation of their governors
- Whether they border oceans, Mexico, Canada, or only other U.S. states

Which of those state features are number line features, and which are categorical?

6. Marketers who survey people to see what they are like and what kinds of products they would like to buy sometimes ask people about their gender, ethnicity, age, income, religion, place of birth, and sometimes even weight. Which of these questions will yield observations that can be modeled with medians?

7. The following table is an abridged version of a table from the Web site of the Centers for Disease Control. This table lists the number of deaths that occurred during 1994 and the age of the people who died. For example, in 1994, in the United States, among the people between 35 and 44 years old, 99,503 died. Altogether, 2,278,580 Americans died in 1994.

AGE	DEATHS (NUMBER)	DEATHS AT EACH AGE (PERCENTAGE)
0–11 months	31,710	1.4%
1–4 years	6,800	0.3%
5–9	3,747	0.2%
10–14	4,717	0.2%
15–19	15,284	0.7%
20–24	19,957	0.9%
25–34	59,273	2.6%
35–44	99,503	4.4%
45–54	137,897	6.1%
55–64	237,119	10.4%
65–74	483,669	21.2%
75–84	640,214	28.1%
Over 84	538,690	23.6%
TOTAL	2,278,580	100%

What can you say about the median age at death?

8. The following table, from the NFL Web site, shows some data about the September 1997 football game between the Dallas Cowboys and the Pittsburgh Steelers. The table shows yards gained with the first 50 passes and first 50 rushes. (A rush is a football play in which the quarterback, or someone to whom he hands the ball, gains yards by running.)

This table shows the yardages sorted from lowest to highest. Each row is numbered. Row 1 is numbered "1" and has the lowest passing yardage and lowest rushing yardage. Row 2 has the second-lowest passing yardage and second-lowest rushing yardage. And so on. The lowest yardages are negative. Those happened when the team lost ground during the play. At the bottom of the table is the sum of each column of numbers.

a. What are the median yards gained by passing?

b. What are the median yards gained by rushing?

PLAY'S SORT POSITION	PASSES	RUSHES	PLAY'S SORT POSITION	PASSES	RUSHES
1	−1	−2	27	5	4
2	0	−2	28	5	4
3	0	−1	29	7	4
4	0	−1	30	7	4
5	0	−1	31	8	4
6	0	0	32	8	4
7	0	0	33	8	4
8	0	0	34	8	5
9	0	0	35	9	5
10	0	1	36	9	5
11	0	1	37	9	5
12	0	1	38	11	5
13	0	2	39	11	6
14	0	2	40	12	6
15	0	2	41	12	6
16	0	2	42	13	6
17	0	2	43	14	8
18	0	2	44	15	8
19	0	2	45	15	8
20	0	3	46	18	8
21	0	3	47	18	9
22	0	3	48	31	9
23	0	3	49	42	11
24	0	3	50	55	13
25	0	3	TOTAL	353	182
26	4	3			

9. Based on the table in Exercise 7, if you took all the ages that Americans were when they died in 1994 and added them together, you would get about 163,969,616. The total number of years lived by Americans who died in 1994 was about 164 million. What is an approximate estimate of the mean age at death in 1994? How does the mean age at death compare to the median age at death (which you calculated in Exercise 7)?

10. Look back at the table in Exercise 8.

   a. What are the mean yards gained by passing?

   b. What are the mean yards gained by rushing?

   c. How do means and medians compare for passing gains and rushing gains?

11. In a survey to set a price on damages caused by letting steam float over the Grand Canyon, researchers showed Americans pictures of the Grand Canyon on regular days and on the days with the steam. The researchers asked how much the survey participants would be willing to pay to prevent that steam from getting to the Grand Canyon. There was so little steam that most people could see no difference between the photographs. More than 95% said they would pay nothing. What was the median payment offered to prevent the steam?

12. In the survey described in Exercise 11, the mean payment offered was $12. How could the mean payment be so much higher than the median payment? Imagine that the researchers surveyed only 20 people. Of these, 95% (19) said they would pay nothing. The average payment was $12. How much did the 20th person offer?

13. What are three numbers whose mean is greater than their median?

14. What are three numbers whose median is greater than their mean?

15. The following figure shows yearly tuition for resident students at a random selection of 25 U.S. colleges and universities listed in the 1996 *Information Please Almanac*. Each bar represents $2,000. The first bar includes tuitions from $0 to $2,000.

Yearly Tuitions for Resident Students

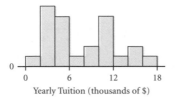

Yearly Tuition (thousands of $)

Estimate the mean and median of those annual tuitions.

16. I have been trying to sell a used car. After spending $200 for ads in the local newspaper, I wondered whether to advertise the car on an Internet newsgroup I found. I wasn't sure that I would be able to sell my car there, however, because someone told me the newsgroup only listed cars being sold for less than $2,000, and I was asking $10,000. To see whether my advertisement would fit in with the rest of the cars listed, I checked the first 20 prices of cars already listed. The following figure shows the prices I found.

Prices of 20 Cars from Newsgroup

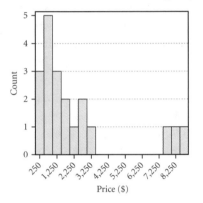

Price ($)

Estimate the mean and median advertised car prices.

17. This exercise may seem odd, but it may reveal something very important.

I painted a 1 on the head side of a coin and a 0 on the tail side. I flipped the coin four times. Here's what I got: 1, 0, 1, and 1. What proportion of those flips gave 1's? What is the mean of those four numbers? I flipped the coin another five times and got 1, 1, 0, 0, and 0. What proportion were 1's? What is the mean of the five numbers? If I have two possible outcomes, and I call one outcome "0" and the other outcome "1," what is the relationship between the mean of the outcomes and the proportions?

Answers to Odd-Numbered Exercises

1. 5.5 million: 11% of 100 million families is 11 million Hispanic families. About half of any set falls above the median, because the median is halfway up a sorted list. Half of the 11 million Hispanic families earned more than $25,000 in 1996. One-half of 11 million is 5.5 million families.

3. The median age for European Americans is somewhere between 15 and 44. The median age is that age below which half of the set falls. Only 22% of

European Americans are younger than 15 years of age, so the median must be older than 14 years. Another 46% are between 15 and 44, so 68% are younger than 45. That leaves 32% that are over 44, so the median must be below 45.

5. Number line features: size, population size, age of consent, year brought into the union. The rest are categorical.

7. In the table, the two proportions for the oldest ages are 28.1% and 23.6%. Together, they tell us that 51.7% died at 75 years or older. The median must be a little above 75 years.

9. The mean is the sum divided by the number of observations. The sum of the ages at death was about 163,969,616. The table reports that 2,278,580 people died. The mean then is 163,969,616 divided by 2,278,580, which is 72 years. The mean age is a little lower than the median age—about 4 or 5 years lower.

11. The median offered payment was nothing. To see this, imagine that there were only 20 payments, and 19 (95%) said they would pay nothing. Here's what the data would look like: 0, 0, 0, 0, 0, 0, 0, 0, 0, 0, 0, 0, 0, 0, 0, 0, 0, 0, 0, and then some other number. If you count up to the 10th and 11th, you see that they are both 0. The median is 0.

13. Any three numbers with a right skew. For example, 1, 1, and 22 would work. Or even 1, 2, and 4.

15. The histogram looks like it would balance around $8,000, so my estimate of the mean is around $8,000. If your estimate for the mean was between $6,000 and $10,000 that would be sensible. The distribution is right skewed, so the mean is greater than the median. The median would be to the left of $8,000. I would guess about $6,000. Estimating from histograms is not an exact business. If you estimated something between $5,000 and $8,000, that would be sensible.

17. The first four flips were 1, 0, 1, and 1. That is 75% 1's. The mean is 0.75. The next five flips were 1, 1, 0, 0, and 0. That is 40% 1's. The mean is 0.4. If I call one outcome "1" and the other outcome "0," the mean is the proportion that are 1's. The important point here is that proportions are a kind of mean.

5.2 Which Tells the Truth—The Mean, the Median . . . or the Weighted Mean?

- Standard Deviation
- Spread
- Weighted Means

The median is considered a more reliable measure than the mean, or average, income, which can be swayed by the gargantuan earnings of a relative few, giving a distorted view of a group's economic circumstances.

—HOLMES, *NEW YORK TIMES*, SEPTEMBER 30, 1997

IN SECTION 5.1, WE SAW THAT the U.S. Census Bureau reported that the median family income in 1996 was $35,492. You may wonder why the Census Bureau reports the median rather than the average we usually think of, the mean. The preceding quote gives some indication of the answer. That's an argument for medians. There are also arguments for means.

Relative Merits of the Mean and Median

When distributions are symmetrical, it doesn't matter whether you use a mean or a median to summarize them. When distributions are skewed, the mean and the median are different, so the mean gives a different impression than the median. Which is better? Each has its own strength.

The median's special strength is that it is more reliable, because mistakes in data collection have little effect on the median. For example, I once studied what people said they would pay for a jar of caviar. This is the kind of thing that helps grocers set prices. Most of the potential offers were between $1 and $10, but when I was done, the mean was over $30. That seemed odd. The median was $2. A histogram showed that one offered price was $900. I checked and found that I had typed "900," when I should have typed "9.00." That kind of data-entry mistake can have a huge impact on the mean and has no effect on the median.

The Median Is Rarely Affected by Data-Entry Mistakes

Because the median is unaffected by numbers at the edges of a distribution, mistakes almost never have a significant effect on the median.

For example, if I have the heights 4 feet, 5 feet, 5 feet, 5 feet, and 6 feet, the median is 5 feet. If I mistakenly add a height of 57 feet, the median is still 5 feet.

Similarly, in the exercises in Section 5.1, I described a study that tried to estimate the cost to Americans of allowing a power plant to release a little steam over the Grand Canyon. More than 95% of the people who were asked said that it was worth nothing to them to prevent the steam, but the mean evaluation was about $12. The mean was at $12 because a few people ignored the photographs and the research documenting that the steam was harmless to the Grand Canyon's flora, fauna, and geology. They saw the word "environment" and offered to pay a million dollars each to prevent the steam. The median could care less about these people, but the mean took them very seriously, and the survey very nearly shut down a power plant in Arizona.

Relation of the Mean to the Total

Sometimes the mean deserves much more attention than the median because the mean is related to the total. That is, the mean is the value you would use to predict what to expect in the long run.

Imagine that someone offers you a simple gambling game. In this game, you will roll a die. If you get a six, you win a dollar. Otherwise, you get nothing. You will get to play this game 10,000 times. How do you figure out how much you will win altogether?

To get an idea of how much you will win, you might go home and roll a die 600 times, playing the game by yourself. On about 500 of those 600 rolls, you will win nothing. On about 100 rolls, you will win a dollar. When you are done, you will have a list of 600 outcomes.

The median winnings would be $0. If you used the median to estimate your winnings, the median would suggest that you win nothing. But your total winnings would be $100.

To find the mean winnings, you would divide that $100 by 600. The mean winnings would be $.17, which is how much you would win per play. To determine how much you would win in 10,000 games, multiply $.17 by 10,000 for a product of $1,700.

To estimate your winnings from the median, you would find that 10,000 times $0 is $0 and expect to win nothing from the game. The median would have misled you. In a situation like this, the mean is more helpful than the median.

Because the median and mean each have their own strengths, the best approach is to report both the mean and the median. Together, they show where the observations are on the number line and reveal the skewness of the observations.

The current Census Bureau strategy is to report medians. That strategy obscures how much richer the wealthiest families are getting. In contrast, if the Census Bureau reported only the mean, it would be misrepresenting what most of us earn. Most American families earn much less than the mean. The most honest approach would be to report both the mean and the median.

Both the Mean and the Median Obscure Variation

Each fall, the Educational Testing Service reports how the previous spring's high school graduates did on the Scholastic Assessment Test (SAT). In its report, the Educational Testing Service reports separately how girls and boys did on the test. For many years, this annual report has produced a flurry of news articles remarking that the math SAT scores are lower for girls than for boys.

The interest in how girls and boys do on the math SATs began in 1980, when a *Newsweek* cover story began like this:

> *Can girls do math as well as boys? All sorts of recent tests have shown that they cannot.*
>
> —WILLIAMS AND KING, *NEWSWEEK*, DECEMBER 15, 1980

The "all sorts of recent tests" that Williams and King were referring to were the SATs. In 1980, the difference between girls' and boys' math SAT scores was larger than it has been more recently. The gap has been shrinking. Here is a report from 1997:

> *Although girls consistently earn higher high school grades, their SAT scores continue to lag behind boys', with the gap reaching 36 points in math.*
>
> —WOO AND SMITH, *LOS ANGELES TIMES*, AUGUST 27, 1997

What does this difference in math scores tell us? If you are a man, does this tell you that the women you meet are worse at math than you? If you are a woman, does this tell you that the men you meet are better at math than you?

First, this difference is a difference in SAT math scores, which are not perfect reflections of math ability. Nonetheless, what about the SAT math scores themselves? When you meet a man and a woman who took the math SATs, does this report tell you that the man had a higher math score?

If you thought that the report was telling you that the man would have a higher math score, you were mistaken, but the mistake is a common one. There is an illusion in averages. The illusion here is that when you find a group of boys and a group of girls, the boys' math SAT scores will be higher than the girls' math SAT scores. The media report that boys have higher scores than girls, so you would think that boys do have higher scores than girls.

The problem is that that is not what the media mean. They mean that, *on the average,* boys have higher scores than girls. That is, many boys have higher scores than many girls, many girls have higher scores than many boys, and if you take the mean of the girls' scores and the mean of the boys' scores, the girls' mean is lower than the boys' mean.

How does this difference in scores happen? Here is the important detail that most news articles omit to tell you about:

> *[On the SATs,] a 500 score represents the average, and each 100 points is a standard deviation above or below that average.*
>
> —*WASHINGTON POST,* MAY 27, 1995

The important detail is the "standard deviation." The standard deviation is close to the average distance from each number to the mean. On the average, a student's math score is about 100 points away from the mean. Some of them are very near the mean. Some are right on top of it. Others are further away, 200 to 300 points away.

The Standard Deviation

The standard deviation is close to the mean distance from each observation to the mean of the observations.

For example, imagine 200 students. Of these, 100 earn math SAT scores of 400, and 100 earn math SAT scores of 600. The mean would be 500, and every score would be 100 points away from the mean. In that case, the standard deviation would be 100.3, very close to 100.

The standard deviation gives you some idea about how the numbers are spread around. For example, Figure 5.2.1 shows how girls' and boys' math SAT scores are spread out.

Figure 5.2.1 **Histograms of Girls' and Boys' Math SAT Scores for 1997**

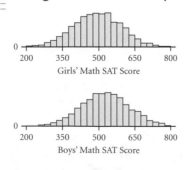

Figure 5.2.2   **Distributions of Girls' and Boys' Math SAT Scores for 1997**

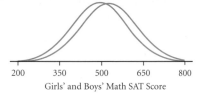

Girls' and Boys' Math SAT Score

Figure 5.2.1 shows two histograms. The top histogram is for girls. SAT scores are roughly normally distributed. That histogram for girls has a mean at 494, which was the average girls' math SAT score in 1997.

The second histogram shows the boys' math scores. The mean of that distribution is at 530, which is where the mean boys' math score was in 1997. The means of those two distributions are 36 points apart. The two distributions in the figure show what is meant when news reports say that girls scored 36 points lower than boys.

Figure 5.2.2 shows the outlines of the SAT math score distributions. The lump on the right is the boys' scores. The lump on the left is the girls' scores.

On the average, girls did score a little lower than boys did. That does not mean that all girls scored lower than all boys. In fact, if you randomly selected pairs of boys and girls from the United States, you would find that about 40% of the time the girl had a higher math SAT score. About 30% of the time the girl would have a score that was 50 points higher than the boy's, and about 20% of the time her math score would be 100 points higher. Not only do many girls have higher math SAT scores than many boys, but many girls have much higher math scores than many boys. (Each year, there are thousands of girls who score more than 100 points higher than thousands of boys.)

When people report a mean or a median by itself, they are omitting to mention that many or all of the observations fell elsewhere. They are not highlighting that things vary around that mean. When you read about a mean, imagine what histogram might lurk behind that average.

Observations Are Spread Out Around Means

When a mean is reported, the observations were probably spread out around that value. For example, if the news reports that the average North Korean uses 4% of the electricity used by the average American, you should consider that there are Americans who use less electricity than that, and there are North Koreans who use more electricity than the average American.

Here is an example for you to practice with. Be wary, because when people are talking about averages, they do not always say so. Commenting on the commotion that came after that 1980 *Newsweek* article, Susan Baxter wrote this:

> *After the girls-can't-do-math flurry, psychologist Jackie Eccles, in a longitudinal study, found that mothers who had read the news reports subsequently had lower expectations of their daughters' math competence than before.*
>
> —BAXTER, *PSYCHOLOGY TODAY*, MARCH 1994

Did the *Newsweek* article convince all mothers that their daughters were less mathematically able? Probably not. Think of a possible histogram of mothers' ratings of their daughters' abilities. It is probably people's mean judgment that was lower after they read the *Newsweek* article. That is usually what news writers would mean by "mothers had lower expectations." Some mothers may have reported higher expectation after reading the article. Our best guess as to what Susan Baxter is telling us is that, *on the average,* mothers' reported expectations were lower. That does not tell us how the mothers' reports were spread out or how often the article raised mothers' expectations of their girls' abilities.

You need to make it a habit to imagine histograms spread out whenever you read about averages. Here are two more quotes to practice on:

> *Despite getting better grades and taking more honors courses in mathematics and sciences, Massachusetts girls nonetheless lagged boys by 39 points on average in their combined scores, mirroring the national gender gap.*
>
> —HART, *BOSTON GLOBE*, AUGUST 27, 1997

> *"Young women earn higher grades than their male counterparts when matched for identical courses in both college and high school, despite their lower scores on the SAT," said Bob Schaeffer of the Boston-based FairTest, referring to studies done by the test makers themselves.*
>
> —BINGHAM, *DENVER POST*, AUGUST 27, 1997

What do these two quotes tell us? Do all girls get higher grades in high school math and college courses than all boys? No. That would be wrong. Girls do get higher grades than boys in high school and college math and science—on the average. However, many boys get higher grades than many girls. It is when you look at only the centers of the distributions that you get the impression of girls doing better than boys.

Differences Compared to Spread

When you look at how boys' and girls' SAT math scores are spread out, the 36-point difference between the boys' mean and the girls' mean does not look very interesting. Sometimes the difference between the means is larger. Table 5.2.1 shows mean scores broken down by family income. The difference between the mean math scores of the richest and poorest teenagers is 125 points.

Table 5.2.1 shows that the mean math score for children from families earning less than $10,000 was 444. Did all of those students get 444 on the math SATs? No. Those students had math scores that were spread out above and below the mean. The Educational Testing Service reports that, overall, the standard deviation is 100 points. If the standard deviation were 100 points for each group in Table 5.2.1, then histograms of the math SAT scores for the richest and poorest students would look something like what is shown in Figure 5.2.3.

Table 5.2.1 SAT Scores for Students from Families with Different Incomes

FAMILY INCOME	MEAN VERBAL SCORE	MEAN MATH SCORE
Less than $10,000	429	444
$10,000–$20,000	456	464
$80,000–$100,000	541	544
More than $100,000	560	569

Source: Data from Anderluh, *Sacramento Bee,* September 23, 1997.

Figure 5.2.3 **Distribution of Math SAT Scores of Students from Low- and High-Income Families**

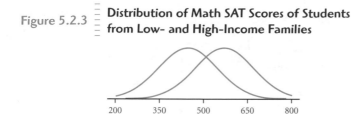

Math SAT Score

In Figure 5.2.3, the lump on the right represents scores for students from families who earned more than $100,000. The lump on the left represents students from families who earned less than $10,000. Notice that the two distributions overlap quite a bit. Some students whose parents earned $8,000 a year got 650, and some students whose parents earned $105,000 a year got 300.

Variation in groups does not always make the difference in means look unimportant, but there is almost always variation within groups, and neither the mean nor median highlight that variation. When summarizing number line observations, it is best to report the mean, the median, and something about how the observations were spread out.

How to Summarize Number Line Measurements

When summarizing number line measurements, remember to report both the mean and the median, along with some indication of how widely spread out the measurements were.

Weighted Means

We have discussed two kinds of averages, the mean and the median. There is another average that shows up in the news, a weighted average:

> *Gasoline prices experienced their biggest jump in nearly a decade. . . . The weighted average, including all grades and taxes, was $1.0869 . . . a gallon Friday, up 8.41 cents from two weeks earlier, according to the Lundberg Survey of 10,000 gas stations nationwide.*
>
> —DETROIT NEWS, MARCH 22, 1999

> *The Illinois economy is on a steady course of growth, thanks to low inflation and low unemployment, the University of Illinois' Flash Economic Index shows. . . . The index is a weighted average of Illinois growth rates in corporate earnings, consumer spending and personal income.*
>
> —CHICAGO SUN-TIMES, MARCH 2, 1999

Shoppers should get some relief from credit card payments this year, as interest rates are starting to go down again. . . . The weighted average annual percentage rate is 18.08 percent this year for standard, gold and platinum cards, compared with 18.11 percent in 1997.

—*Arizona Republic*, November 28, 1998

The usual weighted average is a weighted mean. (There is also a weighted median, but it is not used as often.) The weighted mean gives some measurements more weight and others less when you calculate a mean. If you have ever had a teacher who said that a certain portion of your grade is determined by some work and a larger portion of your grade is determined by some other work, your grade was a weighted mean. The way weighted means work is that every measurement gets multiplied by its weight before you add the measurements. Then, rather than dividing by the number of measurements, you add all the weights and divide by the sum of the weights.

How to Calculate a Weighted Mean

To find a weighted mean, each observation is first multiplied by its weight. All of the observation-weight products are added up. Then the sum is divided by the sum of the weights.

For example, I might like to find the mean length of service in the armed forces for a number of veterans. One group has three veterans with an average of three years of service. Another group has two veterans with an average of seven years. If I wanted to calculate the average of all five veterans, I could weight those lengths by the group sizes. In that case, the products would be 9 and 14. The sum of the products would be 23. The sum of the weights would be 5, and the weighted mean would be 4.6.

Calculating a Weighted Mean with Weights That Sum to 100

	GRADE	NUMERIC GRADE	WEIGHT	GRADE TIMES WEIGHT
MIDTERM	C	2	30	60
FINAL	A	4	70	280
			SUM 100	340

Weighted Mean = 340/100 = 3.4 = B+

In the case of teachers calculating grades, the weights are the portions of your grade that each test determines. For example, let's say that 30% of your grade is determined by your midterm exam and 70% by your final exam. Let's say you get a C on the midterm and an A on the final. Table 5.2.2 is a worksheet your teacher might use to figure out your grade.

To find your weighted mean, the teacher multiplied the weights (30 and 70) by your grades and got 60 and 280. Your weighted mean was then the sum (60 plus 280, which equals 340) divided by the sum of the weights (100).

The weighted mean ended up closer to your final exam grade, because more weight was put on your final exam than on your midterm. In this case, the weights added up to 100, but that is not always the case. Weights can sensibly add up to anything above 0. For example, weights can be decimals. This grading example would come out exactly the same if you considered the weights to be 0.3 and 0.7, as shown in Table 5.2.3.

Weighted means are used to calculate students' GPAs when courses have varying amounts of credits. For example, if a student earned an A in a five-credit course, a B in a three-credit course, and failed a one-credit course, the credits would be the weights for the average, and the calculations would be as you see in Table 5.2.4.

Table 5.2.3 Calculating a Weighted Mean with Weights That Sum to 1

	GRADE	NUMERIC GRADE	WEIGHT	GRADE TIMES WEIGHT
MIDTERM	C	2	0.3	0.6
FINAL	A	4	0.7	2.8
			SUM 1	3.4

Weighted Mean = 3.4/1 = 3.4 = B+

Table 5.2.4 Calculating a Weighted Mean to Find a GPA with Course Credits

NUMERIC GRADE	CREDITS	GRADE TIMES WEIGHT
4	5	20
3	3	9
0	1	0
SUM 9		29

Weighted Mean = 29/9 = 3.22 = B+

Earlier in this section there is a quote about a weighted mean of gasoline prices. Here's the quote again:

> *Gasoline prices experienced their biggest jump in nearly a decade. . . .*
> *The weighted average, including all grades and taxes, was $1.0869 . . .*
> *a gallon Friday, up 8.41 cents from two weeks earlier, according to the*
> *Lundberg Survey of 10,000 gas stations nationwide.*
>
> —DETROIT NEWS, MARCH 22, 1999

You might wonder why the researchers would calculate a weighted mean in this case. The reason is that each brand has a particular price and a particular portion of the market. Rather than calculating the mean, which would give equal attention to every brand, the researchers weighted the brands according to how much they sold. They weighted the prices by the number of gallons sold. For example, let's say that Welsh Standard Oil sells 1,000 gallons at $1.10 per gallon, that CutRite Oil sells 10 gallons at $0.10 a gallon, and Rock Oil sells 2,000 gallons at $1.09 per gallon.

Table 5.2.5 Calculating a Weighted Mean Gasoline Price

BRAND	PRICE	GALLONS SOLD	PRICE TIMES GALLONS SOLD
Welsh Standard	$1.10	1,000	1,100
CutRite	$0.10	10	1
Rock	$1.09	2,000	2,180
		SUM 3,010	3,181

Weighted Mean = 3,181/3,010 = $1.06

Table 5.2.5 shows what our calculations would be.

In this example, even though CutRite had an extremely low price ($0.10), it had little effect on the weighted mean, because its weight (10) was very small compared to that of the other companies.

Another quote earlier in this section was about an index created to represent how the Illinois economy was doing. Here's that quote again:

> The Illinois economy is on a steady course of growth, thanks to low inflation and low unemployment, the University of Illinois' Flash Economic Index shows. . . . The index is a weighted average of Illinois growth rates in corporate earnings, consumer spending and personal income.
>
> —CHICAGO SUN-TIMES, MARCH 2, 1999

In this case, there are three growth rates (corporate earnings, consumer spending, and personal income). If you were a researcher studying the Illinois economy, you might decide that some of these growth areas are more important than others. For example, you might feel that consumer spending is twice as important as corporate earnings. To indicate that, you could use a weight of 2 for consumer spending and a weight of 1 for corporate earnings. If you felt that personal income was three times as important as consumer spending, you would give personal income a weight of 6 (three times as great as your weight for consumer spending).

Let's imagine that corporate earnings has increased 15%, consumer spending has increased 10%, and personal income has increased 5%. In that case, our calculation of the weighted average would be as shown in Table 5.2.6.

Table 5.2.6 Calculating a Weighted Mean Growth Rate

ECONOMIC SECTOR	INCREASE	WEIGHT	WEIGHTED INCREASE
Corporate Earnings	15%	1	0.15
Consumer Spending	10%	2	0.2
Personal Income	5%	6	0.3
		SUM 9	0.65

Weighted Mean $= 0.65/9 = 0.072 = 7.2\%$

Algebra and Greek Symbols

Some standard symbols are used to represent the concepts in this section. The standard deviation in a sample is represented by "s" or "sd." The standard deviation in a population is represented by "σ" (sigma).

Summary

The median is almost immune to errors in data collection, because it is not affected by distributions' tails. A report should provide both the mean and the median.

Observations are usually spread out in a sample. When a mean is reported, you should assume, unless told otherwise, that most of the observations were either above or below the mean. The standard deviation tells you how far observations typically fall away from the sample mean. The standard deviation is close to the mean distance from each observation to the sample mean.

A weighted mean is calculated by first multiplying each observation by its weight to produce a list of products. The weighted mean is the sum of the products divided by the sum of the weights.

Avoiding Common Misunderstandings

The most common misunderstanding of the weighted mean is to think it is not important. Weighted means appear in many places, and we will be using them later in this book.

Computer Project

How are sample means distributed? To find out, have your software take many random samples from the U.S. Representative Sample you looked at in previous computer projects, and save the sample means. Get a histogram of the sample means. How would you describe the distribution? What is the mean? What is the median?

In Section 5.1, it is claimed that a normal distribution is symmetrical. Test that idea by using a simulation to collect a distribution of proportions that are normally distributed. Check the mean and median. Does the distribution appear symmetrical?

Exercises

1. The first table in this exercise shows how many people died of AIDS in the United States during 1994. The table breaks down the death rates by the ages of the people who died. For example, 81 infants died of AIDS, as did 72 teenagers between 15 and 19 years of age. This table also shows the AIDS death rate per 100,000 people in each age group. The table's data are all from the Centers for Disease Control's Web site at *www.cdc.gov.*

   The second table in this exercise shows similar data for heart disease. Some people have argued that government spending on AIDS has been out of proportion, because so many more people die from heart disease than from AIDS, and the ratio of funding levels for the two diseases does not match the ratio of the numbers of deaths. For example, here is a report on what Senator Jesse Helms concluded from this sort of data:

   > The Republican from North Carolina [Jesse Helms] argued that AIDS gets a disproportionately large amount of funding for medical research despite being only the ninth-leading cause of death in the United States. . . . "I'm going to try to get some equity for people who have had heart trouble," said the senator.
   >
   > —ASSOCIATED PRESS, JULY 5, 1995

   Write a brief letter to the editor about what these two tables show about how the two diseases differ and what this should add to the government's deliberations about research funding levels.

AGE AT DEATH	NUMBER OF AIDS DEATHS	AIDS DEATHS PER 100,000
Under 1 Year	81	2.04
1–4 Years	178	1.12
5–9 Years	99	0.52
10–14 Years	64	0.34
15–19 Years	72	0.40
20–24 Years	544	2.96
25–34 Years	11,624	28.10
35–44 Years	17,613	42.27
45–54 Years	7,293	24.41
55–64 Years	2,074	9.86
65–74 Years	553	2.95
75–84 Years	90	0.82
Over 85 Years	9	0.25

AGE AT DEATH	NUMBER OF HEART DISEASE DEATHS	HEART DISEASE DEATHS PER 100,000
Under 1 Year	685	17.32
1–4 Years	285	1.79
5–9 Years	129	0.68
10–14 Years	198	1.05
15–19 Years	376	2.13
20–24 Years	616	3.36
25–34 Years	3,520	8.51
35–44 Years	13,243	31.78
45–54 Years	33,621	112.55
55–64 Years	69,335	329.89
65–74 Years	152,948	817.39
75–84 Years	228,658	2,093.03
Over 85 Years	228,724	6,494.86

2. Here is a report that uses averages to describe immigration rates:

> *The study by Rand Corporation . . . calls on Congress to reduce new legal [immigration] admissions to a "moderate range"—somewhere between the 300,000 annual average of the 1970s and the 1990s median of about 800,000.*
>
> —McDonnell, *Los Angeles Times*, June 23, 1997

The *Statistical Abstract of the United States, 1996* reports that during 1991, 1992, and 1993, a total of 3,705,000 people legally immigrated to the United States. From 1971 to 1980, there were 4,493,000 legal immigrations. Write a brief note explaining what the mean rates of yearly immigration were during the early 1990s and during the 1970s. Note what kind of an average the "300,000 annual average of the 1970s" is. Compare these means to the figures provided by the Rand Corporation. Sketch histograms showing how yearly immigration rates have been distributed during these two time periods. Make a guess as to why the Rand Corporation chose to release the kinds of averages it released, when it could have released other averages.

3. Here is a report using an average to describe children's experiences in foster care:

> *The average time spent by children in foster care more than doubled, to 4.4 years in 1996 from 2.1 years in 1990. But Maggie Lear, a spokeswoman for [New York] city's Administration for Children's Services, said the median stay for children in foster care was 2.5 years.*
>
> —Holloway, *New York Times*, August 12, 1997

Imagine that a reader writes to the newspaper deploring that children are spending four and a half years in foster care. Write a short follow-up letter explaining the reader's mistake and giving a better conception of what is happening. (As you think about this, you might want to sketch a histogram of the length of the foster care stays.)

4. Here is a comment about means and standard deviations from the *London Independent*:

> *The trouble is that arithmetic means make sense only when they come from a distribution with a low standard deviation (the average deflection from the average).*
>
> —Hartston, *London Independent*, October 2, 1997

Imagine that a friend sends you a note asking what Hartston means. Write a brief explanation of this quote.

5. Here are some comments about the standard deviation:

> *Standard deviation, which most investors have heard of, is perhaps the most commonly used measure of volatility.*
>
> —*[LONDON] FINANCIAL TIMES, APRIL 24, 1997*

> *High-yield stocks—ones that pay high dividends as a percentage of their price—returned 13 percent but had a standard deviation of just 17 percent.*
>
> —GLASSMAN, *WASHINGTON POST, SEPTEMBER 14, 1997*

The return is the interest you get from an investment. In the preceding quote, Glassman means that the average return was 13%, but the standard deviation of the returns was 17%. Negative percentages can happen when the percentages are returns on investments. For example, a −10% return means that you lost 10% of your investment. On the average, about how far were the returns from 13%?

6. Here is another report on investing:

> *These results are confirmed by calculating a more direct measure of risk known as standard deviation, which measures the dispersion in returns. The standard deviation of annual stock returns has been 21 per cent historically, compared with 10 per cent on bonds.*
>
> —*[LONDON] FINANCIAL TIMES, JUNE 30, 1997*

Imagine that your Aunt Minnie has retirement money she needs to invest. Write her a brief note explaining what this quote tells you about how stock returns change from year to year. Mention also what this tells you about how bond returns change.

7. Imagine that a student has taken three classes. The following table lists the credits and numerical grade equivalents on the student's record. What is the student's GPA? (Remember that a GPA is a weighted mean of the grades, where the credits are the weights.)

CREDITS	NUMERICAL GRADE EQUIVALENT
5	3
1	4
4	2

8. The following table shows a record for another student. What is this student's GPA?

CREDITS	NUMERICAL GRADE EQUIVALENT
5	4
1	1
4	3
5	4

9. A professor has announced that a midterm exam will count for 20% of students' course grades. The midterm is the first graded work in the class. Imagine that a student makes some mistakes and gets a 0 on the midterm. How much does that restrict the student's grade in the course? Specifically, if the student does A work for the rest of the course, what will the student's course grade be?

10. A professor has announced that a midterm exam will count for 10% of students' course grades. The midterm is the first graded work in the class. Imagine that a student makes mistakes and gets a 0 on the midterm. How much does that restrict the student's grade in the course? Specifically, if the student does A work for the rest of the course, what will the student's course grade be?

11. A company has given two job applicants two tests. Each applicant's performance is rated on a scale of 1 to 10 (10 being best) on each test. The company's previous experience is that test A deserves twice as much attention as test B, because it is twice as accurate in predicting job performance. The following table shows the two applicants' ratings.

	TEST A	TEST B
APPLICANT 1	6	3
APPLICANT 2	2	9

According to the company's standards, what should be the candidates' weighted ratings, and which one should be hired?

12. A company has given two job applicants two tests. Each applicant's performance is rated on a scale of 1 to 10 (10 being best) on each test. The company's previous experience is that test B deserves three times as

much attention as test A, because it is three times as accurate in predicting job performance. The following table shows the two applicants' ratings.

	TEST A	TEST B
APPLICANT 1	10	3
APPLICANT 2	2	6

According to the company's standards, what should be the candidates' weighted ratings, and which one should be hired?

13. A quote earlier in this section about credit card rates is repeated here.

> *Shoppers should get some relief from credit card payments this year, as interest rates are starting to go down again. . . . The weighted average annual percentage rate is 18.08 percent this year for standard, gold and platinum cards, compared with 18.11 percent in 1997.*
>
> —*Arizona Republic*, November 28, 1998

a. What might the researchers have used for weights in this case?

b. Why did the researchers choose to use a weighted average rather than a regular average?

14. If you calculated a weighted mean, and all of the weights were the same, how would the result compare to a regular mean?

Answers to Odd-Numbered Exercises

1. "Dear Editor, This letter is regarding the objection that so much funding goes to AIDS research rather than heart disease research. The most common age of patients who die of AIDS is somewhere between 35 and 44 years, about 25 years before a typical American would expect to die. The mean age at death from AIDS is lower than that. Most deaths from heart disease happen after age 75, which is when people tend to be dying no matter what. Between 25 and 34, the death rate due to AIDS is 28 per 100,000, whereas the death rate due to heart disease in that age bracket is 9 per 100,000. This is not to say that heart disease attacks only the very old. At all ages above 45, heart disease kills more people than does AIDS. My point is only that the consideration of how serious a problem a disease is for society needs to take into account how old people are when they die, not just how many people

are killed by the disease. If some disease is wiping out people over 110, that's not as much of a concern as a disease that kills the same number of infants."

3. "Dear Editor, this letter is in response to the letter about the children spending four and a half years in foster care. That 'four and a half years' is an average. Averages produce the mistaken impression that everyone experienced the average. In fact, experiences are spread around the average. Some children spend one week. Other children spend eight years. Most children, more than half, spend less than three years in foster care. The average stay is 4.4 years, because a few children spend quite a bit more than four years in foster care."

5. 17%. That is the standard deviation.

7.

CREDITS	NUMERICAL GRADE EQUIVALENT	CREDITS TIMES GRADE
5	3	15
1	4	4
4	2	8
SUM 9		27

Weighted Mean = 27/9 = 3 = B

9.

	GRADE	WEIGHT	WEIGHTED GRADE
MIDTERM	0	0.2	0
REST	4	0.8	3.2
	SUM 1.0		3.2

Weighted Mean = 3.2/1 = 3.2 = B+

(Remember that 20% equals 0.2.)

11. Applicant 1

TEST	RATING	WEIGHT	WEIGHTED RATING
A	6	2	12
B	3	1	3
	SUM 3		15

Applicant 1's Weighted Mean Rating = 15/3 = 5

Applicant 2

TEST	RATING	WEIGHT	WEIGHTED RATING
A	2	2	4
B	9	1	9
		SUM 3	13

Applicant 2's Weighted Mean Rating $= 13/3 = 4.33$

According to its standards, the company should hire Applicant 1.

13. a. Their weights could have been the number of dollars charged in a year through each credit card company, the number of dollars left on cards to be charged interest per month at each company, or the number of card holders at each company.

   b. If they had used a regular average, the average would have been overly influenced by tiny credit card companies and not influenced enough by very large credit card companies.

5.3 Inflation and the Consumer Price Index

• Adjusting for Inflation

The rich got richer, the poor got poorer, and the giant middle class did a bit better than treading water last year. . . . For families, the biggest gains were recorded by the richest 20 percent, who had a 2.2 percent increase. Income for the poorest 20 percent fell by 1.8 percent.

—SCHMID, ASSOCIATED PRESS, SEPTEMBER 30, 1997

T HE U.S. CENSUS BUREAU provides yearly reports on how American families are doing financially. These reports allow us to check whether things are getting worse or better for Americans. The preceding quote is about how things looked in the 1997 Census Bureau report.

Schmid reports that, in 1996, incomes rose 2.2% for the richest 20% of American families and fell 1.8% for the poorest 20%. Schmid thinks the rich are getting richer and the poor are getting poorer. Not everyone got that impression of the Census Bureau report:

We have been deluged by the media and a lot of politicians . . . telling us that the rich are getting richer and the poor are getting poorer. . . . But is that information true or is it something of a myth?

—HARWOOD, *WASHINGTON POST*, OCTOBER 21, 1996

These quotes deserve a lot of consideration. Let's start from the top. I think I know what rich and poor are, but I often get confused about who the "middle class" are. Before I could talk about "the rich," "the poor," and "the middle class," I would have to figure out who were and who were not in each group.

In this case, Schmid writes about the richest 20% and the poorest 20%. I would guess that those are "the rich" and "the poor." That leaves the other 60% to be "the middle class."

Schmid reports that his information was from the Census Bureau, which has a Web site for distributing information at *www.census.gov*. That site includes a copy of a press release on U.S. incomes that the Census Bureau gave out on September 29, 1997. Schmid's article came out on September 30, probably reporting on that press release. In that release, the Census Bureau reports that its information came from a survey:

Data from the March Supplement to the Current Population Survey or CPS are the basis for these statistics. The CPS is a sample survey of

> *approximately 50,000 households nationwide, conducted each*
> *month for the Bureau of Labor Statistics. . . . As in all surveys, the*
> *data in these reports are estimates, subject to sampling variability*
> *and response errors.*
>
> —WEINBERG, U.S. CENSUS BUREAU, SEPTEMBER 29, 1997

The CPS is a big survey—about 50,000 households. At its Web site, the Census Bureau provides the full results of the survey. Anyone with the right software can download that data from *www.census.gov,* and check what Weinberg and Schmid said.

In his article for the Associated Press, Schmid writes, "For families, the biggest gains were recorded by the richest 20 percent, who had a 2.2 percent increase." The next sentence makes it somewhat clear that he is talking about an increase in incomes. What are the things that Schmid is omitting here? He omits what the percentage increase was in terms of dollars. He gives us only the percentage change, which is unfortunate. He is also not highlighting the variation between families. Did every rich family get exactly a 2.2% raise? No. Some saw their incomes go down. Some saw their incomes rise much more than 2.2%. That 2.2% change is some sort of average. Schmid omits to say whether it is a median or a mean and provides no indication of how spread out the income changes were from household to household.

Schmid omits some other important information: what inflation was and whether the 2.2% change included inflation. Imagine that I get a 2.2% raise, but inflation is 3%. My paycheck is for more money, but it buys me less than I could buy before.

Although Schmid did not include information about inflation, if it were important to you, you could look elsewhere to fill in the gaps. In this case, we can look at the Census Bureau's Web site. Weinberg at the Census Bureau reports this:

> *All historical income data are expressed in 1996 dollars using the*
> *Consumer Price Index; inflation was 3.0 percent between 1995 and*
> *1996. . . . Median income for all U.S. households rose 1.2 percent or*
> *$410 between 1995 and 1996 to $35,492. . . . Average income in*
> *the lowest quintile fell 1.8 percent, while the average income in the*
> *middle-income quintile rose 1.5 percent, and average income in the*
> *top quintile rose 2.2 percent.*
>
> —WEINBERG, U.S. CENSUS BUREAU, SEPTEMBER 29, 1997

A quintile is one-fifth (20%) of the population. The top quintile is the richest fifth (the richest 20%) of the population. The Census Bureau reports median incomes. The 2.2% rise in the top quintile's incomes was probably a rise in the median income of the top quintile.

In the preceding quote, Weinberg writes, "All historical income data are expressed in 1996 dollars using the Consumer Price Index." This is telling us how inflation was dealt with in creating the report. "1996 dollars" are dollar amounts that have been adjusted for inflation.

Here is what I mean by "adjusted for inflation." In 1967, you could buy a newspaper for a dime. By 1996, some newspapers cost $0.50. We would say that someone with a dime in 1967 had $0.50 in terms of 1996 dollars. When we say "in terms of 1967 dollars" or "in 1996 dollars," we are talking about dollars that are adjusted for inflation.

Another term for dollar amounts that have been adjusted for inflation is "real dollars." For example, the following quote means that in Florida less buying power is available to help a student go to college:

> *The maximum [Florida Student Assistance] grant of $972 is actually $228 less than it was in 1972, when the program started. That is in real dollars.*
>
> —HARPER, St. Petersburg Times, February 9, 1997

All real dollar amounts have been adjusted to some year, such as 1996, 1965, or 1972. When someone writes "1996 dollars," it is shorthand for "real dollars adjusted to 1996." The Census Bureau report used 1996 dollars. The report's 2.2% increase is after adjusting to 1996 dollars. That means that the 2.2% was not just inflation. There was a real 2.2% increase in the buying power of the wealthiest quintile.

Real Dollars

When a report says how much a dollar amount has changed in terms of "real dollars," it means how much the dollar amount has changed after adjusting prices for inflation.

For example, if someone earned $30,000 in 1995 and $33,000 in 1996, that is a 10% increase in raw dollars, but not a 10% increase in that person's buying power. Inflation in 1995 was 3%, so the $30,000 earned in 1995 is like earning 3% more ($30,900) in 1996. The increase in buying power is from $30,900 to $33,000, which is a 7% rise. In terms of real dollars, this person's wages increased 7%, not 10%.

Before you can adjust dollar amounts for inflation, you need to know what inflation was. To measure inflation, the Bureau of Labor Statistics (which is part of the Department of Labor) keeps track of what is called the "Consumer Price Index," or "CPI." To calculate the CPI, the Bureau of Labor Statistics keeps a list of almost 400 goods and services. Each year, the Bureau randomly samples stores and companies, shopping the country to see how much it would cost to buy these 400 items. It averages the prices it finds and then adds up the average costs of the goods and services, as if the surveyors were in a giant supermarket and had put all the goods and services in one market basket. To find the amount of inflation, it divides the change in the market basket's total cost by the basket's total cost the previous year. For example, if the market basket cost $30,000 last year and costs $31,200 this year, then the cost rose $1,200. The increase of $1,200 divided by last year's $30,000 is 4%. That would be 4% inflation, which means that it takes 4% more dollars today to buy the same goods and services we bought last year.

Rather than reporting the total price of the market basket, the Bureau of Labor Statistics divides the cost of the market basket by what the market basket cost in late 1983 and then multiplies by 100. (The Bureau always uses 1983, which is arbitrary, but constant.) What it ends up with is the Consumer Price Index. Because the Bureau divides by the total from the winter of 1983 and multiplies by 100, the CPI for 1983 overall is just a little bit below 100. Table 5.3.1 shows the CPI from 1913 to 2001. Note that the third column shows what inflation was during that year; that is, the percentage change from the beginning of the year listed to the beginning of the next year.

When averages are divided by a constant, such as the price of the 1983 market basket, you get what is called an "index." For example, the Dow Jones Industrial Average is not actually an average. It is an index. The Dow Jones Industrial Average is found by averaging the prices of a set of stocks and then dividing by a constant. At one time, in the 1950s, the constant was selected so that the Dow Jones Industrial Average would be 100. Now the Dow is in the thousands, and has been more than 10,000.

The Consumer Price Index (CPI)

To measure inflation, the Bureau of Labor Statistics shops America finding the average prices of a set of goods and services. The CPI is the cost of this metaphorical market basket of goods divided by the market basket's cost in late 1983 and then multiplied by 100.

You can use the CPI to adjust for inflation. To translate from one year to another, first divide by the CPI of the year from which you are translating and then multiply by the CPI of the year to which you are translating. For example, to translate from 1913 dollars to 1997 dollars, you would divide by 9.9 and then multiply by 160.5. A penny candy bought in 1913 cost about 16 cents in terms of 1997 dollars.

.3.1 The CPI and Inflation

YEAR	CPI	INFLATION	YEAR	CPI	INFLATION	YEAR	CPI	INFLATION
1913	9.9	1.0%	1943	17.3	1.7%	1973	44.4	11.0%
1914	10.0	1.0%	1944	17.6	2.3%	1974	49.3	9.1%
1915	10.1	7.9%	1945	18.0	8.3%	1975	53.8	5.8%
1916	10.9	17.4%	1946	19.5	14.4%	1976	56.9	6.5%
1917	12.8	18.0%	1947	22.3	8.1%	1977	60.6	7.6%
1918	15.1	14.6%	1948	24.1	−1.1%	1978	65.2	11.3%
1919	17.3	15.6%	1949	23.8	1.3%	1979	72.6	13.5%
1920	20.0	−10.4%	1950	24.1	7.9%	1980	82.4	10.3%
1921	17.9	−6.0%	1951	26.0	1.9%	1981	90.9	6.2%
1922	16.8	1.8%	1952	26.5	0.8%	1982	96.5	3.2%
1923	17.1	0.0%	1953	26.7	0.7%	1983	99.6	4.3%
1924	17.1	2.3%	1954	26.9	−0.3%	1984	103.9	3.6%
1925	17.5	1.1%	1955	26.8	1.5%	1985	107.6	1.9%
1926	17.7	−1.6%	1956	27.2	3.3%	1986	109.6	3.6%
1927	17.4	−1.6%	1957	28.1	2.8%	1987	113.6	4.1%
1928	17.1	0.0%	1958	28.9	0.7%	1988	118.3	4.8%
1929	17.1	−2.2%	1959	29.1	1.7%	1989	124.0	5.4%
1930	16.7	−8.9%	1960	29.6	1.0%	1990	130.7	4.2%
1931	15.2	−9.8%	1961	29.9	1.0%	1991	136.2	3.0%
1932	13.7	−5.0%	1962	30.2	1.3%	1992	140.3	3.0%
1933	13.0	3.1%	1963	30.6	1.3%	1993	144.5	2.6%
1934	13.4	2.2%	1964	31.0	1.6%	1994	148.2	2.8%
1935	13.7	1.5%	1965	31.5	2.9%	1995	152.4	3.0%
1936	13.9	3.6%	1966	32.4	3.1%	1996	156.9	2.3%
1937	14.4	−2.0%	1967	33.4	4.2%	1997	160.5	1.6%
1938	14.1	−1.3%	1968	34.8	5.5%	1998	163.0	2.2%
1939	13.9	0.7%	1969	36.7	5.7%	1999	166.6	3.4%
1940	14.0	5.0%	1970	38.8	4.4%	2000	172.2	2.8%
1941	14.7	10.9%	1971	40.5	3.2%	2001	177.1	
1942	16.3	6.1%	1972	41.8	6.2%			

Source: U.S. Bureau of Labor Statistics.

Someone who was a millionaire in 1997 had about as much buying power as someone with 1/16 as much cash in 1913. A million 1997 dollars is only $61,682 in 1913 dollars.

If you have a table of the CPI handy, you can save yourself a lot of silly amazement at how cheap everything used to be. For example, here is a report on how much a hamburger used to cost at McDonald's:

> *McDonald's Corp. is throwing a birthday party for the Big Mac and rolling out promotions harking back to the venerable sandwich's birth in 1968. A three-week retro-style promotion starting Wednesday will bring Big Mac prices back to the 1968 cost—49 cents.*
>
> —MINNEAPOLIS STAR TRIBUNE, SEPTEMBER 11, 1998

How to Adjust for Inflation

To use the CPI to adjust for inflation, divide the raw dollar amount by the CPI of that dollar amount's year. Then multiply by the CPI of the year to which you are adjusting.

For example, in 1955 the CPI was 26.8. In 2001 the CPI was 177.1. In 1955 you could buy a loaf of bread for 10 cents. To adjust the $0.10 to 2001 dollars, we divide by 26.8 (and get 0.3731) and then multiply by 177.1. We find that the 10-cent loaf of bread cost 66 cents in terms of 2001 dollars.

Last time I checked (which was in 1998), a Big Mac cost $2.59. How has the Big Mac changed in price since 1968? To find out, we could transform the 1968 price ($0.49) to 1998 dollars. To do that, we divide by the 1968 CPI and multiply by the 1998 CPI. Here are the calculations:

$$\text{Price in 1998 Dollars} = \frac{\text{Price in 1968 Dollars} \times 1998 \text{ CPI}}{1968 \text{ CPI}}$$

According to Table 5.3.1, in 1968 the CPI was 34.8. In 1998, the CPI was 163.0. We plug in those numbers and the $0.49 for the 1968 price:

$$\text{Price in 1998 Dollars} = \frac{0.49 \times 163.0}{34.8} = \frac{79.87}{34.8} = 2.3$$

$$\text{Price in 1998 Dollars} = \$2.30$$

$2.30 is a little less than the $2.59 that I remember, but not a lot. It looks as though the price of a Big Mac has held pretty steady. The shocking appearance of the 1968 price, $0.49, is mostly just inflation.

Let's use this information to better understand Weinberg's quote from the Census Bureau report on income in 1996. To calculate how the median income had risen from 1995 to 1996, the Census Bureau first translated the 1995 median to 1996 dollars. In 1995 the CPI was 152.4, and in 1996 it was 156.9. To translate from 1995 dollars to 1996 dollars, you divide by 152.4 and then multiply by 156.9. That is the same as multiplying by 1.03. For example, a radio that cost $100 in 1995 would probably cost about $103 in 1996. If its price did go up 3% from 1995 to 1996, then its cost held steady in terms of real dollars. The inflation figure of 3% for 1995 also indicates that the real cost held steady.

The CPI Market Basket

Goods and services vary in how their prices change. Some, such as college tuition, lumber, and real estate, have prices that generally rise faster than inflation. Others, such as personal computers and handheld calculators, have prices that fall. Which goods and services are included in the market basket affect how the CPI changes. For example, if the CPI market basket were only college tuition, lumber, real estate, and health care, the CPI would have risen more quickly than it has. In contrast, if we included only personal computers and handheld calculators, we would find that there had been deflation. The Bureau of Labor Statistics has to deal with the thorny question of which goods and services to include in the CPI market basket, which ultimately can affect government services and economic policy.

Many government benefits, such as social security, are tied to inflation as calculated using the CPI. This can be a big problem for some retired people. Goods, like computers, that get cheaper make little difference in the life of many people on social security, because they are not buying computers. However, such people have seen their medical costs shoot up much more quickly than the CPI market basket. The result is that although their incomes are supposed to be adjusted for inflation, their buying power goes down, because their market basket is different from the CPI market basket.

What to include in the CPI market basket is a serious issue for U.S. policy makers. Some people believe that the CPI should use a market basket that responds

Table 5.3.2 CPI Values and Estimates Based on Prices Doubling Every 20 Years

YEAR	CPI	RULE OF THUMB CPI ESTIMATE
2001	177.1	177.1
1981	90.9	88.6
1961	29.9	44.3
1941	14.7	22.1
1921	17.9	11.1

more to technological advances and reflects the decreasing price of items such as personal computers. This approach would slow the CPI's increase, and therefore slow the increase in benefits for people who live on social security. That reduced cost would help bring down the national debt, but would hurt some seniors. There is no easy answer.

It is difficult to decide which goods and services to include in the CPI market basket. The ones that are included are a sample, and like all samples, they are imperfect. The CPI only gives us a ballpark guess as to the inflation a given person experiences.

Guideline for Estimating Inflation

A fairly accurate rule of thumb is to estimate that prices have doubled every 20 years. That means that $100 now is roughly like $50 of 20 years ago, roughly like $25 of 40 years ago, and roughly like $12.50 of 60 years ago. Table 5.3.2 shows what this rule of thumb would guess for CPI values going back from 2001 along with the actual CPI values. The "doubling in 20 years" rule of thumb is not totally accurate, but it is easy to remember and gives results that aren't too far off.

Geographic CPI

The purchasing power of a dollar varies geographically as well as in time. The most obvious example of this is the cost of renting an apartment. An apartment in a luxury neighborhood in New York City is much more expensive than the same-sized apartment in Jonesboro, Arkansas. To allow for comparisons of money across geography, the Bureau of Labor Statistics creates CPI statistics for geographic areas. Table 5.3.3 shows the CPI values for several metropolitan areas from December 2001 and January 2002.

The CPI values in Table 5.3.3 work the same way as the CPI values for years. For example, if you wanted to translate from Boston dollars to Houston dollars, you would divide by the Boston CPI and multiply by the Houston CPI. For example,

Table 5.3.3 Approximate CPI Values from December 2001 and January 2002

METROPOLITAN AREA	CPI
Houston–Galveston–Brazoria (Texas)	157
Dallas–Fort Worth (Texas)	171
Cleveland–Akron (Ohio)	171
Miami–Fort Lauderdale (Florida)	173
Detroit–Ann Arbor–Flint (Michigan)	174
Atlanta (Georgia)	175
Chicago–Gary–Kenosha (Illinois, Indiana, and Wisconsin)	178
Los Angeles–Riverside–Orange County (California)	178
Philadelphia–Wilmington–Atlantic City (Pennsylvania, Delaware, and New Jersey)	180
Seattle–Tacoma–Bremerton (Washington)	186
New York–Northern New Jersey–Long Island (New York and New Jersey)	188
San Francisco–Oakland–San Jose (California)	191
Boston–Brockton–Nashua (Massachusetts, Maine, and New Hampshire)	193

Janet in Boston is earning $40,000. Susan in Houston is earning $35,000. Who is earning more? In terms of Houston dollars, Janet is earning $40,000 divided by 193 multiplied by 157, which equals $32,539. Susan is earning more.

Another way to think about regional differences is to imagine that Janet's job becomes one of telecommuting over the Internet. It doesn't matter where she lives. If she were to move to Houston, her $40,000 salary would be $40,000 divided by 157 times 193, which equals $49,172 Boston dollars. The move would be nearly a 25% raise.

Algebra and Greek Symbols

This section shows how to adjust for inflation, using the federal Consumer Price Index (CPI). Let the CPI of year X be CPI_X. Let Y dollars adjusted to year X (or in year X) be $\$Y_X$. For example, $10 spent in 1945 would be $\$10_{1945}$.

$$\$Y_X = \$Y_Z \frac{CPI_X}{CPI_Z}$$

For example, $\$Y_{1973}$ equals $\$Y_{1945}$ times CPI_{1973} divided by CPI_{1945}.

Summary

The buying power of a dollar usually drops from year to year due to inflation. The Consumer Price Index (CPI) reveals inflation. The CPI is the typical cost of a particular set of goods and services divided by the cost of that set in late 1983 and then multiplied by 100. To adjust for inflation, divide by the CPI of the raw dollar amount's year and then multiply by the CPI of the year to which you are adjusting. Adjusted dollars are identified by the CPI of the year to which they have been adjusted and are sometimes referred to as "real" dollars. The buying power of a dollar varies with geography, and the Bureau of Labor Statistics provides CPI values for translating between dollar amounts in different places.

Avoiding Common Misunderstandings

Since 1940, inflation has been positive. If you do your calculations, and it appears that goods are costing less money in later years, then you probably divided when you should have multiplied and multiplied when you should have divided. For example, I'm told that in 1940 people could attend the movies for $0.10. If I try to convert that to 2001 dollars and get $0.008, I know I got the multiplication and division backward. When I try again the other way, I get, in 2001 dollars, that the cost was $1.27. That seems cheap, but I can tell that the direction is right.

Computer Project

Have your computer software do the work of Exercises 1 and 2 for this section.

Exercises

1. The following table shows median and mean U.S. household incomes, rounded to the nearest $1,000. The table's medians are from the *Statistical Abstract of the United States, 1996* and are not adjusted for inflation.

YEAR	MEDIAN INCOME	MEAN INCOME	YEAR	MEDIAN INCOME	MEAN INCOME
1967	$7	$8	1984	$22	$27
1968	$8	$9	1985	$24	$29
1969	$8	$10	1986	$25	$31
1970	$9	$10	1987	$26	$32
1971	$9	$10	1988	$27	$34
1972	$10	$11	1989	$29	$37
1973	$11	$12	1990	$30	$37
1974	$11	$13	1991	$30	$38
1975	$12	$14	1992	$31	$39
1976	$13	$15	1993	$31	$41
1977	$14	$16	1994	$32	$43
1978	$15	$18	1995	$34	$45
1979	$16	$20	1996	$35	$47
1980	$18	$21	1997	$37	$50
1981	$19	$23	1998	$39	$52
1982	$20	$24	1999	$41	$55
1983	$21	$25	2000	$42	$57

Source: U.S. Census Bureau.

Make a table showing median U.S. household incomes in real dollars for 1967 to 1983.

2. Using the table in Exercise 1, make a table showing median U.S. household incomes in real dollars for 1983 to 2000.

3. Using the table in Exercise 1, sketch a time-series graph showing the real median U.S. household incomes for 1967 to 1983. Put years on the x-axis and real income on the y-axis.

4. Using the table in Exercise 1, sketch a time-series graph showing the real median U.S. household incomes for 1983 to 2000.

5. A young man in 1967 began paying into a retirement fund. The fund guaranteed that, by 2000, the fund would pay the young man $8,000 a year. How do you think that young man felt about that $8,000? Do you think that he thought it would support him adequately?

6. Imagine that a young couple who are friends of yours began paying into a retirement fund in 2002. The fund guarantees that by 2050 it would pay your friends $57,000 a year. Write your friends a note explaining whether you feel this retirement fund will cover their expenses in their retirement.

7. Here is a report on Tooth Fairy payments:

> *In 1999, the Tooth Fairy is leaving an average of $1.30 per tooth. . . . That's up from $1.25 in 1998. . . . Delta conducts the survey each February. . . . Average rewards: In the 1950s, 19 cents a tooth. In the '60s, 29 cents. In the '70s, 46 cents. In the '80s, 88 cents.*
>
> —UNDERWOOD AND HOLSTON, *MINNEAPOLIS STAR TRIBUNE*, FEBRUARY 24, 1999

The Tooth Fairy payments in the preceding quote are raw dollar amounts. Make a table listing years and payments in real dollars. Use 1955 as the year for the "1950s" payment, 1965 for the "1960s" payment, and so on.

8. Using the quote in Exercise 7, sketch a time-series plot of Tooth Fairy payments in real dollars. Make sure that you are using a number line for your *x*-axis; the years 1998 and 1999 should be closer together than 1975 and 1985, and there should be a gap between 1985 and 1998.

9. The United States has about 100 million households. How many households are there in each class (poorest quintile, middle class, and richest quintile)?

10. The incomes for the richest quintile are right skewed. The incomes for the poorest quintile are left skewed. Explain why those skewnesses probably happen.

11. Why do medians make income inequalities look smaller than means would?

12. Here is some more from the Census Bureau on U.S. incomes:

> *As you can see, average income in the lowest quintile fell 1.8 percent [in real dollars], while the average income in the middle-income quintile rose 1.5 percent, and average income in the top quintile rose 2.2 percent. . . . This is the third consecutive year in which there was* no year-to-year change in overall income inequality—*there was no statistically significant change in quintile income shares between 1995 and 1996.*
>
> —WEINBERG, U.S. CENSUS BUREAU, SEPTEMBER 29, 1997

Weinberg reports that incomes for the poorest quintile fell 1.8% and incomes for the richest quintile rose 2.2%, but that there was no change in income inequality. This is a change in the income inequality seen in the Census Bureau's survey. The rich were richer; the poor were poorer. How can Weinberg say there was no change in income inequality?

13. Your friend is negotiating over salary for a job she has been offered in Seattle. Her mother, who lives in New York City, who knows a lot about

the kind of work that your friend is getting into, advises her to take no less than $40,000. Write a note to your friend explaining why she might want to adjust her mother's advice and explaining what $40,000 in New York translates to in Seattle.

14. Imagine that you are working as a programmer in San Francisco. You're earning $40,000. Your company has decided to save on office space by sending you home. In the future, you will be telecommuting, using e-mail and the Internet. You will never go into the office. You're considering moving to Miami. How will that change your buying power?

Answers to Odd-Numbered Exercises

1. The following table shows calculations to adjust the median incomes to 2001 dollars. To translate each median income to 2001 dollars, I divided it by its year's CPI and then multiplied by 2001's CPI (177.1). You could have adjusted to any year to have comparable values.

YEAR	RAW MEDIAN INCOME (THOUSANDS OF DOLLARS)	YEAR'S CPI	CPI OF 2001	MEDIAN INCOME (THOUSANDS OF 2001 DOLLARS)
1967	$7	33.4	171.1	$36
1968	$8	34.8	171.1	$39
1969	$8	36.7	171.1	$37
1970	$9	38.8	171.1	$40
1971	$9	40.5	171.1	$38
1972	$10	41.8	171.1	$41
1973	$11	44.4	171.1	$42
1974	$11	49.3	171.1	$38
1975	$12	53.8	171.1	$38
1976	$13	56.9	171.1	$39
1977	$14	60.6	171.1	$40
1978	$15	65.2	171.1	$39
1979	$16	72.6	171.1	$38
1980	$18	82.4	171.1	$37
1981	$19	90.9	171.1	$36
1982	$20	96.5	171.1	$35
1983	$21	99.6	171.1	$36

3.

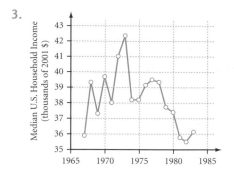

5. He probably thought he was setting himself up to live well. An annual income of $8,000 was the median in 1967. He would have been somewhat surprised to find out that by the time he was getting the $8,000, it was 14% of the median household income, although this would have sunk in sometime in the 1990s.

7.

YEAR	RAW TOOTH FAIRY PAYMENT	YEAR'S CPI	CPI OF 2001	TOOTH FAIRY PAYMENT (2001 DOLLARS)
1955	$0.19	26.8	171.1	$1.21
1965	$0.29	31.5	171.1	$1.58
1975	$0.46	53.8	171.1	$1.46
1985	$0.88	107.6	171.1	$1.40
1998	$1.25	163.0	171.1	$1.31
1999	$1.30	166.6	171.1	$1.34

9. In the United States, there are about 100 million households. The poorest quintile has 20% of the households, which are about 20 million households. The richest quintile also has about 20 million households. The other 60 million households are called the "middle class."

11. Because the incomes in the poorest quintile are left skewed, the median is higher than the mean, making the poorest people look richer than they would if you reported the mean. In the richest quintile, the incomes are right skewed, and the median is lower than the mean. This makes the incomes of the richest quintile look closer to the incomes of the poorest quintile.

13. The buying power of a dollar is different in Seattle than it is in New York. The Bureau of Labor Statistics says that to translate from New York dollars to Seattle dollars, you should multiply by 186 and divide by 188. Your mom's $40,000 in New York is the same buying power as $39,574 in Seattle. So, if they only offer you $39,600, that offer is a little over the $40,000 your mom is talking about.

PART II *Statistics in Science*
Descriptive and Inferential Statistics for Continuous Data

A liberal education includes an introduction to the sciences as well as to the humanities. Liberally educated people can read and learn from reports in biology and anthropology as well as novels. Part I of this text prepared you to read statistics in the news. Part II prepares you to read statistics in the social and natural sciences.

Because chi-square tests and tests of categorical data were covered in Part I, Part II focuses on numeric data, such as temperatures and incomes. Part II presents a test of correlation between categorical measurements and numeric measurements (the ANOVA), and wraps up with a test of correlation between two number line measurements (Pearson's correlation test).

Summaries and Abstracts

In the sciences, it is traditional to provide an abstract at the beginning of a report or article. An abstract is a summary, like the summaries that have appeared at the ends of the sections in Part I. To help you become accustomed to the idea of reading abstracts, for the rest of this book, the section summaries are called abstracts.

CHAPTER 6

What Sample Data Distribution Reveals About the Population

Things vary. For example, different people have different opinions. Different days have different temperatures. Different diseases have different impacts. When we study things, we end up with a variety of measurements—different heights, different prices, or different distances. We need tools to understand the diversity in what we see. Sections 6.1 and 6.2 provide those tools. Section 6.3 explores what the diversity we see tells us about the diversity to expect in the future. Diversity is harder to think about than uniformity, and that's a wonderful challenge.

6.1 Exploratory Data Analysis

- Histograms
- Stem-and-Leaf Plots
- Box Plots

Over a lifetime, a college graduate today will earn an average of $1 million more than a high school graduate, and those with professional degrees increase the gap on average to $3 million.

—YUDOF, *CHANGE*, MARCH 2002

EDUCATION IMPROVES YOUR LIFE in many ways. Being taught not to stick forks into electrical outlets lengthens your life, as does being taught that gasoline vapors are heavier than air. Learning about minimalism and realism can allow you to see beauty in the worst urban blight. What else? Oh, yes, education may affect your income as well.

Yudof reports that college graduates earn $1 million more than high school graduates. What does that come out to per year? Let's say that Americans work 60 years, from age 15 to 75. One-sixtieth of $1 million is a little less than $17,000. The claim is that college graduates earn about $17,000 more per year than high school graduates. If the average American works fewer years, the gap must be larger.

The preceding quote reports that people with professional degrees (for example, doctors, lawyers, and dentists) earn an average of $3 million more than high school graduates. If everyone works 60 years, the doctors and lawyers are earning $50,000 per year more than high school graduates and $34,000 per year more than college graduates.

Before you get too excited about education, consider that economists point out that the pay for a job is related to the supply of workers who can do that work and the demand for that work. For example, I once met a man who could weld the pipes for gasoline pipelines. He had dropped out of high school, but earned more than many lawyers, because his skill was in demand. In contrast, I once met a woman who went to school to learn how to send telegraph messages in Morse code, and there are people who earn their Ph.D.s in classical languages. Both telegraph operators and classicists earn little money, because there is little demand for their services.

I wonder about the relationship between income and education. We can check the relationship ourselves by looking at data from the Census Bureau's Current Population Survey, available through the Census Bureau's Web site at *www.census.gov*. A copy of the data I will be talking about in this section appears in the *Data Matters* Resource Center at *www.keycollege.com/dm*.

To investigate the relationship between income and education, I got data from the March 2001 supplement to the Census Bureau's Current Population Survey. The data are for a representative sample of roughly 120,000 Americans. These data might help reveal the relationship between education and income. Let's see.

I have a hypothesis that more education gets you more income, but, before I leap in with a significance test, I would like to know what the data look like. For example, how many Americans have college educations? How many Americans have professional degrees? Because I am exploring the data without a specific null hypothesis, this kind of work is called "exploratory data analysis." More recently, this sort of work has been called "data mining."

Exploratory Data Analysis

Exploratory data analysis is using statistical techniques to learn about the nature of data without first establishing a null hypothesis.

As a first step in exploratory data analysis, I find out about the general nature of the data. I will be looking at income and education. I will consider age as well, because younger people tend to earn less. In fact, let's start with age.

Histograms

Probably the most powerful exploratory data analysis tool for looking at the nature of a distribution is the histogram. Figure 6.1.1 shows a histogram of the ages in the data. In the figure, each bar of the histogram represents 10 years. The first bar includes ages from 0 to just under 10, the second bar from 10 to just under 20, and so on up to the rightmost bar. The software I used for this histogram includes the maximum in the rightmost bar, so the bar over "85" goes from 80 to 90, including all the 90's.

Each tick along the bottom of Figure 6.1.1 is the midpoint of the range of its bar. The leftmost bar is labeled "5," because 5 is the midpoint between 0 and 10.

In the data, the lowest age is 0. The highest age is 90. The lowest value is called the "minimum," and the highest value is called the "maximum." Table 6.1.1 shows these summary statistics, along with three others that tell a lot about the distribution—the number of observations, the mean, and the median.

The mean is higher than the median, indicating that the distribution is right skewed. The histogram shows us that also.

Summary Statistics

Data can be described with summary statistics, such as the minimum (the lowest value), the maximum (the highest), the mean, the median, and the number of observations.

For example, if a teacher tells a class that the grades on a test had a minimum of 50 out of 100, a maximum of 72, a median of 55, and a mean of 59, the teacher has told the class a lot.

Figure 6.1.1 **Histogram of Age Distribution in the U.S.**

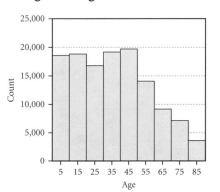

Source: U.S. Census Bureau, Current Population Survey, March 2001 Supplement.

Table 6.1.1 Summary Statistics for American Ages

Number of Observations	126,878
Mean	35.3
Median	35
Minimum	0
Maximum	90

The ages ranged from 0 to 90. (Zero is the age of infants before their first birthdays.) This data goes up to only 90, because it has been top coded by the Census Bureau. "Top coding" is replacing values greater than a chosen top code with the top code itself. For example, in this case, the Census Bureau used 90 as its top code, replacing all values greater than 90 with 90. Anyone who was 100 or 112 was recorded as being 90 years old.

The widths of a histogram's bars can hide or reveal aspects of the data. Figure 6.1.2 is a histogram with a bar for each age (one year old, two years old, and so on). This figure shows the top coding even more. The rightmost bar sticks up oddly, not because there are a lot more 90-year-olds than 89-year-olds, but because that one bar represents everyone who is 90 or more years old.

Histogram Bar Widths

The width of histogram bars affects what the histogram reveals.

For example, the following two histograms are for the same data: 1, 1, 2, 6, 6, 6, and 7.

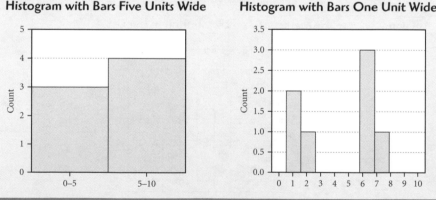

Histogram with Bars Five Units Wide

Histogram with Bars One Unit Wide

Figure 6.1.2 **Histogram of American Ages (Bar Width = 1 Year)**

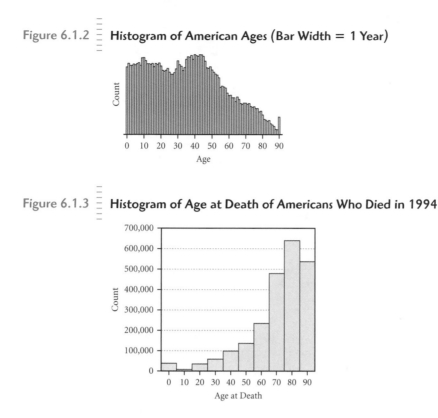

Figure 6.1.3 **Histogram of Age at Death of Americans Who Died in 1994**

The histogram in Figure 6.1.2 has a lump over 35 to 54. That lump represents the baby boom. There's a steep drop from 54 to 55. Americans who were 54 in March 2001 were born in 1946, about nine months after soldiers came back from World War II. Americans who were 55 in this data were conceived just before the war ended. After that drop at 55, there is more drop-off due to Americans dying. Table 5.1.4 contains some data about age at death in 1994. The distribution of ages at death would not have changed much from 1994 to 2001. Figure 6.1.3 shows a histogram of that age-at-death data. So the drop-off in Figure 6.1.2 that starts around 65 is at least partially due to Americans dying.

Figure 6.1.4 shows another way of setting up the histogram of ages. There is a second lump to the left of the baby boomers. That lump has been called the "baby boomlet" because it is formed by the children of baby boomers. People from that group will be entering college over the next eight years, so there will be a rising demand for college classes during that time. Figure 6.1.4 shows a leading edge to the baby boomlet. Neither Figure 6.1.2 nor Figure 6.1.4 makes it easy to tell at what age that edge is. It looks as though people in that group are probably somewhere between 16 and 20. Their age matters quite a bit to college planners, who want to know when to expect the boomlet.

Figure 6.1.4 **Histogram of American Ages (Bar Width = 5 Years)**

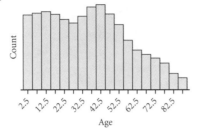

Stem-and-Leaf Plots

Another kind of graphic, a stem-and-leaf plot, makes it easier to read values from histograms. Stem-and-leaf plots were developed for researchers who were not working with computers. Their first step was to sort the data from smallest to largest. If their data ranged from 0 to 90, as ours did, they would write the 10's values in a column (0, 1, 2, 3, and so on up to 9). Those 10's values are the stems. Then the researchers would run their fingers through the data, writing each 1's value next to its 10's value. For example, 23 would show up as a "3" next to the "2" stem. The 1's values are called leaves. In this case, the 3 is the "leaf."

Here are the ages of a random sample of five Americans taken from the March 2001 data: 18, 45, 51, 67, and 75. Figure 6.1.5 is a stem-and-leaf plot of those five ages. In the figure, the first row has a stem of 1 and a leaf of 8 to represent the 18 in the data. Figure 6.1.6 shows a stem-and-leaf plot of the ages of a random sample of 20 Americans. The 20 ages are 1, 1, 2, 6, 12, 23, 28, 35, 38, 39, 40, 41, 44, 44, 44, 47, 48, 52, 68, and 69.

Figure 6.1.5 **Stem-and-Leaf Plot of Five Ages**

```
1 | 8
2 |
3 |
4 | 5
5 | 1
6 | 7
7 | 5
```

Figure 6.1.6 **Stem-and-Leaf Plot of 20 Ages**

```
0 | 1126
1 | 2
2 | 38
3 | 589
4 | 0144478
5 | 2
6 | 89
```

The top row of this stem-and-leaf plot is "0 | 1126." The stem is the "0." The four digits are the two 1's, the 2, and the 6. The baby boom shows up in the row for the forties: "4 | 0144478." That row represents 40, 41, 44, 44, 44, 47, and 48.

Stem-and-Leaf Plot

A stem-and-leaf plot of data lists the highest digit values in a column of what are called "stems." Each observation is represented by the second-highest digit placed to the right of the stem. The lowest digit values can be omitted.

For example, the following figure is a stem-and-leaf plot of these numbers: 1,234, 1,321, 1,345, and 1,555.

```
12 | 3
13 | 24
14 |
15 | 5
```

A stem-and-leaf plot is like a histogram turned on its side. Figure 6.1.7 shows a histogram of the same 20 ages. It's the same shape as the stem-and-leaf plot.

Figure 6.1.7 **Histogram of 20 Ages from Figure 6.1.6**

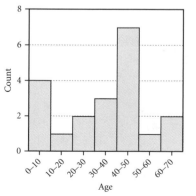

You can decide how wide to make the bars in a histogram. In a stem-and-leaf plot, you can choose how wide a range to include in each stem. For example, rather than having each stem include a range of 10, I could have each stem include a range of 5, as in Figure 6.1.8.

If each observation were represented with its own digit, a stem-and-leaf plot for 140,000 observations would not fit in this book. But a stem-and-leaf plot can be done so that each digit represents multiple observations. For example, in Figure 6.1.9, each digit represents 227 observations; that is, each 1 in the top line means there were 227 1's in the data, each 2 in the third line means there were 227 12's in the data, and so on.

Figure 6.1.8

Stem-and-Leaf Plot of 20 Ages
(Stem Range = 5)

```
0|  112
0|  6
1|  2
1|
2|  3
2|  8
3|
3|  589
4|  01444
4|  78
5|  2
5|
6|
6|  89
```

Figure 6.1.9

Stem-and-Leaf Plot of Ages of 140,000 Americans
(1 Leaf = 227 Observations)

```
0|  00000000111111112222222233333333444444444
0|  5555555566666666777777778888888899999999
1|  00000000111111112222222233333333444444444
1|  555555556666666677777777888888889999999
2|  0000000011111112222222333333334444444444
2|  55555556666666777777788888889999999999
3|  0000000001111111222222223333333344444444
3|  5555555556666666666777777777888888889999999999
4|  000000000111111112222222223333333334444444444
4|  5555555556666666666777777777888888889999999999
5|  000000011111112222222233333334444444444
5|  55555666666677777888889999999
6|  000011111222233334444
6|  5555666677778889999
7|  00001112222333444
7|  555666777888999
8|  0011223344
8|  56789
9|  00
```

Source: U.S. Census Bureau, Current Population Survey, March 2001 Supplement.

Figure 6.1.10 **Histogram of American Ages from 15 to 25**

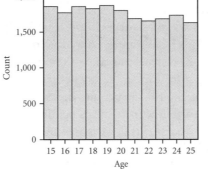

Now we can more easily find out when that boomlet will begin attending college. In Figure 6.1.9, there are eight 15's, 16's, 17's, 18's, 19's, and 20's. There are seven 21's and 22's. The front edge of the boomlet appears to be at 20.

Figure 6.1.10 displays a histogram of the counts of the ages from 15 to 25.

Using histograms and stem-and-leaf plots, we can make a conclusion about when the baby boomlet will begin to attend college: It already has. It began in 2000 or 2001.

Box Plots

To examine the claims about education and income made in the quote at the beginning of the section, we first need to look at data about education levels in the U.S. Figure 6.1.11 is a histogram of the levels of education completed by every

Figure 6.1.11 **Histogram of Level of Education Completed by Americans**

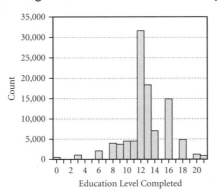

person in the March 2001 Supplement to the U.S. Census Bureau's Current Population Survey. In light of our experience with ages, I have made each bar represent one year of education.

A histogram will often reveal important aspects of the data that you might not think about otherwise. This histogram reveals something about how I translated from the categories that the Census Bureau saved to record education level.

The tallest bar is for grade 12. The 13's are people who attended some college but did not earn a degree. The 14's are people who earned associate's degrees. The Census Bureau didn't record how many years people attended college, so people who deserve a 15 (three years of college) show up as 13 or 14, depending on whether or not they received an associate's degree. The 16's are people who earned bachelor's degrees. The 18's are people who earned master's degrees (including MBAs). The 20's are people with professional degrees (for example, doctors, lawyers, and dentists). The 21's are people who earned doctorates.

The Census Bureau collected educational achievement data only on Americans who were at least 15 years old, and for the lower grades the Census Bureau combined grades. A person with one to four years of schooling appears here as a 3, a person with five or six years of schooling as a 6, and a person with seven or eight years of schooling as an 8.

One way to explore the relationship between education and age is to look at the median education at each age. Figure 6.1.12 shows those medians.

The transitions in Figure 6.1.12 are very abrupt, even spiky. Plots of medians have abrupt transitions like this. The reason is that the median is the middlemost value. If you remove two values from the bottom, the median jumps to the next higher observation. If the values in the middle have gaps between them, that jump sticks out, such as the jumps between 12 years and 13 years in Figure 6.1.12.

Figure 6.1.12 doesn't do much to show the variation at each age. Figure 6.1.13 is a kind of summary chart called a "box plot" that shows both the median and the variation.

Figure 6.1.12 **Median Level of Education for Each Age**

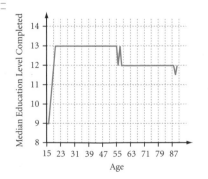

Figure 6.1.13 **Box Plot of Level of Education by Age**

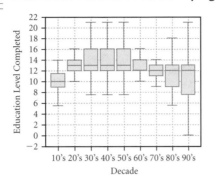

Figure 6.1.13 shows nine boxes, one for each decade of life after the first. First I tried using 75 boxes, but the resulting chart was unreadable. The box on the far left represents people 15 to 19 years old. The second box from the left is for people in their 20's. The next three boxes, which are almost all the same, are for the people in their 30's, 40's, and 50's.

The band in the center of each box is the median for that box. The boxes themselves spread from what is called the "first quartile" to what is called the "third quartile." The first quartile (Q_1) is the median of the lower half of the data. About 25% (or one quarter) of the data fall at or below the first quartile. The third quartile (Q_3) is the median of the higher half of the data, so about 25% of the data fall at or above the third quartile. Each box includes the middle 50% of the data for that age group.

The data in Figure 6.1.14 give an example of quartiles. In the figure, the median is 12, the minimum is 4, and the maximum is 14. The 4, 5, 7, 8, 9, 10, 11, and 12 are the bottom half of the data, because they are the eight lowest values of

Figure 6.1.14 **Level of Education of 16 Hypothetical People and the Corresponding Quartiles**

	Lower Half of Data								Upper Half of Data							
LEVEL	4	5	7	8	9	10	11	12	12	12	12	12	13	14	14	14

QUARTILE	Median of Lower Half = Q_1 = 8.5	Median of Upper Half = Q_3 = 12.5

Figure 6.1.15

Histogram of 16 Observations from Figure 6.1.14

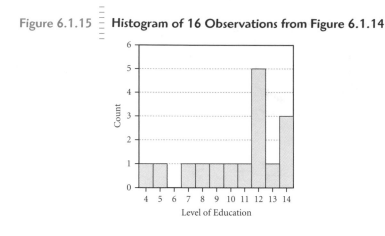

Level of Education

the 16 observations. The median of those values is 8.5, so the first quartile is 8.5. The median of the top half of the data is 12.5, so the third quartile is 12.5. If there are an odd number of observations, the median of the data is included with the lower half when the first quartile is calculated, and is included with the top half when the third quartile is calculated.

Figure 6.1.15 is a histogram of the data in Figure 6.1.14. You can see that the data is left skewed.

Figure 6.1.16 shows a box plot of the data. In the figure, the maximum, 14, is the top of the T on the top. The third quartile, 12.5, is the top of the box. The median, 12, is the thick line across the box. The first quartile, 8.5, is the bottom of the box, and the minimum is the bottom of the bottom T. The T's that stick up and down from the box plot are called its "whiskers." We can see in Figure 6.1.16 that the data is left skewed, because the median is closer to the top of the box and the top whisker is shorter than the bottom whisker. (The bottom of the box plot would be the left side of a distribution graph, and the top would be the right side.)

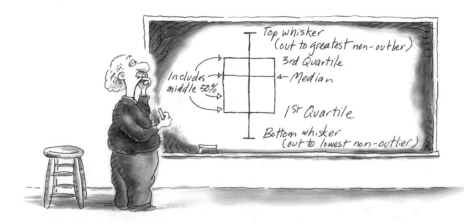

Figure 6.1.16 **Box Plot of Data from Figure 6.1.14**

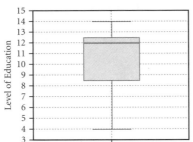

In Figure 6.1.16, the whiskers extend to the minimum and maximum. In box plots, the whiskers extend to the minimum and maximum only if doing so doesn't make the whisker longer than one and a half times the length of the box. For example, the box in Figure 6.1.16 is from 8.5 to 12.5. Its height (from 8.5 to 12.5) represents 4 levels. If the bottom observation were more than 6 levels below 8.5, and the whisker stretched all the way to that lowest observation, the whisker would be more than one and a half times as long as the box. In such a case, the distant observation is called an "outlier" and is either represented with a dot, as in Figure 6.1.17, or left out altogether, as in Figure 6.1.18.

Figure 6.1.17 **Box Plot with Outlier**   Figure 6.1.18 **Box Plot with Outlier Omitted**

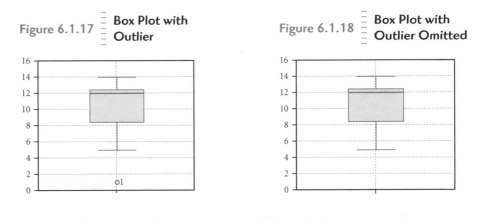

Outliers in Box Plots

In box plots, an outlier is defined as a value for which the distance from the value to the nearest edge of the box plot is more than one and a half times as long as the box.

For example, if the first quartile is 50, and the third quartile is 60, then the box would spread from 50 to 60. One and a half times the length of that box would be 15. Any observation more than 15 above 60 or more than 15 below 50 would be an outlier. That is, any observation more than 75 or less than 35 would be an outlier.

To show you how the box plot and histogram represent the same data, Figure 6.1.19 shows the box plot from Figure 6.1.16 over the histogram of the same data.

To get the box plot and the histogram on the same scale, I had to turn the box plot on its side. Check Figure 6.1.19 to make sure everything is right. The value 12 is the median, and it is the tallest bar in the histogram, and where the dark band in the box plot is. The minimum is 4, which is where the lower whisker stretches to. The maximum is 14, which is where the upper whisker stretches to. The third quartile is at 12.5, which is where the upper edge of the box is, and the first quartile is at 8.5, which is where the lower edge of the box is. Everything checks out.

Figure 6.1.19 **Box Plot and Histogram of Data from Figure 6.1.14**

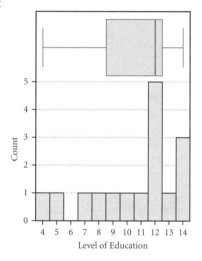

Look at Figure 6.1.13 (shown again on page 333). Notice that the outliers are omitted. Figure 6.1.13 shows us that, generally, people have not graduated from college until they are in their 20's. Then people begin to earn their professional degrees and doctorates (education levels 20 and 21) when they are in their mid- to late 20's. Therefore, professional degrees and doctrates are not as common among the 20's as among the older groups. The figure also shows that college and even a high school diploma are more common for the baby boomers than for older people. Doctorates and professional degrees are uncommon among the pre–baby boom generations, although the spread of education level increases for the oldest Americans.

Now we're ready to look at education level and income. I will let you do that in the exercises.

Figure 6.1.13 **Box Plot of Level of Education by Age**

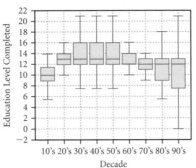

Algebra and Greek Symbols

Exploratory data analysis is an approach to data that does not begin with a specified hypothesis to be tested. The purpose is to find out the nature of the data. Exploratory data analysis tools include histograms, stem-and-leaf plots, and box plots.

The length of a box in a box plot is called the "interquartile range," or "IQR." The IQR is the range from the first quartile (Q_1) to the third quartile (Q_3).

The median is the second quartile (Q_2), and the maximum is the fourth quartile (Q_4). The minimums and the four quartiles make up what is called the "five-number summary."

Abstract

Without starting with specific hypotheses to test, exploratory data analysis looks at the nature of data, using tools such as histograms and summary statistics, such as the minimum, maximum, mean, and median.

Different widths of histogram bars can reveal or hide different aspects of the data.

Stem-and-leaf plots are like histograms turned on their sides, in that each row represents the observations in a range of the data. Stem-and-leaf plots are constructed by listing the largest digits (the stems) of each row's range in a column. For each observation, the observation's next-largest digit (the leaf) is written to the right of the observation's stem. Stem-and-leaf plots combine some strengths of histograms with some strengths of tables of raw counts.

The first quartile is the median of the lower half of the data. The third quartile is the median of the top half of the data. Box plots show the distribution of observations with a vertical scale and a box that has its top at the third quartile and bottom at the first quartile. For a box plot, an outlier is any observation that is more than one and a half times the length of the box away from an edge of the box. A box plot includes a stripe through the box at the median and lines (called "whiskers") extending down to the lowest non-outlier observation and up to the highest non-outlier observation.

Avoiding Common Misunderstandings

Number lines are a big part of the graphics of exploratory data analysis. A histogram is built over a number line. A number line goes up the side of a box plot. The digits that form the stems of a stem-and-leaf plot are actually a number line. This means that, if you are sketching one of these figures, you must use a number line. For example, if you are creating a stem-and-leaf plot of 12, 22, and 55, you need stems for the 30's and 40's, even though there are no numbers in the 30's and 40's. Similarly, a histogram of those numbers would have a gap between the 22 and the 55.

Computer Project

The data explored in this section appear in the *Data Matters* Resource Center at *www.keycollege.com/dm*. These data include income from wages and salaries. They also include income from interest, which indicates savings—people with more savings generally earn more interest. Explore these data also and check for relationships with union membership, being an immigrant, having immigrant parents, and gender.

Exercises

Use the following figure to complete Exercises 1 through 6. This figure is a box plot of American incomes from the U.S. Census Bureau's Current Population Survey, 2001 March Supplement and shows individual income, not household income. Some of the data in the figure reflect half or less of that household's income. This income is not all wages or salary; it also includes income from investments. The figure does not include outliers.

Box Plot of American Incomes from 2000

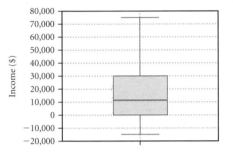

1. About what was the median income in 2000?

2. About what was the first quartile?

3. About how many Americans had incomes lower than the lower quartile?

4. About what was the third quartile?

5. About what was the range of the middle 50% of the incomes?

6. If outliers are not included, what was the range of incomes?

Use the following figure, a stem-and-leaf plot of American incomes, to complete Exercises 7 through 9. Each leaf represents 1,043 observations.

Stem-and-Leaf Plot of American Incomes from $0 to $60,000

```
0 | 000000000000000000000000000000000000000011223344
0 | 55666778899
1 | 00011223344
1 | 55667889
2 | 001234
2 | 556789
3 | 001234
3 | 556789
4 | 0123
4 | 58
5 | 0
5 | 5
6 | 0
```

7. Is the distribution of incomes right skewed, symmetrical, or left skewed?

8. What do all the zeros in the top row of the stem-and-leaf plot mean?

9. About how many people earned $35,000 to $35,999?

10. The following figure shows a histogram of incomes. In this figure, how much money does each bar width represent, and what income values are included in the tall bar over the 5?

Histogram of Incomes from 2000 (from −$10,000 to $170,000)

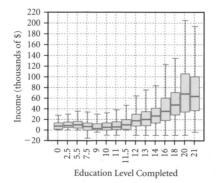

Income (thousands of $)

11. The following table provides summary statistics for the incomes from 2000. How can you tell that the incomes include negative numbers? In terms of annual income, what does a negative number mean?

STATISTIC	VALUE
Mean	$19,707
Median	$11,181
Minimum	−$14,960
Maximum	$169,955
Number of Observations	125,910

12. In the following figure, what is the relationship between education level and income? Describe both the change in median and the change in how spread out the incomes are.

Box Plot of 2000 Incomes at Each Education Level

Income (thousands of $)

Education Level Completed

13. Use the figure in Exercise 12 to complete this exercise. Why might it be sensible to exclude those people who had no income in 2000, and what evidence have we seen that it might change the image we get of the data?

14. Use the figure in Exercise 12 to complete this exercise. Look specifically at the median values for college graduates and high school graduates. Are those medians about $17,000 apart, as was implied by the quote at the beginning of this section?

Answers to Odd-Numbered Exercises

1. It looks as though it's a little over $10,000.

3. 25%, about 64 million.

5. From about $0 to about $30,000.

7. Right skewed. There's a big pile over 0 and then mostly a tail toward the higher values.

9. About 2,000. It says at the bottom that each digit represents 1,043 observations, and there are two 35's in the stem-and-leaf plot.

11. The minimum is −$14,960. A negative income means more money going out than coming in, that is, debt.

13. Many people who are earning zero may not be trying to earn money, or may be incapacitated and unable to earn money, which is unlikely to relate to their education level. Their education may provide them with great opportunities that they are not taking advantage of. We expect that excluding them would change the image, because the stem-and-leaf plot showed that there were a lot of people who earned zero.

6.2 Describing Number Line Variation

- Standard Deviation of Samples
- Variance

Standard deviation is used many times to measure the total risk of a portfolio or money manager. The standard deviation encompasses both market risk and unsystematic risk.

—SHEIN, *FINANCIAL PLANNING*, JUNE 1998

Stock Prices

Over the last few years the stock market has become a bigger and bigger part of the lives of many people. Retirement funds are invested in the stock market, and now there is talk of putting social security money there as well. The problem is that the stock market is risky. It's variable, sometimes going up, other times down. To be able to think about how variable it is, you would need some way to talk about how widely the stock market movements are spread out. For example, do they stay close to a regular 0.03% rise each day? Or do stock prices double some days and get cut in half others? If they are spread widely, that's risky. If they hold pretty much steady, that's more reliable. As Shein points out in the preceding quote, the standard deviation tells us how risky the stock market is.

Table 6.2.1 Changes in the Dow Jones Industrial Average (11/16/98–11/20/98)

DATE	CHANGE
Monday, 11/16/98	Rose 92 points
Tuesday, 11/17/98	Dropped 25 points
Wednesday, 11/18/98	Rose 55 points
Thursday, 11/19/98	Rose 15 points
Friday, 11/20/98	Rose 104 points

To see what the standard deviation is and how to calculate it, consider the data in Table 6.2.1. It shows changes in the Dow Jones Industrial Average from Monday, November 16, 1998, through Friday, November 20, 1998. Every rise is associated with an average rise in people's investments. Every drop is associated with an average drop in investments. At the time, the Dow Jones Industrial Average was at roughly 9,000, so a 90-point rise was a 1% gain.

What can we learn about the Dow's movements from these five days? Quite a bit, but we are going to have to translate the 25-point drop on November 17 so that it is comparable to the other movements. We will call it a change of negative 25 points. Table 6.2.2 shows the same five days of Dow changes.

What do these five days show us about how widely the Dow movements vary from day to day? A statistician would use the standard deviation to find out. Standard deviations describe how number line observations vary. The standard deviation has two special strengths. First, it describes what a sample reveals about variation in the sample's population. Second, the standard error and margin of error of a sample's mean are calculated from the standard deviation.

Small samples tend to be less spread out than the populations from which they are drawn. The standard deviation adjusts for this. The five days of Dow movements in Table 6.2.2 are a very small sample. A larger sample would probably

Table 6.2.2 Point Changes in the Dow Jones Industrial Average (11/16/98–11/20/98)

DATE	POINT CHANGE
Monday, 11/16/98	92
Tuesday, 11/17/98	−25
Wednesday, 11/18/98	55
Thursday, 11/19/98	15
Friday, 11/20/98	104

Figure 6.2.1

95% Confidence Interval for the Population's Mean Point Change (0 to 96)

show the Dow moving around more widely. To show how the standard deviation reveals the wider spread of the full population, I calculated the standard deviation from that sample and then watched what happened over the next several weeks.

The mean of those five observations is 48 points. Their standard deviation is 54 points, and their margin of error is 48 points. Before calculating the standard deviation, let's see how well it works.

Because the sample mean and margin of error are each 48 points, I guessed that the mean of the population from which these observations was drawn is somewhere between 0 and 96 points: that is, from 48 points below the sample mean to 48 points above the sample mean as shown in Figure 6.2.1. (I'll show you how to calculate the confidence interval soon.)

I guessed that, as in a normal distribution, about 95% of the observations would fall within 2 standard deviations of the mean. That would be from 108 points below the population mean to 108 points above. If the population mean were 0, then about 95% of the observations would fall between −108 and 108. If the population mean were 96, then about 95% of the observations would fall between −12 and 204. These possibilities are shown in Figure 6.2.2.

The five Dow changes that I saw ranged from −25 to 104. Because of my work with the standard deviation, I expected that most of the Dow's point changes would fall somewhere in those last two prediction intervals, between −108 and 204. That range is much wider than the range I saw. Table 6.2.3 shows the changes in the Dow that occurred over the following 13 business days.

Table 6.2.4 shows Table 6.2.3's point changes sorted from the lowest to the highest. As Table 6.2.4 shows, 9 out of the following 13 days (70%) had point changes that fell within my expected range. In contrast, only 5 (38%) fell within the range of the point changes I saw in the first week. It was definitely better to guess that stock changes would vary between −108 and 204 than to think that all of the stock movements would be like what I saw in the first week.

Figure 6.2.2

Two Ranges Most Likely to Have Future Point Changes

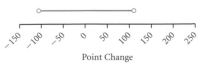

Table 6.2.3 Point Changes in the Dow Jones Industrial Average (11/23/98–12/10/98)

DATE	POINT CHANGE
Monday, 11/23/98	215
Tuesday, 11/24/98	−73
Wednesday, 11/25/98	13
Friday, 11/27/98	19
Monday, 11/30/98	−217
Tuesday, 12/1/98	17
Wednesday, 12/2/98	−69
Thursday, 12/3/98	−185
Friday, 12/4/98	136
Monday, 12/7/98	54
Tuesday, 12/8/98	−42
Wednesday, 12/9/98	−19
Thursday, 12/10/98	−168

Table 6.2.4 Point Changes in the Dow Jones Industrial Average (11/23/98–12/10/98) Sorted from Negative to Positive

DATE	POINT CHANGE
Monday, 11/30/98	−217**
Thursday, 12/3/98	−185**
Thursday, 12/10/98	−168**
Tuesday, 11/24/98	−73*
Wednesday, 12/2/98	−69*
Tuesday, 12/8/98	−42*
Wednesday, 12/9/98	−19
Wednesday, 11/25/98	13
Tuesday, 12/1/98	17
Friday, 11/27/98	19
Monday, 12/7/98	54
Friday, 12/4/98	136*
Monday, 11/23/98	215**

*Outside the range of the first week
**Outside the expected range

You may be wondering why my confidence interval (from -108 to 204) captured only 70% of the observations rather than 95%. There are at least four important reasons. First, the first five observations were a very small sample. Statistical methods become more and more reliable as sample sizes get larger. Second, the first five observations were not a random sample—they were a convenience sample. Third, the test sample (the 13 later days) is also small. With sample sizes like this, all we expect in a confidence interval is roughly the right proportion. Fourth, Dow Jones point changes do not have to be normally distributed. Nonetheless, in spite of these concerns, it was certainly a better idea to calculate that confidence interval than to expect that later days would look like the first five days.

In general, if you have some data, and you want to know where future observations will fall, calculate the standard deviation and the margin of error. You can try this on your own, but you will need to know how to calculate a standard deviation. Table 6.2.5 shows a worksheet I used to find the standard deviation of the first five Dow Jones point changes; the exercises at the end of this section provide practice with the calculations. I will explain these equations and the terms in them in the following pages.

Table 6.2.5   Worksheet for Finding Standard Deviation and Standard Error

OBSERVATION	−	SAMPLE MEAN	=	DEVIATION	SQUARED DEVIATION
92	−	48.2	=	43.8	1,918.44
−25	−	48.2	=	−73.2	5,358.24
55	−	48.2	=	6.8	46.24
15	−	48.2	=	−33.2	1,102.24
104	−	48.2	=	55.8	3,113.64
SUM 241				SUM 0.00	SUM 11,538.80 = SUM OF SQUARES

$$\text{Mean} = \frac{241}{5} = 48.2$$

$$\text{Sample Variance} = \frac{\text{Sum of Squares}}{(\text{Sample Size} - 1)}$$

$$\text{Sample Variance} = \frac{11,538.8}{4} = 2,884.7$$

$$\text{Standard Deviation} = \sqrt{\text{Sample Variance}}$$

$$\text{Standard Deviation} = 53.7$$

$$\text{Standard Error} = \frac{\text{Population Standard Deviation}}{\sqrt{\text{Sample Size}}}$$

Using the sample standard deviation as an estimate of the population standard deviation:

$$\text{Standard Error} = \frac{53.7}{\sqrt{5}} = \frac{53.7}{2.236} = 24$$

$$\text{Margin of Error}^{1} = 2 \text{ Standard Errors} = 48$$

Let's go through the calculations in Table 6.2.5. We will consider later why those calculations are used. The five initial point changes are listed in the Observation column. The first step in finding the standard deviation is to find how much each observation deviates from the sample mean. These are the observations' deviations. To find them, we need to find the mean. The sum of those five observations is 241. The sample mean is the sum of the sample divided by the sample size. There are five observations, so the mean is 241 divided by 5, which gives 48.2.

Each observation's deviation is the distance from that observation to the mean. Figure 6.2.3 shows the five changes (92, −25, 55, 15, and 104) and the deviations from the mean (48.2) for each of the values.

How to Find Deviations

To find each observation's deviation, subtract the sample mean from the observation.

For example, imagine that three runners sprint a 100-yard dash. Their times are 10 seconds, 11 seconds, and 15 seconds. Their mean time was 12 seconds. The following table shows their deviations.

TIME	−	MEAN	=	DEVIATION
10	−	12	=	−2
11	−	12	=	−1
15	−	12	=	3

The Sample Mean column of Table 6.2.5 contains the mean (48.2). To find the deviations, I subtracted that 48.2 from each observation. The Deviation column

---

[1]Two standard errors is a pretty good quick-and-dirty margin of error. It would be a great margin of error if we knew the full nature of the population, but, as you will see later, to adjust for our uncertainty about the population, ideally we would multiply by more than 2 standard errors.

.2.3 Five Values and the Deviations from the Mean (48.2) for Each Value

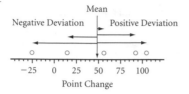

shows the results of that subtraction, the deviations. Observations below the mean have negative deviations, observations above the mean have positive deviations.

The next step in finding the standard deviation is to square all of the deviations. In Table 6.2.5, the squared deviations appear in the Squared Deviation column. The sum of the squared deviations appears below that column. Statisticians do a lot with the sum of the squared deviations; in fact, it has its own name: the "sum of squares." In this case, the sum of squares is 11,538.80.

How to Find the Sum of Squares

The "sum of squares" is the sum of the squares of the deviations.

For example, if the deviations are -2, -1, and 3, then their squares are 4, 1, and 9, and their sum of squares would be 14, as this table shows:

TIME	−	MEAN	=	DEVIATION	SQUARED DEVIATION
10	−	12	=	−2	4
11	−	12	=	−1	1
15	−	12	=	3	9
				SUM OF SQUARES	14

There are a few more steps to calculating the standard deviation. The "sample variance" is found by subtracting 1 from the sample size and then dividing the result into the sum of squares. In this case, there are five observations. One less than the sample size is 4. I divided the sum of squares (11,538.8) by 4 and got 2,884.7, which is the sample variance.

The square root of the sample variance is the sample standard deviation. The square root of 2,884.7 is 53.7, which rounds to 54, so the standard deviation is 54.

In summary, the standard deviation is the square root of a little more than the mean of the squared deviations.

To find the standard error, divide the population standard deviation by the square root of the sample size. Section 6.3 discusses the standard error in more detail. As noted previously, the margin of error is 2 standard errors.

The Thinking Behind How the Standard Deviation Is Calculated

Why does calculating the standard deviation require so many steps? To see why, consider the overall goal. We are looking for something that indicates how far the observations are spread out. But what does "how far the observations are spread out" mean? One interpretation is that it is how far the observations are from the center of the sample. What is the center of the sample? There are a few possibilities. One is that the sample mean is the center. If you look at it this way, then we are looking for how far the observations are from the sample mean, which is a reasonable approach.

Let us say that we are looking for how far our five observations are from the mean. Table 6.2.6 shows the five point changes. The deviations show how far each observation is from the mean.

One way to describe how far the observations are from the mean is to report the deviations, 43.8, −73.2, 6.8, −33.2, and 55.8, but that list of values alone is not very helpful. We would want to summarize those deviations. How would we

Table 6.2.6 Sample of Five Point Changes in the Dow Jones Industrial Average

OBSERVATION	MEAN	DEVIATION
92	48.2	43.8
−25	48.2	−73.2
55	48.2	6.8
15	48.2	−33.2
104	48.2	55.8
SUM 241		0

2.7 The Sample of Five Point Changes and Their Absolute Deviations from the Mean

OBSERVATION	SAMPLE MEAN	DEVIATION	ABSOLUTE DEVIATION
92	48.2	43.8	43.8
−25	48.2	−73.2	73.8
55	48.2	6.8	6.8
15	48.2	−33.2	33.2
104	48.2	55.8	55.8
SUM 241		0.00	213.4
MEAN 48.2		0.00	42.7

do this? One reasonable approach would be to find their mean, but they add up to 0. That always happens with deviations around a mean: The sample mean is that point for which the deviations add up to 0.

What else could we do? We could take the absolute value of all the deviations. Taking the absolute value makes the negative numbers positive. If we did that, the deviations would become the absolute deviations listed in Table 6.2.7.

Table 6.2.7 shows the calculations for finding what would be called the "mean absolute deviation," that is, the sum of the absolute deviations divided by the number of observations. In this case, 42.7 is the mean of the deviations after you take their absolute value.

There are two problems with the mean absolute deviation. The first is that it reflects only how widely the observations are spread in the sample. Observations in the population will probably be more widely spread than observations in the sample. To estimate how widely spread the population was, we would have to make this estimate larger. But how much larger? This brings us to the second problem with the mean absolute deviation. Absolute deviations are not the easiest things to work with in mathematics. Statisticians have preferred working with squares, which are easier to work with mathematically and also make negative values positive. For example, −3 squared is 9. That is why statisticians square the deviations before summing them.

You might think that a statistician would then take the average of the squared deviations. The mean of the squared deviations is in fact the *population* variance. The reason we do not divide by the sample size to find the *sample* variance is that the observations in the sample tend to fall closer together than do the observations in the population. The population variance is usually larger than what you would find if you averaged the sample squared deviations. So, we calculate something a little bit larger than the mean squared deviation. Dividing by 1 less than the sample size gives a result a little bit larger than the mean squared deviation.

Figure 6.2.4 **Histogram with Sample Mean Closer to Observations than Population Mean Would Be If the Population Mean Were 5**

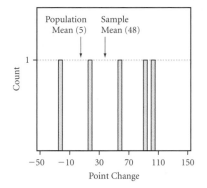

The reason the sample mean squared deviation tends to be smaller than the population variance is that the sample deviations are calculated around the *sample* mean. If you knew the population mean and calculated the sample deviations from that, you would get a good estimate of the population standard deviation. But the sample mean tends to be closer to the sample observations than the population mean is, because the sample mean is calculated from the sample observations. For example, think about the five Dow Jones point changes we were looking at earlier. They could reasonably have come from a population with a mean at 5. Figure 6.2.4 shows what that would look like.

In Figure 6.2.4, on the average, the observations are closer to the sample mean than to the population mean. This is the usual situation. Calculating the deviations from the sample mean produces a smaller mean squared deviation than calculating from the population mean. No matter where the population mean is, the sample mean has to be close to the sample observations, because it is calculated from them. The sample mean is almost always closer to the sample observations than the population mean is.

You can try this for yourself. The computer project at the end of this section tests whether the sample mean squared deviation is typically smaller than the population variance.

I did the test described in the computer project. I was working with a population that had a mean squared deviation of 0.083. I took 10 samples, each with four observations. For each sample, I calculated the mean squared deviation, using the deviations of the sample observations from the sample mean. Table 6.2.8 shows the results for the first 10 samples: 7 out of 10 times, the sample mean squared deviation was less than the population mean squared deviation.

Of course, 10 samples do not give a reliable picture. To get a more reliable idea of what is going on, I reran that program to collect and study 10,000 random

Table 6.2.8 Results of Mean Squared Deviation Tests

SAMPLE SIZE	MEAN SQUARED DEVIATION
4	0.05*
4	0.01*
4	0.12
4	0.09
4	0.03*
4	0.03*
4	0.07*
4	0.04*
4	0.11
4	0.01*

*Estimate below population mean squared deviation

samples. With 10,000 samples, the mean of all the sample mean squared deviations was 0.056, which was less than the actual population mean squared deviation, 0.083. On the average, sample mean squared deviations are less than their population mean squared deviations. If you guessed that the population had the same mean squared deviation as your sample, you would probably underestimate the population mean squared deviation.

You can adjust for this underestimation. To see how, look at Figure 6.2.5, which shows more sample mean squared deviations. For each sample, the mean squared deviation was calculated. I set the program to make 40 tests for each sample size, and I had the sample size increase from 2 to 200. As before, the population mean squared deviation was 0.083. Figure 6.2.5 shows the results.

Figure 6.2.5 **Scatter Plot of Sample Mean Squared Deviation Plotted Against Sample Size**

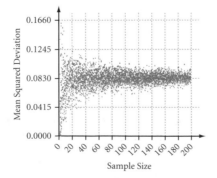

In Figure 6.2.5, each dot represents a single sample mean squared deviation. The value of the mean squared deviation is indicated by how high or low the dot is. The samples ranged in size from 2 to 200. The size of each sample is indicated by how far to the left or right the sample's dot falls.

The first thing to notice about the plot in Figure 6.2.5 is how fuzzy it looks. Every sample was drawn from the same, constant population. In spite of the constancy of the population, the sample mean squared deviations jump around a lot because of random variation due to sampling.

Notice that the sample mean squared deviations jump around more widely for the small sample sizes. As the sample sizes get larger and larger, the sample mean squared deviations tend to stay closer to 0.083. That is the law of large numbers. For random samples, as the sample size gets larger, the aspects of the samples tend to vary more and more closely to the aspects of the population. In this case, the population mean squared deviation (the population variance) is 0.083, and the sample mean squared deviations get closer and closer to that variance.

A reference line in Figure 6.2.5 shows you where the population variance (0.083) is. On the left, where the sample sizes are small, the variances are spread out more widely, but not around 0.083. They are spread around something lower than the population variance.

Figure 6.2.6 shows means for each sample size and makes this distribution pattern more apparent. There were 40 samples taken at each sample size. For example, I had the computer take 40 samples, each with 2 observations. The computer calculated the mean squared deviation of each sample and then found the mean of the 40 results for samples with 2 observations each. That process was repeated for 40 samples with 3 observations in each sample, for 40 samples with 4 observations in each sample, and so on up to 200 observations in each sample. Figure 6.2.6 shows how those means changed as the sample size got larger.

In Figure 6.2.6, the resulting means of sample mean squared deviations were often less than the population variance, but that was a bigger problem for smaller

Figure 6.2.6 **Means of 40 Mean Squared Deviations at Each Sample Size**

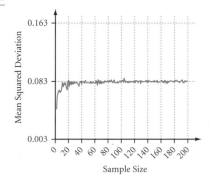

samples. For samples of about 100 or more, the means of the sample mean squared deviations stayed pretty close to the real population variance, 0.083.

Statisticians looked at results like those in Figure 6.2.6 and figured out exactly how much too low the average sample's results would be. That told them how to adjust the sample variance so it would accurately estimate the population variance. When you average the squared deviations, the adjustment is to divide by 1 less than the number of squared deviations. When you divide by something smaller, you end up with a larger result. For example, one-half is bigger than one-third. When you use the adjustment and divide by 1 less than the number of squared deviations, you get something a little larger than the mean squared deviation.

When calculating a sample variance, 1 less than the number of observations is how many observations would be free to vary after you have picked a particular mean. For this reason, 1 less than the number of observations is called the "degrees of freedom." For example, if I am taking two observations, and the mean has to be 4, only one of the observations is free to vary. The second observation is completely determined by the first. If the first is 4, then the second has to be 4 also. If the first is 3, then the second would have to be 5. With only two observations, there is only one degree of freedom. To find the sample variance, we adjust the formula for calculating the variance and divide the sum of squares by the degrees of freedom (sample size minus 1), rather than the sample size.

The sample variance is an unbiased estimate of the population variance (the population mean squared deviation). Figure 6.2.7 shows how well the sample variance does at estimating the population variance. Figure 6.2.7 was produced the same way as Figure 6.2.6, except that the variances were calculated with the adjustment of dividing by the degrees of freedom.

Figure 6.2.7 **Means of 40 Sample Variances (Population Variance = 0.083)**

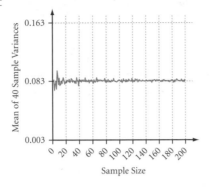

Figure 6.2.7 shows that, with the adjustment, the average sample variance hovers steadily around the population mean squared deviation, 0.083. The sample variance is a good estimate of the population variance.

Degrees of Freedom

The degrees of freedom are how many observations are free to vary, after the mean has been set. If the observations are being modeled with one mean, then the degrees of freedom are 1 less than the number of observations. Sometimes, data are divided into two groups and modeled with two means. In that case, the degrees of freedom would be 2 less than the number of observations.

That is why we divide by the degrees of freedom (1 less than the sample size) when we are finding the sample variance: to adjust for how the variation in samples tends to be smaller than the variation in their populations.

Once I have found the sample variance, I have some sort of indication of how widely observations are spread. Larger sample variances indicate more widely spread observations, but variances are not intuitive. Our five Dow Jones point changes ranged from −25 to 104. On the average, each observation was about 43 points away from the mean. The sample variance of those observations was 2,885. It is hard to see how "2,885" describes what is happening in a set of numbers that covers a range of only 129 points. Why is the sample variance so huge?

The variance is so much larger than the deviations because it is a little more than the average of the squared deviations. To bring the variance back into the range of the original deviations, let's take the square root. The square root of 2,885 is approximately 54, which is quite close to the mean of how far each observation is away from the mean. That is why statisticians typically take the square root of the sample variance; it is the sample standard deviation.

> ## Population Variance and Sample Variance
>
> The population variance is the sum of squares calculated from the entire population divided by the population size.
>
> The sample variance is the sample sum of squares divided by 1 less than the sample size. A sample with only one observation has no sensible sample variance.

It is very rare to work with an entire population. People most commonly calculate standard deviations from samples. Because people almost never calculate population variances or population standard deviations, references to a "standard deviation" almost always mean a sample standard deviation. By "variance," people usually mean the sample variance.

Algebra and Greek Symbols

There are several equations to present the material of this section. Each equation is numbered on the left edge of the page. For example, equation 1 has a (1) next to it.

To present the algebraic representations of the variance and standard deviation, we need to see clearly the algebra of means. A sample mean ($\bar{x}$) is the sum of the observations divided by the number of observations:

(1)
$$\bar{x} = \frac{\sum x}{n}$$

For a finite population, like the current U.S. population, we can say that the population size is N. The population mean (μ) can be calculated by this equation:

(2)
$$\mu = \frac{\sum x}{N}$$

Imagine a population in which 50% of the population is 1's, 25% is 2's, and 25% is 5's. To add all the values in the population, we could recognize that the number of 1's is 50% of N, the number of 2's is 25% of N, and the number of 5's is 25% of N:

(3)
$$\sum x = 0.5N1 + 0.25N2 + 0.25N5$$

That is, the sum of the values is (0.5N times 1) plus (0.25N times 2) plus (0.25N times 5). We can bring the N outside of the parentheses including the sums:

(4)
$$\sum x = N[0.5(1) + 0.25(2) + 0.25(5)]$$

So 0.5 times 1 plus 0.25 times 2 plus 0.25 times 5 is the sum of the proportion of the population that is a value multiplied by that value:

(5) $$\sum x = N\sum_x \Pi_x x$$

where Π_x is the proportion of the population that is x. Equation 5 works for any population. If we substitute the right side of Equation 5 into Equation 2, we get Equation 6:

(6) $$\mu = \frac{N\sum_x \Pi_x x}{N}$$

The N's cancel, so:

(7) $$\mu = \sum_x \Pi_x x$$

Remember, Π_x is the proportion of the population that is x. If you are using random sampling, Π_x is also the probability of drawing x on any draw. This relationship allows us to talk about the mean outcome of a probabilistic system. For example, imagine that we paint a 1 on one side of a coin and a 0 on the other. There is an infinite population of 1's and 0's that could come from that painted coin. In that infinite population, the proportion of each outcome is the probability of that outcome. In that infinite population, the proportion of 1's is 50%, and the proportion of 0's is 50%. For a probability system like this one, Π_x equals θ_x, which is the probability of x. We can substitute that into Equation 7 to get Equation 8:

(8) $$E(x) = \sum_x \theta_x x$$

The left side of Equation 7 is called the "expected value," or "expectation," of x and is represented by "$E(x)$." The population mean, μ, is also the expected value of x.

Traditionally, in statistics, the population standard deviation is represented as σ. The population variance is the square of σ and is represented as σ^2. The value represented by σ^2 is the mean squared deviation of the population's x values from the population mean, μ. That is, it is the expected value of $(x - \mu)^2$. To see what σ^2 is, imagine that we change the population by subtracting its mean from every value in the population and then squaring the differences. To find the mean of these squared differences, we would add them all up and divide by the number in our population to begin with:

(9) $$\sigma^2 = \frac{\sum(x - \mu)^2}{N}$$

Or, if we substitute $(x - \mu)^2$ for x in Equation 7, we get this:

(10) $$\sigma^2 = E[(x - \mu)^2] = \sum_{(x-\mu)^2} \Pi_{(x-\mu)^2}(x - \mu)^2$$

But there is one $(x - \mu)^2$ for each x, so we can sum over x and achieve the same result as summing over $(x - \mu)^2$. Similarly, the proportion of our changed population that is $(x - \mu)^2$ is the same as the proportion in our unchanged population that is x. So $\Pi_{(x-\mu)^2} = \Pi_x$:

$$\sigma^2 = \sum_x \Pi_x (x - \mu)^2 \tag{11}$$

The population standard deviation is the square root of the population variance:

$$\sigma = \sqrt{\sigma^2} \tag{12}$$

In the sciences, the sample standard deviation is abbreviated as SD, and the sample variance is abbreviated as VAR. In mathematics and statistics, the sample standard deviation is traditionally referred to as s, and the sample variance as s^2. The sample variance is the sum of the squared differences between the observations and the sample mean, divided by 1 less than the sample size:

$$s^2 = \frac{\sum (x - \bar{x})^2}{n - 1} \tag{13}$$

$$s = \sqrt{s^2} \tag{14}$$

Estimated statistics are indicated with a circumflex (^). For example, $\hat{\mu}$ is "the estimate of the population mean":

$$\hat{\sigma}^2 = s^2 \tag{15}$$

The estimated population standard deviation is the sample standard deviation.

$$\hat{\sigma} = s \tag{16}$$

Abstract

Follow these steps to find the sample standard deviation: (1) Find the mean. (2) Calculate the deviations by subtracting the mean from each observation. (3) Square the deviations. (4) Sum the squared deviations. (5) Calculate the sample variance by dividing the sum of the squared deviations by 1 less than the number of observations. (6) Calculate the standard deviation by taking the square root of the sample variance.

Avoiding Common Misunderstandings

The calculations for the standard deviation are unusual. You square the differences, then you almost find the mean of the squared differences, then you take the square root. Nonetheless, when you're done, you end up with a value that is close to the average distance from each observation to the mean.

The standard deviation is roughly the average distance from each observation to the center of the data.

Computer Project

Pick a number line measurement in the Representative Sample used in the previous computer projects (from *www.keycollege.com/dm*). For that measurement, calculate the population variance (the population mean squared deviation). Have your software take random samples and calculate their mean squared deviations. Use small sample sizes, such as 2 to 10. Have your computer calculate the sample variances. Notice whether the sample variance is a better estimate of the population variance than the sample mean squared deviation.

Exercises

My wife and I keep track of our expenses with a computerized finance program. I recently asked the program to report how much we had spent on gasoline each week over a five-month period. The following table shows what the program reported. Use this table to complete Exercises 1 through 11.

$53	$12	$46	$22
$26	$10	$27	$25
$14	$14	$25	$30
$15	$14	$21	
$34	$52	$16	

Imagine that we had been keeping track for only a month and had entered only the first four weeks of gasoline payments: $53, $26, $14, and $15. We might want to estimate the range of most of the weekly expenses during the following weeks to forecast future gasoline spending. To complete the following exercises, you will probably want to make a table for calculating the standard deviation as with the tables earlier in this section.

1. What is the mean of the first four payments?
2. What are their deviations?
3. What are the squared deviations?
4. For the first four payments, what is the sum of squares?
5. What are the degrees of freedom?
6. What is the sample variance?
7. What is the sample standard deviation?

8. Because there are four observations, in this case the standard error would be one-half of the standard deviation. Estimate that the margin of error is 2 standard errors. What is the margin of error for the mean?

9. Estimate that the population mean falls within 2 standard errors of the sample mean, and write down your confidence interval for the population mean.

10. Estimate that most future weeks will have expenditures that are within 2 standard deviations of the population mean. Where would you expect future weeks' gasoline expenditures to fall?

11. How does your expected range compare to the rest of the weeks' expenditures?

In November 1998, I visited an Internet newsgroup where people advertise used portable computers that they would like to sell. There were many 233 MHz Pentium laptops. The following table shows the prices that I found that month. Use the information in this table to complete Exercises 12 through 21.

$1,800	$1,550	$1,794	$1,275
$1,950	$1,995	$2,129	$2,700
$1,550	$2,300	$1,609	$2,850
$2,400	$1,350	$2,189	
$1,650	$1,500	$1,392	

Imagine that I had seen only the first three laptop prices: $1,800, $1,950, and $1,550. If I were trying to get a feel for the used laptop market, I might like to know how the prices in the market are spread.

12. What is the mean of those three prices?

13. What are their deviations?

14. What are the squared deviations?

15. For those three prices, what is the sum of squares?

16. How many degrees of freedom are there?

17. What is the sample variance?

18. What is the standard deviation?

19. Because there are three observations, in this case, the standard error would be the standard deviation divided by 1.7. The margin of error would be 2 standard errors. What is the margin of error for the mean?

20. Estimate that the population mean is within a margin of error of the sample mean and that later prices will fall within 2 standard deviations of the population mean. Where would you expect the later laptop prices to fall?

21. How did your expected range do, compared to what I actually found after the first three prices?

The rest of this book talks a lot about variation and sums of squares. It is worthwhile to develop some intuition about sums of squares and standard deviations. For each set of numbers in Exercises 22 through 33, calculate the deviations, the sum of squares, and the standard deviation. Some exercises have additional questions.

22. 1, 2.

23. 1, 3. How does the standard deviation compare to the average distance from the observations to their mean (the mean absolute deviation)?

24. 2, 6. (Note that these numbers are 2 times the numbers in Exercise 23.)

25. 6, 18. (Note that these numbers are 3 times the numbers in Exercise 24.)

26. 12, 36. (Note that these numbers are 2 times the numbers in Exercise 25.)

27. 4, 12. (Note that these numbers are one-third of the numbers in Exercise 26.) What happens to the sample standard deviation when you multiply the observations by some constant (for example, 2, 3, or 1/3)?

28. 5, 13. (Note that these numbers are 1 more than the numbers in Exercise 27.)

29. 3, 11. (Note that these numbers are 2 less than the numbers in Exercise 28.)

30. 103, 111. (Note that these numbers are 100 more than the numbers in Exercise 29.) What happens to the sample standard deviation when you add or subtract some constant?

31. 0, 1.

32. 0, 0, 1, 1.

33. A million 0's and a million 1's. (For this exercise, you have to imagine parts of the table. You won't have space to write it out completely.)

Answers to Odd-Numbered Exercises

1. Mean equals 108 divided by 4, which is 27.

3. Squared deviations: 676, 1, 169, 144.

5. Degrees of freedom equals number of observations minus 1, which is 3.

7. Standard deviation equals 18.2.

9. Confidence interval for the population mean is 9 to 45.

11. My prediction interval for the future weekly payments included all of the later weekly payments. The later gasoline expenses did not vary as widely as I expected. The highest payment, $53, was in my initial set of four weeks. (I think that we were driving to California that week.) The total range of gas expenses was from $10 to $53. The range of the initial sample was a slightly

better indication of how widely the expenses would vary than the prediction interval. It is not always the case that the prediction interval is more accurate, but it is usually more reliable.

13. $33, $183, −$217.

15. $81,666.67.

17. $40,833.33.

19. $237.73.

21. My prediction interval did fairly well. It included 13 of the remaining 15 laptop prices (87%). Not bad for three observations.

23.

OBSERVATION	MEAN	DEVIATION	SQUARED DEVIATION
1	2	−1	1
3	2	1	1

SUM OF SQUARES	2
VARIANCE	2
STANDARD DEVIATION	1.414

With two observations, the standard deviation is 41% larger than the distance from each observation to the sample mean.

25.

OBSERVATION	MEAN	DEVIATION	SQUARED DEVIATION
6	12	−6	36
18	12	6	36

SUM OF SQUARES	72
VARIANCE	72
STANDARD DEVIATION	8.485

27.

OBSERVATION	MEAN	DEVIATION	SQUARED DEVIATION
4	8	−4	16
12	8	4	16

SUM OF SQUARES	32
VARIANCE	32
STANDARD DEVIATION	5.657

When you multiply all of the observations in a set by the same number, you always increase the standard deviation as though you had multiplied the standard deviation by the same number (except for errors due to rounding). For example, imagine that your numbers are 1 and 2. They are 1 away from each other. Multiply both by 2, and you have 2 and 4. Now they are twice as far, and their standard deviation, which represents how spread out they are, is twice as large.

29.

OBSERVATION	MEAN	DEVIATION	SQUARED DEVIATION
3	7	−4	16
11	7	4	16

SUM OF SQUARES 32

VARIANCE 32

STANDARD DEVIATION 5.657

31.

OBSERVATION	MEAN	DEVIATION	SQUARED DEVIATION
0	0.5	−0.5	0.25
1	0.5	0.5	0.25

SUM OF SQUARES 0.5

VARIANCE 0.5

STANDARD DEVIATION 0.707

33.

NUMBER OF ROWS	OBSERVATION	MEAN	DEVIATION	SQUARED DEVIATION
1 million	0	0.5	−0.5	0.25
1 million	1	0.5	0.5	0.25

SUM OF SQUARES 500,000

VARIANCE 500,000/1,999,999 = 0.250000125

STANDARD DEVIATION 0.500

6.3 How to See the Future

- Prediction Intervals for Number Line Observations and Sample Means
- Standard Error of Means
- Confidence Intervals for Population Means
- Central Limit Theorem

For the years 1950 to 1980, the standard deviation in [mean annual] global temperatures is 0.13 deg. C. . . . According to records going back about a century, global temperatures have increased by 0.6 to 0.7 deg. C.

—MONASTERSKY, *SCIENCE NEWS*, JULY 2, 1988

14.4°C . . . is a reasonable value for the modern global average surface temperature.

—REID, *CLIMATIC CHANGE*, 1997, P. 400

ACCORDING TO MONASTERSKY, the standard deviation of the mean annual global temperature between 1950 and 1980 was 0.13°C. (A standard deviation of 0.13°C is 0.2°F.) Researchers looked at mean global temperatures for each of those 31 years. They found the mean of that sample and could find the deviations for each year by subtracting that mean from each year's global temperature. The sum of the squares of those deviations is what statisticians call the "sum of squares." The variance of that sample was the sum of squares divided by 30 (the degrees of freedom are 1 less than the 31 years). The standard deviation, 0.13, must be the square root of that variance.

The temperature 0.13°C may seem low. You may think that temperatures vary more widely. The reason this standard deviation is so small is that it is the standard deviation of observations that are themselves averages of observations taken all over the planet and throughout each year.

Averaging all of the observations in a year makes temperature variations seem smaller than what you experience from hour to hour. For example, last week, where I live, the temperature ranged from below freezing (-1°C) at night to 13°C (55°F) during the day. The variation from hour to hour spanned 14°C. The standard deviation was about 4°C. If I averaged all of the temperature observations of each day in the last week, I would find that each day had a mean temperature of about 6°C. The standard deviation of the daily mean temperatures was only about 1°C. If I looked at the standard deviation of the mean temperatures from day to day around the year, I would see cold days in the winter and warm days in the summer, and the standard deviation of daily means would be well above 5°C. That pattern of colder winters and warmer summers will repeat next year. If I average all of the temperature observations in each year, the variation in the means from year to year would be less than that from season to season.

The quotes at the beginning of this section are referring to temperatures that come from averaging observations not only from all hours and seasons in each year, but also from all over the globe. That is why the standard deviation of the mean annual global temperature is so small, about 0.13°C.

Having a standard deviation of 0.13°C means that the estimated mean annual global temperature jumps around somewhat from year to year. If it held steady, its standard deviation would be 0. Since the temperature does move around, some changes would not be cause for concern, as long as they were within the previous range of movement.

Many researchers claim that recent jumps are not like old jumps and something new is happening—the world is getting hotter. The judgment that the world has gotten hotter is based on a simple statistical trick of seeing the future, and some thought.

Determining a Prediction Interval for the Next Observation

Statisticians have a variety of tricks for telling the future. The most commonly used trick capitalizes on the normal distribution. We used it in the last section. Numbers often tend to fall into roughly normal distributions, and we know a lot about them. For example, two-thirds of the observations in a normal distribution fall within 1 standard deviation of the distribution's mean. About 95% of the observations fall within 2 standard deviations of the mean.

A Prediction Interval for Number Line Observations

To create a prediction interval for naturally occurring number line observations, you can assume that a normal distribution approximates the distribution of those observations. Your 95% prediction interval is within 2 standard deviations of the mean.

For example, when I check the number of pages in four books on my shelves, I find that they have a mean of 477 pages and a standard deviation of 190 pages. Two times 190 is 380. My 95% prediction interval for those page lengths is from 97 to 857 pages. That interval includes all of the four books. Furthermore, the next book I check has 703 pages, which is also within the prediction interval.

This sounds like the relationship between standard errors and the normal distribution. There is a reason: The standard error is a kind of standard deviation which we'll discuss a little later.

To see how we can use the standard deviation, imagine that you were a world climatologist in 1910. From 1880 to 1910, the mean global temperature has been about 13.8°C, with a standard deviation of about 0.13°C. Your friends ask you what the global temperature will be next year. What will you say? You know that about 95% of the time, the annual mean global temperature will be within 2 standard deviations of the population mean. Since 2 standard deviations is 0.26°C, you would guess that in the following year the mean annual global temperature would be somewhere between 13.8°C minus 0.26°C and 13.8°C plus 0.26°C, or between about 13.5°C and 14.1°C.

In that example, you knew that the population's mean temperature was 13.8°C. If you did not know that mean, you would have to take into account your uncertainty. For the moment, let us think about situations in which you know the real mean. How often does this happen? Not often in real life, when we rarely know with absolute certainty the nature of a population. However, we can create a simulation in which we know the real population, and we can learn how random sampling works, by watching how random samples from that population vary. Having learned how random samples compare to a population that we know, we can figure out how random samples compare to populations we do not know.

To check on how random samples from normal distributions behaved, I created a simulation in which the computer takes random samples from a normal distribution with a population mean of 0 and a population standard deviation of 1. When a normal distribution has a mean of 0 and a standard deviation of 1, it is called a "standard" normal distribution, and observations from such a

Figure 6.3.1

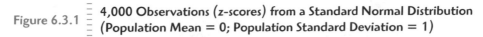

4,000 Observations (z-scores) from a Standard Normal Distribution (Population Mean = 0; Population Standard Deviation = 1)

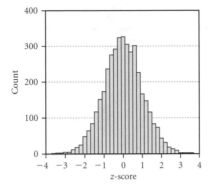

distribution are z-scores. If you are doing the computer projects at the end of each section in this book, you could try it out yourself. Figure 6.3.1 is a histogram of 4,000 observations that the program produced.

For this simulation, 2 standard deviations is 2. The first thing I checked was whether 95% of the time the observations would be within 2 standard deviations of the population mean, or between -2 and 2. Since 95% of 4,000 is 3,800, I was expecting that the middle 3,800 would be above -2 and below 2. The normal distribution is symmetrical, so I expected that about 100 would fall below -2 and about 100 would fall above 2.

I had my computer sort the observations from lowest to highest. After sorting the 4,000 observations, I found that the 100th from the bottom was -1.97. The 93rd from the bottom was -2, and 93 out of 4,000 (2.3%) were at or below -2, close to what I expected. At the other end, the 3,900th was 1.9969; 2.5% fell at 2 or above.

You can try this yourself with your software. In general, you will find that, in a normal distribution, about 95% of the observations fall within 2 standard deviations of the mean, 2.5% fall more than 2 standard deviations above the mean, and about 2.5% fall more than 2 standard deviations below the mean.

Table 6.3.1 shows more about the observations that come from the normal distribution. The table provides information for creating a variety of prediction intervals for observations drawn from a normal distribution. To create a 95% prediction interval, add about 2 standard deviations to and subtract about 2 standard deviations from the population mean. To create a two-thirds (68%) prediction interval, add and subtract about 1 standard deviation. For example, when making random draws from the normal distribution in our simulation, in which the mean is 0 and the standard deviation is 1, a 38% prediction interval for observations would be from $-1/2$ to $1/2$. I would expect 31% to fall below $-1/2$ and

Table 6.3.1 Prediction Intervals for Observations from a Normal Distribution

NUMBER OF STANDARD DEVIATIONS ADDED TO AND SUBTRACTED FROM THE MEAN	PROPORTION INCLUDED IN THE PREDICTION INTERVAL	PROPORTION EXPECTED ABOVE OR BELOW THE PREDICTION INTERVAL
0.5	38%	31%
1	68%	16%
1.5	87%	6.5%
1.96	95%	2.4998%
2	95.45%	2.275%
2.5	99%	.5%
3	99.7%	.15%
3.5	99.9%	.05%
4	99.99%	.005%
4.5	99.999%	.0005%

31% to fall above 1/2. If I drew 100 observations, I would expect that the 32nd would be about −1/2, and the 69th would be about 1/2.

Table 6.3.1 says that going up and down 1 standard deviation includes 68% of the observations. I have been calling that 68% "about two-thirds." Table 6.3.1 also shows you that 1.96 is a more precise number of standard deviations for calculating a 95% prediction interval. The value 1.96 rounds to 2, and for most purposes 2 works fine.

In real life, most of the values in Table 6.3.1 do not work precisely. Most distributions are not normal, or at least you cannot be certain that they are normal. Many distributions have lighter tails than the normal distribution. They do not spread out as widely, so the larger prediction intervals (95%, 99%, or above) will tend to be too large. Often a prediction interval that is too large does well. For example, suppose that your friends ask what the mean global temperature will be next year, and you guess that it will be somewhere between about 13.5°C and 14.1°C. If your estimated range was too large, and the global temperature turns out to be 13.8°C, your range still succeeded in including the actual temperature.

The Central Limit Theorem

Distributions of observations are not always normal, but means become more and more normally distributed as they are calculated from more and more observations. The reason is what is called the "central limit theorem." The central limit theorem says that when you create sums by randomly drawing values from an unchanging distribution and adding them up, as the number of observations

Figure 6.3.2 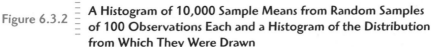 **A Histogram of 10,000 Sample Means from Random Samples of 100 Observations Each and a Histogram of the Distribution from Which They Were Drawn**

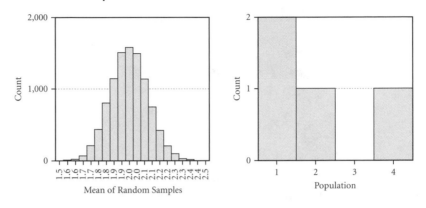

in your sum increases, the distribution of such a sum becomes more and more normally distributed.

Means are sums that have been divided by the number of observations. Dividing by the number of observations shifts the distribution towards zero, but leaves the distribution's shape otherwise unchanged and normally distributed. For example, the left histogram in Figure 6.3.2 shows 10,000 sample means. The samples had 100 observations each. The histogram on the right is the distribution from which the observations were drawn.

Because sample means are more reliably normally distributed than observations, using the normal distribution to calculate prediction intervals for means rather than for single observations produces more reliable prediction intervals.

Imagine that your friends have asked you what the average global temperature will be during the following decade. How would you predict this 10-year average?

Your prediction is going to depend on how widely sample means vary. To see how widely sample means vary, consider Figure 6.3.3, which shows more results of sampling from a normal distribution with a mean of 0 and a standard deviation of 1. Each point in Figure 6.3.3 represents a single random sample. At each sample size 40 samples were taken. For example, 40 samples had 1 observation each. They all appear on the far left. Another 40 samples had 2 observations each, and so on up to 40 samples with 50 observations in each.

Figure 6.3.3 shows several important features of sample means. First, sample means jump around. All of these means were created from observations drawn from the same normal distribution. This jumping around happens simply because of random sampling. Sometimes a random sample has higher numbers; sometimes the numbers are lower. Second, as you might have guessed from the

Figure 6.3.3

Sample Means for Random Samples Drawn from a Normal Distribution (Population Mean = 0; Population Standard Deviation = 1)

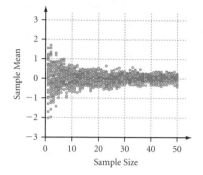

law of large numbers, as the sample sizes get larger, the sample means tend to fall closer and closer to the population mean.

Table 6.3.2 shows the standard deviations of the sort of sample means shown in Figure 6.3.3. To make a clearer picture, for Table 6.3.2, I had my software create 1,000 samples for each sample size. Table 6.3.2 lists only several very interesting sample sizes.

When the standard deviation of the sample means is represented as a fraction, it appears to be related to the sample size. The square root of 1 is 1, and the first line's standard deviation is 1/1. The square root of 4 is 2, and the standard deviation of means from four-observation samples is 1/2. This pattern continues through the table to 49. The square root of 49 is 7, and the standard deviation on the last line is 1/7. The standard deviation of these means seem to be 1 divided by the square root of the sample sizes.

Table 6.3.2

Standard Deviations of Distributions of Means for Random Samples Drawn from a Normal Distribution with a Standard Deviation of 1

SAMPLE SIZE	STANDARD DEVIATION OF THE MEANS	STANDARD DEVIATION OF THE MEANS EXPRESSED AS A FRACTION
1	0.978	1/1
4	0.500	1/2
9	0.334	1/3
16	0.247	1/4
36	0.168	1/6
49	0.142	1/7

For the simulations in Table 6.3.2, the observations had a standard deviation of 1. Let's see if that holds up when we repeat the process using a distribution with a standard deviation of 2. That is, the standard deviation of the observations will be 2, and I will create 4,000 random samples for each sample size.

The relationship holds up, as shown in Table 6.3.3, but the numerator of the fraction is the standard deviation with which we started. This is not coincidence. The standard deviation of the sample means is the population standard deviation divided by the square root of the sample size.

"Standard deviation of sample means" is a mouthful, so statisticians came up with the tradition of saying "standard error" when referring to the standard deviation of means. Here is an equation that shows the relationship between the standard error and the standard deviation:

$$\text{Standard Error} = \frac{\text{Population Standard Deviation}}{\sqrt{\text{Sample Size}}}$$

Standard Error

The standard deviation of sample means is called their "standard error." For sample means, the standard error is the population standard deviation divided by the square root of the sample size.

For example, the standard deviation of U.S. personal incomes is $36,500. If random samples of 100 people were selected from the U.S. population, the standard error of their means would be $3,650, because the square root of 100 is 10, and $3,650 is one-tenth of the population standard deviation.

Table 6.3.3 Standard Deviations of Distributions of Means for Random Samples Drawn from a Normal Distribution with a Standard Deviation of 2

SAMPLE SIZE	STANDARD DEVIATION OF THE MEANS	STANDARD DEVIATION OF THE MEANS EXPRESSED AS A FRACTION
1	1.984944	2/1
4	1.008215	2/2
9	0.684204	2/3
16	0.501069	2/4
25	0.40442	2/5
36	0.340546	2/6
49	0.288794	2/7

For example, imagine that the year is 1920. The mean global temperature has been 13.8°C for years. The standard deviation of those annual global temperatures has been 0.13°C. Now my friends ask me to guess the mean global temperature of all 10 years in the 1920s. I will guess that the decade's mean will be somewhere near 13.8°C. How near? The sample mean will be within about 2 standard errors of the population mean 95% of the time. In this case, what is the standard error? The mean is calculated for 10 years (the 1920s). To find the standard error, we divide the population standard deviation by the square root of 10, which is 3.16. The temperature 0.13°C divided by 3.16 is about 0.04°C.

Two standard errors would be about 0.08°C. I would guess that the decade's mean was somewhere between 13.7°C and 13.9°C, assuming that nothing changes during the decade. Figure 6.3.4 shows how decade means would be distributed in a normal distribution with a mean at 13.8 and a standard deviation of 0.04.

Now jump forward to the late 1990s, when the mean global temperature was about 14.4°C. Compare that to the prediction interval for the 1920s. The value 14.4 would be on the far right in Figure 6.3.4 and is 0.7°C higher than the 1920s mean. The value 0.7 is more than 17 times my standard error for a decade's mean

Figure 6.3.4 **Distribution of Decade Means When the Mean of the Population of Annual Mean Temperatures Is 13.8 and the Standard Error of Decade Means Is 0.04**

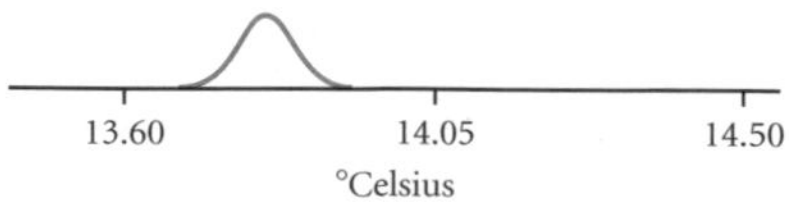

(0.04). It is extremely unlikely for such a 10-year mean to occur simply by random variation. That is part of why people think the Earth is becoming warmer.

Prediction Interval for Sample Means

The 95% prediction interval for the sample means is the population mean plus and minus 2 standard errors. The two-thirds prediction interval is the population mean plus and minus 1 standard error. Other prediction intervals may be created by referring to the normal distribution.

For example, the mean U.S. personal income in 2000 was $22,000. Random samples of 100 people would have a standard error of $3,650. The 95% prediction interval for their mean personal income would be from $14,700 to $29,300.

Calculating a Confidence Interval for the Population Mean

The fact that 95% of the time a sample mean is not more than 2 standard errors away from the population mean leads to an extremely valuable corollary: 95% of the time the population mean is not more than 2 standard errors away from the sample mean. We saw this kind of thinking for proportions earlier. It is like noticing that if you are not more than 50 feet from Joe, then Joe is not more than 50 feet from you. Similarly, if the sample mean is not more than 2 standard errors away from the population mean, then the population mean is not more than 2 standard errors away from the sample mean.

The difficulty in calculating confidence intervals for unknown populations is that we need to calculate the standard error from the population standard deviation. But if the population is unknown, we do not know the population standard deviation. The trick to get around this is to estimate that the population standard deviation is the same as the sample standard deviation. The sample standard deviation is a good estimate of the population standard deviation, and, in the long run, the mean sample standard deviation gets very close to the actual population standard deviation.

Let's calculate a confidence interval for a mean of the population that produced annual mean global temperatures at the turn of the century. From about 1880 to 1920, about 40 years, the mean annual global temperature hovered around roughly 13.8°C. Let's say that the standard deviation from year to year was 0.13°C. We estimate that the population standard deviation was also 0.13°C. The estimated standard error would then be 0.13°C divided by the square root of 40, so the estimated standard error would be 0.02°C.

A 95% confidence interval for the mean of the population from which the globe was then drawing its global temperatures would be from 13.8°C minus 0.04°C to 13.8°C plus 0.04°C, or from 13.76°C to 13.84°C. Rounded to one decimal place, that is from 13.8°C to 13.8°C. That may be why George Reid, the climatologist quoted at the beginning of this section, chose to round to a single digit.

A Confidence Interval for the Population Mean

A 95% confidence interval for the population mean is the sample mean plus and minus 2 estimated standard errors. The estimated standard errors are the standard errors calculated from estimating that the population standard deviation is the same as the sample standard deviation. A two-thirds confidence interval for the population mean is the sample mean plus and minus 1 estimated standard error. Other confidence intervals can be created by reference to the normal distribution.

For example, I sampled four books on my shelves. The mean was 477 pages, and the sample standard deviation was 190 pages. The estimated standard error is 95 pages. I am 95% confident that the mean number of pages of all the books on my shelves is somewhere between 287 and 667 pages.

Algebra and Greek Symbols

The standard error of the sample means is indicated by $\sigma_{\bar{x}}$:

$$(1) \qquad \sigma_{\bar{x}} = \frac{\sigma}{\sqrt{n}}$$

That is, the standard error is the population standard deviation divided by the square root of the sample size:

(2)
$$\hat{\sigma}_{\bar{x}} = \frac{s}{\sqrt{n}}$$

That is, the estimated standard error is the sample standard deviation divided by the square root of the sample size.

A normal distribution with a mean at 0 and a standard deviation of 1 is called a "standard normal distribution." Z_α is the value for which 1 minus α of the standard normal distribution falls below it. For example, let's say that α is 2.5%. Then 1 minus α is 97.5%. $Z_{.025}$ is the value that is greater than 97.5% of the observations in a standard normal distribution. 97.5% of the standard normal distribution falls below 1.96, so $Z_{.025}$ is 1.96. For a normally distributed population, a 1 minus α prediction interval for sample means is the population mean plus and minus $Z_{\alpha/2}$ population standard errors. That is,

(3)
$$P(|\bar{x} - \mu| < Z_{\alpha/2}\sigma_{\bar{x}}) = 1 - \alpha, \text{ if } x \text{ is normally distributed}$$

For data that is skewed or in some other way not normally distributed, this prediction interval tends to be more and more accurate as the sample size increases. That is,

(4)
$$P(|\bar{x} - \mu| < Z_{\alpha/2}\sigma_{\bar{x}}) \to 1 - \alpha; \text{ as } n \to \infty, \text{ for any distribution of } x$$

A 1 minus α confidence interval for the population mean is the sample mean plus and minus $Z_{\alpha/2}$ estimated standard errors. This interval tends to be more and more accurate as the sample size increases. That is,

(5)
$$P(|\bar{x} - \mu| < Z_{\alpha/2}s_{\bar{x}}) \to 1 - \alpha; \text{ as } n \to \infty$$

Equation for the Standard Error of a Proportion

A proportion of events that come up X is the mean of events coded as 1 when they are X, and 0 otherwise. For example, if I got three heads and a tail, the proportion that came up heads is the mean of 1, 1, 1, and 0. The proportion that came up tails is the mean of 0, 0, 0, and 1.

Now imagine that I am going to watch a system for its total trials. These N trials are the total population. By the time we're done, I may need to admit that N is infinity, but we will just call it N for now. The probability of a particular event is P. N is so large that the event happens NP times. The event will not happen $N(1 - P)$ times. I will code the event happening as 1 and the event not happening as 0. When I add up all the 0's and 1's, I will have NP. To find the mean outcome, I divide NP by N and get P. The following table shows my calculations of the standard deviation and the standard error.

PROBABILITY	NUMBER OF ROWS	OBSERVATION	MEAN	DEVIATION	SQUARED DEVIATION
$1 - P$	$N(1 - P)$	0	P	$0 - P = -P$	P^2
P	NP	1	P	$1 - P$	$(1 - P)^2$

Among the squared deviations, there are $N(1 - P)$ P^2's and NP $(1 - P)^2$'s.

The sum of squares is the following:

$$N(1 - P) P^2 + NP(1 - P)^2 = N[P^2 - P^3 + P(1 - 2P + P^2)]$$

$$= N(P^2 - P^3 + P - 2P^2 + P^3)$$

$$= N(P - P^2)$$

$$= N[P(1 - P)]$$

Remember that I'm looking at the population, so the variance is the sum of squares divided by N.

The variance equals $N[P(1 - P)]/N$, which equals $P(1 - P)$.

The population standard deviation equals $\sqrt{P(1 - P)}$.

The sample size is n. The standard error equals $\frac{\sqrt{P(1 - P)}}{\sqrt{n}}$, which equals $\sqrt{\frac{P(1 - P)}{n}}$. Now you know where the equation for the standard error of a proportion comes from.

Abstract

If observations are normally distributed, and you know the mean and standard deviation of the population, the 95% prediction interval for single observations is· from 2 standard deviations below the population mean to 2 standard deviations above the mean. This 95% prediction interval works fairly well for many naturally occurring distributions.

The standard error of a mean is the population standard deviation divided by the square root of the sample size. If the population mean and standard deviation are known, prediction intervals for random sample means can be constructed by starting from the population mean and adding and subtracting enough standard errors to capture the desired proportion of the normal distribution. If the population features are unknown, confidence intervals for the population mean can be constructed around a random sample mean by adding and subtracting estimated standard errors.

Avoiding Common Misunderstandings

Although we use the sample standard deviation to estimate the population standard deviation, they are not the same. You will see later in this text that our use of the sample standard deviation causes some difficulty that we wouldn't have if we knew the population standard deviation.

Computer Project

Use the data in the Representative Sample of 50,000 Americans (from *www.keycollege.com/dm*) that you looked at in previous computer projects. Pick a number line observation with which to work. Have your software calculate the mean and standard deviation of that population. Have your software take random samples and save the means of those samples. Find the standard deviation of those means. Check that the standard deviation of the means is the population standard deviation divided by the square root of your sample size. Make a histogram of the sample means. Is it normally distributed? Sort the sample means and check that 5% fall at least 2 standard errors from the population mean.

Exercises

Nancy Smith and several other researchers tested the possibility that you could treat depression by simply handing depressed people a book about how to cure their own depression (D. D. Burns, *Feeling Good*, 1980).

> *Results and Discussion*
>
> *Means (and standard deviations) for the [Hamilton Rating Scale for Depression] were 19.6 (SD = 4.8), 10.0 (SD = 5.8), and 9.8 (SD = 8.0) for pretreatment, [three months] posttreatment, and 3-year follow-up, respectively.*
>
> —SMITH ET AL., *JOURNAL OF CONSULTING AND CLINICAL PSYCHOLOGY*, 1997, P. 325

The Hamilton Rating Scale for Depression indicates how depressed patients are. Higher scores indicate more depression. The Smith team used the common abbreviation SD to stand for "standard deviation."

Use the preceding information about depression to complete Exercises 1 through 14.

1. Where would you estimate that the middle 95% of the pretreatment Hamilton depression scores were?

2. Elsewhere in their report, the Smith team report that there were 72 people in the study. What is the standard error of the pretreatment scores?

3. What is a two-thirds confidence interval for the mean Hamilton depression score of the population from which the pretreatment scores were drawn?

4. What is a 95% confidence interval for the pretreatment scores' population mean?

5. What is a 99% confidence interval for the pretreatment scores' population mean?

6. If the population mean were at the bottom of your 95% confidence interval for the population mean, what would be a 95% confidence interval for the sample mean of another sample of 72 scores?

7. How do the post-treatment means compare to what you would expect if you drew another 72-score sample from the same distribution that produced the pretreatment scores?

8. Where would you estimate that the middle 95% of the three-year follow-up Hamilton depression scores were?

9. Assuming that there were 72 people in the three-year follow-up sample, what is the standard error of the three-year follow-up scores?

10. What is a two-thirds confidence interval for the mean Hamilton depression score of the population from which the three-year follow-up scores were drawn?

11. What is a 99% confidence interval for the three-year follow-up scores' population mean?

12. What is a 95% confidence interval for the three-year follow-up scores' population mean?

13. If the population mean were at the top of your 95% confidence interval for the population mean, what would be a 95% confidence interval for the sample mean of another sample of 72 scores?

14. How do the pretreatment means compare to what you would expect if you drew another 72-score sample from the same distribution that produced the three-year follow-up scores?

Pao-Shin Chu and Jianxin Wang looked at the number of tropical cyclones that hit Hawaii during El Niño years. During El Niño years, a huge area of the Pacific Ocean gets hotter than usual, and that changes the winds and weather. Pao-Shin Chu and Jianxin Wang found out that one result of El Niño is tropical cyclones that cause heavy damage in Hawaii. Since we know when an El Niño year is happening this is useful information, because it gives Hawaii residents time to prepare for the storms.

The following table gives some of Chu and Wang's data (Chu and Wang, *Journal of Climate,* 1997, p. 2686).

YEAR	NUMBER OF TROPICAL CYCLONES
1951	0
1957	3
1963	1
1965	0
1969	0
1972	2
1976	1
1982	3
1987	0
1991	1

There are 10 El Niño years in the preceding table. You are going to use the first six to predict the mean of the last four. If our methods are sound, you should be able to predict the later mean. Use this information to complete Exercises 15 through 22.

15. What is the mean of the first six El Niño years?
16. What is their sum of squares, variance, and standard deviation?
17. What would you estimate for their standard error?
18. What is a 95% confidence interval for the mean number of tropical cyclones in the population of El Niño years from which this sample was drawn?
19. Now we start to estimate the last four. Assuming that the population standard deviation is the same as what we saw in the first six years, what is the standard error for a sample of four years?
20. Imagine you constructed a 95% prediction interval for the four-year sample on the assumption that the population mean was at the bottom of your 95% confidence interval for the population mean, and imagine that you constructed another such prediction interval on the assumption that the population mean was at the top. What is the interval from the bottom of your lower prediction interval to the top of your higher prediction interval?
21. What is the mean of the last four years?
22. How did your prediction interval do?

If you wanted to tell someone what all 10 years indicated about El Niño patterns, you would use all 10 years. That is what Chu and Wang did. You can summarize what this study indicates. Use this information to complete Exercises 23 through 28.

23. What is the mean of the 10 El Niño years?

24. What is their sum of squares, variance, and standard deviation?

25. What would you estimate for their standard error?

26. What is a 95% confidence interval for the mean number of tropical cyclones in the population of El Niño years from which this sample was drawn?

27. Imagine that someone wanted to know the number of cyclones to expect in two El Niño years. Assuming that the population standard deviation is the same as what we see in those 10 years, what is the standard error for a sample of two years?

28. Imagine you constructed a 95% prediction interval for a two-year sample on the assumption that the population mean was at the bottom of your 95% confidence interval for the population mean, and imagine that you constructed another such prediction interval on the assumption that the population mean was at the top. What is the interval from the bottom of your lower prediction interval to the top of your higher prediction interval?

29. Here is a report on a patient's bones:

    For Bakoulis, the Triad [syndrome] might have been jump-started by simple poor nutrition. . . . Her most recent bone scan was two standard deviations below normal, putting her just short of osteoporosis and at four times greater risk for fracture than a person with healthy bones.

    —DOBIE, *NEWSDAY,* JULY 29, 1997

    Write a short memo explaining what it means that Ms. Bakoulis's bone scan was 2 standard deviations below normal. Give some idea about what proportion of the population you would expect to have worse bones than Ms. Bakoulis does. Mention what assumption about the distribution of bone scans you are making when you make your estimate.

30. Here is a report on the size of a heart in terms of standard deviations:

    When Foker told a visiting cardiac surgeon that McKeely's left ventricle had grown from a severe minus 5.5 standard deviation to normal size in a few short weeks, she said, "No way!"

    —MAJESKI, *CHICAGO TRIBUNE,* JANUARY 17, 1997

    Write a short memo explaining how unusually small McKeely's left ventricle was.

Answers to Odd-Numbered Exercises

1. A 95% prediction interval for single observations is within 2 standard deviations of the mean. The mean is 19.6, and the standard deviation is 4.8. I would expect the middle 95% to range between about 19.6 minus 9.6 and 19.6 plus 9.6—that is, from 10.0 to 29.2.

3. A two-thirds confidence interval for the population mean is within 1 estimated standard error of the sample mean—that is, from 19.0 to 20.2.

5. I look up a 99% interval in Table 6.3.1 and see that I need to add and subtract 2.5 standard errors. My confidence interval is from 19.6 minus (2.5 times 0.57) to 19.6 plus that amount, which equals 18.175 to 21.025.

7. The post-treatment mean (10.0) is below my prediction interval for the sample mean, which was constructed from the bottom of my confidence interval for the population mean.

9. The standard error is 8 divided by the square root of 72, which equals 0.94.

11. The 99% confidence interval is 9.8 plus and minus 2.5 times 0.94, which is a range of 6.862 to 11.562.

13. From 8.988 to 12.748.

15. 1.

17. The standard error equals 1.26 divided by the square root of 6, or 0.5.

19. The standard error equals 1.26 divided by 2, or 0.63.

21. The mean equals (1 plus 3 plus 0 plus 1) divided by 4, which equals 5 divided by 4, or 1.25.

23. 1.1.

25. 0.3786.

27. 1.1 divided by the square root of 2, or 0.78.

29. "Memo: Assuming bone scans come out normally distributed, a bone scan 2 standard deviations below the mean is very unusual. About 95% of the population would have scans closer to the mean. Only 5% would be expected to have more pathological bone scans than Ms. Bakoulis's, with about 2.5% being lower."

CHAPTER 7

Testing Treatments

The 20th century saw an explosion of knowledge about how to influence semi-random events. Farmers learned how to boost yields. Doctors learned how to treat illnesses. Engineers learned how to control production processes enough to produce spare parts that fit in every car a manufacturer makes.

There were, and still are, enormous intellectual obstacles to discovering what treatments work best when chance is involved. For example, imagine the position of a doctor testing a new treatment for high cholesterol. Let's say that the treatment helps the average patient, but it does not work for everyone, and, among the people it does work for, it works different amounts. The doctor doesn't know whether or how well the treatment works. The doctor provides the treatment to four patients. The first patient's cholesterol level rises, the second's level remains constant, the third patient's cholesterol drops a lot, and the last patient's cholesterol drops a little. What can the doctor conclude? All the doctor has is this data to go on. Section 7.1 shows you how she could proceed, by exploring the challenges that William Gosset faced in figuring out how Guinness could make better beer.

There are even worse challenges. Psychiatry has been faced with the overwhelming difficulty that patients often get better on their own. One of the most prevalent psychiatric disorders of our time is depression, which confounds researchers, because the typical depression patient gets better without treatment within three months. To see why this is a problem, consider what happens when a psychiatrist tests a new treatment for depression. The treatment does nothing, but the psychiatrist doesn't know that. The psychiatrist tries the treatment on four patients, and they all get better within about three months! The psychiatrist says, "I've got a treatment for depression that works!" Well, no. The patients probably would have recovered on their own. All that happened was that the psychiatrist was fooled by the results of a research strategy that could not succeed in revealing whether the treatment worked. In Section 7.2 you will learn what research strategy the psychiatrist ought to have used, and Section 7.3 prepares you to understand the statistical test that the ideal research strategy calls for, the analysis of variance.

This book presents three major tests of correlation. The chi-square test checks for a correlation between two sets of categorical measurements. For example, a chi-square test could check for a correlation between profession and political affiliation. Regression tests for a correlation between two sets of number line measurements. For example, regression could be used to check for a correlation between income and age. Chapters 7 and 8 present the analysis of variance, which checks for a correlation between a set of categorical measurements and a set of number line measurements. For example, the analysis of variance could be used to check for a correlation between profession and income, or between age and political affiliation.

7.1 A Cautionary Tale

- William Gosset's Troubles with the Z-Test and the *T*-Distribution
- The *T*-Test

The average rating of . . . external control was [mean +/− SD] 3.53 +/− .83. . . . Internal control ("It is just wrong" and "I would feel guilty") generated an average rating of importance of 3.05 +/− .92. . . . The difference . . . attained high statistical significance (paired t test = 8.75, 386 df, p < .001).

—BERGER AND MARELICH, *JOURNAL OF STUDIES ON ALCOHOL*, 1997, P. 518

WHAT DETERS DRUNK DRIVING? To find out, researchers D. Berger and William Marelich asked drivers to rate statements about why they chose to not drive drunk. Some statements were about avoiding punishments. Others were about living up to ethical standards. The researchers averaged each person's avoid punishment ratings and ethical standards ratings. That gave each person two scores: an avoid punishment ("external control") score and an ethical standards ("internal control") score. Berger and Marelich's results appear in the quote at the beginning of this section. The quote says "paired t test = 8.75, 386 df, p < .001." What does that mean? To find out, we need to see what a *t*-test is.

The *T*-Test

At the turn of the last century, the Guinness Company sent one of its employees, William Gosset, to study with Karl Pearson, one of the people who began the development of modern statistics. It was Pearson who coined the term "standard deviation" and developed the chi-square test.

From Pearson, Gosset learned about the *z*-test presented earlier in this book. Pearson pointed out that because sample means tend to be roughly normally distributed, as are proportions, a *z*-test could be used to check whether a sample of number line observations had a population mean at a particular point. When using a *z*-test to check whether a population proportion is a particular value, we have the advantage of knowing the real standard error, because the standard error of proportions is determined only by the population proportion and the sample size. With samples of number line observations, things are not so easy, because the standard error depends on the *population* standard deviation, and the null hypothesis that Gosset wanted to test could not tell him the population standard deviation. Pearson's solution was to use the sample standard deviation as an estimate of the population standard deviation. So, for such a *z*-test, *z* is the distance from the null hypothesis's population mean to the sample mean divided by the estimated standard error:

$$z = \frac{\text{Sample Mean} - \text{Null Hypothesis's Population Mean}}{\text{Standard Error Estimated from Sample Standard Deviation}}$$

As long as the estimated standard error is consistently near the real standard error, if the null hypothesis is true, *z* will be normally distributed and 95% of the time will fall between −2 and 2. A *z* below −2 or above 2 would be significant if alpha were 5%.

Pearson pointed out to Gosset that, to use the z-test, you had to work with big samples to be sure they were reasonably representative and that your estimated standard error was close to the real standard error. Gosset brought this kind of thinking back to the Guinness brewery, but it was impractical. The Guinness brewers could not try a new method on 400 vats of beer to find out if it worked. Gosset had to test a method after it had been used on only a few vats. He considered trying the z-test, but he quickly found out that with small sample sizes, the z-test was often misleading.

What Gosset was finding was that samples vary, and their standard errors vary too. To see what was happening, we can simulate what happens when you take small random samples and use the z-test. The computer project for this section is to have software pull small samples from a normally distributed population that has a mean at 0 and a standard deviation of 1.

In the simulation, each sample has two observations. If you calculated the standard error from the population standard deviation, you would find that the standard error is 0.71.

Figure 7.1.1 shows a histogram of 5,000 sample means drawn from the simulation. The means in Figure 7.1.1 are normally distributed, because means in general tend to be normally distributed.

For each sample, we could do a z-test. For example, the first sample was 0.36 and -0.7. It had a mean of -0.17 and an estimated standard error of 0.53. If we tested whether that sample came from a distribution with a population mean at 0, the z-value would be -0.17 divided by 0.53, which yields -0.32. More than one-third of z-values fall further from 0 than 0.32. In a z-test, a z of 0.32 has a p-value that is greater than .62. We would retain the null hypothesis that these observations came from a population with a mean at 0. That is good, because they did.

Figure 7.1.1

Histogram of 5,000 Sample Means of Random Samples Drawn from a Standard Normal Distribution (Population Mean = 0; Population Standard Deviation = 1; Sample Size = 2)

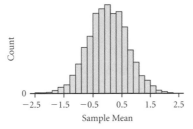

Overall among the 5,000 samples, however, the z-test did not do very well: 31% of the time the calculated z was either greater than 2 or less than -2. For 31% of the samples, the z-test mistakenly rejected the true null hypothesis that the population mean was 0. We do not expect the z-test to be right all the time, but, if we are using an alpha of 5%, we expect it to reject a true null hypothesis about 5% of the time. With small sample sizes, the z-test rejects true null hypotheses too often.

How Often Should a Significance Test Make Mistakes?

If alpha is 5%, and the null hypothesis is true, random variation ought to produce a significant result 5% of the time.

For example, when the null hypothesis is true, the z-test should produce a z-value greater than 2 or less than -2 about 5% of the time, simply by random variation. This will lead the null hypothesis to be wrongly rejected about 5% of the time.

That is the problem that Gosset found. He was testing treatments for which the null hypothesis was often true: There was no benefit in those treatments. For many of the treatments, on the average, vats given the treatment were no better after treatment than before. Gosset's problem was that when there was no effect from the treatment, the z-test was overly enthusiastic about telling him that something important was going on.

Why does the z-test have such a hard time in this situation? The problem that Gosset encountered is that with small samples the estimates of the standard error jump around a lot. Gosset knew that the sample mean was probably not more

Figure 7.1.2

Estimated Standard Errors from 5,000 Samples from a Normal Distribution (Population Standard Deviation = 1; Sample Size = 2)

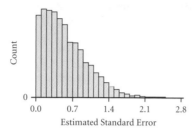

than 2 standard errors away from the population mean. What he did not know was what the standard error really was. In the case of our simulation, we know that the standard error is 0.71, but if you are studying nature, and all you have is your sample, you don't know what the standard error really is. All you have is the *estimated* standard error. That was Gosset's situation.

How does the estimated standard error do? To find out, we can look at estimated standard errors. Figure 7.1.2 shows the estimated standard errors calculated from the 5,000 samples in our simulation.

The most important thing in Figure 7.1.2 is that the estimated standard errors *are* distributed. They vary. They are not all 0.71. Each one is an estimate of that 0.71, but they vary from sample to sample. The estimated standard errors wandered all over between nearly 0 and 2.8.

When the estimated standard error is too high (in this case, above 0.71), that doesn't cause much trouble for the z-test. Having a larger standard error makes the z-test more conservative—less likely to reject the null hypothesis. The problem is when the estimated standard errors are too low (in this case, below 0.71). Too-small standard errors make z too large, because z is calculated by dividing by the standard error. In the earlier simulation, 68% of the estimated standard errors were below 0.71.

Gosset did not know the real standard error. He could have tried using confidence intervals for the standard error, but instead used a more elegant approach that capitalizes on the essence of what a significance test is.

A significance test has four essential elements: (1) You begin with a null hypothesis. (2) You figure out how some relevant statistic is distributed if the null hypothesis is true. (3) Based on the distribution you figured out, you find the p-value, which is the probability of getting a statistic at least as embarrassing for the null hypothesis as the one you got, if the null hypothesis is true. (4) If the p-value is less than your cutoff, alpha, you reject the null hypothesis.

How to Develop Your Own Significance Test

First, state your null hypothesis. Based on your null hypothesis, figure out how a statistic would be distributed if your null hypothesis were true. The statistic is any result you can calculate that in some way reflects how embarrassed the null hypothesis is by the results.

To do the test, collect your sample and calculate the statistic. The *p*-value is the probability of getting a statistic at least as embarrassing for the null hypothesis as the one you calculate from your sample.

To do his *z*-tests, Gosset was taking the difference between the sample mean and the null hypothesis's population mean and dividing it by the estimated standard error. The reason the *z*-test did not work for Gosset was that for small samples that ratio is not normally distributed. The problem was not dividing the difference by the estimated standard error but assuming that the ratio would be normally distributed. Gosset realized that he could continue to look at the difference divided by the estimated standard error. All he had to do was figure out how that ratio would be distributed.

To avoid confusion, Gosset did not use the name "*z*" for the ratio he was calculating. To make it clear that he was talking about something different from the *z* in a *z*-test, Gosset called his statistic "*t*," which is calculated the same way that *z* is calculated. The *t*-value is the difference between the sample mean and the null hypothesis's population mean divided by the sample estimated standard error.

How is *t* distributed if the null hypothesis is true? We can find out from our simulation. For each sample in the simulation, I had the computer divide the sample mean by the sample estimated standard error to produce a *t*-value for each sample. Figure 7.1.3 shows the middle of the distribution of *t*-values.

Figure 7.1.3 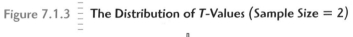 **The Distribution of *T*-Values (Sample Size = 2)**

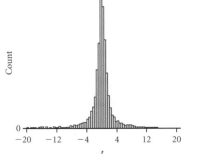

Figure 7.1.3 does not show all of the simulation's t-values, which ranged from $-1,100$ to 800. The middle 95% ranged from -16 to 11. Figure 7.1.3 shows that the distribution of t-values (the t-distribution) has larger tails than the normal distribution. To see where the big tails came from, look again at Figure 7.1.2.

Many estimated standard errors were near 0. When you divide by something close to 0, you get an answer that is far from 0. When the simulation divided the sample mean by the estimated standard error, it often got very extreme t-values.

Gosset did not have the luxury of discovering the distribution of t by running a simulation on a computer. Instead, he figured out mathematically how t would be distributed. To do the mathematics, Gosset had to make an important assumption: that the population from which the observations were drawn was normally distributed. Our population was normal, so Gosset's calculations should have worked for us, and they did, roughly.

A Limit on the Use of the *T*-Test

When figuring out how t would be distributed, Gosset assumed that the population would be normally distributed. If the population is *not* normal, Gosset's calculations about the t-distribution do not apply, and the t-test should not be used.

What we found in our simulation is about what Gosset would have predicted: that t-values are symmetrically distributed around 0, and that in situations like this, if the population is normally distributed and the samples have two observations each, the middle 95% of the t-values fall between about -12.7 and $+12.7$. The t-value is how many estimated standard errors a sample mean is from the population mean, so this 12.7 tells us that 95% of the time the sample mean is not more than 12.7 estimated standard errors away from the population mean.

Once we know something such as "the middle 95% of the t-values will fall between -12.7 and $+12.7$," we have what we need for a significance test. Any t-value closer to 0 than 12.7 would have a p-value over 5% and would not be significant (if alpha is 5%). Any t-value further from 0 than 12.7 would have a p-value below 5% and would be significant (if alpha is 5%).

That is the t-test. It would be very neat and tidy if that were all there was to it, but the test is a little more complicated, because the estimated standard error varies more widely for smaller samples. The distribution's shape depends on how large the samples are. Figure 7.1.4 shows t-distributions for several sample sizes.

Figure 7.1.4 shows something important about how t is distributed. As the sample size gets larger, t becomes less widely distributed because the estimated standard error is constrained to fall closer and closer to the real standard error. The result is that the t-distribution's tails get smaller and smaller as the sample size gets larger. Table 7.1.1 shows the edges of the middle 95% of the t-distribution for several sample sizes.

Figure 7.1.4   **T-Distributions for Sample Sizes 2, 3, 4, 5, and 10**

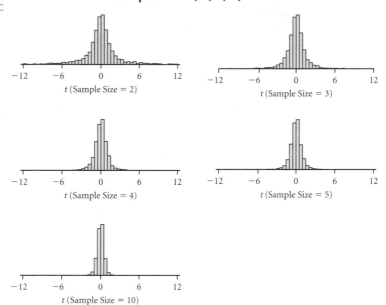

t (Sample Size = 2)

t (Sample Size = 3)

t (Sample Size = 4)

t (Sample Size = 5)

t (Sample Size = 10)

Table 7.1.1   *Edges of the Middle 95% of the T-Distribution*

SAMPLE SIZE	NUMBER OF OBSERVATIONS MINUS NUMBER OF MEANS (df)	LOWER EDGE	UPPER EDGE
2	1	−12.7	12.7
3	2	−4.3	4.3
4	3	−3.2	3.2
5	4	−2.8	2.8
6	5	−2.6	2.6
11	10	−2.2	2.2
21	20	−2.1	2.1
61	60	−2.0	2.0
101	100	−1.98	1.98
1 billion or more	1 billion or more −1	−1.96	1.96

Note: The t-distribution appears in t-statistics calculated from random samples drawn from normal populations. The values in this table were derived from a data-analysis computer program, Systat®.

The *T*-Distribution

The *t*-distribution is the distribution of the difference between sample means and the population mean divided by the sample estimated standard errors, where the samples are random samples from a normal distribution. It is always symmetrical with a mean at the mean of the population from which the observations were drawn. The shape of the *t*-distribution depends on the sample sizes. For small sample sizes, the *t*-distribution is a narrow vertical spike with tails that spread widely. As the sample size increases, the *t*-distribution becomes more and more like the normal distribution. For sample sizes over 60, the *t*-distribution is essentially normal.

For example, consider the following histograms:

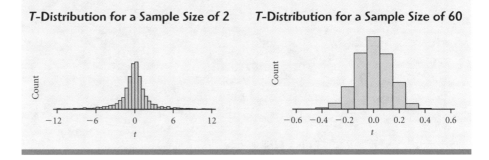

If your sample size is greater than 60, you can add and subtract 2 estimated standard errors, and you will get a fine 95% confidence interval.

The *t*-test is often used to look at differences between multiple measurements taken from each person or thing studied. For example, the study that was quoted at the beginning of this section measured how much people reported being motivated by internal ethics and how much they reported being motivated by fear of external consequences. Here's the quote from that study's report once more:

> *The average rating of . . . external control was [mean +/− SD] 3.53 +/− .83. . . . Internal control ("It is just wrong" and "I would feel guilty") generated an average rating of importance of 3.05 +/− .92. . . . The difference . . . attained high statistical significance (paired t test = 8.75, 386 df, p < .001).*
>
> —BERGER AND MARELICH, *JOURNAL OF STUDIES ON ALCOHOL*, 1997, P. 518

What Berger and Marelich were testing here was a distribution of differences. For each respondent, they subtracted the internal score from the external score. They calculated the mean of those differences and the estimated standard error for those differences. Their null hypothesis was that those differences came from a normally distributed population with a mean at 0. To find *t*, they subtracted 0 from the mean difference and divided by the estimated standard error of the differences. They found that t was 8.75, which they reported at the end of the quote: "(paired t test = 8.75, 386 df, p < .001)."

The p-value was less than .001. That means that *if the null hypothesis were true,* then the chances of getting a t-value at least this far from 0 are less than 1 out of 1,000. That is very embarrassing for the null hypothesis, and Berger and Marelich rejected the idea that people in the population from which the respondents were taken were, on the average, just as enthusiastic about ethical standards as they were about avoiding punishment. According to the study, it seems that external punishments are, on the average, more compelling than internal standards.

Notice that where the t-test is reported, Berger and Marelich say "386 df." There they are telling us that the sample size was 387. The *df*, or degrees of freedom, are reported in the second column of Table 7.1.1; this value is the number of observations minus the number of means. In this case, there were 387 observations, and the researchers checked one mean, so the *df* were 386. In some journals, this would be reported as "$t(386) = 8.75$."

The *df* tell how many observations were free to vary by chance, if you know the mean. For example, if I tell you that there are two observations, and the mean is 10, then the degrees of freedom are only 1, because, if one of the observations is 3, the other observation has to be 17. If chance moved one observation to 8, then the other observation could not change at random, but would have to be 12. With three observations, you could move two observations around however you liked, but, if the mean stays at 10, once you had placed the first two, the third would no longer be free to move around. So, with three observations, there would be two degrees of freedom.

A 95% Confidence Interval Based on the *T*-Distribution

I've been telling you to add and subtract 2 estimated standard errors when you calculate the 95% confidence interval for the population mean. That is good advice if you have large samples, but if you have a small sample, you are going to encounter the same problem that Gosset did.

If your sample is less than 60, use the t-distribution when you calculate your confidence intervals. Rather than multiplying the standard error by 2 to find the margin of error, you multiply by the values in Table 7.1.1. For example, if you have two observations, you add and subtract 12.7 estimated standard errors. If you have three observations, you add and subtract 4.3 standard errors.

I have occasionally worked with very small samples. Recently, my wife and I joined a carpool. Two mornings a week, I have to leave home in time to drop my son at a friend's house by 8:20. I was told that if I could not get there by 8:20, I should just drive my son all the way to school, because my friend's family would leave without him.

Using *T*-Values for Confidence Intervals

For small sample sizes, an interval of 2 estimated standard errors on either side of the sample mean will include the population mean less often than 95% of the time. To create a 95% confidence interval for sample sizes that are less than 60, add and subtract the product of the estimated standard error and the *t*-value from Table 7.1.1 for that sample size.

For example, I took a random sample of the personal annual incomes of two Americans. The incomes were $14,550 and $32,946. The mean was $23,748. The estimated standard error was $9,198. In Table 7.1.1, the *t*-value for a sample size of 2 is 12.7. The amount $9,198 times 12.7 equals $116,814.60. My 95% confidence interval for the mean income is from −$93,066.60 to $140,562.60. The actual mean of the data from which I drew those two incomes was $21,989.93. The confidence interval succeeded in including the actual mean.

My wife told me that it takes only five minutes to get to my son's friend's house. On the first day I left at 8:15 and did get there at 8:20, but the second time I was five minutes late and caught some nasty comments. The third time I left at 8:10, to try to fix things, and got there at 8:18, which was fine, but it raised an alarm for me. I realized that, because of the traffic lights, and because of the random nature of three-year-olds getting into cars, I was dealing with a random system. Normally, I might just leave a half-hour early, but I do not want to get up a half-hour earlier.

I tried to determine more precisely when I should leave. The three trips took 5, 10, and 8 minutes. The mean was 7.7 minutes; the sample standard deviation was 2.5 minutes. The estimated standard error was 1.4 minutes.

$$\text{Mean} = \frac{5 + 10 + 8}{3} = \frac{23}{3} = 7.7$$

$$\text{Estimated Standard Error} = \frac{\text{Standard Deviation}}{\sqrt{\text{Sample Size}}}$$

$$\text{Estimated Standard Error} = \frac{2.5}{\sqrt{3}} = 1.4$$

Using the *t*-distribution, I figured out a 95% confidence interval by adding and subtracting 4.3 estimated standard errors. (Table 7.1.1 shows that, for three observations, the middle 95% of *t*-values fall between −4.3 and 4.3.) Adding and subtracting 6 minutes, I found that, *on the average,* it would take me somewhere between 2 and 14 minutes.

So, 2 to 14 minutes was my confidence interval for the population mean. I needed a prediction interval for single trips. I used the sample standard deviation as an estimate of the population standard deviation and added two of them on either side of my confidence interval for the mean. That meant that one edge of my confidence interval was at 19 minutes. I decided to leave at 8:00, 20 minutes early. That has worked consistently.

If you are trying to figure out a 95% confidence interval for a mean, and you have fewer than 60 observations, do not add and subtract 2 standard errors. Instead look in Table 7.1.1 to figure out how many estimated standard errors you should be adding and subtracting.

Pros and Cons of *T*-Tests

The *t*-test is widely used in the social sciences, even though there are other tests that do the same work and more. The ANOVA test (presented later in this text) can test for differences between two groups and for differences between three or more groups.

Other tests are more reliable than the *t*-test, which assumes a normal distribution and is inaccurate when the population is not normal. Other tests are not fooled if the population is not normal. If you are going to use the *t*-test, you ought to know that your population is normally distributed. Unfortunately, with small sample sizes, you cannot tell from the sample whether it came from a normal population. If you had several hundred observations from the population, you could check whether the population is normally distributed, but if you had that big a sample, you could also do a *z*-test. That means that the *t*-test is rarely justified. Statisticians such as Karl Pearson would suggest that you try to avoid the *t*-test and work with bigger samples instead.

> *Pearson . . . remained firmly in the tradition of mass phenomena. He remarked in a letter of 1912 to Gosset that "only naughty brewers" used numbers so small in their work.*
> —PORTER, *THE RISE OF STATISTICAL THINKING 1820–1900,* 1986, P. 317

If you have no way to gather more data, you may have to be as naughty as Gosset. It turns out that he was successful. It seems that beer is normally distributed. Many things are.

The Moral of Gosset's Story

The caution in this tale is that if you were in Gosset's position, you too might have deduced that the z-test would work fine. Sometimes deductions have errors. You would do well to check your deductions with simulations. You might even want to try your statistical methods and see if they accurately reveal when the null hypothesis is and is not true. These statistical methods will probably mislead you sometimes. That is an important point about the idea of the p-value: It will reject true null hypotheses about 5% of the time (or wherever you set alpha). But if a test misleads you most of the time, maybe it is not because of chance. Maybe some idea behind the test is flawed.

T-Test Summary

Purpose of the T-Test

The t-test can be used to examine a random sample of number line observations to make inferences about the location on the number line of the population mean. The t-test can also be used to check whether evidence exists that a random sample came from a distribution with a population mean different from the population mean designated in the test's null hypothesis.

T-Test Requirements

The population from which the observations come must be normally distributed. The observations must be independent random samples from the population.

T-Test Null Hypothesis

The population mean equals a particular value.

The T-Statistics

The null hypothesis's population mean is subtracted from the sample mean, and the resulting difference is divided by the standard error estimated from the sample standard deviation. These equations summarize the steps:

$$t = \frac{\text{Sample Mean} - \text{Null Hypothesis's Population Mean}}{\text{Estimated Standard Error}}$$

$$\text{Estimated Standard Error} = \frac{\text{Sample Standard Deviation}}{\sqrt{\text{Sample Size}}}$$

The *P*-Value

The distribution of *t* depends on the sample size. To find whether a particular *t* has a *p*-value greater or less than 0, look in a table describing how *t* is distributed, such as this section's Table 7.1.1. Most such tables will describe the *t*-distribution for particular degrees of freedom. In a *t*-test, the degrees of freedom are 1 less than the number of observations. The *p*-value is the proportion of the *t*-distribution that falls at least as far from 0 as the sample's *t*-value.

The Logic of the Inference

There are two possible inferences for the *t*-test. If the *p*-value is below one's cut-off for significance, alpha, then the null hypothesis is rejected. Here is the logic of that inference:

> **If** the null hypothesis that the population mean was a particular stipulated value were true, **then** a *t*-value at least as embarrassing for the null hypothesis as the sample's *t*-value would be very unlikely to appear in a random sample.
>
> The sample's *t*-value appeared in a random sample.
>
> **Therefore,** we reject the null hypothesis (respecting that there is a chance that the null hypothesis is true).

In this case, we would say that the sample mean is significantly greater than (or significantly less than) the null hypothesis's population mean.

If the *p*-value is greater than alpha, then the null hypothesis is retained. Here is the thinking for that situation:

> **If** the null hypothesis were true, **then** a *t*-value at least as embarrassing for the null hypothesis as the sample's *t*-value would be *reasonably likely* to appear in a random sample.
>
> The sample's *t*-value appeared in a random sample.
>
> **Therefore,** the data provide no evidence one way or another about the null hypothesis.
>
> **If** there is no evidence to distinguish between two theories, **then** Occam's razor directs us to proceed with the simpler theory.
>
> The null hypothesis is usually the simpler theory.
>
> **Therefore,** we retain the null hypothesis, if it is the simpler theory.

Note that retaining the null hypothesis is not saying that the null hypothesis was supported by the data.

Correlation Is Not Causation

At first it may be hard to see why a *t*-test checking the location of a population mean is testing for a correlation, but consider Gosset's situation. Let's say that he has tested the acidity of a vat of hops, treated the vat, and then retested the vat's acidity. If the null hypothesis is true, the mean of the population of differences from before and after would be 0. If Gosset rejected the null hypothesis, because the vat was significantly less acidic after treatment, he would be saying that there is a correlation between when the vat was tested and the vat's acidity.

All before-and-after measurements are taken from studies that are at least somewhat correlational, and a significant result would reveal only that knowing when a measurement was taken allowed you to improve your prediction of what the measurement was. But such studies do not let you know what caused the change. The change could be due to the treatment or the passage of time. For example, vats of hops might naturally become less acidic on their own.

Your inability to nail down causation is even more pronounced in studies that do not provide a treatment. For example, if birds in a wildlife refuge are significantly less vigorous at the end of a summer than they were at the beginning, it could be because they are older, because the weather has changed, because there is a pollutant in the refuge, because they are more relaxed after having been at the refuge longer, or because of a multitude of other factors.

Reporting the Results

The popular press would not report anything about the *t*-test other than to say that an average was "statistically significantly higher" or "statistically significantly lower" than some value.

In the sciences, at a minimum, the *p*-value is given. Usually the *t*-value is given as well, as in the following table reporting on a before-and-after study:

(baseline and post intervention; n = 102)

	Baseline mean (sd)	
Dietary Fat servings	7.40 +/− 3.9	
	Post mean (sd)	t value
Dietary Fat servings	5.53 +/− 2.9	4.49 (*)

. . . t-tests were utilized to detect mean differences between baseline and posttime.

(*) p < 0.01

— TREVINO ET AL., *JOURNAL OF SCHOOL HEALTH*, 1998, P. 62

Often the degrees of freedom are provided, as in the following quote:

The difference . . . attained high statistical significance (paired t test = 8.75, 386 df, p < .001).

— BERGER AND MARELICH, *JOURNAL OF STUDIES ON ALCOHOL*, 1997, P. 518

Sometimes the degrees of freedom are reported within parentheses immediately after t, as in the following summary of a t-test in which the degrees of freedom were 648 and the t-value was 3.42:

$$t(648) = 3.42, p < .01$$

Algebra and Greek Symbols

This section introduces the t-value; t is the difference between the sample mean ($\bar{x}$) and a proposed population mean (μ) divided by the standard error estimated from the sample ($s_{\bar{x}}$). That is:

(1)
$$t = \frac{\bar{x} - \mu}{s_{\bar{x}}}$$

The standard error calculated from the sample standard deviation ($s_{\bar{x}}$) is the estimate of the standard error. So:

(2)
$$t = \frac{\bar{x} - \mu}{\text{estimated } \sigma_{\bar{x}}}$$

If observations are drawn from a normal distribution, t-values are distributed in Gosset's t-distribution. The width of Gosset's t-distribution depends on the degrees of freedom (df) in the samples. The degrees of freedom are 1 less than the sample sizes:

(3)
$$df = n - 1$$

To indicate which t-distribution is being referred to, the degrees of freedom are often indicated in parentheses after the t. For example, the t-distribution with 17 degrees of freedom would be indicated by "$t(17)$."

A t-test checks the null hypothesis that the population mean (μ) is a particular value (μ_0): that is, $H_0: \mu = \mu_0$. The alternative hypothesis (H_1) is that the null hypothesis's proposed population mean is not correct. That is, $H_1: \mu \neq \mu_0$. If t is less than $t(df)_{\alpha/2}$ or t is greater than $t(df)_{1-\alpha/2}$, we reject H_0 in favor of H_1. Otherwise, we retain H_0 on the grounds that it is the simpler concept.

A confidence interval for the population mean can be constructed using the critical value of the t-distribution. The critical value is the t-value that falls above all t-values, except half of a chosen proportion (α). With df degrees of freedom, the critical t-value would be written as $t(df)_{1-\alpha/2}$. The critical value is multiplied by the estimated standard error of the mean, and the product is added and subtracted to obtain the desired confidence interval.

Because the t-distribution is symmetrical, subtracting the product of the standard error and $t(df)_{1-\alpha/2}$ is the same as adding the product of the standard error and $t(df)_{\alpha/2}$. For this reason, we can summarize the confidence interval with Equation 4:

(4)
$$P[\mu \in (\bar{x} + t(df)_{\alpha/2}s, \bar{x} + t(df)_{1-\alpha/2}s)] = 1 - \alpha$$

("$\mu \in (a, b)$" means that the population mean is on the number line somewhere between a and b.)

For sample sizes greater than 60, the t-distribution is approximately normally distributed, and as $n \to \infty$, the t-distribution becomes increasingly normally distributed. That is:

(5)   For $n \geq 60, t \sim \mathcal{N},$ approximately

And:

(6)   For $n \geq 60, P[\mu \in (\bar{x} + z_{\alpha/2} \, s, \bar{x} + z_{1-\alpha/2} s)] \approx 1 - \alpha$

The value $z_{\alpha/2}$ is the value below which 1 minus $\alpha/2$ of a standard normal distribution falls. A standard normal distribution is a normal distribution with a mean at 0 and a standard deviation of 1. For example, if α equals 5%, then $z_{\alpha/2}$ equals 1.96.

Abstract

Z-tests done on small samples reject true null hypotheses too often. The t-value is how many estimated standard errors a sample mean is from a null hypothesis's population mean. A t-test calculates t and looks at the distribution of t-values to find the p-value. The t-distribution depends on the sample size.

Avoiding Common Misunderstandings

The t-value is the same as the z-value. If I had 200 observations, and I wanted to do a z-test of whether the population mean is 0, I would divide the sample mean by the sample standard error and call the result a "z-value." If I wanted to do a t-test, I would perform exactly the same calculation and call the result a "t-value."

The reason Gosset changed the name of the statistic from "z" to "t" was only to highlight that the statistic is not normally distributed. When statisticians refer to "z-values," they usually mean that the values are normally distributed. To let people know that his statistic was not normally distributed, Gosset changed its name, even though it is exactly the same statistic, calculated in exactly the same way.

Computer Project

This section claims that when random samples are drawn from a normal distribution, you will get statistics that are distributed like Gosset's t-values if you calculate a statistic by subtracting the population mean from each sample mean and then dividing the difference by the sample standard error. Don't take my word for it. Test it yourself.

Have your computer take random samples of normal distributions. Have the mean of your normal distributions be 0 and the standard error be 1. To start, use sample sizes of 2. Have your software create several hundred samples and calculate the sample mean and sample standard deviation for each one. Save what you get when you divide the sample mean by the sample standard error.

Instructions for doing this project in Fathom™, SPSS®, and Microsoft® Excel can be found in the *Data Matters* Resource Center at *www.keycollege.com/dm*.

Make a histogram of the statistics you calculated and sort the statistics from smallest to largest. Are they distributed as Gosset said they would be? How can you tell?

Try other population standard deviations and other sample sizes. Do Gosset's claims hold up with them?

Exercises

Robert P. Trevino and a group of researchers tested a program designed to encourage fourth-graders to eat a healthier diet. The program included an after-school club devoted to healthy diet. The Trevino team interviewed fourth-graders in September, before the program was begun, and again in May. At both interviews the Trevino team asked the children what they had eaten in the previous 24 hours. Below is an abridged version of a table that the Trevino team used to report their results. The quote says only what they report about how many fat servings the fourth-graders reported in September (the baseline) and May (the posttest).

(baseline and post intervention; n = 102)

	Baseline mean (sd)	
Dietary Fat servings	*7.40 +/− 3.9*	
	Post mean (sd)	t value
Dietary Fat servings	*5.53 +/− 2.9*	*4.49 (*)*

. . . *t-tests were utilized to detect mean differences between baseline and posttime.*

(*) *p < 0.01*

—TREVINO ET AL., *JOURNAL OF SCHOOL HEALTH*, 1998, P. 62

In the quote, the Trevino team writes, "*n* = 102." That means that their sample size was 102.

1. What was the null hypothesis of this *t*-test?

2. What was the *t*-value?

3. What does the quote tell you about the *p*-value?

4. What would you conclude about the null hypothesis in this case? (Be sure to mention your alpha.)

5. Did the children report significantly lower fat servings after the school year was over?

6. In your own words, explain what "significantly lower" means.

7. What were the degrees of freedom of this test?

8. In your own words, what is a *p*-value in general?

9. Does it matter whether the sampled population was normally distributed for this test?

10. In a study with this many observations, about what would be the smallest positive value of *t* that would be significant (at alpha = 5%)?

11. If the null hypothesis were true, and the population normal, what does this quote tell you about how often we would expect a *t*-value of at least 4.49?

12. Did the experimenters need to use a *t*-test? That is, could they have used a *z*-test? Why or why not?

13. When the *t*-test is used this way, why might we call it a "test of location"?

Answers to Odd-Numbered Exercises

1. The differences in fat servings came from a normal population with a mean at 0.

3. The *p*-value was less than .01.

5. Yes.

7. The degrees of freedom are the number of observations minus the number of means. There were 102 fourth-graders in this study, and one mean, so the degrees of freedom are 101.

9. Yes and no. Yes, because the *t*-test requires that the population be normally distributed. No, because with 102 observations, the *t*-test is almost identical to a *z*-test, and the population does not have to be normal for a *z*-test.

11. Less than 1% of the time. (That's what they say about the *p*-value.)

13. It is a test of location in that it is testing the location of the change in population mean. It is testing whether the change in population mean is located at 0 on the number line.

7.2 How to Test Whether a Treatment Works

- The Logic of Experiments
- Correlational Studies

Cognitive behavioral therapy has been shown to be more efficacious than alternative psychosocial interventions for the acute treatment of adolescents with major depressive disorder.

—BIRMAHER ET AL., *ARCHIVES OF GENERAL PSYCHIATRY*, 2000

THERAPISTS HAVE DEVISED SEVERAL THERAPIES to treat depression without drugs. In the 1990s, a group of researchers led by David Brent tested two of these nonpharmaceutical therapies (Brent et al., 1997). The Brent team worked with 107 depressed teenagers. Of these, 37 were given 12 weeks of cognitive-behavioral therapy. In cognitive-behavioral therapy, therapists teach clients about how their assumptions and habits of thinking lead them into depression and teach them new ways of thinking. From the group, 35 teenagers were given systematic behavioral family therapy, in which a therapist works with the entire family, teaching them how to communicate better with one another. Another 35 teens were given nondirective supportive therapy. In nondirective therapy, the therapist is simply a good listener—nonjudgmental but helpful in reflecting back to the client what the client seems to be saying.

The Brent team measured depression by giving the teenagers the Beck Depression Inventory, a questionnaire that asks about the test taker's mood. Higher scores indicate greater depression. Scores can range between 0 and 63. Scores between 0 and 9 are typical among people experiencing no depression. Scores between 10 and 29 indicate moderate depression. Scores above 29 indicate severe depression and are often accompanied with suicidal urges. (For example, one question on the inventory asks whether you feel like killing yourself. Answering that you do raises your depression score.) Table 7.2.1 summarizes the results of the Brent team's study.

Table 7.2.1 lists how many teenagers were in each group in the Brent team's study. In the table, "*n*" stands for "number in group," which is the same as sample size. In the cognitive-behavioral group, two teenagers (5%) dropped out of the study between the baseline and the 12-week retesting. Six (17%) dropped out from the systematic behavioral family therapy, and two (6%) dropped out from the nondirective supportive therapy.

Table 7.2.1 Beck Depression Inventory Scores from a Comparative Study of Three Treatments for Depression

	COGNITIVE-BEHAVIORAL THERAPY	SYSTEMATIC BEHAVIORAL FAMILY THERAPY	NONDIRECTIVE SUPPORTIVE THERAPY
BASELINE	$n = 37$	$n = 35$	$n = 35$
	24.3 (8.1)	22.6 (8.2)	25.7 (7.8)
12 WEEKS	$n = 35$	$n = 29$	$n = 33$
	5.7 (8.6)	9.1 (9.1)	9.8 (11.4)

Note: Values are given as mean (SD).

Let's start by looking at the teenagers in the Brent team's control condition—nondirective supportive therapy. Those teens started with a mean Beck Depression Inventory score of 26, a little under the cutoff for severe depression. The standard deviation for those baseline measurements was 8, so most of the teens in that group had depression scores that fell at roughly 26 plus and minus 16. That is, they ranged between about 10 and 42. After 12 weeks of regular visits to someone who was providing only kind and supportive attention, the teens' mean depression score was 10, just over the lower cutoff for moderate depression. Furthermore, the standard deviation for their 12-week mean was 11. Almost half of them had Beck Depression Inventory scores below 10, which indicates that they no longer had even moderate depression. Two standard deviations above the mean would have been a score of 32, so it's reasonable to guess that one or two still had severe depression.

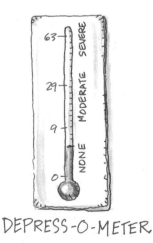

DEPRESS-O-METER

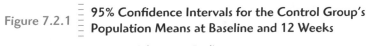

Figure 7.2.1

95% Confidence Intervals for the Control Group's Population Means at Baseline and 12 Weeks

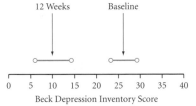

What do you make of this placebo condition? At first glance, it looks as though it works well. Figure 7.2.1 shows the confidence intervals for the before and after means.

This looks good. If Gosset did a *t*-test, he would find a significant improvement in these teenagers. From where does the improvement come? Is it the therapy? Perhaps, although the Brent team picked this therapy to be a placebo. It may be that thinking they are being treated for depression cheers people up.

Another possibility is that depression goes away on its own. The American Psychiatric Association puts out a reference manual about mental illnesses, *The Diagnostic and Statistical Manual IV* (1994). About major depressive episodes, it says this: "an untreated episode typically lasts 6 months or longer" (p. 325). After that, an untreated episode typically clears up on its own. Six months is 26 weeks. The Brent team's study looked at only half that time, and only half of the control condition teenagers had improved. Given that, without any treatment at all, depression goes away on its own in about 26 weeks, it is possible that much of the improvement in the control condition was due to depressions lifting on their own.

This phenomenon reveals a challenge for researchers that has been especially difficult for psychotherapists. Depression goes away on its own. The difficulty is that, for any treatment that is neither harmful nor effective, researchers will find that when they use the treatment, depressed people get better in about six months. If a therapist took this as evidence that the therapy was effective, it would be an invalid conclusion. It would be like poking people who have colds with a stick, noticing that they get better within three weeks, and concluding that poking with a stick cures colds. When the disorder in a study goes away on its own, it can make any treatment look effective. If you are not aware of this difficulty of testing treatments, you're going to end up doing a lot of things similar to poking people with sticks.

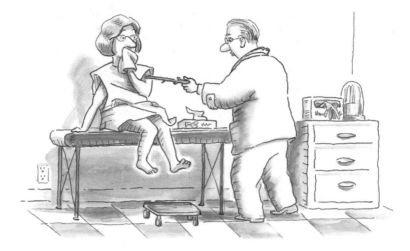

Experiments

How then can you test whether a treatment is helpful? The answer is that you need to conduct an experiment. In an experiment, groups are created in which the members are as close to identical as possible in all ways. The groups are then treated precisely identically, with only one exception. The experimental groups are given experimental treatments, and the control groups are given control treatments. If, at the end of the study, the two groups are significantly different, then something has caused that difference. What could have made them significantly different? There is only one suspect: the difference in their treatments.

How could you find groups that were the same in all ways, even in ways you don't measure? The answer is random sampling. In an experiment, researchers flip a coin or use some similar random device to assign participants to experimental groups. Each group then is a random sample of the same population—the population of people who showed up for the experiment. The law of large numbers tells us that random samples are roughly representative of the population from which they are drawn and that they get more and more representative as the sample size gets larger. Because each group in an experiment is roughly representative of the population that produced the participants to begin with, all of the groups are roughly identical. Because of random variation due to sampling, they aren't completely identical, but our understanding of the standard error allows us to figure out how dissimilar they would be. Figure 7.2.2 diagrams the logic of experiments.

Initially, the two groups will probably not be significantly different. If the two groups are significantly different posttreatment, other than the small risk of rejecting the null hypothesis when it is true, there is only one possible explanation for the change: the difference between their treatments.

Figure 7.2.2 **The Logic of Experiments**

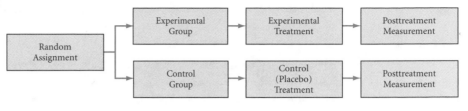

What Is an Experiment?

An experiment is a study in which the objects or people that are studied are randomly assigned to conditions. The conditions differ in that the studied objects or people are treated in different ways. After treatment, identical measurement procedures are used. The only significant difference between the groups is their treatments. If there are significant differences between the measurements, the only reasonable cause is that the differences in the treatments led to the differences in final measurements.

The Brent team did an experiment with two experimental groups. One group was given cognitive-behavioral therapy. The other was given systematic behavioral family therapy. The third group was a control group. It was treated identically to the other two, except that, for the control group, the therapist provided only kind attention. The therapists in the other two conditions also provided kind attention, so any difference in how the teenagers turned out had to be due, not to the kind attention, but to the specific techniques of cognitive-behavioral therapy or systematic behavioral family therapy. Figure 7.2.3 diagrams the logic of the Brent team's study. The last boxes include the mean and standard deviation from Table 7.2.1.

Figure 7.2.3 **The Logic of the Brent Team's Study**

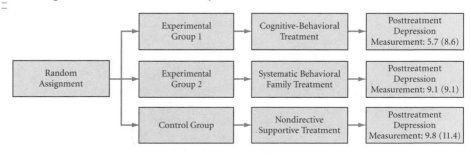

If the three groups were significantly different posttreatment, other than the small risk of rejecting the null hypothesis when it is true, there is only one possible explanation for the change: the difference between their treatments.

Why Experiments Reveal Causation

Random assignment to treatments creates groups that are not significantly different in almost all ways. The only significant difference between the groups is how they are treated. If, at the end of the study, the groups differ significantly, the only respectable theory of cause is that the difference in treatments led to the difference between the groups. Other theories are not sensible, because they would require that something determined the random process that drove the random assignment.

The question is whether those groups are significantly different at the end of the study. Even though the groups have means that are different, it's possible that the difference is due to just random variation in the sampling. For example, imagine that I put slips with numbers in a hat and collect observations for one group by stirring the hat, pulling out a number, recording it, and putting it back. Let's say that while I'm collecting the observations for the first group, I sing "Oh Susannah." Then I use the same hat of numbers to collect observations for the second group. This time I sing "Camptown Races." Will the two groups have identical sample means? No. The sample means will vary. Is it my singing that makes them different? No. The difference is due to random variation. We need some way of testing whether the differences between samples rule out the possibility that all the data came from one hat.

Now consider another possibility. I have two hats. One has slips of paper with a mean of 5. The other has slips of paper with a mean of 500. I will draw a random sample from the first hat. Then I'll draw a random sample from the second hat. We need some way to look at the data and figure out whether the differences are due to random variation when I'm picking from one hat or due to my picking from two hats.

The solution to our problems was developed by Sir Ronald Fisher. His test for these situations is the analysis of variance.

The Strategy of Test Development

When Gosset developed the *t*-test, he realized that all he needed was a statistic that reflected how bad the results made the null hypothesis look. Once he had that statistic and knew how it would be distributed when the null hypothesis was true, he could figure out the *p*-value. The *p*-value was the probability of getting a value for the statistic at least as embarrassing for the null hypothesis as the value that was found, if the null hypothesis is true. In developing the analysis of variance (ANOVA), Fisher knew he needed a measurement of how bad the null hypothesis looked.

For Fisher's test, the null hypothesis was that all of the number line measurements came from a single normal distribution, regardless of which group they were in. Fisher considered what that null hypothesis predicted. What he realized was that he could look at the variation between the means of each group and estimate the single population variance. He could also disregard the variation between the groups and estimate the single population variance from the variation within each group. If the null hypothesis were true, if there were indeed only one population, then the two estimates would not be far from each another. But, if there were multiple populations with means that were different, then the variation between the groups would lead to a larger estimate of the population variance. Fisher decided that his statistic would be the ratio of the variance estimated from the variation between the means and the variance estimated from the variation within each group. The next section will show how those two variances are estimated.

Correlation Is Not Causation

Alternatives to experiments are correlational studies. In a correlational study, the researcher does not do anything to affect the people being studied. A correlational study is a fairly passive activity; the researcher simply gathers data. The drawback in a correlational study is that it doesn't allow you to reach conclusions about whether one thing causes or influences another, because correlation is not causation. All a correlational study allows you to do is to improve your predictions.

What Is a Correlational Study?

In a correlational study, no treatments are provided. Researchers only take measurements.

For example, if the Brent team had done a correlational study, they would have found teenagers who had already been treated for depression. They would have recorded what kind of treatment the teenagers had received and measured the teenagers' depression with the Beck Depression Inventory. Imagine that the depression scores of the teenagers who got cognitive-behavioral therapy were much lower than the rest. With those findings, you could improve your ability to predict how depressed kids were. You would make lower predictions for the kids who got cognitive-behavioral therapy than you would for kids who got other therapies, and your predictions would be more accurate than if you didn't know what kind of therapy the kids got. That's what a correlational study can give you: It improves your ability to predict things if the system doesn't change.

The correlational results would not let you claim that one therapy was better than another, because there would be plenty of other explanations for the correlation. The most obvious would be that more-depressed teenagers preferred one therapy, while less-depressed teenagers preferred another. In such a case, the therapy that the more-depressed teenagers received can end up seeming less effective, but only because it started out working on tougher cases.

Some researchers try to get around the differences between the groups by measuring initial levels of depression. This still does not allow researchers to escape the fact that correlation is not causation. Imagine that all of the groups start out with identical levels of depression, but the group receiving cognitive-behavioral therapy ends up with lower depression levels. It could be that teenagers who are feeling stronger in other ways, perhaps because their parents have more time and attention for them, prefer cognitive-behavioral therapy. Such teenagers might get better more quickly than the other teenagers, even if all of the treatments are only placebos. The problem is that there is no random assignment, and without random assignment, there is no justification for thinking that the groups are identical or even similar in all ways.

Correlation Is Not Causation

Correlational studies never reveal causation, because usually many plausible conceptions exist as to what is affecting what and producing the correlation. Experiments reveal causation, because they are designed so that there is only one plausible explanation as to the cause of the difference between the experimental groups.

Even though correlational studies reveal only how to improve predications (when the system doesn't change), many researchers like correlational studies a lot. One reason is that correlational studies seem so blameless. It seems like a completely valid excuse to say, "I didn't do anything." Many people believe that if they don't act, they remain virtuous. That's what's nice about correlational studies. In doing such a study, researchers don't act in any way. They just collect data. Who could blame them for the outcome? Well, perhaps they could be blamed by parents who come to them asking for help finding an effective treatment for their depressed teenagers. It might be better to do an experiment.

Algebra and Greek Symbols

Let g indicate whether a study participant was assigned to the experimental condition or the control condition in an experiment; x is the measured outcome. In an experiment, because of random assignment, before the study has begun, all of the measured outcomes are independent of the group to which people will be assigned. The probability of any value of x does not depend on g. So, $P(x|g) = P(x)$. That is, the probability of any x, given which group the participants are assigned to, is the same as the probability of that x without any conditions.

If the treatment has no effect, this independence will still exist at the end of the study. To test an experiment we check whether it is still reasonable to conclude that x is independent of group assignment at the end of the experiment. That is, $H_0: P(x|g) = P(x)$.

Abstract

An experiment tests for causal relationships by randomly assigning participants to groups, and treating all groups identically with the exception of the experimental and control treatments. The experimental groups are given specified experimental treatments. The control groups are given specified control treatments, usually placebo treatments. Random assignment will produce significantly different groups as often as is specified by alpha. If the groups are significantly different after the treatments, other than the risk of rejecting a true null hypothesis, the only explanation for the significant difference is the difference in the treatments. One way to measure how much the null hypothesis is embarrassed by the results is to compare what the group means indicate about the population variance to what the group variances indicate about the population variance. If the group means indicate significantly more spread than the group variances, there is a discrepancy that indicates that the groups came from different populations.

Avoiding Common Misunderstandings

In medical research, an experiment is often called a "randomized controlled experiment" or "randomized controlled trial." Whether or not a study is an experiment or a correlational study depends on whether there is random assignment to conditions. If assignment to conditions is not random, then any differences that show up at the end of the study are plausibly due to the nonrandom assignment, and the whole project loses its ability to test the treatments.

Computer Project

Have your software take random samples from a distribution. Pick a single sample size for all the samples. When you have three sample means, find the standard deviation between the sample means. Repeat the process a few times and then try it with distributions with larger or smaller population standard deviations. What we have learned about the standard deviation indicates that when you take samples from a population with a larger population standard deviation, the sample means will be spread further apart. Is that what you saw? Could you use how widely apart the samples fell to estimate what the population standard deviation is? (Before you put too much time into answering that last question, look ahead. It is answered in the next section.)

Exercises

Use the following quote to complete Exercises 1 through 4. The quote is from a study exploring how much Mexican Americans had taken on the values and customs of mainstream America; that is, how much they were acculturated to the United States.

> *This study investigated the effects of skin color on acculturation levels and of both skin color and acculturation on Mexican American students' interest in the Mexican American community. A one-way ANOVA demonstrated that students with the darkest skin had significantly lower levels of acculturation than those with lighter skin.*
> —VASQUEZ ET AL., *HISPANIC JOURNAL OF BEHAVIORAL SCIENCES*, 1977, P. 377

1. The researchers did not look at gradations of skin color. They divided the participants into "dark-skinned" and "light-skinned." Why did they use an analysis of variance (ANOVA) rather than a chi-square test?

2. Was this an experiment or a correlational study? Write out how you deduced your answer.

3. If you wanted to improve your ability to predict which Mexican Americans are more acculturated, would this study be sufficient, or would you need to do another study? Write out how you deduced your answer. If another study is needed, describe it.

4. If you wanted to test whether skin color makes Americans more or less acculturated, would this study be sufficient, or would you need to do some other study? Write out how you deduced your answer. If another study is needed, describe it.

Here is a report on a test of two basketball training programs. Use it to complete Exercises 5 through 7.

> *This study . . . examine[d] the effect of Visuo-Motor Behavior Rehearsal (VMBR) and Videotaped Modeling (VM) on the free throw accuracy of male intercollegiate athletes. . . . Subjects were . . . assigned to one of three experimental conditions. . . . [In all conditions] there was a significant improvement in free throw shooting from pre- to post-assessment.*
>
> —ONESTAK, *JOURNAL OF SPORT BEHAVIOR*, 1997, P. 185

5. What makes the study described in the preceding quote an experiment?

6. Onestak studied each group and compared its posttest scores to its initial scores. To compare the training techniques, what measurements do you need to compare?

7. Why would you use an analysis of variance rather than a chi-square test to compare the training techniques?

Rachel Klein, Ph.D., and a group of researchers (Klein et al., 1997) studied 27 children who exhibited conduct disorder. Children with conduct disorder are confrontational and difficult in the extreme. The Klein team randomly assigned half of the children to a condition in which the children took methylphenidate (sold under the brand name "Ritalin"). The other half took a placebo. Observers who did not know which condition each child exhibited rated the children's behavior. The following table summarizes the Klein team's results. Use it to complete Exercises 8 through 11.

	EXPERIMENTAL GROUP	CONTROL GROUP
N	24	23
OVERALL RATING	0.8 +/− 0.1	1.5 +/− 0.1

8. Which group (the experimental group or the control group) got the methylphenidate and which got the placebo?

9. The Klein team randomly assigned children to groups by doing something like flipping a coin. If methylphenidate might be helpful, why didn't they put the more distressed children in the group that got methylphenidate?

10. The Klein team could have simply contacted pediatricians and found children who were prescribed methylphenidate and children who were not prescribed methylphenidate. If they had compared those children, which test should they have used, the chi-square test or the analysis of variance, and why?

11. Why would the comparison described in Exercise 10 not reveal the effect of methylphenidate?

One difficulty with heart transplants is that patients' bodies tend to recognize the new heart as foreign matter and begin to attack it as though it were an infection. This immune response is very dangerous and can kill the new heart. Such attacks are called "rejection episodes." A group of researchers led by Jon Kobashigawa (Kobashigawa et al., 1999) tested whether exercising the new heart might help in transplant patients' adjustment. The Kobashigawa team randomly assigned heart transplant patients to either an exercise regimen supervised by a physical therapist or a condition in which the patients were left to their doctors' regular treatments. The following table shows the results of the study. Use this information to complete Exercises 12 through 15.

	EXPERIMENTAL GROUP	CONTROL GROUP
N	14	13
REJECTION EPISODES	0.7 +/− 1.0	1.1 +/− 1.8

12. Which group (the experimental group or the control group) participated in the exercise regimen?

13. The Kobashigawa team randomly assigned patients to the two groups by doing something like flipping a coin. If exercise might be helpful, why didn't they put the weaker patients in the group that got exercise?

14. The Kobashigawa team could have simply contacted doctors and found patients who exercised and patients who did not. If they had compared those patients, which test should they have used, the chi-square test or the analysis of variance, and why?

15. Why would such a comparison not reveal the effect of exercise on the frequency of rejection episodes?

Here is a report on research looking at an acupuncture treatment for cocaine addiction. Use it to complete Exercises 16 through 18.

> *Cocaine-dependent adult[s] . . . were randomly assigned to receive auricular acupuncture (n = 222), a needle-insertion control condition (n = 203), or a relaxation control condition (n = 195).*
>
> —MARGOLIN ET AL., *JOURNAL OF THE AMERICAN MEDICAL ASSOCIATION*, 2002, P. 55

16. A friend of yours who is interested in acupuncture writes you about the Margolin team's study described in the preceding quote, saying, "I gather that's an experiment, not a correlational study. How can you tell? I mean, why is it an experiment?" Write your friend a note explaining how you can tell that the study was an experiment.

17. Your friend asks, "Why did the researchers do an experiment?" Write a short note explaining the advantage of an experiment that motivated the Margolin team.

18. Why might the Margolin team have been tempted to do a correlational study rather than an experiment?

Answers to Odd-Numbered Questions

1. This study has a set of categorical measurements, whether the students had light or dark skin color, and a set of number line measurements, the ratings of acculturation. Checking for a correlation between a set of number line measurements and a set of categorical measurements requires the analysis of variance. The chi-square test checks for correlations between two sets of categorical measurements.

3. This study would allow you to improve your predictions. It is a correlational study, and correlational studies with significant results allow you to improve your predictions.

5. Assuming that the assignment to conditions was random, this was an experiment because of the assigning to conditions.

7. The two measurements are the condition to which the players were assigned and free throw accuracy. The first is categorical. The second is a number line measurement. To test for a correlation between a categorical measurement and a number line measurement, you use Fisher's analysis of variance.

9. If they had not used a random assignment, they would have ruined the study's ability to capitalize on the logic of experiments. If the study had resulted in a difference between the two groups, they could not determine why that difference had occurred. It could have been the treatment, or it could have been related to how the two groups differed at the beginning of the study.

11. Such a study would be a correlational study and would not reveal causation. Correlational studies can reveal only how knowing one set of measurements can improve your ability to predict the other measurements.

13. If they had put the weaker patients in one group and the rest of the patients in the other group, then, if the groups turned out to be significantly different, they wouldn't know whether the difference was because of the treatment or the fact that patients started out weaker or stronger.

15. The causation could have been that exercise affects rejection episodes, or that rejection episodes affect exercise, or that some prior health condition affects both rejection episodes and whether people exercise.

17. "A correlational study could not have revealed whether acupuncture was or was not effective in treating cocaine addiction. The reason is that, had the researchers done a correlational study comparing addicts who received acupuncture to addicts who did not, and if the treated group abstained from cocaine more, we couldn't rule out the possibility that the kinds of people who sign up to get poked with needles are the sort of people who will cut their cocaine use no matter what happens to them."

7.3 Variances Between and Within

- Estimating the Population Variance from Variation Within Groups and from Variation Between Group Means

Smokers were randomly assigned to either a . . . program with vigorous exercise ([exercise condition, n = 134]) or to the same program with equal staff contact time ([control condition, n = 147]). . . . Exercise subjects achieved significantly more days of continuous abstinence than control subjects . . . (mean ± SD, 30.1 ± 26.4 vs 17.3 ± 22.4 days, P < .01).

—MARCUS ET AL., ARCHIVES OF INTERNAL MEDICINE, 1999, P. 1229

WHEN SMOKERS TRY TO STOP smoking cigarettes, how long do they typically last without resuming? The preceding quote tells of one study that included exercise in a smoking cessation program. The researchers tested the smokers over 82 days. The study included two groups, and the report includes their mean days of abstinence. One group lasted a mean of 30.1 days (the standard deviation was 26.4 days), and the other group lasted a mean of 17.3 days (the standard deviation was 22.4 days). How long did they last overall?

To find the average number of abstinence days overall, we need to take into account that the experimental group had 134 participants and the control group 147 participants. When the researchers were finding the mean of the experimental group's abstinence days, they added up all the days, divided by 134, and got 30.1. The sum of the days must have been 4,033.4, because 4,033.4 divided by 134 equals 30.1.

The sum of the abstinence days in the control group must have been 2,543.1 days (17.3 times 147).

To find the overall mean, we divide the total number of days (4,033.4 plus 2,543.1) by the total number of participants (134 plus 147). That's 23.4 days.

The result of 23.4 days isn't very encouraging. Did any participants make it all the way to the full 82 days that the researchers tested? To get an idea, you would need to know the standard deviation. The first group's standard deviation was 26.4 days. The second group's standard deviation was 22.4 days. How do we use this information to calculate an overall estimate of the standard deviation? There are two ways: One way looks at the variation within the groups; the other way looks at the variation between the group means.

Estimating the Variance

Before we figure out the standard deviations in the smokers' data, we will see how to estimate the standard deviations by looking at a smaller and simpler situation, one for which we know what's going on in the data. We will look at the data from the roll of six dice. This section will focus on calculating the variance. Once we have the variance, we can get the standard deviation by taking its square root.

First, let's see how to estimate the variance from two groups. Here is what came up in six rolls: 2, 3, 6, 4, 4, and 4. Table 7.3.1 shows the calculations to find the variance from those six observations by treating them as one group.

Table 7.3.1   Calculating the Sample Variance for Six Dice

NUMBER ROLLED	MEAN	DEVIATION	SQUARED DEVIATION
2	3.8333	−1.8333	3.3610
3	3.8333	−0.8333	0.6944
6	3.8333	2.1667	4.6946
4	3.8333	0.1667	0.0278
4	3.8333	0.1667	0.0278
4	3.8333	0.1667	0.0278

SUM 23   SUM OF SQUARES 8.8333

$$\text{Mean} = 23/6 = 3.8333$$

$$df = 5$$

$$\text{Variance} = 8.8333/5 = 1.7667$$

Other samples of dice would produce different estimates of the population variance. Based on a computer simulation, we know that the variance of the full population of all dice rolls is about 2.9. This sample variance, 1.8, is a little low.

Estimating the Population Variance from the Variation Within Groups (The Pooled Variance)

Imagine that we divided those six dice into two groups of three dice each. To estimate the population variance from the variation within each sample, we would do something like estimating the variance within each of the two groups and then somehow summarizing our two estimates. Table 7.3.2 shows what those calculations would be like.

The two estimates of the variance are 4.333 and 0. How should we combine those two estimates? The answer that works well is to go back to before the final steps in calculating the variances. If the sums of squares are added together and the degrees of freedom are added together, the population variance can be estimated from the total of the sums of squares divided by the total of the degrees of freedom. This combination of the variances is called the "pooled variance," because it pools the variation in the two groups.

In this case, the sum of the sums of squares is 8.667 plus 0, which is 8.667. The sum of the degrees of freedom is 4. The estimate of the population variance

Table 7.3.2 Estimating the Population Variance from Two Groups of Three Dice Rolls

GROUP 1

NUMBER ROLLED	MEAN	DEVIATION	SQUARED DEVIATION
2	3.667	−1.667	2.779
3	3.667	−0.667	0.445
6	3.667	2.333	5.443

SUM 11   SUM OF SQUARES 8.667

$$\text{Mean} = 11/3 = 3.667$$

$$df = 2$$

$$\text{Variance} = 8.667/2 = 4.333$$

GROUP 2

NUMBER ROLLED	MEAN	DEVIATION	SQUARED DEVIATION
4	4	0	0
4	4	0	0
4	4	0	0

SUM 12   SUM OF SQUARES 0

$$\text{Mean} = 12/3 = 4$$

$$df = 2$$

$$\text{Variance} = 0/2 = 0$$

would be 8.667 divided by 4, which is 2.17. The population variance is actually 2.9, so this is not a bad estimate.

Table 7.3.3 shows a slightly simpler way of thinking of the calculations. The steps in Table 7.3.3 are very similar to the steps in calculating a single sample variance. The difference is that the deviations are deviations from the group means, and the degrees of freedom are smaller. The degrees of freedom are still the number of observations minus the number of means, but in this case there are two means, so the degrees of freedom are 4 (6 observations minus 2 means).

Table 7.3.3   Estimating the Population Variance from Deviations Within Each Group

NUMBER ROLLED	GROUP MEAN	DEVIATION	SQUARED DEVIATION
2	3.667	−1.667	2.779
3	3.667	−0.667	0.445
6	3.667	2.333	5.443
4	4	0	0
4	4	0	0
4	4	0	0

SUM OF SQUARES 8.667

df = Number of Observations − Number of Groups = 6 − 2 = 4

Estimated Population Variance = 8.667/4 = 2.17

Estimating the Population Variance from the Variation Between the Group Means

In those two groups of three rolls each, the means were 3.667 and 4. That difference between the means reflects the variance in the population, because the variation in the means is related to the standard error, which is itself determined by the sample size and the population variance. What does this difference tell us about the population variance? To find out, we need to consider the deviations in those means. To find the deviation in the means, we can replace each observation with its estimate, its group mean. The deviations of those estimates would then be deviations that arise from the group means. Table 7.3.4 shows these deviations.

Table 7.3.4 Estimating the Population Variance from Deviations of the Group Means

GROUP MEAN	MEAN	DEVIATION	SQUARED DEVIATION
3.667	3.833	−0.167	0.027889
3.667	3.833	−0.167	0.027889
3.667	3.833	−0.167	0.027889
4	3.833	0.167	0.027889
4	3.833	0.167	0.027889
4	3.833	0.167	0.027889

SUM 23 SUM OF SQUARES 0.167334

Mean $= 23/6 = 3.833$

What are the degrees of freedom in this case? There are six numbers, but the first three are all the same, and the last three are all the same. If we have decided that the mean is 3.833, how many are free to vary? Let's say that the first observation is 4. The next two would have to be 4, because all of the estimates for a group are the same. Then the last three would all have to be 3.667. Otherwise, the mean wouldn't work out where it needed to be, at 3.833. In fact, there is only one number that is free to vary. The degree of freedom is 1, which is 1 less than the number of groups, and it is always the case that the degrees of freedom for this variance are 1 less than the number of groups.

Now we can estimate the population variance: 0.167 divided by 1, which is 0.167.

Table 7.3.5 Comparisons of Degrees of Freedom and Sums of Squares from Table 7.3.4

	ALL SIX OBSERVATIONS	VARIATION BETWEEN GROUPS (GROUP MEANS)	VARIATION WITHIN GROUPS
DEGREES OF FREEDOM	5	1	4
SUM OF SQUARES	8.8333	0.167	8.667

The variance 0.167 is low. The actual population variance is 2.9. Later we will try this again with a larger sample, but first notice something about the sums of squares and the degrees of freedom in Table 7.3.5: The sums of squares and the degrees of freedom from between and within add up to the total sum of squares and degrees of freedom.

That means the degrees of freedom from the two estimates (between and within) add up to the degrees of freedom in the original six rolled numbers. And the sums of squares within and between, 8.667 and 0.167, add up to 8.834. Except for rounding that happened in calculating all three numbers, the sums of squares of the two estimates (between and within) add up to the sum of squares for the original numbers (8.8333). You can rely on this regularity. The sum of squares within and the sum of squares between always add up to the total sum of squares.

The reason for this relation is that the deviations in the original numbers have two parts: deviations from the overall mean to the group means and deviations from the group means to the actual observations. Because of this, the sum of squares for the deviations out to the group means can be added to the sum of squares for the deviations from the group means to the actual observations, and the sum will be the sum of squares in the original numbers.

I have a lot of dice. Let's try this again, but with a larger number of dice. Here's what I see when I roll 15 dice: 1, 5, 2, 2, 4, 2, 2, 2, 4, 3, 3, 1, 2, 4, and 3. I have divided the 15 rolls into three groups. The first group is 1 and 5. The second is 2, 2, 4, 2, and 2. Table 7.3.6 shows the three groups.

Table 7.3.7 shows the calculations for estimating the population variance from the variation from the group means, and Table 7.3.8 shows the calculations for estimating the population variance from the variation from the overall mean.

Table 7.3.6 15 Dice Rolls Divided into Three Groups

GROUP 1	GROUP 2	GROUP 3
1, 5	2, 2, 4, 2, 2	2, 4, 3, 3, 1, 2, 4, 3

Table 7.3.7 Estimating the Population Variance from the Variation Within Each Group

	NUMBER ROLLED	GROUP MEAN	DEVIATION	SQUARED DEVIATION
GROUP 1	1	3	−2	4
	5	3	2	4
GROUP 2	2	2.4	−0.4	0.16
	2	2.4	−0.4	0.16
	4	2.4	1.6	2.56
	2	2.4	−0.4	0.16
	2	2.4	−0.4	0.16
GROUP 3	2	2.75	−0.75	0.5625
	4	2.75	1.25	1.5625
	3	2.75	0.25	0.0625
	3	2.75	0.25	0.0625
	1	2.75	1.25	1.5625
	2	2.75	−0.75	0.5625
	4	2.75	1.25	1.5625
	3	2.75	0.25	0.0625

SUM OF SQUARES 17.2

df = Number of Observations − Number of Means

$= 15 - 3 = 12$

Variance Estimated from Variation Within Groups $= 17.2/12 = 1.433$

The two estimates of the variance, 1.43 and 0.32, are somewhat different, and both are low.

Variation in Smoking Abstinence Rates

Now that we know how to estimate the population variance from data in two groups, what can we learn from the smoking cessation study mentioned at the beginning of this section? Table 7.3.9 shows the results from that study.

Table 7.3.8 Estimating the Population Variance from the Variation Between Each Group

	GROUP MEAN	OVERALL MEAN	DEVIATION	SQUARED DEVIATION
GROUP 1	3	2.667	0.333	0.111
	3	2.667	0.333	0.111
GROUP 2	2.4	2.667	−0.267	0.071
	2.4	2.667	−0.267	0.071
	2.4	2.667	−0.267	0.071
	2.4	2.667	−0.267	0.071
	2.4	2.667	−0.267	0.071
GROUP 3	2.75	2.667	0.083	0.007
	2.75	2.667	0.083	0.007
	2.75	2.667	0.083	0.007
	2.75	2.667	0.083	0.007
	2.75	2.667	0.083	0.007
	2.75	2.667	0.083	0.007
	2.75	2.667	0.083	0.007
	2.75	2.667	0.083	0.007

SUM OF SQUARES 0.633

$$df = \text{Number of Means} - 1 = 3 - 1 = 2$$

Variance Estimated from Variation Between Groups $= 0.633/2 = 0.32$

Table 7.3.9 Results of Smoking Cessation Study

	MEAN ABSTINENCE DAYS	STANDARD DEVIATION	NUMBER OF PARTICIPANTS
EXERCISE (EXPERIMENTAL) GROUP	30.1	26.4	134
CONTROL GROUP	17.3	22.4	147
OVERALL	23.4	?	281

Estimating the Variance from Variation Within the Groups

To estimate the variance from variation within the groups, we divide the sum of squares from within the groups by the appropriate degrees of freedom (the number of participants minus the number of groups). The sum of squares within the groups is the sum of the squared deviations of each observation from its group mean. The observations' deviations from the group means were used to calculate the standard deviations of the two groups. We can use that to calculate the sum of squares as shown in Table 7.3.10.

Table 7.3.10 shows that, to find the variance within, we start by squaring the standard deviations to find the variances. The variances are the sum of squares within each group divided by 1 less than the number in each group, so we multiply by 1 less than the number to get the sum of squares within each group. The variance estimated from variation within the groups is 594.8, and the estimated standard deviation is 24.4.

Estimating the Variance from Variation Between the Groups

To estimate the variance from variation between the groups, we would replace each participant's abstinence days with the participant's group mean abstinence days. The deviations would then be deviations from the overall mean. Table 7.3.11 shows the calculations to find the variance from variation between.

Because each respondent's abstinence days are replaced by the group mean, every row would be the same for respondents in one group. Rather than show one row for each respondent, Table 7.3.11 has a row for each group and an indication of how many respondents are represented in that row.

Table 7.3.10 ⫶ Finding the Sum of Squares Within the Groups from the Standard Deviations of the Smoking Cessation Groups

	STANDARD DEVIATION (SD)	VARIANCE = SD^2	NUMBER OF PARTICIPANTS (n)	SUM OF SQUARES = VARIANCE ×(n − 1)
EXERCISE (EXPERIMENTAL) GROUP	26.4	696.96	134	92,695.68
CONTROL GROUP	22.4	501.76	147	73,256.96
			SUM 281	165,952.64
			VARIANCE WITHIN	594.8

Table 7.3.11 Finding the Sum of Squares Between the Groups from the Means of the Smoking Cessation Groups

	NUMBER OF PARTICIPANTS	MEAN ABSTINENCE DAYS	OVERALL MEAN	DEVIATION	SQUARED DEVIATION
EXERCISE (EXPERIMENTAL) GROUP	134	30.1	23.4	6.7	44.89
CONTROL GROUP	147	17.3	23.4	−6.1	37.21
				SUM OF SQUARES	11,485.13

To find the sum of squares in Table 7.3.11, keep in mind that it is as though there were 134 rows for the experimental group and 147 rows for the control group. So the sum of squares is the sum of 134 values of 44.89 and 147 values of 37.21. That is, the sum of squares equals (134 times 44.89) plus (147 times 37.21).

In this case, there is only 1 degree of freedom, so the variance is 11,485.13. The standard deviation is the square root, 107.2.

Testing Whether the Data in Both Groups Came from the Same Population

The variance estimated from the variation within the groups was 594.8. The variance estimated from the variation between the groups was 11,485.13, about 20 times bigger. We have encountered a logical inconsistency that tells us that we made a bad assumption. Here's the thinking:

If all the data came from a single population, **then** the population variance is roughly 594.8.

If all the data came from a single population, **then** the population variance is roughly 11,485.13.

The population variance is only one thing.

Therefore, if all the data came from a single population, then 594.8 is roughly 11,485.13.

The problem here is that 594.8 is *not* roughly 11,485.13. When you follow a line of logic, and the logic is valid, but you end up with an invalid conclusion, that tells you that one of your assumptions was wrong. In this logic we have only one assumption. It is that the data in both groups came from the same population. We can reject that assumption.

By rejecting that assumption, we are doing what the researchers did. Here is part of the quote from the beginning of this section:

> *Exercise subjects achieved significantly more days of continuous abstinence than control subjects . . . (mean ± SD, 30.1 ± 26.4 vs 17.3 ± 22.4 days, P < .01).*
>
> —MARCUS ET AL., *ARCHIVES OF INTERNAL MEDICINE*, 1999, P. 1229

The Marcus team tested a null hypothesis that the data in the two groups came from a single population. Their *p*-value was less than .01, so they rejected that hypothesis and concluded that the participants in the exercise group had significantly longer abstinence durations.

Analysis of Variance

In the early 1900s, Ronald Fisher was faced with similar problems. While playing with the same equations for estimating the variance that we looked at in this section, he had an idea. He wanted to test a null hypothesis that all of the data in multiple groups came from a single population. He realized he could combine the two estimates of the population variance into a single statistic that indicated how embarrassed the null hypothesis was by what happened in the data. Once he knew the distribution of such a statistic, he had the makings of a significance test that could check for a correlation between a set of number line measurements and a set of categorical measurements. In the next chapter, we will see what Fisher came up with.

Algebra and Greek Symbols

Let's say we are looking at data in g groups, where g equals the number of groups. All of the groups are random samples from the same population. x_{ij} is the jth observation in the ith group. $\sum_j x_{2j}$ is the sum of the observations in the second group. n is the total number of observations. n_i is the number of observations in the ith group. $\bar{x}$ is the mean of all the observations. $\bar{x}_i$ is the mean of the observations in the ith group. $\hat{\sigma}_{within}$ is the estimated variance of the population from which all of the data was drawn calculated from variation within each group. $\hat{\sigma}_{between}$ is the estimated population variance calculated from variation between the groups.

$$(1) \qquad \hat{\sigma}_{within} = \frac{\sum_i \sum_j (x_{ij} - \bar{x}_i)^2}{n - g}$$

That is, the population variance estimated from the variation within each group is calculated by summing the squares of the differences between each observation and the observation's group mean, and dividing by the number of observations minus the number of groups.

(2)
$$\hat{\sigma}_{between} = \frac{\sum_j n_i (\bar{x}_i - \bar{x})^2}{g - 1}$$

That is, the population variance estimated from variation between groups is the sum across all the groups of the number of observations in each group times the square of the difference between the group mean and the overall mean, divided by the number of groups minus 1.

Abstract

To estimate the population variance from a sample, you divide the sum of squares by the degrees of freedom.

To estimate the population variance from the variation within each group, you find each observation's deviation from its sample mean. Squaring and summing those deviations gives you the sum of squares. The degrees of freedom are the number of observations minus the number of groups (because there is one sample mean per group).

To estimate the population variance from the variation between the means of each group, you first replace each observation with its estimate, its sample mean. For each observation, the deviation is the overall mean subtracted from the sample mean. The sum of squares is the sum of squared deviations. The degrees of freedom are 1 less than the number of groups.

Avoiding Common Misunderstandings

When estimating the population variance from the variation between the groups, you find the deviations by subtracting the overall mean from each group mean. Each squared deviation then has to be added into the sum of squares once for each observation in that group. For example, if a group has 10 observations, the overall mean is 6, the group mean is 8, the deviation is 2, the squared deviation is 4, and that group has to add 40 to the sum of squares.

One way to keep this straight is to think of the group means as models of the observations, and to construct your tables as in this section, with one row for each observation. Just use the group mean as a substitute for each observation.

Computer Project

Test the two ideas of this section. Pick a population. Have your software take sets of random samples. Calculate the estimated variance both ways and save the estimates. Explore the estimated variances. How do they compare to the real variance of the population? Are the claims in this section about how to estimate the population variance sensible claims? Would you like to propose any warnings for these procedures?

Exercises

The following table contains data that may have all been created by rolling pairs of dice, in which case only a single distribution produced all the data. Or this data may have been created by my rolling a pair of dice for one group, rolling three dice for the other, and discarding all rolls that gave me more than 12. Either all data is from pairs of dice, or one group is from pairs of dice and the other is from three dice. If one of the sets is from three dice, all rolls greater than 12 were removed from the data. Use this information to complete Exercises 1 through 4.

GROUP 1	GROUP 2
9, 6, 9, 9, 6	8, 10, 11, 12, 12

1. Assume that all the data came from a single distribution. What is the estimate of the population variance that you get from the variation within each of the two groups?

2. What is the estimate of the population variance you get from the variation between the two group means?

3. How do the two estimates compare to one another?

4. Turn both estimates into estimates of the population standard deviation. Numbers from rolling pairs of dice are somewhat normally distributed, with a symmetrical distribution around a mean of 7. They can be no lower than 2 and no higher than 12. How do the two estimated variances compare to what you know about the distribution of numbers from rolls of pairs of dice? (Hint: Remember that most of the data will fall within 2 standard deviations of the mean.)

Here is more data. As before, either all this data came from a single distribution, or the data from one of the groups were created by rolling three dice and discarding any rolls greater than 12. Use this information to complete Exercises 5 through 7.

GROUP 1	GROUP 2
8, 9, 12, 5, 11	7, 7, 5, 8, 9

5. Assume that all the data came from a single distribution. What is the estimate of the population variance you get from the variation between the two group means?

6. What is the estimate of the population variance that you get from the variation within each of the two groups?

7. How do the two estimates of the variance compare to one another? What do you think: one distribution or two?

Imagine that you work for the Environmental Protection Agency. You visit four ponds in a neighboring county. You walk around two ponds that are not close to any industry, and see one dead fish floating in one of the ponds and three floating in the other. Then you visit two ponds that are next to a company's factory. You see five dead fish in the first pond and seven in the second.

AWAY FROM INDUSTRY	NEAR INDUSTRY
1, 3	5, 7

You are about to visit the factory to tell the management to clean up their discharges, but you know that they are going to claim that the difference between the ponds is just random variation. To get ready for the visit, you consider a null hypothesis that all of the data came from a single distribution and calculate the estimated variances.

8. What is the population variance estimated from the variation within each group?

9. What is the population variance estimated from the variation between each group?

10. Let's say that you wanted to make a point about how important fish are to you, so you consider each fish to be the equivalent of 100 fish. If you did this, would the world be giving you any different information? That is, as you try to learn from the data, should this recoding change your judgment of whether the null hypothesis is true?

The following table shows your new data about dead fish.

AWAY FROM INDUSTRY	NEAR INDUSTRY
100, 300	500, 700

11. After your recoding, what is the population variance estimated from the variation within each group?

12. What is the population variance estimated from the variation between the groups in the preceding table?

13. I am considering a null hypothesis that all of the data come from a single distribution. If I look at only the two estimates of the population variance, what would be least embarrassing for the null hypothesis?

14. What kinds of patterns in the two variance estimates would be most embarrassing for the null hypothesis?

15. Let's say you are Ronald Fisher. You need to put the two variances together in some way so that you have a statistic that gets larger as the null hypothesis is more embarrassed and gets smaller as the null hypothesis is less embarrassed. How could you combine the two estimates of the population variance to create such a statistic?

Answers to Odd-Numbered Exercises

1.

OBSERVATION	GROUP MEAN	DEVIATION	SQUARED DEVIATION
9	7.8	1.2	1.44
6	7.8	−1.8	3.24
9	7.8	1.2	1.44
9	7.8	1.2	1.44
6	7.8	−1.8	3.24
8	10.6	−2.6	6.76
10	10.6	−0.6	0.36
11	10.6	0.4	0.16
12	10.6	1.4	1.96
12	10.6	1.4	1.96

SUM 92   SUM OF SQUARES 22

$$df = 10 - 2 = 8$$

Variance Estimated from Variation Within Groups $= 22/8 = 2.75$

3. The population variance looks a lot bigger when it's estimated from the variation between the groups—more than six times bigger.

5.

GROUP MEAN	OVERALL MEAN	DEVIATION	SQUARED DEVIATION
9	8.1	0.9	0.81
9	8.1	0.9	0.81
9	8.1	0.9	0.81
9	8.1	0.9	0.81
9	8.1	0.9	0.81
7.2	8.1	−0.9	0.81
7.2	8.1	−0.9	0.81
7.2	8.1	−0.9	0.81
7.2	8.1	−0.9	0.81
7.2	8.1	−0.9	0.81

SUM 81 SUM OF SQUARES 8.1

$$df = 1$$

Variance Estimated from Variation Between Groups $= 8.1/1 = 8.1$

7. The variance estimated from the variation between the groups is a little less than twice as large as the variance estimated from the variation within the groups.

9.

GROUP MEAN	OVERALL MEAN	DEVIATION	SQUARED DEVIATION
2	4	−2	4
2	4	−2	4
6	4	2	4
6	4	2	4

SUM 16 SUM OF SQUARES 16

$$df = 1$$

Variance $= 16$

11.

OBSERVATION	GROUP MEAN	DEVIATION	SQUARED DEVIATION
100	200	−100	10,000
300	200	100	10,000
500	600	−100	10,000
700	600	100	10,000

SUM OF SQUARES 40,000

$$df = 2$$

$$\text{Variance} = 20,000$$

13. What would be absolutely least embarrassing for the null hypothesis is if the two estimates are the same.

15. Subtracting one from the other doesn't seem like a good idea, because it gives different answers as the scale changes. A ratio should work well. That is, I (Fisher) would use the variance from variation between the groups divided by the variance from variation within the groups. When they are the same, the ratio will be 1. As the variation between the groups gets larger, compared to the variation within the groups, the null hypothesis will be more embarrassed, and the ratio will get larger.

CHAPTER 8 | *Analysis of Variance*

Two very different kinds of measurements exist: categorical and numeric. Tests for correlation designed for one type do not work for the other type. To be able to test any kind of correlation, we need to be able to test for three kinds of correlations: categorical-categorical, categorical-numeric, and numeric-numeric.

We have seen how to test for a correlation between two categorical measurements with a chi-square test. In this chapter, in Section 8.1, we will see how to test for a correlation between a categorical and a normally distributed number line measurement with ANOVA. In case you need to read about a study in which the number line measurements were not normally distributed, Section 8.2 presents tests that work for non-normal data.

Having dealt with these problems, the rest of this book focuses on how to test for a correlation between two number line observations with regression. Section 8.3 introduces the task of testing for a correlation between two number line observations.

8.1 Fisher's Analysis of Variance

- Calculating Fisher's *F*-Value

RESULTS . . . Infants' sleep patterns were significantly affected by the interventions: total sleep $F(1,24) = 16.82$, $P < .01$; average duration of sleep bout $F(1,24) = 22.45$, $P < .01$; and longest sleep episode $F(1,24) = 24.29$, $P < .01$.

—PINILLA AND BIRCH, *PEDIATRICS*, 1993, P. 441

ONE OF THE BIGGEST CHALLENGES for parents of new babies is dealing with sleep deprivation. Most babies wake up and wail to be fed several times each night. In the worst cases, the baby sleeps only 20 minutes before wanting to be fed again, all night long.

Two researchers, Teresa Pinilla and Leann Birch, tried to determine whether it might be possible to train infants to sleep longer stretches in the night. Pinilla and Birch randomly assigned 13 families to a treatment condition and 13 families to a control condition. Parents in the treatment condition were taught a variety of methods to encourage infants to sleep through the night. The quote at the beginning of this section shows how Pinilla and Birch reported their findings.

Pinilla and Birch reported on an analysis of variance. Ronald Fisher developed the analysis of variance about 90 years ago. Fisher's test analyzes the kinds of variances we examined in the last chapter, so his test is called an "analysis of variance," or ANOVA (ANalysis Of VAriance). Because Ronald Fisher invented the ANOVA, the statistic of the ANOVA is abbreviated F. Pinilla and Birch are reporting F-values when they write, "$F(1,24) = 16.82$" and "$F(1,24) = 22.45$."

ANOVA

Analysis of variance is abbreviated ANOVA. The ANOVA statistic is F, named after the developer of the ANOVA, Ronald Fisher.

The analysis of variance is used when there are multiple groups and a number line measurement taken for each studied object or person. The ANOVA tests whether all of the groups' number line measurements could be samples from one population. For example, if Pinilla and Birch's treatment had no effect, then all of the sleep durations of all of the infants would be durations drawn from a single baby–sleep-duration distribution. If the treatment worked, then the durations in the treatment group were drawn from a distribution that has longer durations than the distribution that was the origin for the control group's data.

If there is only one population, then there is no reason to make a complicated summary with a mean and standard deviation for each group. A single estimate of the population mean and a single estimate of the population standard deviation would do. For example, if we conclude that the variation in sleep durations from group to group is only random variation, it doesn't make sense to report what that random variation was.

However, if there were reason to suspect that different groups came from different populations, you would want to describe the mean and standard deviation of each group's population. For example, if Pinilla and Birch find that the babies in the treatment group slept significantly longer, then we want to know *how much* longer.

Reporting Group Means

If an analysis of variance reveals no significant differences between the groups, you do not report the group means or standard deviations, because you may be reporting only random variation. If the ANOVA indicates a significant difference, then you do report the group means and might omit the overall mean.

Reporting Group Means (Continued)

For example, if a researcher found no significant relationship between scheduling time for studying and class grades, this would be a fine report: "The average class grade was a 3.0 (a B; SD = 0.87). There was no significant difference in grades between the schedulers and nonschedulers $F(1,34) = 0.58, p = .45$."

If the researcher found a significant relationship, then the report should include the means of each group, as in the following report: "The schedulers had significantly higher grades ($F(1,34) = 6.5, p = .02$). The average grade for schedulers was 3.4 (a B+; SD = 0.93). For nonschedulers, it was 2.5 (a B−; SD = 1.1)."

Calculating F

Fisher sought a test statistic that would be small if the data were similar to what the null hypothesis predicted and would get larger as the data made the null hypothesis look worse. Fisher decided to use a ratio as his statistic. His ratio is the variance estimated from between-group variation divided by the variance estimated from within-group variation. If this ratio, called F, is about 1, the null hypothesis is not at all embarrassed. F can vary somewhat to values greater than 1 due to random variation, but as it gets higher and higher, it embarrasses the null hypothesis more and more. The p-value is the probability of getting an F at least as large as the F that appeared if the null hypothesis is true.

Here is the equation for F:

$$F = \frac{\text{Population Variance Estimated from Variation Between Groups}}{\text{Population Variance Estimated from Variation Within Groups}}$$

F-Value

Fisher's F-value is the variance estimated from variation between the groups divided by the variance estimated from variation within the groups.

F-Value Example

In April 2002, I searched an auction Web site to check the cost of running shoes there. The selling prices of the two most recently completed auctions for the brand and make I wanted were $44 and $55. I searched for retailers selling the same shoes and found two selling them for $110 and $100. Let's use those four prices as our data. Table 8.1.1 shows the calculations to estimate the population variance from the variation between the groups and from the variation within the groups.

Table 8.1.1 Variance Estimated from Variation Between Groups

WEB SITE TYPE	PRICE	GROUP MEAN	OVERALL MEAN	DEVIATION	SQUARED DEVIATION
Auction	$44.00	$49.50	$77.25	−$27.75	770.0625
Auction	$55.00	$49.50	$77.25	−$27.75	770.0625
Retail	$110.00	$105.00	$77.25	$27.75	770.0625
Retail	$100.00	$105.00	$77.25	$27.75	770.0625

$df = 2 - 1 = 1$

SUM OF SQUARES 3,080.25
ESTIMATED VARIANCE 3,080.25

Variance Estimated from Variation Within Groups

WEB SITE TYPE	PRICE	GROUP MEAN	DEVIATION	SQUARED DEVIATION
Auction	$44.00	$49.50	−$5.50	30.25
Auction	$55.00	$49.50	$5.50	30.25
Retail	$110.00	$105.00	$5.00	25
Retail	$100.00	$105.00	−$5.00	25

$df = 4 - 2 = 2$

SUM OF SQUARES 110.5
ESTIMATED VARIANCE 55.25

Inserting the values from the table into the equation to find F, we get the following:

$$F = \frac{3,080.25}{55.25} = 55.75$$

In this case, F is 55.75.

P-Value

Do prices look significantly different on the two types of Web sites? Should we model these data with separate means, one for each group? Or do we have insufficient evidence to justify that complication? The question is whether an F of 55.75 is a *significantly* embarrassing value. To find out, we need the p-value: the probability of getting an F at 55.75 or more embarrassing for the null hypothesis, *if the null hypothesis is true.* To find out, we can run a simulation and see how often F falls at 55.75 or somewhere more embarrassing, when the null hypothesis is true.

The computer project for this section is a simulation that finds F. All observations in the simulation are drawn from a normal population with a mean of 0 and a standard deviation of 1. I had that simulation collect data for 2 groups. Each group had 2 observations. For each set of 2 groups, the simulation calculates the within-group variance, the between-group variance, and F. Figure 8.1.1 is a histogram of most of the 10,000 F-values that came from the simulation.

After sorting those 10,000 observations from lowest to highest, the 9,500th observation from the bottom was 18.56. When the null hypothesis is true, and there are 4 observations divided into 2 groups, the probability of getting an F at least as large as 18.56 is 5%. The probability of getting an F at least as large as 55.75 is less than 5%. In the simulation, 198 out of the 10,000 F-values (2%) fell at 55.75 or greater. The p-value of 55.75 is .02. The auctioned running shoes were significantly less expensive, and it would be worthwhile to summarize the data with a mean auction price ($49.50) and a mean retail price ($105).

Figure 8.1.1

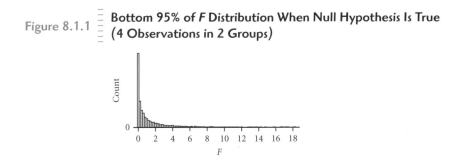

Bottom 95% of F Distribution When Null Hypothesis Is True (4 Observations in 2 Groups)

Degrees of Freedom and the Distribution of F

When we looked at the chi-square test and the t-test, we found that those statistics had distributions that varied, depending on the design of the study. That may be the case for F as well. To find out, I reran the simulation, with 3 groups and with 2 observations in each group. The results are shown in Figure 8.1.2.

Figure 8.1.2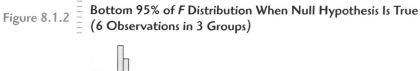

Bottom 95% of F Distribution When Null Hypothesis Is True (6 Observations in 3 Groups)

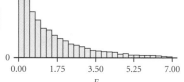

In this second simulation run, the bottom 95% of the *F*-values were 6.6 and less. Only 5% were greater than 6.6. That is different from the results of the simulation when there were 2 observations in each of 2 groups. In fact, the null hypothesis distribution of *F* depends on the degrees of freedom in both estimates of the population variance.

At one time, to find the *p*-value of an ANOVA, you would look in a table reporting *p*-values for a variety of *F*-values. Such tables list the *p*-values according to what they call the "numerator degrees of freedom" and the "denominator degrees of freedom." To see what these two degrees of freedom are, consider the equation for *F*:

$$F = \frac{\text{Between-Group Variance}}{\text{Within-Group Variance}} = \frac{\dfrac{\text{Between-Group Sum of Squares}}{\text{Number of Groups} - 1}}{\dfrac{\text{Within-Group Sum of Squares}}{\text{Number of Observations} - \text{Number of Groups}}}$$

F is actually a ratio of two fractions. The fraction on the top (in the numerator) uses the between-group degrees of freedom, the "numerator degrees of freedom," which are 1 less than the number of groups.

The fraction on the bottom (in the denominator) has the within-group degrees of freedom, the "denominator degrees of freedom," and are the number of observations minus the number of groups.

ANOVA's Degrees of Freedom

The ANOVA has two different degrees of freedom. One is the degrees of freedom associated with the variance estimated from variation between the groups. This *df*(between) is the number of groups minus 1. The other is the degrees of freedom from within the groups, which is the number of observations minus the number of groups.

For example, if there are 24 observations and 3 groups, *df*(between) is 2, and *df*(within) is 21.

You will probably not work much with such tables. Most data analyses are now done by computer programs that calculate F and look up the p-values automatically.

Nonetheless, in case you need to know about an F and do not have access to a statistics reference work or a data-analysis program, it helps to know two rules of thumb. Here is the first:

Rule of Thumb 1: If there are at least 60 observations and fewer than 60 groups, any F greater than 4 will be significant at alpha equal to .05.

Rule of Thumb 1 applies to most studies that use the analysis of variance. It's unusual to have more than five groups, and a study should have at least 60 observations. (Remember that Pearson said "only naughty brewers" would work with small samples.) You may recall that, in a z-test, any z greater than 2 would be significant. To remember Rule of Thumb 1, remember that the square of 2 is 4. Also remember that, with 60 observations, the t-distribution was essentially the same as the z-distribution. Most of the time, an F greater than 4 will be significant. For example, in the last chapter, we looked at how 97 teenagers turned out after one of three kinds of therapy. Our rule of thumb for this many participants is that any F greater than 4 is significant. If F is 4 or less, it might be significant; we would have to look it up to be sure.

Rule of Thumb 2: If there are at least 12 observations and no more than 6 groups, any F greater than 5 will be significant at alpha equal to .05.

Rule of Thumb 2 applies to almost-sensible small studies. There is little point in thinking about a study with fewer than 12 observations. You might consider such a study when you are learning statistics, because the calculations aren't so tedious, but to find out about the world, a study should contain more observations.

Two Rules of Thumb for the Significance of F

The following F-values are significant if alpha equals .05: with 60 or more observations and no more than 59 groups, F greater than 4, and with more than 11 observations and no more than six groups, F greater than 5.

Reporting or Reading an ANOVA

To see how analysis of variance results look, let's return to the report by Teresa Pinilla and Leann Birch:

> RESULTS . . . *Infants' sleep patterns were significantly affected by the interventions: total sleep $F(1,24) = 16.82$, $P < .01$; average duration of sleep bout $F(1,24) = 22.45$, $P < .01$; and longest sleep episode $F(1,24) = 24.29$, $P < .01$.*
>
> —PINILLA AND BIRCH, *PEDIATRICS*, 1993, P. 441

Pinilla and Birch found, averaging across the 13 families in the experimental condition, that the mean longest stretch of sleep was 290 minutes (4 hours and 50 minutes). The mean longest stretch for the control families was 222 minutes (3 hours and 42 minutes). In each group, the standard deviation was about 34 minutes. Was that a significant difference? Pinilla and Birch report, "longest sleep episode $F(1,24) = 24.29$, $P < .01$" for their ANOVA.

Pinilla and Birch write, "$F(1,24) = . . .$" The numbers in the parentheses next to F are the degrees of freedom. The between-group degrees of freedom come first. The degrees of freedom for the between-group estimate are 1 less than the number of groups, so there must have been 2 groups. That makes sense: Pinilla and Birch were comparing 2 groups—an experimental group and a control group. The "24" is the degrees of freedom for the within-group estimate of the population variance, the number of observations minus the number of groups. There were 2 groups, so there must have been 26 families. In fact, there were 13 in each group.

Pinilla and Birch's F-value was 24.29. Following our rule of thumb for when there are more than 12 observations and at most 6 groups, 24.29 must be significant at alpha equal to .05, because it is more than 5. Pinilla and Birch tell us a little more about the p-value: "$P < .01$." So the probability of having an F fall at 24.29 or more, if the null hypothesis is true, and there are 1 and 24 degrees of freedom, must be less than 1%.

Figure 8.1.3 shows F-values from a simulation with 2 groups of 13 observations each. In the simulation, the null hypothesis is true—all observations are drawn from a single normal distribution.

Figure 8.1.3 **Random Sample of 1,000 F-Values, Calculated When Null Hypothesis Is True (26 Observations in 2 Groups)**

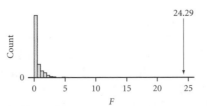

Figure 8.1.3 shows roughly the distribution of F that the null hypothesis predicts. On the far right is the 24.29 that actually appeared, far out of the range that the null hypothesis predicted. The null hypothesis would be badly embarrassed by this result. The actual p-value is close to .00005, which means that, with these degrees of freedom, when the null hypothesis is true, an F will be as much as 24 or more only about 5 times out of 100,000. This result is very much *not* what the null hypothesis was predicting, so we reject the null hypothesis. This training program helps. If you know any parents of infants, you might tell them about the work of Pinilla and Birch.

ANOVA Summary

Purpose of the Analysis of Variance

The analysis of variance is used to test for a correlation between a categorical measurement and a number line measurement.

ANOVA Requirements

The ANOVA is based on the assumptions that the number line measurements are normally distributed and the observations are random samples unaffected by one another.

ANOVA Null Hypothesis

The ANOVA's null hypothesis is that all of the number line observations came from a single, normally distributed population. If most of the groups draw from one population and only one of many groups draws from a different population, that would not be the null hypothesis. The null hypothesis is that *all* of the number line observations are from a single, normally distributed population.

It is a common mistake to think that the ANOVA's null hypothesis is that the population means of all of the groups are the same. This is not true. If the groups come from multiple populations that have the same means, but different variances, the ANOVA would be justified in rejecting its null hypothesis.

The ANOVA Statistic: *F*

F is calculated from two estimates of the variance of the single population that the null hypothesis claims is the source of all of the observations. *F* is the variance estimated from the variation between groups divided by the variance estimated from the variation within the groups:

$$F = \frac{\text{Between-Group Variance}}{\text{Within-Group Variance}}$$

Variances are calculated by dividing sums of squares by degrees of freedom. The between-group sums of squares are the sums of squares found after replacing each observation with an estimate that is its group mean and finding the estimate's deviation from the mean of all of the observations. The between-group degrees of freedom are 1 less than the number of group means:

$$\text{Between Groups Variance} = \frac{\text{Between-Group Sum of Squares}}{\text{Between-Group Degrees of Freedom}}$$

$$= \frac{\text{Sum of Squared Deviations of Each Observation's Group Mean from Overall Mean}}{\text{Number of Groups} - 1}$$

The within-group sum of squares is calculated from the deviations of the observations from their group means. The within-group degrees of freedom are the number of observations minus the number of groups:

$$\text{Within-Group Variance} = \frac{\text{Within-Group Sum of Squares}}{\text{Within-Group Degrees of Freedom}}$$

$$= \frac{\text{Sum of Squared Deviations of Each Observation from Its Group Mean}}{\text{Number of Observations} - \text{Number of Groups}}$$

The *P*-Value

The *p*-value is the probability that *F* would fall at the observed *F*-value or higher, if the null hypothesis were true. The distribution of *F* depends on the two kinds of degrees of freedom. For precise *p*-values, one can look in a table or use a data-analysis computer program. If there are at least 60 observations and fewer than 60 groups, any *F* greater than 4 will be significant at alpha equal to .05. If there are at least 12 observations and fewer than 7 groups, any *F* greater than 5 will be significant at alpha equal to .05.

The Logic of the Inference

There are two possible inferences for the ANOVA. If the p-value is below the cutoff for significance, alpha, then the null hypothesis is rejected. Here is the logic of that inference:

> **If** the null hypothesis that there is only one population were true, **then** the within-group variance would be about the same as the between-group variance, and an F at least as large as the sample's F would be very unlikely to appear in a random sample.
>
> The sample's F did appear in a random sample.
>
> **Therefore,** we reject the null hypothesis of one population (respecting that there is a chance that the null hypothesis is true).

In this case, we would say that there is a significant relationship between the categorical measurements and the number line measurements. The number line measurements in at least one group are significantly greater than (or significantly lower than) the number line measurements in at least one other group.

If the p-value is greater than alpha, then the null hypothesis is retained. Here is the thinking for that situation:

> **If** the null hypothesis were true, **then** an F at least as large and at least as embarrassing for the null hypothesis as the sample's F would be *reasonably likely* to appear in a random sample.
>
> The sample's F is what appeared in a random sample.
>
> **Therefore,** the data provide no evidence one way or another about the null hypothesis.

If there is no evidence to distinguish between two theories, Occam's razor directs us to proceed with the simpler theory:

> The null hypothesis of no correlation is usually the simpler theory. Therefore, we retain the null hypothesis (if it is the simpler theory).

That retaining of the null hypothesis is not saying that the null hypothesis was supported by the data.

Correlation Is Not Causation

With random assignment of participants into groups, ANOVA can reveal how being in a particular group directly or indirectly affects number line measurement. Without random assignment, or without any assignment whatsoever, it is much harder to make judgments about what is causing the correlation, and it is best to consider a significant F as evidence only that knowing one of the measurements can improve your ability to predict the other.

Reporting the Results

The richest style of reporting an ANOVA is what we saw in the Pinilla and Birch quote:

> *RESULTS . . . Infants' sleep patterns were significantly affected by the interventions: total sleep F(1,24) = 16.82, P < .01.*
>
> —Pinilla and Birch, *Pediatrics*, 1993, p. 441

In this case, Pinilla and Birch report that F was 16.82. The between-group degree of freedom was 1. The within-group degrees of freedom were 24. And the p-value was less than .01. Often the degrees of freedom are reported in a less arcane manner, as in this rewrite: "RESULTS . . . Infants' sleep patterns were significantly affected by the interventions; $F = 16.82$; $df = 1$ and 24; $P < .01$." In some fields, researchers omit the degrees of freedom, and in some other fields, researchers omit the F-value as well as the degrees of freedom.

In the popular press, a journalist would report only that a result was statistically significant, as in this rewrite: "Dr. Pinilla and Dr. Birch found that the training program increased the infants' longest block of sleep and that this increase was statistically significant."

Algebra and Greek Symbols

As mathematicians write about the analysis of variance, it is customary to call the variance estimated from the variation between the groups the "mean square between groups," or MS(between), and the sum of squares that went into that estimate the $SS_{between}$. The variance estimated from variation within each group is often called the "mean square within groups," or MS(within), and its sum of squares is often called the SS_{within}.

If you were reporting on a significant analysis of variance, you would summarize the results with the mean of each group. When you do that, you are describing a model of the data in which the group means are the estimates that the model makes for the number line data. The deviations within each group are the errors that those models make. For this reason the "mean square within groups" is sometimes called the "mean squared error," or MSE.

When researchers calculated F-values by hand, they found it was often easier to keep track of what they were doing if they filled in a standard table called an ANOVA table. Most statistical analysis packages still show these tables. Table 8.1.2 shows an ANOVA table for the calculations checking for a relationship between Web site type and running shoe price.

Table 8.1.2 ANOVA Table for Test of Web Site Type and Running Shoe Price

	SUM OF SQUARES	df	MEAN SQUARE	F
BETWEEN GROUPS	3,080.25	1	3,080.25	55.75
WITHIN GROUPS	110.5	2	55.25	
TOTAL	3,190.75	3		

As long as you remember that "mean square" means "estimated variance," the ANOVA table does a nice job of laying out the two estimated variances for easy comparison.

Abstract

The ANOVA (analysis of variance) tests the null hypothesis that all observations in multiple groups come from a single normal distribution. The variance of the single normal distribution can be estimated from variation within the groups and can also be estimated from variation between the means of the groups. The ANOVA's statistic, F, is a ratio—the between-group estimate divided by the within-group estimate. The distribution of F depends on the number of observations and the number of groups. In the ANOVA, the p-value is the probability, at the given number of observations and groups, of getting an F at least as large as the obtained F, if the null hypothesis is true.

Avoiding Common Misunderstandings

As F gets larger, the p-value gets smaller. If the p-value is *less* than alpha, we reject the null hypothesis, and the results are significant. If the p-value is *greater* than alpha, we retain the null hypothesis.

Computer Project

In this project, you will find the critical ANOVA values to fill in the following table. If an ANOVA has an F-value greater than the value in the table, the F is significant.

Critical *F*-Values for the Analysis of Variance

		df OF VARIANCE ESTIMATED FROM BETWEEN-GROUP VARIATION (*df* NUMERATOR: NUMBER OF GROUPS − 1)		
		1	2	3
df OF VARIANCE ESTIMATED FROM WITHIN-GROUP VARIATION (*df* DENOMINATOR: NUMBER OF OBSERVATIONS − NUMBER OF GROUPS)	1			
	2	18.56		
	3			
	4		6.6	
	60			
	100			2.76

Have your software take random samples. Instructions for doing this in Fathom™, SPSS®, and Microsoft® Excel can be found in the *Data Matters* Resource Center at *www.keycollege.com/dm*. Have every sample come from a single normal distribution so that the null hypothesis is true. Have your computer divide the samples into groups to match the cells of the preceding table. For example, the upper-left cell is for 1 degree of freedom for the variation between groups. That means it is for 2 groups. The upper-left cell is for 1 degree of freedom for the variation within groups, so it must have 3 observations, since the degrees of freedom within the groups are the number of observations minus the number of groups.

To make it clearer what this project is supposed to produce, I have filled in the bottom-right cell, which is for 4 groups and 104 observations. When the null hypothesis is true and there are 4 groups and 104 observations, 95% of the time, *F* will fall at 2.76 or less. I have also included the two critical values mentioned in this section.

Exercises

The following table contains some data on letters to the editor published in the *New York Times* and the *San Francisco Chronicle*. Use these data to complete Exercises 1 through 5.

NEWSPAPER	WORDS
New York Times	121
New York Times	297
New York Times	128
San Francisco Chronicle	94
San Francisco Chronicle	244

1. For the data in the table, what is F?

2. What are the between-group degrees of freedom?

3. What are the within-group degrees of freedom?

4. Even though this is not a situation covered by either of the rules of thumb, you can tell something about the p-value. Is it above or below 5%?

5. Report this ANOVA in the style that Pinilla and Birch used.

The following table contains some data I collected when I was house hunting. Use it to complete Exercises 6 through 10.

HOUSE	NEIGHBORHOOD	HOUSE PRICE PER SQUARE FOOT
1	Mays Pond	$99
2	Mays Pond	$91
3	Thrasher's Corner	$66
4	Thrasher's Corner	$92

6. What is F?

7. What are the between-group degrees of freedom?

8. What are the within-group degrees of freedom?

9. In this case, the p-value is .36. Why might you have guessed that the F you calculated wasn't significant?

10. Report this ANOVA in the style that Pinilla and Birch used.

Recall that in Chapter 7 we looked at data from a group experiment that studied the behavior of children with a particular diagnosis. Rachel Klein, Ph.D., and a group of researchers studied 27 children who were diagnosed with conduct disorder. Such children are extremely confrontational and difficult. The Klein team randomly assigned half of the children to an experimental condition in which they took methylphenidate (sold under the brand name "Ritalin"). The other half took a placebo. Observers who did not know which group each child was in rated the children's behavior. The following table summarizes the Klein team's results (Klein et al., 1997). Use it to complete Exercises 11 through 21.

	EXPERIMENTAL GROUP (PRESCRIBED METHYLPHENIDATE)	CONTROL GROUP (PRESCRIBED A PLACEBO)
N	24	23
OVERALL RATING	$0.8 +/- 0.1$	$1.5 +/- 0.1$

11. What was the variance within each group?
12. What were the degrees of freedom within each group from which the two groups' variances would have been calculated?
13. What were the sums of squares of the two groups that went into their variances?
14. Those sums of squares were calculated from the deviations of the observations from their group means. What were the within-group sums of squares?
15. What was the within-group variance?
16. If you were calculating the between-group variance, what would your list of group means be?
17. What was the between-group variance?
18. What was F?
19. What was the null hypothesis of the ANOVA in this case?
20. In this case, there were fewer than 60 observations. Using our rule of thumb, was F significant?
21. Report the results of your ANOVA in the style used by Pinilla and Birch.

Also from Chapter 7, recall that one difficulty with heart transplants is that patients' bodies tend to recognize the new heart as foreign matter and begin to attack it as though it were an infection. This immune response is very dangerous and can kill the new heart. Such attacks are called "rejection episodes." A group of researchers led by Jon Kobashigawa tested whether exercising the new heart might help in transplant patients' adjustment. The Kobashigawa team randomly assigned heart transplant patients to either an exercise regimen supervised by a physical therapist or a control condition. The following table shows the results of the study (Kobashigawa et al., 1999). Use it to complete Exercises 22 through 32.

	EXPERIMENTAL GROUP	CONTROL GROUP
N	14	13
REJECTION EPISODES	$0.7 +/- 1.0$	$1.1 +/- 1.8$

22. What was the variance within each group?

23. What were the degrees of freedom within each group from which the two group variances would have been calculated?

24. What were the sums of squares of the two groups that went into their variances?

25. Those sums of squares were calculated from the deviations of the observations from their group means. What were the within-group sums of squares?

26. What was the within-group variance?

27. If you were calculating the between-group variance, what would your list of group means be?

28. What was the between-group variance?

29. What was F?

30. What was the null hypothesis of the ANOVA in this case?

31. In this case, there were fewer than 60 observations. Using our rule of thumb, was F significant?

32. Report the results of your ANOVA in the style used by Pinilla and Birch.

Answers to Odd-Numbered Questions

1. Calculating Within–Group Variance

PAPER	WORDS	GROUP MEAN	DEVIATION	SQUARED DEVIATION
New York Times	121	182	-61	3,721
New York Times	297	182	115	13,225
New York Times	128	182	-54	2,916
San Francisco Chronicle	94	169	-75	5,625
San Francisco Chronicle	244	169	75	5,625

SUM OF SQUARES $= 31,112$

$$df = 5 - 2 = 3$$

Within-Group Variance $= 31,112/3 = 10,371$

Calculating Between-Group Variance

GROUP MEAN	OVERALL MEAN	DEVIATION	SQUARED DEVIATION
182	176.8	5.2	27
182	176.8	5.2	27
182	176.8	5.2	27
169	176.8	−7.8	60.8
169	176.8	−7.8	60.8
SUM $= 884$			SUM OF SQUARES $= 202.6$

$$df = 2 \text{ groups} - 1 = 1$$

Between-Group Variance $= 202.6$

$$F = 202.6/10,371 = 0.02$$

3. Within groups, there are 3 degrees of freedom.

5. "The data revealed no significant difference between the papers in the length of the letters to the editor $(F(1,3) = 0.02, p > 5\%)$."

7. The between-group degrees of freedom are the number of groups minus 1. There are 2 groups, so there is 1 between-group degree of freedom.

9. Because F was so close to 1, which is very unembarrassing for the null hypothesis.

11. The two standard deviations were both 0.1. The variance is the square of the standard deviation. The two variances were both 0.01.

13. For the experimental group:

$$\text{Sample Variance} = 0.01 = \frac{\text{Sum of Squares}}{23}$$

If we multiply both sides by 23, the 23's cancel on the right, and 0.01 times 23 is 0.23, so 0.23 is the sum of squares.

For the control group:

$$\text{Sample Variance} = 0.01 = \frac{\text{Sum of Squares}}{22}$$

If we multiply both sides by 22, the 22's cancel on the right, and 0.01 times 22 is 0.22, so 0.22 is the sum of squares for the control group.

15. The degrees of freedom for the within-group sum of squares was the number of children minus the number of groups $(47 - 2)$, which is 45:

$$\text{Within-Group Variance} = \frac{\text{Within-Group Sum of Squares}}{\text{Within-Group Degrees of Freedom}} = \frac{0.45}{45} = 0.1$$

17. Calculating the between-group variance:

$$\text{Sum of Group Means} = 24 \times 0.8 + 23 \times 1.5 = 53.7$$

$$\text{Overall Mean} = 53.7/47 = 1.14$$

GROUP MEAN	OVERALL MEAN	DEVIATION	SQUARED DEVIATION
0.8	1.14	-0.34	0.1156

[and 23 more lines like that one just above]

1.5	1.14	0.36	0.1296

[and 22 more lines like that one just above]

$$\text{Between-Group Sum of Squares} = (24 \times 0.1156) + (23 \times 0.1296) = 3.34$$

$$df = 2 \text{ Groups} - 1 = 1$$

$$\text{Between-Group Variance} = 3.34$$

19. The null hypothesis was that the ratings of the children's behavior all came from a single normal population, regardless of whether the children were given methylphenidate.

21. "The children receiving methylphenidate had significantly lower ratings $(F(1,45) = 34.3, p < .05)$."

23. The experimental group had 13 degrees of freedom. The control group had 12.

25. Within-group sum of squares is 51.88.

27. Fourteen 0.7's and thirteen 1.1's.

29. F equals the variance between divided by the variance within, which equals 0.038.

31. No.

8.2 What If the Data Are Not Normally Distributed?

- The Effect of Nonconstant Variances and Non-normality on ANOVA
- Nonparametric Tests

> *Empirical results*
> *[A] non-parametric [test was] used . . . the Kruskal-Wallis test [tested] whether the earnings of promotion employees and those of non-promotion employees are from the same population. . . . [Its value] turned out to be 52.961 . . . implying that the earnings populations in the two sectors are not the same.*
>
> —THEODOSSIOU, *OXFORD ECONOMIC PAPERS*, 1996, P. 456

YOU WOULD EXPECT that career-minded people would be more likely to advance in a career, but do they earn more money? An economist, Ioannis Theodossiou, was interested in how income might be related to whether workers felt their jobs allowed for advancement. To test this, Theodossiou asked a sample of corporate employees two questions: "Do you see yourself as having a career?" and "When a better job becomes available in your organisation, how much of an advantage or a disadvantage is it to be already working in the organisation?" Some employees felt they had a career and that it was a big advantage to be in the organization. Theodossiou considered them to be promotion minded.

As the quote reported, Theodossiou found that the promotion-minded people earned more. This looks like an appropriate situation for an ANOVA. You have a categorical observation: whether or not people are promotion minded. You have a number line variable: how much they earned. But Theodossiou used a "Kruskal-Wallis" test instead.

The Kruskal-Wallis test was developed to cope with a problem in the ANOVA. When Fisher was figuring out the p-values for the ANOVA test, he assumed that the single population from which the data was coming was normal. However, sometimes the data don't seem to have come from a normal distribution. Sometimes you want to test whether different groups came from multiple populations that all have the same mean, and you don't care whether the populations have the same variance or shape. For example, it could be that promotion-minded people earn the same amount on the average, but vary more widely in their earnings. Data from such a situation might cause the ANOVA to reject true null hypotheses too often, even though it is only the mean earnings that Theodossiou cares about. If one group had a larger variance than the other did, even if both groups came from populations that had the same mean, the ANOVA might not reject the null hypothesis as often as it should.

With *large* samples, even if the population is not normally distributed, and even if the variances are different, the ANOVA tends not to reject the null hypothesis too readily. The ANOVA does not work as well when sample sizes are small, in which case violations of Fisher's assumptions can make the ANOVA reject null hypotheses too often.

The preceding section discussed a simulation that created samples and calculated F for each sample. Because the simulation draws all of its observations from a single normal population, the null hypothesis is true. The idea of the ANOVA is that, when the null hypothesis is true, you should get an F large enough to reject the null hypothesis about 5% of the time. As we saw in the last section, that works pretty well when the single population is normal.

We could test how well the ANOVA does with other populations. Let's say that you wanted to test whether two groups came from populations with identical population means. Figures 8.2.1 and 8.2.2 show a pair of populations that would not work well with the ANOVA. Imagine that the first group draws from the population in Figure 8.2.1. The population in that figure is uniform from −0.6 to −0.4 and from 0.4 to 0.6, but has no data from −0.4 to 0.4. Its mean is 0.

The second group draws from the population shown in Figure 8.2.2, which also has a population mean of 0; it is uniform between −2.6 and −2.4 and between 2.4 and 2.6.

Both Population 1 and Population 2 have means at 0. They are a little unusual. You might imagine that they are opinions pro or con on some highly polarized issue, such as whether Mick Jagger is a more impressive singer than Luciano Pavarotti. For Question 1, we ask people to rate these singers' ability on a decimal scale from −0.6 to 0.6. For Question 2, we present exactly the same question, but let people use a scale all the way from –2.6 to 2.6. The two populations have the same mean.

To see how ANOVA dealt with these populations, I ran this through the simulation program. For each test, I took only two observations from each population. According to Fisher, if my alpha is .05, then my cutoff for significance should be 18.51. Figure 8.2.3 shows how the F's came out. In Figure 8.2.3, each bar is 200 units wide. The tall bar on the left represents the range 0 to 200. The very short bars to the right of that bar are so small they hardly show at all. The median was 0.06. More than half of the F's were less than 1, but then there were no F's between 1 and 16.

Violations of the ANOVA's Assumptions

The ANOVA is based on the assumptions that the population is normally distributed and that there is only one population. If there are multiple nonnormal populations, one for each group, and their variances are not equal, the ANOVA may reject the null hypothesis as much as 50% of the time, even if all of the populations have equal means.

Figure 8.2.1 **Population 1: Uniform from −0.6 to −0.4 and 0.4 to 0.6**

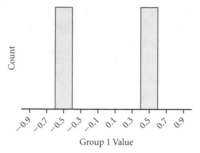

Figure 8.2.2 **Population 2: Uniform from −2.6 to −2.4 and 2.4 to 2.6**

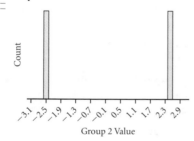

Figure 8.2.3 **Distribution of *F*-Values for Two Groups of Two Observations Each Taken from the Populations in Figures 8.2.1 and 8.2.2**

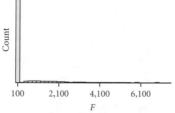

Figure 8.2.4  **A Very Right-Skewed Population (Median = 8; Mean > 3 Million)**

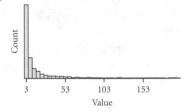

Altogether, 49% of the F's were above 18.51. Unfortunately, 49% is not 5%. For these two populations, the ANOVA would reject the null hypothesis 49% of the time (if you were using an alpha of 5%). That would happen even though both populations had the same mean. If I used an alpha of 1%, I would have rejected the null hypothesis 25% of the time.

The ANOVA is not always too liable to reject true null hypotheses when Fisher's assumptions are violated. Unequal variances tend to make it jump to conclusions too often, but other violations tend to make it too sluggish and conservative. Often when data are not normally distributed, there are tails that extend off one way or another. For example, if you look at how wealthy American families are, you see a right tail going way off to the side before getting to Bill Gates. Skewnesses like that make the ANOVA too conservative. To show you this, I reran the simulation using a very right-skewed population. I used exactly the same population for both groups. Figure 8.2.4 shows part of the distribution. The median is about 8. The minimum is 1, and the mean is greater than three million.

Again, each test had 2 groups of 2 observations. The ANOVA rejected true null hypotheses only 0.25% of the time. That is one-quarter of 1% of the time, 20 times less often than the ANOVA ought to reject the null hypothesis.

Some of the ANOVA's troubles disappear pretty quickly with larger samples. Doing a study with only 4 measurements is pretty silly. It is the kind of thing people used to try in the neurosciences, when testing every participant cost hundreds of thousands of dollars, but it was not a good idea. Not even naughty brewers would be enthusiastic about 4 observations.

Larger sample sizes cut down on the ANOVA's tendency to see things that are not there. To show you this, I went back to the two odd populations that led the ANOVA to reject the null hypothesis 49% of the time. With 10 observations in each group, the ANOVA rejected the null hypotheses (at alpha equal to .05) about 7% of the time. With 30 observations in each group, it rejected the null hypothesis about 5% of the time—pretty good.

Large Sample Sizes Protect the ANOVA

If each group comes from its own non-normal population, and the populations have different variances but equal means, as long as there is a reasonably large sample size, such as 30 per group, the ANOVA will reject the null hypothesis at a rate close to alpha.

Increasing the sample size does not do much to change how the ANOVA responds to skewed populations. I reran the simulation using the very right-skewed distribution in Figure 8.2.4. Even with 100 observations in each group, the ANOVA still rejected the null hypothesis only 0.2% of the time.

Nonparametric Tests

Having seen these troubles with the ANOVA, statisticians developed a variety of ways to test its null hypotheses without making the same assumptions that Fisher used. The assumption that most troubled people was that data were normally distributed.

Tests that make few assumptions about how data are distributed are called "nonparametric" tests. Some nonparametric tests test only whether groups came from one population, without assuming or revealing anything about the distribution of the population. These tests do not guess at the population mean or other population parameters. That's why these tests were originally called "nonparametric." However, other nonparametric tests do reveal some of the parameters of the population. At one time, "nonparametric" meant "no parameters." Now it means "making few assumptions about how the data are distributed, and certainly not assuming that the data are normally distributed."

Nonparametric Tests

Nonparametric tests do not require that the populations that produced the data be normally distributed. Nonparametric tests are developed with efforts to make few assumptions about the populations that produce the data.

This section does not prepare you to do your own nonparametric tests. The goal here is only to give you enough exposure to nonparametrics that you can read a report and understand what null hypothesis was rejected or retained.

Kruskal-Wallis Test

One test that was developed to be an alternative to the ANOVA is the Kruskal-Wallis test that Theodossiou used to test for differences in salaries. Like the ANOVA, the Kruskal-Wallis test checks whether all of the observations came from one distribution, but the Kruskal-Wallis test was developed to cope with populations of any shape.

The first step in the Kruskal-Wallis test is to sort the observations from smallest to largest and then replace them with their positions in the sorted list. That is called replacing them with their "ranks" in the data. For example, given a data set consisting of the three numbers 3, 4, and 60 billion, their ranks are 1, 2, and 3. Analyzing ranks instead of the original numbers kind of evens things out. If there are 40 observations, then the largest is 40 and the smallest is 1. After converting to ranks, you could not have a median at 8 and a mean greater than 3 million.

Like Fisher, Kruskal and Wallis started with the null hypothesis that all of the data came from one population. They were able to figure out how their statistic, H, would be distributed if the null hypothesis were true. When a researcher uses the Kruskal-Wallis test, generally a computer program calculates H and then sees what proportion of H-values would come out at least as embarrassing for the null hypothesis if the null hypothesis were true. That is the p-value.

Theodossiou probably chose to use a Kruskal-Wallis test rather than an ANOVA because salaries are not normally distributed. That is generally true: Dollar figures of any sort tend to be right skewed. The null hypothesis was that, regardless of whether or not people were promotion minded, everyone drew their earnings from the same population of earnings. Theodossiou tells us that the Kruskal-Wallis test rejected the null hypothesis. We can conclude that the two groups had earnings that came from different populations, and we can be pretty sure that we were not misled by the non-normality in the data.

Kruskal-Wallis Test

Use: To test for correlation between a set of categorical observations and a set of number line observations.

Null hypothesis: All of the number line observations came from one population.

P-value: As the Kruskal-Wallis test statistic, H, gets larger, the null hypothesis is more embarrassed. The p-value is the probability of obtaining a Kruskal-Wallis test statistic at least as large as was found if the null hypothesis is true.

Using Both Tests

It can be somewhat confusing figuring out whether to use an ANOVA or a Kruskal-Wallis test. The following report demonstrates one approach:

> *In this study, both ANOVA and Kruskal-Wallis tests are utilized to check on the existence of the day-of-the-week effect over business cycles in the three markets. . . . In [the junk bond] market . . . Friday returns are statistically significantly higher (at the .05 level) than the returns on any other trading day of the week.*
>
> —Kohers and Patel, *Review of Financial Economics*, 1996, p. 31

Kohers and Patel tested to see whether junk bond market returns were greater on particular days. They checked with ANOVA, and they double-checked with the Kruskal-Wallis test. This is not an unusual way to use nonparametric tests. If the analyses come out the same way with both tests, that is reassuring.

Kohers and Patel's result is a little exciting. Maybe we should all start buying stocks on Thursdays and selling late Friday. Unfortunately, broker's fees would probably eat up any profit.

Mann-Whitney *U* Test

Kruskal and Wallis were not the first to create a test that did not make assumptions about the population. They were building on the Mann-Whitney *U* test. The Mann-Whitney *U* test is essentially a Kruskal-Wallis test that can be used only to test whether two groups of data came from the same population. It cannot be used on more than two groups.

Mann-Whitney *U* Test

Use: To test whether a correlation exists between a set of number line observations and a set of categorical observations that have no more than two categories.

Null hypothesis: All number line observations came from one population.

P-value: As the Mann-Whitney *U* statistic gets larger, the null hypothesis is more and more embarrassed. The *p*-value is the probability of obtaining a Mann-Whitney *U* at least as large as the one that was found, if the null hypothesis is true.

In the following quote, biologist Christen Nilsson reports on a study of the plant life along rivers downstream from dams. He compares the plant life along those rivers to the plant life along similar rivers without dams. Nilsson's concern is that dams are used to keep rivers from flooding, and this may affect the plant life on their shores. Nilsson calls the shores "river margins."

> *Compared to similar sites along adjacent, free-flowing rivers, the storage reservoirs had fewer species per 200-m length of river margin (58 versus 83 species; P < 0.0001, Mann-Whitney U test).*
>
> —NILSSON ET AL., SCIENCE, 1997, P. 798

The null hypothesis of the Mann-Whitney *U* test is that the observations in both groups came from one population. In this case, the *p*-value was well under 5%, so we can reject the null hypothesis. Our best model of what is going on is that riverbanks downstream from dams have less biodiversity than do riverbanks on free-flowing rivers.

Wilcoxon Test

Another kind of test looks at changes in an individual's scores. For *t*-tests of changes, each individual's scores are subtracted from one another, and the test looks at the differences. The null hypothesis is that the mean difference is 0. The *t*-test assumes that the differences come from a normal population. The Wilcoxon test's null hypothesis is that the center of the population of differences is at 0, but the Wilcoxon does not assume that the differences are from a normal population.

As with the Kruskal-Wallis test, the Wilcoxon test also works on the ranks of the data rather than on the raw observations. A nice property of the Wilcoxon test is that Wilcoxon's statistic is normally distributed if the null hypothesis is true. The results of the Wilcoxon test are reported as the *z*-values from the test, which can be interpreted the same way as the *z*'s from a *z*-test. Values of *z* that are more than 2 away from 0 are significant (if your alpha is .05).

The following quote is a report of a Wilcoxon test from a team of researchers led by Cheryl King. The King team tested a group of depressed teenagers and one parent for each teenager. Each family was then considered a unit. The King team used a Wilcoxon test to determine whether, on the average, there was no difference in symptom reporting between the parents and teenagers.

> *The Wilcoxon Test for matched samples was used . . .*
> *RESULTS*
> *. . . Across all . . . depressive symptoms, parent and adolescent informants differed significantly in the likelihood with which they reported adolescent depressive symptoms, z = 11.52, p < .0001. Parents endorsed adolescent depressive symptoms more frequently than did adolescents themselves.*
> —KING ET AL., *JOURNAL OF ABNORMAL CHILD PSYCHOLOGY*, 1997, P. 173

In this case the null hypothesis was rejected. The middle of the population that produced the differences was probably not at 0. It appears that parents are better at reporting the symptoms of their teenagers' depression than are the teenagers themselves.

The Wilcoxon Test

Use: To test whether a set of number line observations, such as differences, came from a population with a particular center, such as 0.

Test assumption: The population is symmetrical.

Null hypothesis: The center of the population is a particular value.

Statistic: The Wilcoxon test calculates a value, *z*, that is normally distributed with a mean at 0 and a standard deviation of 1.

P-value: The *p*-value is the probability of obtaining an observation from a normal distribution at least as far from 0 as the one that was found, if the null hypothesis is true.

The Binomial Test

The simplest nonparametric test is the binomial test (also called the "sign test"). The binomial test is a *z*-test of sample proportions. The null hypothesis is usually that the population proportion is 50%. The *p*-value is found by looking at the proportion that was found and seeing how far it is from 50%, in terms of its standard error. If the sample proportion is more than 2 standard errors from 50%, then the results are significant at alpha equal to .05.

Two researchers in Sweden, Drs. Teasdale and Engberg, looked through a database of hospital admissions and found men who were admitted for concussions. Teasdale and Engberg looked at intelligence tests these men had taken as teenagers. Every young man in Sweden has to take a test of cognitive functioning as part of a national draft system. Some of the men who later had concussions scored as having dysfunctional cognitive skills.

> *Of the 520 men who were injured after testing, 158 (30.4%) had a dysfunctional score—significantly above the population rate of 20.4% (binomial test P < 0.001; relative risk 1.49 (95% confidence interval 1.31 to 1.70)).*
>
> —TEASDALE AND ENGBERG, *BRITISH MEDICAL JOURNAL*, 1997, P. 569

Teasdale and Engberg's null hypothesis is that the population proportion for these men was 20.4%. The chances of getting 30.4% in 520 draws from a system with a population proportion of 20.4% are less than .001. That is the *p*-value. The null hypothesis was that these men were as likely as anyone else to have had dysfunctional cognitive skills, and the null hypothesis was rejected.

The Binomial Test

Use: To test whether a proportion came from a population with a specific population proportion.

Null hypothesis: The population proportion is at a particular value.

Statistic: The statistic is found by finding the difference between the sample proportion and the null hypothesis's population proportion. This difference is divided by the standard error calculated from the sample size and the null hypothesis's population proportion. When the null hypothesis is true, the resulting ratio, *z*, is roughly normally distributed with a mean at 0 and a standard deviation of 1.

P-value: The *p*-value is the probability of obtaining an observation from a normal distribution at least as far from 0 as the one that was found, if the null hypothesis is true.

In their study of depressed teens and their parents, the King team could have used a binomial test. A way to do this is to subtract each parent's score from that parent's teen's score, then calculate the proportion of the differences that are positive. The null hypothesis is that the chances of the difference being positive are the same as the chances of its being negative. The null hypothesis says that the population proportion that produced the proportion of positive differences was 50%. Once you have that straight, you do a binomial test. If you do a binomial test on the chances of getting a positive difference, you are doing what is called a "sign test," because you are looking at the signs of the differences.

The Sign Test

Use: To test whether a set of number line observations, such as differences, came from a population with a median at 0.

Null hypothesis: The population median is 0.

Statistic: The statistic is calculated from the proportion of nonzero observations that are positive. This proportion is then examined using the binomial test.

P-value: The p-value is the probability of obtaining an observation from a normal distribution at least as far from 0 as the one that was found, if the null hypothesis is true.

Monte Carlo Simulations

When I did the simulations at the beginning of this section, I started out with particular populations and then did a simulation to find out how F would be distributed. If I were doing a study and knew that the population I used in my simulation was the population from which my data came, I could use my list of F's to figure out the p-value. Let's say that 49% of the F's in the simulation were at or above 18.51. If, in my research, I got an F of 18.51, the p-value would be .49.

This simulation approach is called the "Monte Carlo" method. It does not assume that your data are normally distributed, but it does assume that you know how the population are distributed. Without that information, you cannot set up your simulation properly. For that reason, Monte Carlo simulations are not frequently used.

Monte Carlo Simulation Tests

Use: To test any hypothesis that allows you to calculate a statistic that reflects how embarrassing results are for the null hypothesis.

Test requirements: The null hypothesis states all aspects of the population that are not known, and stipulates distributions for the data.

Null hypothesis: Varies from test to test.

Statistic: Varies from test to test.

P-value: Based on what is known about the population and on the null hypothesis, simulations are run to see how the statistic is distributed when the null hypothesis is true. The p-value is the probability of obtaining a statistic at least as embarrassing for the null hypothesis as the obtained statistic, if the null hypothesis is true.

Resampling

There is an alternative to Monte Carlo simulations that does not make assumptions about the underlying populations. In resampling methods, you randomly mix the observations and keep track of how your measurement of null hypothesis embarrassment is distributed. For example, in the case of an ANOVA, you get the computer to take all the number line observations and randomly assign them to the various groups (without changing the sizes of the groups). An observation that originally appeared in Group 1 could now appear in Group 2. After each remixing, you calculate an F. You would remix many times and keep track of the F's that you calculate. The distribution of those F's then tells you your p-value. For example, if 13% fall above the F from the real data, then your p-value is 13%.

Resampling methods can be used in many situations. With computers, resampling is easy and takes very little time. The statisticians who are working hardest to promote resampling methods feel that eventually all other tests will be replaced with resampling methods. However, resampling methods are quite new. At present many more people use ANOVA's. Even if resampling methods do eventually replace other testing methods, F's and t-values will probably still be useful, if only to be able to read 20th-century research.

> ### Resampling
>
> Use: To test any hypothesis that allows you to calculate a statistic that reflects how embarrassing results are for the null hypothesis.
>
> Null hypothesis: Varies from test to test.
>
> Statistic: Varies from test to test.
>
> *P*-value: The observations are taken as the best approximation of the population from which they came. Using that approximation, one proceeds as with Monte Carlo tests.

ANOVA Versus Nonparametrics

The ANOVA does have some weaknesses. The ANOVA makes two kinds of mistakes when Fisher's assumptions are not valid. One mistake is a tendency to say that there is a significant difference when the population means for the groups are identical. This happens more often than we might like when the groups come from populations with identical means but different variances, and it happens somewhat when the populations have smaller tails than the normal population, but those things only make the ANOVA unreliable when there are not many observations. With at least 30 observations in each group, the *p*-value is probably about right. Nonparametrics might be a better idea when the sample sizes are small, and certainly if there are fewer than 10 in a group.

The other instance when the ANOVA errs is when the population is skewed or has tails that are more spread out than those of the normal population. In these situations, the ANOVA does not reject true null hypotheses as often as it should. At first that makes it seem as though the ANOVA is not going to notice real differences when they appear. But failing to reject true null hypotheses is not the same as failing to notice that the null hypotheses are false.

To give you some idea of what I am talking about, I reran the simulation several times. This time I used normal populations for both groups. The population standard deviations were both 0.914. One way to measure the difference between two groups is to calculate the "effect size," which is the difference between the means of the two groups divided by their standard deviation. To test how well the ANOVA does, I gave it a situation in which the null hypothesis was false. Both groups came from identical populations, except that, for one of the groups, I added 0.2742 to each observation. That is an effect size of 30%, which is small. The question is, how well does the ANOVA notice the effect. Table 8.2.1 shows how often the ANOVA rejected the false null hypotheses in this situation.

Table 8.2.1 reflects the power of the ANOVA. The "power" of a test is its tendency to reject false null hypotheses. We have been talking about how it is not a

Table 8.2.1 — ANOVA Success Rates in Rejecting False Null Hypotheses (Effect Size = 0.30; Two Groups Drawn from Normal Populations)

NUMBER OF OBSERVATIONS PER GROUP	PROPORTION OF FALSE NULL HYPOTHESES REJECTED
2	5%
4	7%
8	9%
16	14%
32	22%
64	39%
128	67%

good idea for a test to be overly jumpy in rejecting true null hypotheses. There is an easy way to get 100% success in testing true null hypotheses: Do not look at the data and simply declare the test inconclusive. In fact, you could simply reject all information: Avoid libraries, books, magazines, and school. The problem with that approach is that it has no power. It is not going to succeed in telling you that important information is available. It will consistently fail to reject null hypotheses that are false and should be rejected. What you want is something that frequently rejects false null hypotheses, while frequently retaining true null hypotheses.

Power

The power of a test is its ability to reject false null hypotheses.

Compare Table 8.2.1 to Table 8.2.2. For Table 8.2.2, I used the right-skewed population shown in Figure 8.2.5. When the null hypothesis is true for the population shown in Figure 8.2.5, ANOVA rejects the null hypothesis only about 2% of the time. The standard deviation of this population is 119. An effect size of 0.30 would be a difference of 35.7 between the means of the groups. Table 8.2.2 shows the power of the means of the ANOVA test with an effect size of 30% for the non-normal distribution in Figure 8.2.5.

Table 8.2.2 shows us that a skewed distribution helps the ANOVA reject a null hypothesis that should be rejected. We saw earlier that a skewed distribution helps the ANOVA retain a null hypothesis that should not be rejected. This is an

| Table 8.2.2 | ANOVA Success Rates in Rejecting False Null Hypotheses (Effect Size = 0.30; Two Samples from Right-Skewed Population) |

NUMBER OF OBSERVATIONS PER GROUP	PROPORTION OF FALSE NULL HYPOTHESES REJECTED
2	81%
4	87%
8	89%
16	89%
32	89%
64	89%
128	89%

argument for the ANOVA. The right skewness makes the ANOVA less likely to reject a true null hypothesis and more likely to reject a false null hypothesis. At least that is how it works in this case. If you change the number of groups or use other right-skewed populations, you might be able to get it to work otherwise.

The Effect of Skewness on the ANOVA

Large tails or skewnesses in the population make the ANOVA less likely to reject the null hypothesis, when there is only one population. It is unclear how skewness affects the ANOVA's power.

Figure 8.2.5

A Right-Skewed Population (Divided by Observations from a Distribution Uniform from 0 to 1)

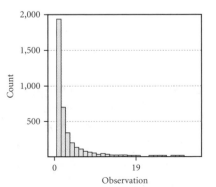

This example raises the question of what comparable amount to add to make the null hypothesis false. For the normal population, I added about 0.3 to each observation in one group. For the right-skewed population, I added 36 to each observation in one of the groups. It is debatable whether the two are comparable. One way to end the argument is simply to use nonparametric tests instead.

As with Kohers and Patel, I run my analyses both ways. If the ANOVA results agree with the nonparametric results, I am happy and feel secure. If they disagree, then I try to determine what is going on by looking at a lot of histograms.

Algebra and Greek Symbols

All of the tests described in this section require that all of the observations be independent. That is, for each observation, that observation was only the result of the trial on which that observation was collected. Independent observations are uncorrelated. That is, knowing one observation does not improve your chances of correctly guessing any other observation.

Table 8.2.3 lists the tests mentioned in this section and the requirements and unique assumptions of each test.

Table 8.2.3 Seven Nonparametric Tests and Their Requirements

TEST	REQUIREMENTS
Kruskal-Wallis	All deviations within each group come from the same continuous population. (For example, if the observations were only whole numbers, that would violate an assumption of the Kruskal-Wallis test.) Also, as with the ANOVA, a variance that is larger in one group than another may lead the test to reject the null hypothesis frequently, even if all populations have equal means.
Mann-Whitney U and Wilcoxon	The differences between the measurements are continuous (all decimal values are possible) and symmetrically distributed.
Binomial and sign	None (other than independence).
Monte Carlo	The population's distribution is known.
Resampling	None (other than independence).

Abstract

Violations of the ANOVA's assumptions of normality sometimes lead the ANOVA to reject true null hypotheses too often and may weaken the ANOVA's power—its ability to recognize false null hypotheses. This is especially a problem with small sample sizes. Other tests, nonparametrics, have been developed to test the hypothesis that all groups came from populations with equal means. These other tests make fewer assumptions and are not misled or weakened by non-normality. The Kruskal-Wallis test can be used to test for a relationship between a set of number line observations and a set of categorical observations and does not assume a normal population. The Mann-Whitney U test can be used the same way, but only if there are only two categories. The Wilcoxon test and sign test can be used to determine whether a set of number line observations came from a population with a specific center. The Wilcoxon test assumes that the population is symmetrically distributed; the sign test does not. The binomial test determines whether a sample proportion came from a population with a specified population proportion by calculating z. The sign test is a binomial test of the proportion of observations that fall above a null hypothesis's population center. The Monte Carlo and resampling methods simulate what would happen if the null hypothesis were true and estimate the p-value by looking at the distribution of statistics that appears in the simulation.

Avoiding Common Misunderstandings

Some people become overly concerned about the whole issue of meeting the requirements of tests. When they learn that a test such as the ANOVA requires a normal distribution, they notice that they cannot be 100% sure that the underlying data are normally distributed and conclude that nothing can be learned. This is a mistake. Not only are there nonparametric tests that might be used, but also, if the sample sizes are large enough, it won't matter that the underlying distribution is not normal.

The null hypothesis of the analysis of variance is that all of the data came from a single distribution. If two groups have data that came from two different normal distributions that have the same mean, but different variances, and the ANOVA rejects the null hypothesis, that is not a mistake on the part of the ANOVA. In that situation, the null hypothesis is not true.

Computer Project

Redo the work of the last section for a particular set of degrees of freedom. Try having the data come from a variety of distributions. Can you beat my populations that led the ANOVA to reject the null hypothesis 49% of the time, even though the means of both populations were the same? Can you find distributions with equal means for which the ANOVA would reject the null hypothesis 50% of the time?

Exercises

1. Teasdale and Engberg (1997) found that 30.4% of the 520 men who later got concussions had had dysfunctional IQ scores when tested as young men. The population proportion of their null hypothesis was 20.4%. What was the z-value of the 30.4% that Teasdale and Engberg found? That is, if they had done a z-test, what would their z-value have been?

2. I used to work at one of three campuses of the University of Washington. An economist I knew wanted to test claims that different campuses have significantly different salaries. He had two sets of measurements for a group of professors. One set was the campus at which each professor works. The other set was the professors' salaries. What two tests might the economist have used if he ignored how the salaries' population was distributed?

3. In the study in Exercise 2 how would you expect salaries to be distributed, and what would that distribution do to the ANOVA?

4. Write to the economist from Exercise 2 about the pros and cons of two tests he might use to determine whether salaries differ between the three campuses. Be sure to address the issue of how many salaries he observes.

5. In the last section, we discussed calculating the sum of squares within and between for a data set with two groups and two observations in each group. Would it ever be sensible in real life to do an ANOVA on such a data set? Write a short note about whether that exercise might have been a little misleading. Explain why you answer as you do. (What would Karl Pearson say about me if he found me doing such an ANOVA in real life?)

6. A friend sends you an e-mail message, complaining, "Not only are the results sections full of complicated tests, but I just realized that sometimes they test the same thing with two different tests. Today I was reading an article, and first they used an ANOVA, then they used something called a Mann-Whitney U test. You have read about stats. What is the deal?" Write a short reply.

A team of biologists studied egg-laying patterns among penguins. Some penguins lay two sets (two clutches) of eggs in a season. Other penguins lay only one set. The biologists checked whether the penguins that lay two sets managed this by laying their first clutch earlier in the breeding season. The following quote is part of their report. Use it to complete Exercises 7 through 9.

> *First clutches of two-clutch breeders (double and replacement brooders) were . . . earlier than those of single brooders (Kruskal-Wallis H = 25.91, P < 0.001 . . .).*
>
> —PAREDES ET AL., *THE AUK*, 2002

7. What test did the biologists use, and why did they use that test?

8. What was the *p*-value, and were the results statistically significant?

9. Should the biologists report the average date of first clutch for the two-clutch breeders separately from the average date of first clutch for the one-clutch breeders? Why or why not?

A biologist in Michigan tracked the growth of trees from 1962 to 1994. The biologist checked whether survival was related to how fast the trees grew. The following quote is part of his report. Use it to complete Exercises 10 through 12.

> *Sugar maple and hemlock trees that died by 1989 grew more slowly during 1962–1967 than did trees that survived (Mann-Whitney tests and resampling comparisons, P < 0.05).*
>
> —WOODS, *ECOLOGY*, 2000, P. 110

10. What tests did Woods use?

11. Why did Woods use two tests rather than one?

12. What was the *p*-value, was the result significant, and what alpha does it seem that Woods was using?

Answers to Odd-Numbered Exercises

1. We would use the null hypothesis's population proportion for estimating the standard error:

$$\text{Standard Error} = \sqrt{\frac{\text{Population Proportion} \times (1 - \text{Population Proportion})}{\text{Sample Size}}}$$

$$\text{Standard Error} = \sqrt{\frac{.204 \times .796}{520}}$$

$$\text{Standard Error} = .018$$

$$z = \frac{\text{Difference}}{\text{Standard Error}}$$

$$\text{Difference} = .304 - .204 = .1$$

$$z = \frac{.1}{.018}$$

$$z = 5.5$$

3. Salaries, as with other dollar amounts, are usually right skewed, which would make the ANOVA less likely to reject a true null hypothesis, but it's unclear exactly what it does when the null hypothesis is false.

5. "Do NOT do an ANOVA on a data set with only four observations. With that small a sample size, violations of the ANOVA's assumptions may interfere with the reliability of the test a lot. You may have a test that would reject a true null hypothesis as much as 50% of the time when you think your alpha is 5%. Doing research like that is what Karl Pearson would call 'being a naughty brewer.'"

7. They used the Kruskal-Wallis test partially because they needed to test for a correlation between a categorical measurement (two-clutch versus one-clutch breeders) and a number line measurement (date). They could have used an ANOVA, but probably decided against it because the dates were not normally distributed.

9. They should report the means separately for the two groups, because the two groups are significantly different in terms of first-clutch date.

11. Probably Woods wanted to double-check that the test would come out significant no matter what assumptions his test was based on.

8.3 American Counties

- Correlation
- Scatter Plots

Violent crime resumed its gradual decrease in the first half of the year despite slightly more murders and robberies. . . . By region, crime totals fell 4% in the Northeast and nearly 2% in the Midwest, but rose 1.6% in the West and 0.8% in the South.

—Jackson, Los Angeles Times, 2001

For more than a decade, violent crime in America has been becoming less common, but the story varies from place to place. To explore this, I visited the Census Bureau's Web site, which reports violent crime statistics by U.S. county. There are more than 3,000 U.S. counties. I used software to randomly select 10 counties, which are listed in Table 8.3.1. (The two counties in Louisiana, Madison and Washington, are called "parishes," the Louisiana term for counties.)

Table 8.3.1 10 Randomly Selected U.S. Counties

COUNTY	COUNTY
Saline, Arkansas	Washington, Louisiana
Tazewell, Illinois	Livingston, Michigan
Pulaski, Indiana	Monmouth, New Jersey
Hickman, Kentucky	Sequoyah, Oklahoma
Madison, Louisiana	Wyoming, West Virginia

Violent Crime and Birth Rate: High Correlation

The Census Bureau also reports the violent crime rates for counties. Table 8.3.2 shows the 1990 violent crime rates for those 10 counties along with the birth rate in each county in 1994. It would be nice to have these data from the same year, but the Census Bureau reports what it has been able to find, and not all statistics are compiled every year. For some reason, the 1990 violent crime rate in Tazewell

Table 8.3.2   Violent Crimes Known to Police in 1990 and Birth Rates in 1994

COUNTY	1990 VIOLENT CRIMES KNOWN TO POLICE PER 1,000 PEOPLE	1994 NUMBER OF BIRTHS PER 1,000 PEOPLE
Saline	2.34	13.1
Tazewell	Not Available	12.8
Pulaski	1.27	14.3
Hickman	0.72	12.3
Madison	18.70	20.4
Washington	7.18	14.5
Livingston	1.58	13.4
Monmouth	2.61	14.3
Sequoyah	2.93	14.6
Wyoming	0.62	11.2

County, Illinois, isn't available, so our analysis of the violent crime rates will leave out Tazewell County.

Figure 8.3.1 shows how the crime rates and birth rates vary across the nine counties. The two charts in Figure 8.3.1 use a number line on the left side (the y-axis). The counties are listed across the bottom (the x-axis), and how high the line is indicates the counties' rates in each graph. For example, Saline County, Arkansas, had a violent crime rate of 2.34 crimes per 1,000 people, and for Saline in the top chart the line is at 2.34. Saline County had a birth rate of 13.1 births per 1,000 people, and for Saline in the bottom chart the line is at 13.1.

Figure 8.3.1 shows a correlation between birth rate and crime rate. As you look from county to county, you can see that the two rates move somewhat together. That is a correlation. Because the rates move together, knowing one tells you something about the other.

Figure 8.3.2 is another way to look at the data in Figure 8.3.1. Figure 8.3.2 is a scatter plot. In a scatter plot, there are two number lines, one along the x-axis and another up the y-axis.

In a scatter plot, each observation's two values are represented by a dot. For example, the upper rightmost dot in Figure 8.3.2 is Madison Parish, Louisiana. To read its birth rate, you can trace down from the dot to the x-axis and see that its birth rate is about 21 births per 1,000 people. To read its violent crime rate, you trace left to the *y*-axis. Its violent crime rate is about 19 crimes per 1,000 people. In fact, if you look back to Table 8.3.2, you will see that Madison Parish's violent crime rate was 18.7 and its birth rate was 20.4.

Figure 8.3.1

1990 Violent Crimes Known to Police per 1,000 and 1994 Birth Rates per 1,000

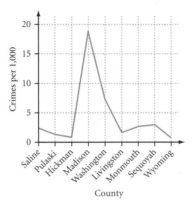

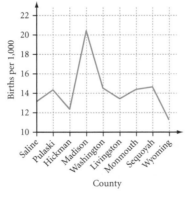

Figure 8.3.2

Scatter Plot of Rates of 1990 Violent Crimes Known to Police and 1994 Birth Rates per 1,000 (Correlation Coefficient = 0.93)

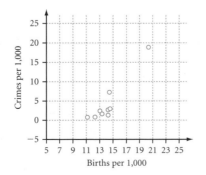

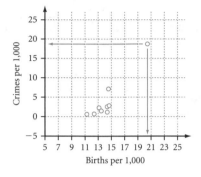

How to Draw a Scatter Plot

Draw two number line segments. One segment, the *x*-axis, is horizontal. The other, the *y*-axis, is vertical. Each axis will represent one measurement for each person or item studied. Each item or person is represented with a dot. The dot's location is found by tracing along the *x*-axis to the item's *x*-axis value and then tracing up until you are level with the item's *y*-axis value.

For example, here are the weights and prices of three packages of hamburger at my local supermarket:

PACKAGE	WEIGHT	PRICE
A	1 lb.	$1.89
B	1.5 lb.	$2.84
C	2 lb.	$3.78

Here is a scatter plot of those three packages:

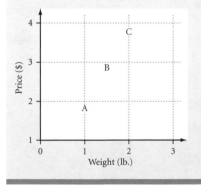

Figure 8.3.3

Scatter Plot of Rates of 1990 Violent Crimes Known to Police and 1994 Birth Rates per 1,000 with Regression Line (Correlation Coefficient = 0.93)

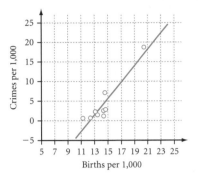

The correlation between number line observations can be described with a statistic called the "correlation coefficient." Correlation coefficients range from -1.0 to 1.0. A correlation of 1.0 is a perfect correlation and means that the points in a scatter plot all fall directly on a line with a positive slope (a diagonal line that goes up and to the right). A correlation coefficient of 0 indicates that there is no correlation between the two sets of measurements. A correlation coefficient of -1.0 indicates that the dots all arrange themselves in a diagonal line with a negative slope (a line that goes down and to the right).

For the data in Figure 8.3.2, the correlation coefficient is 0.93, close to 1. Those rates are highly correlated. To see how correlated, Figure 8.3.3 shows the same scatter plot from Figure 8.3.2 with a line drawn in. That line is called a "regression line." We will get to how to calculate a regression. At this point, the important thing is that the regression line is created to be close to all of the dots on the scatter plot.

Correlation Coefficients

Correlation coefficients range from -1.0 to 1.0, indicating how well you can use a line to predict variations in one set of observations from another set of observations. A correlation coefficient of 0 indicates that, if you use a line on a scatter plot to predict observations, knowing one observation does not at all help predict the other. A correlation of 1.0 or -1.0 indicates that a line would predict a set of observations perfectly.

Violent Crime and Unemployment: Medium Correlation

You might think that unemployment is related to violent crime. Table 8.3.3 shows the violent crime and unemployment rates for the nine counties.

Table 8.3.3 1990 Violent Crimes Known to Police per 1,000 and 1990 Unemployment Rates

COUNTY	1990 VIOLENT CRIMES KNOWN TO POLICE PER 1,000 PEOPLE	1990 UNEMPLOYMENT RATE (%)
Saline	2.34	5.7
Pulaski	1.27	6.2
Hickman	0.72	7.2
Madison	18.70	12.2
Washington	7.18	8.9
Livingston	1.58	5.4
Monmouth	2.61	4.1
Sequoyah	2.93	8.2
Wyoming	0.62	12.0

Figure 8.3.4 shows how the unemployment rate changes from county to county and how those changes match (and don't match) changes in the violent crime rates. Figure 8.3.4 shows that Madison Parish has high unemployment and a high violent crime rate. In contrast, Wyoming County, West Virginia, has equally high unemployment but a quite low violent crime rate. In these nine counties, violent crime and unemployment are less correlated than violent crime and births. Figure 8.3.5 shows this in a scatter plot of violent crime and unemployment.

The data in Figure 8.3.5 has a correlation coefficient of 0.56. That is a positive correlation, but not a very high one. Figure 8.3.6 shows how much the dots diverge from a line. The line in Figure 8.3.6 is a regression line. It doesn't fall as close to some dots as it does to others, because the dots don't fall in a nearly linear arrangement.

Among these nine counties there is some correlation between unemployment and violent crimes.

Violent Crime and Raw Count of Supplemental Social Security: No Correlation

Not everything about the counties is correlated with the violent crime rate. For example, Table 8.3.4 shows the violent crime rate and the number of supplemental social security recipients in each county. Figure 8.3.7 shows how the numbers in Table 8.3.4 vary across the counties.

Figure 8.3.4 **1990 Unemployment Rates and 1990 Violent Crimes Known to Police per 1,000**

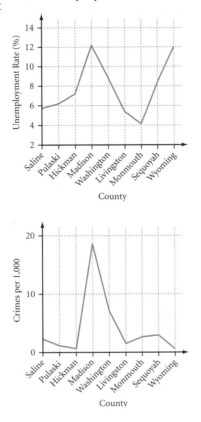

Figure 8.3.5 **Scatter Plot of 1990 Violent Crimes Known to Police per 1,000 and 1990 Unemployment Rates (Correlation Coefficient = 0.56)**

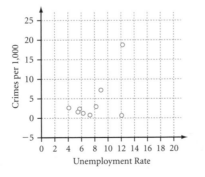

Figure 8.3.6   **Scatter Plot of 1990 Violent Crimes Known to Police per 1,000 and 1990 Unemployment Rates with Regression Line (Correlation Coefficient = 0.56)**

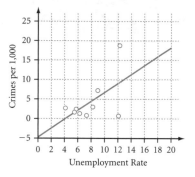

Figure 8.3.7   **Raw Counts of 1996 Supplemental Social Security Recipients and 1990 Violent Crimes Known to Police**

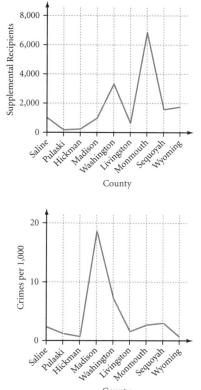

Table 8.3.4

1990 Violent Crimes Known to Police per 1,000 and Number of 1996 Supplemental Social Security Recipients

COUNTY	1990 VIOLENT CRIMES KNOWN TO POLICE PER 1,000 PEOPLE	NUMBER OF 1996 SUPPLEMENTAL SOCIAL SECURITY RECIPIENTS
Saline	2.34	12,411
Pulaski	1.27	2,728
Hickman	0.72	1,189
Madison	18.70	2,296
Washington	7.18	9,385
Livingston	1.58	15,662
Monmouth	2.61	91,400
Sequoyah	2.93	7,435
Wyoming	0.62	7,099

Figure 8.3.7 shows that the counties vary in the number of supplemental social security recipients, but that the number of recipients in 1996 is unrelated to the violent crime rate in 1990. Figure 8.3.8 shows a scatter plot illustrating the lack of relationship between those two measurements.

Figure 8.3.9 shows Figure 8.3.8's scatter plot with a line drawn in that is close to all of the dots.

The line in Figure 8.3.9 is horizontal, because the average violent crime rate is about 4.2 crimes per 1,000 people pretty much all the way along the x-axis. No matter what you told me about the number of supplemental social security recipients, my guess for the violent crime rate would be "4.2 per 1,000." The number

Figure 8.3.8

Scatter Plot of Raw Counts of 1996 Supplemental Social Security Recipients and 1990 Violent Crimes Known to Police per 1,000 (Correlation Coefficient = 0.00)

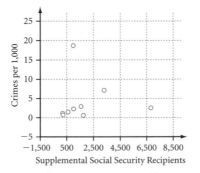

Figure 8.3.9 Scatter Plot of Raw Counts of 1996 Supplemental Social Security Recipients and 1990 Violent Crimes Known to Police per 1,000 with Regression Line (Correlation Coefficient = 0.00)

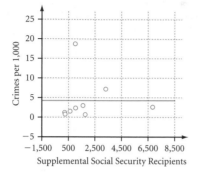

of recipients doesn't help predict the violent crime rate. That is what is meant by "no correlation."

Violent Crime and Median Household Income: Medium Negative Correlation

You might think that, as incomes rise, violent crime goes down. Table 8.3.5 lists the median household incomes of the nine counties in 1993. The county with the highest violent crime rate, Madison, has the lowest median household income, so there might be a correlation in Table 8.3.5. Figure 8.3.10 shows how the incomes vary from county to county compared to how the violent crime rate varies.

Table 8.3.5 1990 Violent Crimes Known to Police per 1,000 and 1993 Median Household Incomes

COUNTY	1990 VIOLENT CRIMES KNOWN TO POLICE PER 1,000 PEOPLE	1993 MEDIAN HOUSEHOLD INCOME
Saline	2.34	$33,020
Pulaski	1.27	$30,426
Hickman	0.72	$24,309
Madison	18.70	$15,324
Washington	7.18	$18,536
Livingston	1.58	$51,167
Monmouth	2.61	$49,048
Sequoyah	2.93	$21,307
Wyoming	0.62	$20,058

Figure 8.3.10 shows that Livingston County and Monmouth County both have high median incomes and low violent crime rates. Figure 8.3.11 is a scatter plot showing the relationship between income and violent crime.

Figure 8.3.10

1993 Median Household Incomes and 1990 Violent Crime Rates

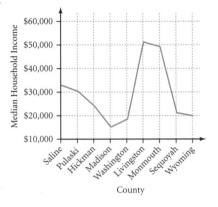

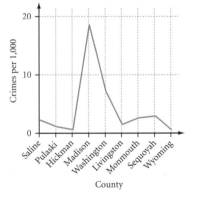

Figure 8.3.11

Scatter Plot of 1993 Median Household Incomes and 1990 Violent Crimes Known to Police per 1,000 (Correlation Coefficient = −0.45)

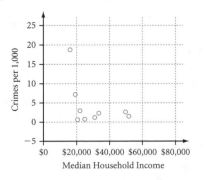

Figure 8.3.12

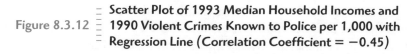

Scatter Plot of 1993 Median Household Incomes and 1990 Violent Crimes Known to Police per 1,000 with Regression Line (Correlation Coefficient = −0.45)

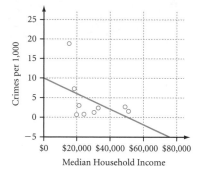

The correlation coefficient reflects how well the dots in the scatter plot line up along a line. Figure 8.3.11 appears to show a strong correlation, but it is not a simple line correlation. It seems to be a drop in violent crime up to a median income of about $20,000, and then no further drop in violent crime. In spite of this relationship in Figure 8.3.11, the dots do not fall very close to a line, as you can see in Figure 8.3.12.

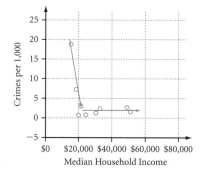

Positive Versus Negative Correlations

In scatter plots, positive correlations have lines that slope up from left to right. That means that as the observations in one set rise, the observations in the other set rise also. Negative correlations have lines that slope downward. That means that as observations in one set rise, the observations in the other set fall.

Violent Crime and Proportion Living Above Poverty Level: Negative Correlation

In the nine counties, the proportion of people in a county who have incomes that keep them above poverty level appears to be related to violent crime, as shown by Table 8.3.6. Living in "poverty" means earning less than the federal government's poverty cutoff for a given family size, which in 2002 was $8,860 for a single person and $18,100 for a family of four.

Figure 8.3.13 shows the percentage of people living above the poverty level in each county compared to the violent crime rates.

Figure 8.3.14 is a scatter plot showing the relationship between violent crime and living above poverty level. The pattern in Figure 8.3.14 shows the same mixed relationship that we saw in the correlation between income and violent crime. Figure 8.3.14's data fall a little closer to a single straight line that angles downward, as is shown in Figure 8.3.15, so the correlation is closer to a negative one.

Table 8.3.6 1990 Violent Crimes Known to Police per 1,000 and 1989 Percentage of the Population Living Above Poverty Level

COUNTY	1990 VIOLENT CRIMES KNOWN TO POLICE PER 1,000 PEOPLE	1989 PERCENTAGE LIVING ABOVE POVERTY LEVEL
Saline	2.34	91%
Pulaski	1.27	89%
Hickman	0.72	80%
Madison	18.70	55%
Washington	7.18	68%
Livingston	1.58	96%
Monmouth	2.61	95%
Sequoyah	2.93	75%
Wyoming	0.62	72%

Figure 8.3.13 **1989 Percentage Living Above Poverty Level and 1990 Violent Crimes Known to Police per 1,000**

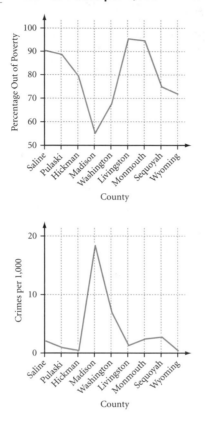

Figure 8.3.14 **Scatter Plot of 1989 Percentage Living Above Poverty Level and 1990 Violent Crimes Known to Police per 1,000 (Correlation Coefficient = −0.74)**

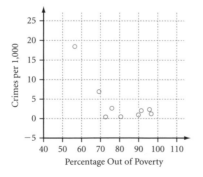

Figure 8.3.15

Scatter Plot of 1989 Percentage Living Above Poverty Level and 1990 Violent Crimes Known to Police per 1,000 with Regression Line (Correlation Coefficient = −0.74)

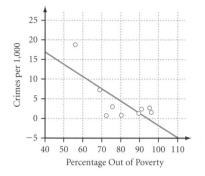

Linear Correlation

The correlation coefficient checks for a linear correlation and tells us whether we can use a line in a scatter plot to improve our ability to predict one set of measurements, given another set of measurements. For example, in these data, the violent crime rates ranged from 0.62 crimes per 1,000 people to 18.7 crimes per 1,000 people, with a mean at 4.2 crimes per 1,000 people. If you told me that you had picked a county at random and asked for my guess for its violent crime rate, I would guess "4.2 per 1,000." The birth rates ranged from 11.2 to 20.4. Figure 8.3.16 shows the relationship between birth rate and violent crime rate again.

If you told me that the county you selected had a birth rate of 13 per 1,000, I would change my guess of the violent crime rate to "1 per 1,000." If you told me that the birth rate was 15 per 1,000, my guess would be "5 per 1,000." Because I can use the birth rate to improve my estimate of the crime rate, the crime rate is

Figure 8.3.16

Scatter Plot of Rates of 1990 Violent Crimes Known to Police per 1,000 and 1994 Birth Rates per 1,000 with Regression Line (Correlation Coefficient = 0.93)

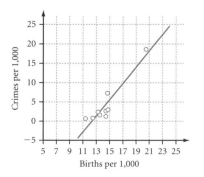

Figure 8.3.17

**Highly Correlated Data Without a Linear Correlation
(Correlation Coefficient = 0.00)**

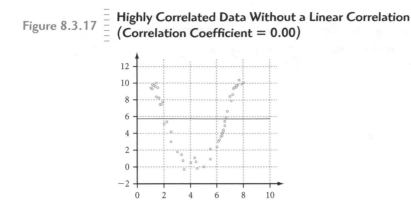

correlated with the birth rate. Because the relationship is a linear relationship—because the dots fall roughly in a straight line on the scatter plot—it is a linear correlation, and it has a high correlation coefficient.

Sometimes measurements are highly correlated, but not linearly correlated. For example, the scatter plot in Figure 8.3.17 is highly correlated, but not in a way that can be summarized by a straight line.

Some of the relationships in this section, such as the relationship between income and violent crime, are stronger correlations than indicated by the correlation coefficient, because they are not linear correlations, and the correlation coefficient reports only the strength of the linear correlation.

Correlation Coefficient Reveals Linear Correlation

The correlation coefficient is a measure of linear correlation. A linear correlation is when you can use a line on a scatter plot to improve your ability to predict one measurement, given another measurement.

For example, this scatter plot shows a high linear correlation:

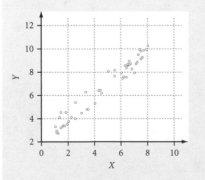

Correlation Coefficient Reveals Linear Correlation *(Continued)*

This scatter plot shows a strong correlation, but no linear correlation:

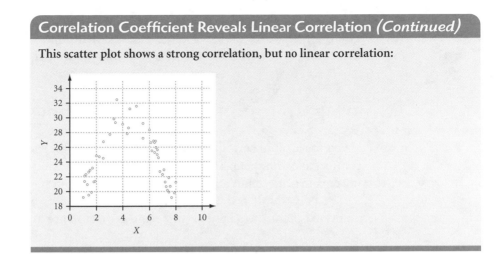

Algebra and Greek Symbols

A linear relationship is one that may be described as $y = b_0 + b_1x$, as we will see in the next chapter. "b_0" is a number, and "b_1" is another number that is multiplied by x in the equation.

Abstract

If a researcher gathers more than one observation from each item or person, the researcher can check for a correlation between the observations. If knowing a randomly chosen item's or person's score for one observation enables researchers to improve their prediction for the other observation, then the two sets of observations are correlated.

If both sets of observations are number line measurements, the data can be depicted in a scatter plot. A scatter plot includes a dot for each item or person studied. The dot's position from left to right indicates its value in terms of the observations being recorded on the *x*-axis. The dot's vertical position indicates that person's or item's value with respect to the *y*-axis observation.

The relationship between two sets of number line observations can be described with a correlation coefficient. Correlation coefficients range from −1.0 to 1.0. A correlation coefficient of 0 means that there is no correlation that can be described with a line. A correlation coefficient of 1.0 means that variations in one set of observations are perfectly predictable from the other observations, and a scatter plot of the data makes a line sloping upward from left to right. A correlation coefficient of -1.0 has a scatter plot line that slopes downward, indicating that as one set of observations goes up, the other set goes down.

Avoiding Common Misunderstandings

If you are at all unsure about scatter plots, take the time to become completely comfortable with them. The rest of this book relies on your comfort with graphing data in scatter plots and thinking about numbers in x-y coordinates.

The two axes of a scatter plot are number lines. For example, the distance on the axis from 1 to 3 has to be the same as the distance from 11 to 13 and from 50 to 52.

A scatter plot can represent two measurements taken from each item or person that was studied. Each studied person or object is represented with a single dot in the scatter plot. The dot's value on the measurement represented on the x-axis is the position on the x-axis that you reach when you trace from the dot directly down to the x-axis. The dot's value on the y-axis is the position on the y-axis that you reach when you trace horizontally from the dot to the y-axis.

Computer Project

Using the Representative Sample of 50,000 Americans from the *Data Matters* Resource Center at *www.keycollege.com/dm,* take random samples of 20 people. Use your software to create scatter plots to check for correlations between measurements. For example, does a scatter plot indicate a correlation between education and income? Take a second random sample and check whether the same image shows up in the scatter plot. Repeat these steps with two random samples of 200 people each. What is the relationship between the image seen in a scatter plot of a sample's data and what would be seen in a scatter plot of the entire population's data?

Exercises

1. A group of researchers grouped families by their income and checked the mean math SAT score for each income level. The following scatter plot shows mean math SAT scores for teenagers from families with various incomes (data from Anderluh, 1997).

Math SATs Plotted Against Family Income

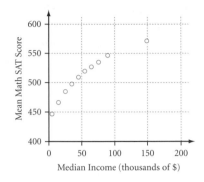

What would be your estimate of the correlation coefficient? Briefly explain how you can guess what the correlation is. Remember to give a range when you are asked to estimate something. You do not know the margin of error here, but do not be fooled into giving a single point answer.

2. Your Aunt Minnie has been reading books suggesting that intelligence is what leads some people to be poor and others wealthy, and she feels that the data from Exercise 1 show that those books are right. Write a short note to Aunt Minnie explaining that correlation is not causation. To illustrate that a correlation does not tell you what is causing what, include three different scenarios that might be producing this particular correlation.

3. The following scatter plot shows data about reading performance and school lunch participation from the *Seattle Times* (Houtz, 1997). Each dot represents a public elementary school in Seattle.

School Lunch Participation and Reading Performance at Seattle Elementary Schools in 1997

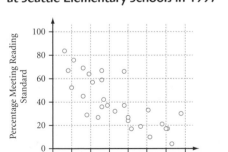

The state had tested all fourth-graders, and the percentage who passed at each school was reported in the newspaper. The article also reported the proportion of students who came from families that were poor enough to qualify for free or reduced-price lunches. Aunt Minnie wants to know whether it is reading skill that affects poverty or whether it is poverty that affects reading skill. Write a short note to answer her.

4. In Exercise 3, what would be your estimate of the correlation coefficient? Briefly explain what in the scatter plot lets you guess what the correlation is.

Here is a report of some sort of correlation between sex education and consequences for young people. Refer to this quote for Exercises 5 through 7.

> *Studies on the efficacy of sex education in preventing early sexual initiation have shown negative correlations. The more sex education a community has, the more trouble with pregnancy, abortion and sexually transmitted diseases.*
>
> —Charen, *St. Louis Post-Dispatch*, 1996, p. 11B

5. Look at the second sentence by itself. Is Charen describing a positive or a negative correlation in that sentence? Explain how sex education and pregnancy trouble might have been measured so that these two sentences are not contradictory. Is it likely that those measurements were done as you describe?

6. Charen is suggesting that sex education is producing the trouble with pregnancy. Write a short note explaining that correlation is not causation. Provide an alternative explanation of what might have produced the correlation. Also, write a sentence explaining what correlations do show.

7. If someone looked at how much sex education was provided and looked at how many teenage pregnancies occurred, what would it mean to say that there was a negative correlation?

8. According to the following quote from the *Wall Street Journal*, if I told you that there was a large rise in temperature, what should you predict about human fertility?

> *[There is a] negative correlation between temperature increases and human fertility.*
>
> —Crispell, *Wall Street Journal*, 1996, p. 9

9. Cousin Fred writes to you about this article:

> *In his 1993 review of four major longitudinal studies of the relationship between spanking and antisocial aggression, Robert E. Larzelere found an average correlation of "about .00."*
>
> —Thomas, *Weekly Standard*, 1997, p. 12

Fred asks, "What does it mean that the average correlation was 'about .00'?" Write a short explanation for Cousin Fred.

10. If the ".00" in the quote in Exercise 9 is referring to a correlation coefficient, does it necessarily mean that there is no correlation between how much parents spank their children and how antisocially aggressive their children turn out? Why or why not?

Exercises 11 through 15 refer to the following quote, which reports on deaths from car accidents and light trucks (including SUV's).

> *Sport-utility vehicle accidents [are correlated with] higher-than-normal liability claims. . . . National Highway Traffic Safety Administration data show more Americans (5,447 in 1996) die in crashes involving a car and a light truck than in crashes involving two cars (4,193). Yet cars account for more than 70 percent of the insured vehicles in the United States.*
>
> —Lubanko, *Hartford Courant*, 1997, p. D1

11. In the preceding quote about sport-utility vehicles (SUV's), what kinds of observations are being correlated, categorical or number line?

12. How do the chances that someone drives a light truck (including the possibility of an SUV) compare to the chances that someone drives a car?

13. How do the chances that someone dies in an accident between a light truck and a car compare to the chances that someone dies in an accident between two cars?

14. How would you estimate the margins of error for each of these chances?

15. Your Auntie Jane sends you a letter including this report and asking whether she is being irresponsible driving her SUV. She wants to know what this report means. Write her a short note clarifying it. Be sure to comment on the issue of how correlation is not causation.

16. In the following quote, what kinds of observations are being correlated, categorical or number line?

> *Women in Japan who eat a traditional Japanese diet have a relatively low rate of breast cancer. But when their diet changes, the breast cancer rate increases. . . . When women from countries with low breast cancer rates migrate to the United States, their chances of developing breast cancer increases.*
>
> —Giuliano, *Los Angeles Times*, 1997, p. S8

17. What would you need to find out before you could estimate the margins of error for each of the chances mentioned in the quote in Exercise 16?

18. Your Auntie Jane wants to know what the report quoted in Exercise 16 means as well. Does it mean that she is making a mistake eating so much barbecue? Write her a short note clarifying the report. Be sure to comment on the issue of how correlation is not causation.

19. In this quote from the *Kansas City Star,* what kind of measurements is Sefton talking about, categorical, number line, or one of each?

> There is a "very high correlation" of women who have had an epidural longer than five hours experiencing a fever, Breedlove said. That, in turn, can raise the baby's temperature and put the newborn in intensive care for evaluation.
>
> —SEFTON, KANSAS CITY STAR, 1997, P. F1

20. In the quote in Exercise 19, Sefton reports a correlation between more than five hours of epidural and a fever. Assume that this data is from a correlational study. What are three different possible directions of causation that might have led to this correlation?

21. Based on the quote in Exercise 19, why might researchers have wanted to avoid doing an experiment on the relationship between epidurals and fevers, and why would it be worthwhile to do that experiment?

Answers to Odd-Numbered Exercises

1. The numbers fall almost in a line. Looks like 0.9 to me; I'd say somewhere between 0.7 and 0.98.

3. "Dear Aunt Minnie, the relationship between percentage on school lunch subsidy and reading scores is telling us only that we can use one to predict the other, given the current situation. It does not tell us why they are related. It could be that being on school lunch subsidy interferes with reading performance. Perhaps the big lunch makes students sleepy. It could be that poverty leads to school lunch subsidies and also interferes with reading achievement. It could be that genetically caused reading difficulties lead to poverty and children's difficulties in reading. It could be that schools that more aggressively seek out support for school lunches have less time to focus on test preparation. The bottom line is that correlation isn't causation. We don't know why these two sets of observations are correlated."

5. The second sentence is describing a positive correlation: *More* sex education appears with *more* trouble. A negative correlation means that as one thing goes up, the other goes down. Perhaps they measured sex education by the

amount of time *not spent on sex education* per week. Then, as the measurement of sex education went down, the amount of sex education went up. Or perhaps they measured how many fewer pregnancies happened than might be expected. Then, as the number of pregnancies went up, this measure went down. It is unlikely that the measurements were done this way.

7. If there were a negative correlation, then as the sex education rose, pregnancy rates would fall.

9. "Cousin Fred, the '.00' is probably the average correlation coefficient. The correlation coefficient represents how correlated two measurements are. A 0 correlation coefficient means that two measurements are not linearly correlated. 'Linearly correlated' means that if you plotted the data on an *x-y* plot, with amount of spanking along the bottom and antisocial behavior ratings up the side, the dots representing each child would fall in roughly a diagonal line. In this case, it appears that spanking and antisocial aggression are not linearly correlated. Correlation is a somewhat complicated thing itself. A correlation means that you can improve your ability to guess one thing from another, so this is saying that (at least using a line on a graph) you could not improve your ability to predict antisocial behavior by knowing how much parents spanked."

11. One set of observations is definitely categorical: whether a sport-utility vehicle is involved in an accident. The other might be number line (insurance payments) or categorical (whether the payments were higher than normal).

13. The chance that a randomly chosen American will die in an accident involving only cars is about 80% of the chance that that American will die in an accident involving a truck.

15. "Dear Auntie Jane, even though most Americans drive cars, most car accident deaths involve a truck. What that means is that, if I had to guess whether your truck was going to kill someone, I would have to say there is a higher chance than if you drove a car. However, I don't know whether your selling it and buying a car would make any difference. This correlation doesn't tell us what is causing the correlation. It could be that truck drivers, on the average, drive more recklessly, not that the trucks are more dangerous. It could be that living in places where the driving is dangerous leads people to buy trucks or sport-utility vehicles, and if they drove cars in those places, their death rates would be even higher."

17. I would need to know the number of women studied.

19. It appears to be two sets of categorical measurements: whether or not the expectant mother had an epidural longer than five hours and whether or not the mother had a fever.

21. One possible reason they might want to avoid the experiment; because an experiment involves doing something, and people worry about liability when they do things. For example, to test whether it is the long epidurals that are causing the fevers, the doctors might randomly assign half of the women to be in a condition in which their prescribing physicians were not allowed to continue the epidural for more than five hours and the other half to have physicians who are not constrained to prescribe less than five hours. If fevers appear more in the second group, the mothers in the second group might try to sue the doctors for putting them at higher risk of a fever. Doing such an experiment would be worthwhile, because, until we do the experiment, we don't know whether it is the long epidurals that lead to the more frequent fevers. (Of course, try explaining that to a jury of people who haven't taken statistics.)

CHAPTER 9

Best Lines

R egression is a statistical method that is used to explore relationships between two sets of numeric (number line) measurements. To see how number line measurements are related, we draw one number line horizontally to be the x-axis and the other number line vertically to be the y-axis. Then we plot each point to create a scatter plot. Correlations between the two sets of measurements show up as patterns in the scatter plot.

In this text, we will focus mostly on linear regression. Linear regression checks for correlations between measurements that can be described with lines in scatter plots. Section 9.1 presents lines and begins to show how a best line can be found.

Picking the ideal line to describe the scatter plot is a little complicated when the dots of the scatter plot are spread out. Each dot seems to pull for its own line. Section 9.2 shows how a compromise line, called a line of best fit, can serve fairly well when no line can go through all the points. The best line turns out to be something of an average, as you will see in Section 9.3.

9.1) Lines

- How to Calculate the Equation of a Line

Schools with more students from low-income families tend to score lower on tests.

—*Seattle Times*, September 17, 1997, p. A12

Poverty and Education

In 1996, Washington State began giving a test with standards in reading, math, writing, and listening skills that are a good guess of what a well-trained and well-motivated fourth-grader might learn. Statewide, about a quarter of fourth-graders exceed the standard in all four tests. Public schools vary in what proportion of the children pass, from lows of only 3% passing all the way up to highs of 95% passing.

The local newspapers reported the schools' test performances in enormous tables because there were lots of percentage *Seattle Times* to report. In the report, there was an interesting and enigmatic footnote to the table of school scores: "Schools with more students from low-income families tend to score lower on tests."

Table 9.1.1 Snohomish County, Washington, School Performances on the 1996 Reading Assessment of Student Learning and School Lunch Subsidy Rates

ELEMENTARY SCHOOL	PERCENTAGE WHO MET STANDARD IN READING	PERCENTAGE WHO QUALIFIED FOR FREE OR REDUCED-PRICE LUNCH
Cascade View	63%	17%
Cathcart	52%	14%
Central	47%	33%
Dutch Hill	63%	14%
Machias	49%	23%
Riverview	52%	20%
Seattle Hill	75%	9%
Totem Falls	68%	4%

Source: *Seattle Times Guide to Schools*, 1997.

The *Seattle Times* based its observation about low-income families on records of the proportion of students in each school that qualify for free or reduced-price lunches. Apparently there is a correlation between a school's passing rate and the proportion of children in that school who come from families poor enough to qualify for a free or reduced-price lunch. If this correlation is strong, it would be interesting in two ways. First, it would indicate something about how well particular schools are doing. For example, a school may have a low pass rate, but that pass rate may be very high given the poverty of its students. If this were the case, we might say that the school was doing a good job given its increased challenge. The second important consideration is about how poverty affects a child's chances in the United States.

What is the effect of having children who are poor enough to get their lunches paid for or at least partially paid for? To get an idea, we can look at the data from Snohomish County. Table 9.1.1 shows how the Snohomish County schools did on the reading test and what percentage of students qualified for the lunch program.

I see no patterns in that table of percentages. To see what's going on, we can make a model of these data. Percentages are calculated from categorical measurements, but the percentages themselves exist on a number line. To summarize these percentages, we would use averages and standard deviations. Table 9.1.2 shows the summary statistics for the two sets of number line measurements.

On the average, in the Snohomish County, Washington, school district, about 59% of the students passed the reading test, and 17% qualified for a lunch subsidy. From school to school, the proportions were only a tiny bit right skewed—the mean and medians are very close to one another. The standard deviations for both sets of measurements were about 10%. Figure 9.1.1 shows histograms of these two sets of number line measurements.

Table 9.1.2 Summary Statistics Describing Satisfactory Reading Rates and School Lunch Subsidy Rates

	PERCENTAGE WHO MET STANDARD IN READING	PERCENTAGE WHO QUALIFIED FOR FREE OR REDUCED-PRICE LUNCH
RANGE	From 47% to 75%	From 4% to 33%
MEAN	59%	17%
MEDIAN	58%	16%
STANDARD DEVIATION	10%	9%
STANDARD ERROR	4%	3%

Is there a relationship between the school lunch rate and the passing rate? To see that, we will need to look at a scatter plot. Figure 9.1.2 shows a scatter plot of the reading test pass rates plotted against the lunch subsidy rates. In Figure 9.1.2, the highest dot in the upper left is Seattle Hill Elementary School (9%, 75%). The dot on the bottom right is Central Elementary School (33%, 47%).

Figure 9.1.2 seems to show a relationship between the proportion of children in the lunch program and the proportion who pass the reading test. From Figure 9.1.2, we can say something about the relationship between poverty and reading performances, but we can't say it with much precision. Figure 9.1.2 shows a trend—as the proportion of the students who qualify for subsidized lunches increases, the proportion passing the test goes down. But just by looking at Figure 9.1.2, we can't say very accurately *how much* the reading test pass rate falls as the subsidized lunch rate increases. It would be nice to be able to say something like, "For each additional 10% on subsidized lunch, the reading test pass rate falls ____%." We will figure out how to find the average reading-rate drop per increase in subsidized lunch.

Figure 9.1.1 **Histograms of Reading Test Pass Rates and School Lunch Subsidy Rates**

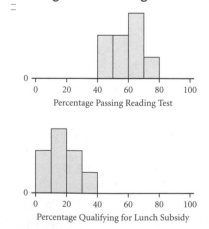

Figure 9.1.2   **Scatter Plot of Reading Test Pass Rates and Lunch Subsidy Rates**

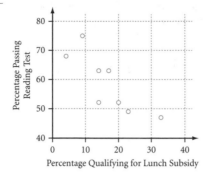

We also might like to use these data to predict what happens in other schools. Simply by looking at Figure 9.1.2, we can say that if 10% of the students qualify for school lunch subsidies, then about 65% to 75% will pass the reading test. If 20% qualify for lunch subsidies, then about 50% will pass the reading test. Now imagine that someone comes to us and says, "I have a school in which 18% qualify for subsidized lunches. What should I expect for the reading test pass rate?" We could estimate, but we would have to look at the figure again. What would be nice is if we could report an easy way to calculate the estimated reading test pass rate from the lunch subsidy rate. For example, it might be that the estimated pass rate could consistently be calculated with this equation:

$$\text{Estimated Pass Rate} = 70\% - \text{Lunch Subsidy Rate}$$

If that were the case, then we could report that equation. With it, someone else could figure out that, when the lunch subsidy rate is 10%, the pass rate will be about 60%. When the lunch subsidy rate is 18%, the pass rate will be about 52%. Regression analysis will show us how to find such an equation.

An equation like the one just given describes a line. Each line in a two-dimensional graph can be described with a short equation. You may have seen an equation of a line that looked like this:

$$y = a + bx$$

Your school may have taught you that the equation of a line is $y = ax + b$, or $y = bx + a$. In any of those cases, the equation of the line is that the y-value is some constant plus another constant times the x-value. That is, no matter where you are on the line, you can find the y-value by multiplying the x-value by b, and then adding a.

In the equation $y = a + bx$, a is the y-intercept, and b is the slope of the line. Another way to write the same equation is like this:

$$y = y\text{-Intercept} + \text{Slope}(x)$$

That is, for any point on the line, y is the y-intercept plus the slope times x.

Equation of a Line

A line is described by this equation:

y-value $= a + (b$ times x-value$)$

For example, $y = 3 + 2x$ is the line in this graph:

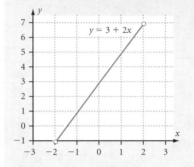

The equation of this line is $y = 3 + 2x$ because all along that line, the y-value of any point is 3 more than 2 times the x-value of that point.

Y-Intercept

The y-intercept is the y-value when the x-value is 0. The slope is how much y increases each time x increases by 1. For example, Figure 9.1.3 shows some lines and their equations.

Figure 9.1.3 allows us to double-check our understanding of the y-intercept and the slope. The y-intercept is the line's y-value when x is 0. To find it, we can trace along the x-axis until we find where x is 0. Then we trace up to the line and check where we are on the y-axis. In the first graph in Figure 9.1.3, the y-intercept is 1. In the second graph, the y-intercept is 2. In the third graph, the y-intercept is -1. These graphs may look unlike graphs you have seen before: There are no bold lines showing where x equals 0 and where y equals 0. These lines are omitted because it is not customary to worry about those lines in scatter plots.

Y-Intercept

The y-intercept is the value of y when x is 0. It is the constant that is not multiplied by x in the equation of the line.

For example, for the line $y = 3 + 2x$, the y-intercept is 3; when x is 0, y is 3 plus 2 times 0, which is 3.

Figure 9.1.3

$y = 1 + 2x$
(y-intercept $= 1$; slope $= 2$)

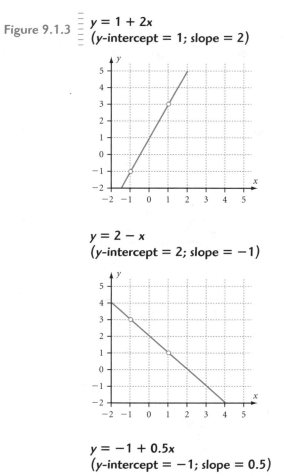

$y = 2 - x$
(y-intercept $= 2$; slope $= -1$)

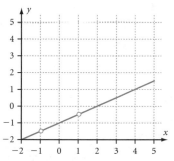

$y = -1 + 0.5x$
(y-intercept $= -1$; slope $= 0.5$)

Slope

The slope of a line is described by the following equation:

$$\text{Slope} = \frac{\text{Rise}}{\text{Run}}$$

That is, when I go from one point on the line to another, there is a rise on the graph. That rise is the change in the y-value. There is also a run, which is the change in the x-value. For example, in the first graph, the line goes through $(0, 1)$.[1] If I trace up and to the right, I get to $(1, 3)$. In that case, the run has been 1 (from 0 to 1), and the rise has been 2 (from 1 to 3). So, I can check the slope:

$$\text{Slope} = \frac{\text{Rise}}{\text{Run}} = \frac{2}{1} = 2$$

That's right. The slope is 2. This highlights another way to think about the slope. It is the change in y that happens each time x increases by 1.

Slope

In the equation of a line, the slope is the constant that is multiplied by x. The slope is the change in y divided by the change in x. Slope can be calculated between any two points on a line by dividing the rise by the run. The rise is one point's y-value minus the second point's y-value. The run is the first point's x-value minus the second point's x-value.

For example, the line $y = 3 + 2x$ goes through $(-2, -1)$ and $(2, 7)$. Those points are $x = -2, y = -1$ and $x = 2, y = 7$, as in this graph:

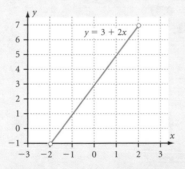

The slope is 2, because that is what is multiplied by x in the equation. The rise is 7 minus (-1), which is 8. The run is 2 minus (-2), which is 4. So if we calculated the slope from the rise and run, we would find the slope was 2 (8 divided by 4), which matches what we see in the equation ($y = 3 + 2x$).

---

[1]When points on a graph are described by their coordinates, we list the x-value first, so $(0,1)$ is where x is 0 and y is 1.

For example, look at the second graph in Figure 9.1.3. The line goes through (1, 1). If I trace 1 unit to the right, the line goes down to (2, 0). That is a drop of 1, or a rise of -1. That means that the slope is -1.

Regression Line

To do the work of the regression analysis, we will find a line that models the relationship in a scatter plot. Our task is to be able to go from a list of points on a scatter plot to a line that does the best job of describing how changes in y can be predicted from changes in x, and that does the best job of allowing us to estimate the y-value at a particular x-value.

Regression Model

The regression model is a line relating the measurements on the x-axis of a scatter plot to the measurements on the y-axis.

For example, the regression model of two points $(-2, -1)$ and $(2, 7)$ is the line through those two points ($y = 3 + 2x$).

To figure out how to find the regression line, we need to retrace the thinking of Carl Gauss and A. M. Legrendre. Gauss and Legrendre independently developed regression at the end of the 18th century (Porter, 1986, p. 95). Before we deal with a lot of observations at once, let us do something with fewer observations. We will come back to the Snohomish County schools later, after we know how to find the regression equation in simpler situations.

The simplest situation is when the scatter plot has only two dots. I was recently challenged with two dots as I was trying to have a conversation about the weather with a friend in England. You would think that the weather is an easy topic, but she wanted to talk in Celsius, and I think in Fahrenheit. After a lot of confusion, I needed an equation to translate from Fahrenheit to Celsius.

I knew that there was a linear relationship between the two, but I did not remember what it was. There were a few things that I did know. In Celsius, water freezes at 0° and boils at 100°. In Fahrenheit, water freezes at 32° and boils at 212°. Table 9.1.3 shows those numbers, and Figure 9.1.4 is a scatter plot of the two points.

Table 9.1.3 Water Temperatures in Celsius and Fahrenheit

	CELSIUS	FAHRENHEIT
FREEZING	0°	32°
BOILING	100°	212°

Figure 9.1.4 **Two Points on the Line Relating Fahrenheit to Celsius**

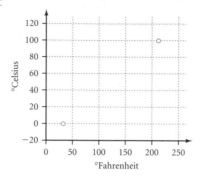

To find the equation, I found the best-fitting line for Figure 9.1.4. The best line is the only line that goes through those two points. To find the equation of that line, I needed to find the slope. I knew two points on the line, (32, 0) and (212, 100). The rise between those two points is 100. The run is 212 minus 32, which is 180.

$$\text{Slope} = \frac{\text{Rise}}{\text{Run}} = \frac{100}{180} = 0.5556 \text{ or } \frac{5}{9}$$

Next, I needed the y-intercept. To get from the freezing point to where x equaled 0°, I had a run of -32°F. Because the slope was 5/9, each time I ran 1° to the left, I would drop 5/9 of a degree. When I ran 32° to the left, the line would drop 32° times 5/9. The total drop would be -17.78°. We had started at 0°C.

When we go down 17.78°, the *y*-intercept is at −17.78°. So to translate from Celsius to Fahrenheit, I can use this equation:

Degrees Celsius = −17.78° + (5/9 × Degrees Fahrenheit)

Does that really work? Let's check. Let's say that I am talking about freezing, which is 32°F. I put that value in my equation, and it tells me that the freezing level in Celsius would have to be −17.78° plus 5/9 of 32°. Except for a little error that arises because of my rounding, that is 0°C. So far so good. Boiling is 212°F. The equation says that, in Celsius, it should be −17.78° plus 5/9 of 212°. In Celsius that would be 100°. Other than the error due to rounding, this equation works.

Before we leave this example, let me point out one neat thing about the regression line for Figure 9.1.4. The two Fahrenheit values were 212° and 32°. The mean Fahrenheit value was (212° plus 32°) divided by 2, or 122°. The mean of the Celsius values is (100° plus 0°) divided by 2, or 50°. If I plug 122° into the equation, Celsius would then be −17.78° plus 5/9 of 122°, or 49.9978°. Other than error due to rounding, that is 50°. The regression line goes through a point at the mean of the values on the two scales. That always happens for lines between two points.

That was a pretty easy situation, because we had only two observations. When there are only two observations, the regression line is the line through the two points. Its slope is the rise between the two points over the run between them.

Regression Lines Between Two Points and the Mean-Mean Point

When the regression line is calculated for two points, it is the line that goes through both points. It also goes through the point for which the coordinates are the mean x-value and the mean y-value.

Two points, $(-2, -1)$ and $(2, 7)$, would have a mean y-value of 0 and a mean y-value of 3. A regression line calculated for those points would go through $(0, 3)$, as in this graph:

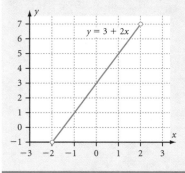

Algebra and Greek Symbols

The regression line is used to estimate y-values. "Estimated y" is indicated by $\hat{y}$. The equation of the regression line is $\hat{y} = b_0 + b_1 x$. Statisticians refer to the y-intercept as b_0 and the slope as b_1. This gives the flexibility to create equations like this: $\hat{y} = b_0 + b_1 x + b_2 x^2 + b_3 z$.

The b-values are coefficients. b_0 is a coefficient that is multiplied by 1. The coefficients you would find if you created a regression equation from all of the objects or people in the population are indicated by the Greek letter beta (β). For the entire population, we would write this:

$$\hat{y} = \beta_0 + \beta_1 x$$

Note that the equation is still an equation that is estimating y, even if we are working with all of the population's data. The reason for this is that, in the population, there may be multiple y-values for a single x-value. The regression equation will report only one as an estimate or model of the values in the population.

Abstract

Regression analysis tests for correlations between number line measurements by modeling points in a scatter plot with the regression line. A line can be described with an equation: $y = y\text{-intercept} + \text{slope}(x)$. The slope is the change in y that accompanies an increase of one unit in x. The y-intercept is the line's y-value when x is 0.

Avoiding Common Misunderstandings

The equation $y = a + bx$ means the same thing as $y = ax + b$. All those equations are saying is that the y-value is some constant multiplied by the x-value plus another constant. When you are adding things together, it doesn't matter which is listed first in the equation, so $b + ax = ax + b$. And whether we call the first "a" and the second "b" or the other way around does not matter.

Computer Project

Set up your software to do Exercises 35 through 38. For each exercise, have your software create a list of possible lunch subsidy rates from 0% to 100% and calculate the reading test pass rates that the equation indicates match each subsidy rate. Plot the points in a scatter plot and notice that you have created a line. You could add more dots between the dots you added by including values between the lunch subsidy rates you worked with. Eventually, the dots merge into a continuous line for which every point is determined by the equation.

Exercises

For the situations in Exercises 1 through 6, which test would you use, the ANOVA or regression, and why would you use that test?

1. You want to test for a correlation between people's religion and how long they live. *ANOVA*

2. You want to test for a correlation between people's wealth and how long they live. *Regression*

3. You want to test for a correlation between job candidates' heights and whether they are hired. *ANOVA*

4. You want to test for a correlation between patients' temperatures and whether blood tests reveal that they have bacterial infections. *ANOVA*

5. You want to test for a correlation between a company's current stock price and that company's last dividend (how much it paid to stockholders). *Regression*

6. You want to test for a correlation between how long customers look at a car before beginning negotiations and how much they end up paying for the car. *Regression*

There are about 90 milligrams of caffeine in a cup of coffee. Use this information to complete Exercises 7 through 11.

7. If you drew a line on a graph to show the relationship between the number of cups of coffee a person drinks and the person's caffeine consumption, what would be the equation of that line? (Assume that this person's only source of caffeine is coffee, so, when the person drinks no coffee, the person consumes no caffeine.)

8. Sketch a graph of the line from Exercise 7, putting cups of coffee on the x-axis and caffeine consumption on the y-axis. Have your x-axis go from 0 to 10 cups of coffee.

9. If someone drank 3 cups of coffee a day, what would that person's caffeine consumption be, according to your graph?

10. What is the slope of your line?

11. What is your line's y-intercept?

An espresso drink, such as a latte, contains about 160 milligrams of caffeine. Use this information to complete Exercises 12 through 16.

12. If you drew a line on a graph to show the relationship between the number of lattes a person drinks and the person's caffeine consumption, what would be the equation of that line? (Assume that this person's only source of caffeine is lattes, so, when the person drinks no lattes, the person consumes no caffeine.)

13. Sketch a graph of the line described in Exercise 12, putting espresso drinks on the x-axis and caffeine consumption on the y-axis. Have your x-axis go from 0 to 5 espresso drinks.

14. If someone drank 4 lattes a day, what would that person's caffeine consumption be, according to your graph?

15. What is the slope of your line?

16. What is your line's y-intercept?

A friend of mine drives a massive station wagon that was built in the 1960s. If he drives it for 7 miles, it uses 4 gallons of gasoline. If he drives it for 15 miles, it uses 8 gallons of gasoline. Assume that the relationship between miles and gasoline fits on a line. Use this information to complete Exercises 17 through 25.

17. Sketch a graph of those two points, (7, 4) and (15, 8). Draw a line showing their relationship. Put miles on the x-axis and have your graph go from 0 miles to 20 miles.

18. Between those two points, what is the run?

19. Between those two points, what is the rise?

20. What is the slope of your line?

21. If you run −7 miles from the leftmost point, you will have gotten to the
    y-axis over 0. What would be the rise that would accompany a run of
    −7 miles?

22. What is the y-intercept of your line from Exercise 21?

23. My friend is going to add 10 miles to his commute each week. How much is
    that going to add to his gasoline consumption?

24. If my friend drives 12 miles, what would his gasoline consumption be?

25. If my friend starts his engine and gets ready to drive away, but then decides
    not to, about how much gasoline do you think he will burn just getting
    warmed up?

In 2000, car manufacturers started selling cars that got very high mileage. If my
friend had bought one of these, he would have been able to drive 35 miles on one-
half gallon of gas and 140 miles on two gallons. Use this information to complete
Exercises 26 through 34.

26. Sketch a graph of those two points, $(35, 0.5)$ and $(140, 2)$. Draw a line
    showing their relationship. Put miles on the x-axis and have your graph go
    from 0 miles to 200 miles.

27. Between those two points, what is the run?

28. Between those two points, what is the rise?

29. What is the slope of your line?

30. If you run −35 miles from the leftmost point, you will have gotten to the
    y-axis over 0. What would be the rise that would accompany a run of
    −35 miles?

31. What is the y-intercept of your line?

32. If my friend already had one of those cars and added 10 miles to his com-
    mute each week, how much would that add to his gasoline consumption?

33. If my friend drove 50 miles, what would his gasoline consumption be?

34. How much gasoline would such cars consume warming up?

The following table shows two schools for each school district in the Seattle area.
The two schools are the school in each district with the highest poverty rate (shown
here as the proportion of students who qualify for lunch subsidies) and the school
with the lowest poverty rate. For each school, the table provides the proportion of
fourth-grade students who met the Washington State standards for reading.

Imagine that each district is plotted on a graph with the poverty rate along the x-axis and the reading test pass rate on the y-axis. For each school district, you could estimate a line to describe the relationship between poverty and reading test pass rates. To find that line, you would need to find the slope of a line between two points describing the two schools in that district. To find the slope, you would need to figure out the rise and run between the two points and the slope. Use the table to complete Exercises 35 through 38.

DISTRICT	SCHOOL	LUNCH SUBSIDY RATE	READING TEST PASS RATE
Auburn	Lake View	19%	59%
	Terminal Park	59%	42%
Bainbridge	Wilkes	4%	63%
	Ordway	8%	77%
Bellevue	Somerset	2%	82%
	Stevenson	49%	49%
Edmonds	Brier	9%	65%
	Cedar Valley	83%	18%

35. What is the equation of the line describing the two points for Auburn School District?

36. What is the equation of the line for Bainbridge School District?

37. What is the equation for Bellevue School District?

38. What is the equation for Edmonds School District?

Answers to Odd-Numbered Exercises

1. Longevity is a number line measurement, and religion is a categorical measurement. You would want to use an ANOVA.

3. Heights fall on a number line, and whether someone is hired is a categorical measurement; use ANOVA.

5. Stock prices and dividends are number line observations; use regression.

7. Caffeine $= 0 + 90x$ cups or $y = 0 + 90x$.

9. Caffeine $= 0 + 90$ cups.

   Caffeine $= 0 + 90 \times 3 = 270$ mg.

11. y-intercept $= 0$.

13. Caffeine from Espresso Drinks

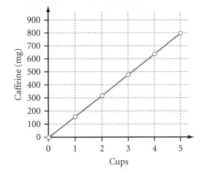

15. 160 mg.

17. Gallons of Gasoline versus Miles Traveled

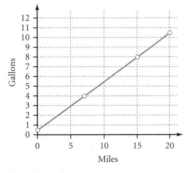

19. $8 - 4 = 4$.

21. If the rise is –7 miles, the run is –3.5 gallons.

23. 5 gallons.

25. Half a gallon; That's how much gasoline is associated with 0 miles.

27. $140 - 35 = 105$.

29. 0.014.

31. 0.0000000000000002.

33. 0.7 gallons.

35. Rise $= -17\%$. Run $= 40\%$. Slope $= -17/40 = -0.425$. Run from 19% to 0% is -19%. Rise $= -19 \times (-0.425) = 8.575\%$. y-intercept $= 59\% + 8.575\% = 67.075\%$.

   Reading Test Pass Rate $= 77.575\% - 0.425 \times$ Lunch Subsidy Rate

37. Rise $= 49\% - 82\% = -33\%$. Run $= 49\% - 2\% = 47\%$. Slope $= -33/47 = -0.70$.

   From 2%, the run to 0% is -2%. The rise is $-2\% \times -0.7 = 1.4\%$. The y-intercept is $82\% + 1.4\% = 83.4\%$.

   Reading Test Pass Rate $= 83.4\% - 0.7 \times$ Lunch Subsidy Rate

9.2 Finding Best-Fitting Lines

• The Least Squares Line

[In Arkansas, the] percent of student participation in free and reduced lunch programs is a prediction of performance on the Fourth Grade Benchmark Exam.

—Mulvenon et al., *Arkansas Educational Research & Policy Studies Journal*, Summer 2001, p. 42

THE RELATIONSHIP BETWEEN SCHOOL LUNCH PARTICIPATION and success on standardized tests that we have been looking at in the Washington State data shows up in Arkansas as well.

Modeling Reading Test Pass Rates

In the last section, we considered how to find the best-fitting line when a scatter plot had only two points. Here is a more difficult situation: Consider just three of the schools in Snohomish County, Washington: Cathcart, Central, and Dutch Hill. Table 9.2.1 shows their reading test pass rates and school lunch subsidy rates.

Figure 9.2.1 shows those points on a scatter plot. How do you figure out a good line to model those three points? When the lunch subsidy rate is 33%, you want the line to go through a reading test pass rate of 47%. What do you want when the lunch subsidy rate is 14%? At 14%, the line is modeling both Cathcart (52%) and Dutch Hill (63%). If you use the mean test pass rate of those two schools, the line will be a good fit for them. Their mean test pass rate is 57.5%. If we use that as the reading test pass rate when the lunch subsidy rate is 14%, then we have two points that we want our line to go through: (14%, 57.5%) and (33%, 47%), as shown in Figure 9.2.2.

Table 9.2.1 | Three Schools in Snohomish County, Washington: 1996 Reading Test Pass Rates and Lunch Subsidy Rates

SCHOOL	LUNCH SUBSIDY RATE	READING TEST PASS RATE
Cathcart	14%	52%
Central	33%	47%
Dutch Hill	14%	63%

Figure 9.2.1

Three Schools' Reading Test Pass Rate Plotted Against Their Lunch Subsidy Rates

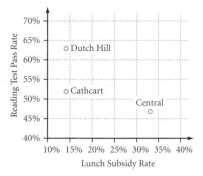

Figure 9.2.2

Three Schools' Reading Test Pass Rates Versus Lunch Subsidy Rates with Regression Line

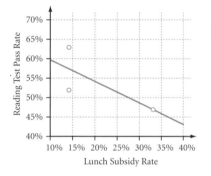

What is the slope of that line? The rise is 57.5% minus 47%, which is 10.5%. The run is 14% minus 33%, which is −19%. So the slope is 10.5% divided by −19%, or −0.55.

What is the y-intercept? From Cathcart and Dutch Hill over to 0% is a run of −14%, which when multiplied by −0.55 gives 7.7%. The y-intercept would be 7.7% up from 57.5%, or 65.2%. The equation of the line is this:

$$\text{Reading Test Pass Rate} = 65\% - 0.55 \times \text{Lunch Subsidy Rate}$$

Regression Line and Mean Values

When there are two x-values, the regression line goes through the mean of the y-values for each x-value.

For example, for the following data, the regression line would go through $(2, 4)$ and $(9, 6)$.

x	y
2	3
2	5
9	4
9	8

One of the regression line's purposes is to allow for predictions of the y-axis values from the x-axis values. In this case, as shown in Figure 9.2.3, the line makes three predictions. It predicts the Central rate is 47%, and makes no error. (Central is the dot on the lower right.) The regression line predicts that the Cathcart and the Dutch Hill rates are both 57.5%. In making those estimates, it is 5.5% too high for Cathcart, and 5.5% too low for Dutch Hill. When it is too high, we say its error is negative, because you would have to go down to get to the real value. The regression line's errors are 0% for Central, 5.5% for Cathcart, and −5.5% for Dutch Hill. If you add the errors, you'll find that they sum to 0. On the average, the regression line makes no error.

Figure 9.2.3  **Errors of Regression Line**

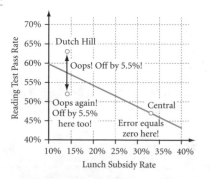

Regression Errors

The regression line estimates *y*-values. It makes an error for each point. The regression line's error is that point's *y*-value minus the regression line's *y*-value at the point's *x*-value. The regression line's errors sum to 0.

For example, for the data in the first two columns of the following table, the regression line would go through (2, 4) and (9, 6) and would make the errors listed in the last column, which sum to 0.

x	*y*	ESTIMATED *y*	ERROR
2	3	4	−1
2	5	4	1
9	4	6	−2
9	8	6	2
		SUM	0

In the Snohomish County school data, the mean lunch subsidy test pass rate was 20.33%. The mean reading pass rate was 54%. Does the line go through that mean-mean point? To find out, plug 20.33% into the equation as the lunch subsidy test pass percentage. When the lunch subsidy rate is 20.33%, the regression line's estimated rate is 65.24% minus (0.55 times 20.33%), or 54.06%—just about 54%. The extra 0.06% has to do with rounding. The line does go through the mean-mean point. Regression lines always go through the mean-mean point.

A second thing to note is the slopes of the lines from the mean-mean point out to the schools' points. Figure 9.2.4 shows the mean-mean point and lines from the mean-mean point out to the schools' points. (Because 0% is not near these numbers, it is not included on the *x*-axis and *y*-axis of Figure 9.2.4.)

Figure 9.2.4   **Slopes from Each Data Point to the Mean-Mean Point**

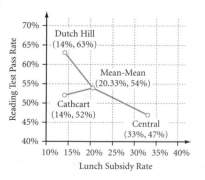

Table 9.2.2 Slope Calculations to Cathcart and Dutch Hill

SCHOOL	READING TEST PASS RATE	MEAN PASS RATE	RISE	LUNCH SUBSIDY RATE	MEAN LUNCH SUBSIDY RATE	RUN	SLOPE
Cathcart	52%	54%	−2	14%	20.33%	−6.33	0.316
Dutch Hill	63%	54%	9	14%	20.33%	−6.33	−1.422

The slope of the line from the mean-mean point down to Central on the lower right is −0.55. We might have expected that, because both Central and the mean-mean point are on the regression line. What about the slopes to the other two schools? Table 9.2.2 will help us figure them out.

At first, 0.316 and −1.422 do not look very interesting, but notice their mean: (−1.422 plus 0.316) divided by 2, which is −0.553. Except for rounding error, it is the same slope as the regression line.

We don't yet know everything there is to know about finding the slope of a regression line, but it involves averaging the slopes from the mean-mean point out to each of the observation's points.

Regression Slope and Slopes to Mean-Mean Point

When only two x-values exist, the regression slope is the mean of the slopes from the mean-mean point to each point.

For example, the following table shows the calculation of the slopes from the mean-mean point to each point and their average, 0.29. The regression line for that data has a slope of 0.29.

x	MEAN x	RUN FROM MEAN-MEAN POINT	y	MEAN y	RISE FROM MEAN-MEAN POINT	SLOPE FROM MEAN-MEAN POINT
2	5.5	−3.5	3	5	−2	4/7
2	5.5	−3.5	5	5	0	0
9	5.5	3.5	4	5	−1	−2/7
9	5.5	3.5	8	5	3	6/7

SUM 8/7

MEAN $2/7 = 0.29$

Algebra and Greek Symbols

The regression line is a series of models of y-values. It estimates where the y-values are for each x-value. As a model, it makes errors, which are the deviations from the line up and down to each point. An error is customarily referred to as e:

$$y_i = (\hat{y} \,|\, x_i) + e_i$$

That is, the actual ith y-value equals the estimated y-value given the ith x-value plus the ith error. The estimated y for a given x is b_0 plus $b_1 x$, so

$$y_i = b_0 + b_1 x_i + e_i$$

When there are only two points, the line goes through them, and the estimated y-values are the same as the actual y-values, and there are no errors. When there are multiple y-values at an x-value, the line cannot go through all of them, and it makes errors. This section suggests that a good line to summarize the position of the dots in a scatter plot is one that goes through the mean y-value for pairs of points that share the same x-value. The regression line is like the mean in that the errors it makes sum to 0, and it minimizes the sum of squared errors. In fact, the regression line is the line that minimizes the squared errors and is called the "least-squares line." That is,

$$\sum\nolimits_{i=1}^{n} e_i = 0,$$

and the least squares regression line is the line that minimizes

$$\sum\nolimits_{i=1}^{n} e_i^2.$$

Abstract

The regression line passes through the mean-mean point, which is a point at the mean x-value and the mean y-value. The regression line is calculated to do the best job of enabling you to estimate y-values from x-values.

Avoiding Common Misunderstandings

As we look for the regression line, we start with a hint: The regression line goes through the mean-mean point, the point found by plotting the mean of the x-values and the mean of the y-values. The lines from the mean-mean point to each observation are *not* the regression lines. They are hints about what kind of regression line should be used. For example, if they are all negative, the regression line should be negative. If they all have the same slope, the regression line should have that slope also.

It can be hard to calculate the slopes of all the lines to the mean-mean point without a table, and it can be hard to understand what you're calculating if you don't sketch a scatter plot of the points and the mean-mean point.

Computer Project

Have your software work with two x-values. Have it select several random y-values for each x-value. Calculate the regression line that goes through the means of the y-values of each x-value. The line is an estimate of the y-values at each x-value. Have your software calculate the mistakes the estimate makes. If the actual y-value is higher than the line's y-value, the mistake is positive. If the actual y-value is lower than the line's y-value, the mistake is negative. Add up all the mistakes the regression line makes. What do they add up to? Does the line go through the mean-mean point? What if you shifted the line by raising one end or lowering the other? How does that affect the sum of the line's mistakes?

Exercises

The following table shows data for four elementary schools. The table shows the percentage of students who passed Washington State's standardized tests in reading and mathematics. Refer to this table for Exercises 1 through 13.

	TEST PASS RATE	
SCHOOL	READING	MATHEMATICS
Cascade View	63%	23%
Cathcart	52%	28%
Dutch Hill	63%	25%
Riverside	52%	12%

1. How are the percentage who passed the reading test and the percentage who passed the mathematics test related? To find out, sketch a scatter plot of the four points. Put the reading test pass rate along the x-axis.

2. For the table, what is the best estimate of the mathematics test pass rate when the reading test pass rate is 52%?

3. For the table, what is the best estimate of the mathematics test pass rate when the reading test pass rate is 63%?

4. For the table, what is the mean-mean point?

5. For the table, what are two points that the regression line would go through other than the mean-mean point?

6. What is the equation of a line through the two points from Exercise 5?

7. Does a line though the two points from Exercise 5 go through the mean-mean point?

8. What is the equation of the regression line for the table?

9. According to the regression equation, for each 1% increase in the reading test pass rate, what is the increase in the mathematics test pass rate?

10. If a school had a 55% reading test pass rate, what would the regression estimate be for the school's mathematics test pass rate?

11. If no one at a school passed the reading test, what would the regression equation have as an estimate of that school's mathematics test pass rate?

12. For the table, what are the four slopes from the mean-mean point out to each of the school's points?

13. What is the mean of those four slopes?

The following table shows data for four elementary schools. The table shows the percentage of students who passed Washington State's standardized tests in reading and the percentage who qualify for lunch subsidies. Refer to this table for Exercises 14 through 24.

SCHOOL	READING TEST PASS RATE	LUNCH SUBSIDY RATE
Clyde Hill	69%	9%
Brier	65%	9%
Sunny Crest	24%	50%
Wildwood	65%	50%

14. Sketch a scatter plot of these four schools. Put the lunch subsidy rate along the x-axis.

15. For the table, what is the best estimate of the reading test pass rate when the lunch subsidy rate is 9%?

16. What is the best estimate of the reading test pass rate when the lunch subsidy rate is 50%?

17. What is the mean-mean point?

18. What are two points that the regression line would go through, other than the mean-mean point, and does a line through those two points go through the mean-mean point?

19. For the table, what is the equation of the regression line?

20. According to the regression equation from Exercise 19, for each 1% increase in the lunch subsidy rate, what is the increase in the reading test pass rate?

21. If 30% of a school's students qualified for lunch subsidies, what would the regression estimate be for the school's reading test pass rate?

22. If no one at a school qualified for lunch subsidies, what would the regression equation estimate to be that school's reading test pass rate?

23. For the table, what are the four slopes from the mean-mean point out to each of the school's points?

24. What is the mean of those four slopes?

When teachers grade quizzes, it is not uncommon to count 85% as a number grade of 3, a numeric "B," and consider 75% a "C," which would be a 2. I often have to do this translation for large numbers of students. I have my computer do it, but I never remember the equation. Instead, I put those two points into my statistical analysis program and ask it to find the regression equation. Use this information to complete Exercises 25 through 27.

25. What is the regression equation?

26. What is the number-grade equivalent of an 81%?

27. If you said that a 0.5 or less was a failing number grade, what is the lowest percentage that would be considered passing?

Answers to Odd-Numbered Exercises

1.

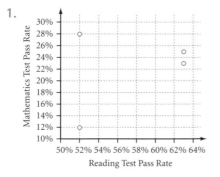

3. 24%.

5. (52, 20) and (63, 24). Those are the mean *y*-values for each of the two *x*-values.

7. Yes, it does.

9. 0.36%, about a third of a percent.

11. 1%.

13. 0.36%, which is the same as the slope of the regression line.

15. 67%.

17. (29.5%, 55.8%).

19. Reading Test Pass Rate $= 0.72 - 0.55 \times$ Lunch Subsidy Rate.

21. $0.72 - (0.55 \times 0.3) = 55.5\%$.

23.

READING TEST PASS RATE	MEAN READING TEST PASS RATE	RISE	LUNCH SUBSIDY RATE	MEAN LUNCH SUBSIDY RATE	RUN	SLOPE (RISE/RUN)
69%	56%	13%	9%	30%	-21%	-0.64%
65%	56%	9%	9%	30%	-21%	-0.45%
24%	56%	-32%	50%	30%	21%	-1.55%
65%	56%	9%	50%	30%	21%	0.45%
					MEAN SLOPE	-0.55%

25. Number-Grade Equivalent $= -5.5 + 10 \times$ Percentage Correct. (For this equation to work, you need to keep in mind that 85% is 0.85.)

27. $10x - 5.5 = 0.5$.

    $10x = 6$.

    $x = 0.6 = 60\%$.

    60% or lower would be considered failing.

9.3 An Excellent Line

- Calculating the Slope of the Regression Equation
- Standard Error and Confidence Interval for the Regression Equation

For a 1% increase in the percentage of students receiving free or reduced school lunch, average mathematics achievement decreases correspondingly by .06 points.

—Roscigno, *Social Forces*, March 1998

In the preceding quote, Roscigno is reporting the slope of a regression equation. Roscigno found that each 1% increase in the lunch subsidy rate was associated with a 0.06-point drop on the mathematics portion of the National Educational Longitudinal Study, which is run by the National Center for Education Statistics. In this section, we will see how a regression equation such as Roscigno's is calculated.

In the last section, we looked at how to find the regression equation when there are only two *x*-values. Table 9.3.1 shows a more difficult case—a set of four schools, each with its own *y*-value. Figure 9.3.1 shows those points plotted in a scatter plot.

Table 9.3.1   Reading Test Pass Rates and Lunch Subsidy Rates for Four Schools in Snohomish Count, Washington

SCHOOL	READING TEST PASS RATE	LUNCH SUBSIDY RATE
Totem Falls	68%	4%
Seattle Hill	75%	9%
Cathcart	52%	14%
Central	47%	33%
MEAN	60.5%	15%

Figure 9.3.1's points almost line up in a line. They look as though they could be well modeled with a diagonal line, but with these four points, it's not as clear exactly where the line should be. There aren't any two points that obviously ought to be on the line. This is a typical situation. Once we know how to find the regression line for this set, we will know how to find the regression line for any set of points.

To get started finding the regression line, let's put in a point that we are sure should be on the line—the mean-mean point. For Table 9.3.1's data, the mean lunch subsidy rate is 15%, and the mean reading test pass rate is 60.5%. Figure 9.3.2 shows the four points along with the mean-mean point, with lines drawn from the mean-mean point out to each school's point.

What should the slope be? As a start, let's consider what would happen if we found the mean slope from the mean-mean point to each school and used that mean slope. Table 9.3.2 shows those calculations.

Something is wrong: The mean of the slopes is positive. That does not seem to be a good regression line, because in Figure 9.3.2 the way the dots are spread

Figure 9.3.1   **Reading Test Pass Rates Plotted Against Lunch Subsidy Rates for Four Schools**

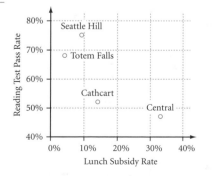

Figure 9.3.2

Reading Test Pass Rates Plotted Against Lunch Subsidy Rates with Lines from Each Point to the Mean-Mean Point

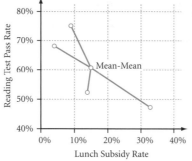

out indicates a negative slope. Figure 9.3.3 shows a line through the mean-mean point with a slope of 1.163. The line that goes from the bottom left of Figure 9.3.3 to the top right has a slope of 1.163. It is not a good regression line.

What went wrong? Only one of the slopes is positive, the slope out to Cathcart, but the mean slope came out positive. This happened because the slope from Cathcart to the mean-mean point (8.5) was so large compared to the other slopes. Cathcart had too much influence, and the rest of the schools had too little influence. We need some way to have the average slope reflect Cathcart less and the others more. We have a way of giving more weight to some values and less to others when calculating the mean: the weighted mean.

Section 5.2 presented how to calculate a weighted mean. GPA's are weighted means, as are class grades when different parts of students' work are given different weights. For example, if Joe has earned an 80 on the midterm and a 100 on the final, and the professor weights the final twice as much as the midterm, Joe's final grade is the sum of the weighted scores divided by the sum of the weights. The calculations for Joe's grade are shown in Table 9.3.3.

Table 9.3.2

Reading Test Pass Rates and Lunch Subsidy Rates for Four Schools in Snohomish County, Washington

SCHOOL	READING TEST PASS RATE	MEAN READING TEST PASS RATE	RISE	LUNCH SUBSIDY RATE	MEAN LUNCH SUBSIDY RATE	RUN	SLOPE
Totem Falls	68%	60.5	7.5	4%	15	−11	−0.682
Seattle Hill	75%	60.5	14.5	9%	15	−6	−2.417
Cathcart	52%	60.5	−8.5	14%	15	−1	8.5
Central	47%	60.5	−13.5	33%	15	18	−0.75

MEAN SLOPE 1.163

Figure 9.3.3 **A Poorly Fitting Line with a Slope of 1.163**

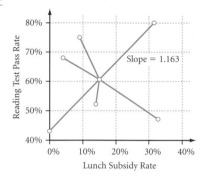

Cathcart's lunch subsidy rate (14%) is very close to the mean lunch subsidy rate (15%). The other schools have rates farther away from the mean lunch subsidy rate. The schools that are further out from the mean rate should have had more weight in determining the slope, and Cathcart should have had less. If we use a weighted mean to find the ideal slope for the regression line, we will need some way to give more weight to slopes going out to points that are further from the mean-mean point.

The runs from the mean-mean point show how far each point is from the mean-mean point. But there is something odd about using the run as a weight. Some of the runs are negative, and the runs from the mean-mean point add up to 0. If we used the runs as weights, we would have to divide by 0, which is not possible. We need something to get all the weights to be positive.

By now, you know what statisticians do when they need to make things positive: They square them. Let's try squaring to see how it works. We will try using the runs squared to calculate the mean slope. Table 9.3.4 shows our calculations.

Table 9.3.3 Calculating a Weighted Mean

SCORE	WEIGHT	WEIGHTED SCORE (WEIGHT TIMES SCORE)
80	1	80
100	2	200
SUM 3		280

Weighted Mean = Sum of Weighted Scores/Sum of Weights

= 280/3 = 93.33

Table 9.3.4 Calculating the Weighted Mean of the Slopes of the Lines from the Mean–Mean Point (15, 60.5) to Each School

SCHOOL	READING TEST PASS RATE	LUNCH SUBSIDY RATE	RISE	RUN	SLOPE	WEIGHTS (RUN SQUARED)	SLOPE TIMES WEIGHT
Totem	68%	4%	7.5	−11	−0.682	121	−82.5
Seattle Hill	75%	9%	14.5	−6	−2.417	36	−87.01
Cathcart	52%	14%	−8.5	−1	8.5	1	8.5
Central	47%	33%	−13.5	18	−0.75	324	−243.0
						SUMS 482	−404

Weighted Mean $= -404/482 = -0.838$

How does a slope of −0.838 work? Figure 9.3.4 shows the slopes out to the four points and a regression line through the mean-mean point, with a slope of −0.838. Figure 9.3.5 shows that same line with only the four points around it.

That line works well. In fact, that is the regression line that was developed more than 100 years ago by Carl Gauss. The regression line's slope is the weighted mean of the slopes from the mean-mean point to the observations' points, using the squared runs as weights.

Figure 9.3.4 **Four Schools with Line Through the Mean-Mean Point with a Slope That Is the Weighted Mean of the Slopes Between Each Point and the Mean-Mean Point**

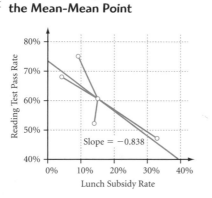

Figure 9.3.5   **Scatter Plot with Regression Line with Slope of −0.838**

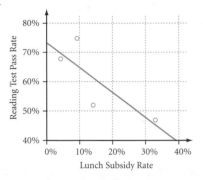

The Slope of the Regression Line

The slope of the regression line is the weighted average of the slopes from the mean-mean point out to each of the points, using the square of each point's run from the mean-mean point as the weight for that point's slope.

You do not have to love Gauss's regression line. Some people use other regression lines, but this one has an interesting property. You use the regression line to predict the *y*-axis measurements from the *x*-axis measurements. The line makes errors predicting the *y*-values. For Gauss's line, the sum of those errors is 0. For example, I would use the regression equation we worked out for these schools to predict reading test pass rates from lunch subsidy rates. For these schools, each time I make that prediction, the model makes an error. Figure 9.3.6 shows those errors, which are the lines that go from the regression line to the actual points.

Figure 9.3.6   **Errors of the Regression Line**

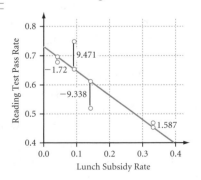

The errors are -1.720, 9.471, -9.338, and 1.587. Add up the errors and you get 0. This is a regular feature of the regression line. When you add up all the errors that Gauss's regression line makes, they always sum to 0.

There is another nice thing about Gauss's regression line. Imagine squaring the errors and adding them up. That would give you the sum of squared errors. Gauss's regression line is the line that has the lowest possible sum of squared errors. If you would like, you may try other lines, but I guarantee you that Gauss found the one that has the smallest sum of squared errors. For that reason, Gauss's regression line is called the "least-squares" line.

The Regression Line's Errors

The distance along the y-axis from the regression line to each point is the deviation of that point from the regression line. When the regression line is a model of the points, the deviations of the points are the errors that the regression line makes. The regression line's deviations add up to 0.

Let's find what the regression equation for all of the schools in Snohomish County would be. There are a lot of steps in finding the regression line, and it is fairly tiresome to do with eight observations. As we go through the steps, you may wonder how people would have the patience to go through this work. The answer is that people do not need that patience. In the past, a variety of computational tricks were found that made the work somewhat easier. Now most of the work is typing the numbers into a computer. Thereafter, the computer can do all the work. I am showing you this work so you can understand what the computer is doing. As we go through the steps, note that only two things are needed for the line's equation: (1) the mean-mean point; and (2) the slope, which is the weighted mean of the slopes from the mean-mean point to the observations' points, where the weights are the squared runs.

The mean-mean point is (16.75, 58.63), as shown in Table 9.3.5.

The first step in Table 9.3.6 is to put the column of mean reading test pass rates next to the actual reading test pass rates. Subtracting the mean reading test pass rates from the actual reading test pass rates produces the column of rises. Then those steps are repeated for the lunch subsidy rates. The mean lunch subsidy rates are subtracted from the actual lunch subsidy rates to figure out the runs. The slopes are the rises divided by the runs. The column of weights is produced by squaring the runs. In Table 9.3.6, the rightmost column of weighted slopes is produced by multiplying the slopes by their weights. The sum of the weights is 551.50. The sum of the weighted slopes is -509.75. The weighted mean is then 551.50 divided by -509.75.

Table 9.3.5   Finding the Mean-Mean Point for the Regression Line Relating Lunch Subsidy Rates and Reading Test Pass Rates

SCHOOL	READING TEST PASS RATE	LUNCH SUBSIDY RATE
Cascade View	63%	17%
Cathcart	52%	14%
Central	47%	33%
Dutch Hill	63%	14%
Machias	49%	23%
Riverview	52%	20%
Seattle Hill	75%	9%
Totem Falls	68%	4%
SUM	469%	134%
MEAN	58.63%	16.75%

Table 9.3.6   Finding the Slope for the Regression Line Relating Lunch Subsidy Rates and Reading Test Pass Rates

READING TEST PASS RATE	MEAN READING TEST PASS RATE	RISE	LUNCH SUBSIDY RATE	MEAN LUNCH SUBSIDY RATE	RUN	SLOPE	WEIGHT (RUN SQUARED)	SLOPE TIMES RUN SQUARED
63	58.63	4.37	17	16.75	0.25	17.48	0.06	1.09
52	58.63	−6.63	14	16.75	−2.75	2.41	7.56	18.23
47	58.63	−11.63	33	16.75	16.25	−0.72	264.06	−188.99
63	58.63	4.37	14	16.75	−2.75	−1.59	7.56	−12.02
49	58.63	−9.63	23	16.75	6.25	−1.54	39.06	−60.19
52	58.63	−6.63	20	16.75	3.25	−2.04	10.56	−21.55
75	58.63	16.37	9	16.75	−7.75	−2.11	60.06	−126.87
68	58.63	9.37	4	16.75	−12.75	−0.73	162.56	−119.47
							SUM 551.50	−509.75

Regression Slope = $551.50/-509.75 = -1.08^2$

---

[2]This slope, −1.08, reflects some of the rounding done during the calculations. When the calculations are done on a computer with much less rounding, the slope turns out to be not much different, −0.92.

A slope of −1.08 is just about 1% more not meeting the standard each time you add 1% to the lunch subsidy rate. It is as though each new child who is eligible for the lunch subsidy does not meet the standard: Add one more lunch subsidy child and you have one more not meeting the standard. Add two more, and you have two more not meeting the standard.

According to the regression model, what proportion of children would pass the reading test if the school had no one who was poor enough to qualify for the lunch subsidy program? The answer would be the *y*-intercept. To find the *y*-intercept, we can start at the mean-mean point (16.75, 58.63) and see what happens when we have a run of −16.75. When we have a run of −16.75, we will have a rise of −16.75 times −1.08, or a rise of 18.09%. The *y*-intercept is 18.09% above the mean reading test pass rate, 58.63%. The *y*-intercept is 76.72%. The regression equation describing what is happening in the Snohomish County schools is this:

Reading Test Pass Rate = 76.72% − 1.08 × Lunch Subsidy Rate

The regression equation says that if there were no children on a lunch subsidy, a school would have about a 77% reading test pass rate. What if 71% of the children qualified for the lunch subsidy program? Then the regression model would predict that the reading test pass rate would be about 76.72 minus (1.08 times 71%), or about 0.

When the Run from the Mean–Mean Point Is 0

Sometimes a point is directly over or under the mean-mean point. In that case, the run from the mean-mean point is 0. That might look as though it would cause a problem, because dividing by 0 doesn't produce an answer that you can work with. It turns out that using the runs squared as the weights deals with this problem.

Each of the weighted slopes is the product of the rise over the run and the runs squared:

$$\text{Weighted Slope} = \frac{\text{Rise}}{\text{Run}} \times \text{Run}^2$$

We can cancel one of the runs in the squared run with the run on the bottom of the equation:

$$\text{Weighted Slope} = \text{Rise} \times \text{Run}$$

Once we see that equation, we have dealt with the infinite slope problem. When the run is 0, the weighted slope is some rise times 0. The product would be 0 as well.

If you were calculating a regression slope by hand, you could save yourself some trouble by remembering that the weighted slopes are all the products of the rise and the run from the mean-mean point.

Confidence Interval for the Regression Slope

The regression slope that comes from a sample is not the regression slope that would be calculated from the population, but the population slope is likely to be somewhere near the sample's regression slope. When you use a regression equation, you want to use a confidence interval for the slope. Otherwise, you would be fooling yourself into thinking you know more than you do.

The regression slope is a kind of mean. Because it is a mean, the central limit theorem tells us that it becomes normally distributed as the sample size gets larger. To figure out a confidence interval for the regression slope, you need the standard error. Then, if your sample size is large enough, you can add and subtract 2 standard errors to find, roughly, the 95% confidence interval.

Almost every time people report a regression slope, they provide a t-value for it. Because regression slopes are normally distributed, one way to test the null hypothesis that the regression slope for the total population is 0 is to divide the slope for the sample by its standard error. That gives you a t-value and you can do a t-test. Most reports include that t-test along with its t-value.

When reading a report, the easiest way to find the standard error is to look at the slope and the t-value. The t-value is the slope divided by the standard error. If you play with that a bit, you will find that the standard error is the slope divided by the t-value.

$$t = \frac{Sample\ Slope}{Standard\ Error}$$

$$t \times Standard\ Error = Sample\ Slope$$

$$Standard\ Error = \frac{Sample\ Slope}{t}$$

The standard error of the slope is calculated pretty much the same way as the standard error of a regular mean. The first step to calculating the slope is to start with the column of slopes that was averaged to find the regression slope. Those are the slopes from the mean-mean point out to each observation's points. The calculations of the standard error begin with the same slopes. The regression slope is subtracted from each slope, and the difference is squared to produce a collection of squared deviations. So far, this is just like calculating the variance.

Because the regression slope is a weighted mean, the squared deviations are weighted also before averaging. The variance of those slopes is the weighted mean of the squared deviations, using the same weights as we used before—the squared runs. You can then take the square root of that mean of squares, producing something like a standard deviation of the slopes.

The slopes are all somewhat related, because they were all taken from the mean-mean point, which itself had been created from the measurements. All of this means that a slight adjustment has to be made in the final step of calculating the standard error. You do not divide by the square root of n (the number of measurements). Instead, you divide by the square root of 2 less than n:

$$Standard\ Error\ of\ Regression\ Slope = \frac{\sqrt{Weighted\ Mean\ of\ Squared\ Slope\ Deviations}}{\sqrt{Sample\ Size - 2}}$$

Table 9.3.7 shows the slopes we used to calculate the regression slope for the relationship between the lunch subsidy rate and the reading test pass rate, and shows the calculations to find the standard error of the slope.

Table 9.3.7 Calculating the Standard Error of the Regression Slope

SLOPE TO POINT	REGRESSION SLOPE	DEVIATION	SQUARED DEVIATION	WEIGHT (RUN SQUARED)	WEIGHTED SQUARED DEVIATION
17.48	−1.08	18.56	344.47	0.06	20.67
2.41	−1.08	3.49	12.18	7.56	92.08
−0.72	−1.08	0.36	0.13	264.06	34.22
−1.59	−1.08	−0.51	0.26	7.56	1.97
−1.54	−1.08	−0.46	0.21	39.06	8.27
−2.04	−1.08	−0.96	0.92	10.56	9.73
−2.11	−1.08	−1.03	1.06	60.06	63.72
−0.73	−1.08	0.35	0.12	162.56	19.91
				SUM 551.50	250.57

$$\text{Standard Error} = \sqrt{\frac{\text{Sum of Weighted Squared Deviations}/\text{Sum of Weights}}{\text{Sample Size} - 2}}$$

$$= \sqrt{\frac{250.57/551.50}{6}} = 0.28$$

The Standard Error of the Regression Slope

The standard error of the regression slope is found by first subtracting the regression slope from each of the slopes calculated from the mean-mean point out to each observation's point. This yields the deviations. The deviations are weighted by the runs squared, and their weighted mean is found. That weighted mean is then divided by 2 less than the sample size, and the square root is taken, which yields the standard error.

This standard error is not the actual standard error in the population, but rather an estimate from the sample. That means that it causes the same trouble that the estimated standard error caused for Gosset. If the number of observations is more than 60, you can add and subtract 2 standard errors to get a 95% confidence interval.

In the case of our regression analysis of the eight Snohomish County schools, our standard error is 0.28. We could add and subtract 2 standard errors, and our 95% confidence interval would be −1.08 plus and minus 0.56, which is from −1.64 to −0.52, but there are far too few observations for us to have much confidence in that interval.

Table 9.3.8   Edges of the Middle 95% of the *T*-Distribution

SAMPLE SIZE	NUMBER OF OBSERVATIONS MINUS NUMBER OF MEANS (*df*)	LOWER EDGE	UPPER EDGE
2	1	-12.7	12.7
3	2	-4.3	4.3
4	3	-3.2	3.2
5	4	-2.8	2.8
6	5	-2.6	2.6
11	10	-2.2	2.2
21	20	-2.1	2.1
61	60	-2.0	2.0
101	100	-1.98	1.98
1 billion or more	1 billion or more $-$ 1	-1.96	1.96

Note: The *t*-distribution appears in *t*-statistics calculated from random samples drawn from normal populations. The values in this table were derived from a data-analysis computer program, Systat®.

It would be better to use Gosset's *t*-distribution. We have eight observations, and only six degrees of freedom. The reason we have six degrees of freedom is that, having set the slope and *y*-intercept, after we have randomly picked the first six observations, the other two would be completely determined by the fact that we have already picked the slope and *y*-intercept. For six degrees of freedom, 95% of the *t*-distribution falls between -2.6 and 2.6, as shown in Table 9.3.8 (copied from Section 7.1). When we are more careful by using the *t*-distribution, our confidence interval is -1.08 plus and minus 2.6 times .28, which is from -1.808 to -0.352.

Take any confidence interval with a grain of salt. Using Gosset's *t*-distribution works well if both sets of measurements are normally distributed. Simulations indicate that the confidence interval works pretty well when the population's regression slope is 0. If the population's regression slope is not 0, and the measurements are badly skewed, the 95% confidence interval might include the population's slope as little as 70% of the time or even less. Even with skewed measurements, if the population's slope is 0 and the samples are large, the 95% confidence interval will include 0 close to 95% of the time.

The most important feature about thinking about a confidence interval for the slope is that it highlights that the slope you see is only a slope in the sample. It is not the slope in the population. The slope in the population is something that you can try to capture in a confidence interval, although that is tricky.

Algebra and Greek Symbols

In the least-squares linear regression equation, each estimated y-value is one constant plus the product of a second constant and the x-value:

$$(1) \qquad \hat{y} = b_0 + b_1 x$$

The least-squares regression slope is the weighted average of the slopes from the mean-mean point to each dot in the scatter plot, where the means are the squares of the runs:

$$(2) \qquad b_1 = \frac{\sum slope_i \times run_i^2}{\sum run_i^2}$$

Each run is the deviation of that observation's x-value from the mean x:

$$(3) \qquad run_i = x_i - \bar{x}$$

When we square the runs and sum them, we are doing the same steps we perform when we start calculating the variance. We are calculating the sum of the squared deviations of the x-values. The sum of squares can be denoted as SS_x:

$$(4) \qquad \sum run_i^2 = \sum_{i=1}^{n}(x_i - \bar{x})^2 = SS_x$$

We can plug that into our equation of the slope:

$$(5) \qquad b_1 = \frac{\sum slope_i \times run_i^2}{SS_x}$$

The slope is the rise over the run, and the slope times the run squared ends up being the rise times the run:

$$(6) \qquad slope \times run^2 = \frac{rise}{run} \times \frac{run \times run}{1} = rise \times run$$

So the sum of the slope times the squared runs is the sum of the rises times the runs. The rise from the mean-mean point to the ith point can be denoted as $rise_i$, and the run to that point can be denoted as run_i:

$$(7) \qquad \sum slope_i \times run_i^2 = \sum_{i=1}^{n} rise_i \times run_i$$

The ith rise is the deviation from the mean y-value to the ith y-value. The ith run is the deviation from the mean x-value to the ith x-value. So:

$$(8) \qquad \sum_{i=1}^{n} rise_i \times run_i = \sum_{i=1}^{n}(y_i - \bar{y})(x_i - \bar{x})$$

The sum of the products of the rises and the runs is similar to the sum of squares, and has its own name, SXY:

$$(9) \qquad b_1 = \frac{\sum_{i=1}^{n}(y_i - \bar{y})(x_i - \bar{x})}{\sum_{i=1}^{n}(x - \bar{x})} = \frac{SXY}{SS_x}$$

The regression slope goes through the mean-mean point $(\bar{x}, \bar{y})$. To find the y-intercept, we start at the mean-mean point and move to where x equals 0. That is a run of $-\bar{x}$. The associated rise is the slope times the run:

$$(10) \qquad b_0 = \bar{y} - b_1\bar{x}$$

Standard Error of Regression Slope

This section emphasizes that the standard error of the regression slope is calculated roughly the same way as the standard error of a mean. The regression slope is a weighted mean, and there are fewer degrees of freedom, because the regression equation has two parameters that are estimated, and the mean has only one. Nonetheless, the slope is a kind of mean, and it makes sense that the calculation of its standard error would be similar to the calculation of the standard error of a mean. We can abbreviate the estimated standard error of the slope as $\hat{\sigma}_{b_1}$:

$$(11) \qquad \hat{\sigma}_{b_1} = \frac{\sqrt{\dfrac{\sum(slope_i - b_1)^2(x_i - \bar{x})^2}{\sum(x - \bar{x})^2}}}{\sqrt{n-2}}$$

In Equation 11, the weight for the ith x-value is $(x_i - \bar{x})^2$.

There is another way to calculate the standard error of the regression slope:

$$(12) \qquad \hat{\sigma}_{b_1} = \frac{\sqrt{\dfrac{\sum(y - \hat{y})^2}{\sum(x - \bar{x})^2}}}{\sqrt{n-2}} = \sqrt{\frac{\sum(y - \hat{y})^2}{(n-2)\sum(x - \bar{x})^2}}$$

The two different calculations are algebraic variations of one another. The difference between the two equations is that where Equation 11 has $(slope_i - b_1)^2$ $(x_i - \bar{x})^2$, Equation 12 has $(y_i - \hat{y}_i)^2$ and $(slope_i - b_1)^2$ times $(x_i - \bar{x})^2$ equals $(y_i - \hat{y}_i)^2$.

The proof that the two ways of calculating the regression slope give the same answers involves many algebraic steps. I include it here to show you that you don't have to take my word for it and also because this gives you a taste of the kind of algebra that you might run into in other statistics books or courses. The rest of the subsection presents this proof.

First, note that the estimated ith y-value is the mean y-value plus the run from the mean x-value to the ith x-value times the slope, b_1. Also, the ith x-value minus the mean x-value is the ith run:

$$(13) \qquad \hat{y} = \bar{y} + b_1(x_i - \bar{x}) = \bar{y} + b_1 run_i$$

When we subtract the mean y-value from each part of that equation, we get an equation that we'll use later:

$$(14) \qquad \hat{y}_i - \bar{y} = b_1(x_i - \bar{x}) = b_1 run_i$$

Here is the proof that $(slope_i - b_1)^2(x_i - \bar{x})^2$ equals $(y_i - \hat{y}_i)^2$. The run is the ith x-value minus the mean x-value, so:

$$(15) \qquad (slope_i - b_1)^2(x_i - \bar{x})^2 = (slope_i - b_1)^2 run_i^2$$

We can square the left expression on the right side of the equation to get this:

$$(16) \qquad = \left(slope_i^2 - 2slope_i b_1 + b_1^2 \right) run_i^2$$

And multiply what is inside the parentheses by the run squared that is outside the parentheses:

$$(17) \qquad = slope_i^2 run_i^2 - 2slope_i b_1 run_i^2 + b_1^2 run_i^2$$

The ith slope is the ith rise over the ith run, and we can substitute using Equation 14 to get this:

$$(18) \qquad = \frac{rise_i^2}{run_i^2} run_i^2 - 2\frac{rise_i}{run_i}(\hat{y}_i - \bar{y})run_i + (\hat{y}_i - \bar{y})^2$$

The runs cancel:

$$(19) \qquad = rise_i^2 - 2rise_i(\hat{y}_i - \bar{y}) + (\hat{y}_i - \bar{y})^2$$

The ith rise is the ith y minus the mean y. We substitute that in:

$$(20) \qquad = (y_i - \bar{y})^2 - 2(y_i - \bar{y})(\hat{y}_i - \bar{y}) + (\hat{y}_i - \bar{y})^2$$

Equation 20 is a square written out. It is the same form as $(a - b)^2$ equals $a^2 - 2ab + b^2$. In this case, a is $(y_i - \bar{y})$ and b is $(\hat{y}_i - \bar{y})$. We can express Equation 20 as a square:

$$(21) \qquad = [(y_i - \bar{y}) - (\hat{y}_i - \bar{y})]^2 = [y_i - \bar{y} - \hat{y}_i + \bar{y}]^2 = (y_i - \hat{y}_i)^2$$

We started with $(slope_i - b_1)^2(x_i - \bar{x})^2$ in Equation 15, and we ended up with $(y_i - \hat{y}_i)^2$, so $(slope_i - b_1)^2(x_i - \bar{x})^2$ equals $(y_i - \hat{y}_i)^2$, and the two equations for calculating the standard error of the regression slope (Equations 11 and 12) are algebraic variations of each other.

Abstract

The regression slope is the weighted mean of the slopes from the mean-mean point out to each observation's point, where the weights are the squared runs. The regression slope is a mean and has a standard error. The standard error of the regression slope is found by examining the slopes from the mean-mean point to each observation's point. The regression slope is subtracted from each slope to find their deviations. The deviations are squared. The standard error is the square root of the weighted mean squared deviation (weights are the runs squared) divided by 2 less than the sample size.

Avoiding Common Misunderstandings

The regression slope is a weighted average of the slopes from the mean-mean point out to each point. Because it is a weighted mean, you find it by multiplying the slopes by the squares of the runs. Then, to find the mean, you add up all the products and divide by the sum of the squares of the runs.

Computer Project

Put the values of the examples in this section into your software and have your software create a regression model. Check that the output of your software matches what is described here. There will be some differences due to rounding, but not large differences.

Work with the Representative Sample of 50,000 Americans data from the *Data Matters* Resource Center at *www.keycollege.com/dm*. Consider those data a population and find the regression equation that describes the relationship between two of the number line observations. Pick a sample size and have your software take a random sample and calculate a confidence interval for the population's slope. Does the interval include the population's slope? Record the estimated standard error of the slope. Repeat these steps, saving the regression slopes and whether the confidence interval includes the population's slope. How often did your confidence interval include the population's slope? How does the standard deviation of the samples' slopes compare to the estimated standard error of the slope that you got in your first sample?

Exercises

It is worthwhile calculating one regression equation on your own. For the rest of your life thereafter you may have a computer calculate regression equations for you, but at least you will know what it is doing. The following questions lead you through the process of finding the equation for the relationship between a school's lunch subsidy program and its mathematics test pass rates.

SCHOOL	LUNCH SUBSIDY RATE	MATHEMATICS TEST PASS RATE
Central	33%	17%
Totem Falls	4%	41%
Cascade View	17%	23%
Riverview	20%	12%
Seattle Hill	9%	51%
Machias	23%	18%
Dutch Hill	14%	25%
Cathcart	14%	28%

For Exercises 1 through 27, use data from just the first three schools (Central, Totem Falls, and Cascade View).

1. Sketch a scatter plot of the data for the first three schools (Central, Totem Falls, and Cascade View).

2. What is the mean-mean point?

3. Make a table listing the rises from the mean-mean point up to each of the points on the scatter plot.

4. Add the runs and the runs squared.

5. Add the slopes and the weighted slopes.

6. What is the sum of the weights?

7. What is the sum of the weighted slopes?

8. What is the weighted mean of the slopes?

9. What is the slope of the regression equation?

10. If you trace along the regression line, what is the run from the mean-mean point to the y-axis?

11. If you trace along the regression line, what is the rise from the mean-mean point to the y-axis?

12. What is the y-intercept of the regression equation?

13. What is the regression equation?

14. To begin figuring out the standard error of the regression slope, make a table of the deviations of the slopes from the regression equation slope.

15. Add the column for the squared deviations.

16. Add the column for the squares of the runs.

17. Add the column for the slope deviations weighted by the runs squared.

18. What is the weighted mean of the squared deviations of the slopes?

19. What is the standard error of the slope?

20. What is a confidence interval for the slope? About how much confidence should you have in that confidence interval?

21. Can you make any conclusions about causation from these data? Why or why not?

22. Correlation is not causation. There are multiple possible causes for that correlation.

    a. What is one line of causation that might be producing that correlation?

    b. What is something else that is very different that might be producing that correlation?

    c. What is a third and different explanation of what might be producing that correlation?

23. Make a table of the regression line's errors. Which schools seem to be doing a good job, given their proportion of poor children, and which schools appear not to be doing such a good job?

24. At each of these schools about 70 children take the test. What is the margin of error for each school? How does the margin of error compare to how much Central's pass rate differs from what the regression equation would predict?

25. Is there any significant evidence here that any of these schools are doing any better or any worse than the pass rates that would be predicted for them by the regression equation?

26. What would Karl Pearson say about us calculating regression equations from three observations?

27. About how many observations would Pearson want us to use, at a minimum?

28. Use the fourth, fifth, and sixth schools in the table (Riverview, Seattle Hill, and Machias). For these three schools, what is the regression equation for predicting mathematics test pass rates from lunch subsidy rates?

29. Using the fourth, fifth, and sixth schools, calculate a confidence interval for the population's regression slope relating mathematics test pass rates and lunch subsidy rates. How much confidence do you have in that interval?

> *Research at the University of Texas indicates a negative correlation between economic growth and the percentage of lawyers in the work force. Predatory litigation lowered GNP by 10% below its potential level during the 1980s.*
>
> —*SOCIETY*, JANUARY–FEBRUARY 1992, P. 2

"GNP" stands for "gross national product," which is the sum of all sales of all goods and services provided or made in the United States. The GNP goes up with inflation. We are more interested in changes in real GNP (the GNP adjusted for inflation). Real GNP goes up simply because there are more people. If 10 people each produce enough for $30,000 in sales, that would be $300,000 total. If the number of people doubled, but nothing else changed, then that would be a total of $600,000. That is not really an interesting change either. What is interesting is the per capita GNP, which is the GNP divided by the size of the population.

The *Statistical Abstract of the U.S.* reports how many people were employed in the legal profession in the United States in 1970, 1980, 1985, and 1990. The following table shows the number of people in the legal profession. Use this table to complete Exercises 30 through 34. As with the GNP, we expect the number of people in the legal profession to go up over time, because the population is changing. Actually, the number of people in the legal profession has increased faster than the population. The third column shows the percentage of the population employed in the legal profession. The fourth column shows how the real per capita GNP changed from that year to the next.

YEAR	NUMBER OF PEOPLE IN LEGAL PROFESSION	PERCENTAGE OF POPULATION IN LEGAL PROFESSION	PERCENTAGE CHANGE IN REAL PER CAPITA GNP
1970	429,000	0.2%	1.6%
1980	776,000	0.3%	0.6%
1985	995,000	0.4%	1.8%
1990	1,217,000	0.5%	−1.8%

30. Sketch a scatter plot of the data in the rightmost two columns of the table.

31. What is the regression equation you would use to estimate the change in the real per capita GNP from the proportion of the population in the legal profession?

32. What is a 95% confidence interval for the slope of the regression equation calculated in Exercise 31?

33. If there were a significant correlation between the proportion of the population in the legal profession and changes in the real per capita GNP, what are three different reasonable possible causes of that correlation?

34. Describe a significance test that you could use to test a null hypothesis that, in the population, the slope of a regression equation would be 0.

Answers to Odd-Numbered Exercises

1.

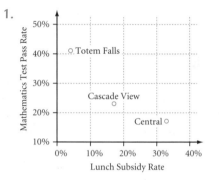

3, 5, 7, and 9.

SCHOOL	LUNCH SUBSIDY RATE	MATHE-MATICS TEST PASS RATE	MEAN LUNCH SUBSIDY RATE	RUN	RUN SQUARED	MEAN MATHEMATICS TEST PASS RATE	RISE	SLOPE	WEIGHTED SLOPE
Central							−0.1000	−0.6667	−0.0150
Totem Falls							0.1400	−1.0000	−0.0196
Cascade View							−0.0400	4.0000	0.0004

SUM	−0.0342
REGRESSION SLOPE	−0.81

11. $-0.81(-0.18) = 0.1458$.

13. Mathematics Test Pass Rate $= 0.42 - 0.81$(Lunch Subsidy Rate). (Notice again that it almost looks as though adding a child who qualifies for a lunch subsidy adds a child who doesn't pass the test.)

15 and 17.

SCHOOL	DEVIATION SQUARED	WEIGHTED SQUARED DEVIATION
Central	0.021	0.0005
Totem Falls	0.036	0.0007
Cascade View	23.140	0.0023

19. 0.29.

21. No, correlation is not causation. We would need an experiment to show causation.

23.

SCHOOL	LUNCH SUBSIDY RATE	MATHEMATICS TEST PASS RATE	ESTIMATED MATHEMATICS TEST PASS RATE	DEVIATION
Central	0.330	0.170	0.1487	0.021
Totem Falls	0.040	0.410	0.3836	0.026
Cascade View	0.170	0.230	0.2783	−0.048

Cascade View would be expected to have a higher pass rate, but it's unclear that this deviation of 5% is significant.

25. No.

27. 60, because then the means behave very similarly to what you would expect if the data were normally distributed, even if they aren't.

29. Using the t-distribution, for a 95% confidence interval: $-3.536 \pm 12.7(0.036)$ equals from -3.99 to -3.08.

31. Change in Real per Capita GNP = $0.037 - 9 \times$ Proportion of Population in Legal Profession.

33. (1) It could be that as the number of people in the legal profession increases, they sue companies, detracting from the companies' ability to do business and diminishing the companies' productivity. (2) It could be that, as things go sour in the economy, people want to sue each other as they blame one another and try to get their badly invested money back, and this inspires more people to go into the legal profession. (3) It could be that both 1 and 2 are right, and that there is a vicious cycle in which increases in the number of people in the legal profession lower the GNP, which raises the number of people in the legal profession, which lowers the GNP further, and so on.

CHAPTER 10

Tests of Regression

There's a world of difference between the nature of a sample and the nature of a population. Usually what happens in a sample is nowhere near as important as what happens in the population. The sample is done. It's over. The nature of the population from which the sample was drawn persists and will continue to affect people in the future.

For example, whether some children in 1996 passed or didn't pass a test isn't very important to anyone outside of their families and friends. But if the nature of education in the United States is that it does not succeed in teaching children whose parents are poor, that is something that will affect all of us eventually.

In Chapter 9, we saw how to find an equation that does an excellent job describing a linear correlation in a sample. In Chapter 10, we will see how to find out what the sample tells us about the population from which the sample was drawn. Section 10.1 presents Karl Pearson's thinking on how to test for a linear correlation in the population. Pearson's system depends on the population's data being normally distributed. Section 10.2 presents Spearman's test for correlation, which does not require the population to be normally distributed.

10.1 How to Test the Regression Models

- R^2
- Pearson's r
- A T-Test for the Regression Slope

In the United States, the coefficient of correlation between education and income within age-sex-race groups never reaches as much as .50 and is typically around .40.

—FUCHS, *AMERICAN ECONOMIST*, 1992, P. 12

IN THE PRECEDING QUOTE, Victor Fuchs summarizes studies of the relationship between education and income, which is not completely consistent. It is not always the case that more education yields more income. Some education prepares people for low-paying work, and not every education is equally effective. Some elementary school students acquire satisfactory skills; others do not. The following table from the *Journal of Political Economy* reports on some of the research that Fuchs was summarizing. ("SES" stands for socioeconomic status—professor and doctor are high-SES occupations; garbage collector is a low-SES occupation.)

Zero-Order Correlations among Measures of Socioeconomic Status, Northeast Census Region, Nonfarm Households Headed by Males, Aged 25–44

VARIABLE	1	2	3	4
1. Income	1.0			
2. Years of Schooling	0.375	1.0		
3. Occupational SES	0.384	0.556	1.0	
4. Net Worth	0.314	0.184	0.177	1.0

Source: . . . Data based on the 1967 Survey of Economic Opportunity tapes made available by the U.S. Office of Economic Opportunity. . . . The sample size is 596.

—BOWLES, *JOURNAL OF POLITICAL ECONOMY*, 1972, P. S219

In 1967, the federal government surveyed U.S. households, asking, among other things, how much education the husband had had and his income. The preceding table is a summary that was published in the *Journal of Political Economy*.

This kind of table is very common. It lists the correlations between all of the measurements in a study. Rather than list the measurements along the top, Bowles has numbered the measurements and listed their numbers across the top. The top "1.0" is the correlation between "income" and "income." A correlation of 1 means that, if you plotted all the points on a scatter plot, they would form a line. In this case, if you plotted each husband's income against his income, the points would all fall along a line with a slope of 1.

The correlation between income and years of schooling is 0.375. Is that good? Does that mean that you will earn more money if you get more education? What is a correlation of 0.375?

The correlation shows how well the regression model does. The correlation is usually represented by the correlation coefficient, Pearson's r, which ranges from -1 to 1. A value of -1 indicates that the observations all fall in a line with a negative slope; a value of 1 indicates that the observations all fall in a line with a positive slope. When the slope of the regression line is 0, r equals 0 also. The null hypothesis of a regression test is that, in the total population, the correlation coefficient is 0. Nothing is less embarrassing for the null hypothesis than when r is 0.

Pearson's r is the square root of another statistic, R^2. R^2 is the proportion of the variation in a measurement that is predictable from the regression model. For an example, think about schools and children on lunch subsidy programs in Snohomish County, Washington. Table 10.1.1 shows the Snohomish County school figures along with some calculations.

The regression equation for all eight schools is 74% minus 0.9 times the percentage on the lunch subsidy program. The second-to-last column in

Table 10.1.1 shows the regression equation's estimated reading test pass rates for each school. Each entry in the Estimated Rate column was calculated by multiplying the lunch subsidy rate by 0.9 and adding 74. The estimates in the Estimated Rate column are the points on the regression line for each school.

The last column in Table 10.1.1 shows the errors each estimate makes. The variance of each column appears at the bottom of Table 10.1.1. The variance is the sum of squared deviations divided by 1 less than the number of observations. In this case, that means dividing by 7. If you wanted to know the sum of squared deviations of any column, you could just multiply the variance by 7.

There is an important relationship in the variances. If you add the variance of the estimates to the variance of the errors, the sum is the variance of the reading test pass rates. One way to think about that relationship is that the variation from the mean reading test pass rate out to each school's reading test pass rate has two parts. One part is the variation out to the regression equation's estimate. The other part is the variation from the regression equation's estimate to the actual reading test pass rate. That second part is the error that the regression equation makes.

Table 10.1.1 Snohomish County School Lunch Subsidy Rates and Reading Test Pass Rates

SCHOOL	LUNCH SUBSIDY RATE	READING TEST PASS RATE	MODEL'S ESTIMATED READING TEST PASS RATE	MODEL'S ERROR
Totem Falls	4%	68%	70.41	−2.41
Seattle Hill	9%	75%	65.79	9.21
Dutch Hill	14%	63%	61.17	1.83
Cathcart	14%	52%	61.17	−9.17
Cascade	17%	63%	58.39	4.61
Riverview	20%	52%	55.62	−3.62
Machias	23%	49%	52.85	−3.85
Central	33%	47%	43.61	3.39
VARIANCE		101.41	67.31	34.10
SD		10.07	8.20	5.84

Model (Regression Equation): Reading Test Pass Rate $= 74\% - 0.9 \times$ Lunch Subsidy Rate

$R^2 =$ Variance of Estimates/Variance of Reading Test Pass Rates

$R^2 = 67.31/101.41 = .66$

$r = \sqrt{R^2} = .81$

The Additivity of Variances

The sum of the variance of the regression estimates and the variance of the errors of the regression estimates equals the variance of the estimated measurements.

For example, the following table shows x-values, y-values, and estimated y-values from a regression model.

x	y	ESTIMATED y	MODEL'S ERROR
2	2	3	−1
4	6	4	2
6	4	5	−1
VARIANCE 4		1	3

The variance of the estimated y-values and the variance of the model's errors add up to the variance of the y-values.

There is variation in the estimates. The estimates move around, because the lunch subsidy rates move around. That means that the variation in the estimates is reading test pass rate variation that is predictable from variation in the lunch subsidy rates. That is, some of the variation from school to school is predictable from lunch subsidy rates. That predictable variation shows up in the estimates, which are essentially reading test pass rates predicted from lunch subsidy rates. The variance of those estimates is the variance in the reading test pass rates that can be predicted from variation in the lunch subsidy rates.

If you are curious about how well the regression model is doing, you might want to see what proportion of the variation in the reading test pass rates is predictable from variation in the lunch subsidy rates.

To find what proportion of the variation in reading test pass rates is predictable from variation in the lunch subsidy rates, keep in mind that the predictable part is the variance in the estimates. The rest of the variance in reading test pass rates is variance of the errors. To find what proportion of the reading test pass rate variance is predictable, you divide the variance of the estimates by the total variance of the reading test pass rates. In this case, that would be 67.31 divided by 101.41, which is .66, or 66%.

Calculating R^2 and r

R^2 is the proportion of the variance of the y-axis measurements that is predictable from the variation in the x-axis measurements. R^2 is the variance of the regression estimates divided by the variance of the y-axis measurements. r is the square root of R^2.

For example, if the variance of the y-values is 4, and the variance of the estimated y-values is 1, R^2 is .25.

The proportion of the total variation that is predictable from the estimates is R^2, a common measure of how well the regression model does. R^2 is a ratio of variances, and variances are peculiar things. The variance is roughly the mean squared deviation. To work with something that is a little more understandable, we tend to take the square root of the variance, which gives us the standard deviation. Similarly, people usually work with the square root of R^2, which is called r.

When you take the square root of something, you need to think a moment about whether what you come up with should be positive or negative. For example, there are two square roots of 4: 2 and -2. When calculating r, you assign a positive or negative to r, depending on the slope of the regression line. If the regression slope is positive, r is positive. If the regression slope is negative, r is negative also.

$$\sqrt{R^2} = \frac{\sqrt{\text{Variance of Estimated } y}}{\sqrt{\text{Variance of } y}} = \frac{\text{Standard Deviation of Estimated } y}{\text{Standard Deviation of } y}$$

If you take the square root of R^2, you are doing the same thing as taking the square root of each of its variances. r is the standard deviation of the estimates divided by the total standard deviation of whatever was being estimated. In the case of the Snohomish County schools, R^2 is .66. The square root of .66 is .81. For the data in Table 10.1.1, r is $-.81$.

It is traditional to refer to R^2 as "the proportion of variance that is explained by" the other measurement. That is an unfortunate and misleading choice of words. If you look up the word "explain" in a dictionary, you will find that it has several definitions, and none of them apply to R^2. My two dictionaries report that the definitions of "explain" are (1) to make something comprehensible, (2) to describe the reasons for or causes of something, and (3) to define or describe something. Usually regression is not used in an experiment. Unless you are talking about an experiment with random assignment of participants, you do not know what causes the correlation. Perhaps the variation in one variable causes or is the reason for the variation in the other, or perhaps not. The variation in either variable does not make anything comprehensible about the variation in the other. All it does is allow you to predict one variable from the other (assuming that the system does not change). Finally, the variation in one variable is not described by the variation in the other. The standard deviation describes the variation.

A better idea would be to say that R^2 is the variation in one variable that is predictable from the variation in the other, but this would only be a valid statement if you kept in mind that we meant "predictable from the other, if the system does not change." To see what I mean, imagine two situations. In one, you are walking along a supermarket aisle. Someone approaches you. You move to the right, and the other person moves the same way. You shift to the left, and the other person shifts the same way. You shift right again, as does the other person. During this effort to avoid a collision, your position and the other person's position are highly correlated, but note that you will be able to get by the other person if you change the system. If you stop long enough, the other person will walk past you and will not remain lined up with you. When you change the system, the correlation disappears.

Imagine another situation. You are dancing with your date, and you are leading. You shift to the right, and your date matches your movement. You shift to the left, and your date shifts too. In this situation, if you stand in one spot, your date will probably stay in that spot as well. In this case, there is a correlation between your position and your date's position, and something else is happening as well. Your position accounts for, or explains, your date's position. In both situations, there is a correlation between your position and the other person's position. In only the second situation does your position explain the other person's position.

That is the case with correlations in general. By itself, a correlation tells us only that, in the system where it was found, variation in one thing was predictable from variation in the other. The correlation could be due to some causation from one of the things to the other, or it might not. Correlation is not causation.

What Does r Tell Us?

R^2 is the variance of the estimates divided by the variance of whatever was being estimated. This relationship works only for R^2, not for r, because, when you take the square root to translate from R^2 to r, you interfere with the additive relationship. You cannot add the standard deviation of the estimates to the standard deviation of the errors and get the total standard deviation of whatever is being estimated. You can see that in Table 10.1.1. The standard deviation of the reading test pass rates is less than the sum of the other two standard deviations.

Nonetheless, r does reflect something understandable about the data: r is the slope of the regression line, in terms of standard deviations. For example, in this case, if you went up 1 standard deviation of the lunch subsidy rates, the regression line would indicate that you should go down 0.81 standard deviations of the reading test pass rates. Figure 10.1.1 shows the scatter plot of the data in Table 10.1.1, along with the regression line.

Figure 10.1.2 is exactly the same plot, except that the axes show how many deviations away from the mean each observation is. For example, look at the mean-mean point in Figure 10.1.2. If you trace to the right 1 standard deviation (of x), the line has you trace down 0.81 standard deviations (of y).

It will always happen that way. If you transform the observations into how many standard deviations they are away from their mean, r is the slope of the regression line. Karl Pearson pointed this out, so r is often called the "Pearson correlation coefficient."

Figure 10.1.1 **Regression Line for Reading Test Pass Rates Plotted Against School Lunch Subsidy Rates from Table 10.1.1**

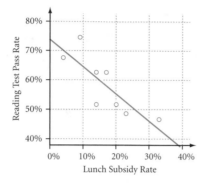

Figure 10.1.2 **The Rise over Run of the Slope of the Regression Line in Figure 10.1.1**

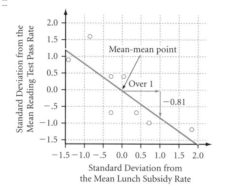

Testing Significance

When is r significant? When can we conclude that there is a relationship in the population that is best described with a line? If we wanted to know whether there was a relationship, we would be testing a null hypothesis of no relationship that ought to be described with a line. The null hypothesis is equivalent to saying that, if you tested the entire population, you would find an r and a regression line slope of 0.

There are several ways to test the null hypothesis. You could even invent another way if you wanted. All you have to do is pick some statistic that gets larger as the null hypothesis is more and more embarrassed by the data.

One way is to find the standard error of the slope. Then you can do a t-test to see whether the slope is significantly greater than 0. That is a common approach of data-analysis computer programs. Another approach that used to be common is to look at r. You can find out how the Pearson correlation coefficient would be distributed, if the null hypothesis were true. To find a *p*-value, you ask the likelihood of getting an *r* at least as far from 0 as the one you got if the null hypothesis were true.

For example, consider our eight schools. Even if the null hypothesis were true, the *r* we got in our sample would not always be 0. Random variation will produce patterns in the data that might look like some relationship existed in the population.

To see where the *r*'s would be, I simulated 3,000 sets of data with eight pairs of observations in each set. Each observation in a pair was drawn from a normal distribution. Across all the simulations, the mean correlation was 0. The correlation in the population I was sampling from was 0. But *r* was not always 0. Figure 10.1.3 shows how the *r*'s were distributed.

Out of the 3,000 *r*'s, 46 were below −.81 or above .81, so the probability of getting at least .81 or something more embarrassing for the null hypothesis is about 46 out of 3,000, or 1.5%. The correlation of −.81 that appears in the school data is significant. Its *p*-value is about .015. (Note that this simulation assumed that both underlying populations were normally distributed.)

In fact, for an alpha of 5%, the cutoff for significance was about .685. Since 75 *r*'s were less than −.685 and 75 were greater than .685, altogether, 150 (5%) were at .685 or further from 0. Any *r* further from 0 than .685 would be significant, if alpha is 5%. At least that is the case with this many observations.

What about the correlation between years of education and income mentioned in the quote at the beginning of this section? Bowles found that the correlation was .375. If there had been only eight observations, that would not be significant, but the distribution of *r* depends on how many observations there are. For example, consider when there are only two observations. In that case, *r* would always be 1, except for the rare cases when the points on the scatter plot fall on a horizontal line. But should the null hypothesis be embarrassed if two points have a correlation of 1? No, because when there are only two observations, correlations of 1 and −1 happen most of the time, even when the null hypothesis is true. The *p*-value for a particular *r* depends on how many observations there are.

Figure 10.1.3 **Distribution of *r* with 3,000 Data Sets (Normally Distributed Population; Population *r* = 0; *n* = 8)**

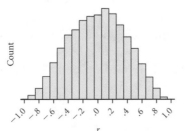

Figure 10.1.4

Distribution of r (x– and y-Values Both Normally Distributed; Population $r = 0$; $n = 596$)

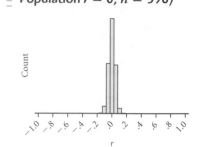

Bowles was reporting on a study with 596 observations. Before we reach a conclusion about Bowles's correlation of .375, we had better check on the distribution of r when there are 596 observations. Figure 10.1.4 shows how r is distributed when the null hypothesis is true, there are 596 observations in each sample, and the measurements come from normally distributed populations.

You can see in Figure 10.1.4 that, with the larger sample size, the correlations in the samples fall closer to the correlation in the population from which the samples were drawn: 5% fell at .085 or further away from 0, so a correlation of .085 would have a p-value of 5%. r's that were further from 0 would have smaller p-values. My simulation with 3,000 samples did not find even one r as large as .375. That would suggest that in the Bowles study the p-value for an r of .375 is less than 1 out of 3,000. My statistical analysis program tells me that, with 596 observations, the p-value of a correlation of .375 would be less than .000005. The correlation that Bowles reports between years of education and income was a significant correlation. The null hypothesis predicts that, with 596 observations, r will fall most of the time between $-.1$ and .1, so .375 is very embarrassing for the null hypothesis. So we discard the null hypothesis.

What does that tell you? Does it prove that education increases your income? No. Bowles did not do an experiment. His study does not tell you what causes what. All it tells you is that, for some unknown reason, education is tied to income. One possibility is that education increases income. Another possibility is that having gotten yourself into a lucrative career, you are more likely to sign up for classes and get more education. That would be the income causing the education. A third possibility is that wealthy parents set you up to earn a high salary by introducing you to their wealthy friends and also pay for you to go to college. That would be a third factor influencing both measurements.

These days, people who test regressions simply ask computer programs what the p-value is. In the past, people looked up critical r's in tables that told how r was distributed for different sample sizes.

Correlation Test Summary

Purpose of Correlation Test

The correlation test checks for a correlation between two number line observations.

Correlation Test Requirements

Number line observations are independent random samples of the population, and each set of measurements comes from a normal distribution.

Correlation Test Null Hypothesis

The null hypothesis is that, in the population, there is no correlation.

The Correlation Statistic

r is the square root of R^2, which is the proportion of the variance of the y-values predictable from the variance in the regression model's estimated y-values. r is negative, if the slope is negative.

The P-Value

When the null hypothesis is true, the distribution of r depends on the sample size. The p-value is the probability of getting an r as far from 0 as the r found in the sample, if the null hypothesis is true, and the measurements come from a normal distribution.

The Logic of the Inference

If the p-value is less than alpha (the cutoff for significance), the null hypothesis is rejected in favor of the alternative that there is a correlation in the population. If the p-value is greater than alpha, the null hypothesis is retained on the grounds that it is the simpler concept.

Correlation Is Not Causation

If neither measurement in a correlation study is a randomly assigned treatment, there are many possible explanations for why a significant correlation exists. For example, if a researcher finds a significant correlation between age and income, it may be that older people earn more, or that richer people live longer, or that a third variable (such as cleverness) improves longevity and income.

A correlation test can be used in an experiment. For example, a researcher could use a random number generator to select how much money to pay students to study. If there is then a correlation between payments and learning, the causation has to flow from the random number generator to the learning.

Reporting the Results

In the popular press, a writer will report at most that a correlation is "statistically significant" and may report only that there is a correlation.

In the sciences, a writer will report at least the p-value. It is usual to report r, as in this quote:

> *Pearson correlation analyses (n = 6, alpha was set at 0.05, two-tailed) showed that several significant relationships were found between patient variables: . . . [between] explanation of care and management of pain and discomfort (r = 0.952, p = .003).*
>
> —TZENG AND KETEFIAN, *JOURNAL OF NURSING CARE QUALITY*, JANUARY 2002

Researchers may report R^2, as in this quote:

> *The 18-h oxidation of protein was significantly correlated with 18-h protein intake (simple linear regression, R² = .46, intercept = 9.99, slope = 0.51, P < 0.001).*
>
> —RUSSELL ET AL., *THE JOURNAL OF NUTRITION*, MARCH 2002

Algebra and Greek Symbols

Additivity of Variances and Sums of Squares

The regression line estimates y-values. The regression line makes mistakes $(y_i - \hat{y}_i)$, which are called "residuals." This section pointed out that the variance of the regression estimates plus the variance of the residuals equals the variance of the y-values. A sample variance is indicated by s^2. A residual is denoted by e:

(1)
$$s_y^2 = s_{\hat{y}}^2 + s_e^2$$

Each sample variance is the sum of squared deviations (SS) divided by 1 less than the number of observations. So Equation 1 can be written like this:

(2)
$$\frac{SS_y}{n-1} = \frac{SS_{\hat{y}}}{n-1} + \frac{SS_e}{n-1}$$

We can multiply both sides of that equation by n minus 1 to get this regularity that is sometimes useful:

(3)
$$SS_y = SS_{\hat{y}} + SS_e$$

That is, the sum of squares of the y-values can be broken into two parts: the sum of squares of the regression estimates and the sum of squares of the residuals.

This highlights why the residuals are called "residuals." The regression model produces the sum of squares of the estimates, which predict as much of the sum of squares of the y-values as possible. The sum of squares of the residuals is all the variation that is left over—all that is residual.

R^2

R^2 is the portion of the variance in the y-values that is predictable from the variance in the y estimates. That is,

(4)
$$R^2 = \frac{s_{\hat{y}}^2}{s_y^2}$$

Both the top and the bottom of Equation 4 are sums of squares divided by n minus 1, which we can show and cancel, like this:

(5)
$$R^2 = \frac{s_{\hat{y}}^2}{s_y^2} = \frac{\dfrac{SS_{\hat{y}}}{n-1}}{\dfrac{SS_y}{n-1}} = \frac{SS_{\hat{y}}}{SS_y}$$

Sometimes it helps to recognize that the variance of the y-values is made up of the variance of the estimates and the variance of the errors, and to write this:

(6)
$$R^2 = \frac{s_{\hat{y}}^2}{s_{\hat{y}}^2 + s_e^2}$$

As in Equation 5, we can cancel the $(n-1)$'s. So,

(7)
$$R^2 = \frac{SS_{\hat{y}}}{SS_{\hat{y}} + SS_e}$$

r

r is the square root of R^2:

(8)
$$r = \sqrt{R^2} = \sqrt{\frac{SS_{\hat{y}}}{SS_y}}$$

Traditional Equation to Calculate r

There is another way to think of r, and another way to calculate it. The calculations start by transforming the x-values into standardized scores by first subtracting $\bar{x}$ and then dividing by the standard deviation of $x(s_x)$. For these calculations, we will not use the estimate of the population standard deviation, which we found by dividing the sum of squares by the degrees of freedom and taking the square root. Instead, we will use the standard deviation calculated as though the sample were the total population, the square root of the mean of the squared deviations. For these calculations, s_x equals $\sqrt{\sum_{i=1}^{n}(x_i - \bar{x})^2/n}$.

We do the same to the y-values, replacing each with $(y - \bar{y})/s_y$. After we have standardized the values, r is the mean of the products of these standardized values:

(9)
$$r = \frac{\sum_{i=1}^{n} \frac{(x_i - \bar{x})}{s_x} \times \frac{(y_i - \bar{y})}{s_y}}{n}$$

The standard deviations of x and y can be moved out of the summation sign and moved to the bottom of the equation:

(10)
$$r = \frac{\frac{1}{s_x s_y}\sum_{i=1}^{n}(x_i - \bar{x})(y_i - \bar{y})}{n} = \frac{\sum_{i}^{n}(x_i - \bar{x})(y_i - \bar{y})}{n s_x s_y}$$

Equation 10 calculates the same value as the square root of R^2, which is the equation for r presented in this section. Below is the proof that the two equations of r are calculating the same value. This proof will show that $\sqrt{SS_{\hat{y}}/SS_y}$ equals $\sum_{i=1}^{n}(x_i - \bar{x})(y_i - \bar{y})/n s_x s_y$. The proof is included here for three reasons. First, you might like to see it to make sure I can prove it. The second reason is that if you find it interesting to read through the proof and think about how these two equations calculate the same value, you will probably enjoy going on to other courses and other books in statistics. You might like further study in statistics even if you do not like such a proof, but if you do, then you will enjoy the kinds of proofs that appear in other books on statistics. The third reason is that, even if you do not want to read through the proof and skip past it, you should be aware that a proof exists for this idea.

Before we begin the proof, here are a few equalities that I will use in it. I'm going to refer to the deviation of the ith x from the mean x as the ith "run." That is, it is the run from the mean-mean point out to the ith point:

(11)
$$run_i = x_i - \bar{x}, \quad \text{and} \quad rise_i = y_i - \bar{y}$$

The ith estimated y is the mean y-value plus the rise associated with going from the mean x-value to the ith x. That is,

(12)
$$\hat{y}_i = \bar{y} + b_1 run_i$$

The mean of the estimated y-values is the mean of the y-values:

(13)
$$mean(\hat{y}) = \frac{\sum_{i=1}^{n}\hat{y}_i}{n} = \frac{\sum_{i=1}^{n}(\bar{y} + b_1 run_i)}{n}$$

There is a general rule about summations:

$$\sum (a + b) = \sum a + \sum b$$

so,

(14)
$$mean(\hat{y}) = \frac{\sum_{i=1}^{n} \bar{y} + \sum_{i=1}^{n} b_1 run_i}{n}$$

The mean y-value doesn't change as we go from one y to another, so the sum of mean y-values from the first observation to the last is the same as the number of observations times the mean y-value:

(15)
$$mean(\hat{y}) = \frac{n\bar{y}}{n} + \frac{\sum_{i=1}^{n} b_1 run_i}{n} = \bar{y} + \frac{\sum_{i=1}^{n} b_1 run_i}{n}$$

We can move that b_1 out of the summation sign, because it is a constant. That is, it is a general rule that $\sum_{i=1} bx_i$ equals $b\sum_{i=1} x_i$. Also, run_i equals $(x_i - \bar{x})$. That's the deviation of x from the mean x-value, and the sum of the deviations is 0.

(16)
$$mean(\hat{y}) = \bar{y} + \frac{b_1 0}{n} = \bar{y} + \frac{b_1 0}{n} = \bar{y}$$

The mean of the estimated y-values is the mean of the y-values.

For the proof that follows, we will need to see that $SS_{\hat{y}}$ equals $b_1^2 \sum_{i=1}^{n} run^2$. By itself, it's not terribly interesting, but we'll use it later. Here is the proof that this equation is true:

(17)
$$SS_{\hat{y}} = \sum_{i=1}^{n} [\hat{y}_i - mean(\hat{y})]^2$$

That's the definition of the sum of squares of the estimated y-values. The mean of the estimated y-values is the mean of the y-values, and we can use Equation 12 to substitute for the estimated y-value:

(18)
$$SS_{\hat{y}} = \sum_{i=1}^{n} (\hat{y}_i - \bar{y})^2 = \sum_{i=1}^{n} (\bar{y} + b_1 run_i - \bar{y})^2$$

Inside the parentheses, the mean y-value and the negative mean y-value cancel each other out. Then we can shift things around to get what we are looking for:

(19)
$$SS_{\hat{y}} = \sum_{i=1}^{n} (b_1 run_i)^2 = \sum_{i=1}^{n} b_1^2 run_i^2 = b_1^2 \sum_{i=1}^{n} run_i^2$$

If you are not comfortable working with square roots, it will help to go over this small proof that $\sqrt{\sum run^2} \sqrt{\sum rise^2}$ equals $n\sqrt{\sum run^2/n} \sqrt{\sum rise^2/n}$. I start by multiplying $\sqrt{a}\sqrt{b}$ by a version of 1, $\sqrt{n}/\sqrt{n}$:

(20)
$$\sqrt{a}\sqrt{b} = \frac{\sqrt{n}\sqrt{a}}{\sqrt{n}} \cdot \frac{\sqrt{n}\sqrt{b}}{\sqrt{n}} = \sqrt{n}\frac{\sqrt{a}}{\sqrt{n}} \sqrt{n}\frac{\sqrt{b}}{\sqrt{n}} = \sqrt{n}\sqrt{n}\frac{\sqrt{a}}{\sqrt{n}}\frac{\sqrt{b}}{\sqrt{n}} = n\sqrt{\frac{a}{n}}\sqrt{\frac{b}{n}}$$

We will use the sum of run^2 for a and the sum of $rise^2$ for b:

$$(21) \qquad \sqrt{\sum run^2} \sqrt{\sum rise^2} = n \sqrt{\frac{\sum run^2}{n}} \sqrt{\frac{\sum rise^2}{n}}$$

We will need to be able to use that equality later.

Now we're ready for the proof. Here's the proof that $\sqrt{SS_{\hat{y}}/SS_y}$ equals $\sum_{i=1}^{n}(x_i - \bar{x})(y_i - \bar{y})/ns_x s_y$. We start with what we know about the regression slope. Remember that the slope to each point from the mean-mean point is the rise over the run:

$$(22) \qquad b_1 = \frac{\sum_{i=1}^{n} slope_i run_i^2}{\sum_{i=1}^{n} run_i^2} = \frac{\sum_{i=1}^{n} \frac{rise_i}{run_i} run_i^2}{\sum_{i=1}^{n} run_i^2} = \frac{\sum_{i=1}^{n} rise_i run_i}{\sum_{i=1}^{n} run_i^2}$$

We can square both sides:

$$(23) \qquad b_1^2 = \frac{\left(\sum_{i=1}^{n} rise_i run_i\right)^2}{\left(\sum_{i=1}^{n} run_i^2\right)^2}$$

And multiply both sides by the sum of squared runs, canceling on the right:

$$(24) \qquad b_1^2 \sum_{i=1}^{n} run_i^2 = \frac{\left(\sum_{i=1}^{n} rise_i run_i\right)^2}{\sum_{i=1}^{n} run_i^2}$$

Equation 19 tells us that the left side of Equation 24 is the sum of squares of the estimated y-values:

$$(25) \qquad SS_{\hat{y}} = \frac{\left(\sum_{i=1}^{n} rise_i run_i\right)^2}{\sum_{i=1}^{n} run_i^2}$$

We can divide both sides by the sum of squares of y:

$$(26) \qquad \frac{SS_{\hat{y}}}{SS_y} = \frac{\left(\sum_{i=1}^{n} rise_i run_i\right)^2}{\left(\sum_{i=1}^{n} run_i^2\right) SS_y}$$

The SS_y is the sum of squared rises:

$$(27) \qquad \frac{SS_{\hat{y}}}{SS_y} = \frac{\left(\sum_{i=1}^{n} rise_i run_i\right)^2}{\sum_{i=1}^{n} run_i^2 \sum_{i=1}^{n} rise_i^2}$$

We can take the square root:

(28)
$$\sqrt{\frac{SS_{\hat{y}}}{SS_y}} = \frac{\sum\limits_{i=1}^{n} rise_i run_i}{\sqrt{\sum\limits_{i=1}^{n} run_i^2}\sqrt{\sum\limits_{i=1}^{n} rise_i^2}}$$

Now we use Equation 21:

(29)
$$\sqrt{\frac{SS_{\hat{y}}}{SS_y}} = \frac{\sum\limits_{i=1}^{n} rise_i run_i}{n\sqrt{\dfrac{\sum\limits_{i=1}^{n} run_i^2}{n}}\sqrt{\dfrac{\sum\limits_{i=1}^{n} rise_i^2}{n}}}$$

The two square roots on the bottom right in Equation 29 are the population-style standard deviations of x and y from the second way of calculating r that appears in Equation 10:

(30)
$$\sqrt{\frac{SS_{\hat{y}}}{SS_y}} = \frac{\sum\limits_{i=1}^{n} (x_i - \bar{x})(y_i - \bar{y})}{n s_x s_y}$$

That is what we were trying to prove. The bottom line here is that these two ways of calculating r are identical:

(31)
$$r = \sqrt{\frac{SS_{\hat{y}}}{SS_y}} = \frac{\sum\limits_{i=1}^{n} (x_i - \bar{x})(y_i - \bar{y})}{n s_x s_y}$$

r is the Regression Slope in Terms of Standard Deviations

r is the regression slope that you would find between the x-values and y-values after you have standardized the values. Standardizing x means transforming each x-value into how far that x is from the mean x-value in terms of the standard deviation of x. When values have been standardized, they are referred to as z-values. I will call the ith standardized value of x "z_{xi}" and the ith standardized value of y "z_{yi}."

Because the first step in standardizing is subtracting the mean, the mean of the standardized values is 0. Because the second step is dividing by the standard deviation (calculated by dividing by n), the standard deviation of the standardized values is 1.

Before we can go through the proof that r is the slope of the standardized values, you need to see that the sum of the squares of the standardized values is n. The first step in seeing this is to replace the z with the equation for calculating z:

$$(32) \qquad \sum_{i=1}^{n} z_{xi}^2 = \sum_{i=1}^{n} \frac{(x_i - \bar{x})^2}{s_x^2}$$

The variance of x is a constant and can be moved outside the summation symbol:

$$(33) \qquad \sum_{i=1}^{n} z_{xi}^2 = \frac{1}{s_x^2} \sum_{i=1}^{n} (x_i - \bar{x})^2$$

We can substitute for s_x and cancel the summations:

$$(34) \qquad \sum_{i=1}^{n} z_{xi} = \frac{n}{\sum_{i=1}^{n} (x_i - \bar{x})^2} \sum_{i=1}^{n} (x_i - \bar{x})^2 = n$$

Here's the proof that r is the regression slope after standardizing. If we calculate the slope of the regression equation after standardizing, this is what we have:

$$(35) \qquad b_1 = \frac{\sum_{i=1}^{n} slope_i run_i^2}{\sum_{i=1}^{n} run_i^2} = \frac{\sum_{i=1}^{n} \frac{rise_i}{run_i} run_i^2}{\sum_{i=1}^{n} (z_{xi} - \bar{z}_x)^2}$$

The runs cancel on the top, and the mean of both standardized values is 0:

$$(36) \qquad b_1 = \frac{\sum_{i=1}^{n} rise_i run_i}{\sum_{i=1}^{n} z_{xi}^2} = \frac{\sum_{i=1}^{n} (z_{yi} - \bar{z}_y)(z_{xi} - \bar{z}_x)}{\sum_{i=1}^{n} z_{xi}^2}$$

As noted earlier, s_{zx} and s_{zy} both equal 1. That means that we can divide by both of them and change nothing. Also, the sum of the squared z-values is n. That can be substituted into the bottom of Equation 36:

$$(37) \qquad b_1 = \frac{\sum_{i=1}^{n} (z_{yi} - \bar{z}_y)(z_{xi} - \bar{z}_x)}{s_{zx} s_{zy} n}$$

According to Equation 31, the right side of Equation 37 is r, where the x-values are z_x and the y-values are z_y. So, after standardizing, b_1 equals r.

Abstract

The regression equation can be used to produce estimates for each y-axis measurement. Each estimate will have some error, called a "residual." The variance of the estimates plus the variance of the residuals add up to the variance of the y-axis measurements. The variance of the estimates is the proportion of the variance of the y-axis measurements predictable from the variation in the x-axis measurements. R^2 is the variance of the estimates divided by the variance of the y-axis measurements. r is the square root of R^2. If the slope is negative, r is negative. To test the significance of r, you look at how r would be distributed if the null hypothesis were true. The p-value is the probability of obtaining an r at least as far from 0 as the r that was found, if the null hypothesis were true.

Avoiding Common Misunderstandings

The distribution of r shown in this section was based on the assumption that the x-values and the y-values both come from normal distributions. If they come from non-normal distributions, r is spread out differently, and this causes problems for the correlation test.

R^2 is a proportion, so it cannot be less than 0 or greater than 1.

Computer Project

Using the Representative Sample of 50,000 Americans from the *Data Matters* Resource Center at *www.keycollege.com/dm,* have your software calculate the correlations between income and education that Fuchs talks about at the beginning of this section. Check whether there is reason to think you could use the correlation test described in this section. If the distributions of the number line observations you were going to work with do not look normal, the significance test of the correlation coefficient is not a good idea. Are there correlations in that data that you could test with the significance test of the correlation coefficient?

Exercises

Here is the table from Bowles again. Use it to complete Exercises 1 through 4.

VARIABLE	1	2	3	4
1. Income	1.0			
2. Years of Schooling	0.375	1.0		
3. Occupational SES	0.384	0.556	1.0	
4. Net Worth	0.314	0.184	0.177	1.0

Source: . . . The sample size is 596.

—BOWLES, *JOURNAL OF POLITICAL ECONOMY,* 1972, P. S219

1. What is R^2 for the relationship between years of schooling and net worth?

2. What is the R^2 for the relationship between income and net worth?

3. Sketch a scatter plot that might have roughly a correlation like that of the relationship between years of schooling and net worth.

4. Sketch a scatter plot that might have roughly a correlation like that of the relationship between income and net worth.

In very small doses, nitrates are not really harmful to people. In large doses, they are poisonous (Fan and Steinberg, 1996). A team of researchers checked the ground water in Pennsylvania and reported the following. Use it to complete Exercises 5 through 10.

> *Median nitrate-N levels significantly increased as the distance to the nearest cornfield decreased. Median nitrate-N concentrations for each county were also positively correlated with percent of agricultural land in use ($r = 0.57$, $p < 0.0014$) and pounds per acre of nitrogen fertilizer used ($r = 0.82$, $p < 0.0001$).*
>
> —SWISTOCK ET AL., JOURNAL OF ENVIRONMENTAL HEALTH, 1993, P. 6

5. With Swistock's sample size, if the null hypothesis were true, what would be the chances of getting a Pearson correlation coefficient, r, greater than .57 or less than −.57? (Hint: The answer is in the quote.)

6. The end of the quote says that $p < .0001$. In this case, what is that "p" that was less than .0001?

7. What do we conclude about the two correlations whose p-values are reported?

8. What was the null hypothesis of those tests?

9. What proportion of the variance in nitrate-N concentrations was predictable from the percentage of agricultural land in use?

10. What proportion of the variance in nitrate-N concentrations was predictable from variation in pounds of nitrogen fertilizer used per acre?

11. The Bowles report on the correlation between education and income was not an experiment. How could you devise an experiment to test whether education causes higher income? Estimate how much your experiment would cost to run.

12. What do you think is causing the link between lunch subsidy rates and reading test pass rates in Snohomish County, Washington? How could you do an experiment to test your theory?

13. Aunt Bessie's well is out by the cornfield. She asks whether the earlier quote from Swistock means that her well water is contaminated. Write a brief note answering her question.

Two economists were exploring what inflation does to the U.S. economy. One thing they looked at was price volatility. You may have seen price volatility at the gas station. When the price jumps up $0.15 a gallon one day and down again the next day, that is price volatility. If the price jumped up and down $0.30, that would be higher price volatility. Use this information and the following quote to complete Exercises 14 through 21.

> *If the 1970s and 1980s data are combined, the correlation coefficient is 0.74 and is statistically significant at less than the 0.1 percent level. . . . Thus, the positive relationship between inflation and relative price variability does not appear to be due to relative price shocks leading to greater inflation.*
>
> —HESS AND MORRIS, *ECONOMIC REVIEW*, 1996, P. 81

14. What alpha were Hess and Morris using?

15. Do you think that these results were significant at alpha equal to .05? Explain your thinking.

16. If Hess and Morris were looking at monthly data, how many observations would they have? And if they were looking at annual data, how many observations would they have?

17. Were Hess and Morris looking at annual or monthly data?

18. Imagine transforming the data into *z*-scores. That would involve replacing each measurement with how many standard deviations it was above 0 (as in Figure 10.1.2). Sketch a scatter plot of the *z*-scores with a regression line.

19. If Hess and Morris had looked at 600 observations and found a correlation of .74, would it have been significant at alpha equal to .05? Explain your thinking.

20. Imagine that the director of the Federal Reserve sees this research and concludes that higher inflation causes higher price volatility. Write him a brief e-mail message explaining what a person can conclude from this correlation.

21. Describe an experiment to test whether higher inflation produces price volatility.

Here is a report of a significant correlation. Refer to this quote to complete Exercises 22 through 24.

> *A new study published in an American Heart Association journal reported a significant correlation between hopelessness and faster progression of atherosclerosis (hardening of the arteries) among 942 middle-aged men.*
>
> —CONDOR, *CHICAGO TRIBUNE*, SEPTEMBER 4, 1997, P. 3

Imagine what this data might look like in a scatter plot. You might guess that hopelessness is measured on a scale of 1 to 10, with 1 being very hopeful, and 10 being very hopeless. Progression of arteriosclerosis is probably measured as a percentage change.

22. What does it mean to say that there was a "significant correlation"?

23. Is the correlation between hopelessness and arteriosclerosis progression necessarily large?

24. Given that this result was statistically significant, does that tell us that it is necessarily important or interesting?

25. In the following quote, what does Emanuel mean by "significant correlation"?

> *[Meteorologist] Kerry Emanuel . . . doubts that this region will see any effect from El Niño. "I have never seen anything to suggest any significant correlation with New England weather," Emanuel said.*
> —CHANDLER, *BOSTON GLOBE*, SEPTEMBER 24, 1997, P. A1

Answers to Odd-Numbered Exercises

1. $.184^2 = 3.3\%$.

3. $r = .18$

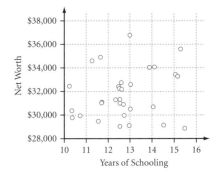

5. It's less than .0014.

7. They are both significant. We reject their null hypotheses.

9. $.57^2 = 32\%$.

11. Randomly assign 60 people to get a college education and 60 people to be put on a waiting list to get the same education after 15 years. See how the two groups compare in terms of income after 15 years. This experiment is going to cost about 120 times the cost of a college education. To make it

less expensive, we could provide no education at all to the control group. With the less expensive design, the experiment would cost something like $2.5 million.

13. "Dear Aunt Bessie, correlation is not causation, but it does allow for predictions. I think you should get your well water tested."

15. Yes. They are significant at alpha equal to .001, which is .1%. That means that the *p*-value was less than .001, so it was less than .05 as well.

17. I bet monthly data. With only 20 observations, an *r* of .74 wouldn't be so significant.

19. Yes. It looks like it's significant with 240 observations. Finding the same correlation with a larger sample size would lower the *p*-value.

21. You would have to do this in a smallish artificial economy, such as a small town, or even a game played by a group of students. You would need to have control of the prices of goods coming into the game or small town. Use multiple towns or multiple games. Have varying levels of inflation in the prices charged for the incoming goods. Check price volatility.

23. No. With 942 people in the sample, the correlation could be quite small and still be significant. In looking at the Bowles data, we found that with 500 observations, .12 would be significant. This correlation could be .11 and still be significant.

25. By "significant correlation," Emanuel is referring to a correlation appearing in data large enough to justify rejecting a null hypothesis that you cannot improve your predictions about New England weather by knowing about the El Niño weather patterns.

10.2 What If the Assumptions of the Regression Test Are Not Valid?

- Spearman's Rho
- Effect of Nonconstant Variances on Correlation Tests
- Effect of Non-normality on Correlation Tests
- Nonlinear Regression

Due to the skewed distributions on the health outcomes, Spearman rank correlations were calculated . . . greater health complaints were linked with greater work-related stress . . . (rs = .21 to .42, all ps < .01) . . . age, education, sex, ethnic group, years in practice, [and] income . . . were not associated with the studied health variables.

—Van Servellen et al., *Hospital Topics*, April 1994, p. 34

CAN STRESS MAKE YOU PHYSICALLY SICK? Van Servellen's research team surveyed 237 nurses, asking them about the stress of their jobs and their health. Both stress and health were measured with number line measurements. Van Servellen's team found a correlation between stress and health, but notice what they used to check for a correlation. They calculated a Spearman rank correlation coefficient, called "rho" to distinguish it from Pearson's correlation coefficient, *r*.

The Spearman rank correlation is the Pearson correlation between measurements after the measurements have been converted to ranks. Converting to ranks is fairly straightforward. The lowest number gets a rank of 1, the next lowest gets a rank of 2, and so on, up to the highest number. For example, Table 10.2.1 shows some health scores and their ranks.

That is all there is to converting to ranks, except for dealing with ties. When two or more observations are equal, they all get the mean of the ranks that could be assigned to them. For example, if the observations were 2, 9, 9, 9, and 10, the ranks would be 1, 3, 3, 3, and 5.

Ranks

To convert to ranks, sort the values from smallest to largest. The smallest gets a rank of 1, the next smallest gets a rank of 2, and so on to the largest. In the event of ties, all of the tied values get the same rank, which is the average of the ranks the tied values would have gotten had they been infinitesimally different from one another but not changed their positions in the ordered list.

For example, 4, 6, 22, 22, 22, and 999 would be ranked as 1, 2, 4, 4, 4, and 6.

Once the numbers are all converted to ranks, all that is left to calculate a Spearman rank correlation is to calculate the Pearson correlation coefficient for those ranks. In Van Servellen's case, for those ranks, the correlation coefficients were all between .21 and .42.

Because of the ranking step, Spearman rank correlations are not distributed exactly the same way that Pearson correlation coefficients are. Figure 10.2.1 shows 3,000 Spearman correlation coefficients that I produced by generating two sets of 237 independent observations drawn from a uniform distribution.

The null hypothesis of a test involving Spearman's correlation coefficient is that there is no correlation in the population. In the population from which I was drawing for the simulation that produced the data for Figure 10.2.1, there was no

Table 10.2.1 Some Health Scores and Their Ranks

SCORE	RANK
2	1
3	2
34	3
99	4

Figure 10.2.1 **Spearman Correlation Coefficients (Population $r = 0$; $n = 237$)**

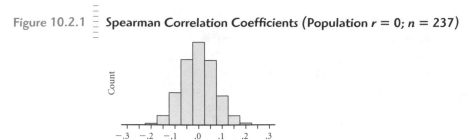

correlation. In that simulation, 5% of the Spearman rho's were at .13 or further from 0. For a sample with 237 observations, the p-value of .13 would be 5%. The Spearman rho-values that Van Servellen reports are all greater than .2. In the simulation, three out of 3,000 Spearman rho-values were greater than .2, so the p-value for Van Servellen's data would be .001 and less.

Spearman's Rho

Spearman's correlation coefficient, rho, is the Pearson correlation coefficient of the data after the data has been converted to ranks.

For example, the following data has a Spearman's rho of .5:

VALUE A	VALUE B
1	2
2	1
300	995

As with Pearson's r, the distribution of Spearman's rho depends on the number of observations, as shown in Table 10.2.2. If the absolute value of Spearman's rho is greater than the critical value, you can reject the null hypothesis of no correlation at alpha equal to 5%.

Why Use the Spearman Rank Correlation Rather Than the Pearson Correlation?

Inaccurate P-Values

There are several reasons to use the Spearman rank correlation rather than a regular Pearson correlation. Two reasons have to do with how the p-values were

Table 10.2.2   Some Critical Values for Spearman's Rho

SAMPLE SIZE	CRITICAL VALUE
3–4	1.00
5	.90
6	.83
7	.75
8	.72
9	.67

figured out for the Pearson correlations. To figure out how r's are distributed when the null hypothesis is true, Karl Pearson had to make some assumption about how the observations were distributed. He made the same assumption as Fisher and Gosset: that the regression model's errors were normally distributed. Sometimes errors are normally distributed; sometimes they are not. There are pros and cons to that assumption.

A second assumption that Pearson made was that the errors made by the regression model were all drawn from a single distribution. If the errors on the left of the scatter plot had a standard deviation of 2, then Pearson assumed that the errors had a standard deviation of 2 all along the regression line. When there is the same standard deviation all along the regression line, the data have constant variances. Nonconstant variances cause problems for Pearson's correlation test.

Nonconstant Variances

The Pearson correlation test assumes the errors around the regression line have an equal variance throughout the data. Nonconstant variances make Pearson's correlation test unreliable, but do not cause trouble for the Spearman correlation test.

Errors are not always equally spread along the regression line. For example, in my own research, I have asked people how much they felt various lottery tickets were worth. The lottery tickets I asked about varied in their prize value and the chances that the lottery ticket would pay off. I asked people for their highest bids to buy the tickets. Figure 10.2.2 shows a scatter plot of their bids and the lottery tickets' potential payoffs. Many of those points represent bids from several people: When several people all made the same bid for the same gamble, they all got plotted as the same point on the scatter plot. The diagonal line is the regression line.

There is an important pattern in these data: People do not bid negative numbers, and people do not bid more than they could win from the lottery. That is what gives the scatter plot its wedge shape.

Where the potential payoffs are \$2, the regression line makes errors between -1 and 1. At the right, where potential payoffs are \$9.50, the regression line makes errors between -3 and 3. That is an example of the errors coming from different distributions as you go along the regression line. Pearson was assuming that the data did not look like that. Pearson's derivation of the p-values was based on an assumption that the errors would be similar all along the regression line, as in Figure 10.2.3.

Figure 10.2.2 **Respondents' Bids to Buy Lottery Tickets Plotted Against the Potential Winnings with a Regression Line**

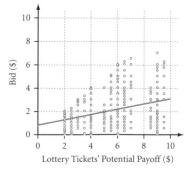

Figure 10.2.3  **Data with Equally Distributed Errors**

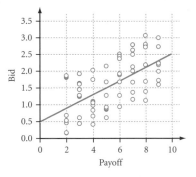

Skewness and the Pearson Correlation Test

The Pearson correlation test is based on an assumption that the data is normally distributed. When the data is skewed, the Pearson correlation test is unreliable.

For Pearson's correlation test, there was another difficulty in bids for lottery tickets. Most of the people who were making bids wanted nothing to do with lottery tickets. Most of the bids were near 0. For any particular gamble, the bids were all very right skewed. That meant that the regression model's errors were all right skewed as well. Pearson assumed that the errors would be normally distributed. In these evaluations of lottery tickets, Pearson's assumptions were violated in two ways.

Because the *p*-values for Pearson correlation coefficients are based on the assumption that the errors are from a single normal distribution, I do not know whether his *p*-values are valid for my data. I might get *p*-values very different from the real *p*-values.

For example, I ran a simulation that took *x*-values and *y*-values from a right-skewed distribution. Figure 10.2.4 shows what the distribution looks like between 0 and 100. To create that histogram, I randomly generated 3,000 values from the distribution. Those 3,000 values ranged from 1 to 5,000. The median was 2, the mean was 11, and the standard deviation was 116. This is a right-skewed distribution.

To create *y*-values, I randomly generated a value from a uniform distribution from −0.5 to 0.5. I then multiplied each of those values by its matched *x*-value. For example, if *x* was 150, and I generated a −0.1, then *y* would be −15. Figure 10.2.5 is a scatter plot of most of the 3,000 observations. In my simulation, the *x*-values actually went all the way up to 5,000, and the *y*-values went up to 2,000.

In the total population of an infinite number of possible values, the relationship is a cone with a tip at (0, 0) that extends to infinity to the right. At any

Figure 10.2.4 **A Very Right-Skewed Distribution**

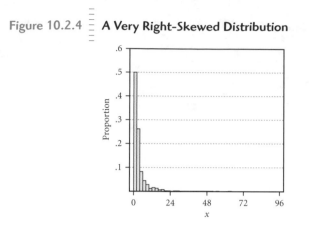

Figure 10.2.5 **A Scatter Plot of Simulated Data that Violates Pearson's Correlation Test Assumptions**

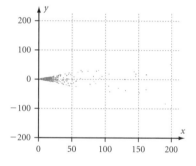

x-value, the slice of the cone goes from negative one-half of x up to positive one-half of x. At every x-value, the mean y-value is 0.

In this simulation, the null hypothesis is true: There is no correlation in the population. Each sample had 200 observations.

Figure 10.2.6 shows how the Pearson r's were distributed. That kind of distribution is *not* what Pearson had in mind! The null hypothesis was rejected 45% of the time, even though alpha was 5%.

The Spearman test was not created with the assumptions Pearson made. Because it first converts to ranks, the Spearman test is protected from the effects of skewed distributions. Changes in the distribution of the errors can still make it inaccurate, but the ranking helps diminish the influence of changes in the error distribution. For example, I reran the simulation that created the correlation coefficients in Figure 10.2.6 using the Spearman correlation test on the same data. For sample sizes between 12 and 62, the rejection rates hovered between 10% and 12%. That is not ideal. Those are not 5%, but they are a lot better than 45%.

Figure 10.2.6

The Distribution of *r* for the Simulation in Figure 10.2.5 (Sample *N* = 200; *X* = 1/uniform(0,1); *Y* = *X* × uniform(−0.5,0.5))

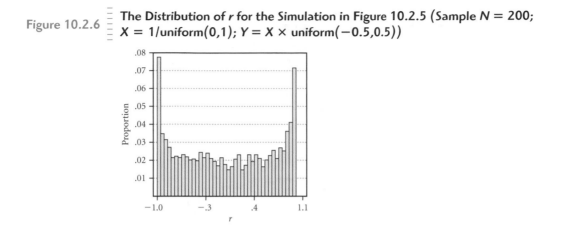

Part of what is misleading about the Pearson correlation test in that simulation is the right skewness of *x*. An important aspect of right skewness is that the values are very sparse on the far right, and they get a lot of weight. Even in a large sample, it would not be unusual to get from that distribution only one observation above 2,000. It could be one *x*-value at 5,000. In the simulation, that observation could have a *y*-value as large as 2,500. Remember that the mean *x*-value is 11, so the run squared out to that observation is 4,989 squared, or 24,890,121. That point gets a huge weight in determining the regression slope and Pearson's *r*.

In contrast, imagine that the *x*-values are not right skewed but are instead uniformly distributed from 0 to 5,000. Imagine that the *y*-values are created the same way as in the last simulation. This is still quite a violation of Pearson's assumptions. Figure 10.2.7 shows a scatter plot of such data. The big difference here is that the points are evenly spread between 0 and 5,000.

This is still very much not what Pearson assumed, which was that the *x*-values would be spread in a normal distribution. The errors in Figure 10.2.7 are spread

Figure 10.2.7

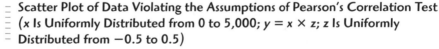

Scatter Plot of Data Violating the Assumptions of Pearson's Correlation Test (*x* Is Uniformly Distributed from 0 to 5,000; *y* = *x* × *z*; *z* Is Uniformly Distributed from −0.5 to 0.5)

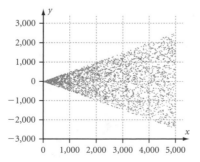

Figure 10.2.8 **Null Hypothesis Rejection Rates for Samples from the Data Shown in Figure 10.2.7**

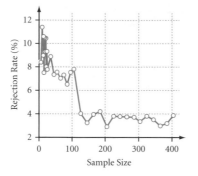

much more widely on the right than on the left. Nonetheless, for sample sizes between 3 and 100, Pearson's regression test rejects the null hypothesis between about 7% and 11% of the time. For sample sizes over 150, the regression test rejects the null hypothesis only 5% of the time or less. Figure 10.2.8 shows how the rejection rate changes with sample size for this strange population. The data in Figure 10.2.8 are from 2,000 simulations at each tested sample size. The point is that, although violations of Pearson's assumptions *can* throw the p-values way off, they do not always do so.

Here is another example of how the test is not always thrown off. This example uses the non-normal distribution that was used for *x* for the first simulation. In that simulation, *x* was drawn from a very right-skewed distribution. *y* is drawn from the same distribution, but is in no way related to *x*. Figure 10.2.9 shows how a part of a scatter plot of the data would look. Both *x* and *y* had values greater than 5,000 in the simulation, but values over 100 were very rare and so are not shown in Figure 10.2.9.

Figure 10.2.9 **Skewed Distributions of x-Values and y-Values (x and y Completely Uncorrelated)**

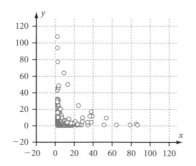

For the data shown in Figure 10.2.9, regardless of sample size, the regression test does not reject the null hypothesis more often than about 9% of the time. Violations of Pearson's assumptions *can* cause trouble, but *may* make only a small difference.

Another Reason to Use Spearman's Test: Low Power

The power of a statistical test is its chances of rejecting the null hypothesis when the null hypothesis is false. When Pearson's assumptions are valid, Pearson's correlation test is fairly powerful. For example, Figure 10.2.10 is a scatter plot of data that meet Pearson's assumptions.

In Figure 10.2.10, the *x*-values are normally distributed. The *y*-values are created by multiplying each *x*-value by one-half and then adding some error. The errors for all of the *y*-values were drawn from a single normal distribution. The regression equation for the full population is *y* equals 0 plus 0.5 times *x* ($y = 0 + 0.5x$), and R^2 is .2. Figure 10.2.11 shows how the power of the test changes with sample size for this population. In this situation, with a sample size of 50 or more, the null hypothesis is rejected at least 90% of the time. By 100 observations, the rejection rate is nearly 100%.

Power

The power of a test is the probability that it will reject the null hypothesis when the null hypothesis is false. Power can be calculated only for specified patterns in the population's data, because the likelihood of rejecting a false null hypothesis depends on how strong the correlation in the population is. A strong correlation leads to frequent rejections of the null hypothesis. A weak correlation makes it less likely that the null hypothesis will be rejected.

Figure 10.2.10 **A Scatter Plot of Data That Fit All of Pearson's Correlation Test Assumptions**

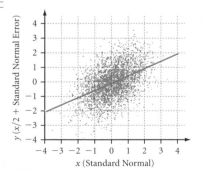

Figure 10.2.11

The Power of Pearson's Correlation Test as a Function of Sample Size for Data Drawn from a Population That Meets the Test's Requirements

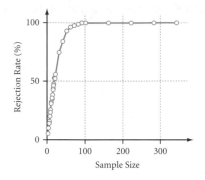

Figure 10.2.12 shows the rejection rates for a simulation that was exactly like that shown in Figure 10.2.11, with one exception. The distribution of x and the distribution of the regression line errors were from the very right-skewed distribution used earlier.

For this simulation, when the sample size is 50, the rejection rate is only about 70%. With 400 observations, the rejection rate is only about 87%. It still has not cleared 90%. Skewed data diminishes the power of the regression test.

Figure 10.2.13 shows the power of the Spearman correlation test for the same data that the Pearson correlation test was facing in Figure 10.2.12. The rejection rate reaches 90% by the time sample sizes get up to 40. That is pretty good for pretty unusual data.

The bottom line here is that violations of Pearson's correlation test assumptions can make the test reject true null hypotheses too often and can also sometimes lower the test's power. Spearman did not make the assumptions Pearson made, so

Figure 10.2.12

The Power of Pearson's Correlation Test as a Function of Sample Size for Data Drawn from a Population That Violates the Test's Requirements

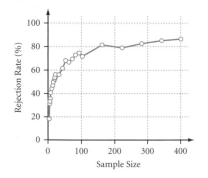

Figure 10.2.13

The Power of Spearman's Correlation Test as a Function of Sample Size for Data Drawn from a Population That Violates the Pearson Test's Requirements

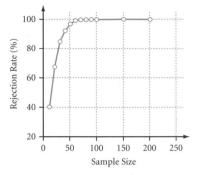

these violations do not throw off his test. That is a big reason to use the Spearman test instead of the regression test.

Some violations increase the power of Pearson's correlation test, and some decrease its tendency to reject true null hypotheses. If statisticians were clear about which kinds of violations improve the correlation test and which kinds interfere with its accuracy, then they would be able to adjust the test in light of the distribution. Unfortunately, there is no general sense of how various violations affect the test. It is well known that you need to worry about changing distributions in the errors and that the errors ought to be normally distributed, but if you sit down with a statistician and sketch a scatter plot for a population, the statistician will not necessarily be able to tell you right off whether the population's characteristics will improve or worsen the performance of Pearson's regression test. That is why some people prefer to work with the Spearman test instead.

However, the correlation test is related to the regression equation, and it allows us to check for a linear model. When a positive Spearman correlation is significant, all we know is that there is a tendency for the y-values to go up when the x-values go up. We do not know how much they change, or even that their change is at all consistent. For example, Figure 10.2.14 shows four sets of data. Each of the sets would have the same Spearman correlation coefficient, 1.0. Their Pearson correlations would range from .57 to 1.00, and the set in Figure 10.2.14a does not have a significant Pearson r.

The data in Figures 10.2.14a, 10.2.14b, and 10.2.14d are the kind of data for which the Spearman correlation coefficient is wonderfully fitted. For the data in Figure 10.2.14c, the relationship between x and y is a line. The other figures have a strong relationship, but it is not linear. It is monotonic, which means that each increase in x is associated with an increase in y. The Spearman correlation picks up that monotonic relationship well.

Figure 10.2.14 **Four Scatter Plots for Which Spearman's Correlation Coefficient is 1.0**

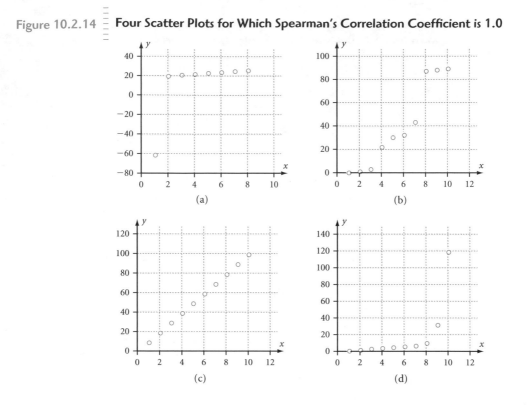

Monotonicity

One measurement has a monotonic relationship with a second measurement if for each rise in the second measurement there is a rise in the first, or if for each rise in the second there is a drop in the first. The Spearman rank order correlation test checks for monotonic relationships. For example, the following numbers are monotonically related:

2   5

3   9

4   99

And the following are also monotonically related:

4   5

3   9

2   99

The following are *not* monotonically related:

1   2

2   1

99   99

Nonlinear Regression

A Spearman correlation test would not work well for the data in Figure 10.2.15, because the relationship in the figure is not monotonic. In Figure 10.2.15, when x goes up, sometimes y goes down and sometimes up. The figure presents data from a study that followed 85,709 women (median age 46) for 12 years (Fuchs et al., 1995). The y-axis in Figure 10.2.15 represents the proportion of women in both groups combined compared to nondrinkers only. You can see that women who did not drink at all died at a higher rate than women who drank an average of a quarter of a drink each day. Heavier drinkers died at higher rates. For example, women who drank an average of 3.5 drinks per day died at a rate 20% greater than those who drank nothing. This is called a U-shaped relationship.

Nonlinear Correlation

Two measurements have a nonlinear correlation if you could use knowledge of one to improve your predictions of the other, and a scatter plot of the data would show that the dots fall in a curve.

A Spearman correlation can reveal monotonic nonlinear correlations, but not U-shaped correlations.

The Spearman correlation coefficient would not do well discerning the U-shaped relationship in Figure 10.2.15. Then again, neither would the Pearson correlation coefficient. The data in Figure 10.2.15 call for nonlinear regression, which is a systematic way to find nonlinear equations that fit the data. Nonlinear equations are equations that do not describe lines; they often include things like x^2, square roots, and logarithms. For example, the relationship in Figure 10.2.15 is pretty well described by this equation:

$$\text{Death Rate} = 1 - (0.2 \times \text{Mean Drinks per Day}) + (0.1 \times \text{Drinks per Day}^2)$$

Figure 10.2.15 **The Relationship Between Drinking and Death Among 85,709 Women**

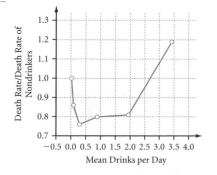

Although some nonlinear relationships do not show up well in a Spearman correlation test, lots of nonlinear relationships are well suited to it. Many things do have monotonic relationships that are not linear. The relationship between how good you feel and how rich you are is probably fairly monotonic, and certainly nonlinear. The nonlinear nature of the relationship is due to the shrinking impact of each additional dollar you own. If you are starving in a Third World country, and we give you $5 worth of food, that makes a huge difference to your happiness. But if you are a doctor, living in the American suburbs, and someone gives you $5, it matters hardly at all. Economists call this phenomenon declining marginal utility. The marginal utility is the additional benefit of getting some more money, given your current wealth. As you get richer, the additional benefit of gaining another single dollar becomes less and less.

There are many declining marginal effects. If you are in a dark room, and you light 1 candle, that makes a huge difference. If you have 20 candles burning, and you light 1 more, it makes hardly any difference at all. My favorite declining marginal effect is the savings in time for each additional 5 miles per hour that you drive. Many commuters speed on their way to work, but I do not think they are aware of how little their speeding benefits them. If you drive 10 miles on a highway, traveling 5 miles per hour faster than 40 miles per hour saves you about 1.7 minutes. But traveling 5 miles per hour faster than 65 miles per hour saves you only 0.6 minutes. Each additional mile per hour buys you less in saved time.

It is nonlinear situations, such as in declining marginal effects, that cry out to be tested with a Spearman correlation, because the Spearman test was designed to check only for monotonicity. In contrast, the Pearson correlation coefficient may be useful in more situations than it was designed for. For example, in Figure 10.2.14, except for the set in Figure 10.2.14a, all of the Pearson correlation coefficients are statistically significant for alpha equal to .01. Even though they are not linear relationships, the fact that you can rule out modeling them with a horizontal line is useful information.

Perhaps a very reasonable approach would be to test your data with both the Pearson test and the Spearman test. If they agree, that is wonderful. If they do not, that makes me nervous, and I would like the researcher to figure out what is going on. Creating many scatter plots and collecting more data would both be good ideas in that case.

Spearman Rank Correlation Test Summary

Purpose of Spearman Rank Correlation Test

The Spearman rank correlation test checks whether there is a monotonic correlation between two sets of measurements.

Spearman Rank Correlation Test Requirements

All measurements are independent random samples of the tested population.

Spearman Rank Correlation Test Null Hypothesis

In the population, it does not help to know one measurement's percentile (the proportion of the population that would fall below that measurement) when predicting the other measurement's percentile, which means that there is no linear correlation in the population and no monotonic correlation in the population.

The Spearman Rank Correlation Statistic

Each set of observations is transformed to ranks, and the Pearson correlation coefficient is calculated from the ranks. The correlation coefficient calculated from the ranks is the Spearman rank order correlation coefficient, rho.

To convert to ranks, the lowest value is assigned a 1, the next lowest a 2, and so on to the highest. In the event of multiple observations with the same value (ties), all of the observations with that value are assigned the mean of the ranks that would have been assigned to those observations had they differed, but remained higher than their nearest lower neighbor and lower than their nearest higher neighbor. For example, ranking would transform 1, 2, 2, 2, and 9 into 1, 3, 3, 3, and 5.

The P-Value

P-values are found by Monte Carlo simulations or by looking up critical values in tables or within statistical analysis computer programs. The p-value is the probability of getting a Spearman rank order correlation coefficient at least as far from 0 as that which was found if the null hypothesis is true.

The Logic of the Inference

If the *p*-value is less than alpha (the cutoff for significance), the null hypothesis of no monotonic correlation in the population is rejected. If the *p*-value is greater than alpha, the null hypothesis is retained on the grounds that it is the simpler concept.

Correlation Is Not Causation

If a significant correlation is found, the causation behind that correlation is unclear, unless one of the measurements is of a treatment that was determined by random assignment.

Algebra and Greek Symbols

The Pearson correlation test was developed with an assumption of bivariate normality, which means that both variables are normally distributed.

Statistical inference can make two kinds of errors. A type I error is rejecting a true null hypothesis. If a statistical test is functioning correctly, and the null hypothesis is true, the test should make type I errors at a rate determined by alpha. If alpha is 5%, then the true null hypothesis should be rejected 5% of the time. A type II error is failing to reject the null hypothesis when it is false. The power of a test is 1 minus the test's probability of committing a type II error.

Abstract

Pearson's regression test assumes that the observations are all distributed around the regression line with one normal distribution. Violations of this assumption can weaken the regression test's power or increase its tendency to reject true null hypotheses. Spearman's rank correlation test does not make these assumptions and is less thrown by violations of Pearson's assumptions. Spearman's correlation test checks only for monotonicity, whereas Pearson's regression test checks for a linear relationship.

Avoiding Common Misunderstandings

The Spearman rank correlation test makes fewer assumptions about the data than does the Pearson correlation test, but Spearman's test does make some assumptions. A common mistake among researchers is to recognize that their data are not independent observations and to use a Spearman rank correlation, in the hope that it will protect them from the dependencies in the data. For example, economists looking at yearly data may recognize that the previous year's data can be used to predict this year's data. That means that each year's x- and y-values are not independent from the previous year's x- and y-values. This dependence between the observations violates Pearson's assumptions, and it violates Spearman's assumptions as well. Neither test provides reliable results in that case.

Computer Project

Using the random number generator in your software, create some distributions that are not normal. For a good skewed distribution, you could start by generating a value from a uniform distribution between 0 and 1, and then square it and divide the square into 1. Or you could try dividing into a second value created by the random number generator. Or you could take a normal distribution and square all the values. Or take a normal distribution with a center near 0 and use the absolute value of each observation.

Have your software create data sets of x-values and y-values with observations from one or more of your distributions. Make sure the values are independent, so that a pair's x-value cannot be used to improve your prediction of the pair's y-value. Have your software calculate the Pearson correlation coefficient. Repeat this several times to collect a sampling distribution of Pearson r's. Compare the distribution you get to the critical values for Pearson correlation coefficients. How do the violations of Pearson's assumptions affect the Pearson correlation test?

For further instructions, see *www.keycollege.com/dm*.

Independence

Use your software to create a series of x- and y-values. Have each x-value be the observation's number in the data set (that is, 1, 2, 3, 4, 5, and so on). Create each y-value by taking the value of the observation before it in the set and adding a random error. Give your random errors a mean of 0. For example, you might use a normal distribution with a mean at 0, or a uniform distribution from 0 to 1 and then subtract 0.5. You will need to select an initial y-value. Generate between 50 and 5,000 observations. Plot your data y against x. Repeat these steps several times to see the patterns that result from this random variation. Neither your x-values nor your y-values are independent. You could improve your predictions of x by looking at the previous x-value, and you could improve your predictions of y by looking at the previous y-value. How would such correlations affect tests of correlation?

Exercises

1. Imagine that a researcher created a policy to reject the null hypothesis only if the Pearson correlation coefficient and the Spearman correlation coefficient *both* exceeded their critical values for alpha equal to 5%.

   a. Would this policy make the researcher more or less likely to reject a true null hypothesis?

   b. How would this policy affect the researcher's power?

2. Imagine that your local college has sent out a survey to college dropouts. The college has noticed that freshmen who are thinking of dropping out are hard to keep in school. Some counselors have come up with the idea that, rather than trying to get the freshman to stick around all the way to graduation, they could just encourage them to make it through their sophomore year. That seems easier. The question is, are you any better off dropping out after your sophomore year than after your freshman year? Or are all college dropouts doing the same, regardless of where in their education they drop out?

   To test this, the college sends out surveys to 10 dropouts, whose time at college ranged from one semester to three and a half years. The college collects information on the dropouts' incomes and finds that the Pearson correlation coefficient relating months at school to income is not significant. Write the college a short note to help with its research.

A team of Australian researchers led by O. F. Dent had records on the 1982 drinking habits of 342 Australian World War II veterans (with a mean age in 1982 of 64.3 years). The Dent team found these veterans in 1991. Many had died. Only 206 were able to participate in testing. The Dent team tested the 206 veterans' thinking abilities and used CAT scans to check on the state of the veterans' brains. The Dent team wanted to check for a correlation between alcohol consumption in 1982 and brain functioning in 1991. Use this information to complete Exercises 3 through 5.

> *In 1982 the average daily consumption of the 178 veterans (85%) who drank alcohol at least once a week ranged from 2 g to 129 g ethanol (mean 38.2 g).*
>
> —DENT ET AL., BRITISH MEDICAL JOURNAL, 1997, P. 1656

3. Why might this information suggest that a Pearson correlation coefficient might not be a good idea to test for a relationship between 1982 drinking and 1991 cognitive functioning?

4. Why might you suspect that this problem for the Pearson correlation might appear in most research on drinking?

5. Sketch a histogram of what the 1982 drinking rates might look like.

Exercises 6 and 7 refer to the following quote, which reports a Spearman correlation test.

> *Correlations with the neuropsychological tests were assessed by both the Spearman rank coefficient ([rho]) on the original values of alcohol intake and the Pearson product moment coefficient (r). . . . The possibility of a non-linear association between alcohol consumption and results of the cognitive function tests was examined by fitting quadratic curves.*
>
> —DENT ET AL., BRITISH MEDICAL JOURNAL, 1997, P. 1656

6. Great Uncle Orville is a regular drinker, and he has found this article in the library. He wants to know what a "nonlinear association" is. Write him a short note explaining it.

7. The quote says that the Dent team did further tests, after the Spearman tests, to check for nonlinear correlations.

   a. What kinds of nonlinear associations would show up in the Spearman test?

   b. What kinds of nonlinear associations would not show up with either test?

Exercises 8 through 13 refer to the following quote, which reports on some estimates of the power of a Pearson correlation test.

> *To estimate the power of the sample we regarded an r of at least 0.2 as the minimum effect size we would wish to identify. At this effect size and with significance set at 0.05 the power of the sample of 209 would be at least 0.8.*
>
> —DENT ET AL., BRITISH MEDICAL JOURNAL, 1997, P. 1656

8. Great Uncle Orville is keen about this too. He writes, "What is 'the power of the sample'?" Please reply.

9. In the simulation described earlier in this section in which Pearson's assumptions were valid, the R^2 for the total population was .20. How does that compare to the effect size for which the Dent team was looking?

10. Would the power of the Dent team's test be greater or less than the power of my test had I used samples with 209 observations?

11. The Dent team looked up the power in a book, which probably based its calculations on Pearson's assumptions. Write the team a short note commenting on their use of the book and describing an alternative approach.

12. Uncle Orville wants to know what it means to set significance at .05. In your reply, let him know what the usual jargon is for significance.

13. Uncle Orville wants to know what it means to say that the power was .8. Write him an explanation.

Exercises 14 through 16 refer to the following quote, which reports on a study of the relationship between age and drinking alcohol.

> *There was no correlation between age and alcohol consumption ([rho] = −0.05, P = 0.39).*
>
> —DENT ET AL., BRITISH MEDICAL JOURNAL, 1997, P. 1656

14. Orville wants to know what the "rho" of −.05 is. Write him a note explaining it.

15. Imagine sorting all the veterans from lightest drinker to heaviest. According to the regression equation behind Spearman's rho, if you went from the youngest veteran to the oldest, how many men would you have moved down in the list of veterans that was sorted by drinking? (That is, in the scatter plot of the ranks, as you go from the youngest to the oldest, how many ranks does the regression line go up?)

16. Uncle Orville asks again, "What is that *p* that is .39? What does it mean that it is .39?"

17. Here is a further report on the effect of drinking alcohol:

> *No significant correlation was found between average daily alcohol consumption in 1982 and any of the cognitive performance measures in 1991 . . . and in no case was there evidence of a significant nonlinear association.*
>
> —DENT ET AL., BRITISH MEDICAL JOURNAL, 1997, P. 1656

Orville asks, "Is alcohol going to rot my brain or what? What are they saying here? And do not pull a fast one on me. Explain what those words mean. I do not want to have to take your word for it. I want to know what they were trying to say." Write him an explanation.

Exercises 18 through 20 refer to the following quote, which reports on a study of men's death rates and drinking alcohol.

> *The proportion of men who died or were not included in the 1991 survey did not differ significantly according to alcohol consumption in 1982.*
>
> —DENT ET AL., BRITISH MEDICAL JOURNAL, 1997, P. 1656

18. What tests do you think the Dent team used to test this? Explain your thinking.

19. Why did the Dent team bother to check for this difference? Consider the three ways the test might have come out. How would your conclusions about the study depend on how this test came out?

20. In what important ways would you expect this sample to be unrepresentative of people like yourself? How might its differences make it inappropriate for you to make inferences about your own drinking from this study?

Use the following information to complete Exercises 21 through 23. You may have heard that children who have been diagnosed with attention deficit disorder are prescribed a stimulant. Two psychiatrists, Dr. Safer and Dr. Krager, checked whether the tendency to prescribe such medications to girls has been rising:

> Between 1971 and 1993, the rate of medication use for [hyperactivity/inattentiveness] in Baltimore County public elementary schools rose from 1.07 to 3.58% ... the female to male on-medication ratio in middle schools was 1:10 to 1:12 in the early and mid 1980s, it narrowed to 1:6 ... (Spearman rank correlation coefficient, rho = .68, n = 7, P < .05).

—SAFER AND KRAGER, PEDIATRICS, 1994, P. 464

Safer and Krager provide their data, which appears in the following table.

YEAR	PROPORTION
1981	7.8%
1983	9.4%
1985	9.1%
1987	14.8%
1989	16.4%
1991	12.4%
1993	13.7%

The mean female proportion is 11.9%; the median is 12.4%.

21. Why do you think that Safer and Krager chose to use a Spearman rank correlation rather than a Pearson correlation?

22. What would Karl Pearson say about the fact that this research is looking at seven observations, and why would he say that?

23. In these data, the x-values of Safer and Krager's analysis are the years. Why are these not data that should be tested with a Spearman rank correlation?

Answers to Odd-Numbered Exercises

1. a. If anything, this policy would lower the chance that she would reject a true null hypothesis.

   b. This policy would lower her power to reject false null hypotheses also.

3. For the daily alcohol consumption, the mean is much closer to the bottom of the range than to the top, so the average daily consumption is right skewed. The Pearson correlation test could be thrown by such non-normality.

5.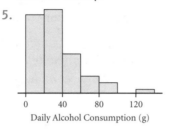

Daily Alcohol Consumption (g)

7. a. Monotonic nonlinear relationships would appear in the Spearman tests.

   b. If the relationship were U shaped or shaped like an upside-down U, that would be a highly predictable relationship that the Spearman test would not pick up.

9. An effect size in which R^2 is .2 is about the same as one in which r equals .45, which is stronger than when r equals .2.

11. Given that the data is not normally distributed, the power calculations would be off. Power calculations for the Spearman correlation test would be more accurate.

13. If the power is .8, then the test will accurately report that there is a correlation in the population 80% of the time.

15. If Spearman's rho is $-.05$, then, on the average, for each age rank we go up, we go *down* .05 ranks in alcohol consumption. If we went up from the rank of 1 all the way to the rank of 178, that would be going down .05 times 178, or about 9 ranks.

17. "Dear Uncle Orville, this study did not find a correlation between drinking and cognitive performance. That is, from how much the men drank in 1982, the researchers could do nothing to improve their predictions of how well the men thought in 1991. However, this doesn't mean that drinking has no effect on cognitive performance. It may be that it does have an effect, but by 1991, those men who could least afford to lose brain cells were already drinking less. If this were the case, by 1991, all of the men would have similar functioning, in spite of their different drinking. Before we draw

conclusions about the effect of drinking, someone is going to have to sign up to participate in an experiment."

19. If it were the case that heavier drinkers were more likely to be dead, that would very much change the conclusions that we might derive from this study. If heavier drinkers were *less* likely to be dead, that too would change our conclusions.

21. The data are not very skewed, but there are so few observations that we can't make much of a guess about what the population distribution is like. Safer and Krager may have used the Spearman correlation test because they didn't have adequate data to test whether the errors were normally distributed. Or they may have used a Spearman test because they were dealing with time-series data for which neither the Pearson test nor the Spearman test should be used, and they suspected that the fewer assumptions of the Spearman test would help.

23. The observations are not independent. Each year is completely predictable from the previous year, and the proportions themselves are correlated from year to year.

A Statistical Life

I N 1997, I WENT SHOPPING FOR A HOME. Living a life with statistical tools is different from a life without them, and my shopping was different from other people's.

Realtors have databases of houses on the market. I found a realtor who was willing to give me access to that data. I asked for a listing of every house that was for sale in the area we were interested in. These days, there are websites that will allow you to get the same data for yourself.

The database that my realtor was tapping into belonged to the Realtors' Association of Puget Sound and is not publicly available. I do not have permission to share data from it with you. But I could get some data to show you what I looked at. Where I live, when a house is for sale, the realtor nails a box on the for sale sign and slips sheets with data about the house into the box. Those data are freely available, and I can share them with you. One morning in 1997, I drove around in the neighborhood near my home, collecting house sale sheets.

I picked up sheets for 11 houses. This is how I began my house search in 1997. Even before I started working with a realtor, I drove around and collected sheets just like this, and even though it is a naughty-brewer sample size, I did look at the first handful to see what was available. Table PS.1 shows the data from the sheets from 1997.

In Table PS.1, I put in that there were half bedrooms. The way the realtors talk about this is to say that there are "three-plus bedrooms" or "three bedrooms and a den." They mean that there are four bedrooms, but one bedroom is small, and you would probably use it as an office or guest bedroom. I note that by calling it 3.5 bedrooms.

The column for bathrooms is strange, and I could figure it out only by asking my realtor. He reported that, at least in Washington State, a toilet and sink without a bath or shower is a quarter bathroom. A toilet, sink, and shower is a half bathroom. A room with a toilet, sink, and bathtub in which you cannot take a shower is a three-quarters bathroom, and a full bathroom has a toilet, sink, bathtub, and shower.

Table PS.1 Data on Available Houses in South Everett in 1997

ASKING PRICE	SQUARE FEET	BEDROOMS	BATHROOMS	GARAGE SPACE
$139,950	1,336	3	2	2
$189,950	2,032	4.5	2.75	3
$239,950	2,600	4.5	2.75	2
$239,500	2,330	4	2.5	3
$197,950	2,051	3.5	2.5	2
$209,500	2,162	4	2.5	2
$189,950	2,032	4.5	2.75	3
$204,500	2,030	4.5	2.5	2
$188,950	1,827	3	2	2
$187,500	1,946	3	2.5	2
$369,950	4,129	5	4	2

Before doing any fancy statistical analysis, I wanted to explore my data. Table PS.2 shows some summary statistics. The garage spaces are essentially categorical: The house has either two or three. All of the data have means reasonably close to their medians.

As a first check on what is going on in these data, I checked the correlations between the variables. Table PS.3 shows the Pearson correlations, and Table PS.4 shows the Spearman correlations.

Except for the garage spaces, all of the measurements are correlated with one another. For both Pearson and Spearman correlations, the p-values for the correlation between square feet and asking price are below .0001.

Table PS.2 Summary Statistics for 11 Houses

	MINIMUM	MAXIMUM	MEDIAN	MEAN	STANDARD ERROR	STANDARD DEVIATION
ASKING PRICE	$139,950	$369,950	$197,950	$214,332	$17,576	$58,293
SQUARE FEET	1,336	4,129	2,032	2,225	212	704
BEDROOMS	3	5	4	4.0	0.2	0.7
BATHROOMS	2	4	3	2.6	0.2	0.5
GARAGE SPACES	2	3	2	2.3	0.1	0.5

Table PS.3 Pearson Correlation Matrix

	ASKING PRICE	SQUARE FEET	BEDROOMS	BATHROOMS
ASKING PRICE	1.00			
SQUARE FEET	0.99	1.00		
BEDROOMS	0.65	0.68	1.00	
BATHROOMS	0.9	0.94	0.77	1.00
GARAGE SPACES	0.09	0.09	0.34	0.06

Here is the regression equation for predicting asking price from square feet:

$$\text{Asking Price} = \$31,510 + \$82 \text{ (Square Feet)}$$

The 95% confidence interval for the slope was from $75 to $89. The 95% confidence interval for the y-intercept was from $15,361 to $47,658. The regression model, then, is roughly that you pay somewhere between $15,000 and $50,000 (with a mean at $32,000) for the plot of land, and $75 to $89 per square foot for the built house.

The R^2 for the regression of asking price onto square feet is .99. It looks as though a linear model describes what is going on well. Figure PS.1 shows the asking prices plotted against square feet.

The regression equation let me know what people in the real estate business would consider a cheap house. A cheap house is one that has a low asking price, given its square feet. I would like someday to be able to get my money back out of my house, if I need to. I would like to buy a house that the industry thinks of as priced cheaply. That way, if I sell it at a medium price, I might even make some money.

The cheapness of a house is determined by the price per square foot. A person might sell a 1,000-square-foot home for $132,000. That would be a low price for this neighborhood, but it would be $100 a square foot (after the $32,000 for

Table PS.4 Spearman Correlation Matrix

	ASKING PRICE	SQUARE FEET	BEDROOMS	BATHROOMS
ASKING PRICE	1.00			
SQUARE FEET	0.94	1.00		
BEDROOMS	0.71	0.67	1.00	
BATHROOMS	0.60	0.71	0.88	1.00
GARAGE SPACES	0.00	0.13	0.30	0.34

Figure PS.1  **Asking Prices Plotted Against Square Feet**

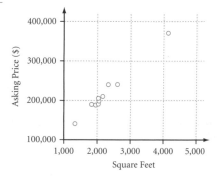

the land). A realtor would price that house at something like $112,000. If I bought a 1,000-square-foot house for $132,000 and then found I had to sell it, I could be looking at a $20,000 loss before I even paid the taxes and realtor fees.

When I was searching, I set a cutoff. I estimated what a good asking price would be. If a house cost less than the good asking price, I would buy it. If it cost more, I would pass it up. I adjusted this cutoff as I got more data, but at any point I knew in advance what would be a good deal. There was a special benefit to this. My realtor was full of hype. According to my realtor, every house was a "hot property" and would be sold that day. If I tried to judge the urgency from what he said, I would have panicked every other hour and ended up in a very expensive shack next to a highway. Having my own way of estimating whether a house was priced cheaply or not, I didn't need to rely on my realtor's claims.

To find what would be a good deal, I used the idea of a 95% confidence interval in a somewhat unusual manner. I paid attention to the outsides of the interval rather than the inside. If 95% of the data fall inside the interval, then 2.5% will fall above (those would be the expensive houses), and 2.5% would fall below. I wanted to get one of those 2.5% below. That would be a reasonably possible asking price, but still a cheap one—it would be more than 2 standard deviations below the mean asking price.

For each house, I subtracted $32,000 for the land and divided the remaining price by the square feet. Figure PS.2 shows the distribution of the asking price per square foot. They ranged from $78 to $89 (mean equal to $82, median equal to $81, standard deviation equal to $3.50). They are a little right skewed.

I wanted to create a prediction interval, but I didn't know the population mean. Rather than using the top or bottom of a confidence interval, I used the sample mean and calculated my prediction interval from that. The standard deviation was $3.50, so a 95% prediction interval based on a normal approximation for single prices is from $75 to $89. I would be interested only in prices at or below $75.

Figure PS.2 **Histogram of the Asking Prices per Square Foot (Minus $32,000 for Land)**

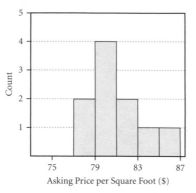

Asking Price per Square Foot ($)

That $75 cutoff is based on the 11 houses in Table PS.1. When I followed the same steps for the database's houses, the bottom of the confidence interval was $72 per square foot.

That modeling gave me a rule for making my decision. I would buy the first house with a view that had an asking price below $72 per square foot (plus the cost of the land) and was large enough for my family (at least 1,300 square feet).

If cost per square foot were normally distributed, the chance that a house would be priced at $72 per square foot or lower was 2.5%. But the data were right skewed. It didn't have much tail on the left, suggesting that the probability of a very low number might be even lower than 2.5%. Knowing this, I waited and searched. Each day, my realtor would telephone or fax me the new listings. I would scan them for my kind of house and then drive out to see houses after work.

There was something else going on in the data that I had not picked up at first, but quickly became apparent. Washington State gets a lot of power from hydro-electric plants in the Cascade Mountains. The lines that bring that power out of the mountains pass right through my neighborhood. I discovered that, if your house was under the power lines, the realtor priced it at or below $72 per square foot. For several months, I saw every house that has been built under the power lines. Nearby power lines can make speakers hum, even when your stereo is off. I was not going to buy any of those houses.

After three months, I was driving out to a house that I assumed was another power line property when I came around a bend in a road, and below me, tucked into the side of the hill, with a massive view of the Cascades, was a house selling for $62 per square foot.

The reason for the low price became apparent when we tried to see inside the house. We were not allowed to visit more than once, and that one time only for one-half hour, while the owner tramped around after us, scowling. After that, we were not allowed in for a second visit. This was an unusual way to have to buy a house, and I was as panicky as a rabbit, but I decided to go with my analysis and the fact that the house inspector saw nothing wrong.

After we moved in, the people who had owned the house continued to be odd. They left no forwarding address. Even their realtor had no idea where they went. They had disappeared, and all their mail still poured into the mailbox.

After two years, the next-door neighbor told us the story. Apparently, the sister of the man from whom we bought the home had divorced her husband and gotten sole custody of her son. The husband was violent and had attempted to kidnap the child. The sister had fled to her brother's house, but the family assumed that it was only a matter of time before the husband figured out where the boy was.

The people we were buying from were afraid that the husband was going to find out the son was living in the house by having a friend pose as a potential buyer. When we visited, there was no sign of a child living there. The neighbor explained that she had spent a day helping the previous owners clean the house to erase any record of the boy before we came to see it, hence the unwillingness to let us come back.

In the end, we capitalized on someone's misfortune. As misfortunes go, this was not the worst. This sister had a brave and intelligent brother, and I am sure that they are all now safe somewhere else. But what does this say about my conception of the costs? I had expected to find a good house at or under $72 per square foot, but I had expected it to appear by random variation. Random variation is not dangerous brothers-in-law trying to kidnap your nephew. Or is it? Is this the random variation we have been talking about?

The answer is "yes." Chances are that your sister will not marry a violent man. Many people do not even have sisters, but for all of us, there was a probability that our parents would provide a sister, and some of us got one or more. For each sister, there is a probability that the sister will marry and have a child, and a probability that the husband will be violent. The probabilities may vary from person to person, but we all run these risks somewhat. With the idea of random variation, sometimes these risks turn out well; sometimes they do not. Overall, they tend to produce data that are kind of normally distributed—lumped in the middle and spread out on either side. That means that someone (anyone in the lower third of the distribution) gets a lot of the bad outcomes.

However, that does not mean that if you tracked down someone in the tail, you would not be able to point to events and decisions that led to their "bad luck." You probably could make up a whole story about their decisions and bad luck. But this kind of storytelling leads to the illusion that somehow the rest of us are not running similar risks. That's a mistake. We all live in risk. We may make decisions that work out. For example, you may buy a lottery ticket, with its infinitesimal chance of paying off, and win money. Or I may drive home on the highway, with its very high chance of not killing me, and not be squashed by a sleeping truck driver. But just because our choices worked out does not mean that you were not running a chance of losing money, or that I was not running a chance of dying on the highway. We were both taking risks. Chance is part of everything we do.

Reality is wrapped up in chances. Nothing is a "sure thing" and uncertainty puts variation into everything. Things vary.

As you live your life, you can work with variation and probability. You can try to see the variation and estimate the probabilities, and you can make decisions in light of what you have learned about the chances. Or you can try to live in an illusion of certainty and stasis. Many people believe in the illusion that things do not vary. This denial of variation can be found in racism when people believe that everyone in a race is the same. It also appears in nationalistic hostilities when people believe that everyone in another country is bad. But life is not like that. Things vary, and people vary too.

References

"Alzheimer's researcher is found slain." *New York Times.* May 10, 1996, A24.

Ames, Genevieve M., Grube, Joel W., & Moore, Roland S. "The relationship of drinking and hangovers to workplace problems: An empirical study." *Journal of Studies on Alcohol,* 1997, 37.

Anderluh, Deborah. "Schools struggle to overcome grim reality of kids' lives." *Sacramento Bee,* Sept. 23, 1997, A1.

Armas, Genaro. "'Go-go 1990s saw living standard rise." *Baton Rouge Advocate,* Aug. 7, 2001.

"Around Texas and Southwest." *Dallas Morning News.* July 25, 1997, 12D.

"Around the AL." *Fort-Lauderdale Sun-Sentinel.* May 26, 1996, 5C.

"Asset allocation—Have investors got it wrong?" *London Financial Times.* June 30, 1997, M2.

Associated Press. "Causes of death in U.S." Dec. 15, 1994.

Associated Press. "Male-female population gap narrows." *Los Angeles Times,* Sept. 10, 2001.

Associated Press. "Midwest leads 1995 real income gains." *Dubuque Telegraph Herald,* Sept. 29, 1996, D7.

Associated Press. "More veterans homeless, survey finds; Shelter: One in three men seeking refuge has been in military. Rise may be linked to downsizing of active-duty forces." *Los Angeles Times,* Nov. 11, 1996, A18.

Associated Press. Report on a study commissioned by the Harvard School of Public Health and reported in *The Journal of the American Medical Association,* Dec. 1994. Jan. 1995.

Associated Press. "Senator Jesse Helms: Cut AIDS Funding," July 5, 1995.

Austin, Harry. "Incomes clash with GOP tax plan." *Chattanooga Times,* Nov. 7, 1995, A4.

Bagnato, Andrew. "They're not just basketball schools; Indiana envies N. Carolina gridiron success." *Chicago Tribune,* Sept. 3, 1997, 10.

Bardwell, S. K. "DARE program to be reviewed for changes." *Houston Chronicle,* Sept. 3, 1998, A31.

Barnes, James. "Polls and the election; Election night heats up—The networks race to make the calls." *The Public Perspective,* Dec.–Jan. 1997, 40.

Baxter, Susan. "The last word on gender differences." *Psychology Today,* Mar. 1994, 50.

Berger, D., & Marelich, William. "Legal and social control of alcohol-impaired driving in California: 1983–1994." *Journal of Studies on Alcohol,* Sept. 1997, 518.

Bingham, Janet. "State's college-bound show testing gains." *Denver Post,* Aug. 27, 1997, B1.

Birmaher, Boris, Brent, David A., Kolko, David, Baugher, Marianne, Bridge, Jeffrey, Holder, Diane, Lyengar, Satish, & Ulloa, Rosa Elena. "Clinical outcome after short-term psychotherapy for adolescents with major depressive disorder." *Archives of General Psychiatry,* vol. 57, no. 1, Jan. 2000.

Blair, Ronnie. "Students give new grading system an A." *Tampa Tribune,* Nov. 25, 2001.

Borst, Don. "Huskies go the distance; 64 percent of '89 recruiting class graduated." *News Tribune,* June 28, 1996, C3.

Bowles, Samuel. "Schooling and inequality from generation to generation." *Journal of Political Economy,* May/June 1972, S219–S251.

"Breakfast Briefing." *Chicago Sun-Times.* Mar. 2, 1999, 38.

Broder, David S. "Still learning to be the opposition." *Washington Post,* Feb. 15, 1981, C7.

Burns, D. D. *Feeling good.* New York: Plume, 1980.

"Business Browser: Technology." *Arizona Republic.* Nov. 28, 1998. E3.

Business Wire, Inc. "NBS Imaging Systems teams with state of Connecticut social services to cut welfare fraud." *Business Wire,* Feb. 6, 1996.

Butterfield, Fox. "'Silent march' on guns talks loudly: 40,000 pairs of shoes, and all empty." *New York Times,* Sept. 21, 1994, A18.

"Byrd feathering a different nest after hitting the heights on court; American in a new ball game as he teams up with London Monarchs." *Daily Telegraph.* Feb. 3, 1997, 9.

Cashnelli, Toni. "Faith finds a home: Interfaith Hospitality Network gives homeless families shelter, food and training." *Cincinnati Enquirer,* Nov. 6, 1995, C1.

Central Intelligence Agency. *The World Factbook 1997.* Available at *www.cia.gov.* Washington, DC: Author.

Chandler, David L. "El Niño is ready to upset weather across the world." *Boston Globe,* Sept. 24, 1997, A1.

Charen, Mona. "Confused message on teen pregnancy." *St. Louis Post-Dispatch,* Feb. 6, 1996, 11B.

Chu, P. S., & Wang, J. "Tropical cyclone occurrences in the vicinity of Hawaii: Are the differences between El Niño and non-El Niño years significant?" *Journal of Climate,* vol. 10, 1997, 2683–2689.

Clancy, Carole. "Convention center building repeat business." *Tampa Bay Business Journal,* June 7, 1996, 1.

Clayton, Mark. "Controversy surrounds gender gap; Fewer males apply, so some schools admit them at higher rates." *Christian Science Monitor,* Nov. 13, 2001.

Cohen, J. *Statistical power analysis for the behavioral sciences* (rev. ed.). San Diego, CA: Academic Press, 1977.

Condor, Bob. "Men and depression; A big stumbling block is that most males are reluctant to talk about it." *Chicago Tribune,* Sept. 4, 1997, 3.

Cook, Derek G., Peacock, Janet L., Feyerabend, Colin, Carey, Iain M., Jarvis, Martin, Anderson, H. Ross, & Bland, J. Martin. "Relation of caffeine intake and blood caffeine concentrations during pregnancy to fetal growth: Prospective population based study." *British Medical Journal,* 1996, 1358.

[Credit Card Rates]. *Arizona Republic.* Nov. 28, 1998.

Crispell, Diane. "More heat, fewer babies." *Wall Street Journal,* Sept. 27, 1996, 9.

Crutsinger, Martin. "Economic reports paint recession." Oct. 25, 2001.

"Demographics: Life expectancy now 76." *Rocky Mountain News,* Dec. 16, 1994, 66A.

Dent, O. F., Sulway, M. R., Broe, G. A., Creasey, H., Kos, S. C., Jorm, A. F., Tennant, C., & Fairley, M. J. "Alcohol consumption and cognitive performance in a random sample of Australian soldiers who served in the Second World War." *British Medical Journal,* 1997, 1656.

Dobie, Michael. "The female athlete triad/case study: Gordon Bakoulis: A runner's race against ignorance." *Newsday,* July 29, 1997, A56.

Durhams, Sharif. "UW graduation rate nears record; University system's officials credit programs that help students make the transition to college life." *Milwaukee Journal Sentinel,* June 2, 2000, 1B.

Eagles, Cynthia. "Bluegrass state poll; Kentuckians give affirmative reaction to affirmative action." *Louisville Courier-Journal,* Oct. 15, 1995, 1A.

Fan, & Steinberg, V. E. "Health implications of nitrate and nitrite in drinking water: An update on methemoglobinemia occurrence and reproductive and developmental toxicity." *Regulatory Toxicology and Pharmacology,* 1996, 35.

Federal Reserve Bank. *Federal Reserve Bulletin.* 1997, no. 1, 1.

Finnigan, Bob, & Sherwin, Bob. "Torres keeps Molitor stalled at no. 2,998." *Seattle Times,* Sept. 16, 1996, C5.

Fiore, Faye, & Brownstein. "Most in U.S. got richer, poor got poorer in 1996." *Los Angeles Times,* Sept. 30, 1997, A1.

Fuchs, C. S., Stampfer, M. J., Colditz, G. A., Giovannucci, E. L., Manson, J. E., Kawachi, I., Hunter, D. J., Hankinson, S. E., Hennekens, C. H., Rosner, B., Speizer, F. E., & Willett, W. C. "Alcohol consumption and mortality among women." *New England Journal of Medicine,* vol. 332, 1995, 1245–1250.

Fuchs, V. R. "Poverty and health: Asking the right questions." *American Economist,* vol. 36, no. 2, 1992, 12.

Garfield, Simon. "This man has AIDS. Nine months ago he was prepared for death. Now, thanks to a new cocktail of drugs, he can prepare for life. He is living proof that a cure is no longer a miracle away; Night and day." *Mail on Sunday,* Mar. 2, 1997, 10.

[Gasoline Prices]. *Detroit News.* Mar. 22, 1999.

Gee, Michael. "BASEBALL; Sox join in the parity; For Pete's sake, this is your average year." *Boston Herald,* May 2, 1997, 104.

Gin, John. "Learn all about life insurers." *New Orleans Times-Picayune,* Sept. 16, 1997, C1.

Giuliano, Armando E. "A high-fiber defense against breast cancer." *Los Angeles Times,* Oct. 20, 1997, S8.

Glassman, James K. "Finding your balance in a volatile market." *Washington Post,* Sept. 14, 1997, H1.

Gorrell, Mike. "Oly organizers can control a lot, but weather has a mind of its own." *Salt Lake Tribune,* Sept. 24, 2001.

Gross, Joe. "Oriole notes." *The Capital,* June 19, 1996, C3.

Gunnison, Robert B. "Lawmakers approve delay in welfare increases." *San Francisco Chronicle,* Mar. 29, 1996, A19.

Harper, James. "To the neediest, goes the least." *St. Petersburg Times,* Feb. 9, 1997, 1D.

Hart, Jordana. "Scores on SAT inch up statewide; Mass. leads nation in rate of test-taking, lags in math." *Boston Globe,* Aug. 27, 1997, A1.

Hartston, William. "Weather: Why we should expect the unexpected." *London Independent,* Oct. 2, 1997, 10.

Harwood, Richard. "The half-full, half-empty economy." *Washington Post,* Oct. 21, 1996, A19.

Havemann, Judith, & Vobejda Barbara. "As welfare cases drop, politicians fight for credit; But experts say reasons for decline are unclear." *Washington Post,* May 13, 1996, A1.

Hess, Gregory D., & Morris, Charles S. "The long-run costs of moderate inflation." *Economic Review,* 1996, 71–88.

Holloway, Lynette. "Report says errors, not fraud, are the biggest reason New York City cuts off welfare." *New York Times,* Aug. 12, 1997, B3.

Holmes, Steven. "New reports say minorities benefit in fiscal recovery." *New York Times,* Sept. 30, 1997, A1.

Houtz, Jolayne. "Tests best where money is—Where income is low, 4th-grade scores dip." *Seattle Times,* Sept. 17, 1997, A1.

"How about queen for a day?" *Columbus Dispatch.* July 18, 1997, 2D.

Howe, Kenneth. "Cars and phones can be hazardous: Study says you run a 34% greater risk of an accident while driving." *San Francisco Chronicle,* Apr. 2, 1996, E3.

Humphreys, Joe. "22% of motorists admitted to driving soon after drinking." *Irish Times,* Mar. 12, 1999.

Hunter, Brian. *The Statesman's Yearbook, 1994–1995.* London: BPC Hazell Books Ltd., 1994.

Jackson, Robert L. "The world and nation: Crime rate continues downward trend in '01. Statistics: Decrease comes even as murders, robberies rise slightly. Los Angeles goes against the grain as violent incidents rise." *Los Angeles Times,* Dec. 18, 2001.

Kerr, J. B., & McElroy, C. T. "Evidence for large upward trends of ultraviolet-B radiation linked to ozone depletion." *Science,* 1993, 1032.

King, A., Katz, Steven H., Ghaziuddin, Neera, Brand, Elena, Hill, Elizabeth, & McGovern, Laurie King. "Diagnosis and assessment of depression and suicidality using the NIMH Diagnostic Interview Schedule for Children DISC-2.3." *Journal of Abnormal Child Psychology,* 1997, 173.

Kirk, Laura Meade. "Where the boys are." *Providence Journal,* Jan. 13, 2002.

Klein, R. G., Abikoff, H., Klass, E., Ganeles, D., Seese, L. M., & Pollack, S. "Clinical efficacy of methylphenidate in conduct disorder with and without attention deficit hyperactivity disorder." *Archives of General Psychiatry,* vol. 54, 1997, 1073–1080.

Kobashigawa, Jon A., Leaf, David A., Lee, Nancy, Gleeson, Michael P., Liu, Hong Hu, Hamilton, Michele A., Moriguchi, Jaime D., Kawata, Nobuyuki, Einhorn, Kim, Herlihy, Elise, & Laks, Hillel. "A controlled trial of exercise rehabilitation after heart transplantation." *The New England Journal of Medicine,* vol. 340, 1999, 272–277.

Kohers, & Patel. "An examination of the day-of-the-week effect in junk bond returns over business cycles." *Review of Financial Economics,* 1996, 31.

Landers, Ann. *Seattle Post-Intelligencer,* Oct. 17, 1996.

"Lawyers and the GNP." *Society.* Jan.–Feb. 1992, 2.

Lewis, Greg. "Referee draws criticism from UCLA with questionable calls." *UCLA Daily Bruin,* Feb. 3, 1999.

Lindberg, Tod. "The rise and fall of Pitchfork Pat." *Washington Times,* Mar. 20, 1996, A17.

Loury, Linda Datcher. "The gender earnings gap among college-educated workers." *Industrial and Labor Relations Review,* 1997, 580.

Lubanko, Matthew. "Red tape buys time; Sport-utility premiums in state won't rise soon." *Hartford Courant,* Oct. 21, 1997, D1.

Majeski, Tom. "Heart repair." *Chicago Tribune,* Jan. 17, 1997, 7.

Marcus, Bess H., Albrecht, Anna E., King, Teresa K., Parisi, Alfred F., Pinto, Bernardine M., Roberts, Mary, Niaura, Raymond S., & Abrams, David B. "The efficacy of exercise as an aid for smoking cessation in women: A randomized controlled trial." *Archives of Internal Medicine,* vol. 159, June 14, 1999, 1229–1234.

Margolin, Arthur, Kleber, Herbert D., Avants, S. Kelly, Konefal, Janet, Gawin, Frank, Stark, Elena, Sorensen, James, Midkiff, Eleanor, Wells, Elizabeth, Jackson, T. Ron, Bullock, Milton, Culliton, Patricia D., Boles, Sharon, & Vaughan, Roger. "Acupuncture for the treatment of cocaine addiction: A randomized controlled trial." *Journal of the American Medical Association,* vol. 287, no. 1, Jan. 2, 2002, 55–63.

Martin, Stump. "New Orleans knows how to throw a Super Bowl party!" *Chattanooga Free Press,* Jan. 26, 1997, I4.

Mason-Draffen, Carrie. "The news en Espanol: As immigrant population grows, so does Spanish-language press." *Newsday,* Mar. 23, 1998, C10.

"McDonald's Marks Big Mac's Birthday," [Minneapolis] *Star Tribune.* Sept. 11, 1998.

McDonnell, Patrick J. "Deportation of criminals, INS fugitives at new high; Immigration: The total is expected to reach 93,000 this fiscal year, including a significant number picked up in orange county." *Los Angeles Times,* June 23, 1997, A1.

Mehren, Elizabeth. "Education: Smart resources for students and parents. Still giving it the old college cry: Drink! Study: Despite well-publicized problems and efforts to combat them, bingeing and abstaining are both reported up on U.S. campuses." *Los Angeles Times,* Sept. 28, 1998.

Mestel, Rosie. "The nation: Adolescents' TV watching is linked to violent behavior psychology: A 17-year study tracked 700 young people into their adult lives. Hours of viewing were correlated with acts of aggression." *Los Angeles Times,* Mar. 29, 2002.

Monastersky, Richard. "Scientist says greenhouse warming is here." *Science News,* July 2, 1988, 4.

Montagne, Renee. "Profile: Non-aligned movement meets in Johannesburg to condemn lawsuit by drug companies to prevent South Africa from importing generic AIDS drugs." National Public Radio, *Morning Edition,* Mar. 29, 2001.

Morin, Richard. "Who's in control? Many don't know or care; Knowledge gap affects attitudes and participation." *Washington Post,* Jan. 29, 1996, A6.

Mulvenon, Sean W., Ganley, Barbara J., & Fritts-Scott, Kristina. "The impact of socioeconomic status on performance: A case study of Arkansas schools." *Arkansas Educational Research & Policy Studies Journal,* vol. 1, no. 1, Summer 2001, 42–61.

Nakamura, David, & Asher, Mark. "Graduation rates steady for college programs; Two area basketball teams show decline." *Washington Post,* June 28, 1996, B01.

Nesland, Matt. "Power customers favor a coal-burning plant in Las Animas, Colo., area." *Pueblo [Colorado] Chieftain,* Nov. 27, 2001.

Newnham, Blaine. "Rodriguez finds focus in blur of pennant race." *Seattle Times,* Aug. 8, 1996, C1.

New York Times News Service. "Car phone use raises risk of accident, study asserts; Danger equated to driving while slightly intoxicated." *Chicago Tribune,* Feb. 13, 1997, 3.

Nilsson, Jansson, Roland, & Zinko. "Long-term responses of river-margin vegetation to water-level regulation." *Science,* 1997, 798.

Nisbett, Richard, & Ross, Lee. *Human Inference: Strategies and Shortcomings of Social Judgment.* Hillsdale, NJ: Lawrence Erlbaum, 1980.

Nolan, Martin F. "Revenge of the science nerds." *Tampa Tribune,* July 15, 1997, 7.

"On personal finance." *Chicago Tribune.* Oct. 2, 1994, 3.

Onestak, David. "The effect of visuo-motor behavior rehearsal (VMBR) and videotaped modeling on the free-throw performance of intercollegiate athletes." *Journal of Sport Behavior,* 1997, 185.

Ostrom, Carol. "Washington State slips in health insurance coverage." *Seattle Times,* Sept. 28, 2001.

Padawer, Ruth. "Gay couples, at long last feel acknowledged." *[Bergen County, NJ] Record,* Aug. 15, 2001.

Paredes, Rosana, Zavalaga, Carlos B, & Boness, Daryl J. "Patterns of egg laying and breeding success in Humboldt penguins (*Spheniscus humboldti*) at Punta San Juan, Peru." *The Auk,* Jan. 2002.

Pearson, Karl. *The Life, Letters and Labours of Francis Galton, Vol. 2.* Cambridge, England: Cambridge University Press, 1924.

Pedulla, Tom. "Isringhausen prevails vs. Giants 15–6." *USA Today,* Aug. 28, 1997, 6C.

Peterson, Karen S. "Neighborly neighbors are the norm, poll says." *USA Today,* July 14, 1997, 1D.

Peterson, Peter G. "Facing up; Causes of federal budget deficit." *The Atlantic Monthly,* Oct. 1993, 77.

Peyser, James A. "Charter school myths dispelled." *Boston Herald,* July 10, 1998, 25.

Pinilla, Teresa, & Birch, Leann L. "Help me make it through the night: Behavioral entrainment of breast-fed infants' sleep patterns." *Pediatrics,* 1993, 436–444.

Pinzur, Matthew. "Political sway of First Baptist with several elected officials among its congregants, many feel church has clout, but members say that isn't true." *Florida Times Union,* Aug. 26, 2001.

"Plans put profits before patients." *USA Today*. May 1, 1997, 14A.

Porter, Theodore M. *The Rise of Statistical Thinking 1820–1900*, Princeton, NJ: Princeton University Press, 1986.

Quinn, Jane Bryant. "Top-rated funds aren't always best bet." *Washington Post,* Oct. 2, 1994, H2.

Reid, G. C. "Solar forcing of global climate change since the mid-17th century." *Climatic Change,* vol. 37, 1997, 391–405.

Reuters. "AIDS spreading rapidly among women; Blacks and Hispanics more likely to contract disease, report says." *Rocky Mountain News,* Feb. 10, 1995, 40A.

Reuters Financial Service. "Paris commuter train drivers begin strike." May 15, 1996.

Rew, Resnick, & Blum. "An exploration of help-seeking behaviors in female Hispanic adolescents." *Family and Community Health,* Oct. 1997, 1.

"Risk assessment." *London Financial Times*. Apr. 24, 1997, G3.

Rockne, Dick. "M's power takes over as Sox unravel—Griffey, Rodriguez rip homers in Seattle's comeback surge." *Seattle Times,* June 1, 1996. B1.

Roscigno, Vincent J. "Race and reproduction of educational disadvantage." *Social Forces,* Mar. 1998.

Rosenblatt, Robert A. "Jobless rate slips to 4.8%, a 23-year low; Employment: The good news arrives with negligible inflation and helps lead to a surge in the stock market." *Los Angeles Times,* June 7, 1997, D1.

Ruelas, Richard. "10% in state look to skies, see UFOs." *Arizona Republic,* July 26, 1997, A1.

Russell, Kim, Murgatroyd, Peter R., & Batt, Roger M. "Net protein oxidation is adapted to dietary protein intake in domestic cats (*Felis silvestris catus*)." *The Journal of Nutrition,* Mar. 2002.

Sable, Marjorie R., & Herman, Allen A. "The relationship between prenatal health behavior advice and low birth weight." *Public Health Reports,* 1997, 332.

Safer, Daniel J., & Krager, John M. "The increased rate of stimulant treatment for hyperactive/inattentive students in secondary schools." *Pediatrics,* 1994, 462–464.

Schmid, Randolph E. "Americans' income up—but not for poor." *Chattanooga Times,* Sept. 30, 1997.

Sefton, Dru. "Epidurals popular with moms-to-be painkiller may not be as risky as once thought." *Kansas City Star,* Oct. 23, 1997, F1.

"Sex and the Joneses." *Sacramento Bee*. Oct. 11, 1994, B6.

Shanahan, Michael, & Benson, Miles. "GOP's Medicare stance could doom Dole; Older voters get big share of last word on presidency." *New Orleans Times-Picayune,* Apr. 28, 1996, A20.

Shein, Jay L. "It seems unfair to compare a money manager who does not invest in large-cap stocks to the S&P 500, a large-cap stock index with a weighting toward growth." *Financial Planning,* June 1998.

Sherwin, Bob. "Rodriguez lifts average to .358, second in AL." *Seattle Times,* Aug. 2, 1996, C7.

Shields, Todd. "Survey hits a nerve in Charles; Teachers say classes among most crowded." *Washington Post,* June 14, 1998, M1.

Simon, Scott. National Public Radio, *All Things Considered.* May 4, 1996.

Singletary, Michelle. "Helping Blacks overcome barriers to home ownership." *Washington Post,* Oct. 14, 2001.

Sklar, Jeff. "U. Arizona president authorizes contracts for part-time instructors." *Arizona Daily Wildcat (University Wire),* Nov. 16, 2001.

Smith, N., Floyd, M., Scogin, F., & Jamison, C. "A three-year follow-up of cognitive bibliotherapy for depression." *Journal of Consulting and Clinical Psychology,* vol. 65, 1997, 324–327.

Stolberg, Sheryl Gay. "Epidemic of silence: A special report; Eyes shut, Black America is being ravaged by AIDS." *New York Times,* June 29, 1998, A1.

"Stonewalling on AIDS." *Montreal Gazette.* Aug. 27, 2001.

"Study links car phones to higher risk of wrecks." [Greensboro, NC] *News & Records.* Mar. 19, 1996, A1.

Swistock, Bryan R., Sharpe, William E., & Robillard, Paul D. "A survey of lead, nitrate and radon contamination of private individual water systems in Pennsylvania." *Journal of Environmental Health,* 1993, 6.

Talan, Jamie, & Brown, Peggy. "Second-hand drinking collegians who binge may affect peers, study says." *Newsday,* Dec. 7, 1994.

Tasker, Fred. "Living to 100: Good genes, good habits or good luck?" *Miami Herald,* Oct. 7, 2001.

Teasdale, Thomas W., & Engberg, Aase. "Duration of cognitive dysfunction after concussion, and cognitive dysfunction as a risk factor: A population study of young men." *British Medical Journal,* 1997, 569.

"Test cases." *Washington Post.* May 27, 1995, A27.

Theodossiou, Ioannis. "Promotions, job seniority, and product demand effects on earnings." *Oxford Economic Papers,* 1996, 456.

Thomas, Andrew Peyton. "Spanking the anti-spankers." *Weekly Standard,* Sept. 8, 1997, 12.

Trevino, Robert P., Pugh, Jacqueline A., Hernandez, Arthur E., Menchaca, Velma D., Ramirez, Robert R., & Mendoza, Monica. "Bienestar: A diabetes risk-factor prevention program." *Journal of School Health,* 1998, 62.

Tzeng, Huey-Ming, & Ketefian, Shake. "The relationship between nurses' job satisfaction and inpatient satisfaction: An exploratory study in a Taiwan teaching hospital." *Journal of Nursing Care Quality,* Jan. 2002.

"UK opens market for maintenance of call-routing equipment." *Telecom Markets.* Sept. 12, 1996.

"Underground economy." *The Nation.* Jan. 12/19, 1998, 3.

Underwood, Lynn, & Holston, Noel. "FYI: Speaking of teeth, [Minneapolis] *Star Tribune,* Feb. 24, 1999, 1E.

United States Bureau of the Census. *Historical Statistics, Colonial Times to 1970.* Washington, DC: U.S. Government Printing Office, 1989.

United States Bureau of the Census. *Statistical Abstract of the United States 1996*. Austin, TX: Hoover's Business Press.

"U.S. schools in crisis; So what else is new?" *Chicago Sun-Times*. Nov. 22, 1996, 39.

Van Servellen, Gwen, Topf, Margaret, et al. "Personality hardiness, work-related stress, and health in hospital nurses." *Hospital Topics,* Apr. 1994, 34–39.

Vasquez, Luis A., Garcia, Vasquez Enedina, Bauman, Sheri A., & Sierra, Arturo S. "Skin color, acculturation, and community interest among Mexican American students: A research note." *Hispanic Journal of Behavioral Sciences,* 1997, 377.

Vobejda, & Chandler. "Household incomes rise again; Women catching up; Rich–poor pay gap continues to widen." *Washington Post,* Sept. 30, 1997, A1.

Walter, Bob. "Sacramento, Calif.–area firm creates solid waste empire." *Sacramento Bee,* Aug. 17, 2001.

Webster, Guy. "Minority graduates declining; Goals for Blacks, Indians go unmet." *Arizona Republic,* Feb. 22, 1996, A1.

Wechsler, Henry, Davenport, Andrea, Dowdall, George, Moeykens, Barbara, & Castillo, Sonya. "Health and behavioral consequences of binge drinking in college: A national survey of students at 140 campuses." *Journal of the American Medical Association,* 1994, 1672.

Weinberg, Daniel H. "Press briefing on 1996 income, poverty, and health insurance estimates." Washington, DC: U.S. Census Bureau, Sept. 29, 1997.

Williams, Dennis, & King, Patricia. "Do males have a math gene?" *Newsweek,* Dec. 15, 1980, 73.

Wise, Daniel. "Minority enrollment at CUNY Law soars." *New York Law Journal,* Aug. 15, 1996, 1.

Woo, Elaine, & Smith, Doug. "California and the West; SAT scores rise, but trouble spots remain; Education: California's test-takers are enrolling in fewer college prep courses than the national average, official says." *Los Angeles Times,* Aug. 27, 1997, A3.

Woods, Kerry D. "Dynamics in late-successional hemlock-hardwood forests over three decades." *Ecology,* vol. 81, no. 1, Jan. 2000, 110–126.

World Almanac Books. *The World Almanac and Book of Facts.* Mahwah, NJ: Author, 1996.

Wyatt, Edward. "Mutual funds; A top performing fund that Santa Claus could love." *New York Times,* May 14, 1995, sec. 3, 8.

Yudof, Mark. "Higher tuitions." *Change,* Mar. 2002.

Index

T

Some Useful Equations

Proportional Change

When a measure increases from x_1 to x_2,

$$\text{Proportional Change} = \frac{x_2 - x_1}{x_1}$$

Prediction Intervals

$$\text{Standard Error of Sample Proportions} = \sqrt{\frac{\text{Probability} \times (1 - \text{Probability})}{\text{Sample Size}}}$$

A 95% prediction interval for a proportion of a sample that is x is the range from the probability of x minus 2 standard errors to the probability of x plus 2 standard errors.

A two-thirds prediction interval for a proportion of a sample that is x is the range from the probability of x minus 1 standard error to the probability of x plus 1 standard error.

Confidence Intervals

$$\text{Estimated Standard Error of Sample Proportions}$$
$$= \sqrt{\frac{\text{Sample Proportion} \times (1 - \text{Sample Proportion})}{\text{Sample Size}}}$$

$$\text{Margin of Error} = 2 \text{ Estimated Standard Errors}$$

$$\text{95\% Confidence Interval for Population Proportion} = \text{Sample Proportion} +/- \text{Margin of Error}$$

Z-Value in a Z-Test of Location of a Population Proportion or Probability

$$z\text{-value} = \frac{\text{Sample Proportion} - \text{Null Hypothesis's Claimed Population Proportion}}{\text{Standard Error}}$$

Chi-Square Value

Chi-square (χ^2) equals the sum of the relative squared differences between the expected and observed counts in a cross-tab. Each cell's expected count equals the product of the row proportion and the column total.

Summarizing Number Line (Numeric) Data

$$\text{Mean} = \frac{\text{Sum of Observations}}{\text{Number of Observations}}$$

$$\text{Estimated Population Standard Deviation} = \sqrt{\frac{\text{Sum of Squared Deviations}}{\text{Sample Size} - 1}}$$

The deviations are the differences between the observations and the sample mean.

$$\text{Estimated Standard Error of Sample Means} = \frac{\text{Estimated Population Standard Deviation}}{\sqrt{\text{Sample Size}}}$$

$$\text{95\% Prediction Interval for Sample Means} = \text{Population Mean} +/- 2 \text{ Standard Errors}$$

$$\text{95\% Confidence Interval for Population Mean} = \text{Sample Mean} +/- 2 \text{ Estimated Standard Errors}$$